1

Fundamental Concepts of Algebra

The word *algebra* comes from *ilm al-jabr w'al muqabala,* the title of a book written in the ninth century by the Arabian mathematician al-Khworizimi. The title has been translated as the science of restoration and reduction, which means transposing and combining similar terms (of an equation). The Latin transliteration of al-jabr led to the name of the branch of mathematics we now call algebra.

In algebra we use symbols or letters—such as a, b, c, d, x, y—to denote arbitrary numbers. This general nature of algebra is illustrated by the many formulas used in science and industry. As you proceed through this text and go on either to more advanced courses in mathematics or to fields that employ mathematics, you will become more and more aware of the importance and the power of algebraic techniques.

1.1

Real Numbers

Real numbers are used throughout mathematics, and you should be acquainted with symbols that represent them, such as

$$1, \quad 73, \quad -5, \quad \tfrac{49}{12}, \quad \sqrt{2}, \quad 0, \quad \sqrt[3]{-85}, \quad 0.33333\ldots, \quad 596.25,$$

and so on. The **positive integers,** or **natural numbers,** are

$$1, \quad 2, \quad 3, \quad 4, \quad \ldots.$$

The **whole numbers** (or *nonnegative integers*) are the natural numbers combined with the number 0. The **integers** are often listed as follows:

$$\ldots, \quad -4, \quad -3, \quad -2, \quad -1, \quad 0, \quad 1, \quad 2, \quad 3, \quad 4, \quad \ldots$$

Throughout this text lowercase letters a, b, c, x, y, $\ldots$ represent arbitrary real numbers (also called *variables*). If a and b denote the same real number, we write $a = b$, which is read "a **is equal to** b" and is called an **equality.** The notation $a \neq b$ is read "a **is *not* equal to** b."

If a, b, and c are integers and $c = ab$, then a and b are **factors,** or **divisors,** of c. For example, since

$$6 = 2 \cdot 3 = (-2)(-3) = 1 \cdot 6 = (-1)(-6),$$

we know that $1, -1, 2, -2, 3, -3, 6$, and -6 are factors of 6.

A positive integer p different from 1 is **prime** if its only positive factors are 1 and p. The first few primes are 2, 3, 5, 7, 11, 13, 17, and 19. The **Fundamental Theorem of Arithmetic** states that every positive integer different from 1 can be expressed as a product of primes in one and only one way (except for order of factors). Some examples are

$$12 = 2 \cdot 2 \cdot 3, \quad 126 = 2 \cdot 3 \cdot 3 \cdot 7, \quad 540 = 2 \cdot 2 \cdot 3 \cdot 3 \cdot 3 \cdot 5.$$

A **rational number** is a real number that can be expressed in the form a/b, where a and b are integers and $b \neq 0$. Note that every integer a is a rational number, since it can be expressed in the form $a/1$. Every real number can be expressed as a decimal, and the decimal representations for rational numbers are either *terminating* or *nonterminating and repeating*. For example, we can show by using the arithmetic process of division that

$$\tfrac{5}{4} = 1.25 \quad \text{and} \quad \tfrac{177}{55} = 3.2181818\ldots,$$

where the digits 1 and 8 in the representation of $\tfrac{177}{55}$ repeat indefinitely (sometimes written $3.2\overline{18}$).

FORMULAS FROM GEOMETRY

area A perimeter P circumference C volume V curved surface area S altitude h radius r

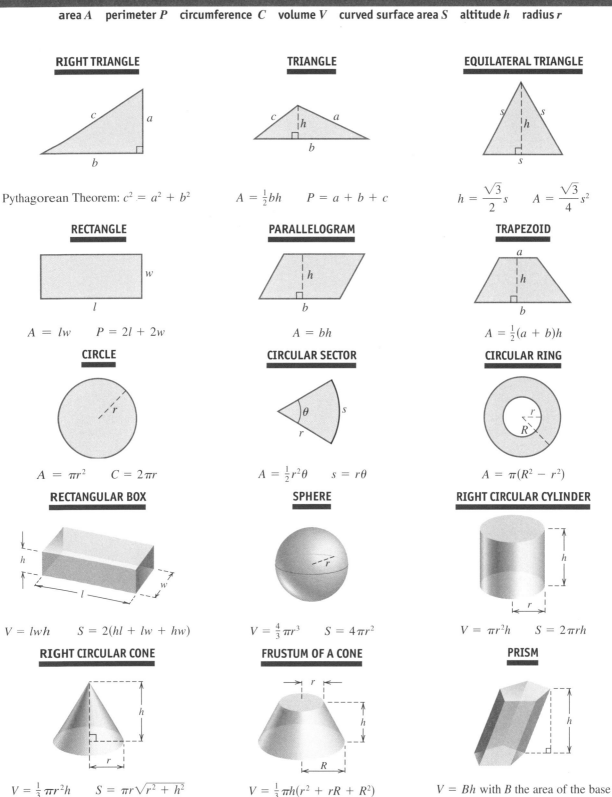

RIGHT TRIANGLE

Pythagorean Theorem: $c^2 = a^2 + b^2$

TRIANGLE

$A = \frac{1}{2}bh$ $P = a + b + c$

EQUILATERAL TRIANGLE

$h = \frac{\sqrt{3}}{2}s$ $A = \frac{\sqrt{3}}{4}s^2$

RECTANGLE

$A = lw$ $P = 2l + 2w$

PARALLELOGRAM

$A = bh$

TRAPEZOID

$A = \frac{1}{2}(a + b)h$

CIRCLE

$A = \pi r^2$ $C = 2\pi r$

CIRCULAR SECTOR

$A = \frac{1}{2}r^2\theta$ $s = r\theta$

CIRCULAR RING

$A = \pi(R^2 - r^2)$

RECTANGULAR BOX

$V = lwh$ $S = 2(hl + lw + hw)$

SPHERE

$V = \frac{4}{3}\pi r^3$ $S = 4\pi r^2$

RIGHT CIRCULAR CYLINDER

$V = \pi r^2 h$ $S = 2\pi rh$

RIGHT CIRCULAR CONE

$V = \frac{1}{3}\pi r^2 h$ $S = \pi r\sqrt{r^2 + h^2}$

FRUSTUM OF A CONE

$V = \frac{1}{3}\pi h(r^2 + rR + R^2)$

PRISM

$V = Bh$ with B the area of the base

ANALYTIC GEOMETRY

DISTANCE FORMULA

$$d(P_1, P_2) = \sqrt{(x_2 - x_1)^2 + (y_2 - y_1)^2}$$

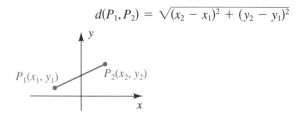

SLOPE m OF A LINE

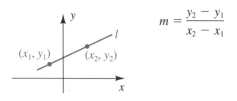

$$m = \frac{y_2 - y_1}{x_2 - x_1}$$

POINT-SLOPE FORM OF A LINE

$$y - y_1 = m(x - x_1)$$

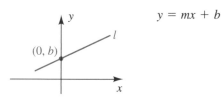

SLOPE-INTERCEPT FORM OF A LINE

$$y = mx + b$$

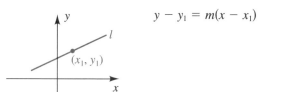

INTERCEPT FORM OF A LINE

$$\frac{x}{a} + \frac{y}{b} = 1 \quad (a \neq 0, b \neq 0)$$

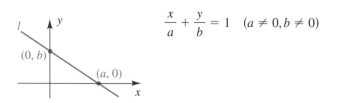

EQUATION OF A CIRCLE

$$(x - h)^2 + (y - k)^2 = r^2$$

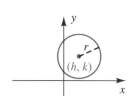

GRAPH OF A QUADRATIC FUNCTION

$$y = ax^2,\ a > 0 \qquad y = ax^2 + bx + c,\ a > 0$$

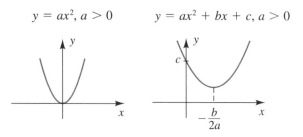

CONSTANTS

$\pi \approx 3.14159$

$e \approx 2.71828$

CONVERSIONS

1 centimeter $\approx$ 0.3937 inch

1 meter $\approx$ 3.2808 feet

1 kilometer $\approx$ 0.6214 mile

1 gram $\approx$ 0.0353 ounce

1 kilogram $\approx$ 2.2046 pounds

1 liter $\approx$ 0.2642 gallon

1 milliliter $\approx$ 0.0381 fluid ounce

1 joule $\approx$ 0.7376 foot-pound

1 newton $\approx$ 0.2248 pound

1 lumen $\approx$ 0.0015 watt

1 acre = 43,560 square feet

College Algebra

Custom Edition

Earl W. Swokowski | Jeffery A. Cole

CENGAGE
Learning™

Australia • Brazil • Japan • Korea • Mexico • Singapore • Spain • United Kingdom • United States

CENGAGE
Learning™

College Algebra

Custom Edition

Earl W. Swokowski | Jeffery A. Cole

Executive Editors:
Maureen Staudt
Michael Stranz

Project Development Manager:
Linda deStefano

Senior Marketing Coordinators:
Sara Mercurio

Senior Production / Manufacturing Manager:
Donna M. Brown

PreMedia Services Supervisor:
Joel Brennecke

Rights & Permissions Specialist:
Kalina Hintz
Todd Osborne

Cover Image:

Getty Images*

For product information and technology assistance, contact us at
Cengage Learning Customer & Sales Support, 1-800-354-9706

For permission to use material from this text or product,
submit all requests online at **cengage.com/permissions**
Further permissions questions can be emailed to
permissionrequest@cengage.com

ISBN-13: 978-1-4240-8427-2

ISBN-10: 1-4240-8427-X

Cengage Learning
5191 Natorp Boulevard
Mason, Ohio 45040
USA

Cengage Learning is a leading provider of customized learning solutions with office locations around the globe, including Singapore, the United Kingdom, Australia, Mexico, Brazil, and Japan. Locate your local office at:
international.cengage.com/region

Cengage Learning products are represented in Canada by Nelson Education, Ltd.

For your lifelong learning solutions, visit **custom.cengage.com**

Visit our corporate website at **cengage.com**

Printed in the United States of America

Brief Contents

Real numbers that are not rational are **irrational numbers.** Decimal representations for irrational numbers are always *nonterminating and nonrepeating.* One common irrational number, denoted by π, is the ratio of the circumference of a circle to its diameter. We sometimes use the notation $\pi \approx 3.1416$ to indicate that π **is approximately equal to** 3.1416.

There is no *rational* number b such that $b^2 = 2$, where b^2 denotes $b \cdot b$. However, there is an *irrational* number, denoted by $\sqrt{2}$ (the **square root** of 2), such that $\left(\sqrt{2}\right)^2 = 2$.

The system of **real numbers** consists of all rational and irrational numbers. Relationships among the types of numbers used in algebra are illustrated in the diagram in Figure 1, where a line connecting two rectangles means that the numbers named in the higher rectangle include those in the lower rectangle. The complex numbers, discussed in Section 2.4, contain all real numbers.

In technical writing, the use of the symbol $\doteq$ for is approximately equal to is convenient.

Figure 1   Types of numbers used in algebra

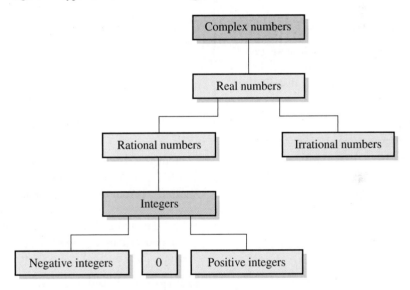

The real numbers are **closed relative to the operation of addition** (denoted by $+$); that is, to every pair a, b of real numbers there corresponds exactly one real number $a + b$ called the **sum** of a and b. The real numbers are also **closed relative to multiplication** (denoted by $\cdot$); that is, to every pair a, b of real numbers there corresponds exactly one real number $a \cdot b$ (also denoted by ab) called the **product** of a and b.

Important properties of addition and multiplication of real numbers are listed in the following chart.

Properties of Real Numbers

Terminology	General case	Meaning
(1) Addition is **commutative**.	$a + b = b + a$	Order is immaterial when adding two numbers.
(2) Addition is **associative**.	$a + (b + c) = (a + b) + c$	Grouping is immaterial when adding three numbers.
(3) 0 is the **additive identity**.	$a + 0 = a$	Adding 0 to any number yields the same number.
(4) $-a$ is the **additive inverse,** or **negative,** of a.	$a + (-a) = 0$	Adding a number and its negative yields 0.
(5) Multiplication is **commutative**.	$ab = ba$	Order is immaterial when multiplying two numbers.
(6) Multiplication is **associative**.	$a(bc) = (ab)c$	Grouping is immaterial when multiplying three numbers.
(7) 1 is the **multiplicative identity**.	$a \cdot 1 = a$	Multiplying any number by 1 yields the same number.
(8) If $a \neq 0$, $\dfrac{1}{a}$ is the **multiplicative inverse,** or **reciprocal,** of a.	$a\left(\dfrac{1}{a}\right) = 1$	Multiplying a nonzero number by its reciprocal yields 1.
(9) Multiplication is **distributive** over addition.	$a(b + c) = ab + ac$ and $(a + b)c = ac + bc$	Multiplying a number and a sum of two numbers is equivalent to multiplying each of the two numbers by the number and then adding the products.

Since $a + (b + c)$ and $(a + b) + c$ are always equal, we may use $a + b + c$ to denote this real number. We use abc for either $a(bc)$ or $(ab)c$. Similarly, if four or more real numbers a, b, c, d are added or multiplied, we may write $a + b + c + d$ for their sum and $abcd$ for their product, regardless of how the numbers are grouped or interchanged.

The distributive properties are useful for finding products of many types of expressions involving sums. The next example provides one illustration.

EXAMPLE 1 Using distributive properties

If p, q, r, and s denote real numbers, show that

$$(p + q)(r + s) = pr + ps + qr + qs.$$

SOLUTION We use both of the distributive properties listed in (9) of the preceding chart:

$$
\begin{aligned}
(p + q)(r + s) & \\
= p(r + s) + q(r + s) \quad & \text{second distributive property, with } c = r + s \\
= (pr + ps) + (qr + qs) \quad & \text{first distributive property} \\
= pr + ps + qr + qs \quad & \text{remove parentheses}
\end{aligned}
$$

The following are basic properties of equality.

Properties of Equality	If $a = b$ and c is any real number, then
	
	    (1) $a + c = b + c$
	    (2) $ac = bc$

Properties 1 and 2 state that the same number may be added to both sides of an equality, and both sides of an equality may be multiplied by the same number. We will use these properties extensively throughout the text to help find solutions of equations.

The next result can be proved.

Products Involving Zero	**(1)** $a \cdot 0 = 0$ for every real number a. **(2)** If $ab = 0$, then either $a = 0$ or $b = 0$.

When we use the word *or* as we do in (2), we mean that *at least* one of the factors a and b is 0. We will refer to (2) as the *zero factor theorem* in future work.

Some properties of negatives are listed in the following chart.

Properties of Negatives

Property	Illustration
(1) $-(-a) = a$	$-(-3) = 3$
(2) $(-a)b = -(ab) = a(-b)$	$(-2)3 = -(2 \cdot 3) = 2(-3)$
(3) $(-a)(-b) = ab$	$(-2)(-3) = 2 \cdot 3$
(4) $(-1)a = -a$	$(-1)3 = -3$

The reciprocal $\dfrac{1}{a}$ of a nonzero real number a is often denoted by a^{-1}, as in the next chart.

Notation for Reciprocals

Definition	Illustrations
If $a \neq 0$, then $a^{-1} = \dfrac{1}{a}$.	$2^{-1} = \dfrac{1}{2}$ $\left(\dfrac{3}{4}\right)^{-1} = \dfrac{1}{3/4} = \dfrac{4}{3}$

Note that if $a \neq 0$, then

$$a \cdot a^{-1} = a\left(\frac{1}{a}\right) = 1.$$

The operations of **subtraction** $(-)$ and **division** $(\div)$ are defined as follows.

Subtraction and Division

Definition	Meaning	Illustration
$a - b = a + (-b)$	To subtract one number from another, add the negative.	$3 - 7 = 3 + (-7)$
$a \div b = a \cdot \left(\dfrac{1}{b}\right)$ $= a \cdot b^{-1};\ b \neq 0$	To divide one number by a nonzero number, multiply by the reciprocal.	$3 \div 7 = 3 \cdot \left(\dfrac{1}{7}\right)$ $= 3 \cdot 7^{-1}$

We use either a/b or $\dfrac{a}{b}$ for $a \div b$ and refer to a/b as the **quotient of a and b** or the **fraction a over b.** The numbers a and b are the **numerator** and **denominator,** respectively, of a/b. Since 0 has no multiplicative inverse, a/b is not defined if $b = 0$; that is, *division by zero is not defined.* It is for this reason that the real numbers are not closed relative to division. Note that

$$1 \div b = \frac{1}{b} = b^{-1} \quad \text{if} \quad b \neq 0.$$

The following properties of quotients are true, provided all denominators are nonzero real numbers.

Properties of Quotients

Property	Illustration
(1) $\dfrac{a}{b} = \dfrac{c}{d}$ if $ad = bc$	$\dfrac{2}{5} = \dfrac{6}{15}$ because $2 \cdot 15 = 5 \cdot 6$
(2) $\dfrac{ad}{bd} = \dfrac{a}{b}$	$\dfrac{2 \cdot 3}{5 \cdot 3} = \dfrac{2}{5}$
(3) $\dfrac{a}{-b} = \dfrac{-a}{b} = -\dfrac{a}{b}$	$\dfrac{2}{-5} = \dfrac{-2}{5} = -\dfrac{2}{5}$
(4) $\dfrac{a}{b} + \dfrac{c}{b} = \dfrac{a+c}{b}$	$\dfrac{2}{5} + \dfrac{9}{5} = \dfrac{2+9}{5} = \dfrac{11}{5}$
(5) $\dfrac{a}{b} + \dfrac{c}{d} = \dfrac{ad+bc}{bd}$	$\dfrac{2}{5} + \dfrac{4}{3} = \dfrac{2 \cdot 3 + 5 \cdot 4}{5 \cdot 3} = \dfrac{26}{15}$
(6) $\dfrac{a}{b} \cdot \dfrac{c}{d} = \dfrac{ac}{bd}$	$\dfrac{2}{5} \cdot \dfrac{7}{3} = \dfrac{2 \cdot 7}{5 \cdot 3} = \dfrac{14}{15}$
(7) $\dfrac{a}{b} \div \dfrac{c}{d} = \dfrac{a}{b} \cdot \dfrac{d}{c} = \dfrac{ad}{bc}$	$\dfrac{2}{5} \div \dfrac{7}{3} = \dfrac{2}{5} \cdot \dfrac{3}{7} = \dfrac{6}{35}$

Real numbers may be represented by points on a line l such that to each real number a there corresponds exactly one point on l and to each point P on l there corresponds one real number. This is called a **one-to-one correspondence.** We first choose an arbitrary point O, called the **origin,** and associate with it the real number 0. Points associated with the integers are then determined by laying off successive line segments of equal length on either side of O, as illustrated in Figure 2. The point corresponding to a rational number, such as $\frac{23}{5}$, is obtained by subdividing these line segments. Points associated with certain irrational numbers, such as $\sqrt{2}$, can be found by construction (see Exercise 45).

Figure 2

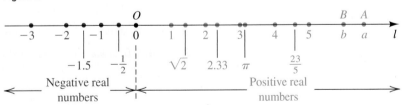

The number a that is associated with a point A on l is the **coordinate** of A. We refer to these coordinates as a **coordinate system** and call l a **coordinate line** or a **real line.** A direction can be assigned to l by taking the **positive direction** to the right and the **negative direction** to the left. The positive direction is noted by placing an arrowhead on l, as shown in Figure 2.

The numbers that correspond to points to the right of O in Figure 2 are **positive real numbers.** Numbers that correspond to points to the left of O are **negative real numbers.** *The real number 0 is neither positive nor negative.*

Note the difference between a negative real number and the *negative of* a real number. In particular, the negative of a real number a can be positive. For example, if a is negative, say $a = -3$, then the negative of a is $-a = -(-3) = 3$, which is positive. In general, we have the following relationships.

Relationships Between a and $-a$	(1) If a is positive, then $-a$ is negative.
	(2) If a is negative, then $-a$ is positive.

In the following chart we define the notions of **greater than** and **less than** for real numbers a and b. The symbols $>$ and $<$ are **inequality signs,** and the expressions $a > b$ and $a < b$ are called **(strict) inequalities.**

Greater Than or Less Than

Notation	Definition	Terminology
$a > b$	$a - b$ is positive	a is greater than b
$a < b$	$a - b$ is negative	a is less than b

If points A and B on a coordinate line have coordinates a and b, respectively, then $a > b$ is equivalent to the statement "A is to the *right* of B," whereas $a < b$ is equivalent to "A is to the *left* of B."

ILLUSTRATION   Greater Than (>) and Less Than (<)

- $5 > 3$, since $5 - 3 = 2$ is positive.
- $-6 < -2$, since $-6 - (-2) = -6 + 2 = -4$ is negative.
- $\frac{1}{3} > 0.33$, since $\frac{1}{3} - 0.33 = \frac{1}{3} - \frac{33}{100} = \frac{1}{300}$ is positive.
- $7 > 0$, since $7 - 0 = 7$ is positive.
- $-4 < 0$, since $-4 - 0 = -4$ is negative.

The next law enables us to compare, or *order*, any two real numbers.

Trichotomy Law	If a and b are real numbers, then exactly one of the following is true:
	$$a = b, \qquad a > b, \qquad \text{or} \qquad a < b$$

We refer to the **sign** of a real number as positive if the number is positive, or negative if the number is negative. Two real numbers have *the same sign* if both are positive or both are negative. The numbers have *opposite signs* if one is positive and the other is negative. The following results about the signs of products and quotients of two real numbers a and b can be proved using properties of negatives and quotients.

Laws of Signs	
	(1) If a and b have the same sign, then ab and $\dfrac{a}{b}$ are positive.
	(2) If a and b have opposite signs, then ab and $\dfrac{a}{b}$ are negative.

The **converses*** of the laws of signs are also true. For example, if a quotient is negative, then the numerator and denominator have opposite signs.

The notation $a \geq b$, read "a **is greater than or equal to** b," means that either $a > b$ or $a = b$ (but not both). For example, $a^2 \geq 0$ for every real number a. The symbol $a \leq b$, which is read "a **is less than or equal to** b," means that either $a < b$ or $a = b$. Expressions of the form $a \geq b$ and $a \leq b$ are called **nonstrict inequalities,** since a may be equal to b. As with the equality symbol, we may negate any inequality symbol by putting a slash through it—that is, $\not>$ means not greater than.

An expression of the form $a < b < c$ is called a **continued inequality** and means that both $a < b$ *and* $b < c$; we say "b **is between** a and c." Similarly, the expression $c > b > a$ means that both $c > b$ and $b > a$.

ILLUSTRATION **Ordering Three Real Numbers**

- $1 < 5 < \frac{11}{2}$
- $-4 < \frac{2}{3} < \sqrt{2}$
- $3 > -6 > -10$

There are other types of inequalities. For example, $a < b \leq c$ means both $a < b$ and $b \leq c$. Similarly, $a \leq b < c$ means both $a \leq b$ and $b < c$. Finally, $a \leq b \leq c$ means both $a \leq b$ and $b \leq c$.

EXAMPLE 2   Determining the sign of a real number

If $x > 0$ and $y < 0$, determine the sign of $\dfrac{x}{y} + \dfrac{y}{x}$.

SOLUTION   Since x is a positive number and y is a negative number, x and y have opposite signs. Thus, both x/y and y/x are negative. The sum of two negative numbers is a negative number, so

$$\text{the sign of} \quad \frac{x}{y} + \frac{y}{x} \quad \text{is negative.}$$

*If a theorem is written in the form "if P, then Q," where P and Q are mathematical statements called the *hypothesis* and *conclusion,* respectively, then the *converse* of the theorem has the form "if Q, then P." If both the theorem and its converse are true, we often write "P if and only if Q" (denoted P iff Q).

Figure 3

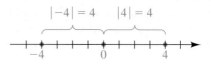

If a is an integer, then it is the coordinate of some point A on a coordinate line, and the symbol $|a|$ denotes the number of units between A and the origin, without regard to direction. The nonnegative number $|a|$ is called the *absolute value of a.* Referring to Figure 3, we see that for the point with coordinate -4 we have $|-4| = 4$. Similarly, $|4| = 4$. In general, *if a is negative, we change its sign to find* $|a|$; *if a is nonnegative, then* $|a| = a$. The next definition extends this concept to every real number.

Definition of Absolute Value	The **absolute value** of a real number a, denoted by $|a|$, is defined as follows.
	(1) If $a \geq 0$, then $|a| = a$.
	(2) If $a < 0$, then $|a| = -a$.

Since a is negative in part (2) of the definition, $-a$ represents a *positive* real number. Some special cases of this definition are given in the following illustration.

ILLUSTRATION   **The Absolute Value Notation** $|a|$

- ■ $|3| = 3$, since $3 > 0$.
- ■ $|-3| = -(-3)$, since $-3 < 0$. Thus, $|-3| = 3$.
- ■ $|2 - \sqrt{2}| = 2 - \sqrt{2}$, since $2 - \sqrt{2} > 0$.
- ■ $|\sqrt{2} - 2| = -(\sqrt{2} - 2)$, since $\sqrt{2} - 2 < 0$.
     Thus, $|\sqrt{2} - 2| = 2 - \sqrt{2}$.

In the preceding illustration, $|3| = |-3|$ and $|2 - \sqrt{2}| = |\sqrt{2} - 2|$. In general, we have the following:

$$|a| = |-a|, \text{ for every real number } a$$

EXAMPLE 3   Removing an absolute value symbol

If $x < 1$, rewrite $|x - 1|$ without using the absolute value symbol.

SOLUTION   If $x < 1$, then $x - 1 < 0$; that is, $x - 1$ is negative. Hence, by part (2) of the definition of absolute value,

$$|x - 1| = -(x - 1) = -x + 1 = 1 - x.$$

Figure 4

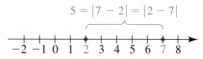

We shall use the concept of absolute value to define the distance between any two points on a coordinate line. First note that the distance between the points with coordinates 2 and 7, shown in Figure 4, equals 5 units. This distance is the difference obtained by subtracting the smaller (leftmost) coordinate from the larger (rightmost) coordinate ($7 - 2 = 5$). If we use absolute values, then, since $|7 - 2| = |2 - 7|$, it is unnecessary to be concerned about the order of subtraction. This fact motivates the next definition.

Definition of the Distance Between Points on a Coordinate Line	Let a and b be the coordinates of two points A and B, respectively, on a co-ordinate line. The **distance between A and B,** denoted by $d(A, B)$, is defined by $$d(A, B) = |b - a|.$$

The number $d(A, B)$ is the length of the line segment AB.

Since $d(B, A) = |a - b|$ and $|b - a| = |a - b|$, we see that

$$d(A, B) = d(B, A).$$

Note that the distance between the origin O and the point A is

$$d(O, A) = |a - 0| = |a|,$$

which agrees with the geometric interpretation of absolute value illustrated in Figure 4. The formula $d(A, B) = |b - a|$ is true regardless of the signs of a and b, as illustrated in the next example.

EXAMPLE 4   Finding distances between points

Figure 5

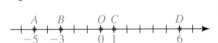

Let A, B, C, and D have coordinates -5, -3, 1, and 6, respectively, on a coordinate line, as shown in Figure 5. Find $d(A, B)$, $d(C, B)$, $d(O, A)$, and $d(C, D)$.

SOLUTION   Using the definition of the distance between points on a coordinate line, we obtain the distances:

$$d(A, B) = |-3 - (-5)| = |-3 + 5| = |2| = 2$$
$$d(C, B) = |-3 - 1| = |-4| = 4$$
$$d(O, A) = |-5 - 0| = |-5| = 5$$
$$d(C, D) = |6 - 1| = |5| = 5$$

The concept of absolute value has uses other than finding distances between points; it is employed whenever we are interested in the magnitude or numerical value of a real number without regard to its sign.

In the next section we shall discuss the *exponential notation a^n*, where a is a real number (called the *base*) and n is an integer (called an *exponent*). In particular, for base 10 we have

$$10^0 = 1, \quad 10^1 = 10, \quad 10^2 = 10 \cdot 10 = 100, \quad 10^3 = 10 \cdot 10 \cdot 10 = 1000,$$

and so on. For negative exponents we use the reciprocal of the corresponding positive exponent, as follows:

$$10^{-1} = \frac{1}{10^1} = \frac{1}{10}, \quad 10^{-2} = \frac{1}{10^2} = \frac{1}{100}, \quad 10^{-3} = \frac{1}{10^3} = \frac{1}{1000}$$

We can use this notation to write any finite decimal representation of a real number as a sum of the following type:

$$437.56 = 4(100) + 3(10) + 7(1) + 5\left(\tfrac{1}{10}\right) + 6\left(\tfrac{1}{100}\right)$$
$$= 4(10^2) + 3(10^1) + 7(10^0) + 5(10^{-1}) + 6(10^{-2})$$

In the sciences it is often necessary to work with very large or very small numbers and to compare the relative magnitudes of very large or very small quantities. We usually represent a large or small positive number a in *scientific form*, using the symbol $\times$ to denote multiplication.

Scientific Form	$a = c \times 10^n$, where $1 \le c < 10$ and n is an integer

The distance a ray of light travels in one year is approximately 5,900,000,000,000 miles. This number may be written in scientific form as 5.9×10^{12}. The positive exponent 12 indicates that the decimal point should be moved 12 places to the *right*. The notation works equally well for small numbers. The weight of an oxygen molecule is estimated to be

0.000 000 000 000 000 000 000 053 gram,

or, in scientific form, 5.3×10^{-23} gram. The negative exponent indicates that the decimal point should be moved 23 places to the *left*.

ILLUSTRATION Scientific Form

- $513 = 5.13 \times 10^2$
- $93,000,000 = 9.3 \times 10^7$
- $0.000\,000\,000\,43 = 4.3 \times 10^{-10}$

- $7.3 = 7.3 \times 10^0$
- $20,700 = 2.07 \times 10^4$
- $0.000\,648 = 6.48 \times 10^{-4}$

Figure 6

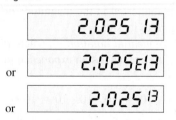

or

or

Many calculators use scientific form in their display panels. For the number $c \times 10^n$, the 10 is suppressed and the exponent is often shown preceded by the letter E. For example, to find $(4,500,000)^2$ on a scientific calculator, we could enter the integer 4,500,000 and press the $\boxed{x^2}$ (or squaring) key, obtaining a display similar to one of those in Figure 6. We would translate this as 2.025×10^{13}. Thus,

$$(4,500,000)^2 = 20,250,000,000,000.$$

Calculators may also use scientific form in the entry of numbers. The user's manual for your calculator should give specific details.

Before we conclude this section, we should briefly consider the issue of rounding off results. Applied problems often include numbers that are obtained by various types of measurements and, hence, are *approximations* to exact values. Such answers should be rounded off, since the final result of a calculation cannot be more accurate than the data that have been used. For example, if the length and width of a rectangle are measured to two-decimal-place accuracy, we cannot expect more than two-decimal-place accuracy in the calculated value of the area of the rectangle. For purely *mathematical* work, if values of the length and width of a rectangle are given, we assume that the dimensions are *exact,* and no rounding off is required.

If a number a is written in scientific form as $a = c \times 10^n$ for $1 \le c < 10$ and if c is rounded off to k decimal places, then we say that a is accurate (or has been rounded off) to $k + 1$ **significant figures,** or **digits.** For example, 37.2638 rounded to 5 significant figures is 3.7264×10^1, or 37.264; to 3 significant figures, 3.73×10^1, or 37.3; and to 1 significant figure, 4×10^1, or 40.

1.1 Exercises

Exer. 1–2: If $x < 0$ and $y > 0$, determine the sign of the real number.

1 (a) xy (b) x^2y (c) $\dfrac{x}{y} + x$ (d) $y - x$

2 (a) $\dfrac{x}{y}$ (b) xy^2 (c) $\dfrac{x - y}{xy}$ (d) $y(y - x)$

Exer. 3–6: Replace the symbol □ with either <, >, or = to make the resulting statement true.

3 ·(a) $-7 \,\square\, -4$ (b) $\dfrac{\pi}{2} \,\square\, 1.57$ (c) $\sqrt{225} \,\square\, 15$

4 (a) $-3 \,\square\, -5$ (b) $\dfrac{\pi}{4} \,\square\, 0.8$ (c) $\sqrt{289} \,\square\, 17$

5 (a) $\frac{1}{11} \,\square\, 0.09$ (b) $\frac{2}{3} \,\square\, 0.6666$ (c) $\frac{22}{7} \,\square\, \pi$

6 (a) $\frac{1}{7} \,\square\, 0.143$ (b) $\frac{5}{6} \,\square\, 0.833$ (c) $\sqrt{2} \,\square\, 1.4$

Exer. 7–8: Express the statement as an inequality.

7 (a) x is negative.

(b) y is nonnegative.

(c) q is less than or equal to π.

(d) d is between 4 and 2.

(e) t is not less than 5.

(f) The negative of z is not greater than 3.

(g) The quotient of p and q is at most 7.

(h) The reciprocal of w is at least 9.

(i) The absolute value of x is greater than 7.

8 (a) b is positive.

(b) s is nonpositive.

(c) w is greater than or equal to -4.

(d) c is between $\frac{1}{5}$ and $\frac{1}{3}$.

(e) p is not greater than -2.

(f) The negative of m is not less than -2.

(g) The quotient of r and s is at least $\frac{1}{5}$.

(h) The reciprocal of f is at most 14.

(i) The absolute value of x is less than 4.

Exer. 9–14: Rewrite the number without using the absolute value symbol, and simplify the result.

9 (a) $|-3 - 2|$ (b) $|-5| - |2|$ (c) $|7| + |-4|$

10 (a) $|-11 + 1|$ (b) $|6| - |-3|$ (c) $|8| + |-9|$

11 (a) $(-5)|3 - 6|$ (b) $|-6|/(-2)$ (c) $|-7| + |4|$

12 (a) $(4)|6 - 7|$ (b) $5/|-2|$ (c) $|-1| + |-9|$

13 (a) $|4 - \pi|$ (b) $|\pi - 4|$ (c) $|\sqrt{2} - 1.5|$

14 (a) $|\sqrt{3} - 1.7|$ (b) $|1.7 - \sqrt{3}|$ (c) $|\frac{1}{5} - \frac{1}{3}|$

Exer. 15–18: The given numbers are coordinates of points A, B, and C, respectively, on a coordinate line. Find the distance.

(a) $d(A, B)$ (b) $d(B, C)$

(c) $d(C, B)$ (d) $d(A, C)$

15 $3, 7, -5$ 16 $-6, -2, 4$

17 $-9, 1, 10$ 18 $8, -4, -1$

Exer. 19–24: The two given numbers are coordinates of points A and B, respectively, on a coordinate line. Express the indicated statement as an inequality involving the absolute value symbol.

19 x,   7; $d(A, B)$ is less than 5

20 x, $-\sqrt{2}$; $d(A, B)$ is greater than 1

21 x, -3; $d(A, B)$ is at least 8

22 x,   4; $d(A, B)$ is at most 2

23 4, x; $d(A, B)$ is not greater than 3

24 -2, x; $d(A, B)$ is not less than 2

Exer. 25–32: Rewrite the expression without using the absolute value symbol, and simplify the result.

25 $|3 + x|$ if $x < -3$ 26 $|5 - x|$ if $x > 5$

27 $|2 - x|$ if $x < 2$ 28 $|7 + x|$ if $x \geq -7$

29 $|a - b|$ if $a < b$ 30 $|a - b|$ if $a > b$

31 $|x^2 + 4|$ 32 $|-x^2 - 1|$

Exer. 33–40: Replace the symbol □ with either = or ≠ to make the resulting statement true for all real numbers a, b, c, and d, whenever the expressions are defined.

33 $\dfrac{ab + ac}{a} \ \square \ b + ac$ 34 $\dfrac{ab + ac}{a} \ \square \ b + c$

35 $\dfrac{b + c}{a} \ \square \ \dfrac{b}{a} + \dfrac{c}{a}$ 36 $\dfrac{a + c}{b + d} \ \square \ \dfrac{a}{b} + \dfrac{c}{d}$

37 $(a \div b) \div c \ \square \ a \div (b \div c)$

38 $(a - b) - c \ \square \ a - (b - c)$

39 $\dfrac{a - b}{b - a} \ \square \ -1$ 40 $-(a + b) \ \square \ -a + b$

Exer. 41–42: Approximate the real-number expression to four decimal places.

41 (a) $|3.2^2 - \sqrt{3.15}|$

    (b) $\sqrt{(15.6 - 1.5)^2 + (4.3 - 5.4)^2}$

42 (a) $\dfrac{3.42 - 1.29}{5.83 + 2.64}$

    (b) π^3

Exer. 43–44: Approximate the real-number expression. Express the answer in scientific notation accurate to four significant figures.

43 (a) $\dfrac{1.2 \times 10^3}{3.1 \times 10^2 + 1.52 \times 10^3}$

    (b) $(1.23 \times 10^{-4}) + \sqrt{4.5 \times 10^3}$

44 (a) $\sqrt{|3.45 - 1.2 \times 10^4| + 10^5}$

    (b) $(1.791 \times 10^2) \times (9.84 \times 10^3)$

45 The point on a coordinate line corresponding to $\sqrt{2}$ may be determined by constructing a right triangle with sides of length 1, as shown in the figure. Determine the points that correspond to $\sqrt{3}$ and $\sqrt{5}$, respectively. (*Hint:* Use the Pythagorean theorem.)

Exercise 45

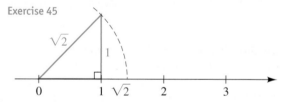

46 A circle of radius 1 rolls along a coordinate line in the positive direction, as shown in the figure. If point P is initially at the origin, find the coordinate of P after one, two, and ten complete revolutions.

Exercise 46

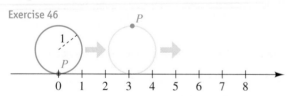

47 Geometric proofs of properties of real numbers were first given by the ancient Greeks. In order to establish the distributive property $a(b + c) = ab + ac$ for positive real numbers a, b, and c, find the area of the rectangle shown in the figure on the next page in two ways.

Exercise 47

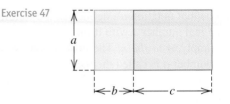

48 Rational approximations to square roots can be found using a formula discovered by the ancient Babylonians. Let x_1 be the first rational approximation for $\sqrt{n}$. If we let

$$x_2 = \frac{1}{2}\left(x_1 + \frac{n}{x_1}\right),$$

then x_2 will be a better approximation for $\sqrt{n}$, and we can repeat the computation with x_2 replacing x_1. Starting with $x_1 = \frac{3}{2}$, find the next two rational approximations for $\sqrt{2}$.

Exer. 49–50: Express the number in scientific form.

49 (a) 427,000   (b) 0.000 000 098   (c) 810,000,000

50 (a) 85,200   (b) 0.000 005 5   (c) 24,900,000

Exer. 51–52: Express the number in decimal form.

51 (a) 8.3×10^5 (b) 2.9×10^{-12} (c) 5.63×10^8

52 (a) 2.3×10^7 (b) 7.01×10^{-9} (c) 1.23×10^{10}

53 Mass of a hydrogen atom The mass of a hydrogen atom is approximately

0.000 000 000 000 000 000 000 001 7 gram.

Express this number in scientific form.

54 Mass of an electron The mass of an electron is approximately 9.1×10^{-31} kilogram. Express this number in decimal form.

55 Light year In astronomy, distances to stars are measured in light years. One light year is the distance a ray of light travels in one year. If the speed of light is approximately 186,000 miles per second, estimate the number of miles in one light year.

56 Milky Way galaxy

(a) Astronomers have estimated that the Milky Way galaxy contains 100 billion stars. Express this number in scientific form.

(b) The diameter d of the Milky Way galaxy is estimated as 100,000 light years. Express d in miles. (Refer to Exercise 55.)

57 Avogadro's number The number of hydrogen atoms in a mole is Avogadro's number, 6.02×10^{23}. If one mole of the gas has a mass of 1.01 grams, estimate the mass of a hydrogen atom.

58 Fish population The population dynamics of many fish are characterized by extremely high fertility rates among adults and very low survival rates among the young. A mature halibut may lay as many as 2.5 million eggs, but only 0.00035% of the offspring survive to the age of 3 years. Use scientific form to approximate the number of offspring that live to age 3.

59 Frames in a movie film One of the longest movies ever made is a 1970 British film that runs for 48 hours. Assuming that the film speed is 24 frames per second, approximate the total number of frames in this film. Express your answer in scientific form.

60 Large prime numbers The number $2^{44,497} - 1$ is prime. At the time that this number was determined to be prime, it took one of the world's fastest computers about 60 days to verify that it was prime. This computer was capable of performing 2×10^{11} calculations per second. Use scientific form to estimate the number of calculations needed to perform this computation. (More recently, in 2005, $2^{30,402,457} - 1$, a number containing 9,152,052 digits, was shown to be prime.)

61 Tornado pressure When a tornado passes near a building, there is a rapid drop in the outdoor pressure and the indoor pressure does not have time to change. The resulting difference is capable of causing an outward pressure of 1.4 lb/in² on the walls and ceiling of the building.

(a) Calculate the force in pounds exerted on 1 square foot of a wall.

(b) Estimate the tons of force exerted on a wall that is 8 feet high and 40 feet wide.

62 Cattle population A rancher has 750 head of cattle consisting of 400 adults (aged 2 or more years), 150 yearlings, and 200 calves. The following information is known about this particular species. Each spring an adult female gives birth to a single calf, and 75% of these calves will survive the first year. The yearly survival percentages for yearlings and adults are 80% and 90%, respectively. The male-female ratio is one in all age classes. Estimate the population of each age class

(a) next spring   (b) last spring

1.2

Exponents and Radicals

If n is a positive integer, the exponential notation a^n, defined in the following chart, represents the product of the real number a with itself n times. We refer to a^n as ***a* to the *n*th power** or, simply, *a to the n*. The positive integer n is called the **exponent,** and the real number a is called the **base.**

Exponential Notation

General case (n is any positive integer)	Special cases
$a^n = \underbrace{a \cdot a \cdot a \cdot \cdots \cdot a}_{n \text{ factors of } a}$	$a^1 = a$ $a^2 = a \cdot a$ $a^3 = a \cdot a \cdot a$ $a^6 = a \cdot a \cdot a \cdot a \cdot a \cdot a$

The next illustration contains several numerical examples of exponential notation.

ILLUSTRATION   **The Exponential Notation a^n**

- $5^4 = 5 \cdot 5 \cdot 5 \cdot 5 = 625$
- $\left(\frac{1}{2}\right)^5 = \frac{1}{2} \cdot \frac{1}{2} \cdot \frac{1}{2} \cdot \frac{1}{2} \cdot \frac{1}{2} = \frac{1}{32}$
- $(-3)^3 = (-3)(-3)(-3) = -27$
- $\left(-\frac{1}{3}\right)^4 = \left(-\frac{1}{3}\right)\left(-\frac{1}{3}\right)\left(-\frac{1}{3}\right)\left(-\frac{1}{3}\right) = \left(\frac{1}{9}\right)\left(\frac{1}{9}\right) = \frac{1}{81}$

It is important to note that if n is a positive integer, then an expression such as $3a^n$ means $3(a^n)$, *not* $(3a)^n$. The real number 3 is the **coefficient** of a^n in the expression $3a^n$. Similarly, $-3a^n$ means $(-3)a^n$, *not* $(-3a)^n$.

ILLUSTRATION   **The Notation ca^n**

- $5 \cdot 2^3 = 5 \cdot 8 = 40$
- $-5 \cdot 2^3 = -5 \cdot 8 = -40$
- $-2^4 = -(2^4) = -16$
- $3(-2)^3 = 3(-2)(-2)(-2) = 3(-8) = -24$

We next extend the definition of a^n to nonpositive exponents.

Zero and Negative (Nonpositive) Exponents

Definition ($a \neq 0$)	Illustrations
$a^0 = 1$	$3^0 = 1, \qquad \left(-\sqrt{2}\right)^0 = 1$
$a^{-n} = \dfrac{1}{a^n}$	$5^{-3} = \dfrac{1}{5^3}, \qquad (-3)^{-5} = \dfrac{1}{(-3)^5}$

If m and n are positive integers, then

$$a^m a^n = \underbrace{a \cdot a \cdot a \cdot \; \cdots \; \cdot a}_{m \text{ factors of } a} \cdot \underbrace{a \cdot a \cdot a \cdot \; \cdots \; \cdot a}_{n \text{ factors of } a}.$$

Since the total number of factors of a on the right is $m + n$, this expression is equal to a^{m+n}; that is,

$$a^m a^n = a^{m+n}.$$

We can extend this formula to $m \leq 0$ or $n \leq 0$ by using the definitions of the zero exponent and negative exponents. This gives us law 1, stated in the next chart.

To prove law 2, we may write, for m and n positive,

$$(a^m)^n = \underbrace{a^m \cdot a^m \cdot a^m \cdot \; \cdots \; \cdot a^m}_{n \text{ factors of } a^m}$$

and count the number of times a appears as a factor on the right-hand side. Since $a^m = a \cdot a \cdot a \cdot \; \cdots \; \cdot a$, with a occurring as a factor m times, and since the number of such groups of m factors is n, the total number of factors of a is $m \cdot n$. Thus,

$$(a^m)^n = a^{mn}.$$

The cases $m \leq 0$ and $n \leq 0$ can be proved using the definition of nonpositive exponents. The remaining three laws can be established in similar fashion by counting factors. In laws 4 and 5 we assume that denominators are not 0.

Laws of Exponents for Real Numbers a and b and Integers m and n

Law	Illustration
(1) $a^m a^n = a^{m+n}$	$2^3 \cdot 2^4 = 2^{3+4} = 2^7 = 128$
(2) $(a^m)^n = a^{mn}$	$(2^3)^4 = 2^{3 \cdot 4} = 2^{12} = 4096$
(3) $(ab)^n = a^n b^n$	$(20)^3 = (2 \cdot 10)^3 = 2^3 \cdot 10^3 = 8 \cdot 1000 = 8000$
(4) $\left(\dfrac{a}{b}\right)^n = \dfrac{a^n}{b^n}$	$\left(\dfrac{2}{5}\right)^3 = \dfrac{2^3}{5^3} = \dfrac{8}{125}$
(5) (a) $\dfrac{a^m}{a^n} = a^{m-n}$	$\dfrac{2^5}{2^3} = 2^{5-3} = 2^2 = 4$
(b) $\dfrac{a^m}{a^n} = \dfrac{1}{a^{n-m}}$	$\dfrac{2^3}{2^5} = \dfrac{1}{2^{5-3}} = \dfrac{1}{2^2} = \dfrac{1}{4}$

We usually use 5(a) if $m > n$ and 5(b) if $m < n$.

We can extend laws of exponents to obtain rules such as $(abc)^n = a^n b^n c^n$ and $a^m a^n a^p = a^{m+n+p}$. Some other examples of the laws of exponents are given in the next illustration.

ILLUSTRATION   **Laws of Exponents**

■ $x^5 x^6 x^2 = x^{5+6+2} = x^{13}$ ■ $(y^5)^7 = y^{5 \cdot 7} = y^{35}$

■ $(3st)^4 = 3^4 s^4 t^4 = 81 s^4 t^4$ ■ $\left(\dfrac{p}{2}\right)^5 = \dfrac{p^5}{2^5} = \dfrac{p^5}{32}$

■ $\dfrac{c^8}{c^3} = c^{8-3} = c^5$ ■ $\dfrac{u^3}{u^8} = \dfrac{1}{u^{8-3}} = \dfrac{1}{u^5}$

To **simplify** an expression involving powers of real numbers means to change it to an expression in which each real number appears only once and all exponents are positive. *We shall assume that denominators always represent nonzero real numbers.*

EXAMPLE 1   **Simplifying expressions containing exponents**

Use laws of exponents to simplify each expression:

(a) $(3x^3 y^4)(4xy^5)$ (b) $(2a^2 b^3 c)^4$ (c) $\left(\dfrac{2r^3}{s}\right)^2 \left(\dfrac{s}{r^3}\right)^3$ (d) $(u^{-2} v^3)^{-3}$

SOLUTION

(a) $(3x^3 y^4)(4xy^5) = (3)(4)x^3 x y^4 y^5$ rearrange factors

$\qquad = 12x^4 y^9$ law 1

(b) $\quad (2a^2 b^3 c)^4 = 2^4 (a^2)^4 (b^3)^4 c^4$ law 3

$\qquad = 16 a^8 b^{12} c^4$ law 2

(c) $\left(\dfrac{2r^3}{s}\right)^2 \left(\dfrac{s}{r^3}\right)^3 = \dfrac{(2r^3)^2}{s^2} \cdot \dfrac{s^3}{(r^3)^3}$ law 4

$\qquad = \dfrac{2^2 (r^3)^2}{s^2} \cdot \dfrac{s^3}{(r^3)^3}$ law 3

$\qquad = \left(\dfrac{4r^6}{s^2}\right)\left(\dfrac{s^3}{r^9}\right)$ law 2

$\qquad = 4\left(\dfrac{r^6}{r^9}\right)\left(\dfrac{s^3}{s^2}\right)$ rearrange factors

$\qquad = 4\left(\dfrac{1}{r^3}\right)(s)$ laws 5(b) and 5(a)

$\qquad = \dfrac{4s}{r^3}$ rearrange factors

(d) $\quad (u^{-2} v^3)^{-3} = (u^{-2})^{-3}(v^3)^{-3}$ law 3

$\qquad = u^6 v^{-9}$ law 2

$\qquad = \dfrac{u^6}{v^9}$ definition of a^{-n}

The following theorem is useful for problems that involve negative exponents.

Theorem on Negative Exponents	**(1)** $\dfrac{a^{-m}}{b^{-n}} = \dfrac{b^n}{a^m}$ **(2)** $\left(\dfrac{a}{b}\right)^{-n} = \left(\dfrac{b}{a}\right)^n$

PROOFS   Using properties of negative exponents and quotients, we obtain

(1) $\dfrac{a^{-m}}{b^{-n}} = \dfrac{1/a^m}{1/b^n} = \dfrac{1}{a^m} \cdot \dfrac{b^n}{1} = \dfrac{b^n}{a^m}$

(2) $\left(\dfrac{a}{b}\right)^{-n} = \dfrac{a^{-n}}{b^{-n}} = \dfrac{b^n}{a^n} = \left(\dfrac{b}{a}\right)^n$

EXAMPLE 2   Simplifying expressions containing negative exponents

Simplify:

(a) $\dfrac{8x^3 y^{-5}}{4x^{-1} y^2}$ **(b)** $\left(\dfrac{u^2}{2v}\right)^{-3}$

SOLUTION   We apply the theorem on negative exponents and the laws of exponents.

(a) $\dfrac{8x^3 y^{-5}}{4x^{-1} y^2} = \dfrac{8x^3}{4y^2} \cdot \dfrac{y^{-5}}{x^{-1}}$ rearrange quotients so that negative exponents are in one fraction

$= \dfrac{8x^3}{4y^2} \cdot \dfrac{x^1}{y^5}$ theorem on negative exponents (1)

$= \dfrac{2x^4}{y^7}$ law 1 of exponents

(b) $\left(\dfrac{u^2}{2v}\right)^{-3} = \left(\dfrac{2v}{u^2}\right)^3$ theorem on negative exponents (2)

$= \dfrac{2^3 v^3}{(u^2)^3}$ laws 4 and 3 of exponents

$= \dfrac{8v^3}{u^6}$ law 2 of exponents

We next define the **principal nth root** $\sqrt[n]{a}$ of a real number a.

Definition of $\sqrt[n]{a}$	Let n be a positive integer greater than 1, and let a be a real number.
	(1) If $a = 0$, then $\sqrt[n]{a} = 0$.
	(2) If $a > 0$, then $\sqrt[n]{a}$ is the *positive* real number b such that $b^n = a$.
	(3) (a) If $a < 0$ and n is odd, then $\sqrt[n]{a}$ is the *negative* real number b such that $b^n = a$.
	(b) If $a < 0$ and n is even, then $\sqrt[n]{a}$ is not a real number.

Complex numbers, discussed in Section 2.4, are needed to define $\sqrt[n]{a}$ if $a < 0$ and n is an *even* positive integer, because for all real numbers b, $b^n \geq 0$ whenever n is even.

If $n = 2$, we write $\sqrt{a}$ instead of $\sqrt[2]{a}$ and call $\sqrt{a}$ the **principal square root** of a or, simply, the **square root** of a. The number $\sqrt[3]{a}$ is the (principal) **cube root** of a.

ILLUSTRATION   **The Principal nth Root $\sqrt[n]{a}$**

-    $\sqrt{16} = 4$, since $4^2 = 16$.
-    $\sqrt[5]{\frac{1}{32}} = \frac{1}{2}$, since $\left(\frac{1}{2}\right)^5 = \frac{1}{32}$.
-    $\sqrt[3]{-8} = -2$, since $(-2)^3 = -8$.
-    $\sqrt[4]{-16}$ is not a real number.

Note that $\sqrt{16} \neq \pm 4$, since, by definition, roots of positive real numbers are positive. The symbol $\pm$ is read "plus or minus."

To complete our terminology, the expression $\sqrt[n]{a}$ is a **radical,** the number a is the **radicand,** and n is the **index** of the radical. The symbol $\sqrt{}$ is called a **radical sign.**

If $\sqrt{a} = b$, then $b^2 = a$; that is, $\left(\sqrt{a}\right)^2 = a$. If $\sqrt[3]{a} = b$, then $b^3 = a$, or $\left(\sqrt[3]{a}\right)^3 = a$. Generalizing this pattern gives us property 1 in the next chart.

Properties of $\sqrt[n]{a}$ (n is a positive integer)

Property	Illustrations	
(1) $\left(\sqrt[n]{a}\right)^n = a$ if $\sqrt[n]{a}$ is a real number	$\left(\sqrt{5}\right)^2 = 5,$	$\left(\sqrt[3]{-8}\right)^3 = -8$
(2) $\sqrt[n]{a^n} = a$ if $a \geq 0$	$\sqrt{5^2} = 5,$	$\sqrt[3]{2^3} = 2$
(3) $\sqrt[n]{a^n} = a$ if $a < 0$ and n is odd	$\sqrt[3]{(-2)^3} = -2,$	$\sqrt[5]{(-2)^5} = -2$
(4) $\sqrt[n]{a^n} = |a|$ if $a < 0$ and n is even	$\sqrt{(-3)^2} = |-3| = 3,$	$\sqrt[4]{(-2)^4} = |-2| = 2$

If $a \geq 0$, then property 4 reduces to property 2. We also see from property 4 that

$$\sqrt{x^2} = |x|$$

for every real number x. In particular, if $x \geq 0$, then $\sqrt{x^2} = x$; however, if $x < 0$, then $\sqrt{x^2} = -x$, which is positive.

The three laws listed in the next chart are true for positive integers m and n, *provided the indicated roots **exist***—that is, provided the roots are real numbers.

Laws of Radicals

Law	Illustrations
(1) $\sqrt[n]{ab} = \sqrt[n]{a}\,\sqrt[n]{b}$	$\sqrt{50} = \sqrt{25 \cdot 2} = \sqrt{25}\,\sqrt{2} = 5\sqrt{2}$
	$\sqrt[3]{-108} = \sqrt[3]{(-27)(4)} = \sqrt[3]{-27}\,\sqrt[3]{4} = -3\sqrt[3]{4}$
(2) $\sqrt[n]{\dfrac{a}{b}} = \dfrac{\sqrt[n]{a}}{\sqrt[n]{b}}$	$\sqrt[3]{\dfrac{5}{8}} = \dfrac{\sqrt[3]{5}}{\sqrt[3]{8}} = \dfrac{\sqrt[3]{5}}{2}$
(3) $\sqrt[m]{\sqrt[n]{a}} = \sqrt[mn]{a}$	$\sqrt{\sqrt[3]{64}} = \sqrt[2(3)]{64} = \sqrt[6]{2^6} = 2$

The radicands in laws 1 and 2 involve products and quotients. Care must be taken if sums or differences occur in the radicand. The following chart contains two particular warnings concerning commonly made mistakes.

◥ Warning! ◣

If $a \neq 0$ and $b \neq 0$	Illustration
(1) $\sqrt{a^2 + b^2} \neq a + b$	$\sqrt{3^2 + 4^2} = \sqrt{25} = 5 \neq 3 + 4 = 7$
(2) $\sqrt{a + b} \neq \sqrt{a} + \sqrt{b}$	$\sqrt{4 + 9} = \sqrt{13} \neq \sqrt{4} + \sqrt{9} = 5$

If c is a real number and c^n occurs as a factor in a radical of index n, then we can remove c from the radicand if the sign of c is taken into account. For example, if $c > 0$ or if $c < 0$ and n is *odd*, then

$$\sqrt[n]{c^n d} = \sqrt[n]{c^n}\,\sqrt[n]{d} = c\sqrt[n]{d},$$

provided $\sqrt[n]{d}$ exists. If $c < 0$ and n is *even,* then

$$\sqrt[n]{c^n d} = \sqrt[n]{c^n}\,\sqrt[n]{d} = |c|\sqrt[n]{d},$$

provided $\sqrt[n]{d}$ exists.

ILLUSTRATION   Removing nth Powers from $\sqrt[n]{}$

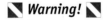

- $\sqrt[5]{x^7} = \sqrt[5]{x^5 \cdot x^2} = \sqrt[5]{x^5}\,\sqrt[5]{x^2} = x\sqrt[5]{x^2}$
- $\sqrt[3]{x^7} = \sqrt[3]{x^6 \cdot x} = \sqrt[3]{(x^2)^3 x} = \sqrt[3]{(x^2)^3}\,\sqrt[3]{x} = x^2\sqrt[3]{x}$
- $\sqrt{x^2 y} = \sqrt{x^2}\,\sqrt{y} = |x|\sqrt{y}$
- $\sqrt{x^6} = \sqrt{(x^3)^2} = |x^3|$
- $\sqrt[4]{x^6 y^3} = \sqrt[4]{x^4 \cdot x^2 y^3} = \sqrt[4]{x^4}\,\sqrt[4]{x^2 y^3} = |x|\sqrt[4]{x^2 y^3}$

Note: To avoid considering absolute values, *in examples and exercises involving radicals in this chapter, we shall assume that all letters—a, b, c, d, x, y,* *and so on—that appear in radicands represent positive real numbers, unless otherwise specified.*

As shown in the preceding illustration and in the following examples, if the index of a radical is n, then we rearrange the radicand, isolating a factor of the form p^n, where p may consist of several letters. We then remove $\sqrt[n]{p^n} = p$ from the radical, as previously indicated. Thus, in Example 3(b) the index of the radical is 3 and we rearrange the radicand into *cubes*, obtaining a factor p^3, with $p = 2xy^2z$. In part (c) the index of the radical is 2 and we rearrange the radicand into *squares*, obtaining a factor p^2, with $p = 3a^3b^2$.

To *simplify a radical* means to remove factors from the radical until no factor in the radicand has an exponent greater than or equal to the index of the radical and the index is as low as possible.

EXAMPLE 3   Removing factors from radicals

Simplify each radical (all letters denote positive real numbers):

(a) $\sqrt[3]{320}$ (b) $\sqrt[3]{16x^3y^8z^4}$ (c) $\sqrt{3a^2b^3}\sqrt{6a^5b}$

SOLUTION

(a) $\sqrt[3]{320} = \sqrt[3]{64 \cdot 5}$ factor out the largest cube in 320

$\qquad = \sqrt[3]{4^3}\,\sqrt[3]{5}$ law 1 of radicals

$\qquad = 4\sqrt[3]{5}$ property 2 of $\sqrt[n]{\ }$

(b) $\sqrt[3]{16x^3y^8z^4} = \sqrt[3]{(2^3x^3y^6z^3)(2y^2z)}$ rearrange radicand into cubes

$\qquad = \sqrt[3]{(2xy^2z)^3(2y^2z)}$ laws 2 and 3 of exponents

$\qquad = \sqrt[3]{(2xy^2z)^3}\,\sqrt[3]{2y^2z}$ law 1 of radicals

$\qquad = 2xy^2z\,\sqrt[3]{2y^2z}$ property 2 of $\sqrt[n]{\ }$

(c) $\sqrt{3a^2b^3}\sqrt{6a^5b} = \sqrt{3a^2b^3 \cdot 2 \cdot 3a^5b}$ law 1 of radicals

$\qquad = \sqrt{(3^2a^6b^4)(2a)}$ rearrange radicand into squares

$\qquad = \sqrt{(3a^3b^2)^2(2a)}$ laws 2 and 3 of exponents

$\qquad = \sqrt{(3a^3b^2)^2}\,\sqrt{2a}$ law 1 of radicals

$\qquad = 3a^3b^2\sqrt{2a}$ property 2 of $\sqrt[n]{\ }$

If the denominator of a quotient contains a factor of the form $\sqrt[n]{a^k}$, with $k < n$ and $a > 0$, then multiplying the numerator and denominator by $\sqrt[n]{a^{n-k}}$ will eliminate the radical from the denominator, since

$$\sqrt[n]{a^k}\,\sqrt[n]{a^{n-k}} = \sqrt[n]{a^{k+n-k}} = \sqrt[n]{a^n} = a.$$

This process is called **rationalizing a denominator.** Some special cases are listed in the following chart.

Rationalizing Denominators of Quotients ($a > 0$)

Factor in denominator	Multiply numerator and denominator by	Resulting factor
$\sqrt{a}$	$\sqrt{a}$	$\sqrt{a}\,\sqrt{a} = \sqrt{a^2} = a$
$\sqrt[3]{a}$	$\sqrt[3]{a^2}$	$\sqrt[3]{a}\,\sqrt[3]{a^2} = \sqrt[3]{a^3} = a$
$\sqrt[7]{a^3}$	$\sqrt[7]{a^4}$	$\sqrt[7]{a^3}\,\sqrt[7]{a^4} = \sqrt[7]{a^7} = a$

The next example illustrates this technique.

EXAMPLE 4   Rationalizing denominators

Rationalize each denominator:

(a) $\dfrac{1}{\sqrt{5}}$ (b) $\dfrac{1}{\sqrt[3]{x}}$ (c) $\sqrt{\dfrac{2}{3}}$ (d) $\sqrt[5]{\dfrac{x}{y^2}}$

SOLUTION

(a) $\dfrac{1}{\sqrt{5}} = \dfrac{1}{\sqrt{5}}\dfrac{\sqrt{5}}{\sqrt{5}} = \dfrac{\sqrt{5}}{\sqrt{5^2}} = \dfrac{\sqrt{5}}{5}$

(b) $\dfrac{1}{\sqrt[3]{x}} = \dfrac{1}{\sqrt[3]{x}}\dfrac{\sqrt[3]{x^2}}{\sqrt[3]{x^2}} = \dfrac{\sqrt[3]{x^2}}{\sqrt[3]{x^3}} = \dfrac{\sqrt[3]{x^2}}{x}$

(c) $\sqrt{\dfrac{2}{3}} = \dfrac{\sqrt{2}}{\sqrt{3}} = \dfrac{\sqrt{2}}{\sqrt{3}}\dfrac{\sqrt{3}}{\sqrt{3}} = \dfrac{\sqrt{2 \cdot 3}}{\sqrt{3^2}} = \dfrac{\sqrt{6}}{3}$

(d) $\sqrt[5]{\dfrac{x}{y^2}} = \dfrac{\sqrt[5]{x}}{\sqrt[5]{y^2}} = \dfrac{\sqrt[5]{x}}{\sqrt[5]{y^2}}\dfrac{\sqrt[5]{y^3}}{\sqrt[5]{y^3}} = \dfrac{\sqrt[5]{xy^3}}{\sqrt[5]{y^5}} = \dfrac{\sqrt[5]{xy^3}}{y}$

If we use a calculator to find decimal approximations of radicals, there is no advantage in rationalizing denominators, such as $1/\sqrt{5} = \sqrt{5}/5$ or $\sqrt{2/3} = \sqrt{6}/3$, as we did in Example 4(a) and (c). However, for *algebraic* simplifications, changing expressions to such forms is sometimes desirable. Similarly, in advanced mathematics courses such as calculus, changing $1/\sqrt[3]{x}$ to $\sqrt[3]{x^2}/x$, as in Example 4(b), could make a problem *more* complicated. In such courses it is simpler to work with the expression $1/\sqrt[3]{x}$ than with its rationalized form.

We next use radicals to define *rational exponents*.

Definition of Rational Exponents	Let m/n be a rational number, where n is a positive integer greater than 1. If a is a real number such that $\sqrt[n]{a}$ exists, then **(1)** $a^{1/n} = \sqrt[n]{a}$ **(2)** $a^{m/n} = \left(\sqrt[n]{a}\right)^m = \sqrt[n]{a^m}$ **(3)** $a^{m/n} = (a^{1/n})^m = (a^m)^{1/n}$

When evaluating $a^{m/n}$ in (2), we usually use $\left(\sqrt[n]{a}\right)^{m}$; that is, we take the nth root of a first and then raise that result to the mth power, as shown in the following illustration.

ILLUSTRATION **The Exponential Notation $a^{m/n}$**

- $x^{1/3} = \sqrt[3]{x}$ ▪ $x^{3/5} = \left(\sqrt[5]{x}\right)^{3} = \sqrt[5]{x^{3}}$
- $125^{2/3} = \left(\sqrt[3]{125}\right)^{2} = \left(\sqrt[3]{5^{3}}\right)^{2} = 5^{2} = 25$
- $\left(\frac{32}{243}\right)^{3/5} = \left(\sqrt[5]{\frac{32}{243}}\right)^{3} = \left(\sqrt[5]{\left(\frac{2}{3}\right)^{5}}\right)^{3} = \left(\frac{2}{3}\right)^{3} = \frac{8}{27}$

The laws of exponents are true for rational exponents and also for *irrational* exponents, such as $3^{\sqrt{2}}$ or 5^{π}, considered in Chapter 5.

To simplify an expression involving rational powers of letters that represent real numbers, we change it to an expression in which each letter appears only once and all exponents are positive. As we did with radicals, we shall assume that all letters represent positive real numbers unless otherwise specified.

EXAMPLE 5 Simplifying rational powers

Simplify:

(a) $(-27)^{2/3}(4)^{-5/2}$ (b) $(r^{2}s^{6})^{1/3}$ (c) $\left(\dfrac{2x^{2/3}}{y^{1/2}}\right)^{2}\left(\dfrac{3x^{-5/6}}{y^{1/3}}\right)$

SOLUTION

(a) $(-27)^{2/3}(4)^{-5/2} = \left(\sqrt[3]{-27}\right)^{2}\left(\sqrt{4}\right)^{-5}$ definition of rational exponents

$= (-3)^{2}(2)^{-5}$ take roots

$= \dfrac{(-3)^{2}}{2^{5}}$ definition of negative exponents

$= \dfrac{9}{32}$ take powers

(b) $(r^{2}s^{6})^{1/3} = (r^{2})^{1/3}(s^{6})^{1/3}$ law 3 of exponents

$= r^{2/3}s^{2}$ law 2 of exponents

(c) $\left(\dfrac{2x^{2/3}}{y^{1/2}}\right)^{2}\left(\dfrac{3x^{-5/6}}{y^{1/3}}\right) = \left(\dfrac{4x^{4/3}}{y}\right)\left(\dfrac{3x^{-5/6}}{y^{1/3}}\right)$ laws of exponents

$= \dfrac{(4 \cdot 3)x^{4/3-5/6}}{y^{1+(1/3)}}$ law 1 of exponents

$= \dfrac{12x^{8/6-5/6}}{y^{4/3}}$ common denominator

$= \dfrac{12x^{1/2}}{y^{4/3}}$ simplify

Rational exponents are useful for problems involving radicals that do not have the same index, as illustrated in the next example.

EXAMPLE 6   Combining radicals

Change to an expression containing one radical of the form $\sqrt[n]{a^m}$:

(a) $\sqrt[3]{a}\sqrt{a}$ (b) $\dfrac{\sqrt[4]{a}}{\sqrt[3]{a^2}}$

SOLUTION   Introducing rational exponents, we obtain

(a) $\sqrt[3]{a}\sqrt{a} = a^{1/3}a^{1/2} = a^{(1/3)+(1/2)} = a^{5/6} = \sqrt[6]{a^5}$

(b) $\dfrac{\sqrt[4]{a}}{\sqrt[3]{a^2}} = \dfrac{a^{1/4}}{a^{2/3}} = a^{(1/4)-(2/3)} = a^{-5/12} = \dfrac{1}{a^{5/12}} = \dfrac{1}{\sqrt[12]{a^5}}$

In Exercises 1.2, whenever an index of a radical is even (or a rational exponent m/n with n even is employed), assume that the letters that appear in the radicand denote positive real numbers unless otherwise specified.

1.2   *Exercises*

Exer. 1–10: Express the number in the form a/b, where a and b are integers.

1 $\left(-\frac{2}{3}\right)^4$ 2 $(-3)^3$

3 $\dfrac{2^{-3}}{3^{-2}}$ 4 $\dfrac{2^0 + 0^2}{2 + 0}$

5 $-2^4 + 3^{-1}$ 6 $\left(-\frac{3}{2}\right)^4 - 2^{-4}$

7 $16^{-3/4}$ 8 $9^{5/2}$

9 $(-0.008)^{2/3}$ 10 $(0.008)^{-2/3}$

Exer. 11–46: Simplify.

11 $\left(\frac{1}{2}x^4\right)(16x^5)$ 12 $(-3x^{-2})(4x^4)$

13 $\dfrac{(2x^3)(3x^2)}{(x^2)^3}$ 14 $\dfrac{(2x^2)^3}{4x^4}$

15 $\left(\frac{1}{6}a^5\right)(-3a^2)(4a^7)$ 16 $(-4b^3)\left(\frac{1}{6}b^2\right)(-9b^4)$

17 $\dfrac{(6x^3)^2}{(2x^2)^3}\cdot(3x^2)^0$ 18 $\dfrac{(3y^3)(2y^2)^2}{(y^4)^3}\cdot(y^3)^0$

19 $(3u^7v^3)(4u^4v^{-5})$ 20 $(x^2yz^3)(-2xz^2)(x^3y^{-2})$

21 $(8x^4y^{-3})\left(\frac{1}{2}x^{-5}y^2\right)$ 22 $\left(\dfrac{4a^2b}{a^3b^2}\right)\left(\dfrac{5a^2b}{2b^4}\right)$

23 $\left(\frac{1}{3}x^4y^{-3}\right)^{-2}$ 24 $(-2xy^2)^5\left(\dfrac{x^7}{8y^3}\right)$

25 $(3y^3)^4(4y^2)^{-3}$ 26 $(-3a^2b^{-5})^3$

27 $(-2r^4s^{-3})^{-2}$ 28 $(2x^2y^{-5})(6x^{-3}y)\left(\frac{1}{3}x^{-1}y^3\right)$

29 $(5x^2y^{-3})(4x^{-5}y^4)$ 30 $(-2r^2s)^5(3r^{-1}s^3)^2$

31 $\left(\dfrac{3x^5y^4}{x^0y^{-3}}\right)^2$ 32 $(4a^2b)^4\left(\dfrac{-a^3}{2b}\right)^2$

33 $(4a^{3/2})(2a^{1/2})$ 34 $(-6x^{7/5})(2x^{8/5})$

35 $(3x^{5/6})(8x^{2/3})$ 36 $(8r)^{1/3}(2r^{1/2})$

37 $(27a^6)^{-2/3}$ 38 $(25z^4)^{-3/2}$

39 $(8x^{-2/3})x^{1/6}$ 40 $(3x^{1/2})(-2x^{5/2})$

41 $\left(\dfrac{-8x^3}{y^{-6}}\right)^{2/3}$ 42 $\left(\dfrac{-y^{3/2}}{y^{-1/3}}\right)^3$

43 $\left(\dfrac{x^6}{9y^{-4}}\right)^{-1/2}$ 44 $\left(\dfrac{c^{-4}}{16d^8}\right)^{3/4}$

45 $\dfrac{(x^6y^3)^{-1/3}}{(x^4y^2)^{-1/2}}$ 46 $a^{4/3}a^{-3/2}a^{1/6}$

Exer. 47–52: Rewrite the expression using rational exponents.

47 $\sqrt[4]{x^3}$ 48 $\sqrt[3]{x^5}$

49 $\sqrt[3]{(a+b)^2}$ 50 $\sqrt{a} + \sqrt{b}$

51 $\sqrt{x^2 + y^2}$ 52 $\sqrt[3]{r^3 - s^3}$

Exer. 53–56: Rewrite the expression using a radical.

53 (a) $4x^{3/2}$ (b) $(4x)^{3/2}$

54 (a) $4 + x^{3/2}$ (b) $(4 + x)^{3/2}$

55 (a) $8 - y^{1/3}$ (b) $(8 - y)^{1/3}$

56 (a) $8y^{1/3}$ (b) $(8y)^{1/3}$

Exer. 57–80: Simplify the expression, and rationalize the denominator when appropriate.

57 $\sqrt{81}$ 58 $\sqrt[3]{-125}$

59 $\sqrt[3]{-64}$ 60 $\sqrt[4]{256}$

61 $\dfrac{1}{\sqrt[3]{2}}$ 62 $\sqrt{\dfrac{1}{7}}$

63 $\sqrt{9x^{-4}y^6}$ 64 $\sqrt{16a^8b^{-2}}$

65 $\sqrt[3]{8a^6b^{-3}}$ 66 $\sqrt[4]{81r^5s^8}$

67 $\sqrt{\dfrac{3x}{2y^3}}$ 68 $\sqrt{\dfrac{1}{3x^3y}}$

69 $\sqrt[3]{\dfrac{2x^4y^4}{9x}}$ 70 $\sqrt[3]{\dfrac{3x^2y^5}{4x}}$

71 $\sqrt[4]{\dfrac{5x^8y^3}{27x^2}}$ 72 $\sqrt[4]{\dfrac{x^7y^{12}}{125x}}$

73 $\sqrt[5]{\dfrac{5x^7y^2}{8x^3}}$ 74 $\sqrt[5]{\dfrac{3x^{11}y^3}{9x^2}}$

75 $\sqrt[4]{(3x^5y^{-2})^4}$ 76 $\sqrt[6]{(2u^{-3}v^4)^6}$

77 $\sqrt[5]{\dfrac{8x^3}{y^4}}\ \sqrt[5]{\dfrac{4x^4}{y^2}}$ 78 $\sqrt{5xy^7}\ \sqrt{10x^3y^3}$

79 $\sqrt[3]{3t^4v^2}\ \sqrt[3]{-9t^{-1}v^4}$ 80 $\sqrt[3]{(2r - s)^3}$

Exer. 81–84: Simplify the expression, assuming x and y may be negative.

81 $\sqrt{x^6y^4}$ 82 $\sqrt{x^4y^{10}}$

83 $\sqrt[4]{x^8(y - 1)^{12}}$ 84 $\sqrt[4]{(x + 2)^{12}y^4}$

Exer. 85–90: Replace the symbol $\square$ with either $=$ or $\neq$ to make the resulting statement true, whenever the expression has meaning. Give a reason for your answer.

85 $(a^r)^2 \ \square \ a^{(r^2)}$ 86 $(a^2 + 1)^{1/2} \ \square \ a + 1$

87 $a^xb^y \ \square \ (ab)^{xy}$ 88 $\sqrt{a^r} \ \square \ (\sqrt{a})^r$

89 $\sqrt[n]{\dfrac{1}{c}} \ \square \ \dfrac{1}{\sqrt[n]{c}}$ 90 $a^{1/k} \ \square \ \dfrac{1}{a^k}$

Exer. 91–92: In evaluating negative numbers raised to fractional powers, it may be necessary to evaluate the root and integer power separately. For example, $(-3)^{2/5}$ can be evaluated successfully as $[(-3)^{1/5}]^2$ or $[(-3)^2]^{1/5}$, whereas an error message might otherwise appear. Approximate the real-number expression to four decimal places.

91 (a) $(-3)^{2/5}$ (b) $(-5)^{4/3}$

92 (a) $(-1.2)^{3/7}$ (b) $(-5.08)^{7/3}$

Exer. 93–94: Approximate the real-number expression to four decimal places.

93 (a) $\sqrt{\pi + 1}$ (b) $\sqrt[3]{15.1} + 5^{1/4}$

94 (a) $(2.6 - 1.9)^{-2}$ (b) $5^{\sqrt{7}}$

95 **Savings account** One of the oldest banks in the United States is the Bank of America, founded in 1812. If $200 had been deposited at that time into an account that paid 4% annual interest, then 180 years later the amount would have grown to $200(1.04)^{180}$ dollars. Approximate this amount to the nearest cent.

96 **Viewing distance** On a clear day, the distance d (in miles) that can be seen from the top of a tall building of height h (in feet) can be approximated by $d = 1.2\sqrt{h}$. Approximate the distance that can be seen from the top of the Chicago Sears Tower, which is 1454 feet tall.

97 **Length of a halibut** The length-weight relationship for Pacific halibut can be approximated by the formula $L = 0.46\sqrt[3]{W}$, where W is in kilograms and L is in meters. The largest documented halibut weighed 230 kilograms. Estimate its length.

98 **Weight of a whale** The length-weight relationship for the sei whale can be approximated by $W = 0.0016L^{2.43}$, where W is in tons and L is in feet. Estimate the weight of a whale that is 25 feet long.

99 **Weight lifters' handicaps** O'Carroll's formula is used to handicap weight lifters. If a lifter who weighs b kilograms lifts w kilograms of weight, then the handicapped weight W is given by

$$W = \frac{w}{\sqrt[3]{b - 35}}.$$

Suppose two lifters weighing 75 kilograms and 120 kilograms lift weights of 180 kilograms and 250 kilograms, respectively. Use O'Carroll's formula to determine the superior weight lifter.

100 **Body surface area** A person's body surface area S (in square feet) can be approximated by

$$S = (0.1091)w^{0.425}h^{0.725},$$

where height h is in inches and weight w is in pounds.

(a) Estimate S for a person 6 feet tall weighing 175 pounds.

(b) If a person is 5 feet 6 inches tall, what effect does a 10% increase in weight have on S?

101 **Men's weight** The average weight W (in pounds) for men with height h between 64 and 79 inches can be approximated using the formula $W = 0.1166h^{1.7}$. Construct a table for W by letting $h = 64, 65, \ldots, 79$. Round all weights to the nearest pound.

Height	Weight	Height	Weight
64		72	
65		73	
66		74	
67		75	
68		76	
69		77	
70		78	
71		79	

102 **Women's weight** The average weight W (in pounds) for women with height h between 60 and 75 inches can be approximated using the formula $W = 0.1049h^{1.7}$. Construct a table for W by letting $h = 60, 61, \ldots, 75$. Round all weights to the nearest pound.

Height	Weight	Height	Weight
60		68	
61		69	
62		70	
63		71	
64		72	
65		73	
66		74	
67		75	

1.3

Algebraic Expressions

We sometimes use the notation and terminology of sets to describe mathematical relationships. A **set** is a collection of objects of some type, and the objects are called **elements** of the set. Capital letters $R, S, T, \ldots$ are often used to denote sets, and lowercase letters $a, b, x, y, \ldots$ usually represent elements of sets. Throughout this book, $\mathbb{R}$ denotes the set of real numbers and $\mathbb{Z}$ denotes the set of integers.

Two sets S and T are **equal,** denoted by $S = T$, if S and T contain exactly the same elements. We write $S \neq T$ if S and T are not equal. Additional notation and terminology are listed in the following chart.

Notation or terminology	Meaning	Illustrations
$a \in S$	a is an element of S	$3 \in \mathbb{Z}$
$a \notin S$	a is not an element of S	$\frac{3}{5} \notin \mathbb{Z}$
S is a **subset** of T	Every element of S is an element of T	$\mathbb{Z}$ is a subset of $\mathbb{R}$
Constant	A letter or symbol that represents a *specific* element of a set	$5, -\sqrt{2}, \pi$
Variable	A letter or symbol that represents *any* element of a set	Let x denote any real number

We usually use letters near the end of the alphabet, such as x, y, and z, for variables and letters near the beginning of the alphabet, such as a, b, and c, for constants. Throughout this text, unless otherwise specified, variables represent real numbers.

If the elements of a set S have a certain property, we sometimes write $S = \{x: \}$ and state the property describing the variable x in the space after the colon. The expression involving the braces and colon is read "the set of all x such that . . . ," where we complete the phrase by stating the desired property.

$\{x \mid x > 3\}$ is an equivalent notation.

For example, $\{x: x > 3\}$ is read "the set of all x such that x is greater than 3."

For finite sets, we sometimes list all the elements of the set within braces. Thus, if the set T consists of the first five positive integers, we may write $T = \{1, 2, 3, 4, 5\}$. When we describe sets in this way, the order used in listing the elements is irrelevant, so we could also write $T = \{1, 3, 2, 4, 5\}$, $T = \{4, 3, 2, 5, 1\}$, and so on.

If we begin with any collection of variables and real numbers, then an **algebraic expression** is the result obtained by applying additions, subtractions, multiplications, divisions, powers, or the taking of roots to this collection. If specific numbers are substituted for the variables in an algebraic expression, the resulting number is called the **value** of the expression for these numbers. The **domain** of an algebraic expression consists of all real numbers that may represent the variables. Thus, unless otherwise specified, *we assume that the domain consists of the real numbers that, when substituted for the variables, do not make the expression meaningless, in the sense that denominators cannot equal zero and roots always exist.* Two illustrations are given in the following chart.

Algebraic Expressions

Illustration	Domain	Typical value
$x^3 - 5x + \dfrac{6}{\sqrt{x}}$	all $x > 0$	At $x = 4$: $4^3 - 5(4) + \dfrac{6}{\sqrt{4}} = 64 - 20 + 3 = 47$
$\dfrac{2xy + (3/x^2)}{\sqrt[3]{y} - 1}$	all $x \neq 0$ and all $y \neq 1$	At $x = 1$ and $y = 9$: $\dfrac{2(1)(9) + (3/1^2)}{\sqrt[3]{9} - 1} = \dfrac{18 + 3}{\sqrt[3]{8}} = \dfrac{21}{2}$

If x is a variable, then a **monomial** in x is an expression of the form ax^n, where a is a real number and n is a nonnegative integer. A **binomial** is a sum of two monomials, and a **trinomial** is a sum of three monomials. A *polynomial in x* is a sum of any number of monomials in x. Another way of stating this is as follows.

SOLUTION

(a) We use product formula 1, with $x = 2r^2$ and $y = \sqrt{s}$:

$$\left(2r^2 - \sqrt{s}\right)\left(2r^2 + \sqrt{s}\right) = (2r^2)^2 - \left(\sqrt{s}\right)^2$$
$$= 4r^4 - s$$

(b) We use product formula 2, with $x = \sqrt{c}$ and $y = \dfrac{1}{\sqrt{c}}$:

$$\left(\sqrt{c} + \frac{1}{\sqrt{c}}\right)^2 = \left(\sqrt{c}\right)^2 + 2 \cdot \sqrt{c} \cdot \frac{1}{\sqrt{c}} + \left(\frac{1}{\sqrt{c}}\right)^2$$

$$= c + 2 + \frac{1}{c}$$

Note that the last expression is *not* a polynomial.

(c) We use product formula 3, with $x = 2a$ and $y = 5b$:

$$(2a - 5b)^3 = (2a)^3 - 3(2a)^2(5b) + 3(2a)(5b)^2 - (5b)^3$$
$$= 8a^3 - 60a^2b + 150ab^2 - 125b^3$$

If a polynomial is a product of other polynomials, then each polynomial in the product is a **factor** of the original polynomial. **Factoring** is the process of expressing a sum of terms as a product. For example, since $x^2 - 9 = (x + 3)(x - 3)$, the polynomials $x + 3$ and $x - 3$ are factors of $x^2 - 9$.

Factoring is an important process in mathematics, since it may be used to reduce the study of a complicated expression to the study of several simpler expressions. For example, properties of the polynomial $x^2 - 9$ can be determined by examining the factors $x + 3$ and $x - 3$. As we shall see in Chapter 2, another important use for factoring is in finding solutions of equations.

We shall be interested primarily in **nontrivial factors** of polynomials — that is, factors that contain polynomials of positive degree. However, if the coefficients are restricted to *integers,* then we usually remove a common integral factor from each term of the polynomial. For example,

$$4x^2y + 8z^3 = 4(x^2y + 2z^3).$$

A polynomial with coefficients in some set S of numbers is **prime,** or **irreducible** over S, if it cannot be written as a product of two polynomials of positive degree with coefficients in S. A polynomial may be irreducible over one set S but not over another. For example, $x^2 - 2$ is irreducible over the rational numbers, since it cannot be expressed as a product of two polynomials of positive degree that have *rational* coefficients. However, $x^2 - 2$ is *not* irreducible over the real numbers, since we can write

$$x^2 - 2 = \left(x + \sqrt{2}\right)\left(x - \sqrt{2}\right).$$

Similarly, $x^2 + 1$ is irreducible over the real numbers, but, as we shall see in Section 2.4, not over the complex numbers.

Every polynomial $ax + b$ of degree 1 is irreducible.

Before we factor a polynomial, we must specify the number system (or set) from which the coefficients of the factors are to be chosen. In this chapter we shall use the rule that *if a polynomial has integral coefficients, then the factors should be polynomials with integral coefficients*. To **factor a polynomial** means to express it as a product of irreducible polynomials.

The **greatest common factor (gcf)** of an expression is the product of the factors that appear in each term, with each of these factors raised to the smallest nonzero exponent appearing in any term. In factoring polynomials, it is advisable to first factor out the gcf, as shown in the following illustration.

ILLUSTRATION Factored Polynomials

- $8x^2 + 4xy = 4x(2x + y)$
- $25x^2 + 25x - 150 = 25(x^2 + x - 6) = 25(x + 3)(x - 2)$
- $4x^5y - 9x^3y^3 = x^3y(4x^2 - 9y^2) = x^3y(2x + 3y)(2x - 3y)$

It is usually difficult to factor polynomials of degree greater than 2. In simple cases, the following factoring formulas may be useful. Each formula can be verified by multiplying the factors on the right-hand side of the equals sign. It can be shown that the factors $x^2 + xy + y^2$ and $x^2 - xy + y^2$ in the difference and sum of two cubes, respectively, are irreducible over the real numbers.

Factoring Formulas

Formula	Illustration
(1) Difference of two squares: $x^2 - y^2 = (x + y)(x - y)$	$9a^2 - 16 = (3a)^2 - (4)^2 = (3a + 4)(3a - 4)$
(2) Difference of two cubes: $x^3 - y^3 = (x - y)(x^2 + xy + y^2)$	$8a^3 - 27 = (2a)^3 - (3)^3$ $= (2a - 3)[(2a)^2 + (2a)(3) + (3)^2]$ $= (2a - 3)(4a^2 + 6a + 9)$
(3) Sum of two cubes: $x^3 + y^3 = (x + y)(x^2 - xy + y^2)$	$125a^3 + 1 = (5a)^3 + (1)^3$ $= (5a + 1)[(5a)^2 - (5a)(1) + (1)^2]$ $= (5a + 1)(25a^2 - 5a + 1)$

Several other illustrations of the use of factoring formulas are given in the next two examples.

EXAMPLE 6   Difference of two squares

Factor each polynomial:

(a) $25r^2 - 49s^2$ (b) $81x^4 - y^4$ (c) $16x^4 - (y - 2z)^2$

SOLUTION

(a) We apply the difference of two squares formula, with $x = 5r$ and $y = 7s$:

$$25r^2 - 49s^2 = (5r)^2 - (7s)^2 = (5r + 7s)(5r - 7s)$$

(b) We write $81x^4 = (9x^2)^2$ and $y^4 = (y^2)^2$ and apply the difference of two squares formula twice:

$$81x^4 - y^4 = (9x^2)^2 - (y^2)^2$$
$$= (9x^2 + y^2)(9x^2 - y^2)$$
$$= (9x^2 + y^2)[(3x)^2 - (y)^2]$$
$$= (9x^2 + y^2)(3x + y)(3x - y)$$

(c) We write $16x^4 = (4x^2)^2$ and apply the difference of two squares formula:

$$16x^4 - (y - 2z)^2 = (4x^2)^2 - (y - 2z)^2$$
$$= [(4x^2) + (y - 2z)][(4x^2) - (y - 2z)]$$
$$= (4x^2 + y - 2z)(4x^2 - y + 2z)$$

EXAMPLE 7   Sum and difference of two cubes

Factor each polynomial:

(a) $a^3 + 64b^3$ (b) $8c^6 - 27d^9$

SOLUTION

(a) We apply the sum of two cubes formula, with $x = a$ and $y = 4b$:

$$a^3 + 64b^3 = a^3 + (4b)^3$$
$$= (a + 4b)[a^2 - a(4b) + (4b)^2]$$
$$= (a + 4b)(a^2 - 4ab + 16b^2)$$

(b) We apply the difference of two cubes formula, with $x = 2c^2$ and $y = 3d^3$:

$$8c^6 - 27d^9 = (2c^2)^3 - (3d^3)^3$$
$$= (2c^2 - 3d^3)[(2c^2)^2 + (2c^2)(3d^3) + (3d^3)^2]$$
$$= (2c^2 - 3d^3)(4c^4 + 6c^2d^3 + 9d^6)$$

A factorization of a trinomial $px^2 + qx + r$, where p, q, and r are integers, must be of the form

$$px^2 + qx + r = (ax + b)(cx + d),$$

where a, b, c, and d are integers. It follows that

$$ac = p, \quad bd = r, \quad \text{and} \quad ad + bc = q.$$

Only a limited number of choices for a, b, c, and d satisfy these conditions. If none of the choices work, then $px^2 + qx + r$ is irreducible. Trying the various possibilities, as depicted in the next example, is called the **method of trial and error.** This method is also applicable to trinomials of the form $px^2 + qxy + ry^2$, in which case the factorization must be of the form $(ax + by)(cx + dy)$.

EXAMPLE 8   Factoring a trinomial by trial and error

Factor $6x^2 - 7x - 3$.

SOLUTION If we write

$$6x^2 - 7x - 3 = (ax + b)(cx + d),$$

then the following relationships must be true:

$$ac = 6, \quad bd = -3, \quad \text{and} \quad ad + bc = -7$$

If we assume that a and c are both positive, then all possible values are given in the following table:

a	1	6	2	3
c	6	1	3	2

Thus, if $6x^2 - 7x - 3$ is factorable, then one of the following is true:

$$6x^2 - 7x - 3 = (x + b)(6x + d)$$
$$6x^2 - 7x - 3 = (6x + b)(x + d)$$
$$6x^2 - 7x - 3 = (2x + b)(3x + d)$$
$$6x^2 - 7x - 3 = (3x + b)(2x + d)$$

We next consider all possible values for b and d. Since $bd = -3$, these are as follows:

b	1	−1	3	−3
d	−3	3	−1	1

Trying various (possibly all) values, we arrive at $b = -3$ and $d = 1$; that is,

$$6x^2 - 7x - 3 = (2x - 3)(3x + 1).$$

As a check, you should multiply the final factorization to see whether the original polynomial is obtained.

The method of trial and error illustrated in Example 8 can be long and tedious if the coefficients of the polynomial are large and have many prime factors. We will show a factoring method in Section 2.3 that can be used to factor any trinomial of the form of the one in Example 8—regardless of the size of the coefficients. For simple cases, it is often possible to arrive at the correct choice rapidly.

EXAMPLE 9 Factoring polynomials

Factor:

(a) $12x^2 - 36xy + 27y^2$ **(b)** $4x^4y - 11x^3y^2 + 6x^2y^3$

SOLUTION

(a) Since each term has 3 as a factor, we begin by writing

$$12x^2 - 36xy + 27y^2 = 3(4x^2 - 12xy + 9y^2).$$

A factorization of $4x^2 - 12xy + 9y^2$ as a product of two first-degree polynomials must be of the form

$$4x^2 - 12xy + 9y^2 = (ax + by)(cx + dy),$$

with $\quad ac = 4, \quad bd = 9, \quad$ and $\quad ad + bc = -12.$

Using the method of trial and error, as in Example 8, we obtain

$$4x^2 - 12xy + 9y^2 = (2x - 3y)(2x - 3y) = (2x - 3y)^2.$$

Thus, $\quad 12x^2 - 36xy + 27y^2 = 3(4x^2 - 12xy + 9y^2) = 3(2x - 3y)^2.$

(b) Since each term has x^2y as a factor, we begin by writing

$$4x^4y - 11x^3y^2 + 6x^2y^3 = x^2y(4x^2 - 11xy + 6y^2).$$

By trial and error, we obtain the factorization

$$4x^4y - 11x^3y^2 + 6x^2y^3 = x^2y(4x - 3y)(x - 2y).$$

If a sum contains four or more terms, it may be possible to group the terms in a suitable manner and then find a factorization by using distributive properties. This technique, called **factoring by grouping,** is illustrated in the next example.

EXAMPLE 10 Factoring by grouping

Factor:

(a) $4ac + 2bc - 2ad - bd$ (b) $3x^3 + 2x^2 - 12x - 8$

(c) $x^2 - 16y^2 + 10x + 25$

SOLUTION

(a) We group the first two terms and the last two terms and then proceed as follows:

$$4ac + 2bc - 2ad - bd = (4ac + 2bc) - (2ad + bd)$$
$$= 2c(2a + b) - d(2a + b)$$

At this stage we have not factored the given expression because the right-hand side has the form

$$2ck - dk \quad \text{with } k = 2a + b.$$

However, if we factor out k, then

$$2ck - dk = (2c - d)k = (2c - d)(2a + b).$$

Hence,

$$4ac + 2bc - 2ad - bd = 2c(2a + b) - d(2a + b)$$
$$= (2c - d)(2a + b).$$

Note that if we factor $2ck - dk$ as $k(2c - d)$, then the last expression is $(2a + b)(2c - d)$.

(b) We group the first two terms and the last two terms and then proceed as follows:

$$3x^3 + 2x^2 - 12x - 8 = (3x^3 + 2x^2) - (12x + 8)$$
$$= x^2(3x + 2) - 4(3x + 2)$$
$$= (x^2 - 4)(3x + 2)$$

Finally, using the difference of two squares formula for $x^2 - 4$, we obtain the factorization:

$$3x^3 + 2x^2 - 12x - 8 = (x + 2)(x - 2)(3x + 2)$$

(c) First we rearrange and group terms, and then we apply the difference of two squares formula, as follows:

$$x^2 - 16y^2 + 10x + 25 = (x^2 + 10x + 25) - 16y^2$$
$$= (x + 5)^2 - (4y)^2$$
$$= [(x + 5) + 4y][(x + 5) - 4y]$$
$$= (x + 4y + 5)(x - 4y + 5)$$

1.3 *Exercises*

Exer. 1–44: Express as a polynomial.

1 $(3x^3 + 4x^2 - 7x + 1) + (9x^3 - 4x^2 - 6x)$

2 $(7x^3 + 2x^2 - 11x) + (-3x^3 - 2x^2 + 5x - 3)$

3 $(4x^3 + 5x - 3) - (3x^3 + 2x^2 + 5x - 7)$

4 $(6x^3 - 2x^2 + x - 2) - (8x^2 - x - 2)$

5 $(2x + 5)(3x - 7)$ 6 $(3x - 4)(2x + 9)$

7 $(5x + 7y)(3x + 2y)$ 8 $(4x - 3y)(x - 5y)$

9 $(2u + 3)(u - 4) + 4u(u - 2)$

10 $(3u - 1)(u + 2) + 7u(u + 1)$

11 $(3x + 5)(2x^2 + 9x - 5)$ 12 $(7x - 4)(x^3 - x^2 + 6)$

13 $(t^2 + 2t - 5)(3t^2 - t + 2)$

14 $(r^2 - 8r - 2)(-r^2 + 3r - 1)$

15 $(x + 1)(2x^2 - 2)(x^3 + 5)$ 16 $(2x - 1)(x^2 - 5)(x^3 - 1)$

17 $\dfrac{8x^2y^3 - 10x^3y}{2x^2y}$

18 $\dfrac{6a^3b^3 - 9a^2b^2 + 3ab^4}{3ab^2}$

19 $\dfrac{3u^3v^4 - 2u^5v^2 + (u^2v^2)^2}{u^3v^2}$

20 $\dfrac{6x^2yz^3 - xy^2z}{xyz}$

21 $(2x + 3y)(2x - 3y)$ 22 $(5x + 4y)(5x - 4y)$

23 $(x^2 + 2y)(x^2 - 2y)$ 24 $(3x + y^3)(3x - y^3)$

25 $(x^2 + 9)(x^2 - 4)$ 26 $(x^2 + 1)(x^2 - 16)$

27 $(3x + 2y)^2$ 28 $(5x - 4y)^2$

29 $(x^2 - 3y^2)^2$ 30 $(2x^2 + 5y^2)^2$

31 $(x + 2)^2(x - 2)^2$ 32 $(x + y)^2(x - y)^2$

33 $\left(\sqrt{x} + \sqrt{y}\right)\left(\sqrt{x} - \sqrt{y}\right)$

34 $\left(\sqrt{x} + \sqrt{y}\right)^2\left(\sqrt{x} - \sqrt{y}\right)^2$

35 $(x^{1/3} - y^{1/3})(x^{2/3} + x^{1/3}y^{1/3} + y^{2/3})$

36 $(x^{1/3} + y^{1/3})(x^{2/3} - x^{1/3}y^{1/3} + y^{2/3})$

37 $(x - 2y)^3$ 38 $(x + 3y)^3$

39 $(2x + 3y)^3$ 40 $(3x - 4y)^3$

41 $(a + b - c)^2$ 42 $(x^2 + x + 1)^2$

43 $(2x + y - 3z)^2$ 44 $(x - 2y + 3z)^2$

Exer. 45–102: Factor the polynomial.

45 $rs + 4st$ 46 $4u^2 - 2uv$

47 $3a^2b^2 - 6a^2b$ 48 $10xy + 15xy^2$

49 $3x^2y^3 - 9x^3y^2$ 50 $16x^5y^2 + 8x^3y^3$

51 $15x^3y^5 - 25x^4y^2 + 10x^6y^4$ 52 $121r^3s^4 + 77r^2s^4 - 55r^4s^3$

53 $8x^2 - 53x - 21$ 54 $7x^2 + 10x - 8$

55 $x^2 + 3x + 4$ 56 $3x^2 - 4x + 2$

57 $6x^2 + 7x - 20$ 58 $12x^2 - x - 6$

59 $12x^2 - 29x + 15$ 60 $21x^2 + 41x + 10$

61 $4x^2 - 20x + 25$ 62 $9x^2 + 24x + 16$

63 $25z^2 + 30z + 9$ 64 $16z^2 - 56z + 49$

65 $45x^2 + 38xy + 8y^2$ 66 $50x^2 + 45xy - 18y^2$

67 $36r^2 - 25t^2$ 68 $81r^2 - 16t^2$

69 $z^4 - 64w^2$ 70 $9y^4 - 121x^2$

71 $x^4 - 4x^2$ 72 $x^3 - 25x$

73 $x^2 + 25$ 74 $4x^2 + 9$

75 $75x^2 - 48y^2$ 76 $64x^2 - 36y^2$

77 $64x^3 + 27$ 78 $125x^3 - 8$

79 $64x^3 - y^6$ 80 $216x^9 + 125y^3$

81 $343x^3 + y^9$ 82 $x^6 - 27y^3$

83 $125 - 27x^3$ 84 $x^3 + 64$

85 $2ax - 6bx + ay - 3by$ 86 $2ay^2 - axy + 6xy - 3x^2$

87 $3x^3 + 3x^2 - 27x - 27$ 88 $5x^3 + 10x^2 - 20x - 40$

89 $x^4 + 2x^3 - x - 2$ 90 $x^4 - 3x^3 + 8x - 24$

91 $a^3 - a^2b + ab^2 - b^3$ 92 $6w^8 + 17w^4 + 12$

93 $a^6 - b^6$ 94 $x^8 - 16$

95 $x^2 + 4x + 4 - 9y^2$ 96 $x^2 - 4y^2 - 6x + 9$

97 $y^2 - x^2 + 8y + 16$ 98 $y^2 + 9 - 6y - 4x^2$

99 $y^6 + 7y^3 - 8$

100 $8c^6 + 19c^3 - 27$

101 $x^{16} - 1$

102 $4x^3 + 4x^2 + x$

Exer. 103–104: The ancient Greeks gave geometric proofs of the factoring formulas for the difference of two squares and the difference of two cubes. Establish the formula for the special case described.

103 Find the areas of regions I and II in the figure to establish the difference of two squares formula for the special case $x > y$.

Exercise 103

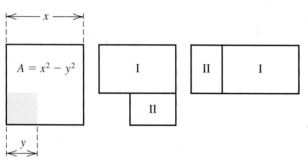

104 Find the volumes of boxes I, II, and III in the figure to establish the difference of two cubes formula for the special case $x > y$.

Exercise 104

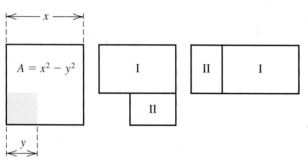

$V = x^3 - y^3$

105 Calorie requirements The basal energy requirement for an individual indicates the minimum number of calories necessary to maintain essential life-sustaining processes such as circulation, regulation of body temperature, and respiration. Given a person's sex, weight w (in kilograms), height h (in centimeters), and age y (in years), we can estimate the basal energy requirement in calories using the following formulas, where C_f and C_m are the calories necessary for females and males, respectively:

$$C_f = 66.5 + 13.8w + 5h - 6.8y$$
$$C_m = 655 + 9.6w + 1.9h - 4.7y$$

(a) Determine the basal energy requirements first for a 25-year-old female weighing 59 kilograms who is 163 centimeters tall and then for a 55-year-old male weighing 75 kilograms who is 178 centimeters tall.

(b) Discuss why, in both formulas, the coefficient for y is negative but the other coefficients are positive.

1.4

Fractional Expressions

A **fractional expression** is a quotient of two algebraic expressions. As a special case, a **rational expression** is a quotient p/q of two *polynomials p* and *q*. Since division by zero is not allowed, the domain of p/q consists of all real numbers except those that make the denominator zero. Two illustrations are given in the chart.

Rational Expressions

Quotient	Denominator is zero if	Domain
$\dfrac{6x^2 - 5x + 4}{x^2 - 9}$	$x = \pm 3$	All $x \neq \pm 3$
$\dfrac{x^3 - 3x^2y + 4y^2}{y - x^3}$	$y = x^3$	All x and y such that $y \neq x^3$

In most of our work we will be concerned with rational expressions in which both numerator and denominator are polynomials in only one variable.

Since the variables in a rational expression represent real numbers, we may use the properties of quotients in Section 1.1, replacing the letters a, b, c, and d with polynomials. The following property is of particular importance, where $bd \neq 0$:

$$\frac{ad}{bd} = \frac{a}{b} \cdot \frac{d}{d} = \frac{a}{b} \cdot 1 = \frac{a}{b}$$

We sometimes describe this simplification process by saying that *a common nonzero factor in the numerator and denominator of a quotient may be canceled*. In practice, we usually show this cancellation by means of a slash through the common factor, as in the following illustration, where all denominators are assumed to be nonzero.

ILLUSTRATION   **Canceled Common Factors**

■ $\dfrac{\cancel{a}d}{\cancel{b}d} = \dfrac{a}{b}$ ■ $\dfrac{m\cancel{n}}{\cancel{n}pq} = \dfrac{m}{pq}$ ■ $\dfrac{\cancel{p}q\cancel{r}}{\cancel{r}p\cancel{v}} = \dfrac{q}{v}$

A rational expression is *simplified,* or *reduced to lowest terms,* if the numerator and denominator have no common polynomial factors of positive degree and no common integral factors greater than 1. To simplify a rational expression, we factor both the numerator and the denominator into prime factors and then, assuming the factors in the denominator are not zero, cancel common factors, as in the following illustration.

ILLUSTRATION   **Simplified Rational Expressions**

$$\text{if } x \neq 2$$

■ $\dfrac{3x^2 - 5x - 2}{x^2 - 4} = \dfrac{(3x + 1)(x - 2)}{(x + 2)(x - 2)} \overset{\downarrow}{=} \dfrac{3x + 1}{x + 2}$ $\text{if } x \neq 2/3$

■ $\dfrac{2 - x - 3x^2}{6x^2 - x - 2} = \dfrac{-(3x^2 + x - 2)}{6x^2 - x - 2} = -\dfrac{(3x - 2)(x + 1)}{(3x - 2)(2x + 1)} \overset{\downarrow}{=} -\dfrac{x + 1}{2x + 1}$

$$\text{if } x \neq 5, x \neq -4$$

■ $\dfrac{(x^2 + 8x + 16)(x - 5)}{(x^2 - 5x)(x^2 - 16)} = \dfrac{(x + 4)^{\overset{1}{\cancel{2}}}(x - 5)}{x(x - 5)(x + 4)(x - 4)} \overset{\downarrow}{=} \dfrac{x + 4}{x(x - 4)}$

As shown in the next example, when simplifying a product or quotient of rational expressions, we often use properties of quotients to obtain one rational expression. Then we factor the numerator and denominator and cancel common factors, as we did in the preceding illustration.

EXAMPLE 1   Products and quotients of rational expressions

Perform the indicated operation and simplify:

(a) $\dfrac{x^2 - 6x + 9}{x^2 - 1} \cdot \dfrac{2x - 2}{x - 3}$ (b) $\dfrac{x + 2}{2x - 3} \div \dfrac{x^2 - 4}{2x^2 - 3x}$

SOLUTION

(a) $\dfrac{x^2 - 6x + 9}{x^2 - 1} \cdot \dfrac{2x - 2}{x - 3} = \dfrac{(x^2 - 6x + 9)(2x - 2)}{(x^2 - 1)(x - 3)}$ property of quotients

$= \dfrac{(x - 3)^{\cancel{2}^{1}} \cdot 2(\cancel{x - 1})}{(x + 1)(\cancel{x - 1})(\cancel{x - 3})}$ factor all polynomials

$\qquad\qquad$ if $x \neq 3, x \neq 1$

$\downarrow = \dfrac{2(x - 3)}{x + 1}$ cancel common factors

(b) $\dfrac{x + 2}{2x - 3} \div \dfrac{x^2 - 4}{2x^2 - 3x} = \dfrac{x + 2}{2x - 3} \cdot \dfrac{2x^2 - 3x}{x^2 - 4}$ property of quotients

$= \dfrac{(\cancel{x + 2})x(\cancel{2x - 3})}{(\cancel{2x - 3})(\cancel{x + 2})(x - 2)}$ property of quotients; factor all polynomials

$\qquad\qquad$ if $x \neq -2, x \neq 3/2$

$\downarrow = \dfrac{x}{x - 2}$ cancel common factors

To add or subtract two rational expressions, we usually find a *common denominator* and use the following properties of quotients:

$$\frac{a}{d} + \frac{c}{d} = \frac{a + c}{d} \qquad \text{and} \qquad \frac{a}{d} - \frac{c}{d} = \frac{a - c}{d}$$

If the denominators of the expressions are not the same, we may obtain a common denominator by multiplying the numerator and denominator of each fraction by a suitable expression. We usually use the *least* **common denominator** **(lcd)** of the two quotients. To find the lcd, we factor each denominator into primes and then form the product of the different prime factors, using the *largest* exponent that appears with each prime factor. Let us begin with a numerical example of this technique.

EXAMPLE 2   Adding fractions using the lcd

Express as a simplified rational number:

$$\frac{7}{24} + \frac{5}{18}$$

SOLUTION   The prime factorizations of the denominators 24 and 18 are $24 = 2^3 \cdot 3$ and $18 = 2 \cdot 3^2$. To find the lcd, we form the product of the different prime factors, using the largest exponent associated with each factor. This gives us $2^3 \cdot 3^2$. We now change each fraction to an equivalent fraction with denominator $2^3 \cdot 3^2$ and add:

$$\frac{7}{24} + \frac{5}{18} = \frac{7}{2^3 \cdot 3} + \frac{5}{2 \cdot 3^2}$$

$$= \frac{7}{2^3 \cdot 3} \cdot \frac{3}{3} + \frac{5}{2 \cdot 3^2} \cdot \frac{2^2}{2^2}$$

$$= \frac{21}{2^3 \cdot 3^2} + \frac{20}{2^3 \cdot 3^2}$$

$$= \frac{41}{2^3 \cdot 3^2}$$

$$= \frac{41}{72}$$

The method for finding the lcd for rational expressions is analogous to the process illustrated in Example 2. The only difference is that we use factorizations of polynomials instead of integers.

EXAMPLE 3   Sums and differences of rational expressions

Perform the operations and simplify:

$$\frac{6}{x(3x - 2)} + \frac{5}{3x - 2} - \frac{2}{x^2}$$

SOLUTION   The denominators are already in factored form. The lcd is $x^2(3x - 2)$. To obtain three quotients having the denominator $x^2(3x - 2)$, we multiply the numerator and denominator of the first quotient by x, those of the second by x^2, and those of the third by $3x - 2$, which gives us

$$\frac{6}{x(3x - 2)} + \frac{5}{3x - 2} - \frac{2}{x^2} = \frac{6}{x(3x - 2)} \cdot \frac{x}{x} + \frac{5}{3x - 2} \cdot \frac{x^2}{x^2} - \frac{2}{x^2} \cdot \frac{3x - 2}{3x - 2}$$

$$= \frac{6x}{x^2(3x - 2)} + \frac{5x^2}{x^2(3x - 2)} - \frac{2(3x - 2)}{x^2(3x - 2)}$$

$$= \frac{6x + 5x^2 - 2(3x - 2)}{x^2(3x - 2)}$$

$$= \frac{5x^2 + 4}{x^2(3x - 2)}.$$

EXAMPLE 4 Simplifying sums of rational expressions

Perform the operations and simplify:

$$\frac{2x + 5}{x^2 + 6x + 9} + \frac{x}{x^2 - 9} + \frac{1}{x - 3}$$

SOLUTION We begin by factoring denominators:

$$\frac{2x + 5}{x^2 + 6x + 9} + \frac{x}{x^2 - 9} + \frac{1}{x - 3} = \frac{2x + 5}{(x + 3)^2} + \frac{x}{(x + 3)(x - 3)} + \frac{1}{x - 3}$$

Since the lcd is $(x + 3)^2(x - 3)$, we multiply the numerator and denominator of the first quotient by $x - 3$, those of the second by $x + 3$, and those of the third by $(x + 3)^2$ and then add:

$$\frac{(2x + 5)(x - 3)}{(x + 3)^2(x - 3)} + \frac{x(x + 3)}{(x + 3)^2(x - 3)} + \frac{(x + 3)^2}{(x + 3)^2(x - 3)}$$

$$= \frac{(2x^2 - x - 15) + (x^2 + 3x) + (x^2 + 6x + 9)}{(x + 3)^2(x - 3)}$$

$$= \frac{4x^2 + 8x - 6}{(x + 3)^2(x - 3)} = \frac{2(2x^2 + 4x - 3)}{(x + 3)^2(x - 3)}$$

A **complex fraction** is a quotient in which the numerator and/or the denominator is a fractional expression. Certain problems in calculus require simplifying complex fractions of the type given in the next example.

EXAMPLE 5 Simplifying a complex fraction

Simplify the complex fraction:

$$\frac{\dfrac{2}{x + 3} - \dfrac{2}{a + 3}}{x - a}$$

SOLUTION We change the numerator of the given expression into a single quotient and then use a property for simplifying quotients:

$$\frac{\dfrac{2}{x + 3} - \dfrac{2}{a + 3}}{x - a} = \frac{\dfrac{2(a + 3) - 2(x + 3)}{(x + 3)(a + 3)}}{x - a} \quad \text{combine fractions in the numerator}$$

$$= \frac{2a - 2x}{(x + 3)(a + 3)} \cdot \frac{1}{x - a} \quad \text{simplify; property of quotients}$$

$$= \frac{2(a - x)}{(x + 3)(a + 3)(x - a)} \quad \begin{array}{l}\text{factor } 2a - 2x; \text{ property of}\\ \text{quotients}\end{array}$$

$$\text{if } x \neq a$$

$$\underset{\downarrow}{=} -\frac{2}{(x + 3)(a + 3)} \quad \text{replace } \dfrac{a - x}{x - a} \text{ with } -1$$

An alternative method is to multiply the numerator and denominator of the given expression by $(x + 3)(a + 3)$, the lcd of the numerator and denominator, and then simplify the result.

Some quotients that are not rational expressions contain denominators of the form $a + \sqrt{b}$ or $\sqrt{a} + \sqrt{b}$; as in the next example, these quotients can be simplified by multiplying the numerator and denominator by the **conjugate** $a - \sqrt{b}$ or $\sqrt{a} - \sqrt{b}$, respectively. Of course, if $a - \sqrt{b}$ appears, multiply by $a + \sqrt{b}$ instead.

EXAMPLE 6   Rationalizing a denominator

Rationalize the denominator:

$$\frac{1}{\sqrt{x} + \sqrt{y}}$$

SOLUTION

$$\frac{1}{\sqrt{x} + \sqrt{y}} = \frac{1}{\sqrt{x} + \sqrt{y}} \cdot \frac{\sqrt{x} - \sqrt{y}}{\sqrt{x} - \sqrt{y}}$$ multiply numerator and denominator by the conjugate of $\sqrt{x} + \sqrt{y}$

$$= \frac{\sqrt{x} - \sqrt{y}}{\left(\sqrt{x}\right)^2 - \left(\sqrt{y}\right)^2}$$ property of quotients and difference of squares

$$= \frac{\sqrt{x} - \sqrt{y}}{x - y}$$ law of radicals

In calculus it is sometimes necessary to rationalize the *numerator* of a quotient, as shown in the following example.

EXAMPLE 7   Rationalizing a numerator

If $h \neq 0$, rationalize the numerator of

$$\frac{\sqrt{x + h} - \sqrt{x}}{h}.$$

SOLUTION

$$\frac{\sqrt{x + h} - \sqrt{x}}{h} = \frac{\sqrt{x + h} - \sqrt{x}}{h} \cdot \frac{\sqrt{x + h} + \sqrt{x}}{\sqrt{x + h} + \sqrt{x}}$$ multiply numerator and denominator by the conjugate of $\sqrt{x + h} - \sqrt{x}$

$$= \frac{\left(\sqrt{x + h}\right)^2 - \left(\sqrt{x}\right)^2}{h\left(\sqrt{x + h} + \sqrt{x}\right)}$$ property of quotients and difference of squares

$$= \frac{(x + h) - x}{h\left(\sqrt{x + h} + \sqrt{x}\right)}$$ law of radicals

$$= \frac{h}{h\left(\sqrt{x + h} + \sqrt{x}\right)}$$ simplify

$$= \frac{1}{\sqrt{x + h} + \sqrt{x}}$$ cancel $h \neq 0$

(continued)

It may seem as though we have accomplished very little, since radicals occur in the denominator. In calculus, however, it is of interest to determine what is true if h is very close to zero. Note that if we use the *given* expression we obtain the following:

$$\text{If} \quad h \approx 0, \quad \text{then} \quad \frac{\sqrt{x + h} - \sqrt{x}}{h} \approx \frac{\sqrt{x + 0} - \sqrt{x}}{0} = \frac{0}{0},$$

a meaningless expression. If we use the *rationalized* form, however, we obtain the following information:

$$\text{If} \quad h \approx 0, \quad \text{then} \quad \frac{\sqrt{x + h} - \sqrt{x}}{h} = \frac{1}{\sqrt{x + h} + \sqrt{x}}$$

$$\approx \frac{1}{\sqrt{x} + \sqrt{x}} = \frac{1}{2\sqrt{x}}.$$

Certain problems in calculus require simplifying expressions of the type given in the next example.

EXAMPLE 8   Simplifying a fractional expression

Simplify, if $h \neq 0$:

$$\frac{\dfrac{1}{(x + h)^2} - \dfrac{1}{x^2}}{h}$$

SOLUTION

$$\frac{\dfrac{1}{(x + h)^2} - \dfrac{1}{x^2}}{h} = \frac{\dfrac{x^2 - (x + h)^2}{(x + h)^2 x^2}}{h} \qquad \text{combine quotients in numerator}$$

$$= \frac{x^2 - (x^2 + 2xh + h^2)}{(x + h)^2 x^2} \cdot \frac{1}{h} \qquad \begin{array}{l}\text{square } x + h; \text{ property of}\\ \text{quotients}\end{array}$$

$$= \frac{x^2 - x^2 - 2xh - h^2}{(x + h)^2 x^2 h} \qquad \text{remove parentheses}$$

$$= \frac{-h(2x + h)}{(x + h)^2 x^2 h} \qquad \text{simplify; factor out } -h$$

$$= -\frac{2x + h}{(x + h)^2 x^2} \qquad \text{cancel } h \neq 0$$

Problems of the type given in the next example also occur in calculus.

EXAMPLE 9   Simplifying a fractional expression

Simplify:

$$\frac{3x^2(2x + 5)^{1/2} - x^3\left(\frac{1}{2}\right)(2x + 5)^{-1/2}(2)}{[(2x + 5)^{1/2}]^2}$$

SOLUTION   One way to simplify the expression is as follows:

$$\frac{3x^2(2x+5)^{1/2} - x^3\left(\frac{1}{2}\right)(2x+5)^{-1/2}(2)}{[(2x+5)^{1/2}]^2}$$

$$= \frac{3x^2(2x+5)^{1/2} - \dfrac{x^3}{(2x+5)^{1/2}}}{2x+5}$$ definition of negative exponents

$$= \frac{\dfrac{3x^2(2x+5) - x^3}{(2x+5)^{1/2}}}{2x+5}$$ combine terms in numerator

$$= \frac{6x^3 + 15x^2 - x^3}{(2x+5)^{1/2}} \cdot \frac{1}{2x+5}$$ property of quotients

$$= \frac{5x^3 + 15x^2}{(2x+5)^{3/2}}$$ simplify

$$= \frac{5x^2(x+3)}{(2x+5)^{3/2}}$$ factor numerator

An alternative simplification is to eliminate the negative power, $-\frac{1}{2}$, in the given expression, as follows:

$$\frac{3x^2(2x+5)^{1/2} - x^3\left(\frac{1}{2}\right)(2x+5)^{-1/2}(2)}{[(2x+5)^{1/2}]^2} \cdot \frac{(2x+5)^{1/2}}{(2x+5)^{1/2}}$$ multiply numerator and denominator by $(2x+5)^{1/2}$

$$= \frac{3x^2(2x+5) - x^3}{(2x+5)(2x+5)^{1/2}}$$ property of quotients and law of exponents

The remainder of the simplification is similar.

A third method of simplification is to first factor out the gcf. In this case, the common factors are x and $(2x+5)$, and the smallest exponents are 2 and $-\frac{1}{2}$, respectively. Thus, the gcf is $x^2(2x+5)^{-1/2}$, and we factor the numerator and simplify as follows:

$$\frac{x^2(2x+5)^{-1/2}[3(2x+5)^1 - x]}{(2x+5)^1} = \frac{x^2(5x+15)}{(2x+5)^{3/2}} = \frac{5x^2(x+3)}{(2x+5)^{3/2}}$$

One of the problems in calculus is determining the values of x that make the numerator equal to zero. The simplified form helps us answer this question with relative ease—the values are 0 and -3.

1.4 Exercises

Exer. 1–4: Write the expression as a simplified rational number.

1 $\dfrac{3}{50} + \dfrac{7}{30}$

2 $\dfrac{4}{63} + \dfrac{5}{42}$

3 $\dfrac{5}{24} - \dfrac{3}{20}$

4 $\dfrac{11}{54} - \dfrac{7}{72}$

Exer. 5–48: Simplify the expression.

5 $\dfrac{2x^2 + 7x + 3}{2x^2 - 7x - 4}$

6 $\dfrac{2x^2 + 9x - 5}{3x^2 + 17x + 10}$

7 $\dfrac{y^2 - 25}{y^3 - 125}$

8 $\dfrac{y^2 - 9}{y^3 + 27}$

9 $\dfrac{12 + r - r^2}{r^3 + 3r^2}$

10 $\dfrac{10 + 3r - r^2}{r^4 + 2r^3}$

11 $\dfrac{9x^2 - 4}{3x^2 - 5x + 2} \cdot \dfrac{9x^4 - 6x^3 + 4x^2}{27x^4 + 8x}$

12 $\dfrac{4x^2 - 9}{2x^2 + 7x + 6} \cdot \dfrac{4x^4 + 6x^3 + 9x^2}{8x^7 - 27x^4}$

13 $\dfrac{5a^2 + 12a + 4}{a^4 - 16} \div \dfrac{25a^2 + 20a + 4}{a^2 - 2a}$

14 $\dfrac{a^3 - 8}{a^2 - 4} \div \dfrac{a}{a^3 + 8}$

15 $\dfrac{6}{x^2 - 4} - \dfrac{3x}{x^2 - 4}$

16 $\dfrac{15}{x^2 - 9} - \dfrac{5x}{x^2 - 9}$

17 $\dfrac{2}{3s + 1} - \dfrac{9}{(3s + 1)^2}$

18 $\dfrac{4}{(5s - 2)^2} + \dfrac{s}{5s - 2}$

19 $\dfrac{2}{x} + \dfrac{3x + 1}{x^2} - \dfrac{x - 2}{x^3}$

20 $\dfrac{5}{x} - \dfrac{2x - 1}{x^2} + \dfrac{x + 5}{x^3}$

21 $\dfrac{3t}{t + 2} + \dfrac{5t}{t - 2} - \dfrac{40}{t^2 - 4}$

22 $\dfrac{t}{t + 3} + \dfrac{4t}{t - 3} - \dfrac{18}{t^2 - 9}$

23 $\dfrac{4x}{3x - 4} + \dfrac{8}{3x^2 - 4x} + \dfrac{2}{x}$

24 $\dfrac{12x}{2x + 1} - \dfrac{3}{2x^2 + x} + \dfrac{5}{x}$

25 $\dfrac{2x}{x + 2} - \dfrac{8}{x^2 + 2x} + \dfrac{3}{x}$

26 $\dfrac{5x}{2x + 3} - \dfrac{6}{2x^2 + 3x} + \dfrac{2}{x}$

27 $\dfrac{p^4 + 3p^3 - 8p - 24}{p^3 - 2p^2 - 9p + 18}$

28 $\dfrac{2ac + bc - 6ad - 3bd}{6ac + 2ad + 3bc + bd}$

29 $3 + \dfrac{5}{u} + \dfrac{2u}{3u + 1}$

30 $4 + \dfrac{2}{u} - \dfrac{3u}{u + 5}$

31 $\dfrac{2x + 1}{x^2 + 4x + 4} - \dfrac{6x}{x^2 - 4} + \dfrac{3}{x - 2}$

32 $\dfrac{2x + 6}{x^2 + 6x + 9} + \dfrac{5x}{x^2 - 9} + \dfrac{7}{x - 3}$

33 $\dfrac{\dfrac{b}{a} - \dfrac{a}{b}}{\dfrac{1}{a} - \dfrac{1}{b}}$

34 $\dfrac{\dfrac{1}{x + 2} - 3}{\dfrac{4}{x} - x}$

35 $\dfrac{\dfrac{x}{y^2} - \dfrac{y}{x^2}}{\dfrac{1}{y^2} - \dfrac{1}{x^2}}$

36 $\dfrac{\dfrac{r}{s} + \dfrac{s}{r}}{\dfrac{r^2}{s^2} - \dfrac{s^2}{r^2}}$

37 $\dfrac{y^{-1} + x^{-1}}{(xy)^{-1}}$

38 $\dfrac{y^{-2} - x^{-2}}{y^{-2} + x^{-2}}$

39 $\dfrac{\dfrac{5}{x + 1} + \dfrac{2x}{x + 3}}{\dfrac{x}{x + 1} + \dfrac{7}{x + 3}}$

40 $\dfrac{\dfrac{3}{w} - \dfrac{6}{2w + 1}}{\dfrac{5}{w} + \dfrac{8}{2w + 1}}$

41 $\dfrac{\dfrac{3}{x - 1} - \dfrac{3}{a - 1}}{x - a}$

42 $\dfrac{\dfrac{x + 2}{x} - \dfrac{a + 2}{a}}{x - a}$

43 $\dfrac{(x + h)^2 - 3(x + h) - (x^2 - 3x)}{h}$

44 $\dfrac{(x + h)^3 + 5(x + h) - (x^3 + 5x)}{h}$

45 $\dfrac{\dfrac{1}{(x + h)^3} - \dfrac{1}{x^3}}{h}$

46 $\dfrac{\dfrac{1}{x + h} - \dfrac{1}{x}}{h}$

47 $\dfrac{\dfrac{4}{3x + 3h - 1} - \dfrac{4}{3x - 1}}{h}$

48 $\dfrac{\dfrac{5}{2x + 2h + 3} - \dfrac{5}{2x + 3}}{h}$

Exer. 49–54: Rationalize the denominator.

49 $\dfrac{\sqrt{t} + 5}{\sqrt{t} - 5}$

50 $\dfrac{\sqrt{t} - 4}{\sqrt{t} + 4}$

51 $\dfrac{81x^2 - 16y^2}{3\sqrt{x} - 2\sqrt{y}}$

52 $\dfrac{16x^2 - y^2}{2\sqrt{x} - \sqrt{y}}$

53 $\dfrac{1}{\sqrt[3]{a} - \sqrt[3]{b}}$ (*Hint:* Multiply numerator and denominator by $\sqrt[3]{a^2} + \sqrt[3]{ab} + \sqrt[3]{b^2}$.)

54 $\dfrac{1}{\sqrt[3]{x} + \sqrt[3]{y}}$

Exer. 55–60: Rationalize the numerator.

55 $\dfrac{\sqrt{a} - \sqrt{b}}{a^2 - b^2}$

56 $\dfrac{\sqrt{b} + \sqrt{c}}{b^2 - c^2}$

57 $\dfrac{\sqrt{2(x + h) + 1} - \sqrt{2x + 1}}{h}$

58 $\dfrac{\sqrt{x} - \sqrt{x + h}}{h\sqrt{x}\sqrt{x + h}}$

59 $\dfrac{\sqrt{1 - x - h} - \sqrt{1 - x}}{h}$

60 $\dfrac{\sqrt[3]{x + h} - \sqrt[3]{x}}{h}$ (*Hint:* Compare with Exercise 53.)

Exer. 61–64: Express as a sum of terms of the form ax^r, where r is a rational number.

61 $\dfrac{4x^2 - x + 5}{x^{2/3}}$

62 $\dfrac{x^2 + 4x - 6}{\sqrt{x}}$

63 $\dfrac{(x^2 + 2)^2}{x^5}$

64 $\dfrac{\left(\sqrt{x} - 3\right)^2}{x^3}$

Exer. 65–68: Express as a quotient.

65 $x^{-3} + x^2$

66 $x^{-4} - x$

67 $x^{-1/2} - x^{3/2}$

68 $x^{-2/3} + x^{7/3}$

Exer. 69–82: Simplify the expression.

69 $(2x^2 - 3x + 1)(4)(3x + 2)^3(3) + (3x + 2)^4(4x - 3)$

70 $(6x - 5)^3(2)(x^2 + 4)(2x) + (x^2 + 4)^2(3)(6x - 5)^2(6)$

71 $(x^2 - 4)^{1/2}(3)(2x + 1)^2(2) + (2x + 1)^3(\tfrac{1}{2})(x^2 - 4)^{-1/2}(2x)$

72 $(3x + 2)^{1/3}(2)(4x - 5)(4) + (4x - 5)^2(\tfrac{1}{3})(3x + 2)^{-2/3}(3)$

73 $(3x + 1)^6(\tfrac{1}{2})(2x - 5)^{-1/2}(2) + (2x - 5)^{1/2}(6)(3x + 1)^5(3)$

74 $(x^2 + 9)^4\left(-\tfrac{1}{3}\right)(x + 6)^{-4/3} + (x + 6)^{-1/3}(4)(x^2 + 9)^3(2x)$

75 $\dfrac{(6x + 1)^3(27x^2 + 2) - (9x^3 + 2x)(3)(6x + 1)^2(6)}{(6x + 1)^6}$

76 $\dfrac{(x^2 - 1)^4(2x) - x^2(4)(x^2 - 1)^3(2x)}{(x^2 - 1)^8}$

77 $\dfrac{(x^2 + 2)^3(2x) - x^2(3)(x^2 + 2)^2(2x)}{[(x^2 + 2)^3]^2}$

78 $\dfrac{(x^2 - 5)^4(3x^2) - x^3(4)(x^2 - 5)^3(2x)}{[(x^2 - 5)^4]^2}$

79 $\dfrac{(x^2 + 4)^{1/3}(3) - (3x)(\tfrac{1}{3})(x^2 + 4)^{-2/3}(2x)}{[(x^2 + 4)^{1/3}]^2}$

80 $\dfrac{(1 - x^2)^{1/2}(2x) - x^2(\tfrac{1}{2})(1 - x^2)^{-1/2}(-2x)}{[(1 - x^2)^{1/2}]^2}$

81 $\dfrac{(4x^2 + 9)^{1/2}(2) - (2x + 3)(\tfrac{1}{2})(4x^2 + 9)^{-1/2}(8x)}{[(4x^2 + 9)^{1/2}]^2}$

82 $\dfrac{(3x + 2)^{1/2}(\tfrac{1}{3})(2x + 3)^{-2/3}(2) - (2x + 3)^{1/3}(\tfrac{1}{2})(3x + 2)^{-1/2}(3)}{[(3x + 2)^{1/2}]^2}$

CHAPTER 1 REVIEW EXERCISES

1 Express as a simplified rational number:

(a) $\left(\tfrac{2}{3}\right)\left(-\tfrac{5}{8}\right)$ (b) $\tfrac{3}{4} + \tfrac{6}{5}$ (c) $\tfrac{5}{8} - \tfrac{6}{7}$ (d) $\tfrac{3}{4} \div \tfrac{6}{5}$

2 Replace the symbol $\square$ with either $<$, $>$, or $=$ to make the resulting statement true.

(a) $-0.1 \ \square \ -0.001$ (b) $\sqrt{9} \ \square \ -3$

(c) $\tfrac{1}{6} \ \square \ 0.166$

3 Express the statement as an inequality.

(a) x is negative.

(b) a is between $\tfrac{1}{2}$ and $\tfrac{1}{3}$.

(c) The absolute value of x is not greater than 4.

4 Rewrite without using the absolute value symbol, and simplify:

(a) $|-7|$ (b) $\dfrac{|-5|}{-5}$ (c) $|3^{-1} - 2^{-1}|$

5 If points A, B, and C on a coordinate line have coordinates -8, 4, and -3, respectively, find the distance:

(a) $d(A, C)$ (b) $d(C, A)$ (c) $d(B, C)$

6 Express the indicated statement as an inequality involving the absolute value symbol.

(a) $d(x, -2)$ is at least 7.

(b) $d(4, x)$ is less than 4.

Exer. 7–8: Rewrite the expression without using the absolute value symbol, and simplify the result.

7 $|x + 3|$ if $x \le -3$

8 $|(x - 2)(x - 3)|$ if $2 < x < 3$

9 Determine whether the expression is true for all values of the variables, whenever the expression is defined.

(a) $(x + y)^2 = x^2 + y^2$ (b) $\dfrac{1}{\sqrt{x + y}} = \dfrac{1}{\sqrt{x}} + \dfrac{1}{\sqrt{y}}$

(c) $\dfrac{1}{\sqrt{c} - \sqrt{d}} = \dfrac{\sqrt{c} + \sqrt{d}}{c - d}$

10 Express the number in scientific form.

(a) 93,700,000,000   (b) 0.000 004 02

11 Express the number in decimal form.

(a) 6.8×10^7 (b) 7.3×10^{-4}

12 (a) Approximate $|\sqrt{5} - 17^2|$ to four decimal places.

(b) Express the answer in part (a) in scientific notation accurate to four significant figures.

Exer. 13–14: Express the number in the form a/b, where a and b are integers.

13 $-3^2 + 2^0 + 27^{-2/3}$ 14 $\left(\frac{1}{2}\right)^0 - 1^2 + 16^{-3/4}$

Exer. 15–40: Simplify the expression, and rationalize the denominator when appropriate.

15 $(3a^2b)^2(2ab^3)$

16 $\dfrac{6r^3y^2}{2r^5y}$

17 $\dfrac{(3x^2y^{-3})^{-2}}{x^{-5}y}$

18 $\left(\dfrac{a^{2/3}b^{3/2}}{a^2b}\right)^6$

19 $(-2p^2q)^3\left(\dfrac{p}{4q^2}\right)^2$

20 $c^{-4/3}c^{3/2}c^{1/6}$

21 $\left(\dfrac{xy^{-1}}{\sqrt{z}}\right)^4 \div \left(\dfrac{x^{1/3}y^2}{z}\right)^3$

22 $\left(\dfrac{-64x^3}{z^6y^9}\right)^{2/3}$

23 $[(a^{2/3}b^{-2})^3]^{-1}$

24 $\dfrac{(3u^2v^5w^{-4})^3}{(2uv^{-3}w^2)^4}$

25 $\dfrac{r^{-1} + s^{-1}}{(rs)^{-1}}$

26 $(u + v)^3(u + v)^{-2}$

27 $s^{5/2}s^{-4/3}s^{-1/6}$

28 $x^{-2} - y^{-1}$

29 $\sqrt[3]{(x^4y^{-1})^6}$

30 $\sqrt[3]{8x^5y^3z^4}$

31 $\dfrac{1}{\sqrt[3]{4}}$

32 $\sqrt{\dfrac{a^2b^3}{c}}$

33 $\sqrt[3]{4x^2y}\ \sqrt[3]{2x^5y^2}$

34 $\sqrt[4]{(-4a^3b^2c)^2}$

35 $\dfrac{1}{\sqrt{t}}\left(\dfrac{1}{\sqrt{t}} - 1\right)$

36 $\sqrt{\sqrt[3]{(c^3d^6)^4}}$

37 $\dfrac{\sqrt{12x^4y}}{\sqrt{3x^2y^5}}$

38 $\sqrt[3]{(a + 2b)^3}$

39 $\sqrt[3]{\dfrac{1}{2\pi^2}}$

40 $\sqrt[3]{\dfrac{x^2}{9y}}$

Exer. 41–44: Rationalize the denominator.

41 $\dfrac{1 - \sqrt{x}}{1 + \sqrt{x}}$

42 $\dfrac{1}{\sqrt{a} + \sqrt{a - 2}}$

43 $\dfrac{81x^2 - y^2}{3\sqrt{x} + \sqrt{y}}$

44 $\dfrac{3 + \sqrt{x}}{3 - \sqrt{x}}$

Exer. 45–62: Express as a polynomial.

45 $(3x^3 - 4x^2 + x - 7) + (x^4 - 2x^3 + 3x^2 + 5)$

46 $(4z^4 - 3z^2 + 1) - z(z^3 + 4z^2 - 4)$

47 $(x + 4)(x + 3) - (2x - 1)(x - 5)$

48 $(4x - 5)(2x^2 + 3x - 7)$

49 $(3y^3 - 2y^2 + y + 4)(y^2 - 3)$

50 $(3x + 2)(x - 5)(5x + 4)$

51 $(a - b)(a^3 + a^2b + ab^2 + b^3)$

52 $\dfrac{9p^4q^3 - 6p^2q^4 + 5p^3q^2}{3p^2q^2}$

53 $(3a - 5b)(2a + 7b)$ 54 $(4r^2 - 3s)^2$

55 $(13a^2 + 4b)(13a^2 - 4b)$ 56 $(a^3 - a^2)^2$

57 $(3y + x)^2$ 58 $(c^2 - d^2)^3$

59 $(2a + b)^3$ 60 $(x^2 - 2x + 3)^2$

61 $(3x + 2y)^2(3x - 2y)^2$ 62 $(a + b + c + d)^2$

Exer. 63–78: Factor the polynomial.

63 $60xw + 70w$ 64 $2r^4s^3 - 8r^2s^5$

65 $28x^2 + 4x - 9$ 66 $16a^4 + 24a^2b^2 + 9b^4$

67 $2wy + 3yx - 8wz - 12zx$ 68 $2c^3 - 12c^2 + 3c - 18$

69 $8x^3 + 64y^3$ 70 $u^3v^4 - u^6v$

71 $p^8 - q^8$ 72 $x^4 - 8x^3 + 16x^2$

73 $w^6 + 1$ 74 $3x + 6$

75 $x^2 + 36$ 76 $x^2 - 49y^2 - 14x + 49$

77 $x^5 - 4x^3 + 8x^2 - 32$ 78 $4x^4 + 12x^3 + 20x^2$

Exer. 79–90: Simplify the expression.

79 $\dfrac{6x^2 - 7x - 5}{4x^2 + 4x + 1}$

80 $\dfrac{r^3 - t^3}{r^2 - t^2}$

81 $\dfrac{6x^2 - 5x - 6}{x^2 - 4} \div \dfrac{2x^2 - 3x}{x + 2}$

82 $\dfrac{2}{4x - 5} - \dfrac{5}{10x + 1}$

83 $\dfrac{7}{x + 2} + \dfrac{3x}{(x + 2)^2} - \dfrac{5}{x}$

84 $\dfrac{x + x^{-2}}{1 + x^{-2}}$

85 $\dfrac{1}{x} - \dfrac{2}{x^2 + x} - \dfrac{3}{x + 3}$

86 $(a^{-1} + b^{-1})^{-1}$

87 $\dfrac{x + 2 - \dfrac{3}{x + 4}}{\dfrac{x}{x + 4} + \dfrac{1}{x + 4}}$

88 $\dfrac{\dfrac{x}{x + 2} - \dfrac{4}{x + 2}}{x - 3 - \dfrac{6}{x + 2}}$

89 $(x^2 + 1)^{3/2}(4)(x + 5)^3 + (x + 5)^4\left(\frac{3}{2}\right)(x^2 + 1)^{1/2}(2x)$

90 $\dfrac{(4 - x^2)\left(\frac{1}{3}\right)(6x + 1)^{-2/3}(6) - (6x + 1)^{1/3}(-2x)}{(4 - x^2)^2}$

91 Express $\dfrac{(x + 5)^2}{\sqrt{x}}$ as a sum of terms of the form ax^r, where r is a rational number.

92 Express $x^3 + x^{-1}$ as a quotient.

93 Red blood cells in a body The body of an average person contains 5.5 liters of blood and about 5 million red blood cells per cubic millimeter of blood. Given that $1 \text{ L} = 10^6 \text{ mm}^3$, estimate the number of red blood cells in an average person's body.

94 Heartbeats in a lifetime A healthy heart beats 70 to 90 times per minute. Estimate the number of heartbeats in the lifetime of an individual who lives to age 80.

95 Body surface area At age 2 years, a typical boy is 91.2 centimeters tall and weighs 13.7 kilograms. Use the DuBois and DuBois formula, $S = (0.007184)w^{0.425}h^{0.725}$, where w is weight and h is height, to find the body surface area S (in square meters).

96 Adiabatic expansion A gas is said to expand *adiabatically* if there is no loss or gain of heat. The formula for the adiabatic expansion of air is $pv^{-1.4} = c$, where p is the pressure, v is the volume, and c is a constant. If, at a certain instant, the pressure is 40 dyne/cm^2 and the volume is 60 cm^3, find the value of c (a *dyne* is the unit of force in the cgs system).

CHAPTER 1 DISCUSSION EXERCISES

1 Credit card cash back For every \$10 charged to a particular credit card, 1 point is awarded. At the end of the year, 100 points can be exchanged for \$1 in cash back. What percent discount does this cash back represent in terms of the amount of money charged to the credit card?

2 Determine the conditions under which $\sqrt{a^2 + b^2} = a + b$.

3 Show that the sum of squares $x^2 + 25$ can be factored by adding and subtracting a particular term and following the method demonstrated in Example 10(c) of Section 1.3.

4 What is the difference between the expressions $\dfrac{1}{x + 1}$ and $\dfrac{x - 1}{x^2 - 1}$?

5 Write the quotient of two arbitrary second-degree polynomials in x, and evaluate the quotient with several large values of x. What general conclusion can you reach about such quotients?

6 Simplify the expression $\dfrac{3x^2 - 5x - 2}{x^2 - 4}$. Now evaluate both expressions with a value of x ($x \neq \pm 2$). Discuss what this evaluation proves (or doesn't) and what your simplification proves (or doesn't).

7 Party trick To guess your partner's age and height, have him/her do the following:

 1 Write down his/her age.

 2 Multiply it by 2.

 3 Add 5.

 4 Multiply this sum by 50.

 5 Subtract 365.

 6 Add his/her height (in inches).

 7 Add 115.

The first two digits of the result equal his/her age, and the last two digits equal his/her height. Explain why this is true.

8 Circuits problem In a particular circuits problem, the output voltage is defined by

$$V_{\text{out}} = I_{\text{in}}\left(-\frac{RXi}{R - Xi}\right),$$

where $I_{\text{in}} = \dfrac{V_{\text{in}}}{Z_{\text{in}}}$ and $Z_{\text{in}} = \dfrac{R^2 - X^2 - 3RXi}{R - Xi}$. Find a formula for V_{out} in terms of V_{in} when R is equal to X.

9 Relating baseball records Based on the number of runs scored (S) and runs allowed (A), the Pythagorean winning percentage estimates what a baseball team's winning percentage should be. This formula, developed by baseball statistician Bill James, has the form

$$\frac{S^x}{S^x + A^x}.$$

James determined that $x = 1.83$ yields the most accurate results.

 The 1927 New York Yankees are generally regarded as one of the best teams in baseball history. Their record was 110 wins and 44 losses. They scored 975 runs while allowing only 599.

 (a) Find their Pythagorean win–loss record.

 (b) Estimate the value of x (to the nearest 0.01) that best predicts the 1927 Yankees' actual win–loss record.

2

Equations and Inequalities

Methods for solving equations date back to the Babylonians (2000 B.C.), who described equations in words instead of the variables—x, y, and so on—that we use today. Major advances in finding solutions of equations then took place in Italy in the sixteenth century and continued throughout the world well into the nineteenth century. In modern times, computers are used to approximate solutions of very complicated equations.

Inequalities that involve variables have now attained the same level of importance as equations, and they are used extensively in applications of mathematics. In this chapter we shall discuss several methods for solving basic equations and inequalities.

2.1

Equations

An **equation** (or **equality**) is a statement that two quantities or expressions are equal. Equations are employed in every field that uses real numbers. As an illustration, the equation

$$d = rt, \quad \text{or} \quad \text{distance} = (\text{rate})(\text{time}),$$

is used in solving problems involving an object moving at a constant rate of speed. If the rate r is 45 mi/hr (miles per hour), then the distance d (in miles) traveled after time t (in hours) is given by

$$d = 45t.$$

For example, if $t = 2$ hr, then $d = 45 \cdot 2 = 90$ mi. If we wish to find how long it takes the object to travel 75 miles, we let $d = 75$ and *solve* the equation

$$75 = 45t \quad \text{or, equivalently,} \quad 45t = 75.$$

Dividing both sides of the last equation by 45, we obtain

$$t = \frac{75}{45} = \frac{5}{3}.$$

Thus, if $r = 45$ mi/hr, then the time required to travel 75 miles is $1\frac{2}{3}$ hours, or 1 hour and 40 minutes.

Note that the equation $d = rt$ contains three variables: d, r, and t. In much of our work in this chapter we shall consider equations that contain only one variable. The following chart applies to a variable x, but any other variable may be considered. The abbreviations LS and RS in the second illustration stand for the equation's left side and right side, respectively.

Terminology	Definition	Illustration
Equation in x	A statement of equality involving one variable, x	$x^2 - 5 = 4x$
Solution, or **root,** of an equation in x	A number b that yields a true statement when substituted for x	5 is a solution of $x^2 - 5 = 4x$, since substitution gives us LS: $5^2 - 5 = 25 - 5 = 20$ and RS: $4 \cdot 5 = 20$, and $20 = 20$ is a true statement.
A number b **satisfies** an equation in x	b is a solution of the equation	5 satisfies $x^2 - 5 = 4x$.
Equivalent equations	Equations that have exactly the same solutions	$2x + 1 = 7$ $2x = 7 - 1$ $2x = 6$ $x = 3$
Solve an equation in x	Find all solutions of the equation	To solve $(x + 3)(x - 5) = 0$, set each factor equal to 0: $x + 3 = 0, x - 5 = 0$, obtaining the solutions -3 and 5.

An **algebraic equation** in x contains only algebraic expressions such as polynomials, rational expressions, radicals, and so on. An equation of this type is called a **conditional equation** if there are numbers in the domains of the expressions that are not solutions. For example, the equation $x^2 = 9$ is conditional, since the number $x = 4$ (and others) is not a solution. If *every* number in the domains of the expressions in an algebraic equation is a solution, the equation is called an **identity.**

Sometimes it is difficult to determine whether an equation is conditional or an identity. An identity will often be indicated when, after properties of real numbers are applied, an equation of the form $p = p$ is obtained, where p is some expression. To illustrate, if we multiply both sides of the equation

$$\frac{x}{x^2 - 4} = \frac{x}{(x + 2)(x - 2)}$$

by $x^2 - 4$, we obtain $x = x$. This alerts us to the fact that we may have an identity on our hands; it does not, however, prove anything. A standard method for verifying that an equation is an identity is to show, using properties of real numbers, that the expression which appears on one side of the given equation can be transformed into the expression which appears on the other side of the given equation. That is easy to do in the preceding illustration, since we know that $x^2 - 4 = (x + 2)(x - 2)$. Of course, to show that an equation is not an identity, we need only find one real number in the domain of the variable that fails to satisfy the original equation.

The most basic equation in algebra is the *linear equation,* defined in the next chart, where a and b denote real numbers.

Terminology	Definition	Illustration
Linear equation in x	An equation that can be written in the form $ax + b = 0$, where $a \neq 0$	$4x + 5 = 0$ $4x = -5$ $x = -\frac{5}{4}$

The illustration in the preceding chart indicates a typical method of solving a linear equation. Following the same procedure, we see that

$$\text{if} \quad ax + b = 0, \quad \text{then} \quad x = -\frac{b}{a},$$

provided $a \neq 0$. Thus, a linear equation has exactly one solution.

We sometimes solve an equation by making a list of equivalent equations, each in some sense simpler than the preceding one, ending the list with an equation from which the solutions can be easily obtained. We often simplify an equation by adding the same expression to both sides or subtracting the same expression from both sides. We can also multiply or divide both sides of an equation by an expression that represents a *nonzero* real number. In the following examples, the phrases in color indicate how an equivalent equation was obtained from the preceding equation. To shorten these phrases we have, as in Example 1, used "add 7" instead of the more accurate but lengthy *add 7 to both sides.* Similarly, "subtract $2x$" is used for *subtract $2x$ from both sides,* and "divide by 4" means *divide both sides by* 4.

EXAMPLE 1 Solving a linear equation

Solve the equation $6x - 7 = 2x + 5$.

SOLUTION   The equations in the following list are equivalent:

$$
\begin{array}{ll}
6x - 7 = 2x + 5 & \text{given} \\
(6x - 7) + 7 = (2x + 5) + 7 & \text{add 7} \\
6x = 2x + 12 & \text{simplify} \\
6x - 2x = (2x + 12) - 2x & \text{subtract } 2x \\
4x = 12 & \text{simplify} \\
\dfrac{4x}{4} = \dfrac{12}{4} & \text{divide by 4} \\
x = 3 & \text{simplify}
\end{array}
$$

✔ Check $x = 3$ LS: $6(3) - 7 = 18 - 7 = 11$
RS: $2(3) + 5 = 6 + 5 = 11$

Since $11 = 11$ is a true statement, $x = 3$ checks as a solution.

As indicated in the preceding example, we often check a solution by substituting it into the given equation. Such checks may detect errors introduced through incorrect manipulations or mistakes in arithmetic.

We say that the equation given in Example 1 *has the solution* $x = 3$. Similarly, we would say that the equation $x^2 = 4$ *has solutions* $x = 2$ *and* $x = -2$.

The next example illustrates that a seemingly complicated equation may simplify to a linear equation.

EXAMPLE 2 Solving an equation

Solve the equation $(8x - 2)(3x + 4) = (4x + 3)(6x - 1)$.

SOLUTION   The equations in the following list are equivalent:

$$
\begin{array}{ll}
(8x - 2)(3x + 4) = (4x + 3)(6x - 1) & \text{given} \\
24x^2 + 26x - 8 = 24x^2 + 14x - 3 & \text{multiply factors} \\
26x - 8 = 14x - 3 & \text{subtract } 24x^2 \\
12x - 8 = -3 & \text{subtract } 14x \\
12x = 5 & \text{add 8} \\
x = \frac{5}{12} & \text{divide by 12}
\end{array}
$$

Hence, the solution of the given equation is $\frac{5}{12}$.

We did not check the preceding solution because each step yields an equivalent equation; however, when you are working exercises or taking a test, it is always a good idea to check answers to guard against errors.

If an equation contains rational expressions, we often eliminate denominators by multiplying both sides by the lcd of these expressions. If we multiply both sides by an expression that equals zero for some value of x, then the resulting equation may *not* be equivalent to the original equation, as illustrated in the following example.

EXAMPLE 3   An equation with no solutions

Solve the equation $\dfrac{3x}{x-2} = 1 + \dfrac{6}{x-2}$.

SOLUTION

$$\frac{3x}{x-2} = 1 + \frac{6}{x-2} \qquad \text{given}$$

$$\left(\frac{3x}{x-2}\right)(x-2) = (1)(x-2) + \left(\frac{6}{x-2}\right)(x-2) \quad \text{multiply by } x-2$$

$$3x = (x-2) + 6 \qquad \text{simplify}$$

$$3x = x + 4 \qquad \text{simplify}$$

$$2x = 4 \qquad \text{subtract } x$$

$$x = 2 \qquad \text{divide by 2}$$

✔ Check $x = 2$ LS: $\dfrac{3(2)}{(2)-2} = \dfrac{6}{0}$

Since division by 0 is not permissible, $x = 2$ is not a solution. Hence, *the given equation has no solutions.*   ◪

In the process of solving an equation, we may obtain, as a *possible* solution, a number that is *not* a solution of the given equation. Such a number is called an **extraneous solution** or **extraneous root** of the given equation. In Example 3, $x = 2$ is an extraneous solution (root) of the given equation.

The following guidelines may also be used to solve the equation in Example 3. In this case, observing guideline 2 would make it unnecessary to check the extraneous solution $x = 2$.

Guidelines for Solving an Equation Containing Rational Expressions	1 Determine the lcd of the rational expressions. 2 Find the values of the variable that make the lcd zero. These are *not* solutions, because they yield at least one zero denominator when substituted into the given equation. 3 Multiply each term of the equation by the lcd and simplify, thereby eliminating all of the denominators. 4 Solve the equation obtained in guideline 3. 5 The solutions of the given equation are the solutions found in guideline 4, with the exclusion of the values found in guideline 2.

We shall follow these guidelines in the next example.

EXAMPLE 4   An equation containing rational expressions

Solve the equation $\dfrac{3}{2x-4} - \dfrac{5}{x+3} = \dfrac{2}{x-2}$.

SOLUTION

Guideline 1   Rewriting the denominator $2x - 4$ as $2(x - 2)$, we see that the lcd of the three rational expressions is $2(x - 2)(x + 3)$.

Guideline 2   The values of x that make the lcd $2(x - 2)(x + 3)$ zero are 2 and -3, so these numbers cannot be solutions of the equation.

Guideline 3   Multiplying each term of the equation by the lcd and simplifying gives us the following:

$$\frac{3}{2(x-2)}2(x-2)(x+3) - \frac{5}{x+3}2(x-2)(x+3) = \frac{2}{x-2}2(x-2)(x+3)$$

$$3(x+3) - 10(x-2) = 4(x+3) \qquad \text{cancel like factors}$$

$$3x + 9 - 10x + 20 = 4x + 12 \qquad \text{multiply factors}$$

Guideline 4   We solve the last equation obtained in guideline 3.

$$3x - 10x - 4x = 12 - 9 - 20 \qquad \text{subtract } 4x, 9, \text{ and } 20$$

$$-11x = -17 \qquad \text{combine like terms}$$

$$x = \tfrac{17}{11} \qquad \text{divide by } -11$$

Guideline 5   Since $\tfrac{17}{11}$ is not included among the values (2 and -3) that make the lcd zero (guideline 2), we see that $x = \tfrac{17}{11}$ is a solution of the given equation.

We shall not check the solution $x = \tfrac{17}{11}$ by substitution, because the arithmetic involved is complicated. It is simpler to carefully check the algebraic manipulations used in each step. However, a calculator check is recommended.

Formulas involving several variables occur in many applications of mathematics. Sometimes it is necessary to solve for a specific variable in terms of the remaining variables that appear in the formula, as the next two examples illustrate.

Figure 1

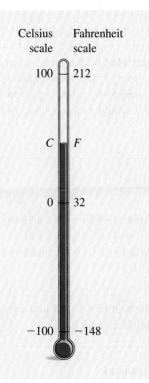

Celsius scale   Fahrenheit scale

100   212

C F

0   32

-100 -148

EXAMPLE 5   Relationship between temperature scales

The Celsius and Fahrenheit temperature scales are shown on the thermometer in Figure 1. The relationship between the temperature readings C and F is given by $C = \tfrac{5}{9}(F - 32)$. Solve for F.

SOLUTION   To *solve for F* we must obtain a formula that has F by itself on one side of the equals sign and does not have F on the other side. We may do this as follows:

$$C = \tfrac{5}{9}(F - 32) \qquad \text{given}$$

$$\tfrac{9}{5}C = F - 32 \qquad \text{multiply by } \tfrac{9}{5}$$

$$\tfrac{9}{5}C + 32 = F \qquad \text{add 32}$$

$$F = \tfrac{9}{5}C + 32 \qquad \text{equivalent equation}$$

We can make a simple check of our result in Example 5 as follows. Start with $C = \tfrac{5}{9}(F - 32)$ and substitute 212 (an arbitrary choice) for F to obtain 100 for C. Now let $C = 100$ in $F = \tfrac{9}{5}C + 32$ to get $F = 212$. Again, this check does not *prove* we are correct, but certainly lends credibility to our result.

EXAMPLE 6   Resistors connected in parallel

In electrical theory, the formula

$$\frac{1}{R} = \frac{1}{R_1} + \frac{1}{R_2}$$

is used to find the total resistance R when two resistors R_1 and R_2 are connected in parallel, as illustrated in Figure 2. Solve for R_1.

SOLUTION   We first multiply both sides of the given equation by the lcd of the three fractions and then solve for R_1, as follows:

$$\frac{1}{R} = \frac{1}{R_1} + \frac{1}{R_2} \qquad \text{given}$$

$$\frac{1}{R} \cdot RR_1R_2 = \frac{1}{R_1} \cdot RR_1R_2 + \frac{1}{R_2} \cdot RR_1R_2 \qquad \text{multiply by the lcd, } RR_1R_2$$

$$R_1R_2 = RR_2 + RR_1 \qquad \text{cancel common factors}$$

$$R_1R_2 - RR_1 = RR_2 \qquad \text{collect terms with } R_1 \text{ on one side}$$

$$R_1(R_2 - R) = RR_2 \qquad \text{factor out } R_1$$

$$R_1 = \frac{RR_2}{R_2 - R} \qquad \text{divide by } R_2 - R$$

An alternative method of solution is to first solve for $\dfrac{1}{R_1}$:

$$\frac{1}{R} = \frac{1}{R_1} + \frac{1}{R_2} \qquad \text{given}$$

$$\frac{1}{R_1} + \frac{1}{R_2} = \frac{1}{R} \qquad \text{equivalent equation}$$

$$\frac{1}{R_1} = \frac{1}{R} - \frac{1}{R_2} \qquad \text{subtract } \frac{1}{R_2}$$

$$\frac{1}{R_1} = \frac{R_2 - R}{RR_2} \qquad \text{combine fractions}$$

If two nonzero numbers are equal, then so are their reciprocals. Hence,

$$R_1 = \frac{RR_2}{R_2 - R}.$$

Figure 2

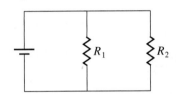

2.1 Exercises

Exer. 1–44: Solve the equation.

1 $-3x + 4 = -1$

2 $2x - 2 = -9$

3 $4x - 3 = -5x + 6$

4 $5x - 4 = 2(x - 2)$

5 $4(2y + 5) = 3(5y - 2)$

6 $6(2y + 3) - 3(y - 5) = 0$

7 $\frac{1}{5}x + 2 = 3 - \frac{2}{7}x$

8 $\frac{5}{3}x - 1 = 4 + \frac{2}{3}x$

9 $0.3(3 + 2x) + 1.2x = 3.2$

10 $1.5x - 0.7 = 0.4(3 - 5x)$

11 $\frac{3 + 5x}{5} = \frac{4 - x}{7}$

12 $\frac{2x - 9}{4} = 2 + \frac{x}{12}$

13 $\frac{13 + 2x}{4x + 1} = \frac{3}{4}$

14 $\frac{3}{7x - 2} = \frac{9}{3x + 1}$

15 $8 - \frac{5}{x} = 2 + \frac{3}{x}$

16 $\frac{3}{y} + \frac{6}{y} - \frac{1}{y} = 11$

17 $(3x - 2)^2 = (x - 5)(9x + 4)$

18 $(x + 5)^2 + 3 = (x - 2)^2$

19 $(5x - 7)(2x + 1) - 10x(x - 4) = 0$

20 $(2x + 9)(4x - 3) = 8x^2 - 12$

21 $\frac{3x + 1}{6x - 2} = \frac{2x + 5}{4x - 13}$

22 $\frac{5x + 2}{10x - 3} = \frac{x - 8}{2x + 3}$

23 $\frac{2}{5} + \frac{4}{10x + 5} = \frac{7}{2x + 1}$

24 $\frac{-5}{3x - 9} + \frac{4}{x - 3} = \frac{5}{6}$

25 $\frac{3}{2x - 4} - \frac{5}{3x - 6} = \frac{3}{5}$

26 $\frac{9}{2x + 6} - \frac{7}{5x + 15} = \frac{2}{3}$

27 $2 - \frac{5}{3x - 7} = 2$

28 $\frac{6}{2x + 11} + 5 = 5$

29 $\frac{1}{2x - 1} = \frac{4}{8x - 4}$

30 $\frac{4}{5x + 2} - \frac{12}{15x + 6} = 0$

31 $\frac{7}{y^2 - 4} - \frac{4}{y + 2} = \frac{5}{y - 2}$

32 $\frac{4}{2u - 3} + \frac{10}{4u^2 - 9} = \frac{1}{2u + 3}$

33 $(x + 3)^3 - (3x - 1)^2 = x^3 + 4$

34 $(x - 1)^3 = (x + 1)^3 - 6x^2$

35 $\frac{9x}{3x - 1} = 2 + \frac{3}{3x - 1}$

36 $\frac{2x}{2x + 3} + \frac{6}{4x + 6} = 5$

37 $\frac{1}{x + 4} + \frac{3}{x - 4} = \frac{3x + 8}{x^2 - 16}$

38 $\frac{2}{2x + 3} + \frac{4}{2x - 3} = \frac{5x + 6}{4x^2 - 9}$

39 $\frac{4}{x + 2} + \frac{1}{x - 2} = \frac{5x - 6}{x^2 - 4}$

40 $\frac{2}{2x + 5} + \frac{3}{2x - 5} = \frac{10x + 5}{4x^2 - 25}$

41 $\frac{2}{2x + 1} - \frac{3}{2x - 1} = \frac{-2x + 7}{4x^2 - 1}$

42 $\frac{3}{2x + 5} + \frac{4}{2x - 5} = \frac{14x + 3}{4x^2 - 25}$

43 $\frac{5}{2x + 3} + \frac{4}{2x - 3} = \frac{14x + 3}{4x^2 - 9}$

44 $\frac{-3}{x + 4} + \frac{7}{x - 4} = \frac{-5x + 4}{x^2 - 16}$

Exer. 45–50: Show that the equation is an identity.

45 $(4x - 3)^2 - 16x^2 = 9 - 24x$

46 $(3x - 4)(2x + 1) + 5x = 6x^2 - 4$

47 $\frac{x^2 - 9}{x + 3} = x - 3$

48 $\frac{x^3 + 8}{x + 2} = x^2 - 2x + 4$

49 $\frac{3x^2 + 8}{x} = \frac{8}{x} + 3x$

50 $\frac{49x^2 - 25}{7x - 5} = 7x + 5$

Exer. 51–52: For what value of c is the number a a solution of the equation?

51 $4x + 1 + 2c = 5c - 3x + 6$; $a = -2$

52 $3x - 2 + 6c = 2c - 5x + 1$; $a = 4$

Exer. 53–54: Determine whether the two equations are equivalent.

53 (a) $\dfrac{7x}{x-5} = \dfrac{42}{x-5}$, $\quad x = 6$

(b) $\dfrac{7x}{x-5} = \dfrac{35}{x-5}$, $\quad x = 5$

54 (a) $\dfrac{8x}{x-7} = \dfrac{72}{x-7}$, $\quad x = 9$

(b) $\dfrac{8x}{x-7} = \dfrac{56}{x-7}$, $\quad x = 7$

Exer. 55–56: Determine values for a and b such that $\frac{5}{3}$ is a solution of the equation.

55 $ax + b = 0$

56 $ax^2 + bx = 0$

Exer. 57–58: Determine which equation is not equivalent to the equation preceding it.

57 $\quad x^2 - x - 2 = x^2 - 4$
$\quad (x + 1)(x - 2) = (x + 2)(x - 2)$
$\quad\quad\quad x + 1 = x + 2$
$\quad\quad\quad\quad 1 = 2$

58 $\quad\quad 5x + 6 = 4x + 3$
$\quad x^2 + 5x + 6 = x^2 + 4x + 3$
$\quad (x + 2)(x + 3) = (x + 1)(x + 3)$
$\quad\quad\quad x + 2 = x + 1$
$\quad\quad\quad\quad 2 = 1$

Exer. 59–62: Solve the formula for the specified variable.

59 $EK + L = D - TK$ for K

60 $CD + C = PC + N$ for C

61 $M = \dfrac{Q+1}{Q}$ for Q

62 $\beta = \dfrac{\alpha}{1-\alpha}$ for α

Exer. 63–76: The formula occurs in the indicated application. Solve for the specified variable.

63 $I = Prt$ for P (simple interest)

64 $C = 2\pi r$ for r (circumference of a circle)

65 $A = \frac{1}{2}bh$ for h (area of a triangle)

66 $V = \frac{1}{3}\pi r^2 h$ for h (volume of a cone)

67 $F = g\dfrac{mM}{d^2}$ for m (Newton's law of gravitation)

68 $R = \dfrac{V}{I}$ for I (Ohm's law in electrical theory)

69 $P = 2l + 2w$ for w (perimeter of a rectangle)

70 $A = P + Prt$ for r (principal plus interest)

71 $A = \frac{1}{2}(b_1 + b_2)h$ for b_1 (area of a trapezoid)

72 $s = \frac{1}{2}gt^2 + v_0 t$ for v_0 (distance an object falls)

73 $S = \dfrac{p}{q + p(1 - q)}$ for q (Amdahl's law for supercomputers)

74 $S = 2(lw + hw + hl)$ for h (surface area of a rectangular box)

75 $\dfrac{1}{f} = \dfrac{1}{p} + \dfrac{1}{q}$ for q (lens equation)

76 $\dfrac{1}{R} = \dfrac{1}{R_1} + \dfrac{1}{R_2} + \dfrac{1}{R_3}$ for R_2 (three resistors connected in parallel)

2.2
Applied Problems

Equations are often used to solve *applied problems*—that is, problems that involve applications of mathematics to other fields. Because of the unlimited variety of applied problems, it is difficult to state specific rules for finding solutions. The following guidelines may be helpful, provided the problem can be formulated in terms of an equation in one variable.

Guidelines for Solving Applied Problems	*1* If the problem is stated in writing, read it carefully several times and think about the given facts, together with the unknown quantity that is to be found.
	2 Introduce a letter to denote the unknown quantity. This is one of the most crucial steps in the solution. Phrases containing words such as *what, find, how much, how far,* or *when* should alert you to the unknown quantity.
	3 If appropriate, draw a picture and label it.
	4 List the known facts, together with any relationships that involve the unknown quantity. A relationship may be described by an equation in which written statements, instead of letters or numbers, appear on one or both sides of the equals sign.
	5 After analyzing the list in guideline 4, formulate an equation that describes precisely what is stated in words.
	6 Solve the equation formulated in guideline 5.
	7 Check the solutions obtained in guideline 6 by referring to the original statement of the problem. Verify that the solution agrees with the stated conditions.

The use of these guidelines is illustrated in the next example.

EXAMPLE 1　Test average

A student in an algebra course has test scores of 64 and 78. What score on a third test will give the student an average of 80?

SOLUTION

Guideline 1　Read the problem at least one more time.

Guideline 2　The unknown quantity is the score on the third test, so we let

$$x = \text{score on the third test.}$$

Guideline 3　A picture or diagram is unnecessary for this problem.

Guideline 4　Known facts are scores of 64 and 78 on the first two tests. A relationship that involves x is the average score of 64, 78, and x. Thus,

$$\text{average score} = \frac{64 + 78 + x}{3}.$$

Guideline 5　Since the average score in guideline 4 is to be 80, we consider the equation

$$\frac{64 + 78 + x}{3} = 80.$$

Guideline 6 We solve the equation formulated in guideline 5:

$$64 + 78 + x = 80 \cdot 3 \qquad \text{multiply by 3}$$
$$142 + x = 240 \qquad \text{simplify}$$
$$x = 98 \qquad \text{subtract 142}$$

Guideline 7 Check If the three test scores are 64, 78, and 98, then the average is

$$\frac{64 + 78 + 98}{3} = \frac{240}{3} = 80,$$

as desired.

In the remaining examples, try to identify the explicit guidelines that are used in the solutions.

EXAMPLE 2 Calculating a presale price

A clothing store holding a clearance sale advertises that all prices have been discounted 20%. If a shirt is on sale for $28, what was its presale price?

SOLUTION Since the unknown quantity is the presale price, we let

$$x = \text{presale price}.$$

We next note the following facts:

$$0.20x = \text{discount of 20\% on presale price}$$
$$28 = \text{sale price}$$

The sale price is determined as follows:

$$(\text{presale price}) - (\text{discount}) = \text{sale price}$$

Translating the last equation into symbols and then solving gives us

$$x - 0.20x = 28 \qquad \text{formulate an equation}$$
$$0.80x = 28 \qquad \text{subtract } 0.20x \text{ from } 1x$$
$$x = \frac{28}{0.80} = 35. \qquad \text{divide by } 0.80$$

The presale price was $35.

Check If a $35 shirt is discounted 20%, then the discount (in dollars) is $(0.20)(35) = 7$ and the sale price is $35 - 7$, or $28.

Banks and other financial institutions pay interest on investments. Usually this interest is *compounded* (as described in Section 5.2); however, if money is invested or loaned for a short period of time, *simple interest* may be paid, using the following formula.

Simple Interest Formula	If a sum of money P (the **principal**) is invested at a simple interest rate r (expressed as a decimal), then the **simple interest** I at the end of t years is $$I = Prt.$$

The following table illustrates simple interest for three cases.

Principal P	Interest rate r	Number of years t	Interest $I = Prt$
$1000	$8\% = 0.08$	1	$1000(0.08)(1) = \$80$
$2000	$6\% = 0.06$	$1\frac{1}{2}$	$2000(0.06)(1.5) = \$180$
$3200	$5\frac{1}{2}\% = 0.055$	2	$3200(0.055)(2) = \$352$

EXAMPLE 3 Investing money in two stocks

An investment firm has $100,000 to invest for a client and decides to invest it in two stocks, A and B. The expected annual rate of return, or simple interest, for stock A is 15%, but there is some risk involved, and the client does not wish to invest more than $50,000 in this stock. The annual rate of return on the more stable stock B is anticipated to be 10%. Determine whether there is a way of investing the money so that the annual interest is

(a) $12,000   **(b)** $13,000

SOLUTION   The annual interest is given by $I = Pr$, which comes from the simple interest formula $I = Prt$ with $t = 1$. If we let x denote the amount invested in stock A, then $100,000 - x$ will be invested in stock B. This leads to the following equalities:

$$x = \text{amount invested in stock A at } 15\%$$
$$100,000 - x = \text{amount invested in stock B at } 10\%$$
$$0.15x = \text{annual interest from stock A}$$
$$0.10(100,000 - x) = \text{annual interest from stock B}$$

Adding the interest from both stocks, we obtain

$$\text{total annual interest} = 0.15x + 0.10(100,000 - x).$$

Simplifying the right-hand side gives us

$$\text{total annual interest} = 10,000 + 0.05x. \qquad (*)$$

(a) The total annual interest is $12,000 if

$$10,000 + 0.05x = 12,000 \qquad \text{from (*)}$$

$$0.05x = 2000 \qquad \text{subtract } 10,000$$

$$x = \frac{2000}{0.05} = 40,000. \qquad \text{divide by } 0.05$$

Thus, $40,000 should be invested in stock A, and the remaining $60,000 should be invested in stock B. Since the amount invested in stock A is not more than $50,000, this manner of investing the money meets the requirement of the client.

✔ Check   If $40,000 is invested in stock A and $60,000 in stock B, then the total annual interest is

$$40,000(0.15) + 60,000(0.10) = 6000 + 6000 = 12,000.$$

(b) The total annual interest is $13,000 if

$$10,000 + 0.05x = 13,000 \qquad \text{from (*)}$$

$$0.05x = 3000 \qquad \text{subtract } 10,000$$

$$x = \frac{3000}{0.05} = 60,000. \qquad \text{divide by } 0.05$$

Thus, $60,000 should be invested in stock A and the remaining $40,000 in stock B. This plan does *not* meet the client's requirement that no more than $50,000 be invested in stock A. Hence, the firm cannot invest the client's money in stocks A and B such that the total annual interest is $13,000.   ◢

In certain applications, it is necessary to combine two substances to obtain a prescribed mixture, as illustrated in the next two examples.

EXAMPLE 4   Mixing chemicals

A chemist has 10 milliliters of a solution that contains a 30% concentration of acid. How many milliliters of pure acid must be added in order to increase the concentration to 50%?

SOLUTION   Since the unknown quantity is the amount of pure acid to add, we let

$$x = \text{number of mL of pure acid to be added.}$$

To help visualize the problem, let us draw a picture, as in Figure 1, and attach appropriate labels.

(continued)

Figure 1

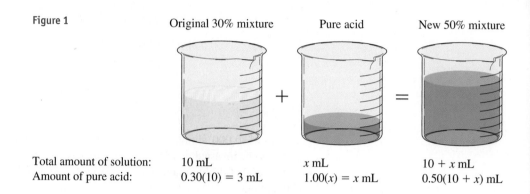

Original 30% mixture   Pure acid   New 50% mixture

Total amount of solution:	10 mL	x mL		$10 + x$ mL
Amount of pure acid:	$0.30(10) = 3$ mL	$1.00(x) = x$ mL		$0.50(10 + x)$ mL

Since we can express the amount of pure acid in the final solution as either $3 + x$ (from the first two beakers) or $0.50(10 + x)$, we obtain the equation

$$3 + x = 0.50(10 + x).$$

We now solve for x:

$$3 + x = 5 + 0.5x \qquad \text{multiply factors}$$
$$0.5x = 2 \qquad \text{subtract } 0.5x \text{ and } 3$$
$$x = \frac{2}{0.5} = 4 \qquad \text{divide by } 0.5$$

Hence, 4 milliliters of pure acid should be added to the original solution.

✔ Check If 4 milliliters of acid is added to the original solution, then the new solution contains 14 milliliters, 7 milliliters of which is pure acid. This is the desired 50% concentration.

EXAMPLE 5 Replacing antifreeze

A radiator contains 8 quarts of a mixture of water and antifreeze. If 40% of the mixture is antifreeze, how much of the mixture should be drained and replaced by pure antifreeze so that the resultant mixture will contain 60% antifreeze?

SOLUTION Let

$$x = \text{number of qt of mixture to be drained.}$$

Since there were 8 quarts in the original 40% mixture, we may depict the problem as in Figure 2.

Figure 2

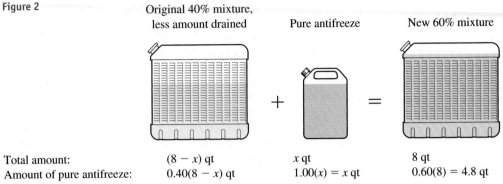

Original 40% mixture,
less amount drained   Pure antifreeze   New 60% mixture

Total amount:	$(8 - x)$ qt	x qt	8 qt
Amount of pure antifreeze:	$0.40(8 - x)$ qt	$1.00(x) = x$ qt	$0.60(8) = 4.8$ qt

Since the number of quarts of pure antifreeze in the final mixture can be expressed as either $0.40(8 - x) + x$ or 4.8, we obtain the equation

$$0.40(8 - x) + x = 4.8.$$

We now solve for x:

$3.2 - 0.4x + x = 4.8$	multiply factors
$0.6x = 1.6$	combine x terms and subtract 3.2
$x = \dfrac{1.6}{0.6} = \dfrac{16}{6} = \dfrac{8}{3}$	divide by 0.6

Thus, $\frac{8}{3}$ quarts should be drained from the original mixture.

✔ Check   Let us first note that the amount of antifreeze in the original 8-quart mixture was 0.4(8), or 3.2 quarts. In draining $\frac{8}{3}$ quarts of the original 40% mixture, we lose $0.4\left(\frac{8}{3}\right)$ quarts of antifreeze, and so $3.2 - 0.4\left(\frac{8}{3}\right)$ quarts of antifreeze remain after draining. If we then add $\frac{8}{3}$ quarts of pure antifreeze, the amount of antifreeze in the final mixture is

$$3.2 - 0.4\left(\tfrac{8}{3}\right) + \tfrac{8}{3} = 4.8 \text{ qt.}$$

This number, 4.8, is 60% of 8.

EXAMPLE 6   Comparing times traveled by cars

Two cities are connected by means of a highway. A car leaves city B at 1:00 P.M. and travels at a constant rate of 40 mi/hr toward city C. Thirty minutes later, another car leaves B and travels toward C at a constant rate of 55 mi/hr. If the lengths of the cars are disregarded, at what time will the second car reach the first car?

SOLUTION   Let t denote the number of hours after 1:00 P.M. traveled by the first car. Since the second car leaves B at 1:30 P.M., it has traveled $\frac{1}{2}$ hour less than the first. This leads to the following table.

(continued)

Car	Rate (mi/hr)	Hours traveled	Miles traveled
First car	40	t	$40t$
Second car	55	$t - \frac{1}{2}$	$55\left(t - \frac{1}{2}\right)$

The schematic drawing in Figure 3 illustrates possible positions of the cars t hours after 1:00 P.M. The second car reaches the first car when the number of miles traveled by the two cars is equal—that is, when

$$55\left(t - \tfrac{1}{2}\right) = 40t.$$

Figure 3

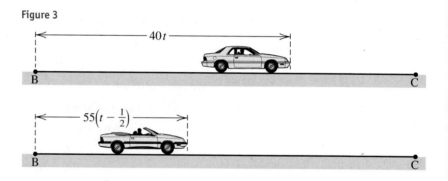

We now solve for t:

$$55t - \tfrac{55}{2} = 40t \qquad \text{multiply factors}$$
$$15t = \tfrac{55}{2} \qquad \text{subtract } 40t \text{ and add } \tfrac{55}{2}$$
$$t = \tfrac{55}{30} = \tfrac{11}{6} \qquad \text{divide by 15}$$

Thus, t is $1\frac{5}{6}$ hours or, equivalently, 1 hour 50 minutes after 1:00 P.M. Consequently, the second car reaches the first at 2:50 P.M.

Figure 4

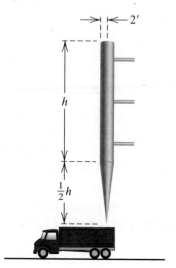

✔ Check At 2:50 P.M. the first car has traveled for $1\frac{5}{6}$ hours, and its distance from B is $40\left(\frac{11}{6}\right) = \frac{220}{3}$ mi. At 2:50 P.M. the second car has traveled for $1\frac{1}{3}$ hours and is $55\left(\frac{4}{3}\right) = \frac{220}{3}$ mi from B. Hence, they are together at 2:50 P.M. ✏

EXAMPLE 7 Constructing a grain-elevator hopper

A grain-elevator hopper is to be constructed as shown in Figure 4, with a right circular cylinder of radius 2 feet and altitude h feet on top of a right circular cone whose altitude is one-half that of the cylinder. What value of h will make the total volume V of the hopper 500 ft³?

SOLUTION   If $V_{cylinder}$ and V_{cone} denote the volumes (in ft³) and $h_{cylinder}$ and h_{cone} denote the heights (in feet) of the cylinder and cone, respectively, then, using the formulas for volume stated on the endpapers at the front of the text, we obtain the following:

$$V_{cylinder} = \pi r^2 h_{cylinder} = \pi(2)^2 h = 4\pi h$$
$$V_{cone} = \tfrac{1}{3}\pi r^2 h_{cone} = \tfrac{1}{3}\pi(2)^2\left(\tfrac{1}{2}h\right) = \tfrac{2}{3}\pi h$$

Since the total volume V of the hopper is to be 500 ft³, we must have

$4\pi h + \tfrac{2}{3}\pi h = 500$	$V_{cylinder} + V_{cone} = V_{total}$
$12\pi h + 2\pi h = 1500$	multiply by 3
$14\pi h = 1500$	combine terms
$h = \dfrac{1500}{14\pi} \approx 34.1 \text{ ft.}$	divide by 14π

EXAMPLE 8   Time required to do a job

Two pumps are available for filling a gasoline storage tank. Pump A, used alone, can fill the tank in 3 hours, and pump B, used alone, can fill it in 4 hours. If both pumps are used simultaneously, how long will it take to fill the tank?

SOLUTION   Let t denote the number of hours needed for A and B to fill the tank if used simultaneously. It is convenient to introduce the *part* of the tank filled in 1 hour as follows:

$$\tfrac{1}{3} = \text{part of the tank filled by A in 1 hr}$$
$$\tfrac{1}{4} = \text{part of the tank filled by B in 1 hr}$$
$$\frac{1}{t} = \text{part of the tank filled by A } and \text{ B in 1 hr}$$

Using the fact that

$$\begin{pmatrix} \text{part filled by} \\ \text{A in 1 hr} \end{pmatrix} + \begin{pmatrix} \text{part filled by} \\ \text{B in 1 hr} \end{pmatrix} = \begin{pmatrix} \text{part filled by} \\ \text{A } and \text{ B in 1 hr} \end{pmatrix},$$

we obtain

$$\frac{1}{3} + \frac{1}{4} = \frac{1}{t}, \qquad \text{or} \qquad \frac{7}{12} = \frac{1}{t}.$$

Taking the reciprocal of each side of the last equation gives us $t = \tfrac{12}{7}$. Thus, if pumps A and B are used simultaneously, the tank will be filled in $1\tfrac{5}{7}$ hours, or approximately 1 hour 43 minutes.

2.2   Exercises

1 Test scores A student in an algebra course has test scores of 75, 82, 71, and 84. What score on the next test will raise the student's average to 80?

2 Final class average Before the final exam, a student has test scores of 72, 80, 65, 78, and 60. If the final exam counts as one-third of the final grade, what score must the student receive in order to have a final average of 76?

3 Gross pay A worker's take-home pay is $492, after deductions totaling 40% of the gross pay have been subtracted. What is the gross pay?

4 Cost of dining out A couple does not wish to spend more than $70 for dinner at a restaurant. If a sales tax of 6% is added to the bill and they plan to tip 15% after the tax has been added, what is the most they can spend for the meal?

5 Intelligence quotient A person's intelligence quotient (IQ) is determined by multiplying the quotient of his or her mental age and chronological age by 100.

   (a) Find the IQ of a 12-year-old child whose mental age is 15.

   (b) Find the mental age of a person 15 years old whose IQ is 140.

6 Earth's surface area Water covers 70.8%, or about 361×10^6 km², of Earth's surface. Approximate the total surface area of Earth.

7 Cost of insulation The cost of installing insulation in a particular two-bedroom home is $2400. Present monthly heating costs average $200, but the insulation is expected to reduce heating costs by 10%. How many months will it take to recover the cost of the insulation?

8 Overtime pay A workman's basic hourly wage is $10, but he receives one and a half times his hourly rate for any hours worked in excess of 40 per week. If his paycheck for the week is $595, how many hours of overtime did he work?

9 Savings accounts An algebra student has won $100,000 in a lottery and wishes to deposit it in savings accounts in two financial institutions. One account pays 8% simple interest, but deposits are insured only to $50,000. The second

account pays 6.4% simple interest, and deposits are insured up to $100,000. Determine whether the money can be deposited so that it is fully insured and earns annual interest of $7500.

10 Municipal funding A city government has approved the construction of an $800 million sports arena. Up to $480 million will be raised by selling bonds that pay simple interest at a rate of 6% annually. The remaining amount (up to $640 million) will be obtained by borrowing money from an insurance company at a simple interest rate of 5%. Determine whether the arena can be financed so that the annual interest is $42 million.

11 Movie attendance Six hundred people attended the premiere of a motion picture. Adult tickets cost $9, and children were admitted for $6. If box office receipts totaled $4800, how many children attended the premiere?

12 Hourly pay A consulting engineer's time is billed at $60 per hour, and her assistant's is billed at $20 per hour. A customer received a bill for $580 for a certain job. If the assistant worked 5 hours less than the engineer, how much time did each bill on the job?

13 Preparing a glucose solution In a certain medical test designed to measure carbohydrate tolerance, an adult drinks 7 ounces of a 30% glucose solution. When the test is administered to a child, the glucose concentration must be decreased to 20%. How much 30% glucose solution and how much water should be used to prepare 7 ounces of 20% glucose solution?

14 Preparing eye drops A pharmacist is to prepare 15 milliliters of special eye drops for a glaucoma patient. The eye-drop solution must have a 2% active ingredient, but the pharmacist only has 10% solution and 1% solution in stock. How much of each type of solution should be used to fill the prescription?

15 Preparing an alloy British sterling silver is a copper-silver alloy that is 7.5% copper by weight. How many grams of pure copper and how many grams of British sterling silver should be used to prepare 200 grams of a copper-silver alloy that is 10% copper by weight?

16 **Drug concentration** Theophylline, an asthma medicine, is to be prepared from an elixir with a drug concentration of 5 mg/mL and a cherry-flavored syrup that is to be added to hide the taste of the drug. How much of each must be used to prepare 100 milliliters of solution with a drug concentration of 2 mg/mL?

17 **Walking rates** Two children, who are 224 meters apart, start walking toward each other at the same instant at rates of 1.5 m/sec and 2 m/sec, respectively (see the figure).

(a) When will they meet?

(b) How far will each have walked?

Exercise 17

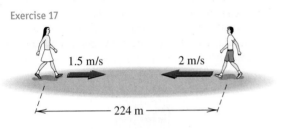

18 **Running rates** A runner starts at the beginning of a runners' path and runs at a constant rate of 6 mi/hr. Five minutes later a second runner begins at the same point, running at a rate of 8 mi/hr and following the same course. How long will it take the second runner to reach the first?

19 **Snowplow speed** At 6 A.M. a snowplow, traveling at a constant speed, begins to clear a highway leading out of town. At 8 A.M. an automobile begins traveling the highway at a speed of 30 mi/hr and reaches the plow 30 minutes later. Find the speed of the snowplow.

20 **Two-way radio range** Two children own two-way radios that have a maximum range of 2 miles. One leaves a certain point at 1:00 P.M., walking due north at a rate of 4 mi/hr. The other leaves the same point at 1:15 P.M., traveling due south at 6 mi/hr. When will they be unable to communicate with one another?

21 **Rowing rate** A boy can row a boat at a constant rate of 5 mi/hr in still water, as indicated in the figure. He rows upstream for 15 minutes and then rows downstream, returning to his starting point in another 12 minutes.

Exercise 21

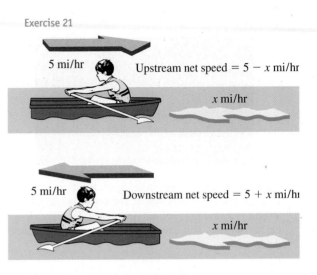

(a) Find the rate of the current.

(b) Find the total distance traveled.

22 **Gas mileage** A salesperson purchased an automobile that was advertised as averaging 25 mi/gal in the city and 40 mi/gal on the highway. A recent sales trip that covered 1800 miles required 51 gallons of gasoline. Assuming that the advertised mileage estimates were correct, how many miles were driven in the city?

23 **Distance to a target** A bullet is fired horizontally at a target, and the sound of its impact is heard 1.5 seconds later. If the speed of the bullet is 3300 ft/sec and the speed of sound is 1100 ft/sec, how far away is the target?

24 **Jogging rates** A woman begins jogging at 3:00 P.M., running due north at a 6-minute-mile pace. Later, she reverses direction and runs due south at a 7-minute-mile pace. If she returns to her starting point at 3:45 P.M., find the total number of miles run.

25 **Fencing a region** A farmer plans to use 180 feet of fencing to enclose a rectangular region, using part of a straight river bank instead of fencing as one side of the rectangle, as shown in the figure on the next page. Find the area of the region if the length of the side parallel to the river bank is

(a) twice the length of an adjacent side.

(b) one-half the length of an adjacent side.

(c) the same as the length of an adjacent side.

Exercise 25

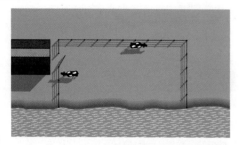

26 House dimensions Shown in the figure is a cross section of a design for a two-story home. The center height h of the second story has not yet been determined. Find h such that the second story will have the same cross-sectional area as the first story.

Exercise 26

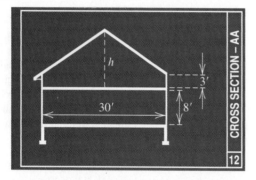

27 Window dimensions A stained-glass window is being designed in the shape of a rectangle surmounted by a semicircle, as shown in the figure. The width of the window is to be 3 feet, but the height h is yet to be determined. If 24 ft² of glass is to be used, find the height h.

Exercise 27

28 Drainage ditch dimensions Every cross section of a drainage ditch is an isosceles trapezoid with a small base of 3 feet and a height of 1 foot, as shown in the figure. Determine the width of the larger base that would give the ditch a cross-sectional area of 5 ft².

Exercise 28

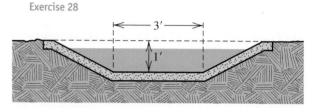

29 Constructing a silo A large grain silo is to be constructed in the shape of a circular cylinder with a hemisphere attached to the top (see the figure). The diameter of the silo is to be 30 feet, but the height is yet to be determined. Find the height h of the silo that will result in a capacity of $11{,}250\pi$ ft³.

Exercise 29

30 Dimensions of a cone The wafer cone shown in the figure is to hold 8 in³ of ice cream when filled to the bottom. The diameter of the cone is 2 inches, and the top of the ice cream has the shape of a hemisphere. Find the height h of the cone.

Exercise 30

31 Lawn mowing rates It takes a boy 90 minutes to mow the lawn, but his sister can mow it in 60 minutes. How long would it take them to mow the lawn if they worked together, using two lawn mowers?

32 Filling a swimming pool With water from one hose, a swimming pool can be filled in 8 hours. A second, larger hose used alone can fill the pool in 5 hours. How long would it take to fill the pool if both hoses were used simultaneously?

33 Delivering newspapers It takes a girl 45 minutes to deliver the newspapers on her route; however, if her brother helps, it takes them only 20 minutes. How long would it take her brother to deliver the newspapers by himself?

34 Emptying a tank A water tank can be emptied by using one pump for 5 hours. A second, smaller pump can empty the tank in 8 hours. If the larger pump is started at 1:00 P.M., at what time should the smaller pump be started so that the tank will be emptied at 5:00 P.M.?

35 Grade point average (GPA) A college student has finished 48 credit hours with a GPA of 2.75. To get into the program she wishes to enter, she must have a GPA of 3.2. How many additional credit hours of 4.0 work will raise her GPA to 3.2?

36 Ohm's law In electrical theory, Ohm's law states that $I = V/R$, where I is the current in amperes, V is the electromotive force in volts, and R is the resistance in ohms. In a certain circuit $V = 110$ and $R = 50$. If V and R are to be changed by the same numerical amount, what change in them will cause I to double?

37 Air temperature Below the cloud base, the air temperature T (in °F) at height h (in feet) can be approximated by the equation $T = T_0 - \left(\frac{5.5}{1000}\right)h$, where T_0 is the temperature at ground level.

(a) Determine the air temperature at a height of 1 mile if the ground temperature is 70°F.

(b) At what altitude is the temperature freezing?

38 Height of a cloud The height h (in feet) of the cloud base can be estimated using $h = 227(T - D)$, where T is the ground temperature and D is the dew point.

(a) If the temperature is 70°F and the dew point is 55°F, find the height of the cloud base.

(b) If the dew point is 65°F and the cloud base is 3500 feet, estimate the ground temperature.

39 A cloud's temperature The temperature T within a cloud at height h (in feet) above the cloud base can be approximated using the equation $T = B - \left(\frac{3}{1000}\right)h$, where B is the temperature of the cloud at its base. Determine the temperature at 10,000 feet in a cloud with a base temperature of 55°F and a base height of 4000 feet. **Note:** For an interesting application involving the three preceding exercises, see Exercise 6 in the Discussion Exercises at the end of the chapter.

40 Bone-height relationship Archeologists can determine the height of a human without having a complete skeleton. If an archeologist finds only a humerus, then the height of the individual can be determined by using a simple linear relationship. (The humerus is the bone between the shoulder and the elbow.) For a female, if x is the length of the humerus (in centimeters), then her height h (in centimeters) can be determined using the formula $h = 65 + 3.14x$. For a male, $h = 73.6 + 3.0x$ should be used.

(a) A female skeleton having a 30-centimeter humerus is found. Find the woman's height at death.

(b) A person's height will typically decrease by 0.06 centimeter each year after age 30. A complete male skeleton is found. The humerus is 34 centimeters, and the man's height was 174 centimeters. Determine his approximate age at death.

2.3
Quadratic Equations

A toy rocket is launched vertically upward from level ground, as illustrated in Figure 1. If its initial speed is 120 ft/sec and the only force acting on it is gravity, then the rocket's height h (in feet) above the ground after t seconds is given by

$$h = -16t^2 + 120t.$$

Some values of h for the first 7 seconds of flight are listed in the following table.

t (sec)	0	1	2	3	4	5	6	7
h (ft)	0	104	176	216	224	200	144	56

Figure 1

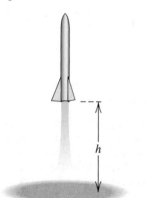

We see from the table that, as it ascended, the rocket was 180 feet above the ground at some time between $t = 2$ and $t = 3$. As it descended, the rocket was 180 feet above the ground at some time between $t = 5$ and $t = 6$. To find the exact values of t for which $h = 180$ ft, we must solve the equation

$$180 = -16t^2 + 120t,$$

or

$$16t^2 - 120t + 180 = 0.$$

As indicated in the next chart, an equation of this type is called a *quadratic equation* in t. After developing a formula for solving such equations, we will return to this problem in Example 13 and find the exact times at which the rocket was 180 feet above the ground.

Terminology	Definition	Illustrations
Quadratic equation in x	An equation that can be written in the form $ax^2 + bx + c = 0,$ where $a \neq 0$	$4x^2 = 8 - 11x$ $x(3 + x) = 5$ $4x = x^2$

To enable us to solve many types of equations, we will make use of the next theorem.

Zero Factor Theorem	If p and q are algebraic expressions, then $$pq = 0 \quad \text{if and only if} \quad p = 0 \quad \text{or} \quad q = 0.$$

The zero factor theorem can be extended to any number of algebraic expressions—that is,

$$pqr = 0 \quad \text{if and only if} \quad p = 0 \quad \text{or} \quad q = 0 \quad \text{or} \quad r = 0,$$

and so on. It follows that if $ax^2 + bx + c$ can be written as a product of two first-degree polynomials, then solutions can be found by setting each factor equal to 0, as illustrated in the next two examples. This technique is called the **method of factoring.**

EXAMPLE 1 Solving an equation by factoring

Solve the equation $3x^2 = 10 - x$.

SOLUTION   To use the method of factoring, *it is essential that only the number 0 appear on one side of the equation.* Thus, we proceed as follows:

$$3x^2 = 10 - x \quad \text{given}$$
$$3x^2 + x - 10 = 0 \quad \text{add } x - 10$$
$$(3x - 5)(x + 2) = 0 \quad \text{factor}$$
$$3x - 5 = 0, \quad x + 2 = 0 \quad \text{zero factor theorem}$$
$$x = \tfrac{5}{3}, \quad\quad x = -2 \quad \text{solve for } x$$

Hence, the solutions of the given equation are $\tfrac{5}{3}$ and -2.

EXAMPLE 2   Solving an equation by factoring

Solve the equation $x^2 + 16 = 8x$.

SOLUTION   We proceed as in Example 1:

$$x^2 + 16 = 8x \quad \text{given}$$
$$x^2 - 8x + 16 = 0 \quad \text{subtract } 8x$$
$$(x - 4)(x - 4) = 0 \quad \text{factor}$$
$$x - 4 = 0, \quad x - 4 = 0 \quad \text{zero factor theorem}$$
$$x = 4, \quad\quad x = 4 \quad \text{solve for } x$$

Thus, the given quadratic equation has one solution, 4.

Since $x - 4$ appears as a factor twice in the previous solution, we call 4 a **double root** or **root of multiplicity 2** of the equation $x^2 + 16 = 8x$.

If a quadratic equation has the form $x^2 = d$ for some number $d > 0$, then $x^2 - d = 0$ or, equivalently,

$$\left(x + \sqrt{d}\right)\left(x - \sqrt{d}\right) = 0.$$

Setting each factor equal to zero gives us the solutions $-\sqrt{d}$ and $\sqrt{d}$. We frequently use the symbol $\pm\sqrt{d}$ (*plus or minus* $\sqrt{d}$) to represent both $\sqrt{d}$ and $-\sqrt{d}$. Thus, for $d > 0$, we have proved the following result. (The case $d < 0$ requires the system of complex numbers discussed in Section 2.4.)

A Special Quadratic Equation	If $x^2 = d$, then $x = \pm\sqrt{d}$.

Note on Notation: It is common practice to allow one variable to represent more than one value, as in $x = \pm 3$. A more descriptive notation is $x_{1,2} = \pm 3$, implying that $x_1 = 3$ and $x_2 = -3$.

The process of solving $x^2 = d$ as indicated in the preceding box is referred to as *taking the square root of both sides of the equation.* Note that if

$d > 0$ we obtain both a positive square root and a negative square root, not just the principal square root defined in Section 1.2.

EXAMPLE 3 Solving equations of the form $x^2 = d$

Solve the equations:

(a) $x^2 = 5$ (b) $(x + 3)^2 = 5$

SOLUTION

(a) $x^2 = 5$ given

       $x = \pm\sqrt{5}$ take the square root

Thus, the solutions are $\sqrt{5}$ and $-\sqrt{5}$.

(b) $(x + 3)^2 = 5$ given

       $x + 3 = \pm\sqrt{5}$ take the square root

          $x = -3 \pm \sqrt{5}$ subtract 3

Thus, the solutions are $-3 + \sqrt{5}$ and $-3 - \sqrt{5}$.

In the work that follows we will replace an expression of the form $x^2 + kx$ by $(x + d)^2$, where k and d are real numbers. This procedure, called **completing the square** for $x^2 + kx$, calls for adding $(k/2)^2$, as described in the next box. (The same procedure is used for $x^2 - kx$.)

Completing the Square	To complete the square for $x^2 + kx$ or $x^2 - kx$, add $\left(\dfrac{k}{2}\right)^2$; that is, *add the square of half the coefficient of* x.

$$\textbf{(1)} \quad x^2 + kx + \left(\frac{k}{2}\right)^2 = \left(x + \frac{k}{2}\right)^2$$

$$\textbf{(2)} \quad x^2 - kx + \left(\frac{k}{2}\right)^2 = \left(x - \frac{k}{2}\right)^2$$

EXAMPLE 4 Completing the square

Determine the value or values of d that complete the square for each expression. Write the trinomial and the square of the binomial it represents.

(a) $x^2 - 3x + d$ (b) $x^2 + dx + 64$

SOLUTION

(a) The square of half the coefficient of x is $\left(-\frac{3}{2}\right)^2 = \frac{9}{4}$. Thus, $d = \frac{9}{4}$ and

$$x^2 - 3x + \tfrac{9}{4} = \left(x - \tfrac{3}{2}\right)^2.$$

(b)   If $(x + c)^2 = x^2 + dx + 64$, then $x^2 + 2cx + c^2 = x^2 + dx + 64$, so c^2 must equal 64 and $2c$ must equal d. Hence, c must equal 8 or -8, and since $d = 2c$, d could equal 16 or -16. So we could have

$$x^2 + 16x + 64 = (x + 8)^2 \quad \text{or} \quad x^2 - 16x + 64 = (x - 8)^2.$$

In the next example we solve a quadratic equation by completing a square.

EXAMPLE 5   Solving a quadratic equation by completing the square

Solve the equation $x^2 - 5x + 3 = 0$.

SOLUTION   It is convenient to first rewrite the equation so that only terms involving x are on the left-hand side, as follows:

$$x^2 - 5x + 3 = 0 \qquad\qquad \text{given}$$

$$x^2 - 5x = -3 \qquad\qquad \text{subtract 3}$$

$$x^2 - 5x + \left(\tfrac{5}{2}\right)^2 = -3 + \left(\tfrac{5}{2}\right)^2 \qquad \text{complete the square,}$$
$$\text{adding } \left(\tfrac{5}{2}\right)^2 \text{ to } both \text{ sides}$$

$$\left(x - \tfrac{5}{2}\right)^2 = \tfrac{13}{4} \qquad\qquad \text{equivalent equation}$$

$$x - \tfrac{5}{2} = \pm\sqrt{\tfrac{13}{4}} \qquad\qquad \text{take the square root}$$

$$x = \frac{5}{2} \pm \frac{\sqrt{13}}{2} = \frac{5 \pm \sqrt{13}}{2} \quad \text{add } \tfrac{5}{2}$$

Thus, the solutions of the equation are $\left(5 + \sqrt{13}\right)/2 \approx 4.3$ and $\left(5 - \sqrt{13}\right)/2 \approx 0.7$.

In Example 5, we solved a quadratic equation of the form $ax^2 + bx + c = 0$ with $a = 1$. If $a \neq 1$, we can solve the quadratic equation by adding a step to the procedure used in the preceding example. After rewriting the equation so that only terms involving x are on the left-hand side,

$$ax^2 + bx = -c,$$

we divide both sides by a, obtaining

$$x^2 + \frac{b}{a}x = -\frac{c}{a}.$$

We then complete the square by adding $\left(\dfrac{b}{2a}\right)^2$ to both sides. This technique is used in the proof of the following important formula.

Quadratic Formula	If $a \neq 0$, the roots of $ax^2 + bx + c = 0$ are given by $$x = \frac{-b \pm \sqrt{b^2 - 4ac}}{2a}.$$

The quadratic formula gives us two solutions of the equation

$$ax^2 + bx + c = 0.$$

They are $x = x_1, x_2$, where

$$x_1 = \frac{-b + \sqrt{b^2 - 4ac}}{2a}$$

and

$$x_2 = \frac{-b - \sqrt{b^2 - 4ac}}{2a}.$$

PROOF   We shall assume that $b^2 - 4ac \geq 0$ so that $\sqrt{b^2 - 4ac}$ is a real number. (The case in which $b^2 - 4ac < 0$ will be discussed in the next section.) Let us proceed as follows:

$$ax^2 + bx + c = 0 \qquad \text{given}$$

$$ax^2 + bx = -c \qquad \text{subtract } c$$

$$x^2 + \frac{b}{a}x = -\frac{c}{a} \qquad \text{divide by } a$$

$$x^2 + \frac{b}{a}x + \left(\frac{b}{2a}\right)^2 = \left(\frac{b}{2a}\right)^2 - \frac{c}{a} \qquad \text{complete the square}$$

$$\left(x + \frac{b}{2a}\right)^2 = \frac{b^2 - 4ac}{4a^2} \qquad \text{equivalent equation}$$

$$x + \frac{b}{2a} = \pm\sqrt{\frac{b^2 - 4ac}{4a^2}} \qquad \text{take the square root}$$

$$x = -\frac{b}{2a} \pm \sqrt{\frac{b^2 - 4ac}{4a^2}} \qquad \text{subtract } \frac{b}{2a}$$

We may write the radical in the last equation as

$$\pm\sqrt{\frac{b^2 - 4ac}{4a^2}} = \pm\frac{\sqrt{b^2 - 4ac}}{\sqrt{(2a)^2}} = \pm\frac{\sqrt{b^2 - 4ac}}{|2a|}.$$

Since $|2a| = 2a$ if $a > 0$ or $|2a| = -2a$ if $a < 0$, we see that in all cases

$$x = -\frac{b}{2a} \pm \frac{\sqrt{b^2 - 4ac}}{2a} = \frac{-b \pm \sqrt{b^2 - 4ac}}{2a}.$$

Note that if the quadratic formula is executed properly, it is unnecessary to check the solutions.

The number $b^2 - 4ac$ under the radical sign in the quadratic formula is called the **discriminant** of the quadratic equation. The discriminant can be used to determine the nature of the roots of the equation, as in the following chart.

Value of the discriminant $b^2 - 4ac$	Nature of the roots of $ax^2 + bx + c = 0$
Positive value	Two real and unequal roots
0	One root of multiplicity 2
Negative value	No real root

The discriminant in the next two examples is positive. In Example 8 the discriminant is 0.

EXAMPLE 6   Using the quadratic formula

Solve the equation $4x^2 + x - 3 = 0$.

SOLUTION   Let $a = 4$, $b = 1$, and $c = -3$ in the quadratic formula:

$$x = \frac{-1 \pm \sqrt{(1)^2 - 4(4)(-3)}}{2(4)} \qquad x = \frac{-b \pm \sqrt{b^2 - 4ac}}{2a}$$

$$= \frac{-1 \pm \sqrt{49}}{8} \qquad\qquad \text{simplify the discriminant}$$

$$= \frac{-1 \pm 7}{8} \qquad\qquad \sqrt{49} = 7$$

Hence, the solutions are

$$x = \frac{-1 + 7}{8} = \frac{3}{4} \quad \text{and} \quad x = \frac{-1 - 7}{8} = -1.$$

Example 6 can also be solved by factoring. Writing $(4x - 3)(x + 1) = 0$ and setting each factor equal to zero gives us $x = \frac{3}{4}$ and $x = -1$.

EXAMPLE 7   Using the quadratic formula

Solve the equation $2x(3 - x) = 3$.

SOLUTION   To use the quadratic formula, we must write the equation in the form $ax^2 + bx + c = 0$. The following equations are equivalent:

$$2x(3 - x) = 3 \quad \text{given}$$
$$6x - 2x^2 = 3 \quad \text{multiply factors}$$
$$-2x^2 + 6x - 3 = 0 \quad \text{subtract 3}$$
$$2x^2 - 6x + 3 = 0 \quad \text{multiply by } -1$$

We now let $a = 2$, $b = -6$, and $c = 3$ in the quadratic formula, obtaining

$$x = \frac{-(-6) \pm \sqrt{(-6)^2 - 4(2)(3)}}{2(2)} = \frac{6 \pm \sqrt{12}}{4} = \frac{6 \pm 2\sqrt{3}}{4}.$$

Note that

$$\frac{3 \pm \sqrt{3}}{2} \neq \frac{3}{2} \pm \sqrt{3}.$$

*The 2 in the denominator must be divided into **both** terms of the numerator, so*

$$\frac{3 \pm \sqrt{3}}{2} = \frac{3}{2} \pm \frac{1}{2}\sqrt{3}.$$

Since 2 is a factor of the numerator and denominator, we can simplify the last fraction as follows:

$$\frac{2(3 \pm \sqrt{3})}{2 \cdot 2} = \frac{3 \pm \sqrt{3}}{2}$$

Hence, the solutions are

$$\frac{3 + \sqrt{3}}{2} \approx 2.37 \quad \text{and} \quad \frac{3 - \sqrt{3}}{2} \approx 0.63.$$

The following example illustrates the case of a double root.

EXAMPLE 8   Using the quadratic formula

Solve the equation $9x^2 - 30x + 25 = 0$.

SOLUTION   Let $a = 9$, $b = -30$, and $c = 25$ in the quadratic formula:

$$x = \frac{-(-30) \pm \sqrt{(-30)^2 - 4(9)(25)}}{2(9)} \qquad x = \frac{-b \pm \sqrt{b^2 - 4ac}}{2a}$$

$$= \frac{30 \pm \sqrt{900 - 900}}{18} \qquad \text{simplify}$$

$$= \frac{30 \pm 0}{18} = \frac{5}{3}$$

Consequently, the equation has one (double) root, $\frac{5}{3}$.

EXAMPLE 9   Clearing an equation of fractions

Solve the equation $\dfrac{2x}{x - 3} + \dfrac{5}{x + 3} = \dfrac{36}{x^2 - 9}$.

SOLUTION   Using the guidelines stated in Section 2.1 for solving an equation containing rational expressions, we multiply by the lcd, $(x + 3)(x - 3)$, remembering that, by guideline 2, the numbers (-3 and 3) that make the lcd zero cannot be solutions. Thus, we proceed as follows:

$$\frac{2x}{x - 3} + \frac{5}{x + 3} = \frac{36}{x^2 - 9} \qquad \text{given}$$

$$2x(x + 3) + 5(x - 3) = 36 \qquad \text{multiply by the lcd, } (x + 3)(x - 3)$$

$$2x^2 + 6x + 5x - 15 - 36 = 0 \qquad \text{multiply factors and subtract 36}$$

$$2x^2 + 11x - 51 = 0 \qquad \text{simplify}$$

$$(2x + 17)(x - 3) = 0 \qquad \text{factor}$$

$$2x + 17 = 0, \quad x - 3 = 0 \qquad \text{zero factor theorem}$$

$$x = -\tfrac{17}{2}, \quad x = 3 \qquad \text{solve for } x$$

Since $x = 3$ cannot be a solution, we see that $x = -\frac{17}{2}$ is the only solution of the given equation.

The next example shows how the quadratic formula can be used to help factor trinomials.

EXAMPLE 10   Factoring with the quadratic formula

Factor the polynomial $21x^2 - 13x - 20$.

SOLUTION   We solve the associated quadratic equation,

$$21x^2 - 13x - 20 = 0,$$

by using the quadratic formula:

$$x = \frac{-(-13) \pm \sqrt{(-13)^2 - 4(21)(-20)}}{2(21)}$$

$$= \frac{13 \pm \sqrt{169 + 1680}}{42} = \frac{13 \pm \sqrt{1849}}{42}$$

$$= \frac{13 \pm 43}{42} = \frac{56}{42}, -\frac{30}{42} = \frac{4}{3}, -\frac{5}{7}$$

We now write the equation as a product of linear factors, both of the form $(x - \text{solution})$:

$$\left(x - \tfrac{4}{3}\right)\left(x - \left(-\tfrac{5}{7}\right)\right) = 0$$

Eliminate the denominators by multiplying both sides by $3 \cdot 7$:

$$3 \cdot 7\left(x - \tfrac{4}{3}\right)\left(x + \tfrac{5}{7}\right) = 0 \cdot 3 \cdot 7$$

$$3\left(x - \tfrac{4}{3}\right) \cdot 7\left(x + \tfrac{5}{7}\right) = 0$$

$$(3x - 4)(7x + 5) = 0$$

The left side is the desired factoring—that is,

$$21x^2 - 13x - 20 = (3x - 4)(7x + 5).$$

In the next example, we use the quadratic formula to solve an equation that contains more than one variable.

EXAMPLE 11   Using the quadratic formula

Solve $y = x^2 - 6x + 5$ for x, where $x \leq 3$.

SOLUTION   The equation can be written in the form

$$x^2 - 6x + 5 - y = 0,$$

so it is a quadratic equation in x with coefficients $a = 1$, $b = -6$, and

(continued)

$c = 5 - y$. Notice that y is considered to be a constant since we are solving for the variable x. Now we use the quadratic formula:

$$x = \frac{-(-6) \pm \sqrt{(-6)^2 - 4(1)(5 - y)}}{2(1)} \qquad x = \frac{-b \pm \sqrt{b^2 - 4ac}}{2a}$$

$$= \frac{6 \pm \sqrt{16 + 4y}}{2} \qquad \text{simplify } b^2 - 4ac$$

$$= \frac{6 \pm \sqrt{4}\sqrt{4 + y}}{2} \qquad \text{factor out } \sqrt{4}$$

$$= \frac{6 \pm 2\sqrt{4 + y}}{2} \qquad \sqrt{4} = 2$$

$$= 3 \pm \sqrt{4 + y} \qquad \text{divide 2 into } both \text{ terms}$$

Since $\sqrt{4 + y}$ is nonnegative, $3 + \sqrt{4 + y}$ is greater than or equal to 3 and $3 - \sqrt{4 + y}$ is less than or equal to 3. Because the given restriction is $x \le 3$, we have

$$x = 3 - \sqrt{4 + y}. \qquad \text{✎}$$

Many applied problems lead to quadratic equations. One is illustrated in the following example.

Figure 2

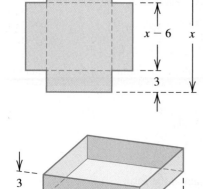

EXAMPLE 12 Constructing a rectangular box

A box with a square base and no top is to be made from a square piece of tin by cutting out a 3-inch square from each corner and folding up the sides. If the box is to hold 48 in³, what size piece of tin should be used?

SOLUTION   We begin by drawing the picture in Figure 2, letting x denote the unknown length of the side of the piece of tin. Subsequently, each side of the base of the box will have length $x - 3 - 3 = x - 6$.

Since the area of the base of the box is $(x - 6)^2$ and the height is 3, we obtain

$$\text{volume of box} = 3(x - 6)^2.$$

Since the box is to hold 48 in³,

$$3(x - 6)^2 = 48.$$

We now solve for x:

$$(x - 6)^2 = 16 \qquad \text{divide by 3}$$

$$x - 6 = \pm 4 \qquad \text{take the square root}$$

$$x = 6 \pm 4 \qquad \text{add 6}$$

Consequently,

$$x = 10 \quad \text{or} \quad x = 2.$$

✔ Check   Referring to Figure 2, we see that $x = 2$ is unacceptable, since no box is possible in this case. However, if we begin with a 10-inch square of tin, cut out 3-inch corners, and fold, we obtain a box having dimensions 4 inches, 4 inches, and 3 inches. The box has the desired volume of 48 in³. Thus, a 10-inch square is the answer to the problem.   ◢

As illustrated in Example 12, even though an equation is formulated correctly, it is possible to arrive at meaningless solutions because of the physical nature of a given problem. Such solutions should be discarded. For example, we would not accept the answer -7 years for the age of an individual or $\sqrt{50}$ for the number of automobiles in a parking lot.

In the next example we solve the applied problem discussed at the beginning of this section.

EXAMPLE 13   Finding the height of a toy rocket

The height above ground h (in feet) of a toy rocket, t seconds after it is launched, is given by $h = -16t^2 + 120t$. When will the rocket be 180 feet above the ground?

SOLUTION   Using $h = -16t^2 + 120t$, we obtain the following:

$$180 = -16t^2 + 120t \qquad \text{let } h = 180$$

$$16t^2 - 120t + 180 = 0 \qquad \text{add } 16t^2 - 120t$$

$$4t^2 - 30t + 45 = 0 \qquad \text{divide by 4}$$

Note that the equation is quadratic in t, so the quadratic formula is solved for t.

Applying the quadratic formula with $a = 4$, $b = -30$, and $c = 45$ gives us

$$t = \frac{-(-30) \pm \sqrt{(-30)^2 - 4(4)(45)}}{2(4)}$$

$$= \frac{30 \pm \sqrt{180}}{8} = \frac{30 \pm 6\sqrt{5}}{8} = \frac{15 \pm 3\sqrt{5}}{4}.$$

Hence, the rocket is 180 feet above the ground at the following times:

$$t = \frac{15 - 3\sqrt{5}}{4} \approx 2.07 \text{ sec}$$

$$t = \frac{15 + 3\sqrt{5}}{4} \approx 5.43 \text{ sec}$$ ◢

2.3 Exercises

Exer. 1–14: Solve the equation by factoring.

1 $6x^2 + x - 12 = 0$

2 $4x^2 + x - 14 = 0$

3 $15x^2 - 12 = -8x$

4 $15x^2 - 14 = 29x$

5 $2x(4x + 15) = 27$

6 $x(3x + 10) = 77$

7 $75x^2 + 35x - 10 = 0$

8 $48x^2 + 12x - 90 = 0$

9 $12x^2 + 60x + 75 = 0$

10 $4x^2 - 72x + 324 = 0$

11 $\dfrac{2x}{x + 3} + \dfrac{5}{x} - 4 = \dfrac{18}{x^2 + 3x}$

12 $\dfrac{5x}{x - 2} + \dfrac{3}{x} + 2 = \dfrac{-6}{x^2 - 2x}$

13 $\dfrac{5x}{x - 3} + \dfrac{4}{x + 3} = \dfrac{90}{x^2 - 9}$

14 $\dfrac{3x}{x - 2} + \dfrac{1}{x + 2} = \dfrac{-4}{x^2 - 4}$

Exer. 15–16: Determine whether the two equations are equivalent.

15 (a) $x^2 = 16, x = 4$

(b) $x = \sqrt{9}, x = 3$

16 (a) $x^2 = 25, x = 5$

(b) $x = \sqrt{64}, x = 8$

Exer. 17–24: Solve the equation by using the special quadratic equation on page 75.

17 $x^2 = 169$

18 $x^2 = 361$

19 $25x^2 = 9$

20 $16x^2 = 49$

21 $(x - 3)^2 = 17$

22 $(x + 4)^2 = 31$

23 $4(x + 2)^2 = 11$

24 $9(x - 1)^2 = 7$

Exer. 25–26: Determine the value or values of d that complete the square for the expression.

25 (a) $x^2 + 9x + d$

(b) $x^2 - 8x + d$

(c) $x^2 + dx + 36$

(d) $x^2 + dx + \frac{49}{4}$

26 (a) $x^2 + 13x + d$

(b) $x^2 - 6x + d$

(c) $x^2 + dx + 25$

(d) $x^2 + dx + \frac{81}{4}$

Exer. 27–30: Solve by completing the square. (*Note:* See the discussion after Example 5 for help in solving Exercises 29 and 30.)

27 $x^2 + 6x + 7 = 0$

28 $x^2 - 8x + 11 = 0$

29 $4x^2 - 12x - 11 = 0$

30 $4x^2 + 20x + 13 = 0$

Exer. 31–44: Solve by using the quadratic formula.

31 $6x^2 - x = 2$

32 $5x^2 + 13x = 6$

33 $x^2 + 4x + 2 = 0$

34 $x^2 - 6x - 3 = 0$

35 $2x^2 - 3x - 4 = 0$

36 $3x^2 + 5x + 1 = 0$

37 $\frac{3}{2}z^2 - 4z - 1 = 0$

38 $\frac{5}{3}s^2 + 3s + 1 = 0$

39 $\dfrac{5}{w^2} - \dfrac{10}{w} + 2 = 0$

40 $\dfrac{x + 1}{3x + 2} = \dfrac{x - 2}{2x - 3}$

41 $4x^2 + 81 = 36x$

42 $24x + 9 = -16x^2$

43 $\dfrac{5x}{x^2 + 9} = -1$

44 $\frac{1}{7}x^2 + 1 = \frac{4}{7}x$

Exer. 45–48: Use the quadratic formula to factor the expressions.

45 $x^2 + x - 30$

46 $x^2 + 7x$

47 $12x^2 - 16x - 3$

48 $15x^2 + 34x - 16$

Exer. 49–50: Use the quadratic formula to solve the equation for (a) x in terms of y and (b) y in terms of x.

49 $4x^2 - 4xy + 1 - y^2 = 0$

50 $2x^2 - xy = 3y^2 + 1$

Exer. 51–54: Solve for the specified variable.

51 $K = \frac{1}{2}mv^2$ for v (kinetic energy)

52 $F = g\dfrac{mM}{d^2}$ for d (Newton's law of gravitation)

53 $A = 2\pi r(r + h)$ for r (surface area of a closed cylinder)

54 $s = \frac{1}{2}gt^2 + v_0 t$ for t (distance an object falls)

55 Velocity of a gas When a hot gas exits a cylindrical smokestack, its velocity varies throughout a circular cross section of the smokestack, with the gas near the center of the cross section having a greater velocity than the gas near the perimeter. This phenomenon can be described by the formula

$$V = V_{max}\left[1 - \left(\frac{r}{r_0}\right)^2\right],$$

where V_{max} is the maximum velocity of the gas, r_0 is the radius of the smokestack, and V is the velocity of the gas at a distance r from the center of the circular cross section. Solve this formula for r.

56 Density of the atmosphere For altitudes h up to 10,000 meters, the density D of Earth's atmosphere (in kg/m³) can be approximated by the formula

$$D = 1.225 - (1.12 \times 10^{-4})h + (3.24 \times 10^{-9})h^2.$$

Approximate the altitude if the density of the atmosphere is 0.74 kg/m³.

57 Dimensions of a tin can A manufacturer of tin cans wishes to construct a right circular cylindrical can of height 20 centimeters and capacity 3000 cm³ (see the figure). Find the inner radius r of the can.

Exercise 57

20 cm

CORN

r

58 Constructing a rectangular box Refer to Example 12. A box with an open top is to be constructed by cutting 3-inch squares from the corners of a rectangular sheet of tin whose length is twice its width. What size sheet will produce a box having a volume of 60 in³?

59 Baseball toss A baseball is thrown straight upward with an initial speed of 64 ft/sec. The number of feet s above the ground after t seconds is given by the equation $s = -16t^2 + 64t$.

(a) When will the baseball be 48 feet above the ground?

(b) When will it hit the ground?

60 Braking distance The distance that a car travels between the time the driver makes the decision to hit the brakes and the time the car actually stops is called the braking distance. For a certain car traveling v mi/hr, the braking distance d (in feet) is given by $d = v + (v^2/20)$.

(a) Find the braking distance when v is 55 mi/hr.

(b) If a driver decides to brake 120 feet from a stop sign, how fast can the car be going and still stop by the time it reaches the sign?

61 Temperature of boiling water The temperature T (in °C) at which water boils is related to the elevation h (in meters above sea level) by the formula

$$h = 1000(100 - T) + 580(100 - T)^2$$

for $95 \le T \le 100$.

(a) At what elevation does water boil at a temperature of 98°C?

(b) The elevation of Mt. Everest is approximately 8840 meters. Estimate the temperature at which water boils at the top of this mountain. (*Hint:* Use the quadratic formula with $x = 100 - T$.)

62 Coulomb's law A particle of charge -1 is located on a coordinate line at $x = -2$, and a particle of charge -2 is located at $x = 2$, as shown in the figure. If a particle of charge $+1$ is located at a position x between -2 and 2, Coulomb's law in electrical theory asserts that the net force F acting on this particle is given by

$$F = \frac{-k}{(x + 2)^2} + \frac{2k}{(2 - x)^2}$$

for some constant $k > 0$. Determine the position at which the net force is zero.

Exercise 62

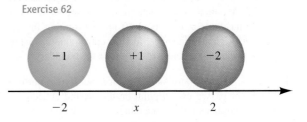

-1 $+1$ -2

-2 x 2

63 Dimensions of a sidewalk A rectangular plot of ground having dimensions 26 feet by 30 feet is surrounded by a walk of uniform width. If the area of the walk is 240 ft², what is its width?

64 Designing a poster A 24-by-36-inch sheet of paper is to be used for a poster, with the shorter side at the bottom. The margins at the sides and top are to have the same width, and the bottom margin is to be twice as wide as the other margins. Find the width of the margins if the printed area is to be 661.5 in².

65 Fencing a garden A square vegetable garden is to be tilled and then enclosed with a fence. If the fence costs $1 per foot and the cost of preparing the soil is $0.50 per ft², determine the size of the garden that can be enclosed for $120.

66 Fencing a region A farmer plans to enclose a rectangular region, using part of his barn for one side and fencing for the other three sides. If the side parallel to the barn is to be twice the length of an adjacent side, and the area of the region is to be 128 ft², how many feet of fencing should be purchased?

67 Planning a freeway The boundary of a city is a circle of diameter 5 miles. As shown in the figure, a straight highway runs through the center of the city from *A* to *B*. The highway department is planning to build a 6-mile-long freeway from *A* to a point *P* on the outskirts and then to *B*. Find the distance from *A* to *P*. (*Hint: APB* is a right triangle.)

Exercise 67

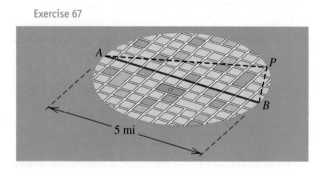

68 City expansion The boundary of a city is a circle of diameter 10 miles. Within the last decade, the city has grown in area by approximately 16π mi² (about 50 mi²). Assuming the city was always circular in shape, find the corresponding change in distance from the center of the city to the boundary.

69 Distance between airplanes An airplane flying north at 200 mi/hr passed over a point on the ground at 2:00 P.M. Another airplane at the same altitude passed over the point at 2:30 P.M., flying east at 400 mi/hr (see the figure).

(a) If *t* denotes the time in hours after 2:30 P.M., express the distance *d* between the airplanes in terms of *t*.

(b) At what time after 2:30 P.M. were the airplanes 500 miles apart?

Exercise 69

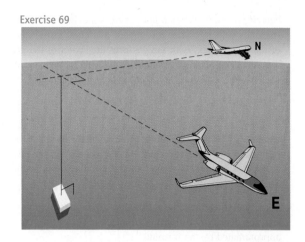

70 Two-way radio range Two surveyors with two-way radios leave the same point at 9:00 A.M., one walking due south at 4 mi/hr and the other due west at 3 mi/hr. How long can they communicate with one another if each radio has a maximum range of 2 miles?

71 Constructing a pizza box A pizza box with a square base is to be made from a rectangular sheet of cardboard by cutting six 1-inch squares from the corners and the middle sections and folding up the sides (see the figure). If the area of the base is to be 144 in², what size piece of cardboard should be used?

Exercise 71

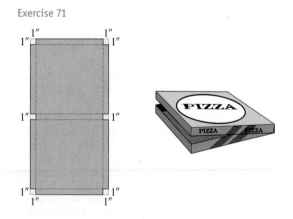

72 Constructing wire frames Two square wire frames are to be constructed from a piece of wire 100 inches long. If the area enclosed by one frame is to be one-half the area enclosed by the other, find the dimensions of each frame. (Disregard the thickness of the wire.)

73 Canoeing rate The speed of the current in a stream is 5 mi/hr. It takes a canoeist 30 minutes longer to paddle 1.2 miles upstream than to paddle the same distance downstream. What is the canoeist's rate in still water?

74 Height of a cliff When a rock is dropped from a cliff into an ocean, it travels approximately $16t^2$ feet in t seconds. If the splash is heard 4 seconds later and the speed of sound is 1100 ft/sec, approximate the height of the cliff.

75 Quantity discount A company sells running shoes to dealers for $40 per pair if less than 50 pairs are ordered. If 50 or more pairs are ordered (up to 600), the price per pair is reduced at a rate of $0.04 times the number ordered. How many pairs can a dealer purchase for $8400?

76 Price of a CD player When a popular brand of CD player is priced at $300 per unit, a store sells 15 units per week. Each time the price is reduced by $10, however, the sales increase by 2 per week. What selling price will result in weekly revenues of $7000?

77 Dimensions of an oil drum A closed right circular cylindrical oil drum of height 4 feet is to be constructed so that the total surface area is 10π ft^2. Find the diameter of the drum.

78 Dimensions of a vitamin tablet The rate at which a tablet of vitamin C begins to dissolve depends on the surface area of the tablet. One brand of tablet is 2 centimeters long and is in the shape of a cylinder with hemispheres of diameter 0.5 centimeter attached to both ends, as shown in the figure. A second brand of tablet is to be manufactured in the shape of a right circular cylinder of altitude 0.5 centimeter.

(a) Find the diameter of the second tablet so that its surface area is equal to that of the first tablet.

(b) Find the volume of each tablet.

Exercise 78

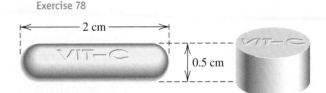

Exer. 79–80: During a nuclear explosion, a fireball will be produced having a maximum volume V_0. For temperatures below 2000 K and a given explosive force, the volume V of the fireball t seconds after the explosion can be estimated using the given formula. (Note that the kelvin is abbreviated as K, not °K.) Approximate t when V is 95% of V_0.

79 $V/V_0 = 0.8197 + 0.007752t + 0.0000281t^2$
   (20-kiloton explosion)

80 $V/V_0 = 0.831 + 0.00598t + 0.0000919t^2$
   (10-megaton explosion)

Exer. 81–82: When computations are carried out on a calculator, the quadratic formula will not always give accurate results if b^2 is large in comparison to ac, because one of the roots will be close to zero and difficult to approximate.

(a) Use the quadratic formula to approximate the roots of the given equation.

(b) To obtain a better approximation for the root near zero, rationalize the numerator to change

$$x = \frac{-b \pm \sqrt{b^2 - 4ac}}{2a} \quad \text{to} \quad x = \frac{2c}{-b \mp \sqrt{b^2 - 4ac}},$$

and use the second formula.

81 $x^2 + 4{,}500{,}000x - 0.96 = 0$

82 $x^2 - 73{,}000{,}000x + 2.01 = 0$

2.4

Complex Numbers

Complex numbers are needed to find solutions of equations that cannot be solved using only the set $\mathbb{R}$ of real numbers. The following chart illustrates several simple quadratic equations and the types of numbers required for solutions.

Equation	Solutions	Type of numbers required
$x^2 = 9$	$3, -3$	Integers
$x^2 = \frac{9}{4}$	$\frac{3}{2}, -\frac{3}{2}$	Rational numbers
$x^2 = 5$	$\sqrt{5}, -\sqrt{5}$	Irrational numbers
$x^2 = -9$	?	Complex numbers

The solutions of the first three equations in the chart are in $\mathbb{R}$; however, since squares of real numbers are never negative, $\mathbb{R}$ does not contain the solutions of $x^2 = -9$. To solve this equation, we need the **complex number system** $\mathbb{C}$, which contains both $\mathbb{R}$ and numbers whose squares are negative.

We begin by introducing the **imaginary unit,** denoted by i, which has the following properties.

Properties of i	$i = \sqrt{-1}, \qquad i^2 = -1$

Because its square is negative, the letter i does not represent a real number. It is a new mathematical entity that will enable us to obtain $\mathbb{C}$. Since i, together with $\mathbb{R}$, is to be contained in $\mathbb{C}$, we must consider products of the form bi for a real number b and also expressions of the form $a + bi$ for real numbers a and b. The next chart provides definitions we shall use.

Terminology	Definition	Examples
Complex number	$a + bi$, where a and b are real numbers and $i^2 = -1$	$3, 2 + i, 2i$
Imaginary number	$a + bi$ with $b \neq 0$	$3 + 2i, -4i$
Pure imaginary number	bi with $b \neq 0$	$-4i, \sqrt{3}\,i, i$
Equality	$a + bi = c + di$ if and only if $a = c$ and $b = d$	$x + yi = 3 + 4i$ iff $x = 3$ and $y = 4$
Sum	$(a + bi) + (c + di) = (a + c) + (b + d)i$	see Example 1(a)
Product	$(a + bi)(c + di) = (ac - bd) + (ad + bc)i$	see Example 1(b)

Note that the pure imaginary numbers are a subset of the imaginary numbers and the imaginary numbers are a subset of the complex numbers. We use the phrase *nonreal complex number* interchangeably with *imaginary number*.

It is not necessary to memorize the definitions of addition and multiplication of complex numbers given in the preceding chart. Instead, *we may treat all symbols as having properties of real numbers, with exactly one exception: We replace i^2 by -1.* Thus, for the product $(a + bi)(c + di)$ we simply use the distributive laws and the fact that

$$(bi)(di) = bdi^2 = bd(-1) = -bd.$$

EXAMPLE 1 Addition and multiplication of complex numbers

Express in the form $a + bi$, where a and b are real numbers:

(a) $(3 + 4i) + (2 + 5i)$ **(b)** $(3 + 4i)(2 + 5i)$

SOLUTION

(a) $(3 + 4i) + (2 + 5i) = (3 + 2) + (4 + 5)i = 5 + 9i$

(b) $(3 + 4i)(2 + 5i) = (3 + 4i)(2) + (3 + 4i)(5i)$

$$= 6 + 8i + 15i + 20i^2$$

$$= 6 + 23i + 20(-1)$$

$$= -14 + 23i$$

The set $\mathbb{R}$ of real numbers may be identified with the set of complex numbers of the form $a + 0i$. It is also convenient to denote the complex number $0 + bi$ by bi. Thus,

$$(a + 0i) + (0 + bi) = (a + 0) + (0 + b)i = a + bi.$$

Hence, we may regard $a + bi$ as the sum of two complex numbers a and bi (that is, $a + 0i$ and $0 + bi$). For the complex number $a + bi$, we call a the **real part** and b the **imaginary part.**

EXAMPLE 2   Equality of complex numbers

Find the values of x and y, where x and y are real numbers:

$$(2x - 4) + 9i = 8 + 3yi$$

SOLUTION   We begin by equating the real parts and the imaginary parts of each side of the equation:

$$2x - 4 = 8 \quad \text{and} \quad 9 = 3y$$

Since $2x - 4 = 8$, $2x = 12$ and $x = 6$. Since $9 = 3y$, $y = 3$. The values of x and y that make the complex numbers equal are

$$x = 6 \quad \text{and} \quad y = 3.$$

With complex numbers, we are now able to solve an equation such as $x^2 = -9$. Specifically, since

$$(3i)(3i) = 3^2 i^2 = 9(-1) = -9,$$

we see that one solution is $3i$ and another is $-3i$.

In the next chart we define the difference of complex numbers and multiplication of a complex number by a real number.

Terminology	Definition
Difference	$(a + bi) - (c + di) = (a - c) + (b - d)i$
Multiplication by a real number k	$k(a + bi) = ka + (kb)i$

If we are asked to write an expression in the form $a + bi$, the form $a - di$ is acceptable, since $a - di = a + (-d)i$.

EXAMPLE 3 Operations with complex numbers

Express in the form $a + bi$, where a and b are real numbers:

(a) $4(2 + 5i) - (3 - 4i)$ (b) $(4 - 3i)(2 + i)$ (c) $i(3 - 2i)^2$

(d) i^{51} (e) i^{-13}

SOLUTION

(a) $4(2 + 5i) - (3 - 4i) = 8 + 20i - 3 + 4i = 5 + 24i$

(b) $(4 - 3i)(2 + i) = 8 - 6i + 4i - 3i^2 = 11 - 2i$

(c) $i(3 - 2i)^2 = i(9 - 12i + 4i^2) = i(5 - 12i) = 5i - 12i^2 = 12 + 5i$

(d) Taking successive powers of i, we obtain

$$i^1 = i, \quad i^2 = -1, \quad i^3 = -i, \quad i^4 = 1,$$

and then the cycle starts over:

$$i^5 = i, \quad i^6 = i^2 = -1, \quad \text{and so on.}$$

In particular,

$$i^{51} = i^{48}i^3 = (i^4)^{12}i^3 = (1)^{12}i^3 = (1)(-i) = -i.$$

(e) In general, multiply i^{-a} by i^b, where $a \le b \le a + 3$ and b is a multiple of 4 (so that $i^b = 1$). For i^{-13}, choose $b = 16$.

$$i^{-13} \cdot i^{16} = i^3 = -i$$

The following concept has important uses in working with complex numbers.

Definition of the Conjugate of a Complex Number	If $z = a + bi$ is a complex number, then its **conjugate,** denoted by $\bar{z}$, is $a - bi$.

Since $a - bi = a + (-bi)$, it follows that the conjugate of $a - bi$ is

$$a - (-bi) = a + bi.$$

Therefore, $a + bi$ *and* $a - bi$ *are conjugates of each other.* Some properties of conjugates are given in Exercises 57–62.

ILLUSTRATION   Conjugates

Complex number	Conjugate
■ $5 + 7i$	$5 - 7i$
■ $5 - 7i$	$5 + 7i$
■ $4i$	$-4i$
■ 3	3

The following two properties are consequences of the definitions of the sum and the product of complex numbers.

Properties of conjugates	Illustration
$(a + bi) + (a - bi) = 2a$	$(4 + 3i) + (4 - 3i) = 4 + 4 = 2 \cdot 4$
$(a + bi)(a - bi) = a^2 + b^2$	$(4 + 3i)(4 - 3i) = 4^2 - (3i)^2 = 4^2 - 3^2i^2 = 4^2 + 3^2$

Note that *the sum and the product of a complex number and its conjugate are real numbers.* Conjugates are useful for finding the **multiplicative inverse** of $a + bi$, $1/(a + bi)$, or for simplifying the quotient of two complex numbers. As illustrated in the next example, we may think of these types of simplifications as merely *rationalizing the denominator,* since we are multiplying the quotient by the conjugate of the denominator divided by itself.

EXAMPLE 4 Quotients of complex numbers

Express in the form $a + bi$, where a and b are real numbers:

(a) $\dfrac{1}{9 + 2i}$ (b) $\dfrac{7 - i}{3 - 5i}$

SOLUTION

(a) $\dfrac{1}{9 + 2i} = \dfrac{1}{9 + 2i} \cdot \dfrac{9 - 2i}{9 - 2i} = \dfrac{9 - 2i}{81 + 4} = \dfrac{9}{85} - \dfrac{2}{85}i$

(b) $\dfrac{7 - i}{3 - 5i} = \dfrac{7 - i}{3 - 5i} \cdot \dfrac{3 + 5i}{3 + 5i} = \dfrac{21 + 35i - 3i - 5i^2}{9 + 25}$

$= \dfrac{26 + 32i}{34} = \dfrac{13}{17} + \dfrac{16}{17}i$

If p is a positive real number, then the equation $x^2 = -p$ has solutions in $\mathbb{C}$. One solution is $\sqrt{p}\,i$, since

$$\left(\sqrt{p}\,i\right)^2 = \left(\sqrt{p}\right)^2 i^2 = p(-1) = -p.$$

Similarly, $-\sqrt{p}\,i$ is also a solution.

The definition of $\sqrt{-r}$ in the next chart is motivated by $\left(\sqrt{r}\,i\right)^2 = -r$ for $r > 0$. When using this definition, take care *not* to write $\sqrt{r}i$ when $\sqrt{r}\,i$ is intended.

Terminology	Definition	Illustrations
Principal square root $\sqrt{-r}$ for $r > 0$	$\sqrt{-r} = \sqrt{r}\,i$	$\sqrt{-9} = \sqrt{9}\,i = 3i$ $\sqrt{-5} = \sqrt{5}\,i$ $\sqrt{-1} = \sqrt{1}\,i = i$

The radical sign must be used with caution when the radicand is negative. For example, the formula $\sqrt{a}\,\sqrt{b} = \sqrt{ab}$, which holds for positive real numbers, is *not* true when a and b are both negative, as shown below:

$$\sqrt{-3}\,\sqrt{-3} = \left(\sqrt{3}\,i\right)\left(\sqrt{3}\,i\right) = \left(\sqrt{3}\right)^2 i^2 = 3(-1) = -3$$

But
$$\sqrt{(-3)(-3)} = \sqrt{9} = 3.$$

Hence,
$$\sqrt{-3}\,\sqrt{-3} \neq \sqrt{(-3)(-3)}.$$

If only *one* of a or b is negative, then $\sqrt{a}\,\sqrt{b} = \sqrt{ab}$. In general, we shall not apply laws of radicals if radicands are negative. Instead, we shall change the form of radicals before performing any operations, as illustrated in the next example.

EXAMPLE 5 Working with square roots of negative numbers

Express in the form $a + bi$, where a and b are real numbers:

$$\left(5 - \sqrt{-9}\right)\left(-1 + \sqrt{-4}\right)$$

SOLUTION First we use the definition $\sqrt{-r} = \sqrt{r}\,i$, and then we simplify:

$$\left(5 - \sqrt{-9}\right)\left(-1 + \sqrt{-4}\right) = \left(5 - \sqrt{9}\,i\right)\left(-1 + \sqrt{4}\,i\right)$$
$$= (5 - 3i)(-1 + 2i)$$
$$= -5 + 10i + 3i - 6i^2$$
$$= -5 + 13i + 6 = 1 + 13i$$

In Section 2.3 we stated that if the discriminant $b^2 - 4ac$ of the quadratic equation $ax^2 + bx + c = 0$ is negative, then there are no real roots of the equation. In fact, the solutions of the equation are two *imaginary* numbers. Moreover, the solutions are conjugates of each other, as shown in the next example.

EXAMPLE 6 A quadratic equation with complex solutions

Solve the equation $5x^2 + 2x + 1 = 0$.

SOLUTION Applying the quadratic formula with $a = 5$, $b = 2$, and $c = 1$, we see that

$$x = \frac{-2 \pm \sqrt{2^2 - 4(5)(1)}}{2(5)}$$
$$= \frac{-2 \pm \sqrt{-16}}{10} = \frac{-2 \pm 4i}{10} = \frac{-1 \pm 2i}{5} = -\frac{1}{5} \pm \frac{2}{5}i.$$

Thus, the solutions of the equation are $-\frac{1}{5} + \frac{2}{5}i$ and $-\frac{1}{5} - \frac{2}{5}i$.

EXAMPLE 7 An equation with complex solutions

Solve the equation $x^3 - 1 = 0$.

Difference of two cubes:

$$a^3 - b^3 = (a - b)(a^2 + ab + b^2)$$

SOLUTION Using the difference of two cubes factoring formula with $a = x$ and $b = 1$, we write $x^3 - 1 = 0$ as

$$(x - 1)(x^2 + x + 1) = 0.$$

Setting each factor equal to zero and solving the resulting equations, we obtain the solutions

$$1, \quad \frac{-1 \pm \sqrt{1 - 4}}{2} = \frac{-1 \pm \sqrt{3}\,i}{2}$$

or, equivalently,

$$1, \quad -\frac{1}{2} + \frac{\sqrt{3}}{2}i, \quad -\frac{1}{2} - \frac{\sqrt{3}}{2}i.$$

Since the number 1 is called the **unit real number** and the given equation may be written as $x^3 = 1$, we call these three solutions the **cube roots of unity.**

In Section 1.3 we mentioned that $x^2 + 1$ is irreducible over the *real* numbers. However, if we factor over the *complex* numbers, then $x^2 + 1$ may be factored as follows:

$$x^2 + 1 = (x + i)(x - i)$$

2.4 Exercises

Exer. 1–34: Write the expression in the form $a + bi$, where a and b are real numbers.

1 $(5 - 2i) + (-3 + 6i)$

2 $(-5 + 7i) + (4 + 9i)$

3 $(7 - 6i) - (-11 - 3i)$

4 $(-3 + 8i) - (2 + 3i)$

5 $(3 + 5i)(2 - 7i)$

6 $(-2 + 6i)(8 - i)$

7 $(1 - 3i)(2 + 5i)$

8 $(8 + 2i)(7 - 3i)$

9 $(5 - 2i)^2$

10 $(6 + 7i)^2$

11 $i(3 + 4i)^2$

12 $i(2 - 7i)^2$

13 $(3 + 4i)(3 - 4i)$

14 $(4 + 9i)(4 - 9i)$

15 (a) i^{43} (b) i^{-20}

16 (a) i^{92} (b) i^{-33}

17 (a) i^{73} (b) i^{-46}

18 (a) i^{66} (b) i^{-55}

19 $\dfrac{3}{2 + 4i}$

20 $\dfrac{5}{2 - 7i}$

21 $\dfrac{1 - 7i}{6 - 2i}$

22 $\dfrac{2 + 9i}{-3 - i}$

23 $\dfrac{-4 + 6i}{2 + 7i}$

24 $\dfrac{-3 - 2i}{5 + 2i}$

25 $\dfrac{4 - 2i}{-5i}$

26 $\dfrac{-2 + 6i}{3i}$

27 $(2 + 5i)^3$

28 $(3 - 2i)^3$

29 $\left(2 - \sqrt{-4}\right)\left(3 - \sqrt{-16}\right)$

30 $\left(-3 + \sqrt{-25}\right)\left(8 - \sqrt{-36}\right)$

31 $\dfrac{4 + \sqrt{-81}}{7 - \sqrt{-64}}$

32 $\dfrac{5 - \sqrt{-121}}{1 + \sqrt{-25}}$

33 $\dfrac{\sqrt{-36}\,\sqrt{-49}}{\sqrt{-16}}$

34 $\dfrac{\sqrt{-25}}{\sqrt{-16}\,\sqrt{-81}}$

Exer. 35–38: Find the values of x and y, where x and y are real numbers.

35 $4 + (x + 2y)i = x + 2i$ 36 $(x - y) + 3i = 7 + yi$

37 $(2x - y) - 16i = 10 + 4yi$

38 $8 + (3x + y)i = 2x - 4i$

Exer. 39–56: Find the solutions of the equation.

39 $x^2 - 6x + 13 = 0$ 40 $x^2 - 2x + 26 = 0$

41 $x^2 + 4x + 13 = 0$ 42 $x^2 + 8x + 17 = 0$

43 $x^2 - 5x + 20 = 0$ 44 $x^2 + 3x + 6 = 0$

45 $4x^2 + x + 3 = 0$ 46 $-3x^2 + x - 5 = 0$

47 $x^3 + 125 = 0$ 48 $x^3 - 27 = 0$

49 $27x^3 = (x + 5)^3$ 50 $16x^4 = (x - 4)^4$

51 $x^4 = 256$ 52 $x^4 = 81$

53 $4x^4 + 25x^2 + 36 = 0$ 54 $27x^4 + 21x^2 + 4 = 0$

55 $x^3 + 3x^2 + 4x = 0$

56 $8x^3 - 12x^2 + 2x - 3 = 0$

Exer. 57–62: Verify the property.

57 $\overline{z + w} = \bar{z} + \bar{w}$ 58 $\overline{z - w} = \bar{z} - \bar{w}$

59 $\overline{z \cdot w} = \bar{z} \cdot \bar{w}$ 60 $\overline{z/w} = \bar{z}/\bar{w}$

61 $\bar{z} = z$ if and only if z is real.

62 $\overline{z^2} = (\bar{z})^2$

2.5

Other Types of Equations

The equations considered in previous sections are inadequate for many problems. For example, in applications it is often necessary to consider powers x^k with $k > 2$. Some equations involve absolute values or radicals. In this section we give examples of equations of these types that can be solved using elementary methods.

EXAMPLE 1 Solving an equation containing an absolute value

Solve the equation $|x - 5| = 3$.

SOLUTION   If a and b are real numbers with $b > 0$, then $|a| = b$ if and only if $a = b$ or $a = -b$. Hence, if $|x - 5| = 3$, then either

$$x - 5 = 3 \quad \text{or} \quad x - 5 = -3.$$

Solving for x gives us

$$x = 5 + 3 = 8 \quad \text{or} \quad x = 5 - 3 = 2.$$

Thus, the given equation has two solutions, 8 and 2.

For an equation such as

$$2|x - 5| + 3 = 11,$$

we first isolate the absolute value expression by subtracting 3 and dividing by 2 to obtain

$$|x - 5| = \frac{11 - 3}{2} = 4,$$

and then we proceed as in Example 1.

If an equation is in factored form *with zero on one side,* then we may obtain solutions by setting each factor equal to zero. For example, if *p*, *q*, and *r* are expressions in *x* and if $pqr = 0$, then either $p = 0$, $q = 0$, or $r = 0$. In the next example we factor by grouping terms.

EXAMPLE 2   Solving an equation using grouping

Solve the equation $x^3 + 2x^2 - x - 2 = 0$.

SOLUTION
$$x^3 + 2x^2 - x - 2 = 0 \qquad \text{given}$$
$$x^2(x + 2) - 1(x + 2) = 0 \qquad \text{group terms}$$
$$(x^2 - 1)(x + 2) = 0 \qquad \text{factor out } x + 2$$
$$(x + 1)(x - 1)(x + 2) = 0 \qquad \text{factor } x^2 - 1$$
$$x + 1 = 0, \quad x - 1 = 0, \quad x + 2 = 0 \qquad \text{zero factor theorem}$$
$$x = -1, \qquad x = 1, \qquad x = -2 \qquad \text{solve for } x$$

EXAMPLE 3   Solving an equation containing rational exponents

Solve the equation $x^{3/2} = x^{1/2}$.

SOLUTION
$$x^{3/2} = x^{1/2} \qquad \text{given}$$
$$x^{3/2} - x^{1/2} = 0 \qquad \text{subtract } x^{1/2}$$
$$x^{1/2}(x - 1) = 0 \qquad \text{factor out } x^{1/2}$$
$$x^{1/2} = 0, \quad x - 1 = 0 \qquad \text{zero factor theorem}$$
$$x = 0, \qquad x = 1 \qquad \text{solve for } x$$

In Example 3 it would have been incorrect to divide both sides of the equation $x^{3/2} = x^{1/2}$ by $x^{1/2}$, obtaining $x = 1$, since the solution $x = 0$ would be lost. In general, *avoid dividing both sides of an equation by an expression that contains variables*—always *factor* instead.

If an equation involves radicals or fractional exponents, we often raise both sides to a positive power. The solutions of the new equation always contain the solutions of the given equation. For example, the solutions of

$$2x - 3 = \sqrt{x + 6}$$

are also solutions of

$$(2x - 3)^2 = \left(\sqrt{x + 6}\right)^2.$$

*Raising both sides of an equation to an **odd** power can introduce imaginary solutions. For example, cubing both sides of $x = 1$ gives us $x^3 = 1$, which is equivalent to $x^3 - 1 = 0$. This equation has three solutions, of which two are imaginary (see Example 7 in Section 2.4).*

In some cases the new equation has *more* solutions than the given equation. To illustrate, if we are given the equation $x = 3$ and we square both sides, we obtain $x^2 = 9$. Note that the given equation $x = 3$ has only one solution, 3, but the new equation $x^2 = 9$ has two solutions, 3 and -3. Any solution of the new equation that is not a solution of the given equation is an extraneous solution. Since extraneous solutions may occur, *it is absolutely essential to check all solutions obtained after raising both sides of an equation to an even power.* Such checks are unnecessary if both sides are raised to an *odd* power, because in this case extraneous (real number) solutions are not introduced.

EXAMPLE 4 Solving an equation containing a radical

Solve the equation $\sqrt[3]{x^2 - 1} = 2$.

SOLUTION

$$\sqrt[3]{x^2 - 1} = 2 \qquad \text{given}$$
$$\left(\sqrt[3]{x^2 - 1}\right)^3 = 2^3 \qquad \text{cube both sides}$$
$$x^2 - 1 = 8 \qquad \text{property of } \sqrt[n]{}$$
$$x^2 = 9 \qquad \text{add 1}$$
$$x = \pm 3 \qquad \text{take the square root}$$

Thus, the given equation has two solutions, 3 and -3. Except to detect algebraic errors, a check is unnecessary, since we raised both sides to an odd power.

In the last solution we used the phrase *cube both sides* of $\sqrt[3]{x^2 - 1} = 2$. In general, for the equation $x^{m/n} = a$, where x is a real number, we raise both sides to the power n/m (the reciprocal of m/n) to solve for x. If m is odd, we obtain $x = a^{n/m}$, but if m is even, we have $x = \pm a^{n/m}$. If n is even, extraneous solutions may occur—for example, if $x^{3/2} = -8$, then $x = (-8)^{2/3} = \left(\sqrt[3]{-8}\right)^2 = (-2)^2 = 4$. However, 4 is not a solution of $x^{3/2} = -8$ since $4^{3/2} = 8$, not -8.

ILLUSTRATION   Solving $x^{m/n} = a$, m odd, x real

Equation	**Solution**
■ $x^{3/1} = 64$	$x = 64^{1/3} = \sqrt[3]{64} = 4$
■ $x^{3/2} = 64$	$x = 64^{2/3} = \left(\sqrt[3]{64}\right)^2 = 4^2 = 16$

ILLUSTRATION   Solving $x^{m/n} = a$, m even, x real

Equation	**Solution**
■ $x^{4/1} = 16$	$x = \pm 16^{1/4} = \pm \sqrt[4]{16} = \pm 2$
■ $x^{2/3} = 16$	$x = \pm 16^{3/2} = \pm\left(\sqrt{16}\right)^3 = \pm 4^3 = \pm 64$

In the next two examples, before we raise both sides of the equation to a power, we *isolate a radical*—that is, we consider an equivalent equation in which only the radical appears on one side.

EXAMPLE 5 Solving an equation containing a radical

Solve the equation $3 + \sqrt{3x + 1} = x$.

SOLUTION

$$3 + \sqrt{3x + 1} = x \qquad \text{given}$$
$$\sqrt{3x + 1} = x - 3 \qquad \text{isolate the radical}$$
$$\left(\sqrt{3x + 1}\right)^2 = (x - 3)^2 \qquad \text{square both sides}$$
$$3x + 1 = x^2 - 6x + 9 \qquad \text{simplify}$$
$$x^2 - 9x + 8 = 0 \qquad \text{subtract } 3x + 1$$
$$(x - 1)(x - 8) = 0 \qquad \text{factor}$$
$$x - 1 = 0, \quad x - 8 = 0 \qquad \text{zero factor theorem}$$
$$x = 1, \qquad x = 8 \qquad \text{solve for } x$$

We raised both sides to an even power, so checks are required.

✔ Check $x = 1$ LS: $3 + \sqrt{3(1) + 1} = 3 + \sqrt{4} = 3 + 2 = 5$
RS: 1

Since $5 \neq 1$, $x = 1$ is not a solution.

✔ Check $x = 8$ LS: $3 + \sqrt{3(8) + 1} = 3 + \sqrt{25} = 3 + 5 = 8$
RS: 8

Since $8 = 8$ is a true statement, $x = 8$ is a solution.
Hence, the given equation has one solution, $x = 8$.

In order to solve an equation involving several radicals, it may be necessary to raise both sides to powers two or more times, as in the next example.

EXAMPLE 6 Solving an equation containing radicals

Solve the equation $\sqrt{2x - 3} - \sqrt{x + 7} + 2 = 0$.

SOLUTION

$$\begin{aligned}
\sqrt{2x - 3} - \sqrt{x + 7} + 2 &= 0 && \text{given} \\
\sqrt{2x - 3} &= \sqrt{x + 7} - 2 && \text{isolate } \sqrt{2x - 3} \\
2x - 3 &= (x + 7) - 4\sqrt{x + 7} + 4 && \text{square both sides} \\
x - 14 &= -4\sqrt{x + 7} && \text{isolate the radical} \\
&&& \text{term} \\
x^2 - 28x + 196 &= 16(x + 7) && \text{square both sides} \\
x^2 - 28x + 196 &= 16x + 112 && \text{multiply factors} \\
x^2 - 44x + 84 &= 0 && \text{subtract } 16x + 112 \\
(x - 42)(x - 2) &= 0 && \text{factor} \\
x - 42 = 0, \quad x - 2 &= 0 && \text{zero factor theorem} \\
x = 42, \qquad x &= 2 && \text{solve for } x
\end{aligned}$$

A check is required, since both sides were raised to an even power.

✔ Check $x = 42$ LS: $\sqrt{84 - 3} - \sqrt{42 + 7} + 2 = 9 - 7 + 2 = 4$
RS: 0

Since $4 \neq 0$, $x = 42$ is not a solution.

✔ Check $x = 2$ LS: $\sqrt{4 - 3} - \sqrt{2 + 7} + 2 = 1 - 3 + 2 = 0$
RS: 0

Since $0 = 0$ is a true statement, $x = 2$ is a solution.
Hence, the given equation has one solution, $x = 2$.

An equation is of **quadratic type** if it can be written in the form

$$au^2 + bu + c = 0,$$

where $a \neq 0$ and u is an expression in some variable. If we find the solutions in terms of u, then the solutions of the given equation can be obtained by referring to the specific form of u.

EXAMPLE 7 Solving an equation of quadratic type

Solve the equation $x^{2/3} + x^{1/3} - 6 = 0$.

SOLUTION Since $x^{2/3} = (x^{1/3})^2$, the form of the equation suggests that we let $u = x^{1/3}$, as in the second line below:

$$
\begin{array}{ll}
x^{2/3} + x^{1/3} - 6 = 0 & \text{given} \\
u^2 + u - 6 = 0 & \text{let } u = x^{1/3} \\
(u + 3)(u - 2) = 0 & \text{factor} \\
u + 3 = 0, \quad u - 2 = 0 & \text{zero factor theorem} \\
u = -3, \quad u = 2 & \text{solve for } u \\
x^{1/3} = -3, \quad x^{1/3} = 2 & u = x^{1/3} \\
x = -27, \quad x = 8 & \text{cube both sides}
\end{array}
$$

A check is unnecessary, since we did not raise both sides to an even power. Hence, the given equation has two solutions, -27 and 8.

An alternative method is to factor the left side of the given equation as follows:

$$x^{2/3} + x^{1/3} - 6 = (x^{1/3} + 3)(x^{1/3} - 2)$$

By setting each factor equal to 0, we obtain the solutions.

EXAMPLE 8 Solving an equation of quadratic type

Solve the equation $x^4 - 3x^2 + 1 = 0$.

SOLUTION Since $x^4 = (x^2)^2$, the form of the equation suggests that we let $u = x^2$, as in the second line below:

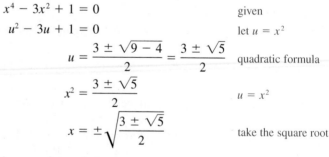

$$
\begin{array}{ll}
x^4 - 3x^2 + 1 = 0 & \text{given} \\
u^2 - 3u + 1 = 0 & \text{let } u = x^2 \\
u = \dfrac{3 \pm \sqrt{9 - 4}}{2} = \dfrac{3 \pm \sqrt{5}}{2} & \text{quadratic formula} \\
x^2 = \dfrac{3 \pm \sqrt{5}}{2} & u = x^2 \\
x = \pm\sqrt{\dfrac{3 \pm \sqrt{5}}{2}} & \text{take the square root}
\end{array}
$$

Thus, there are four solutions:

$$\sqrt{\frac{3 + \sqrt{5}}{2}}, \quad -\sqrt{\frac{3 + \sqrt{5}}{2}}, \quad \sqrt{\frac{3 - \sqrt{5}}{2}}, \quad -\sqrt{\frac{3 - \sqrt{5}}{2}}$$

Using a calculator, we obtain the approximations ± 1.62 and ± 0.62. A check is unnecessary because we did not raise both sides of an equation to an even power.

EXAMPLE 9 Determining the route of a ferry

A passenger ferry makes trips from a town to an island community that is 7 miles downshore from the town and 3 miles off a straight shoreline. As shown in Figure 1, the ferry travels along the shoreline to some point and then proceeds directly to the island. If the ferry travels 12 mi/hr along the shoreline and 10 mi/hr as it moves out to sea, determine the routes that have a travel time of 45 minutes.

SOLUTION   Let x denote the distance traveled along the shoreline. This leads to the sketch in Figure 2, where d is the distance from a point on the shoreline to the island. Refer to the indicated right triangle:

$$d^2 = (7 - x)^2 + 3^2 \qquad \text{Pythagorean theorem}$$
$$= 49 - 14x + x^2 + 9 \qquad \text{square terms}$$
$$= x^2 - 14x + 58 \qquad \text{simplify}$$

Taking the square root of both sides and noting that $d > 0$, we obtain

$$d = \sqrt{x^2 - 14x + 58}.$$

Using distance = (rate)(time) or, equivalently, time = (distance)/(rate) gives us the following table.

	Along the shoreline	Away from shore
Distance (mi)	x	$\sqrt{x^2 - 14x + 58}$
Rate (mi/hr)	12	10
Time (hr)	$\dfrac{x}{12}$	$\dfrac{\sqrt{x^2 - 14x + 58}}{10}$

The time for the complete trip is the sum of the two expressions in the last row of the table. Since the rate is in mi/hr, we must, for consistency, express this time (45 minutes) as $\frac{3}{4}$ hour. Thus, we have the following:

$$\frac{x}{12} + \frac{\sqrt{x^2 - 14x + 58}}{10} = \frac{3}{4} \qquad \text{total time for trip}$$

$$\frac{\sqrt{x^2 - 14x + 58}}{10} = \frac{3}{4} - \frac{x}{12} \qquad \text{subtract } \frac{x}{12}$$

$$6\sqrt{x^2 - 14x + 58} = 45 - 5x \qquad \text{multiply by the lcd, 60}$$

$$6\sqrt{x^2 - 14x + 58} = 5(9 - x) \qquad \text{factor}$$

$$36(x^2 - 14x + 58) = 25(9 - x)^2 \qquad \text{square both sides}$$

$$36x^2 - 504x + 2088 = 2025 - 450x + 25x^2 \qquad \text{multiply terms}$$

$$11x^2 - 54x + 63 = 0 \qquad \text{simplify}$$

(continued)

Figure 1

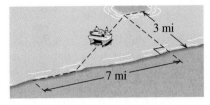

Figure 2

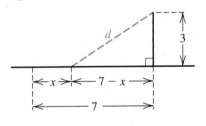

$$(x - 3)(11x - 21) = 0 \qquad \text{factor}$$

$$x - 3 = 0, \quad 11x - 21 = 0 \qquad \text{zero factor theorem}$$

$$x = 3, \qquad x = \frac{21}{11} \qquad \text{solve for } x$$

A check verifies that these numbers are also solutions of the original equation. Hence, there are two possible routes with a travel time of 45 minutes: the ferry may travel along the shoreline either 3 miles or $\frac{21}{11} \approx 1.9$ miles before proceeding to the island.

2.5 Exercises

Exer. 1–50: Solve the equation.

1 $|x + 4| = 11$

2 $|x - 5| = 2$

3 $|3x - 2| + 3 = 7$

4 $2|5x + 2| - 1 = 5$

5 $3|x + 1| - 2 = -11$

6 $|x - 2| + 5 = 5$

7 $9x^3 - 18x^2 - 4x + 8 = 0$

8 $3x^3 - 4x^2 - 27x + 36 = 0$

9 $4x^4 + 10x^3 = 6x^2 + 15x$

10 $15x^5 - 20x^4 = 6x^3 - 8x^2$

11 $y^{3/2} = 5y$

12 $y^{4/3} = -3y$

13 $\sqrt{7 - 5x} = 8$

14 $\sqrt{2x - 9} = \frac{1}{3}$

15 $2 + \sqrt[3]{1 - 5t} = 0$

16 $\sqrt[3]{6 - s^2} + 5 = 0$

17 $\sqrt[5]{2x^2 + 1} - 2 = 0$

18 $\sqrt[4]{2x^2 - 1} = x$

19 $\sqrt{7 - x} = x - 5$

20 $\sqrt{3 - x} - x = 3$

21 $3\sqrt{2x - 3} + 2\sqrt{7 - x} = 11$

22 $\sqrt{2x + 15} - 2 = \sqrt{6x + 1}$

23 $x = 4 + \sqrt{4x - 19}$

24 $x = 3 + \sqrt{5x - 9}$

25 $x + \sqrt{5x + 19} = -1$

26 $x - \sqrt{-7x - 24} = -2$

27 $\sqrt{7 - 2x} - \sqrt{5 + x} = \sqrt{4 + 3x}$

28 $4\sqrt{1 + 3x} + \sqrt{6x + 3} = \sqrt{-6x - 1}$

29 $\sqrt{11 + 8x} + 1 = \sqrt{9 + 4x}$

30 $2\sqrt{x} - \sqrt{x - 3} = \sqrt{5 + x}$

31 $\sqrt{2\sqrt{x + 1}} = \sqrt{3x - 5}$

32 $\sqrt{5\sqrt{x}} = \sqrt{2x - 3}$

33 $\sqrt{1 + 4\sqrt{x}} = \sqrt{x} + 1$

34 $\sqrt{x + 1} = \sqrt{x - 1}$

35 $x^4 - 25x^2 + 144 = 0$

36 $2x^4 - 10x^2 + 8 = 0$

37 $5y^4 - 7y^2 + 1 = 0$

38 $3y^4 - 5y^2 + 1 = 0$

39 $36x^{-4} - 13x^{-2} + 1 = 0$

40 $x^{-2} - 2x^{-1} - 35 = 0$

41 $3x^{2/3} + 4x^{1/3} - 4 = 0$

42 $2y^{1/3} - 3y^{1/6} + 1 = 0$

43 $6w + 7w^{1/2} - 20 = 0$

44 $8t - 22t^{1/2} - 21 = 0$

45 $2x^{-2/3} - 7x^{-1/3} - 15 = 0$

46 $6u^{-1/2} - 13u^{-1/4} + 6 = 0$

47 $\left(\dfrac{t}{t + 1}\right)^2 - \dfrac{2t}{t + 1} - 8 = 0$

48 $\left(\dfrac{x}{x - 2}\right)^2 - \dfrac{2x}{x - 2} - 15 = 0$

49 $\sqrt[3]{x} = 2\sqrt[4]{x}$ (*Hint:* Raise both sides to the least common multiple of 3 and 4.)

50 $\sqrt{x + 3} = \sqrt[4]{2x + 6}$

Exer. 51–52: Find the real solutions of the equation.

51 (a) $x^{5/3} = 32$ 　　　　(b) $x^{4/3} = 16$

(c) $x^{2/3} = -36$ 　　　　(d) $x^{3/4} = 125$

(e) $x^{3/2} = -27$

52 (a) $x^{3/5} = -27$ 　　　　(b) $x^{2/3} = 25$

(c) $x^{4/3} = -49$ 　　　　(d) $x^{3/2} = 27$

(e) $x^{3/4} = -8$

Exer. 53–56: Solve for the specified variable.

53 $T = 2\pi\sqrt{\dfrac{l}{g}}$ for l (period of a pendulum)

54 $d = \frac{1}{2}\sqrt{4R^2 - C^2}$ for C (segments of circles)

55 $S = \pi r\sqrt{r^2 + h^2}$ for h (surface area of a cone)

56 $\omega = \dfrac{1}{\sqrt{LC}}$ for C (alternating-current circuits)

57 Ladder height The recommended distance d that a ladder should be placed away from a vertical wall is 25% of its length L. Approximate the height h that can be reached by relating h as a percentage of L.

Exercise 57

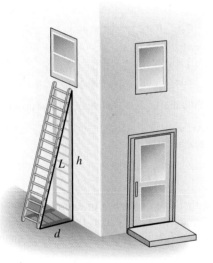

58 Nuclear experiments Nuclear experiments performed in the ocean vaporize large quantities of salt water. Salt boils and turns into vapor at 1738 K. After being vaporized by a 10-megaton force, the salt takes at least 8–10 seconds to cool enough to crystallize. The amount of salt A that has crystallized t seconds after an experiment is sometimes calculated using $A = k\sqrt{t/T}$, where k and T are constants. Solve this equation for t.

59 Windmill power The power P (in watts) generated by a windmill that has efficiency E is given by the formula $P = 0.31ED^2V^3$, where D is the diameter (in feet) of the windmill blades and V is the wind velocity (in ft/sec). Approximate the wind velocity necessary to generate 10,000 watts if $E = 42\%$ and $D = 10$.

60 Withdrawal resistance of nails The *withdrawal resistance* of a nail indicates its holding strength in wood. A formula that is used for bright common nails is $P = 15{,}700S^{5/2}RD$, where P is the maximum withdrawal resistance (in pounds), S is the specific gravity of the wood at 12% moisture content, R is the radius of the nail (in inches), and D is the depth (in inches) that the nail has penetrated the wood. A 6d (sixpenny) bright, common nail of length 2 inches and diameter 0.113 inch is driven completely into a piece of Douglas fir. If it requires a maximum force of 380 pounds to remove the nail, approximate the specific gravity of Douglas fir.

61 The effect of price on demand The demand for a commodity usually depends on its price. If other factors do not affect the demand, then the quantity Q purchased at price P (in cents) is given by $Q = kP^{-c}$, where k and c are positive constants. If $k = 10^5$ and $c = \frac{1}{2}$, find the price that will result in the purchase of 5000 items.

62 The urban heat island Urban areas have higher average air temperatures than rural areas, as a result of the presence of buildings, asphalt, and concrete. This phenomenon has become known as the *urban heat island*. The temperature difference T (in °C) between urban and rural areas near Montreal, with a population P between 1000 and 1,000,000, can be described by the formula $T = 0.25P^{1/4}/\sqrt{v}$, where v is the average wind speed (in mi/hr) and $v \geq 1$. If $T = 3$ and $v = 5$, find P.

63 Dimensions of a sand pile As sand leaks out of a certain container, it forms a pile that has the shape of a right circular cone whose altitude is always one-half the diameter d of the base. What is d at the instant at which 144 cm³ of sand has leaked out?

Exercise 63

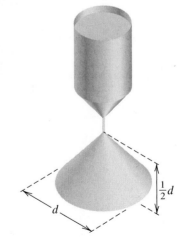

64 **Inflating a weather balloon** The volume of a spherical weather balloon is $10\frac{2}{3}$ ft³. In order to lift a transmitter and meteorological equipment, the balloon is inflated with an additional $25\frac{1}{3}$ ft³ of helium. How much does its diameter increase?

65 **The cube rule in political science** The cube rule in political science is an empirical formula that is said to predict the percentage y of seats in the U.S. House of Representatives that will be won by a political party from the popular vote for the party's presidential candidate. If x denotes the percentage of the popular vote for a party's presidential candidate, then the cube rule states that

$$y = \frac{x^3}{x^3 + (1-x)^3}.$$

What percentage of the popular vote will the presidential candidate need in order for the candidate's party to win 60% of the House seats?

66 **Dimensions of a conical cup** A conical paper cup is to have a height of 3 inches. Find the radius of the cone that will result in a surface area of 6π in².

67 **Installing a power line** A power line is to be installed across a river that is 1 mile wide to a town that is 5 miles downstream (see the figure). It costs $7500 per mile to lay the cable underwater and $6000 per mile to lay it overland. Determine how the cable should be installed if $35,000 has been allocated for this project.

Exercise 67

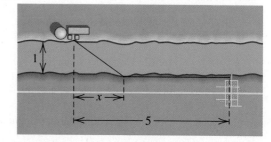

68 **Calculating human growth** Adolphe Quetelet (1796–1874), the director of the Brussels Observatory from 1832 to 1874, was the first person to attempt to fit a mathematical expression to human growth data. If h denotes height in meters and t denotes age in years, Quetelet's formula for males in Brussels can be expressed as

$$h + \frac{h}{h_M - h} = at + \frac{h_0 + t}{1 + \frac{4}{3}t},$$

with $h_0 = 0.5$, the height at birth; $h_M = 1.684$, the final adult male height; and $a = 0.545$.

(a) Find the expected height of a 12-year-old male.

(b) At what age should 50% of the adult height be reached?

2.6

Inequalities

An **inequality** is a statement that two quantities or expressions are not equal. It may be the case that one quantity is less than ($<$), less than or equal to ($\leq$), greater than ($>$), or greater than or equal to ($\geq$) another quantity. Consider the inequality

$$2x + 3 > 11,$$

where x is a variable. As illustrated in the following table, certain numbers yield true statements when substituted for x, and others yield false statements.

x	$2x + 3 > 11$	Conclusion
3	$9 > 11$	False statement
4	$11 > 11$	False statement
5	$13 > 11$	True statement
6	$15 > 11$	True statement

If a true statement is obtained when a number b is substituted for x, then b is a **solution** of the inequality. Thus, $x = 5$ is a solution of $2x + 3 > 11$

since $13 > 11$ is true, but $x = 3$ is not a solution since $9 > 11$ is false. To **solve** an inequality means to find *all* solutions. Two inequalities are **equivalent** if they have exactly the same solutions.

Most inequalities have an infinite number of solutions. To illustrate, the solutions of the inequality

$$2 < x < 5$$

consist of *every* real number x between 2 and 5. We call this set of numbers an **open interval** and denote it by $(2, 5)$. The **graph** of the open interval $(2, 5)$ is the set of all points on a coordinate line that lie between—but do not include—the points corresponding to $x = 2$ and $x = 5$. The graph is represented by shading an appropriate part of the axis, as shown in Figure 1. We refer to this process as **sketching the graph** of the interval. The numbers 2 and 5 are called the **endpoints** of the interval $(2, 5)$. The parentheses in the notation $(2, 5)$ and in Figure 1 are used to indicate that the endpoints of the interval are not included.

If we wish to include an endpoint, we use a bracket instead of a parenthesis. For example, the solutions of the inequality $2 \leq x \leq 5$ are denoted by $[2, 5]$ and are referred to as a **closed interval.** The graph of $[2, 5]$ is sketched in Figure 2, where brackets indicate that endpoints are included. We shall also consider **half-open intervals** $[a, b)$ and $(a, b]$ and **infinite intervals,** as described in the following chart. The symbol ∞ (read "infinity") used for infinite intervals is merely a notational device and does *not* represent a real number.

Figure 1

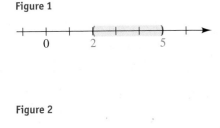

Figure 2

Intervals

Notation	Inequality	Graph
(1) (a, b)	$a < x < b$	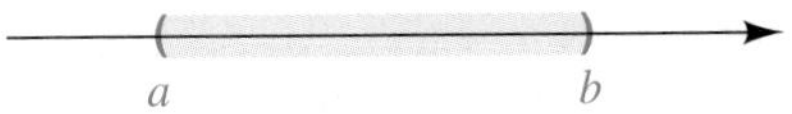
(2) $[a, b]$	$a \leq x \leq b$	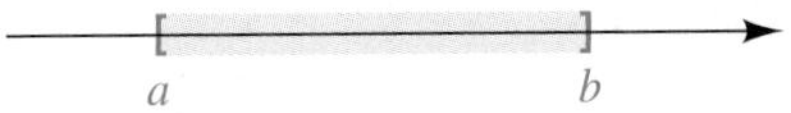
(3) $[a, b)$	$a \leq x < b$	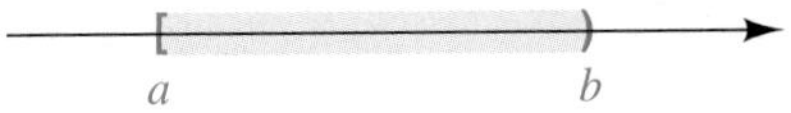
(4) $(a, b]$	$a < x \leq b$	
(5) (a, ∞)	$x > a$	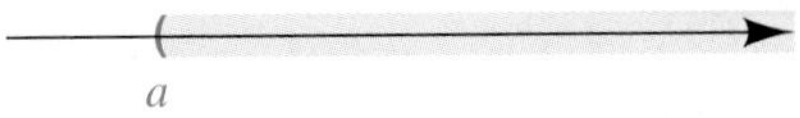
(6) $[a, \infty)$	$x \geq a$	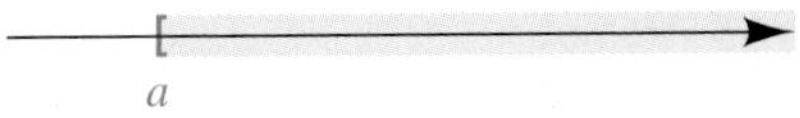
(7) $(-\infty, b)$	$x < b$	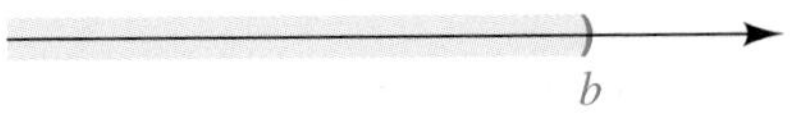
(8) $(-\infty, b]$	$x \leq b$	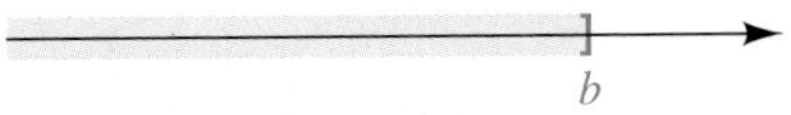
(9) $(-\infty, \infty)$	$-\infty < x < \infty$	

Methods for solving inequalities in x are similar to those used for solving equations. In particular, we often use properties of inequalities to replace a given inequality with a list of equivalent inequalities, ending with an inequality from which solutions are easily obtained. The properties in the following chart can be proved for real numbers $a, b, c,$ and d.

Properties of Inequalities

Property	Illustration
(1) If $a < b$ and $b < c$, then $a < c$.	$2 < 5$ and $5 < 9$, so $2 < 9$.
(2) If $a < b$, then $a + c < b + c$ and $a - c < b - c$.	$2 < 7$, so $2 + 3 < 7 + 3$ and $2 - 3 < 7 - 3$.
(3) If $a < b$ and $c > 0$, then $ac < bc$ and $\dfrac{a}{c} < \dfrac{b}{c}$.	$2 < 5$ and $3 > 0$, so $2 \cdot 3 < 5 \cdot 3$ and $\dfrac{2}{3} < \dfrac{5}{3}$.
(4) If $a < b$ and $c < 0$, then $ac > bc$ and $\dfrac{a}{c} > \dfrac{b}{c}$.	$2 < 5$ and $-3 < 0$, so $2(-3) > 5(-3)$ and $\dfrac{2}{-3} > \dfrac{5}{-3}$.

Reverse the inequality when multiplying or dividing by a negative number.

It is important to remember that multiplying or dividing both sides of an inequality by a negative real number *reverses* the inequality sign (see property 4). Properties similar to those above are true for other inequalities and for $\leq$ and $\geq$. Thus, if $a > b$, then $a + c > b + c$; if $a \geq b$ and $c < 0$, then $ac \leq bc$; and so on.

If x represents a real number, then, by property 2, adding or subtracting the same expression containing x on both sides of an inequality yields an equivalent inequality. By property 3, we may multiply or divide both sides of an inequality by an expression containing x if we are certain that the expression is positive for all values of x under consideration. To illustrate, multiplication or division by $x^4 + 3x^2 + 5$ would be permissible, since this expression is always positive. If we multiply or divide both sides of an inequality by an expression that is always negative, such as $-7 - x^2$, then, by property 4, the inequality is reversed.

In examples we shall describe solutions of inequalities by means of intervals and also represent them graphically.

EXAMPLE 1 Solving an inequality

Solve the inequality $-3x + 4 < 11$.

SOLUTION

$$-3x + 4 < 11 \qquad \text{given}$$
$$(-3x + 4) - 4 < 11 - 4 \qquad \text{subtract 4}$$
$$-3x < 7 \qquad \text{simplify}$$
$$\frac{-3x}{-3} > \frac{7}{-3} \qquad \text{divide by } -3; \text{ reverse the inequality sign}$$
$$x > -\tfrac{7}{3} \qquad \text{simplify}$$

Figure 3

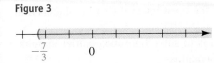

$-\frac{7}{3}$ 0

Thus, the solutions of $-3x + 4 < 11$ consist of all real numbers x such that $x > -\frac{7}{3}$. This is the interval $\left(-\frac{7}{3}, \infty\right)$ sketched in Figure 3.

EXAMPLE 2 **Solving an inequality**

Solve the inequality $4x - 3 < 2x + 5$.

SOLUTION

$$
\begin{array}{ll}
4x - 3 < 2x + 5 & \text{given} \\
(4x - 3) + 3 < (2x + 5) + 3 & \text{add 3} \\
4x < 2x + 8 & \text{simplify} \\
4x - 2x < (2x + 8) - 2x & \text{subtract } 2x \\
2x < 8 & \text{simplify} \\
\dfrac{2x}{2} < \dfrac{8}{2} & \text{divide by 2} \\
x < 4 & \text{simplify}
\end{array}
$$

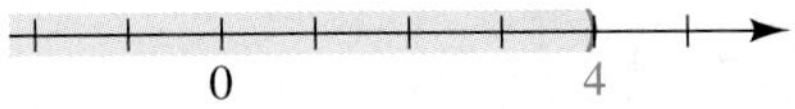

Hence, the solutions of the given inequality consist of all real numbers x such that $x < 4$. This is the interval $(-\infty, 4)$ sketched in Figure 4.

Figure 4

0 4

EXAMPLE 3 **Solving an inequality**

Solve the inequality $-6 < 2x - 4 < 2$.

SOLUTION A real number x is a solution of the given inequality if and only if it is a solution of *both* of the inequalities

$$-6 < 2x - 4 \quad \text{and} \quad 2x - 4 < 2.$$

This first inequality is solved as follows:

$$
\begin{array}{ll}
-6 < 2x - 4 & \text{given} \\
-6 + 4 < (2x - 4) + 4 & \text{add 4} \\
-2 < 2x & \text{simplify} \\
\dfrac{-2}{2} < \dfrac{2x}{2} & \text{divide by 2} \\
-1 < x & \text{simplify} \\
x > -1 & \text{equivalent inequality}
\end{array}
$$

The second inequality is then solved:

$$
\begin{array}{ll}
2x - 4 < 2 & \text{given} \\
2x < 6 & \text{add 4} \\
x < 3 & \text{divide by 2}
\end{array}
$$

Thus, x is a solution of the given inequality if and only if *both*

$$x > -1 \quad \text{and} \quad x < 3;$$

that is,

$$-1 < x < 3.$$

(continued)

Figure 5

Hence, the solutions are all numbers in the open interval $(-1, 3)$ sketched in Figure 5.

An alternative (and shorter) method is to solve both inequalities simultaneously—that is, solve the continued inequality:

$$
\begin{array}{ll}
-6 < 2x - 4 < 2 & \text{given} \\
-6 + 4 < 2x \qquad < 2 + 4 & \text{add 4} \\
-2 < 2x \qquad < 6 & \text{simplify} \\
-1 < \ x \qquad < 3 & \text{divide by 2}
\end{array}
$$

EXAMPLE 4 Solving a continued inequality

Solve the continued inequality $-5 \le \dfrac{4 - 3x}{2} < 1$.

SOLUTION   A number x is a solution of the given inequality if and only if

$$
-5 \le \frac{4 - 3x}{2} \quad \text{and} \quad \frac{4 - 3x}{2} < 1.
$$

We can either work with each inequality separately or solve both inequalities simultaneously, as follows (keep in mind that our goal is to isolate x):

$$
\begin{array}{ll}
-5 \le \dfrac{4 - 3x}{2} < 1 & \text{given} \\[2mm]
-10 \le 4 - 3x < 2 & \text{multiply by 2} \\[1mm]
-10 - 4 \le \quad -3x < 2 - 4 & \text{subtract 4} \\[1mm]
-14 \le \quad -3x < -2 & \text{simplify} \\[1mm]
\dfrac{-14}{-3} \ge \quad \dfrac{-3x}{-3} > \dfrac{-2}{-3} & \text{divide by } -3;\ \text{reverse} \\
& \text{the inequality signs} \\[1mm]
\frac{14}{3} \ge \quad x \quad > \frac{2}{3} & \text{simplify} \\[1mm]
\frac{2}{3} < \quad x \quad \le \frac{14}{3} & \text{equivalent inequality}
\end{array}
$$

Figure 6

Thus, the solutions of the inequality are all numbers in the half-open interval $\left(\frac{2}{3}, \frac{14}{3}\right]$ sketched in Figure 6.

EXAMPLE 5 Solving a rational inequality

Solve the inequality $\dfrac{1}{x - 2} > 0$.

Figure 7

SOLUTION   Since the numerator is positive, the fraction is positive if and only if the denominator, $x - 2$, is also positive. Thus, $x - 2 > 0$ or, equivalently, $x > 2$, and the solutions are all numbers in the infinite interval $(2, \infty)$ sketched in Figure 7.

EXAMPLE 6 Using a lens formula

As illustrated in Figure 8, if a convex lens has focal length f centimeters and if an object is placed a distance p centimeters from the lens with $p > f$, then the distance q from the lens to the image is related to p and f by the formula

$$\frac{1}{p} + \frac{1}{q} = \frac{1}{f}.$$

If $f = 5$ cm, how close must the object be to the lens for the image to be more than 12 centimeters from the lens?

SOLUTION   Since $f = 5$, the given formula may be written as

$$\frac{1}{p} + \frac{1}{q} = \frac{1}{5}.$$

We wish to determine the values of q such that $q > 12$. Let us first solve the equation for q:

$$5q + 5p = pq \qquad \text{multiply by the lcd, } 5pq$$
$$q(5 - p) = -5p \qquad \text{collect } q \text{ terms on one side and factor}$$
$$q = -\frac{5p}{5 - p} = \frac{5p}{p - 5} \qquad \text{divide by } 5 - p$$

To solve the inequality $q > 12$, we proceed as follows:

$$\frac{5p}{p - 5} > 12 \qquad\qquad q = \frac{5p}{p - 5}$$
$$5p > 12(p - 5) \qquad \text{allowable, since } p > f \text{ implies } p - 5 > 0$$
$$-7p > -60 \qquad \text{multiply factors and collect } p \text{ terms on one side}$$
$$p < \tfrac{60}{7} \qquad \text{divide by } -7; \text{ reverse the inequality}$$

Combining the last inequality with the fact that p is greater than 5, we obtain the solution

$$5 < p < \tfrac{60}{7}. \qquad\qquad ◪$$

If a point X on a coordinate line has coordinate x, as shown in Figure 9, then X is to the right of the origin O if $x > 0$ and to the left of O if $x < 0$. From Section 1.1, the distance $d(O, X)$ between O and X is the *nonnegative* real number given by

$$d(O, X) = |x - 0| = |x|.$$

It follows that the solutions of an inequality such as $|x| < 3$ consist of the coordinates of all points whose distance from O is less than 3. This is the open interval $(-3, 3)$ sketched in Figure 10. Thus,

$$|x| < 3 \quad \text{is equivalent to} \quad -3 < x < 3.$$

Figure 8

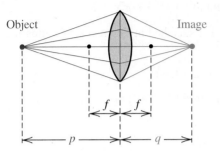

Object   Image

Figure 9

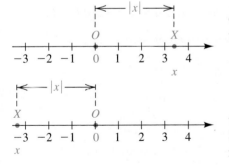

Figure 10

Similarly, for $|x| > 3$, the distance between O and a point with coordinate x is greater than 3; that is,

$$|x| > 3 \quad \text{is equivalent to} \quad x < -3 \text{ or } x > 3.$$

Figure 11

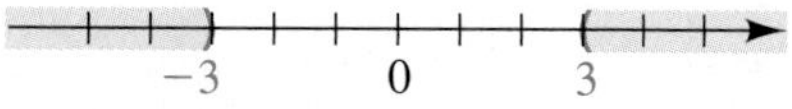

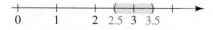

The graph of the solutions to $|x| > 3$ is sketched in Figure 11. We often use the **union symbol** $\cup$ and write

$$(-\infty, -3) \cup (3, \infty)$$

to denote all real numbers that are in either $(-\infty, -3)$ or $(3, \infty)$.

The notation

$$(-\infty, 2) \cup (2, \infty)$$

represents the set of all real numbers except 2.

The **intersection symbol** $\cap$ is used to denote the elements that are *common* to two sets. For example,

$$(-\infty, 3) \cap (-3, \infty) = (-3, 3),$$

since the intersection of $(-\infty, 3)$ and $(-3, \infty)$ consists of all real numbers x such that both $x < 3$ *and* $x > -3$.

The preceding discussion may be generalized to obtain the following properties of absolute values.

Properties of Absolute Values ($b > 0$)	
	(1) $\|a\| < b$ is equivalent to $-b < a < b$.
	(2) $\|a\| > b$ is equivalent to $a < -b$ or $a > b$.

In the next example we use property 1 with $a = x - 3$ and $b = 0.5$.

EXAMPLE 7 Solving an inequality containing an absolute value

Solve the inequality $|x - 3| < 0.5$.

SOLUTION

$$
\begin{array}{ll}
|x - 3| < 0.5 & \text{given} \\
-0.5 < x - 3 < 0.5 & \text{property 1} \\
-0.5 + 3 < (x - 3) + 3 < 0.5 + 3 & \text{isolate } x \text{ by adding 3} \\
2.5 < x < 3.5 & \text{simplify}
\end{array}
$$

Figure 12

Thus, the solutions are the real numbers in the open interval $(2.5, 3.5)$. The graph is sketched in Figure 12.

In the next example we use property 2 with $a = 2x + 3$ and $b = 9$.

EXAMPLE 8   Solving an inequality containing an absolute value

Solve the inequality $|2x + 3| > 9$.

SOLUTION

$$|2x + 3| > 9 \qquad \text{given}$$

$$2x + 3 < -9 \quad \text{or} \quad 2x + 3 > 9 \quad \text{property 2}$$

$$2x < -12 \quad \text{or} \qquad 2x > 6 \quad \text{subtract 3}$$

$$x < -6 \quad \text{or} \qquad x > 3 \quad \text{divide by 2}$$

Figure 13

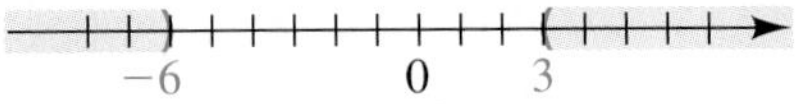

Consequently, the solutions of the inequality $|2x + 3| > 9$ consist of the numbers in $(-\infty, -6) \cup (3, \infty)$. The graph is sketched in Figure 13.

The trichotomy law in Section 1.1 states that for any real numbers a and b exactly one of the following is true:

$$a > b, \qquad a < b, \qquad \text{or} \qquad a = b$$

Thus, after solving $|2x + 3| > 9$ in Example 8, we readily obtain the solutions for $|2x + 3| < 9$ and $|2x + 3| = 9$—namely, $(-6, 3)$ and $\{-6, 3\}$, respectively. Note that the union of these three sets of solutions is necessarily the set $\mathbb{R}$ of real numbers.

When using the notation $a < x < b$, we must have $a < b$. Thus, *it is incorrect to write the solution $x < -6$ or $x > 3$ (in Example 8) as $3 < x < -6$.* Another misuse of inequality notation is to write $a < x > b$, since when several inequality symbols are used in one expression, *they must point in the same direction.*

2.6   *Exercises*

1 Given $-7 < -3$, determine the inequality obtained if

(a) 5 is added to both sides

(b) 4 is subtracted from both sides

(c) both sides are multiplied by $\frac{1}{3}$

(d) both sides are multiplied by $-\frac{1}{3}$

2 Given $4 > -5$, determine the inequality obtained if

(a) 7 is added to both sides

(b) -5 is subtracted from both sides

(c) both sides are divided by 6

(d) both sides are divided by -6

Exer. 3–12: Express the inequality as an interval, and sketch its graph.

3 $x < -2$

4 $x \le 5$

5 $x \ge 4$

6 $x > -3$

7 $-2 < x \le 4$

8 $-3 \le x < 5$

9 $3 \le x \le 7$

10 $-3 < x < -1$

11 $5 > x \ge -2$

12 $-3 \ge x > -5$

Exer. 13–20: Express the interval as an inequality in the variable x.

13 $(-5, 8]$

14 $[0, 4)$

15 $[-4, -1]$

16 $(3, 7)$

17 $[4, \infty)$

18 $(-3, \infty)$

19 $(-\infty, -5)$

20 $(-\infty, 2]$

Exer. 21–70: Solve the inequality, and express the solutions in terms of intervals whenever possible.

21 $3x - 2 > 14$

22 $2x + 5 \leq 7$

23 $-2 - 3x \geq 2$

24 $3 - 5x < 11$

25 $2x + 5 < 3x - 7$

26 $x - 8 > 5x + 3$

27 $9 + \frac{1}{3}x \geq 4 - \frac{1}{2}x$

28 $\frac{1}{4}x + 7 \leq \frac{1}{3}x - 2$

29 $-3 < 2x - 5 < 7$

30 $4 \geq 3x + 5 > -1$

31 $3 \leq \frac{2x - 3}{5} < 7$

32 $-2 < \frac{4x + 1}{3} \leq 0$

33 $4 > \frac{2 - 3x}{7} \geq -2$

34 $5 \geq \frac{6 - 5x}{3} > 2$

35 $0 \leq 4 - \frac{1}{3}x < 2$

36 $-2 < 3 + \frac{1}{4}x \leq 5$

37 $(2x - 3)(4x + 5) \leq (8x + 1)(x - 7)$

38 $(x - 3)(x + 3) \geq (x + 5)^2$

39 $(x - 4)^2 > x(x + 12)$

40 $2x(6x + 5) < (3x - 2)(4x + 1)$

41 $\frac{4}{3x + 2} \geq 0$

42 $\frac{3}{2x + 5} \leq 0$

43 $\frac{-2}{4 - 3x} > 0$

44 $\frac{-3}{2 - x} < 0$

45 $\frac{2}{(1 - x)^2} > 0$

46 $\frac{4}{x^2 + 4} < 0$

47 $|x| < 3$

48 $|x| \leq 7$

49 $|x| \geq 5$

50 $|-x| > 2$

51 $|x + 3| < 0.01$

52 $|x - 4| \leq 0.03$

53 $|x + 2| + 0.1 \geq 0.2$

54 $|x - 3| - 0.3 > 0.1$

55 $|2x + 5| < 4$

56 $|3x - 7| \geq 5$

57 $-\frac{1}{3}|6 - 5x| + 2 \geq 1$

58 $2|-11 - 7x| - 2 > 10$

59 $|7x + 2| > -2$

60 $|6x - 5| \leq -2$

61 $|3x - 9| > 0$

62 $|5x + 2| \leq 0$

63 $\left|\frac{2 - 3x}{5}\right| \geq 2$

64 $\left|\frac{2x + 5}{3}\right| < 1$

65 $\frac{3}{|5 - 2x|} < 2$

66 $\frac{2}{|2x + 3|} \geq 5$

67 $-2 < |x| < 4$

68 $1 < |x| < 5$

69 $1 < |x - 2| < 4$

70 $2 < |2x - 1| < 3$

Exer. 71–72: Solve part (a) and use that answer to determine the answers to parts (b) and (c).

71 (a) $|x + 5| = 3$ (b) $|x + 5| < 3$

   (c) $|x + 5| > 3$

72 (a) $|x - 3| < 2$ (b) $|x - 3| = 2$

   (c) $|x - 3| > 2$

Exer. 73–76: Express the statement in terms of an inequality involving an absolute value.

73 The weight w of a wrestler must be within 2 pounds of 148 pounds.

74 The radius r of a ball bearing must be within 0.01 centimeter of 1 centimeter.

75 The difference of two temperatures T_1 and T_2 within a chemical mixture must be between 5°C and 10°C.

76 The arrival time t of train B must be at least 5 minutes different from the 4:00 P.M. arrival time of train A.

77 Temperature scales Temperature readings on the Fahrenheit and Celsius scales are related by the formula $C = \frac{5}{9}(F - 32)$. What values of F correspond to the values of C such that $30 \leq C \leq 40$?

78 Hooke's law According to Hooke's law, the force F (in pounds) required to stretch a certain spring x inches beyond its natural length is given by $F = (4.5)x$ (see the figure). If $10 \le F \le 18$, what are the corresponding values for x?

Exercise 78

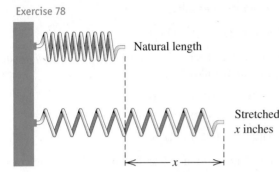

Natural length

Stretched x inches

79 Ohm's law Ohm's law in electrical theory states that if R denotes the resistance of an object (in ohms), V the potential difference across the object (in volts), and I the current that flows through it (in amperes), then $R = V/I$. If the voltage is 110, what values of the resistance will result in a current that does not exceed 10 amperes?

80 Electrical resistance If two resistors R_1 and R_2 are connected in parallel in an electrical circuit, the net resistance R is given by

$$\frac{1}{R} = \frac{1}{R_1} + \frac{1}{R_2}.$$

If $R_1 = 10$ ohms, what values of R_2 will result in a net resistance of less than 5 ohms?

81 Linear magnification Shown in the figure is a simple magnifier consisting of a convex lens. The object to be magnified is positioned so that the distance p from the lens is less than the focal length f. The linear magnification M is the ratio of the image size to the object size. It is shown in physics that $M = f/(f - p)$. If $f = 6$ cm, how far should the object be placed from the lens so that its image appears at least three times as large? (Compare with Example 6.)

Exercise 81

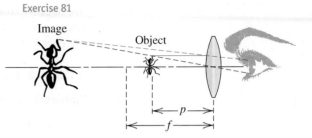

Image   Object

p

f

82 Drug concentration To treat arrhythmia (irregular heartbeat), a drug is fed intravenously into the bloodstream. Suppose that the concentration c of the drug after t hours is given by $c = 3.5t/(t + 1)$ mg/L. If the minimum therapeutic level is 1.5 mg/L, determine when this level is exceeded.

83 Business expenditure A construction firm is trying to decide which of two models of a crane to purchase. Model A costs $100,000 and requires $8000 per year to maintain. Model B has an initial cost of $80,000 and a maintenance cost of $11,000 per year. For how many years must model A be used before it becomes more economical than B?

84 Buying a car A consumer is trying to decide whether to purchase car A or car B. Car A costs $20,000 and has an mpg rating of 30, and insurance is $1000 per year. Car B costs $24,000 and has an mpg rating of 50, and insurance is $1200 per year. Assume that the consumer drives 15,000 miles per year and that the price of gas remains constant at $3 per gallon. Based only on these facts, determine how long it will take for the total cost of car B to become less than that of car A.

85 Decreasing height A person's height will typically decrease by 0.024 inch each year after age 30.

(a) If a woman was 5 feet 9 inches tall at age 30, predict her height at age 70.

(b) A 50-year-old man is 5 feet 6 inches tall. Determine an inequality for the range of heights (in inches) that this man will experience between the ages of 30 and 70.

2.7

More on Inequalities

To solve an inequality involving polynomials of degree greater than 1, we shall express each polynomial as a product of linear factors $ax + b$ and/or irreducible quadratic factors $ax^2 + bx + c$. If any such factor is not zero in an interval, then it is either positive throughout the interval or negative throughout the interval. Hence, if we choose any k in the interval and if the factor is positive (or negative) for $x = k$, then it is positive (or negative) throughout the interval. The value of the factor at $x = k$ is called a **test value** of the factor at the test number k. This concept is exhibited in the following example.

EXAMPLE 1 Solving a quadratic inequality

Solve the inequality $2x^2 - x < 3$.

SOLUTION   To use test values, *it is essential to have* 0 *on one side of the inequality sign.* Thus, we proceed as follows:

$$2x^2 - x < 3 \qquad \text{given}$$
$$2x^2 - x - 3 < 0 \qquad \text{make one side 0}$$
$$(x + 1)(2x - 3) < 0 \qquad \text{factor}$$

Figure 1

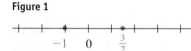

The factors $x + 1$ and $2x - 3$ are zero at -1 and $\frac{3}{2}$, respectively. The corresponding points on a coordinate line (see Figure 1) determine the nonintersecting intervals

$$(-\infty, -1), \quad \left(-1, \tfrac{3}{2}\right), \quad \text{and} \quad \left(\tfrac{3}{2}, \infty\right).$$

We may find the signs of $x + 1$ and $2x - 3$ in each interval by using a test value taken from each interval. To illustrate, if we choose $k = -10$ in $(-\infty, -1)$, the values of both $x + 1$ and $2x - 3$ are negative, and hence they are negative throughout $(-\infty, -1)$. A similar procedure for the remaining two intervals gives us the following *sign chart,* where the term *resulting sign* in the last row refers to the sign obtained by applying laws of signs to the product of the factors. Note that the resulting sign is positive or negative according to whether the number of negative signs of factors is even or odd, respectively.

Interval	$(-\infty, -1)$	$\left(-1, \tfrac{3}{2}\right)$	$\left(\tfrac{3}{2}, \infty\right)$
Sign of $x + 1$	$-$	$+$	$+$
Sign of $2x - 3$	$-$	$-$	$+$
Resulting sign	$+$	$-$	$+$

Sometimes it is convenient to represent the signs of $x + 1$ and $2x - 3$ by using a coordinate line and a *sign diagram,* of the type illustrated in Figure 2. The vertical lines indicate where the factors are zero, and signs of factors are shown above the coordinate line. The resulting signs are shown in red.

Figure 2

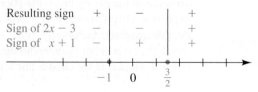

Resulting sign $+$ $-$ $+$
Sign of $2x - 3$ $-$ $-$ $+$
Sign of $x + 1$ $-$ $+$ $+$

The solutions of $(x + 1)(2x - 3) < 0$ are the values of x for which the product of the factors is *negative*—that is, where the resulting sign is negative. This corresponds to the open interval $\left(-1, \frac{3}{2}\right)$.

Back on page 74, we discussed the zero factor theorem, which dealt with *equalities*. It is a common mistake to extend this theorem to *inequalities*. The following warning shows this incorrect extension applied to the inequality in Example 1.

 **Warning!**

$(x + 1)(2x - 3) < 0$ is **not** equivalent to $x + 1 < 0$ or $2x - 3 < 0$

In future examples we will use either a sign chart or a sign diagram, but not both. When working exercises, you should choose the method of solution with which you feel most comfortable.

EXAMPLE 2   Solving a quadratic inequality

Solve the inequality $-3x^2 < -21x + 30$.

SOLUTION

$-3x^2 < -21x + 30$	given
$-3x^2 + 21x - 30 < 0$	make one side 0
$x^2 - 7x + 10 > 0$	divide by the common factor -3; reverse the inequality
$(x - 2)(x - 5) > 0$	factor

The factors are zero at 2 and 5. The corresponding points on a coordinate line (see Figure 3) determine the nonintersecting intervals

$$(-\infty, 2), \quad (2, 5), \quad \text{and} \quad (5, \infty).$$

Figure 3

As in Example 1, we may use test values from each interval to obtain the following sign chart.

Interval	$(-\infty, 2)$	$(2, 5)$	$(5, \infty)$
Sign of $x - 2$	−	+	+
Sign of $x - 5$	−	−	+
Resulting sign	+	−	+

The solutions of $(x - 2)(x - 5) > 0$ are the values of x for which the resulting sign is *positive*. Thus, the solution of the given inequality is the union $(-\infty, 2) \cup (5, \infty)$.

EXAMPLE 3   Using a sign diagram to solve an inequality

Solve the inequality $\dfrac{(x + 2)(3 - x)}{(x + 1)(x^2 + 1)} \leq 0$.

SOLUTION   Since 0 is already on the right side of the inequality and the left side is factored, we may proceed directly to the sign diagram in Figure 4, where the vertical lines indicate the zeros (-2, -1, and 3) of the factors.

Figure 4

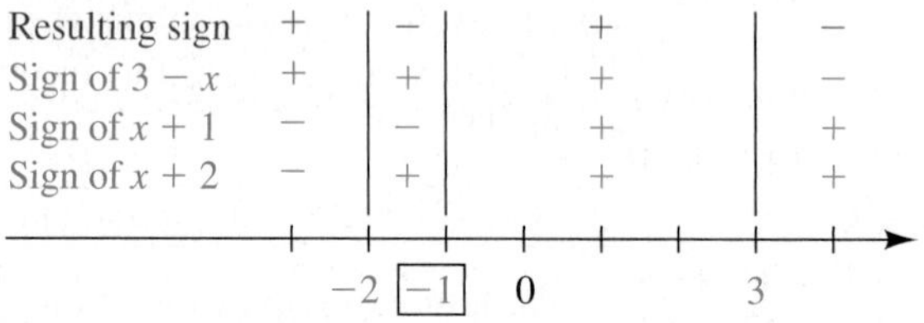

Resulting sign	+		$-$		+		$-$
Sign of $3 - x$	+		+		+		$-$
Sign of $x + 1$	$-$		$-$		+		+
Sign of $x + 2$	$-$		+		+		+

$$-2 \quad \boxed{-1} \quad 0 \qquad 3$$

The frame around the -1 indicates that -1 makes a factor in the denominator of the original inequality equal to 0. Since the quadratic factor $x^2 + 1$ is always positive, it has no effect on the sign of the quotient and hence may be omitted from the diagram.

The various signs of the factors can be found using test values. Alternatively, we need only remember that as x increases, the sign of a linear factor $ax + b$ changes from negative to positive if the coefficient a of x is positive, and the sign changes from positive to negative if a is negative.

To determine where the quotient is less than or equal to 0, we first note from the sign diagram that it is *negative* for numbers in $(-2, -1) \cup (3, \infty)$. Since the quotient is 0 at $x = -2$ and $x = 3$, the numbers -2 and 3 are also solutions and must be *included* in our solution. Lastly, the quotient is *undefined* at $x = -1$, so -1 must be *excluded* from our solution. Thus, the solutions of the given inequality are given by

$$[-2, -1) \cup [3, \infty).$$

EXAMPLE 4   Using a sign diagram to solve an inequality

Solve the inequality $\dfrac{(2x + 1)^2(x - 1)}{x(x^2 - 1)} \geq 0$.

SOLUTION   Rewriting the inequality as

$$\frac{(2x + 1)^2(x - 1)}{x(x + 1)(x - 1)} \geq 0,$$

we see that $x - 1$ is a factor of both the numerator and the denominator. Thus, *assuming that* $x - 1 \neq 0$ (that is, $x \neq 1$), we may cancel this factor and reduce our search for solutions to the case

$$\frac{(2x + 1)^2}{x(x + 1)} \geq 0 \qquad \text{and} \qquad x \neq 1.$$

We next observe that this quotient is 0 if $2x + 1 = 0$ $\left(\text{that is, if } x = -\frac{1}{2}\right)$. Hence, $-\frac{1}{2}$ is a solution. To find the remaining solutions, we construct the sign

Figure 5

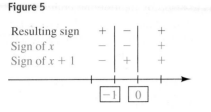

diagram in Figure 5. We do not include $(2x + 1)^2$ in the sign diagram, since this expression is always positive if $x \neq -\frac{1}{2}$ and so has no effect on the sign of the quotient. Referring to the resulting sign and remembering that $-\frac{1}{2}$ is a solution but 1 is *not* a solution, we see that the solutions of the given inequality are given by

$$(-\infty, -1) \cup \left\{-\tfrac{1}{2}\right\} \cup (0, 1) \cup (1, \infty).$$

EXAMPLE 5 Using a sign diagram to solve an inequality

Solve the inequality $\dfrac{x + 1}{x + 3} \leq 2$.

SOLUTION A common mistake in solving such an inequality is to first multiply both sides by $x + 3$. If we did so, we would have to consider two cases, since $x + 3$ may be positive or negative (assuming $x + 3 \neq 0$), and we might have to reverse the inequality. A simpler method is to first obtain an equivalent inequality that has 0 on the right side and proceed from there:

$$\frac{x + 1}{x + 3} \leq 2 \quad \text{given}$$

$$\frac{x + 1}{x + 3} - 2 \leq 0 \quad \text{make one side 0}$$

$$\frac{x + 1 - 2(x + 3)}{x + 3} \leq 0 \quad \text{combine into one fraction}$$

$$\frac{-x - 5}{x + 3} \leq 0 \quad \text{simplify}$$

$$\frac{x + 5}{x + 3} \geq 0 \quad \text{multiply by } -1$$

Note that the direction of the inequality is changed in the last step, since we multiplied by a negative number. This multiplication was performed for convenience, so that all factors would have positive coefficients of x.

The factors $x + 5$ and $x + 3$ are 0 at $x = -5$ and $x = -3$, respectively. This leads to the sign diagram in Figure 6, where the signs are determined as in previous examples. We see from the diagram that the resulting sign, and hence the sign of the quotient, is positive in $(-\infty, -5) \cup (-3, \infty)$. The quotient is 0 at $x = -5$ (include -5) and undefined at $x = -3$ (exclude -3). Hence, the solution of $(x + 5)/(x + 3) \geq 0$ is $(-\infty, -5] \cup (-3, \infty)$.

Figure 6

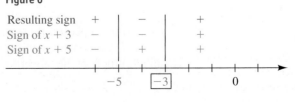

(continued)

An alternative method of solution is to begin by multiplying both sides of the given inequality by $(x + 3)^2$, *assuming that* $x \neq -3$. In this case, $(x + 3)^2 > 0$ and the multiplication is permissible; however, after the resulting inequality is solved, the value $x = -3$ must be excluded. ◢

EXAMPLE 6 Determining minimum therapeutic levels

For a drug to have a beneficial effect, its concentration in the bloodstream must exceed a certain value, which is called the *minimum therapeutic level.* Suppose that the concentration c (in mg/L) of a particular drug t hours after it is taken orally is given by

$$c = \frac{20t}{t^2 + 4}.$$

If the minimum therapeutic level is 4 mg/L, determine when this level is exceeded.

SOLUTION   The minimum therapeutic level, 4 mg/L, is exceeded if $c > 4$. Thus, we must solve the inequality

$$\frac{20t}{t^2 + 4} > 4.$$

Since $t^2 + 4 > 0$ for every t, we may multiply both sides by $t^2 + 4$ and proceed as follows:

$$20t > 4t^2 + 16 \qquad \text{allowable, since } t^2 + 4 > 0$$

$$-4t^2 + 20t - 16 > 0 \qquad \text{make one side 0}$$

$$t^2 - 5t + 4 < 0 \qquad \text{divide by the common factor } -4$$

$$(t - 1)(t - 4) < 0 \qquad \text{factor}$$

The factors in the last inequality are 0 when $t = 1$ and $t = 4$. These are the times at which c is *equal to* 4. As in previous examples, we may use a sign chart or sign diagram (with $t \geq 0$) to show that $(t - 1)(t - 4) < 0$ for every t in the interval $(1, 4)$. Hence, the minimum therapeutic level is exceeded if $1 < t < 4$. ◢

Some basic properties of inequalities were stated at the beginning of the last section. The following additional properties are helpful for solving certain inequalities. Proofs of the properties are given after the chart.

Additional Properties of Inequalities

Property	Illustration
(1) If $0 < a < b$, then $\dfrac{1}{a} > \dfrac{1}{b}$.	If $0 < \dfrac{1}{x} < 4$, then $\dfrac{1}{1/x} > \dfrac{1}{4}$, or $x > \dfrac{1}{4}$.
(2) If $0 < a < b$, then $0 < a^2 < b^2$.	If $0 < \sqrt{x} < 4$, then $0 < (\sqrt{x})^2 < 4^2$, or $0 < x < 16$.
(3) If $0 < a < b$, then $0 < \sqrt{a} < \sqrt{b}$.	If $0 < x^2 < 4$, then $0 < \sqrt{x^2} < \sqrt{4}$, or $0 < |x| < 2$.

PROOFS

(1) If $0 < a < b$, then multiplying by $1/(ab)$ yields

$$a \cdot \frac{1}{ab} < b \cdot \frac{1}{ab}, \quad \text{or} \quad \frac{1}{b} < \frac{1}{a}; \qquad \text{that is,} \quad \frac{1}{a} > \frac{1}{b}.$$

(2) If $0 < a < b$, then multiplying by a yields $a \cdot a < a \cdot b$ and multiplying by b yields $b \cdot a < b \cdot b$, so $a^2 < ab < b^2$ and hence $a^2 < b^2$.

(3) If $0 < a < b$, then $b - a > 0$ or, equivalently,

$$\left(\sqrt{b} + \sqrt{a}\right)\left(\sqrt{b} - \sqrt{a}\right) > 0.$$

Dividing both sides of the last inequality by $\sqrt{b} + \sqrt{a}$, we obtain $\sqrt{b} - \sqrt{a} > 0$; that is, $\sqrt{b} > \sqrt{a}$. ◢

2.7   *Exercises*

Exer. 1–40: Solve the inequality, and express the solutions in terms of intervals whenever possible.

1 $(3x + 1)(5 - 10x) > 0$

2 $(2 - 3x)(4x - 7) \geq 0$

3 $(x + 2)(x - 1)(4 - x) \leq 0$

4 $(x - 5)(x + 3)(-2 - x) < 0$

5 $x^2 - x - 6 < 0$

6 $x^2 + 4x + 3 \geq 0$

7 $x^2 - 2x - 5 > 3$

8 $x^2 - 4x - 17 \leq 4$

9 $x(2x + 3) \geq 5$

10 $x(3x - 1) \leq 4$

11 $6x - 8 > x^2$

12 $x + 12 \leq x^2$

13 $x^2 < 16$

14 $x^2 > 9$

15 $25x^2 - 9 < 0$

16 $25x^2 - 9x < 0$

17 $16x^2 \geq 9x$

18 $16x^2 > 9$

19 $x^4 + 5x^2 \geq 36$

20 $x^4 + 15x^2 < 16$

21 $x^3 + 2x^2 - 4x - 8 \geq 0$

22 $2x^3 - 3x^2 - 2x + 3 \leq 0$

23 $\dfrac{x^2(x + 2)}{(x + 2)(x + 1)} \leq 0$

24 $\dfrac{(x^2 + 1)(x - 3)}{x^2 - 9} \geq 0$

25 $\dfrac{x^2 - x}{x^2 + 2x} \leq 0$

26 $\dfrac{(x + 3)^2(2 - x)}{(x + 4)(x^2 - 4)} \leq 0$

27 $\dfrac{x - 2}{x^2 - 3x - 10} \geq 0$

28 $\dfrac{x + 5}{x^2 - 7x + 12} \leq 0$

29 $\dfrac{-3x}{x^2 - 9} > 0$

30 $\dfrac{2x}{16 - x^2} < 0$

31 $\dfrac{x + 1}{2x - 3} > 2$

32 $\dfrac{x - 2}{3x + 5} \leq 4$

33 $\dfrac{1}{x - 2} \geq \dfrac{3}{x + 1}$

34 $\dfrac{2}{2x + 3} \leq \dfrac{2}{x - 5}$

35 $\dfrac{4}{3x - 2} \leq \dfrac{2}{x + 1}$

36 $\dfrac{3}{5x + 1} \geq \dfrac{1}{x - 3}$

37 $\dfrac{x}{3x - 5} \leq \dfrac{2}{x - 1}$

38 $\dfrac{x}{2x - 1} \geq \dfrac{3}{x + 2}$

39 $x^3 > x$

40 $x^4 \geq x^2$

Exer. 41–42: As a particle moves along a straight path, its speed v (in cm/sec) at time t (in seconds) is given by the equation. For what subintervals of the given time interval $[a, b]$ will its speed be at least k cm/sec?

41 $v = t^3 - 3t^2 - 4t + 20$; $[0, 5]$; $k = 8$

42 $v = t^4 - 4t^2 + 10$; $[1, 6]$; $k = 10$

43 Vertical leap record *Guinness Book of World Records* reports that German shepherds can make vertical leaps of over 10 feet when scaling walls. If the distance s (in feet) off the ground after t seconds is given by the equation $s = -16t^2 + 24t + 1$, for how many seconds is the dog more than 9 feet off the ground?

44 Height of a projected object If an object is projected vertically upward from ground level with an initial velocity of 320 ft/sec, then its distance s above the ground after t seconds is given by $s = -16t^2 + 320t$. For what values of t will the object be more than 1536 feet above the ground?

45 Braking distance The braking distance d (in feet) of a certain car traveling v mi/hr is given by the equation $d = v + (v^2/20)$. Determine the velocities that result in braking distances of less than 75 feet.

46 Gas mileage The number of miles M that a certain compact car can travel on 1 gallon of gasoline is related to its speed v (in mi/hr) by

$$M = -\tfrac{1}{30}v^2 + \tfrac{5}{2}v \quad \text{for} \quad 0 < v < 70.$$

For what speeds will M be at least 45?

47 Salmon propagation For a particular salmon population, the relationship between the number S of spawners and the number R of offspring that survive to maturity is given by the formula $R = 4500S/(S + 500)$. Under what conditions is $R > S$?

48 Population density The population density D (in people/mi^2) in a large city is related to the distance x from the center of the city by $D = 5000x/(x^2 + 36)$. In what areas of the city does the population density exceed 400 people/mi^2?

49 Weight in space After an astronaut is launched into space, the astronaut's weight decreases until a state of weightlessness is achieved. The weight of a 125-pound astronaut at an altitude of x kilometers above sea level is given by

$$W = 125\left(\dfrac{6400}{6400 + x}\right)^2.$$

At what altitudes is the astronaut's weight less than 5 pounds?

50 Lorentz contraction formula The Lorentz contraction formula in relativity theory relates the length L of an object moving at a velocity of v mi/sec with respect to an observer to its length L_0 at rest. If c is the speed of light, then

$$L^2 = L_0^2\left(1 - \dfrac{v^2}{c^2}\right).$$

For what velocities will L be less than $\tfrac{1}{2}L_0$? State the answer in terms of c.

51 Aircraft's landing speed In the design of certain small turbo-prop aircraft, the landing speed V (in ft/sec) is determined by the formula $W = 0.00334V^2S$, where W is the gross weight (in pounds) of the aircraft and S is the surface area (in ft^2) of the wings. If the gross weight of the aircraft is between 7500 pounds and 10,000 pounds and $S = 210$ ft^2, determine the range of the landing speeds in miles per hour.

73 **Speedboat rates** A speedboat leaves a dock traveling east at 30 mi/hr. Another speedboat leaves from the same dock 20 minutes later, traveling west at 24 mi/hr. How long after the first speedboat departs will the speedboats be 37 miles apart?

74 **Jogging rates** A girl jogs 5 miles in 24 minutes less than she can jog 7 miles. Assuming she jogs at a constant rate, find her jogging rate in miles per hour.

75 **Filling a bin** An extruder can fill an empty bin in 2 hours, and a packaging crew can empty a full bin in 5 hours. If a bin is half full when an extruder begins to fill it and a crew begins to empty it, how long will it take to fill the bin?

76 **Gasoline mileage** A sales representative for a company estimates that her automobile gasoline consumption averages 28 mpg on the highway and 22 mpg in the city. A recent trip covered 627 miles, and 24 gallons of gasoline was used. How much of the trip was spent driving in the city?

77 **City expansion** The longest drive to the center of a square city from the outskirts is 10 miles. Within the last decade the city has expanded in area by 50 mi². Assuming the city has always been square in shape, find the corresponding change in the longest drive to the center of the city.

78 **Dimensions of a cell membrane** The membrane of a cell is a sphere of radius 6 microns. What change in the radius will increase the surface area of the membrane by 25%?

79 **Highway travel** A north-south highway intersects an east-west highway at a point P. An automobile crosses P at 10 A.M., traveling east at a constant rate of 20 mi/hr. At the same instant another automobile is 2 miles north of P, traveling south at 50 mi/hr.

(a) Find a formula for the distance d between the automobiles t hours after 10:00 A.M.

(b) At approximately what time will the automobiles be 104 miles apart?

80 **Fencing a kennel** A kennel owner has 270 feet of fencing material to be used to divide a rectangular area into 10 equal pens, as shown in the figure. Find dimensions that would allow 100 ft² for each pen.

Exercise 80

81 **Dimensions of an aquarium** An open-topped aquarium is to be constructed with 6-foot-long sides and square ends, as shown in the figure.

(a) Find the height of the aquarium if the volume is to be 48 ft³.

(b) Find the height if 44 ft² of glass is to be used.

Exercise 81

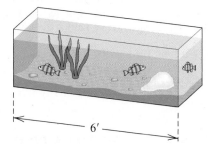

6'

82 **Dimensions of a pool** The length of a rectangular pool is to be four times its width, and a sidewalk of width 6 feet will surround the pool. If a total area of 1440 ft² has been set aside for construction, what are the dimensions of the pool?

83 **Dimensions of a bath** A contractor wishes to design a rectangular sunken bath with 40 ft² of bathing area. A 1-foot-wide tile strip is to surround the bathing area. The total length of the tiled area is to be twice the width. Find the dimensions of the bathing area.

84 **Population growth** The population P (in thousands) of a small town is expected to increase according to the formula

$$P = 15 + \sqrt{3t + 2},$$

where t is time in years. When will the population be 20,000?

85 **Boyle's law** Boyle's law for a certain gas states that if the temperature is constant, then $pv = 200$, where p is the pressure (in lb/in²) and v is the volume (in in³). If $25 \le v \le 50$, what is the corresponding range for p?

86 **Sales commission** A recent college graduate has job offers for a sales position in two computer firms. Job A pays $50,000 per year plus 10% commission. Job B pays only $40,000 per year, but the commission rate is 20%. How much yearly business must the salesman do for the second job to be more lucrative?

87 **Speed of sound** The speed of sound in air at 0°C (or 273 K) is 1087 ft/sec, but this speed increases as the temperature rises. The speed v of sound at temperature T in K is given by $v = 1087\sqrt{T/273}$. At what temperatures does the speed of sound exceed 1100 ft/sec?

88 **Period of a pendulum** If the length of the pendulum in a grandfather clock is l centimeters, then its period T (in seconds) is given by $T = 2\pi\sqrt{l/g}$, where g is a gravitational constant. If, under certain conditions, $g = 980$ and $98 \le l \le 100$, what is the corresponding range for T?

89 **Orbit of a satellite** For a satellite to maintain an orbit of altitude h kilometers, its velocity (in km/sec) must equal $626.4/\sqrt{h + R}$, where $R = 6372$ km is the radius of the earth. What velocities will result in orbits with an altitude of more than 100 kilometers from Earth's surface?

90 **Fencing a region** There is 100 feet of fencing available to enclose a rectangular region. For what widths will the fenced region contain at least 600 ft²?

91 **Planting an apple orchard** The owner of an apple orchard estimates that if 24 trees are planted per acre, then each mature tree will yield 600 apples per year. For each additional tree planted per acre, the number of apples produced by each tree decreases by 12 per year. How many trees should be planted per acre to obtain at least 16,416 apples per year?

92 **Apartment rentals** A real estate company owns 218 efficiency apartments, which are fully occupied when the rent is $940 per month. The company estimates that for each $25 increase in rent, 5 apartments will become unoccupied. What rent should be charged in order to pay the monthly bills, which total $205,920?

CHAPTER 2 DISCUSSION EXERCISES

1 When we factor the sum or difference of cubes, $x^3 \pm y^3$, is the factor $(x^2 \mp xy + y^2)$ ever factorable over the real numbers?

2 What is the average of the two solutions of the arbitrary quadratic equation $ax^2 + bx + c = 0$? Discuss how this knowledge can help you easily check the solutions to a quadratic equation.

3 (a) Find an expression of the form $p + qi$ for the multiplicative inverse of $\dfrac{a + bi}{c + di}$, where a, b, c, and d are real numbers.

   (b) Does the expression you found apply to real numbers of the form a/c?

   (c) Are there any restrictions on your answer for part (a)?

4 In solving the inequality $\dfrac{x - 1}{x - 2} \ge 3$, what is wrong with employing $x - 1 \ge 3(x - 2)$ as a first step?

5 Consider the inequality $ax^2 + bx + c \ge 0$, where a, b, and c are real numbers with $a \ne 0$. Suppose the associated equality $ax^2 + bx + c = 0$ has discriminant D. Categorize the solutions of the inequality according to the signs of a and D.

6 **Freezing level in a cloud** Refer to Exercises 37–39 in Section 2.2.

   (a) Approximate the height of the freezing level in a cloud if the ground temperature is 80°F and the dew point is 68°F.

   (b) Find a formula for the height h of the freezing level in a cloud for ground temperature G and dew point D.

7 Explain why you should not try to solve one of these equations.

$$\sqrt{2x - 3} + \sqrt{x + 5} = 0$$
$$\sqrt[3]{2x - 3} + \sqrt[3]{x + 5} = 0$$

8 Solve the equation

$$\sqrt{x} = cx - 2/c$$

for x, where $c = 2 \times 10^{500}$. Discuss why one of your positive solutions is extraneous.

9 **Surface area of a tank** You know that a spherical tank holds 10,000 gallons of water. What do you need to know to determine the surface area of the tank? Estimate the surface area of the tank.

3

Functions
and Graphs

The mathematical term *function* (or its Latin equivalent) dates back to the late seventeenth century, when calculus was in the early stages of development. This important concept is now the backbone of advanced courses in mathematics and is indispensable in every field of science.

In this chapter we study properties of functions using algebraic and graphical methods that include plotting points, determining symmetries, and making horizontal and vertical shifts. These techniques are adequate for obtaining rough sketches of graphs that help us understand properties of functions; modern-day methods, however, employ sophisticated computer software and advanced mathematics to generate extremely accurate graphical representations of functions.

3.1

Rectangular Coordinate Systems

In Section 1.1 we discussed how to assign a real number (coordinate) to each point on a line. We shall now show how to assign an **ordered pair** (a, b) of real numbers to each point in a plane. Although we have also used the notation (a, b) to denote an open interval, there is little chance for confusion, since it should always be clear from our discussion whether (a, b) represents a point or an interval.

We introduce a **rectangular,** or **Cartesian,* coordinate system** in a plane by means of two perpendicular coordinate lines, called **coordinate axes,** that intersect at the **origin** O, as shown in Figure 1. We often refer to the horizontal line as the **x-axis** and the vertical line as the **y-axis** and label them x and y, respectively. The plane is then a **coordinate plane,** or an **xy-plane.** The coordinate axes divide the plane into four parts called the **first, second, third,** and **fourth quadrants,** labeled I, II, III, and IV, respectively (see Figure 1). Points on the axes do not belong to any quadrant.

Each point P in an xy-plane may be assigned an ordered pair (a, b), as shown in Figure 1. We call a the **x-coordinate** (or **abscissa**) of P, and b the **y-coordinate** (or **ordinate**). We say that P *has coordinates* (a, b) and refer to the *point* (a, b) or the *point* $P(a, b)$. Conversely, every ordered pair (a, b) determines a point P with coordinates a and b. We **plot a point** by using a dot, as illustrated in Figure 2.

Figure 1

Figure 2

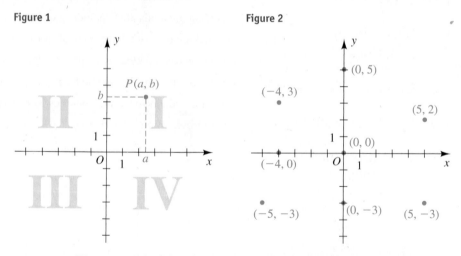

We may use the following formula to find the distance between two points in a coordinate plane.

Distance Formula	The distance $d(P_1, P_2)$ between any two points $P_1(x_1, y_1)$ and $P_2(x_2, y_2)$ in a coordinate plane is $$d(P_1, P_2) = \sqrt{(x_2 - x_1)^2 + (y_2 - y_1)^2}.$$

*The term *Cartesian* is used in honor of the French mathematician and philosopher René Descartes (1596–1650), who was one of the first to employ such coordinate systems.

Figure 3

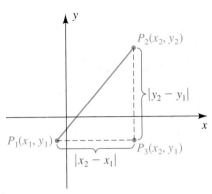

PROOF If $x_1 \neq x_2$ and $y_1 \neq y_2$, then, as illustrated in Figure 3, the points P_1, P_2, and $P_3(x_2, y_1)$ are vertices of a right triangle. By the Pythagorean theorem,

$$[d(P_1, P_2)]^2 = [d(P_1, P_3)]^2 + [d(P_3, P_2)]^2.$$

From the figure we see that

$$d(P_1, P_3) = |x_2 - x_1| \quad \text{and} \quad d(P_3, P_2) = |y_2 - y_1|.$$

Since $|a|^2 = a^2$ for every real number a, we may write

$$[d(P_1, P_2)]^2 = (x_2 - x_1)^2 + (y_2 - y_1)^2.$$

Taking the square root of each side of the last equation and using the fact that $d(P_1, P_2) \geq 0$ gives us the distance formula.

If $y_1 = y_2$, the points P_1 and P_2 lie on the same horizontal line, and

$$d(P_1, P_2) = |x_2 - x_1| = \sqrt{(x_2 - x_1)^2}.$$

Similarly, if $x_1 = x_2$, the points are on the same vertical line, and

$$d(P_1, P_2) = |y_2 - y_1| = \sqrt{(y_2 - y_1)^2}.$$

These are special cases of the distance formula.

Although we referred to the points shown in Figure 3, our proof is independent of the positions of P_1 and P_2. ◢

When applying the distance formula, note that $d(P_1, P_2) = d(P_2, P_1)$ and, hence, the order in which we subtract the x-coordinates and the y-coordinates of the points is immaterial. We may think of the distance between two points as the length of the hypotenuse of a right triangle.

Figure 4

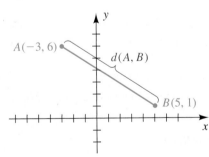

EXAMPLE 1 Finding the distance between points

Plot the points $A(-3, 6)$ and $B(5, 1)$, and find the distance $d(A, B)$.

SOLUTION The points are plotted in Figure 4. By the distance formula,

$$d(A, B) = \sqrt{[5 - (-3)]^2 + (1 - 6)^2}$$
$$= \sqrt{8^2 + (-5)^2}$$
$$= \sqrt{64 + 25} = \sqrt{89} \approx 9.43.$$

◢

EXAMPLE 2 Showing that a triangle is a right triangle

(a) Plot $A(-1, -3)$, $B(6, 1)$, and $C(2, -5)$, and show that triangle ABC is a right triangle.

(b) Find the area of triangle ABC.

Figure 5

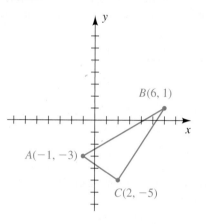

Area of a triangle:

$$A = \tfrac{1}{2}bh$$

SOLUTION

(a) The points are plotted in Figure 5. From geometry, triangle ABC is a right triangle if the sum of the squares of two of its sides is equal to the square of the remaining side. By the distance formula,

$$d(A, B) = \sqrt{(6 + 1)^2 + (1 + 3)^2} = \sqrt{49 + 16} = \sqrt{65}$$
$$d(B, C) = \sqrt{(2 - 6)^2 + (-5 - 1)^2} = \sqrt{16 + 36} = \sqrt{52}$$
$$d(A, C) = \sqrt{(2 + 1)^2 + (-5 + 3)^2} = \sqrt{9 + 4} = \sqrt{13}.$$

Since $d(A, B) = \sqrt{65}$ is the largest of the three values, the condition to be satisfied is

$$[d(A, B)]^2 = [d(B, C)]^2 + [d(A, C)]^2.$$

Substituting the values found using the distance formula, we obtain

$$[d(A, B)]^2 = \left(\sqrt{65}\right)^2 = 65$$

and $\;\;[d(B, C)]^2 + [d(A, C)]^2 = \left(\sqrt{52}\right)^2 + \left(\sqrt{13}\right)^2 = 52 + 13 = 65.$
Thus, the triangle is a right triangle with hypotenuse AB.

(b) The area of a triangle with base b and altitude h is $\tfrac{1}{2}bh$. Referring to Figure 5, we let

$$b = d(B, C) = \sqrt{52} \quad \text{and} \quad h = d(A, C) = \sqrt{13}.$$

Hence, the area of triangle ABC is

$$\tfrac{1}{2}bh = \tfrac{1}{2}\sqrt{52}\,\sqrt{13} = \tfrac{1}{2} \cdot 2\sqrt{13}\,\sqrt{13} = 13.$$

EXAMPLE 3 Applying the distance formula

Given $A(1, 7)$, $B(-3, 2)$, and $C\!\left(4, \tfrac{1}{2}\right)$, prove that C is on the perpendicular bisector of segment AB.

SOLUTION   The points A, B, C and the *perpendicular bisector l* are illustrated in Figure 6. From plane geometry, l can be characterized by either of the following conditions:

(1) l is the line perpendicular to segment AB at its midpoint.

(2) l is the set of all points equidistant from the endpoints of segment AB.

We shall use condition 2 to show that C is on l by verifying that

$$d(A, C) = d(B, C).$$

We apply the distance formula:

$$d(A, C) = \sqrt{(4 - 1)^2 + \left(\tfrac{1}{2} - 7\right)^2} = \sqrt{3^2 + \left(-\tfrac{13}{2}\right)^2} = \sqrt{9 + \tfrac{169}{4}} = \sqrt{\tfrac{205}{4}}$$

$$d(B, C) = \sqrt{[4 - (-3)]^2 + \left(\tfrac{1}{2} - 2\right)^2} = \sqrt{7^2 + \left(-\tfrac{3}{2}\right)^2} = \sqrt{49 + \tfrac{9}{4}} = \sqrt{\tfrac{205}{4}}$$

Thus, C is equidistant from A and B, and the verification is complete.

Figure 6

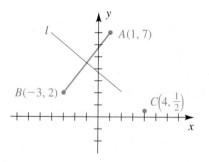

EXAMPLE 4   Finding a formula that describes
a perpendicular bisector

Given $A(1, 7)$ and $B(-3, 2)$, find a formula that expresses the fact that an arbitrary point $P(x, y)$ is on the perpendicular bisector l of segment AB.

SOLUTION   By condition 2 of Example 3, $P(x, y)$ is on l if and only if $d(A, P) = d(B, P)$; that is,

$$\sqrt{(x - 1)^2 + (y - 7)^2} = \sqrt{[x - (-3)]^2 + (y - 2)^2}.$$

To obtain a simpler formula, let us square both sides and simplify terms of the resulting equation, as follows:

$$(x - 1)^2 + (y - 7)^2 = [x - (-3)]^2 + (y - 2)^2$$
$$x^2 - 2x + 1 + y^2 - 14y + 49 = x^2 + 6x + 9 + y^2 - 4y + 4$$
$$-2x + 1 - 14y + 49 = 6x + 9 - 4y + 4$$
$$-8x - 10y = -37$$
$$8x + 10y = 37$$

Note that, in particular, the last formula is true for the coordinates of the point $C\left(4, \frac{1}{2}\right)$ in Example 3, since if $x = 4$ and $y = \frac{1}{2}$, substitution in $8x + 10y$ gives us

$$8 \cdot 4 + 10 \cdot \tfrac{1}{2} = 37.$$

In Example 9 of Section 3.3, we will find a formula for the perpendicular bisector of a segment using condition 1 of Example 3.   ◢

We can find the midpoint of a line segment by using the following formula.

Midpoint Formula	The midpoint M of the line segment from $P_1(x_1, y_1)$ to $P_2(x_2, y_2)$ is $$\left(\frac{x_1 + x_2}{2}, \frac{y_1 + y_2}{2}\right).$$

PROOF   The lines through P_1 and P_2 parallel to the y-axis intersect the x-axis at $A_1(x_1, 0)$ and $A_2(x_2, 0)$. From plane geometry, the line through the midpoint M parallel to the y-axis bisects the segment A_1A_2 at point M_1 (see Figure 7). If $x_1 < x_2$, then $x_2 - x_1 > 0$, and hence $d(A_1, A_2) = x_2 - x_1$. Since M_1 is halfway from A_1 to A_2, the x-coordinate of M_1 is equal to the x-coordinate of A_1 plus one-half the distance from A_1 to A_2; that is,

$$x\text{-coordinate of } M_1 = x_1 + \tfrac{1}{2}(x_2 - x_1).$$

(continued)

Figure 7

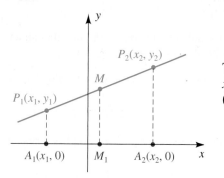

The expression on the right side of the last equation simplifies to

$$\frac{x_1 + x_2}{2}.$$

This quotient is the *average* of the numbers x_1 and x_2. It follows that the x-coordinate of M is also $(x_1 + x_2)/2$. Similarly, the y-coordinate of M is $(y_1 + y_2)/2$. These formulas hold for all positions of P_1 and P_2.

To apply the midpoint formula, it may suffice to remember that

the x-coordinate of the midpoint = the *average* of the x-coordinates,

and that

the y-coordinate of the midpoint = the *average* of the y-coordinates.

EXAMPLE 5 **Finding a midpoint**

Find the midpoint M of the line segment from $P_1(-2, 3)$ to $P_2(4, -2)$, and verify that $d(P_1, M) = d(P_2, M)$.

SOLUTION By the midpoint formula, the coordinates of M are

$$\left(\frac{-2 + 4}{2}, \frac{3 + (-2)}{2}\right), \quad \text{or} \quad \left(1, \frac{1}{2}\right).$$

Figure 8

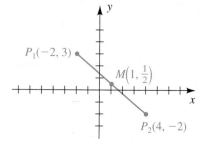

The three points P_1, P_2, and M are plotted in Figure 8. By the distance formula,

$$d(P_1, M) = \sqrt{(1 + 2)^2 + \left(\frac{1}{2} - 3\right)^2} = \sqrt{9 + \frac{25}{4}}$$

$$d(P_2, M) = \sqrt{(1 - 4)^2 + \left(\frac{1}{2} + 2\right)^2} = \sqrt{9 + \frac{25}{4}}.$$

Hence, $d(P_1, M) = d(P_2, M)$.

3.1 Exercises

1 Plot the points $A(5, -2)$, $B(-5, -2)$, $C(5, 2)$, $D(-5, 2)$, $E(3, 0)$, and $F(0, 3)$ on a coordinate plane.

2 Plot the points $A(-3, 1)$, $B(3, 1)$, $C(-2, -3)$, $D(0, 3)$, and $E(2, -3)$ on a coordinate plane. Draw the line segments AB, BC, CD, DE, and EA.

3 Plot the points $A(0, 0)$, $B(1, 1)$, $C(3, 3)$, $D(-1, -1)$, and $E(-2, -2)$. Describe the set of all points of the form (a, a), where a is a real number.

4 Plot the points $A(0, 0)$, $B(1, -1)$, $C(3, -3)$, $D(-1, 1)$, and $E(-3, 3)$. Describe the set of all points of the form $(a, -a)$, where a is a real number.

Exer. 5–6: Find the coordinates of the points A–F.

5

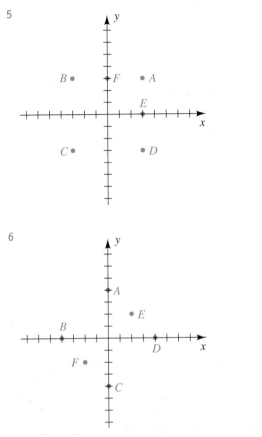

6

Exer. 15–16: Show that the triangle with vertices A, B, and C is a right triangle, and find its area.

15

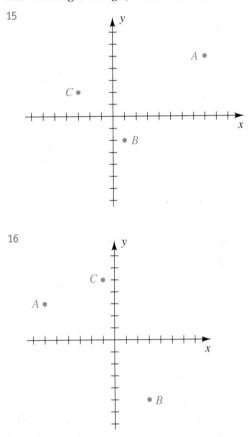

16

Exer. 7–8: Describe the set of all points P(x, y) in a coordinate plane that satisfy the given condition.

7 (a) $x = -2$ (b) $y = 3$ (c) $x \geq 0$

  (d) $xy > 0$ (e) $y < 0$ (f) $x = 0$

8 (a) $y = -2$ (b) $x = -4$ (c) $x/y < 0$

  (d) $xy = 0$ (e) $y > 1$ (f) $y = 0$

Exer. 9–14: (a) Find the distance d(A, B) between A and B. (b) Find the midpoint of the segment AB.

9   $A(4, -3),$ $B(6, 2)$ 10 $A(-2, -5),$ $B(4, 6)$

11   $A(-5, 0),$ $B(-2, -2)$ 12 $A(6, 2),$ $B(6, -2)$

13   $A(7, -3),$ $B(3, -3)$ 14 $A(-4, 7),$ $B(0, -8)$

17   Show that $A(-4, 2)$, $B(1, 4)$, $C(3, -1)$, and $D(-2, -3)$ are vertices of a square.

18   Show that $A(-4, -1)$, $B(0, -2)$, $C(6, 1)$, and $D(2, 2)$ are vertices of a parallelogram.

19   Given $A(-3, 8)$, find the coordinates of the point B such that $C(5, -10)$ is the midpoint of segment AB.

20   Given $A(5, -8)$ and $B(-6, 2)$, find the point on segment AB that is three-fourths of the way from A to B.

Exer. 21–22: Prove that C is on the perpendicular bisector of segment AB.

21   $A(-4, -3),$ $B(6, 1),$ $C(5, -11)$

22   $A(-3, 2),$ $B(5, -4),$ $C(7, 7)$

Exer. 23–24: Find a formula that expresses the fact that an arbitrary point $P(x, y)$ is on the perpendicular bisector l of segment AB.

23 $A(-4, -3)$, $B(6, 1)$ 24 $A(-3, 2)$, $B(5, -4)$

25 Find a formula that expresses the fact that $P(x, y)$ is a distance 5 from the origin. Describe the set of all such points.

26 Find a formula that states that $P(x, y)$ is a distance $r > 0$ from a fixed point $C(h, k)$. Describe the set of all such points.

27 Find all points on the y-axis that are a distance 6 from $P(5, 3)$.

28 Find all points on the x-axis that are a distance 5 from $P(-2, 4)$.

29 Find the point with coordinates of the form $(2a, a)$ that is in the third quadrant and is a distance 5 from $P(1, 3)$.

30 Find all points with coordinates of the form (a, a) that are a distance 3 from $P(-2, 1)$.

31 For what values of a is the distance between $P(a, 3)$ and $Q(5, 2a)$ greater than $\sqrt{26}$?

32 Given $A(-2, 0)$ and $B(2, 0)$, find a formula not containing radicals that expresses the fact that the sum of the distances from $P(x, y)$ to A and to B, respectively, is 5.

33 Prove that the midpoint of the hypotenuse of any right triangle is equidistant from the vertices. (*Hint:* Label the vertices of the triangle $O(0, 0)$, $A(a, 0)$, and $B(0, b)$.)

34 Prove that the diagonals of any parallelogram bisect each other. (*Hint:* Label three of the vertices of the parallelogram $O(0, 0)$, $A(a, b)$, and $C(0, c)$.)

3.2
Graphs of Equations

Graphs are often used to illustrate changes in quantities. A graph in the business section of a newspaper may show the fluctuation of the Dow-Jones average during a given month; a meteorologist might use a graph to indicate how the air temperature varied throughout a day; a cardiologist employs graphs (electrocardiograms) to analyze heart irregularities; an engineer or physicist may turn to a graph to illustrate the manner in which the pressure of a confined gas increases as the gas is heated. Such visual aids usually reveal the behavior of quantities more readily than a long table of numerical values.

Two quantities are sometimes related by means of an equation or formula that involves two variables. In this section we discuss how to represent such an equation geometrically, by a graph in a coordinate plane. The graph may then be used to discover properties of the quantities that are not evident from the equation alone. The following chart introduces the basic concept of the graph of an equation in two variables x and y. Of course, other letters can also be used for the variables.

Terminology	Definition	Illustration
Solution of an equation in x and y	An ordered pair (a, b) that yields a true statement if $x = a$ and $y = b$	$(2, 3)$ is a solution of $y^2 = 5x - 1$, since substituting $x = 2$ and $y = 3$ gives us LS: $3^2 = 9$ RS: $5(2) - 1 = 10 - 1 = 9$.

For each solution (a, b) of an equation in x and y there is a point $P(a, b)$ in a coordinate plane. The set of all such points is called the **graph** of the equation. To *sketch the graph of an equation,* we illustrate the significant features of the graph in a coordinate plane. In simple cases, a graph can be sketched by plotting few, if any, points. For a complicated equation, plotting points may give very little information about the graph. In such cases, methods of calculus or computer graphics are often employed. Let us begin with a simple example.

EXAMPLE 1   Sketching a simple graph by plotting points

Sketch the graph of the equation $y = 2x - 1$.

SOLUTION   We wish to find the points (x, y) in a coordinate plane that correspond to the solutions of the equation. It is convenient to list coordinates of several such points in a table, where for each x we obtain the value for y from $y = 2x - 1$:

x	-3	-2	-1	0	1	2	3
y	-7	-5	-3	-1	1	3	5

Figure 1

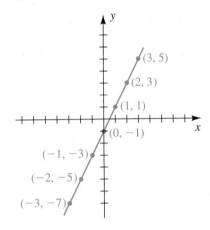

The points with these coordinates appear to lie on a line, and we can sketch the graph in Figure 1. Ordinarily, the few points we have plotted would not be enough to illustrate the graph of an equation; however, in this elementary case we can be reasonably sure that the graph is a line. In the next section we will establish this fact.

It is impossible to sketch the entire graph in Example 1, because we can assign values to x that are numerically as large as desired. Nevertheless, we call the drawing in Figure 1 *the graph of the equation* or *a sketch of the graph.* In general, the sketch of a graph should illustrate its essential features so that the remaining (unsketched) parts are self-evident. For instance, in Figure 1, the **end behavior**—the pattern of the graph as x assumes large positive and negative values (that is, the shape of the right and left ends)—is apparent to the reader.

If a graph terminates at some point (as would be the case for a half-line or line segment), we place a dot at the appropriate *endpoint* of the graph. As a final general remark, *if ticks on the coordinate axes are not labeled (as in Figure 1), then each tick represents one unit.* We shall label ticks only when different units are used on the axes. For *arbitrary* graphs, where units of measurement are irrelevant, we omit ticks completely (see, for example, Figures 5 and 6).

EXAMPLE 2   Sketching the graph of an equation

Sketch the graph of the equation $y = x^2 - 3$.

Figure 2

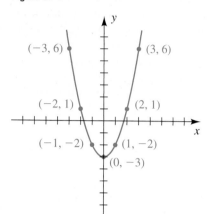

SOLUTION   Substituting values for x and finding the corresponding values of y using $y = x^2 - 3$, we obtain a table of coordinates for several points on the graph:

x	-3	-2	-1	0	1	2	3
y	6	1	-2	-3	-2	1	6

Larger values of $|x|$ produce larger values of y. For example, the points $(4, 13)$, $(5, 22)$, and $(6, 33)$ are on the graph, as are $(-4, 13)$, $(-5, 22)$, and $(-6, 33)$. Plotting the points given by the table and drawing a smooth curve through these points (in the order of increasing values of x) gives us the sketch in Figure 2.

The graph in Figure 2 is a **parabola,** and the y-axis is the **axis of the parabola.** The lowest point $(0, -3)$ is the **vertex** of the parabola, and we say that the parabola *opens upward.* If we invert the graph, then the parabola *opens downward* and the vertex is the highest point on the graph. In general, the graph of *any* equation of the form $y = ax^2 + c$ with $a \neq 0$ is a parabola with vertex $(0, c)$, opening upward if $a > 0$ or downward if $a < 0$. If $c = 0$, the equation reduces to $y = ax^2$ and the vertex is at the origin $(0, 0)$. Parabolas may also open to the right or to the left (see Example 4) or in other directions.

We shall use the following terminology to describe where the graph of an equation in x and y intersects the x-axis or the y-axis.

Intercepts of the Graph of an Equation in x and y

Terminology	Definition	Graphical interpretation	How to find
x-intercepts	The x-coordinates of points where the graph intersects the x-axis		Let $y = 0$ and solve for x. Here, a and c are x-intercepts.
y-intercepts	The y-coordinates of points where the graph intersects the y-axis		Let $x = 0$ and solve for y. Here, b is the y-intercept.

An x-intercept is sometimes referred to as a *zero* of the graph of an equation or as a *root* of an equation.

EXAMPLE 3 Finding x-intercepts and y-intercepts

Find the x- and y-intercepts of the graph of $y = x^2 - 3$.

SOLUTION   The graph is sketched in Figure 2 (Example 2). We find the intercepts as stated in the preceding chart.

(1) x-intercepts:

$$y = x^2 - 3 \qquad \text{given}$$

$$0 = x^2 - 3 \qquad \text{let } y = 0$$

$$x^2 = 3 \qquad \text{equivalent equation}$$

$$x = \pm\sqrt{3} \approx \pm 1.73 \qquad \text{take the square root}$$

Thus, the x-intercepts are $-\sqrt{3}$ and $\sqrt{3}$. The points at which the graph crosses the x-axis are $\left(-\sqrt{3}, 0\right)$ and $\left(\sqrt{3}, 0\right)$.

(2) y-intercepts:

$$y = x^2 - 3 \qquad \text{given}$$

$$y = 0 - 3 = -3 \qquad \text{let } x = 0$$

Thus, the y-intercept is -3, and the point at which the graph crosses the y-axis is $(0, -3)$.

If the coordinate plane in Figure 2 is folded along the y-axis, the graph that lies in the left half of the plane coincides with that in the right half, and we say that *the graph is symmetric with respect to the y-axis*. A graph is symmetric with respect to the y-axis provided that the point $(-x, y)$ is on the graph whenever (x, y) is on the graph. The graph of $y = x^2 - 3$ in Example 2 has this property, since substitution of $-x$ for x yields the same equation:

$$y = (-x)^2 - 3 = x^2 - 3$$

This substitution is an application of symmetry test 1 in the following chart. Two other types of symmetry and the appropriate tests are also listed. The graphs of $x = y^2$ and $4y = x^3$ in the illustration column are discussed in Examples 4 and 5, respectively.

Symmetries of Graphs of Equations in x and y

Terminology	Graphical interpretation	Test for symmetry	Illustration
The graph is symmetric with respect to the y-axis.	$(-x, y)$ (x, y)	(1) Substitution of $-x$ for x leads to the same equation.	$y = x^2 - 3$
The graph is symmetric with respect to the x-axis.	(x, y) $(x, -y)$	(2) Substitution of $-y$ for y leads to the same equation.	$x = y^2$
The graph is symmetric with respect to the origin.	(x, y) $(-x, -y)$	(3) Simultaneous substitution of $-x$ for x and $-y$ for y leads to the same equation.	$4y = x^3$

If a graph is symmetric with respect to an axis, it is sufficient to determine the graph in half of the coordinate plane, since we can sketch the remainder of the graph by taking a *mirror image,* or *reflection,* through the appropriate axis.

EXAMPLE 4 A graph that is symmetric with respect to the x-axis

Sketch the graph of the equation $y^2 = x$.

SOLUTION Since substitution of $-y$ for y does not change the equation, the graph is symmetric with respect to the x-axis (see symmetry test 2). Hence, if the point (x, y) is on the graph, then the point $(x, -y)$ is on the graph. Thus, it

Figure 3

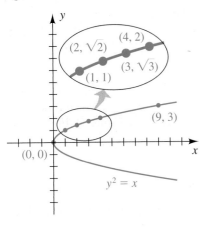

$y^2 = x$

is sufficient to find points with nonnegative y-coordinates and then reflect through the x-axis. The equation $y^2 = x$ is equivalent to $y = \pm\sqrt{x}$. The y-coordinates of points *above* the x-axis (y is *positive*) are given by $y = \sqrt{x}$, whereas the y-coordinates of points *below* the x-axis (y is *negative*) are given by $y = -\sqrt{x}$. Coordinates of some points on the graph are listed below. The graph is sketched in Figure 3.

x	0	1	2	3	4	9
y	0	1	$\sqrt{2} \approx 1.4$	$\sqrt{3} \approx 1.7$	2	3

The graph is a parabola that opens to the right, with its vertex at the origin. In this case, the x-axis is the axis of the parabola.

EXAMPLE 5 A graph that is symmetric with respect to the origin

Sketch the graph of the equation $4y = x^3$.

SOLUTION   If we simultaneously substitute $-x$ for x and $-y$ for y, then

$$4(-y) = (-x)^3 \qquad \text{or, equivalently,} \qquad -4y = -x^3.$$

Figure 4

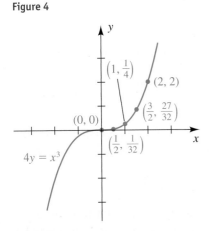

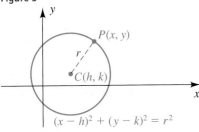

$4y = x^3$

Multiplying both sides by -1, we see that the last equation has the same solutions as the equation $4y = x^3$. Hence, from symmetry test 3, the graph is symmetric with respect to the origin—and if the point (x, y) is on the graph, then the point $(-x, -y)$ is on the graph. The following table lists coordinates of some points on the graph.

x	0	$\frac{1}{2}$	1	$\frac{3}{2}$	2	$\frac{5}{2}$
y	0	$\frac{1}{32}$	$\frac{1}{4}$	$\frac{27}{32}$	2	$\frac{125}{32}$

Because of the symmetry, we can see that the points $\left(-1, -\frac{1}{4}\right)$, $(-2, -2)$, and so on, are also on the graph. The graph is sketched in Figure 4.

Figure 5

$(x - h)^2 + (y - k)^2 = r^2$

If $C(h, k)$ is a point in a coordinate plane, then a circle with center C and radius $r > 0$ consists of all points in the plane that are r units from C. As shown in Figure 5, a point $P(x, y)$ is on the circle provided $d(C, P) = r$ or, by the distance formula,

$$\sqrt{(x - h)^2 + (y - k)^2} = r.$$

The above equation is equivalent to the following equation, which we will refer to as the **standard equation of a circle.**

Standard Equation of a Circle with Center (h, k) and Radius r	$(x - h)^2 + (y - k)^2 = r^2$

Figure 6

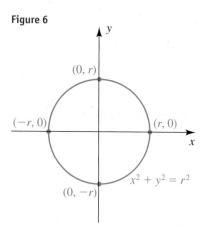

If $h = 0$ and $k = 0$, this equation reduces to $x^2 + y^2 = r^2$, which is an equation of a circle of radius r with center at the origin (see Figure 6). If $r = 1$, we call the graph a **unit circle.**

EXAMPLE 6 Finding an equation of a circle

Find an equation of the circle that has center $C(-2, 3)$ and contains the point $D(4, 5)$.

SOLUTION The circle is shown in Figure 7. Since D is on the circle, the radius r is $d(C, D)$. By the distance formula,

$$r = \sqrt{(4 + 2)^2 + (5 - 3)^2} = \sqrt{36 + 4} = \sqrt{40}.$$

Using the standard equation of a circle with $h = -2$, $k = 3$, and $r = \sqrt{40}$, we obtain

$$(x + 2)^2 + (y - 3)^2 = 40.$$

By squaring terms and simplifying the last equation, we may write it as

$$x^2 + y^2 + 4x - 6y - 27 = 0.$$

Figure 7

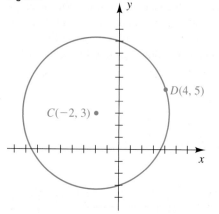

As in the solution to Example 6, squaring terms of an equation of the form $(x - h)^2 + (y - k)^2 = r^2$ and simplifying leads to an equation of the form

$$x^2 + y^2 + ax + by + c = 0,$$

where a, b, and c are real numbers. Conversely, if we begin with this equation, it is always possible, by *completing squares,* to obtain an equation of the form

$$(x - h)^2 + (y - k)^2 = d.$$

This method will be illustrated in Example 7. If $d > 0$, the graph is a circle with center (h, k) and radius $r = \sqrt{d}$. If $d = 0$, the graph consists of only the point (h, k). Finally, if $d < 0$, the equation has no real solutions, and hence there is no graph.

EXAMPLE 7   Finding the center and radius of a circle

Find the center and radius of the circle with equation

$$3x^2 + 3y^2 - 12x + 18y = 9.$$

SOLUTION   Since it is easier to complete the square if the coefficients of x^2 and y^2 are 1, we begin by dividing the given equation by 3, obtaining

$$x^2 + y^2 - 4x + 6y = 3.$$

Next, we rewrite the equation as follows, where the underscored spaces represent numbers to be determined:

$$(x^2 - 4x + \underline{\ \ }) + (y^2 + 6y + \underline{\ \ }) = 3 + \underline{\ \ } + \underline{\ \ }$$

We then complete the squares for the expressions within parentheses, taking care to add the appropriate numbers to *both* sides of the equation. To complete the square for an expression of the form $x^2 + ax$, we add the square of half the coefficient of x (that is, $(a/2)^2$) to both sides of the equation. Similarly, for $y^2 + by$, we add $(b/2)^2$ to both sides. In this example, $a = -4$, $b = 6$, $(a/2)^2 = (-2)^2 = 4$, and $(b/2)^2 = 3^2 = 9$. These additions lead to

$$(x^2 - 4x + \underline{4}) + (y^2 + 6y + \underline{9}) = 3 + \underline{4} + \underline{9} \quad \text{completing the squares}$$

$$(x - 2)^2 + (y + 3)^2 = 16. \quad \text{equivalent equation}$$

Comparing the last equation with the standard equation of a circle, we see that $h = 2$ and $k = -3$ and conclude that the circle has center $(2, -3)$ and radius $\sqrt{16} = 4$. A sketch of this circle is shown in Figure 8. ▰

In some applications it is necessary to work with only one-half of a circle—that is, a **semicircle.** The next example indicates how to find equations of semicircles for circles with centers at the origin.

EXAMPLE 8   Finding equations of semicircles

Find equations for the upper half, lower half, right half, and left half of the circle $x^2 + y^2 = 81$.

SOLUTION   The graph of $x^2 + y^2 = 81$ is a circle of radius 9 with center at the origin (see Figure 9). To find equations for the upper and lower halves, we solve for y in terms of x:

$$x^2 + y^2 = 81 \qquad \text{given}$$

$$y^2 = 81 - x^2 \qquad \text{subtract } x^2$$

$$y = \pm\sqrt{81 - x^2} \qquad \text{take the square root}$$

Since $\sqrt{81 - x^2} \geq 0$, it follows that the upper half of the circle has the equation $y = \sqrt{81 - x^2}$ (y is positive) and the lower half is given by $y = -\sqrt{81 - x^2}$ (y is negative), as illustrated in Figure 10(a) and (b).

(continued)

Figure 8

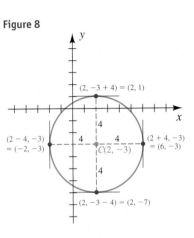

*Recall that a **tangent line** to a circle is a line that contains exactly one point of the circle. Every circle has four points of tangency associated with horizontal and vertical lines. It is helpful to plot these points when sketching the graph of a circle.*

Figure 9

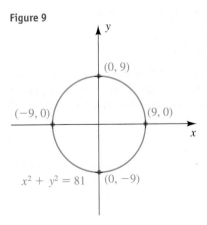

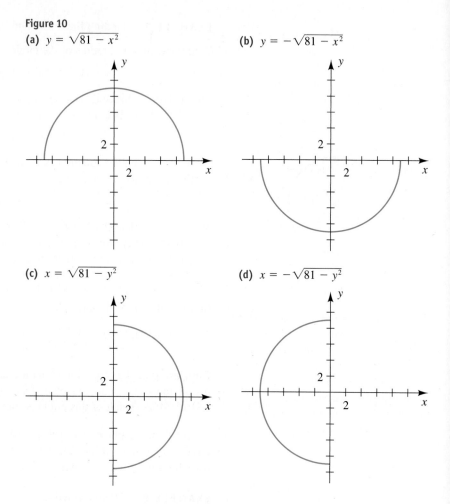

Figure 10

(a) $y = \sqrt{81 - x^2}$

(b) $y = -\sqrt{81 - x^2}$

(c) $x = \sqrt{81 - y^2}$

(d) $x = -\sqrt{81 - y^2}$

Similarly, to find equations for the right and left halves, we solve $x^2 + y^2 = 81$ for x in terms of y, obtaining

$$x = \pm\sqrt{81 - y^2}.$$

Since $\sqrt{81 - y^2} \geq 0$, it follows that the right half of the circle has the equation $x = \sqrt{81 - y^2}$ (x is positive) and the left half is given by the equation $x = -\sqrt{81 - y^2}$ (x is negative), as illustrated in Figure 10(c) and (d).

3.2 *Exercises*

Exer. 1–20: Sketch the graph of the equation, and label the x- and y-intercepts.

1 $y = 2x - 3$

2 $y = 3x + 2$

3 $y = -x + 1$

4 $y = -2x - 3$

5 $y = -4x^2$

6 $y = \frac{1}{3}x^2$

7 $y = 2x^2 - 1$

8 $y = -x^2 + 2$

9 $x = \frac{1}{4}y^2$

10 $x = -2y^2$

11 $x = -y^2 + 3$

12 $x = 2y^2 - 4$

13 $y = -\frac{1}{2}x^3$

14 $y = \frac{1}{2}x^3$

15 $y = x^3 - 8$

16 $y = -x^3 + 1$

17 $y = \sqrt{x}$

18 $y = \sqrt{-x}$

19 $y = \sqrt{x} - 4$

20 $y = \sqrt{x - 4}$

Exer. 21–22: Use tests for symmetry to determine which graphs in the indicated exercises are symmetric with respect to (a) the y-axis, (b) the x-axis, and (c) the origin.

21 The odd-numbered exercises in 1–20

22 The even-numbered exercises in 1–20

Exer. 23–34: Sketch the graph of the circle or semicircle.

23 $x^2 + y^2 = 11$

24 $x^2 + y^2 = 7$

25 $(x + 3)^2 + (y - 2)^2 = 9$

26 $(x - 4)^2 + (y + 2)^2 = 4$

27 $(x + 3)^2 + y^2 = 16$

28 $x^2 + (y - 2)^2 = 25$

29 $4x^2 + 4y^2 = 25$

30 $9x^2 + 9y^2 = 1$

31 $y = -\sqrt{16 - x^2}$

32 $y = \sqrt{4 - x^2}$

33 $x = \sqrt{9 - y^2}$

34 $x = -\sqrt{25 - y^2}$

Exer. 35–46: Find an equation of the circle that satisfies the stated conditions.

35 Center $C(2, -3)$, radius 5

36 Center $C(-4, 1)$, radius 3

37 Center $C\left(\frac{1}{4}, 0\right)$, radius $\sqrt{5}$

38 Center $C\left(\frac{3}{4}, -\frac{2}{3}\right)$, radius $3\sqrt{2}$

39 Center $C(-4, 6)$, passing through $P(1, 2)$

40 Center at the origin, passing through $P(4, -7)$

41 Center $C(-3, 6)$, tangent to the y-axis

42 Center $C(4, -1)$, tangent to the x-axis

43 Tangent to both axes, center in the second quadrant, radius 4

44 Tangent to both axes, center in the fourth quadrant, radius 3

45 Endpoints of a diameter $A(4, -3)$ and $B(-2, 7)$

46 Endpoints of a diameter $A(-5, 2)$ and $B(3, 6)$

Exer. 47–56: Find the center and radius of the circle with the given equation.

47 $x^2 + y^2 - 4x + 6y - 36 = 0$

48 $x^2 + y^2 + 8x - 10y + 37 = 0$

49 $x^2 + y^2 + 4y - 117 = 0$

50 $x^2 + y^2 - 10x + 18 = 0$

51 $2x^2 + 2y^2 - 12x + 4y - 15 = 0$

52 $9x^2 + 9y^2 + 12x - 6y + 4 = 0$

53 $x^2 + y^2 + 4x - 2y + 5 = 0$

54 $x^2 + y^2 - 6x + 4y + 13 = 0$

55 $x^2 + y^2 - 2x - 8y + 19 = 0$

56 $x^2 + y^2 + 4x + 6y + 16 = 0$

Exer. 57–60: Find equations for the upper half, lower half, right half, and left half of the circle.

57 $x^2 + y^2 = 36$

58 $(x + 3)^2 + y^2 = 64$

59 $(x - 2)^2 + (y + 1)^2 = 49$

60 $(x - 3)^2 + (y - 5)^2 = 4$

Exer. 61–64: Find an equation for the circle or semicircle.

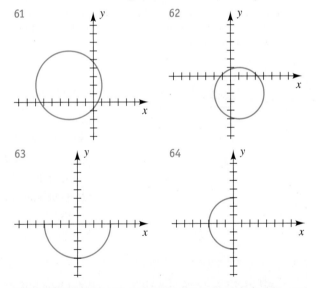

61

62

63

64

Exer. 65–66: Determine whether the point P is inside, outside, or on the circle with center C and radius r.

65 (a) $P(2, 3)$, $C(4, 6)$, $r = 4$

    (b) $P(4, 2)$, $C(1, -2)$, $r = 5$

    (c) $P(-3, 5)$, $C(2, 1)$, $r = 6$

66 (a) $P(3, 8)$, $C(-2, -4)$, $r = 13$

(b) $P(-2, 5)$, $C(3, 7)$, $r = 6$

(c) $P(1, -2)$, $C(6, -7)$, $r = 7$

Exer. 67–68: For the given circle, find (a) the x-intercepts and (b) the y-intercepts.

67 $x^2 + y^2 - 4x - 6y + 4 = 0$

68 $x^2 + y^2 - 10x + 4y + 13 = 0$

69 Find an equation of the circle that is concentric (has the same center) with $x^2 + y^2 + 4x - 6y + 4 = 0$ and passes through $P(2, 6)$.

70 **Radio broadcasting ranges** The signal from a radio station has a circular range of 50 miles. A second radio station, located 100 miles east and 80 miles north of the first station, has a range of 80 miles. Are there locations where signals can be received from both radio stations? Explain your answer.

71 A circle C_1 of radius 5 has its center at the origin. Inside this circle there is a first-quadrant circle C_2 of radius 2 that is tangent to C_1. The y-coordinate of the center of C_2 is 2. Find the x-coordinate of the center of C_2.

72 A circle C_1 of radius 5 has its center at the origin. Outside this circle is a first-quadrant circle C_2 of radius 2 that is tangent to C_1. The y-coordinate of the center of C_2 is 3. Find the x-coordinate of the center of C_2.

Exer. 73–76: Express, in interval form, the x-values such that $y_1 < y_2$. Assume all points of intersection are shown on the interval $(-\infty, \infty)$.

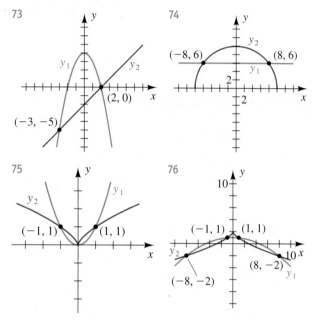

3.3

Lines

One of the basic concepts in geometry is that of a *line*. In this section we will restrict our discussion to lines that lie in a coordinate plane. This will allow us to use algebraic methods to study their properties. Two of our principal objectives may be stated as follows:

(1) Given a line l in a coordinate plane, find an equation whose graph corresponds to l.

(2) Given an equation of a line l in a coordinate plane, sketch the graph of the equation.

The following concept is fundamental to the study of lines.

Definition of Slope of a Line	Let l be a line that is not parallel to the y-axis, and let $P_1(x_1, y_1)$ and $P_2(x_2, y_2)$ be distinct points on l. The **slope m** of l is

$$m = \frac{y_2 - y_1}{x_2 - x_1}.$$

If l is parallel to the y-axis, then the slope of l is not defined.

The Greek letter Δ (delta) is used in mathematics to denote "change in." Thus, we can think of the slope m as

$$m = \frac{\Delta y}{\Delta x} = \frac{\text{change in } y}{\text{change in } x}.$$

Figure 1

(a) Positive slope (line rises)

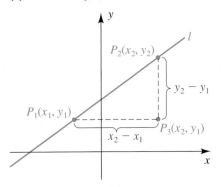

(b) Negative slope (line falls)

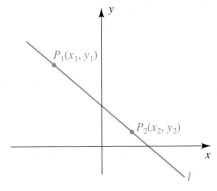

Typical points P_1 and P_2 on a line l are shown in Figure 1. The numerator $y_2 - y_1$ in the formula for m is the vertical change in direction from P_1 to P_2 and may be positive, negative, or zero. The denominator $x_2 - x_1$ is the horizontal change from P_1 to P_2, and it may be positive or negative, but never zero, because l is not parallel to the y-axis if a slope exists. In Figure 1(a) the slope is positive, and we say that the line *rises*. In Figure 1(b) the slope is negative, and the line *falls*.

In finding the slope of a line it is immaterial which point we label as P_1 and which as P_2, since

$$\frac{y_2 - y_1}{x_2 - x_1} = \frac{y_2 - y_1}{x_2 - x_1} \cdot \frac{(-1)}{(-1)} = \frac{y_1 - y_2}{x_1 - x_2}.$$

If the points are labeled so that $x_1 < x_2$, as in Figure 1, then $x_2 - x_1 > 0$, and hence the slope is positive, negative, or zero, depending on whether $y_2 > y_1$, $y_2 < y_1$, or $y_2 = y_1$, respectively.

The definition of slope is independent of the two points that are chosen on l. If other points $P_1'(x_1', y_1')$ and $P_2'(x_2', y_2')$ are used, then, as in Figure 2, the triangle with vertices P_1', P_2', and $P_3'(x_2', y_1')$ is similar to the triangle with vertices P_1, P_2, and $P_3(x_2, y_1)$. Since the ratios of corresponding sides of similar triangles are equal,

$$\frac{y_2 - y_1}{x_2 - x_1} = \frac{y_2' - y_1'}{x_2' - x_1'}.$$

Figure 2

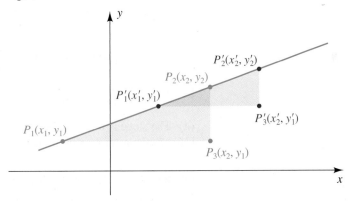

EXAMPLE 1 Finding slopes

Sketch the line through each pair of points, and find its slope m:

(a) $A(-1, 4)$ and $B(3, 2)$ **(b)** $A(2, 5)$ and $B(-2, -1)$

(c) $A(4, 3)$ and $B(-2, 3)$ **(d)** $A(4, -1)$ and $B(4, 4)$

SOLUTION   The lines are sketched in Figure 3. We use the definition of slope to find the slope of each line.

(continued)

Figure 3

(a) $m = -\frac{1}{2}$

(b) $m = \frac{3}{2}$

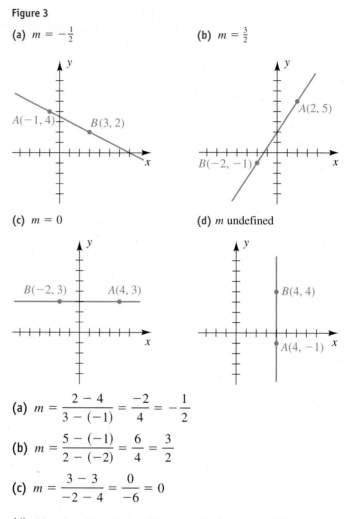

(c) $m = 0$

(d) m undefined

(a) $m = \dfrac{2 - 4}{3 - (-1)} = \dfrac{-2}{4} = -\dfrac{1}{2}$

(b) $m = \dfrac{5 - (-1)}{2 - (-2)} = \dfrac{6}{4} = \dfrac{3}{2}$

(c) $m = \dfrac{3 - 3}{-2 - 4} = \dfrac{0}{-6} = 0$

(d) The slope is undefined because the line is parallel to the y-axis. Note that if the formula for m is used, the denominator is zero.

EXAMPLE 2 Sketching a line with a given slope

Sketch a line through $P(2, 1)$ that has

(a) slope $\frac{5}{3}$ (b) slope $-\frac{5}{3}$

SOLUTION   If the slope of a line is a/b and b is positive, then for every change of b units in the horizontal direction, the line rises or falls $|a|$ units, depending on whether a is positive or negative, respectively.

(a) If $P(2, 1)$ is on the line and $m = \frac{5}{3}$, we can obtain another point on the line by starting at P and moving 3 units to the right and 5 units *upward*. This gives us the point $Q(5, 6)$, and the line is determined as in Figure 4(a).

(b) If $P(2, 1)$ is on the line and $m = -\frac{5}{3}$, we move 3 units to the right and 5 units *downward*, obtaining the line through $Q(5, -4)$, as in Figure 4(b).

Figure 4
(a) $m = \frac{5}{3}$ **(b)** $m = -\frac{5}{3}$

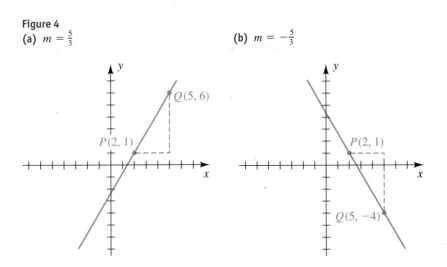

The diagram in Figure 5 indicates the slopes of several lines through the origin. The line that lies on the *x*-axis has slope $m = 0$. If this line is rotated about *O* in the *counterclockwise* direction (as indicated by the blue arrow), the slope is positive and increases, reaching the value 1 when the line bisects the first quadrant and continuing to increase as the line gets closer to the *y*-axis. If we rotate the line of slope $m = 0$ in the *clockwise* direction (as indicated by the red arrow), the slope is negative, reaching the value -1 when the line bisects the second quadrant and becoming large and negative as the line gets closer to the *y*-axis.

Figure 5

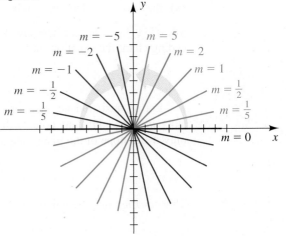

Lines that are horizontal or vertical have simple equations, as indicated in the following chart.

Terminology	Definition	Graph	Equation	Slope
Horizontal line	A line parallel to the x-axis	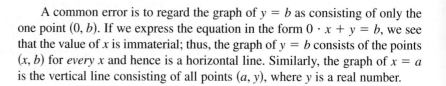	$y = b$ y-intercept is b	Slope is 0
Vertical line	A line parallel to the y-axis	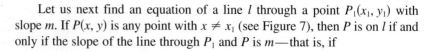	$x = a$ x-intercept is a	Slope is undefined

Figure 6

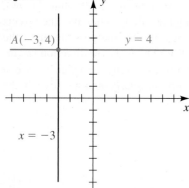

A common error is to regard the graph of $y = b$ as consisting of only the one point $(0, b)$. If we express the equation in the form $0 \cdot x + y = b$, we see that the value of x is immaterial; thus, the graph of $y = b$ consists of the points (x, b) for *every* x and hence is a horizontal line. Similarly, the graph of $x = a$ is the vertical line consisting of all points (a, y), where y is a real number.

EXAMPLE 3 Finding equations of horizontal and vertical lines

Find an equation of the line through $A(-3, 4)$ that is parallel to

(a) the x-axis   **(b)** the y-axis

SOLUTION   The two lines are sketched in Figure 6. As indicated in the preceding chart, the equations are $y = 4$ for part (a) and $x = -3$ for part (b).

Figure 7

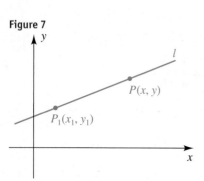

Let us next find an equation of a line l through a point $P_1(x_1, y_1)$ with slope m. If $P(x, y)$ is any point with $x \neq x_1$ (see Figure 7), then P is on l if and only if the slope of the line through P_1 and P is m—that is, if

$$\frac{y - y_1}{x - x_1} = m.$$

This equation may be written in the form

$$y - y_1 = m(x - x_1).$$

Note that (x_1, y_1) is a solution of the last equation, and hence the points on l are precisely the points that correspond to the solutions. This equation for l is referred to as the **point-slope form.**

Point-Slope Form for the Equation of a Line	An equation for the line through the point (x_1, y_1) with slope m is $$y - y_1 = m(x - x_1).$$

The point-slope form is only one possibility for an equation of a line. There are many equivalent equations. We sometimes simplify the equation obtained using the point-slope form to either

$$ax + by = c \quad \text{or} \quad ax + by + d = 0,$$

where a, b, and c are integers with no common factor, $a > 0$, and $d = -c$.

EXAMPLE 4 Finding an equation of a line through two points

Find an equation of the line through $A(1, 7)$ and $B(-3, 2)$.

Figure 8

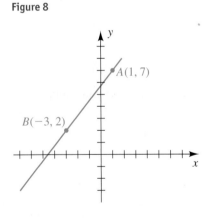

SOLUTION   The line is sketched in Figure 8. The formula for the slope m gives us

$$m = \frac{7 - 2}{1 - (-3)} = \frac{5}{4}.$$

We may use the coordinates of either A or B for (x_1, y_1) in the point-slope form. Using $A(1, 7)$ gives us the following:

$$\begin{aligned}
y - 7 &= \tfrac{5}{4}(x - 1) &&\text{point-slope form} \\
4(y - 7) &= 5(x - 1) &&\text{multiply by 4} \\
4y - 28 &= 5x - 5 &&\text{multiply factors} \\
-5x + 4y &= 23 &&\text{subtract } 5x \text{ and add 28} \\
5x - 4y &= -23 &&\text{multiply by } -1
\end{aligned}$$

The last equation is one of the desired forms for an equation of a line. Another is $5x - 4y + 23 = 0$.

Figure 9

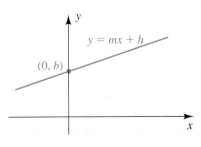

The point-slope form for the equation of a line may be rewritten as $y = mx - mx_1 + y_1$, which is of the form

$$y = mx + b$$

with $b = -mx_1 + y_1$. The real number b is the y-intercept of the graph, as indicated in Figure 9. Since the equation $y = mx + b$ displays the slope m and

y-intercept b of l, it is called the **slope-intercept form** for the equation of a line. Conversely, if we start with $y = mx + b$, we may write

$$y - b = m(x - 0).$$

Comparing this equation with the point-slope form, we see that the graph is a line with slope m and passing through the point $(0, b)$. We have proved the following result.

Slope-Intercept Form for the Equation of a Line	The graph of $y = mx + b$ is a line having slope m and y-intercept b.

EXAMPLE 5   Expressing an equation in slope-intercept form

Express the equation $2x - 5y = 8$ in slope-intercept form.

SOLUTION   Our goal is to solve the given equation for y to obtain the form $y = mx + b$. We may proceed as follows:

$$2x - 5y = 8 \qquad \text{given}$$
$$-5y = -2x + 8 \qquad \text{subtract } 2x$$
$$y = \left(\frac{-2}{-5}\right)x + \left(\frac{8}{-5}\right) \qquad \text{divide by } -5$$
$$y = \tfrac{2}{5}x + \left(-\tfrac{8}{5}\right) \qquad \text{equivalent equation}$$

The last equation is the slope-intercept form $y = mx + b$ with slope $m = \tfrac{2}{5}$ and y-intercept $b = -\tfrac{8}{5}$.

It follows from the point-slope form that every line is a graph of an equation

$$ax + by = c,$$

where a, b, and c are real numbers and a and b are not both zero. We call such an equation a **linear equation** in x and y. Let us show, conversely, that the graph of $ax + by = c$, with a and b not both zero, is always a line. If $b \neq 0$, we may solve for y, obtaining

$$y = \left(-\frac{a}{b}\right)x + \frac{c}{b},$$

which, by the slope-intercept form, is an equation of a line with slope $-a/b$ and y-intercept c/b. If $b = 0$ but $a \neq 0$, we may solve for x, obtaining $x = c/a$, which is the equation of a vertical line with x-intercept c/a. This discussion establishes the following result.

General Form for the Equation of a Line	The graph of a linear equation $ax + by = c$ is a line, and conversely, every line is the graph of a linear equation.

For simplicity, we use the terminology *the line $ax + by = c$* rather than *the line with equation $ax + by = c$.*

EXAMPLE 6   Sketching the graph of a linear equation

Sketch the graph of $2x - 5y = 8$.

Figure 10

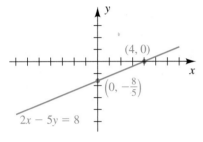

SOLUTION   We know from the preceding discussion that the graph is a line, so it is sufficient to find two points on the graph. Let us find the x- and y-intercepts by substituting $y = 0$ and $x = 0$, respectively, in the given equation, $2x - 5y = 8$.

x-intercept: If $y = 0$, then $2x = 8$, or $x = 4$.

y-intercept: If $x = 0$, then $-5y = 8$, or $y = -\frac{8}{5}$.

Plotting the points $(4, 0)$ and $\left(0, -\frac{8}{5}\right)$ and drawing a line through them gives us the graph in Figure 10.

The following theorem specifies the relationship between **parallel lines** (lines in a plane that do not intersect) and slope.

Theorem on Slopes of Parallel Lines	Two nonvertical lines are parallel if and only if they have the same slope.

Figure 11

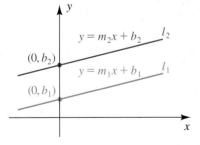

PROOF   Let l_1 and l_2 be distinct lines of slopes m_1 and m_2, respectively. If the y-intercepts are b_1 and b_2 (see Figure 11), then, by the slope-intercept form, the lines have equations

$$y = m_1x + b_1 \quad \text{and} \quad y = m_2x + b_2.$$

The lines intersect at some point (x, y) if and only if the values of y are equal for some x—that is, if

$$m_1x + b_1 = m_2x + b_2,$$

or

$$(m_1 - m_2)x = b_2 - b_1.$$

The last equation can be solved for x if and only if $m_1 - m_2 \neq 0$. We have shown that the lines l_1 and l_2 intersect if and only if $m_1 \neq m_2$. Hence, they do *not* intersect (are parallel) if and only if $m_1 = m_2$.

EXAMPLE 7 Finding an equation of a line parallel to a given line

Find an equation of the line through $P(5, -7)$ that is parallel to the line $6x + 3y = 4$.

SOLUTION We first express the given equation in slope-intercept form:

$$6x + 3y = 4 \qquad \text{given}$$
$$3y = -6x + 4 \qquad \text{subtract } 6x$$
$$y = -2x + \tfrac{4}{3} \qquad \text{divide by 3}$$

The last equation is in slope-intercept form, $y = mx + b$, with slope $m = -2$ and y-intercept $\tfrac{4}{3}$. Since parallel lines have the same slope, the required line also has slope -2. Using the point $P(5, -7)$ gives us the following:

$$y - (-7) = -2(x - 5) \qquad \text{point-slope form}$$
$$y + 7 = -2x + 10 \qquad \text{simplify}$$
$$y = -2x + 3 \qquad \text{subtract 7}$$

The last equation is in slope-intercept form and shows that the parallel line we have found has y-intercept 3. This line and the given line are sketched in Figure 12.

As an alternative solution, we might use the fact that lines of the form $6x + 3y = k$ have the same slope as the given line and hence are parallel to it. Substituting $x = 5$ and $y = -7$ into the equation $6x + 3y = k$ gives us $6(5) + 3(-7) = k$ or, equivalently, $k = 9$. The equation $6x + 3y = 9$ is equivalent to $y = -2x + 3$.

If the slopes of two nonvertical lines are not the same, then the lines are not parallel and intersect at exactly one point.

The next theorem gives us information about **perpendicular lines** (lines that intersect at a right angle).

Figure 12

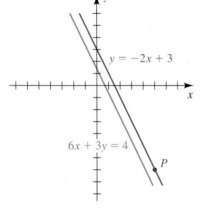

Theorem on Slopes of Perpendicular Lines	Two lines with slope m_1 and m_2 are perpendicular if and only if $$m_1 m_2 = -1.$$

Figure 13

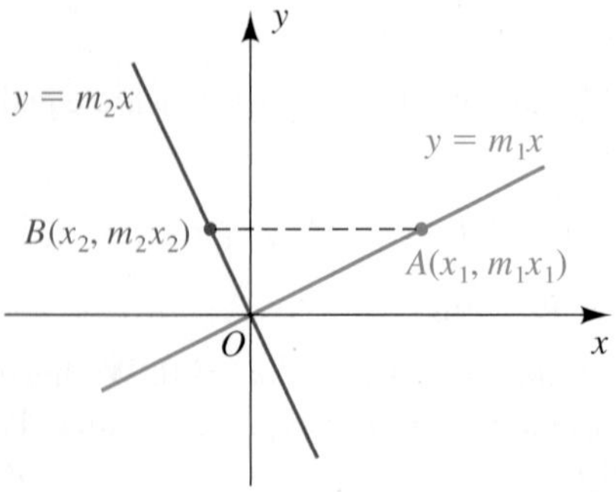

PROOF For simplicity, let us consider the special case of two lines that intersect at the origin O, as illustrated in Figure 13. Equations of these lines are $y = m_1 x$ and $y = m_2 x$. If, as in the figure, we choose points $A(x_1, m_1 x_1)$ and $B(x_2, m_2 x_2)$ different from O on the lines, then the lines are perpendicular if and only if angle AOB is a right angle. Applying the Pythagorean theorem, we know that angle AOB is a right angle if and only if

$$[d(A, B)]^2 = [d(O, B)]^2 + [d(O, A)]^2$$

or, by the distance formula,

$$(x_2 - x_1)^2 + (m_2 x_2 - m_1 x_1)^2 = x_2^2 + (m_2 x_2)^2 + x_1^2 + (m_1 x_1)^2.$$

Figure 14

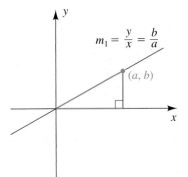

Figure 15

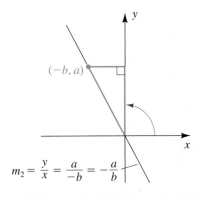

Figure 16

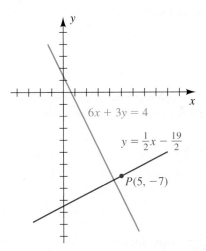

Squaring terms, simplifying, and factoring gives us

$$-2m_1m_2x_1x_2 - 2x_1x_2 = 0$$

$$-2x_1x_2(m_1m_2 + 1) = 0.$$

Since both x_1 and x_2 are not zero, we may divide both sides by $-2x_1x_2$, obtaining $m_1m_2 + 1 = 0$. Thus, the lines are perpendicular if and only if $m_1m_2 = -1$.

The same type of proof may be given if the lines intersect at *any* point (a, b).

A convenient way to remember the conditions on slopes of perpendicular lines is to note that m_1 and m_2 must be *negative reciprocals* of each other— that is, $m_1 = -1/m_2$ and $m_2 = -1/m_1$.

We can visualize the result of the last theorem as follows. Draw a triangle as in Figure 14; the line containing its hypotenuse has slope $m_1 = b/a$. Now rotate the triangle 90° as in Figure 15. The line now has slope $m_2 = a/(-b)$, the negative reciprocal of m_1.

EXAMPLE 8 Finding an equation of a line perpendicular to a given line

Find the slope-intercept form for the line through $P(5, -7)$ that is perpendicular to the line $6x + 3y = 4$.

SOLUTION We considered the line $6x + 3y = 4$ in Example 7 and found that its slope is -2. Hence, the slope of the required line is the negative reciprocal $-[1/(-2)]$, or $\frac{1}{2}$. Using $P(5, -7)$ gives us the following:

$$y - (-7) = \tfrac{1}{2}(x - 5) \quad \text{point-slope form}$$

$$y + 7 = \tfrac{1}{2}x - \tfrac{5}{2} \quad \text{simplify}$$

$$y = \tfrac{1}{2}x - \tfrac{19}{2} \quad \text{put in slope-intercept form}$$

The last equation is in slope-intercept form and shows that the perpendicular line has y-intercept $-\frac{19}{2}$. This line and the given line are sketched in Figure 16.

EXAMPLE 9 Finding an equation of a perpendicular bisector

Given $A(-3, 1)$ and $B(5, 4)$, find the general form of the perpendicular bisector l of the line segment AB.

Figure 17

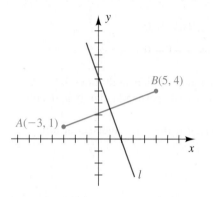

SOLUTION The line segment AB and its perpendicular bisector l are shown in Figure 17. We calculate the following, where M is the midpoint of AB:

Coordinates of M: $\left(\dfrac{-3+5}{2}, \dfrac{1+4}{2}\right) = \left(1, \dfrac{5}{2}\right)$ midpoint formula

Slope of AB: $\dfrac{4-1}{5-(-3)} = \dfrac{3}{8}$ slope formula

Slope of l: $-\dfrac{1}{\frac{3}{8}} = -\dfrac{8}{3}$ negative reciprocal of $\frac{3}{8}$

Using the point $M\left(1, \frac{5}{2}\right)$ and slope $-\frac{8}{3}$ gives us the following equivalent equations for l:

$$y - \tfrac{5}{2} = -\tfrac{8}{3}(x - 1) \quad \text{point-slope form}$$
$$6y - 15 = -16(x - 1) \quad \text{multiply by the lcd, 6}$$
$$6y - 15 = -16x + 16 \quad \text{multiply}$$
$$16x + 6y = 31 \quad \text{put in general form}$$

Two variables x and y are **linearly related** if $y = ax + b$, where a and b are real numbers and $a \neq 0$. Linear relationships between variables occur frequently in applied problems. The following example gives one illustration.

EXAMPLE 10   Relating air temperature to altitude

The relationship between the air temperature T (in °F) and the altitude h (in feet above sea level) is approximately linear for $0 \le h \le 20{,}000$. If the temperature at sea level is 60°, an increase of 5000 feet in altitude lowers the air temperature about 18°.

(a) Express T in terms of h, and sketch the graph on an hT-coordinate system.

(b) Approximate the air temperature at an altitude of 15,000 feet.

(c) Approximate the altitude at which the temperature is 0°.

SOLUTION

(a) If T is linearly related to h, then

$$T = ah + b$$

for some constants a and b (a represents the slope and b the T-intercept). Since $T = 60°$ when $h = 0$ ft (sea level), the T-intercept is 60, and the temperature T for $0 \le h \le 20{,}000$ is given by

$$T = ah + 60.$$

From the given data, we note that when the altitude $h = 5000$ ft, the temperature $T = 60° - 18° = 42°$. Hence, we may find a as follows:

$$42 = a(5000) + 60 \quad \text{let } T = 42 \text{ and } h = 5000$$
$$a = \frac{42 - 60}{5000} = -\frac{9}{2500} \quad \text{solve for } a$$

Figure 18

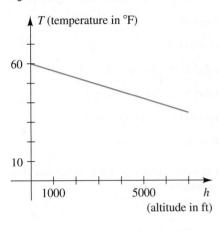

Substituting for a in $T = ah + 60$ gives us the following formula for T:

$$T = -\frac{9}{2500}h + 60$$

The graph is sketched in Figure 18, with different scales on the axes.

(b) Using the last formula for T obtained in part (a), we find that the temperature (in °F) when $h = 15{,}000$ is

$$T = -\frac{9}{2500}(15{,}000) + 60 = -54 + 60 = 6.$$

(c) To find the altitude h that corresponds to $T = 0°$, we proceed as follows:

$$T = -\frac{9}{2500}h + 60 \qquad \text{from part (a)}$$

$$0 = -\frac{9}{2500}h + 60 \qquad \text{let } T = 0$$

$$\frac{9}{2500}h = 60 \qquad \text{add } \frac{9}{2500}h$$

$$h = 60 \cdot \frac{2500}{9} \qquad \text{multiply by } \frac{2500}{9}$$

$$h = \frac{50{,}000}{3} \approx 16{,}667 \text{ ft} \quad \text{simplify and approximate}$$

A **mathematical model** is a mathematical description of a problem. For our purposes, these descriptions will be graphs and equations. In the last example, the equation $T = -\frac{9}{2500}h + 60$ *models* the relationship between air temperature and altitude.

3.3 *Exercises*

Exer. 1–6: Sketch the line through A and B, and find its slope m.

1 $A(-3, 2)$, $B(5, -4)$ 2 $A(4, -1)$, $B(-6, -3)$

3 $A(2, 5)$, $B(-7, 5)$ 4 $A(5, -1)$, $B(5, 6)$

5 $A(-3, 2)$, $B(-3, 5)$ 6 $A(4, -2)$, $B(-3, -2)$

Exer. 7–10: Use slopes to show that the points are vertices of the specified polygon.

7 $A(-3, 1)$, $B(5, 3)$, $C(3, 0)$, $D(-5, -2)$; parallelogram

8 $A(2, 3)$, $B(5, -1)$, $C(0, -6)$, $D(-6, 2)$; trapezoid

9 $A(6, 15)$, $B(11, 12)$, $C(-1, -8)$, $D(-6, -5)$; rectangle

10 $A(1, 4)$, $B(6, -4)$, $C(-15, -6)$; right triangle

11 If three consecutive vertices of a parallelogram are $A(-1, -3)$, $B(4, 2)$, and $C(-7, 5)$, find the fourth vertex.

12 Let $A(x_1, y_1)$, $B(x_2, y_2)$, $C(x_3, y_3)$, and $D(x_4, y_4)$ denote the vertices of an arbitrary quadrilateral. Show that the line segments joining midpoints of adjacent sides form a parallelogram.

Exer. 13–14: Sketch the graph of $y = mx$ for the given values of m.

13 $m = 3, -2, \frac{2}{3}, -\frac{1}{4}$ 14 $m = 5, -3, \frac{1}{2}, -\frac{1}{3}$

Exer. 15–16: Sketch the graph of the line through P for each value of m.

15 $P(3, 1)$; $m = \frac{1}{2}, -1, -\frac{1}{5}$

16 $P(-2, 4)$; $m = 1, -2, -\frac{1}{2}$

Exer. 17–18: Write equations of the lines.

17

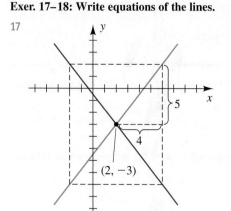

18

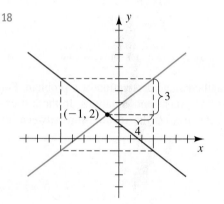

Exer. 19–20: Sketch the graphs of the lines on the same coordinate plane.

19 $y = x + 3,$ $\quad y = x + 1,$ $\quad y = -x + 1$

20 $y = -2x - 1,$ $\quad y = -2x + 3,$ $\quad y = \frac{1}{2}x + 3$

Exer. 21–32: Find a general form of an equation of the line through the point A that satisfies the given condition.

21 $A(5, -2)$

    (a) parallel to the y-axis

    (b) perpendicular to the y-axis

22 $A(-4, 2)$

    (a) parallel to the x-axis

    (b) perpendicular to the x-axis

23 $A(5, -3);$ slope -4 24 $A(-1, 4);$ slope $\frac{2}{3}$

25 $A(4, 0);$ slope -3 26 $A(0, -2);$ slope 5

27 $A(4, -5);$ through $B(-3, 6)$

28 $A(-1, 6);$ x-intercept 5

29 $A(2, -4);$ parallel to the line $5x - 2y = 4$

30 $A(-3, 5);$ parallel to the line $x + 3y = 1$

31 $A(7, -3);$ perpendicular to the line $2x - 5y = 8$

32 $A(4, 5);$ perpendicular to the line $3x + 2y = 7$

Exer. 33–36: Find the slope-intercept form of the line that satisfies the given conditions.

33 x-intercept 4, y-intercept -3

34 x-intercept -5, y-intercept -1

35 Through $A(5, 2)$ and $B(-1, 4)$

36 Through $A(-2, 1)$ and $B(3, 7)$

Exer. 37–38: Find a general form of an equation for the perpendicular bisector of the segment AB.

37 $A(3, -1), B(-2, 6)$ 38 $A(4, 2), B(-2, 10)$

Exer. 39–40: Find an equation for the line that bisects the given quadrants.

39 II and IV   40 I and III

Exer. 41–44: Use the slope-intercept form to find the slope and y-intercept of the given line, and sketch its graph.

41 $2x = 15 - 3y$ 42 $7x = -4y - 8$

43 $4x - 3y = 9$ 44 $x - 5y = -15$

Exer. 45–46: Find an equation of the line shown in the figure.

45 (a)   (b)

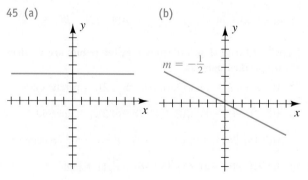

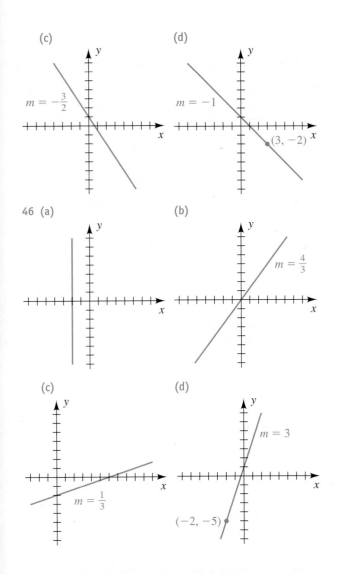

(c) $m = -\dfrac{3}{2}$

(d) $m = -1$ (3, −2)

46 (a)

(b) $m = \dfrac{4}{3}$

(c) $m = \dfrac{1}{3}$

(d) $m = 3$ (−2, −5)

Exer. 47–48: If a line *l* has nonzero *x*- and *y*-intercepts *a* and *b*, respectively, then its *intercept form* is

$$\frac{x}{a} + \frac{y}{b} = 1.$$

Find the intercept form for the given line.

47 $4x - 2y = 6$

48 $x - 3y = -2$

49 Find an equation of the circle that has center $C(3, -2)$ and is tangent to the line $y = 5$.

50 Find an equation of the line that is tangent to the circle $x^2 + y^2 = 25$ at the point $P(3, 4)$.

51 **Fetal growth** The growth of a fetus more than 12 weeks old can be approximated by the formula $L = 1.53t - 6.7$, where L is the length (in centimeters) and t is the age (in weeks). Prenatal length can be determined by ultrasound. Approximate the age of a fetus whose length is 28 centimeters.

52 **Estimating salinity** Salinity of the ocean refers to the amount of dissolved material found in a sample of seawater. Salinity S can be estimated from the amount C of chlorine in seawater using $S = 0.03 + 1.805C$, where S and C are measured by weight in parts per thousand. Approximate C if S is 0.35.

53 **Weight of a humpback whale** The expected weight W (in tons) of a humpback whale can be approximated from its length L (in feet) by using $W = 1.70L - 42.8$ for $30 \le L \le 50$.

(a) Estimate the weight of a 40-foot humpback whale.

(b) If the error in estimating the length could be as large as 2 feet, what is the corresponding error for the weight estimate?

54 **Growth of a blue whale** Newborn blue whales are approximately 24 feet long and weigh 3 tons. Young whales are nursed for 7 months, and by the time of weaning they often are 53 feet long and weigh 23 tons. Let L and W denote the length (in feet) and the weight (in tons), respectively, of a whale that is t months of age.

(a) If L and t are linearly related, express L in terms of t.

(b) What is the daily increase in the length of a young whale? (Use 1 month = 30 days.)

(c) If W and t are linearly related, express W in terms of t.

(d) What is the daily increase in the weight of a young whale?

55 **Baseball stats** Suppose a major league baseball player has hit 5 home runs in the first 14 games, and he keeps up this pace throughout the 162-game season.

(a) Express the number y of home runs in terms of the number x of games played.

(b) How many home runs will the player hit for the season?

56 **Cheese production** A cheese manufacturer produces 18,000 pounds of cheese from January 1 through March 24. Suppose that this rate of production continues for the remainder of the year.

(a) Express the number y of pounds of cheese produced in terms of the number x of the day in a 365-day year.

(b) Predict, to the nearest pound, the number of pounds produced for the year.

57 **Childhood weight** A baby weighs 10 pounds at birth, and three years later the child's weight is 30 pounds. Assume that childhood weight W (in pounds) is linearly related to age t (in years).

(a) Express W in terms of t.

(b) What is W on the child's sixth birthday?

(c) At what age will the child weigh 70 pounds?

(d) Sketch, on a tW-plane, a graph that shows the relationship between W and t for $0 \le t \le 12$.

58 **Loan repayment** A college student receives an interest-free loan of $8250 from a relative. The student will repay $125 per month until the loan is paid off.

(a) Express the amount P (in dollars) remaining to be paid in terms of time t (in months).

(b) After how many months will the student owe $5000?

(c) Sketch, on a tP-plane, a graph that shows the relationship between P and t for the duration of the loan.

59 **Vaporizing water** The amount of heat H (in joules) required to convert one gram of water into vapor is linearly related to the temperature T (in °C) of the atmosphere. At 10°C this conversion requires 2480 joules, and each increase in temperature of 15°C lowers the amount of heat needed by 40 joules. Express H in terms of T.

60 **Aerobic power** In exercise physiology, aerobic power P is defined in terms of maximum oxygen intake. For altitudes up to 1800 meters, aerobic power is optimal—that is, 100%. Beyond 1800 meters, P decreases linearly from the maximum of 100% to a value near 40% at 5000 meters.

(a) Express aerobic power P in terms of altitude h (in meters) for $1800 \le h \le 5000$.

(b) Estimate aerobic power in Mexico City (altitude: 2400 meters), the site of the 1968 Summer Olympic Games.

61 **Urban heat island** The urban heat island phenomenon has been observed in Tokyo. The average temperature was 13.5°C in 1915, and since then has risen 0.032°C per year.

(a) Assuming that temperature T (in °C) is linearly related to time t (in years) and that $t = 0$ corresponds to 1915, express T in terms of t.

(b) Predict the average temperature in the year 2010.

62 **Rising ground temperature** In 1870 the average ground temperature in Paris was 11.8°C. Since then it has risen at a nearly constant rate, reaching 13.5°C in 1969.

(a) Express the temperature T (in °C) in terms of time t (in years), where $t = 0$ corresponds to the year 1870 and $0 \le t \le 99$.

(b) During what year was the average ground temperature 12.5°C?

63 **Business expenses** The owner of an ice cream franchise must pay the parent company $1000 per month plus 5% of the monthly revenue R. Operating cost of the franchise includes a fixed cost of $2600 per month for items such as utilities and labor. The cost of ice cream and supplies is 50% of the revenue.

(a) Express the owner's monthly expense E in terms of R.

(b) Express the monthly profit P in terms of R.

(c) Determine the monthly revenue needed to break even.

64 **Drug dosage** Pharmacological products must specify recommended dosages for adults and children. Two formulas for modification of adult dosage levels for young children are

$$\text{Cowling's rule:} \quad y = \tfrac{1}{24}(t + 1)a$$

and $\quad$ Friend's rule: $\quad y = \tfrac{2}{25}ta,$

where a denotes adult dose (in milligrams) and t denotes the age of the child (in years).

(a) If $a = 100$, graph the two linear equations on the same coordinate plane for $0 \le t \le 12$.

(b) For what age do the two formulas specify the same dosage?

65 **Video game** In the video game shown in the figure, an airplane flies from left to right along the path given by $y = 1 + (1/x)$ and shoots bullets in the tangent direction at creatures placed along the x-axis at $x = 1, 2, 3, 4$.

Exercise 65

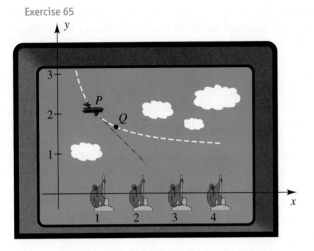

From calculus, the slope of the tangent line to the path at $P(1, 2)$ is $m = -1$ and at $Q\left(\frac{3}{2}, \frac{5}{3}\right)$ is $m = -\frac{4}{9}$. Determine whether a creature will be hit if bullets are shot when the airplane is at

(a) P (b) Q

66 Temperature scales The relationship between the temperature reading F on the Fahrenheit scale and the temperature reading C on the Celsius scale is given by $C = \frac{5}{9}(F - 32)$.

(a) Find the temperature at which the reading is the same on both scales.

(b) When is the Fahrenheit reading twice the Celsius reading?

67 Vertical wind shear Vertical wind shear occurs when wind speed varies at different heights above the ground. Wind shear is of great importance to pilots during takeoffs and landings. If the wind speed is v_1 at height h_1 and v_2 at height h_2, then the average wind shear s is given by the slope formula

$$s = \frac{v_2 - v_1}{h_2 - h_1}.$$

If the wind speed at ground level is 22 mi/hr and s has been determined to be 0.07, find the wind speed 185 feet above the ground.

68 Vertical wind shear In the study of vertical wind shear, the formula

$$\frac{v_1}{v_2} = \left(\frac{h_1}{h_2}\right)^P$$

is sometimes used, where P is a variable that depends on the terrain and structures near ground level. In Montreal, the average daytime value for P with north winds over 29 mi/hr was determined to be 0.13. If a 32 mi/hr north wind is measured 20 feet above the ground, approximate the average wind shear (see Exercise 67) between 20 feet and 200 feet.

Exer. 69–70: The given points were found using empirical methods. Determine whether they lie on the same line $y = ax + b$, and if so, find the values of a and b.

69 $A(-1.3, -1.3598)$, $B(-0.55, -1.11905)$,

   $C(1.2, -0.5573)$, $D(3.25, 0.10075)$

70 $A(-0.22, 1.6968)$, $B(-0.12, 1.6528)$,

   $C(1.3, 1.028)$ $D(1.45, 0.862)$

3.4

Definition of Function

The notion of **correspondence** occurs frequently in everyday life. Some examples are given in the following illustration.

ILLUSTRATION   **Correspondence**

■   To each book in a library there corresponds the number of pages in the book.

■   To each human being there corresponds a birth date.

■   If the temperature of the air is recorded throughout the day, then to each instant of time there corresponds a temperature.

Each correspondence in the previous illustration involves two sets, D and E. In the first illustration, D denotes the set of books in a library and E the set of positive integers. To each book x in D there corresponds a positive integer y in E—namely, the number of pages in the book.

We sometimes depict correspondences by diagrams of the type shown in Figure 1, where the sets D and E are represented by points within regions in a plane. The curved arrow indicates that the element y of E corresponds to the element x of D. The two sets may have elements in common. As a matter of fact, we often have $D = E$. It is important to note that *to each x in D there corresponds exactly one y in E.* However, the same element of E may correspond to different elements of D. For example, two books may have the same number of pages, two people may have the same birthday, and the temperature may be the same at different times.

In most of our work, D and E will be sets of numbers. To illustrate, let both D and E denote the set $\mathbb{R}$ of real numbers, and to each real number x let us assign its square x^2. This gives us a correspondence from $\mathbb{R}$ to $\mathbb{R}$.

Each of our illustrations of a correspondence is a *function,* which we define as follows.

Figure 1

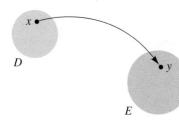

Definition of Function	A **function** f from a set D to a set E is a correspondence that assigns to each element x of D exactly one element y of E.

---

*For many cases, we can simply remember that the **domain** is the set of x-values and the **range** is the set of y-values.*

The element x of D is the **argument** of f. The set D is the **domain** of the function. The element y of E is the **value** of f at x (or the **image** of x under f) and is denoted by $f(x)$, read "f of x." The **range** of f is the subset R of E consisting of all possible values $f(x)$ for x in D. Note that there may be elements in the set E that are not in the range R of f.

Consider the diagram in Figure 2. The curved arrows indicate that the elements $f(w)$, $f(z)$, $f(x)$, and $f(a)$ of E correspond to the elements w, z, x, and a of D. *To each element in D there is assigned exactly one function value in E;* however, different elements of D, such as w and z in Figure 2, may have the same value in E.

The symbols

$$D \xrightarrow{f} E, \qquad f : D \rightarrow E, \qquad \text{and}$$

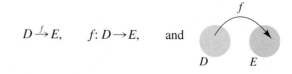

signify that f is a function from D to E, and we say that f **maps** D *into* E. Initially, the notations f and $f(x)$ may be confusing. Remember that f is used to represent the function. It is neither in D nor in E. However, $f(x)$ is an element

Figure 2

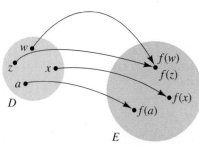

of the range R—the element that the function f assigns to the element x, which is in the domain D.

Two functions f and g from D to E are **equal,** and we write

$$f = g \quad \text{provided} \quad f(x) = g(x) \quad \text{for every } x \text{ in } D.$$

For example, if $g(x) = \frac{1}{2}(2x^2 - 6) + 3$ and $f(x) = x^2$ for every x in $\mathbb{R}$, then $g = f$.

EXAMPLE 1   Finding function values

Let f be the function with domain $\mathbb{R}$ such that $f(x) = x^2$ for every x in $\mathbb{R}$.

(a) Find $f(-6)$, $f(\sqrt{3})$, $f(a + b)$, and $f(a) + f(b)$, where a and b are real numbers.

(b) What is the range of f?

SOLUTION

(a) We find values of f by substituting for x in the equation $f(x) = x^2$:

$$f(-6) = (-6)^2 = 36$$
$$f(\sqrt{3}) = (\sqrt{3})^2 = 3$$

Note that, in general,

$$f(a + b) \neq f(a) + f(b).$$

$$f(a + b) = (a + b)^2 = a^2 + 2ab + b^2$$
$$f(a) + f(b) = a^2 + b^2$$

(b) By definition, the range of f consists of all numbers of the form $f(x) = x^2$ for x in $\mathbb{R}$. Since the square of every real number is nonnegative, the range is contained in the set of all nonnegative real numbers. Moreover, every nonnegative real number c is a value of f, since $f(\sqrt{c}) = (\sqrt{c})^2 = c$. Hence, the range of f is the set of all nonnegative real numbers.

If a function is defined as in Example 1, the symbols used for the function and variable are immaterial; that is, expressions such as $f(x) = x^2$, $f(s) = s^2$, $g(t) = t^2$, and $k(r) = r^2$ all define the same function. This is true because if a is any number in the domain, then the same value a^2 is obtained regardless of which expression is employed.

In the remainder of our work, the phrase f is a function will mean that the domain and range are sets of real numbers. If a function is defined by means of an expression, as in Example 1, and the domain D is not stated, then we will consider D to be the totality of real numbers x such that $f(x)$ is real. This is sometimes called the **implied domain** of f. To illustrate, if $f(x) = \sqrt{x - 2}$, then the implied domain is the set of real numbers x such that $\sqrt{x - 2}$ is real—that is, $x - 2 \geq 0$, or $x \geq 2$. Thus, the domain is the infinite interval $[2, \infty)$. If x is in the domain, we say that f is defined at x or that $f(x)$ exists. If a set S is contained in the domain, f *is defined on S*. The terminology *f is undefined at x* means that x is not in the domain of f.

EXAMPLE 2 Finding function values

Let $g(x) = \dfrac{\sqrt{4 + x}}{1 - x}$.

(a) Find the domain of g.

(b) Find $g(5)$, $g(-2)$, $g(-a)$, and $-g(a)$.

SOLUTION

(a) The expression $\sqrt{4 + x}/(1 - x)$ is a real number if and only if the radicand $4 + x$ is nonnegative and the denominator $1 - x$ is not equal to 0. Thus, $g(x)$ exists if and only if

$$4 + x \geq 0 \quad \text{and} \quad 1 - x \neq 0$$

or, equivalently,

$$x \geq -4 \quad \text{and} \quad x \neq 1.$$

We may express the domain in terms of intervals as $[-4, 1) \cup (1, \infty)$.

(b) To find values of g, we substitute for x:

$$g(5) = \frac{\sqrt{4 + 5}}{1 - 5} = \frac{\sqrt{9}}{-4} = -\frac{3}{4}$$

$$g(-2) = \frac{\sqrt{4 + (-2)}}{1 - (-2)} = \frac{\sqrt{2}}{3}$$

$$g(-a) = \frac{\sqrt{4 + (-a)}}{1 - (-a)} = \frac{\sqrt{4 - a}}{1 + a}$$

$$-g(a) = -\frac{\sqrt{4 + a}}{1 - a} = \frac{\sqrt{4 + a}}{a - 1}$$

Functions are commonplace in everyday life and show up in a variety of forms. For instance, the menu in a restaurant (Figure 3) can be considered to be a function f from a set of items to a set of prices. Note that f is given in a table format. Here $f(\text{Hamburger}) = 1.69$, $f(\text{French fries}) = 0.99$, and $f(\text{Soda}) = 0.79$.

An example of a function given by a rule can be found in the federal tax tables (Figure 4). Specifically, in 2006, for a single person with a taxable income of $120,000, the tax due was given by the rule

$15,107.50 plus 28% of the amount over $74,200.

Figure 3

MENU	
Hamburger	$1.69
French fries	$0.99
Soda	$0.79

Figure 4

2006 Federal Tax Rate Schedules

Schedule X –Use if your Filing status is **single**

If taxable income is over–	But not over–	The tax is:	of the amount over–
$0	$7,550	- - - - - - - - 10%	$0
7,550	30,650	$755.00 + 15%	7,550
30,650	74,200	$4,220.00 + 25%	30,650
74,200	154,800	15,107.50 + 28%	74,200
154,800	336,550	37,675.50 + 33%	154,800
336,550	- - - - - - -	97,653.00 + 35%	336,550

In this case, the tax would be

$$\$15,107.50 + 0.28(\$120,000 - \$74,200) = \$27,931.50.$$

Graphs are often used to describe the variation of physical quantities. For example, a scientist may use the graph in Figure 5 to indicate the temperature T of a certain solution at various times t during an experiment. The sketch shows that the temperature increased gradually for time $t = 0$ to time $t = 5$, did not change between $t = 5$ and $t = 8$, and then decreased rapidly from $t = 8$ to $t = 9$.

Similarly, if f is a function, we may use a graph to indicate the change in $f(x)$ as x varies through the domain of f. Specifically, we have the following definition.

Figure 5

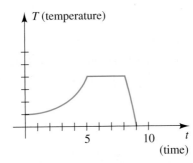

Definition of Graph of a Function	The **graph of a function** f is the graph of the equation $y = f(x)$ for x in the domain of f.

We often attach the label $y = f(x)$ to a sketch of the graph. If $P(a, b)$ is a point on the graph, then the y-coordinate b is the function value $f(a)$, as illustrated in Figure 6 on the next page. The figure displays the domain of f (the set of possible values of x) and the range of f (the corresponding values of y). Although we have pictured the domain and range as closed intervals, they may be infinite intervals or other sets of real numbers.

Since there is exactly one value $f(a)$ for each a in the domain of f, only *one* point on the graph of f has x-coordinate a. In general, we may use the following graphical test to determine whether a graph is the graph of a function.

Vertical Line Test	The graph of a set of points in a coordinate plane is the graph of a function if every vertical line intersects the graph in at most one point.

Figure 6

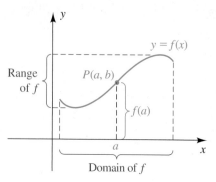

Thus, *every vertical line intersects the graph of a function in at most one point.* Consequently, the graph of a function cannot be a figure such as a circle, in which a vertical line may intersect the graph in more than one point.

The x-intercepts of the graph of a function f are the solutions of the equation $f(x) = 0$. These numbers are called the **zeros** of the function. The y-intercept of the graph is $f(0)$, if it exists.

EXAMPLE 3 Sketching the graph of a function

Let $f(x) = \sqrt{x - 1}$.

(a) Sketch the graph of f.

(b) Find the domain and range of f.

SOLUTION

(a) By definition, the graph of f is the graph of the equation $y = \sqrt{x - 1}$. The following table lists coordinates of several points on the graph.

Figure 7

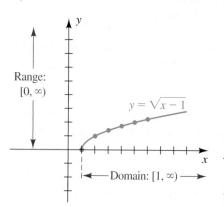

x	1	2	3	4	5	6
$y = f(x)$	0	1	$\sqrt{2} \approx 1.4$	$\sqrt{3} \approx 1.7$	2	$\sqrt{5} \approx 2.2$

Plotting points, we obtain the sketch shown in Figure 7. Note that the x-intercept is 1 and there is no y-intercept.

(b) Referring to Figure 7, note that the domain of f consists of all real numbers x such that $x \geq 1$ or, equivalently, the interval $[1, \infty)$. The range of f is the set of all real numbers y such that $y \geq 0$ or, equivalently, $[0, \infty)$.

The **square root function,** defined by $f(x) = \sqrt{x}$, has a graph similar to the one in Figure 7, but the endpoint is at $(0, 0)$. The y-value of a point on this graph is the number displayed on a calculator when a square root is requested. This graphical relationship may help you remember that $\sqrt{9}$ is 3 and that $\sqrt{9}$ is *not* ± 3. Similarly, $f(x) = x^2$, $f(x) = x^3$, and $f(x) = \sqrt[3]{x}$ are often referred to as the **squaring function,** the **cubing function,** and the **cube root function,** respectively.

In Example 3, as x increases, the function value $f(x)$ also increases, and we say that the graph of f *rises* (see Figure 7). A function of this type is said to be *increasing.* For certain functions, $f(x)$ decreases as x increases. In this case the graph *falls,* and *f* is a *decreasing* function. In general, we shall consider functions that increase or decrease on an interval *I,* as described in the following chart, where x_1 and x_2 denote numbers in *I.*

Increasing, Decreasing, and Constant Functions

Terminology	Definition	Graphical interpretation
f is **increasing** on an interval *I*	$f(x_1) < f(x_2)$ whenever $x_1 < x_2$	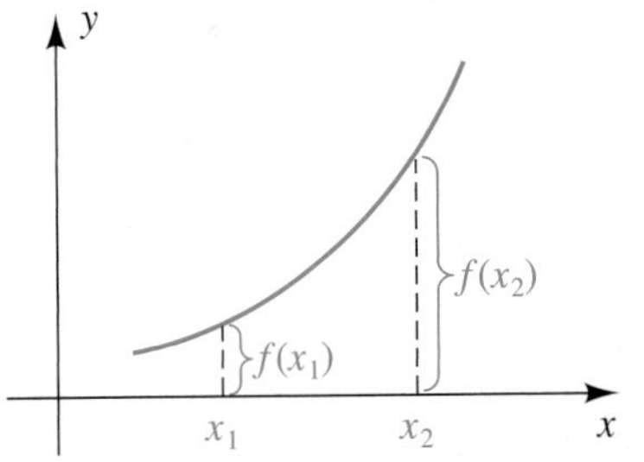
f is **decreasing** on an interval *I*	$f(x_1) > f(x_2)$ whenever $x_1 < x_2$	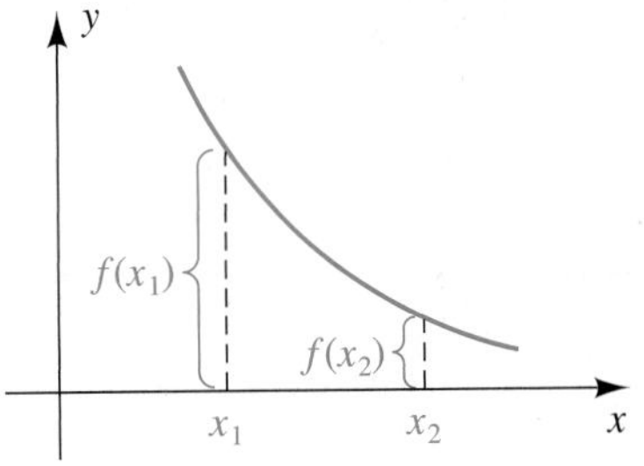
f is **constant** on an interval *I*	$f(x_1) = f(x_2)$ for every x_1 and x_2	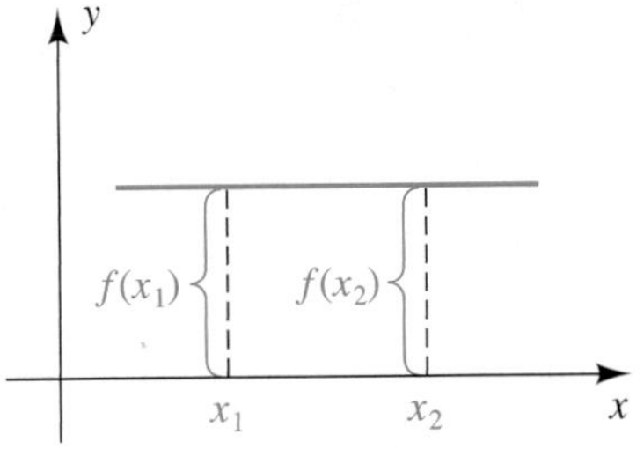

An example of an *increasing function* is the **identity function,** whose equation is $f(x) = x$ and whose graph is the line through the origin with slope 1. An example of a *decreasing function* is $f(x) = -x$, an equation of the line through the origin with slope -1. If $f(x) = c$ for every real number *x,* then *f* is called a *constant function.*

We shall use the phrases *f is increasing* and *f(x) is increasing* interchangeably. We shall do the same with the terms *decreasing* and *constant*.

EXAMPLE 4 Using a graph to find domain, range, and where a function increases or decreases

Let $f(x) = \sqrt{9 - x^2}$.

(a) Sketch the graph of f.

(b) Find the domain and range of f.

(c) Find the intervals on which f is increasing or is decreasing.

SOLUTION

(a) By definition, the graph of f is the graph of the equation $y = \sqrt{9 - x^2}$. We know from our work with circles in Section 3.2 that the graph of $x^2 + y^2 = 9$ is a circle of radius 3 with center at the origin. Solving the equation $x^2 + y^2 = 9$ for y gives us $y = \pm\sqrt{9 - x^2}$. It follows that the graph of f is the *upper half* of the circle, as illustrated in Figure 8.

(b) Referring to Figure 8, we see that the domain of f is the closed interval $[-3, 3]$, and the range of f is the interval $[0, 3]$.

(c) The graph rises as x increases from -3 to 0, so f is increasing on the closed interval $[-3, 0]$. Thus, as shown in the preceding chart, if $x_1 < x_2$ in $[-3, 0]$, then $f(x_1) < f(x_2)$ (note that *possibly* $x_1 = -3$ or $x_2 = 0$).

The graph falls as x increases from 0 to 3, so f is decreasing on the closed interval $[0, 3]$. In this case, the chart indicates that if $x_1 < x_2$ in $[0, 3]$, then $f(x_1) > f(x_2)$ (note that *possibly* $x_1 = 0$ or $x_2 = 3$). ◢

Figure 8

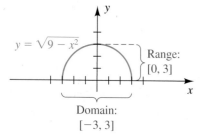

$y = \sqrt{9 - x^2}$

Range: [0, 3]

Domain: [−3, 3]

Of special interest in calculus is a problem of the following type.

Problem: Find the slope of the secant line through the points P and Q shown in Figure 9.

Figure 9

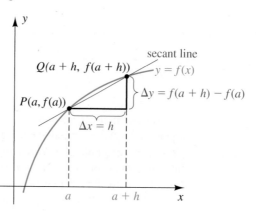

$Q(a + h, f(a + h))$

secant line

$y = f(x)$

$\Delta y = f(a + h) - f(a)$

$P(a, f(a))$

$\Delta x = h$

a $a + h$ x

The slope m_{PQ} is given by

$$m_{PQ} = \frac{\Delta y}{\Delta x} = \frac{f(a + h) - f(a)}{h}.$$

The last expression (with $h \neq 0$) is commonly called a **difference quotient.** Let's take a look at the algebra involved in simplifying a difference quotient. (See Discussion Exercise 5 at the end of the chapter for a related problem.)

EXAMPLE 5   Simplifying a difference quotient

Simplify the difference quotient

$$\frac{f(x + h) - f(x)}{h}$$

using the function $f(x) = x^2 + 6x - 4$.

SOLUTION

$$\frac{f(x + h) - f(x)}{h} = \frac{[(x + h)^2 + 6(x + h) - 4] - [x^2 + 6x - 4]}{h}$$

definition of f

$$= \frac{(x^2 + 2xh + h^2 + 6x + 6h - 4) - (x^2 + 6x - 4)}{h}$$

expand numerator

$$= \frac{(x^2 + 2xh + h^2 + \cancel{6x} + 6h - \cancel{4}) - (\cancel{x^2} + \cancel{6x} - \cancel{4})}{h}$$

subtract terms

$$= \frac{2xh + h^2 + 6h}{h}$$

simplify

$$= \frac{h(2x + h + 6)}{h}$$

factor out h

$$= 2x + h + 6$$

cancel $h \neq 0$

The following type of function is one of the most basic in algebra.

Definition of Linear Function	A function f is a **linear function** if
	$$f(x) = ax + b,$$
	where x is any real number and a and b are constants.

The graph of f in the preceding definition is the graph of $y = ax + b$, which, by the slope-intercept form, is a line with slope a and y-intercept b.

Thus, *the graph of a linear function is a line.* Since $f(x)$ exists for every x, the domain of f is $\mathbb{R}$. As illustrated in the next example, if $a \neq 0$, then the range of f is also $\mathbb{R}$.

EXAMPLE 6 Sketching the graph of a linear function

Let $f(x) = 2x + 3$.

(a) Sketch the graph of f.

(b) Find the domain and range of f.

(c) Determine where f is increasing or is decreasing.

Figure 10

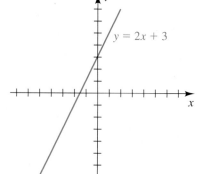

SOLUTION

(a) Since $f(x)$ has the form $ax + b$, with $a = 2$ and $b = 3$, f is a linear function. The graph of $y = 2x + 3$ is the line with slope 2 and y-intercept 3, illustrated in Figure 10.

(b) We see from the graph that x and y may be any real numbers, so both the domain and the range of f are $\mathbb{R}$.

(c) Since the slope a is positive, the graph of f rises as x increases; that is, $f(x_1) < f(x_2)$ whenever $x_1 < x_2$. Thus, f is increasing throughout its domain.

In applications it is sometimes necessary to determine a specific linear function from given data, as in the next example.

EXAMPLE 7 Finding a linear function

If f is a linear function such that $f(-2) = 5$ and $f(6) = 3$, find $f(x)$, where x is any real number.

Figure 11

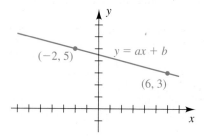

SOLUTION By the definition of linear function, $f(x) = ax + b$, where a and b are constants. Moreover, the given function values tell us that the points $(-2, 5)$ and $(6, 3)$ are on the graph of f—that is, on the line $y = ax + b$ illustrated in Figure 11. The slope a of this line is

$$a = \frac{5 - 3}{-2 - 6} = \frac{2}{-8} = -\frac{1}{4},$$

and hence $f(x)$ has the form

$$f(x) = -\tfrac{1}{4}x + b.$$

To find the value of b, we may use the fact that $f(6) = 3$, as follows:

$$f(6) = -\tfrac{1}{4}(6) + b \qquad \text{let } x = 6 \text{ in } f(x) = -\tfrac{1}{4}x + b$$
$$3 = -\tfrac{3}{2} + b \qquad f(6) = 3$$
$$b = 3 + \tfrac{3}{2} = \tfrac{9}{2} \qquad \text{solve for } b$$

Thus, the linear function satisfying $f(-2) = 5$ and $f(6) = 3$ is

$$f(x) = -\tfrac{1}{4}x + \tfrac{9}{2}.$$

Many formulas that occur in mathematics and the sciences determine functions. For instance, the formula $A = \pi r^2$ for the area A of a circle of radius r assigns to each positive real number r exactly one value of A. This determines a function f such that $f(r) = \pi r^2$, and we may write $A = f(r)$. The letter r, which represents an arbitrary number from the domain of f, is called an **independent variable.** The letter A, which represents a number from the range of f, is a **dependent variable,** since its value depends on the number assigned to r. If two variables r and A are related in this manner, we say that A *is a function of r.* In applications, the independent variable and dependent variable are sometimes referred to as the **input variable** and **output variable,** respectively. As another example, if an automobile travels at a uniform rate of 50 mi/hr, then the distance d (miles) traveled in time t (hours) is given by $d = 50t$, and hence *the distance d is a function of time t.*

EXAMPLE 8 Expressing the volume of a tank as a function of its radius

A steel storage tank for propane gas is to be constructed in the shape of a right circular cylinder of altitude 10 feet with a hemisphere attached to each end. The radius r is yet to be determined. Express the volume V (in ft³) of the tank as a function of r (in feet).

Figure 12

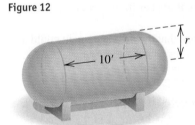

SOLUTION The tank is illustrated in Figure 12. We may find the volume of the cylindrical part of the tank by multiplying the altitude 10 by the area πr^2 of the base of the cylinder. This gives us

$$\text{volume of cylinder} = 10(\pi r^2) = 10\pi r^2.$$

The two hemispherical ends, taken together, form a sphere of radius r. Using the formula for the volume of a sphere, we obtain

$$\text{volume of the two ends} = \tfrac{4}{3}\pi r^3.$$

Thus, the volume V of the tank is

$$V = \tfrac{4}{3}\pi r^3 + 10\pi r^2.$$

This formula expresses V as a function of r. In factored form,

$$V(r) = \tfrac{1}{3}\pi r^2(4r + 30) = \tfrac{2}{3}\pi r^2(2r + 15).$$

EXAMPLE 9 Expressing a distance as a function of time

Two ships leave port at the same time, one sailing west at a rate of 17 mi/hr and the other sailing south at 12 mi/hr. If t is the time (in hours) after their departure, express the distance d between the ships as a function of t.

Figure 13

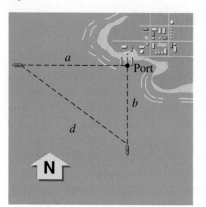

SOLUTION   To help visualize the problem, we begin by drawing a picture and labeling it, as in Figure 13. By the Pythagorean theorem,

$$d^2 = a^2 + b^2, \quad \text{or} \quad d = \sqrt{a^2 + b^2}.$$

Since distance = (rate)(time) and the rates are 17 and 12, respectively,

$$a = 17t \quad \text{and} \quad b = 12t.$$

Substitution in $d = \sqrt{a^2 + b^2}$ gives us

$$d = \sqrt{(17t)^2 + (12t)^2} = \sqrt{289t^2 + 144t^2} = \sqrt{433t^2} \approx (20.8)t.$$

Ordered pairs can be used to obtain an alternative approach to functions. We first observe that a function f from D to E determines the following set W of ordered pairs:

$$W = \{(x, f(x)) : x \text{ is in } D\}$$

Thus, W consists of all ordered pairs such that the first number x is in D and the second number is the function value $f(x)$. In Example 1, where $f(x) = x^2$, W is the set of all ordered pairs of the form (x, x^2). It is important to note that, *for each x, there is exactly one ordered pair (x, y) in W having x in the first position.*

Conversely, if we begin with a set W of ordered pairs such that each x in D appears exactly once in the first position of an ordered pair, then W determines a function. Specifically, for each x in D there is exactly one pair (x, y) in W, and by letting y correspond to x, we obtain a function with domain D. The range consists of all real numbers y that appear in the second position of the ordered pairs.

It follows from the preceding discussion that the next statement could also be used as a definition of function.

Alternative Definition of Function	A **function** with domain D is a set W of ordered pairs such that, for each x in D, there is exactly one ordered pair (x, y) in W having x in the first position.

In terms of the preceding definition, the ordered pairs $\left(x, \sqrt{x - 1}\right)$ determine the function of Example 3 given by $f(x) = \sqrt{x - 1}$. Note, however, that if

$$W = \{(x, y) : x^2 = y^2\},$$

then W is *not* a function, since for a given x there may be more than one pair in W with x in the first position. For example, if $x = 2$, then both $(2, 2)$ and $(2, -2)$ are in W.

As a reference aid, some common graphs and their equations are listed in Appendix I. Many of these graphs are graphs of functions.

3.4   Exercises

1 If $f(x) = -x^2 - x - 4$, find $f(-2)$, $f(0)$, and $f(4)$.

2 If $f(x) = -x^3 - x^2 + 3$, find $f(-3)$, $f(0)$, and $f(2)$.

3 If $f(x) = \sqrt{x - 4} - 3x$, find $f(4)$, $f(8)$, and $f(13)$.

4 If $f(x) = \dfrac{x}{x - 3}$, find $f(-2)$, $f(0)$, and $f(3)$.

Exer. 5–10: If a and h are real numbers, find
(a) $f(a)$ (b) $f(-a)$ (c) $-f(a)$ (d) $f(a + h)$

(e) $f(a) + f(h)$ (f) $\dfrac{f(a + h) - f(a)}{h}$, if $h \neq 0$

5 $f(x) = 5x - 2$

6 $f(x) = 3 - 4x$

7 $f(x) = -x^2 + 4$

8 $f(x) = 3 - x^2$

9 $f(x) = x^2 - x + 3$

10 $f(x) = 2x^2 + 3x - 7$

Exer. 11–14: If a is a positive real number, find
(a) $g\left(\dfrac{1}{a}\right)$ (b) $\dfrac{1}{g(a)}$ (c) $g(\sqrt{a})$ (d) $\sqrt{g(a)}$

11 $g(x) = 4x^2$

12 $g(x) = 2x - 5$

13 $g(x) = \dfrac{2x}{x^2 + 1}$

14 $g(x) = \dfrac{x^2}{x + 1}$

Exer. 15–16: Explain why the graph is or is not the graph of a function.

15

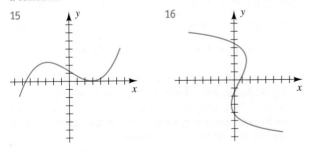

16

Exer. 17–18: Determine the domain D and range R of the function shown in the figure.

17

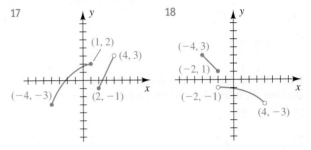

18

Exer. 19–20: For the graph of the function f sketched in the figure, determine
(a) the domain   (b) the range   (c) $f(1)$
(d) all x such that $f(x) = 1$
(e) all x such that $f(x) > 1$

19

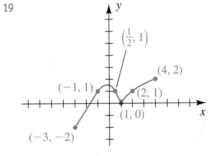

20

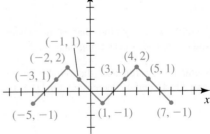

Exer. 21–32: Find the domain of f.

21 $f(x) = \sqrt{2x + 7}$

22 $f(x) = \sqrt{8 - 3x}$

23 $f(x) = \sqrt{9 - x^2}$

24 $f(x) = \sqrt{x^2 - 25}$

25 $f(x) = \dfrac{x + 1}{x^3 - 4x}$

26 $f(x) = \dfrac{4x}{6x^2 + 13x - 5}$

27 $f(x) = \dfrac{\sqrt{2x - 3}}{x^2 - 5x + 4}$

28 $f(x) = \dfrac{\sqrt{4x - 3}}{x^2 - 4}$

29 $f(x) = \dfrac{x - 4}{\sqrt{x - 2}}$

30 $f(x) = \dfrac{1}{(x - 3)\sqrt{x + 3}}$

31 $f(x) = \sqrt{x + 2} + \sqrt{2 - x}$

32 $f(x) = \sqrt{(x - 2)(x - 6)}$

Exer. 33–34: (a) Find the domain D and range R of f. (b) Find the intervals on which f is increasing, is decreasing, or is constant.

33
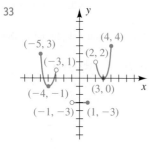

34
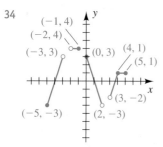

35 Sketch the graph of a function that is increasing on $(-\infty, -3]$ and $[2, \infty)$ and is decreasing on $[-3, 2]$.

36 Sketch the graph of a function that is decreasing on $(-\infty, -2]$ and $[1, 4]$ and is increasing on $[-2, 1]$ and $[4, \infty)$.

Exer. 37–46: (a) Sketch the graph of f. (b) Find the domain D and range R of f. (c) Find the intervals on which f is increasing, is decreasing, or is constant.

37 $f(x) = 3x - 2$

38 $f(x) = -2x + 3$

39 $f(x) = 4 - x^2$

40 $f(x) = x^2 - 1$

41 $f(x) = \sqrt{x + 4}$

42 $f(x) = \sqrt{4 - x}$

43 $f(x) = -2$

44 $f(x) = 3$

45 $f(x) = -\sqrt{36 - x^2}$

46 $f(x) = \sqrt{16 - x^2}$

Exer. 47–48: Simplify the difference quotient $\dfrac{f(2 + h) - f(2)}{h}$ if $h \neq 0$.

47 $f(x) = x^2 - 3x$

48 $f(x) = -2x^2 + 3$

Exer. 49–50: Simplify the difference quotient $\dfrac{f(x + h) - f(x)}{h}$ if $h \neq 0$.

49 $f(x) = x^2 + 5$

50 $f(x) = 1/x^2$

Exer. 51–52: Simplify the difference quotient $\dfrac{f(x) - f(a)}{x - a}$ if $x \neq a$.

51 $f(x) = \sqrt{x - 3}$ (*Hint:* Rationalize the numerator.)

52 $f(x) = x^3 - 2$

Exer. 53–54: If a linear function f satisfies the given conditions, find $f(x)$.

53 $f(-3) = 1$ and $f(3) = 2$

54 $f(-2) = 7$ and $f(4) = -2$

Exer. 55–64: Determine whether the set W of ordered pairs is a function in the sense of the alternative definition of function on page 166.

55 $W = \{(x, y): 2y = x^2 + 5\}$

56 $W = \{(x, y): x = 3y + 2\}$

57 $W = \{(x, y): x^2 + y^2 = 4\}$

58 $W = \{(x, y): y^2 - x^2 = 1\}$

59 $W = \{(x, y): y = 3\}$

60 $W = \{(x, y): x = 3\}$

61 $W = \{(x, y): xy = 0\}$

62 $W = \{(x, y): x + y = 0\}$

63 $W = \{(x, y): |y| = |x|\}$

64 $W = \{(x, y): y < x\}$

65 Constructing a box From a rectangular piece of cardboard having dimensions 20 inches × 30 inches, an open box is to be made by cutting out an identical square of area x^2 from each corner and turning up the sides (see the figure). Express the volume V of the box as a function of x.

Exercise 65

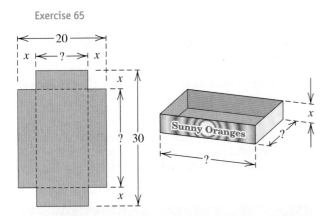

66 **Constructing a storage tank** Refer to Example 8. A steel storage tank for propane gas is to be constructed in the shape of a right circular cylinder of altitude 10 feet with a hemisphere attached to each end. The radius r is yet to be determined. Express the surface area S of the tank as a function of r.

67 **Dimensions of a building** A small office unit is to contain 500 ft^2 of floor space. A simplified model is shown in the figure.

(a) Express the length y of the building as a function of the width x.

(b) If the walls cost $100 per running foot, express the cost C of the walls as a function of the width x. (Disregard the wall space above the doors and the thickness of the walls.)

Exercise 67

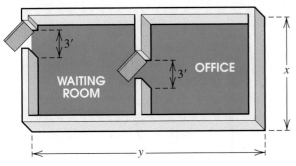

68 **Dimensions of an aquarium** An aquarium of height 1.5 feet is to have a volume of 6 ft^3. Let x denote the length of the base and y the width (see the figure).

(a) Express y as a function of x.

(b) Express the total number S of square feet of glass needed as a function of x.

Exercise 68

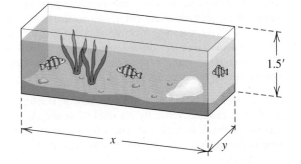

69 **Skyline ordinance** A city council is proposing a new skyline ordinance. It would require the setback S for any building from a residence to be a minimum of 100 feet, plus an additional 6 feet for each foot of height above 25 feet. Find a linear function for S in terms of h.

Exercise 69

70 **Energy tax** A proposed energy tax T on gasoline, which would affect the cost of driving a vehicle, is to be computed by multiplying the number x of gallons of gasoline that you buy by 125,000 (the number of BTUs per gallon of gasoline) and then multiplying the total BTUs by the tax—34.2 cents per million BTUs. Find a linear function for T in terms of x.

71 **Childhood growth** For children between ages 6 and 10, height y (in inches) is frequently a linear function of age t (in years). The height of a certain child is 48 inches at age 6 and 50.5 inches at age 7.

(a) Express y as a function of t.

(b) Sketch the line in part (a), and interpret the slope.

(c) Predict the height of the child at age 10.

72 **Radioactive contamination** It has been estimated that 1000 curies of a radioactive substance introduced at a point on the surface of the open sea would spread over an area of 40,000 km² in 40 days. Assuming that the area covered by the radioactive substance is a linear function of time t and is always circular in shape, express the radius r of the contamination as a function of t.

73 **Distance to a hot-air balloon** A hot-air balloon is released at 1:00 P.M. and rises vertically at a rate of 2 m/sec. An observation point is situated 100 meters from a point on the ground directly below the balloon (see the figure). If t denotes the time (in seconds) after 1:00 P.M., express the distance d between the balloon and the observation point as a function of t.

Exercise 73

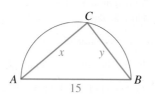

74 Triangle ABC is inscribed in a semicircle of diameter 15 (see the figure).

(a) If x denotes the length of side AC, express the length y of side BC as a function of x. (*Hint:* Angle ACB is a right angle.)

(b) Express the area $\mathcal{A}$ of triangle ABC as a function of x, and state the domain of this function.

Exercise 74

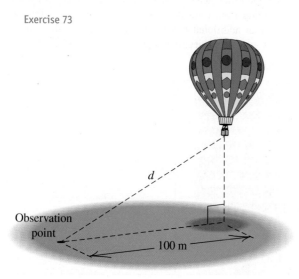

75 **Distance to Earth** From an exterior point P that is h units from a circle of radius r, a tangent line is drawn to the circle (see the figure). Let y denote the distance from the point P to the point of tangency T.

(a) Express y as a function of h. (*Hint:* If C is the center of the circle, then PT is perpendicular to CT.)

(b) If r is the radius of Earth and h is the altitude of a space shuttle, then y is the maximum distance to Earth that an astronaut can see from the shuttle. In particular, if $h = 200$ mi and $r \approx 4000$ mi, approximate y.

Exercise 75

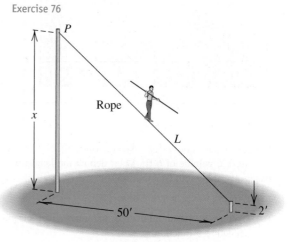

76 **Length of a tightrope** The figure illustrates the apparatus for a tightrope walker. Two poles are set 50 feet apart, but the point of attachment P for the rope is yet to be determined.

(a) Express the length L of the rope as a function of the distance x from P to the ground.

(b) If the total walk is to be 75 feet, determine the distance from P to the ground.

Exercise 76

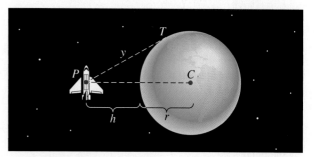

77 Airport runway The relative positions of an aircraft runway and a 20-foot-tall control tower are shown in the figure. The beginning of the runway is at a perpendicular distance of 300 feet from the base of the tower. If x denotes the distance an airplane has moved down the runway, express the distance d between the airplane and the top of the control tower as a function of x.

Exercise 77

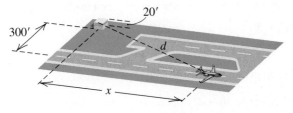

78 Destination time A man in a rowboat that is 2 miles from the nearest point A on a straight shoreline wishes to reach a house located at a point B that is 6 miles farther down the shoreline (see the figure). He plans to row to a point P that is between A and B and is x miles from the house, and then he will walk the remainder of the distance. Suppose he can row at a rate of 3 mi/hr and can walk at a rate of 5 mi/hr. If T is the total time required to reach the house, express T as a function of x.

Exercise 78

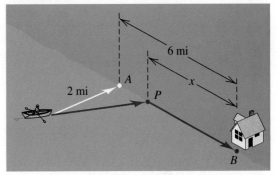

3.5

Graphs of Functions

In this section we discuss aids for sketching graphs of certain types of functions. In particular, a function f is called **even** if $f(-x) = f(x)$ for every x in its domain. In this case, the equation $y = f(x)$ is not changed if $-x$ is substituted for x, and hence, from symmetry test 1 of Section 3.2, the graph of an even function is symmetric with respect to the y-axis.

A function f is called **odd** if $f(-x) = -f(x)$ for every x in its domain. If we apply symmetry test 3 of Section 3.2 to the equation $y = f(x)$, we see that the graph of an odd function is symmetric with respect to the origin.

These facts are summarized in the first two columns of the next chart.

Even and Odd Functions

Terminology	Definition	Illustration	Type of symmetry of graph
f is an *even* **function.**	$f(-x) = f(x)$ for every x in the domain.	$y = f(x) = x^2$	with respect to the y-axis
f is an *odd* **function.**	$f(-x) = -f(x)$ for every x in the domain.	$y = f(x) = x^3$	with respect to the origin

EXAMPLE 1 Determining whether a function is even or odd

Determine whether f is even, odd, or neither even nor odd.

(a) $f(x) = 3x^4 - 2x^2 + 5$ (b) $f(x) = 2x^5 - 7x^3 + 4x$

(c) $f(x) = x^3 + x^2$

SOLUTION   In each case the domain of f is $\mathbb{R}$. To determine whether f is even or odd, we begin by examining $f(-x)$, where x is any real number.

(a) $f(-x) = 3(-x)^4 - 2(-x)^2 + 5$ substitute $-x$ for x in $f(x)$

$ = 3x^4 - 2x^2 + 5$ simplify

$ = f(x)$ definition of f

Since $f(-x) = f(x)$, f is an even function.

(b) $f(-x) = 2(-x)^5 - 7(-x)^3 + 4(-x)$ substitute $-x$ for x in $f(x)$

$ = -2x^5 + 7x^3 - 4x$ simplify

$ = -(2x^5 - 7x^3 + 4x)$ factor out -1

$ = -f(x)$ definition of f

Since $f(-x) = -f(x)$, f is an odd function.

(c) $f(-x) = (-x)^3 + (-x)^2$ substitute $-x$ for x in $f(x)$

$ = -x^3 + x^2$ simplify

Since $f(-x) \neq f(x)$, and $f(-x) \neq -f(x)$ (note that $-f(x) = -x^3 - x^2$), the function f is neither even nor odd.

In the next example we consider the **absolute value function** f, defined by $f(x) = |x|$.

EXAMPLE 2 Sketching the graph of the absolute value function

Let $f(x) = |x|$.

(a) Determine whether f is even or odd.

(b) Sketch the graph of f.

(c) Find the intervals on which f is increasing or is decreasing.

SOLUTION

(a) The domain of f is $\mathbb{R}$, because the absolute value of x exists for every real number x. If x is in $\mathbb{R}$, then

$$f(-x) = |-x| = |x| = f(x).$$

Thus, f is an even function, since $f(-x) = f(x)$.

(b) Since f is even, its graph is symmetric with respect to the y-axis. If $x \geq 0$, then $|x| = x$, and therefore the first quadrant part of the graph coincides with the line $y = x$. Sketching this half-line and using symmetry gives us Figure 1.

Figure 1

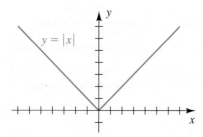

(c) Referring to the graph, we see that f is decreasing on $(-\infty, 0]$ and is increasing on $[0, \infty)$.

If we know the graph of $y = f(x)$, it is easy to sketch the graphs of

$$y = f(x) + c \qquad \text{and} \qquad y = f(x) - c$$

for any positive real number c. As in the next chart, for $y = f(x) + c$, we add c to the y-coordinate of each point on the graph of $y = f(x)$. This *shifts* the graph of f *upward* a distance c. For $y = f(x) - c$ with $c > 0$, we subtract c from each y-coordinate, thereby shifting the graph of f a distance c *downward*. These are called **vertical shifts** of graphs.

Vertically Shifting the Graph of $y = f(x)$

Equation	$y = f(x) + c$ with $c > 0$	$y = f(x) - c$ with $c > 0$
Effect on graph	The graph of f is shifted vertically upward a distance c.	The graph of f is shifted vertically downward a distance c.
Graphical interpretation		

EXAMPLE 3 **Vertically shifting a graph**

Sketch the graph of f:

(a) $f(x) = x^2$ **(b)** $f(x) = x^2 + 4$ **(c)** $f(x) = x^2 - 4$

SOLUTION We shall sketch all graphs on the same coordinate plane.

(a) Since

$$f(-x) = (-x)^2 = x^2 = f(x),$$

the function f is even, and hence its graph is symmetric with respect to the y-axis. Several points on the graph of $y = x^2$ are $(0, 0)$, $(1, 1)$, $(2, 4)$, and $(3, 9)$. Drawing a smooth curve through these points and reflecting through the y-axis gives us the sketch in Figure 2. The graph is a parabola with vertex at the origin and opening upward.

(continued)

Figure 2

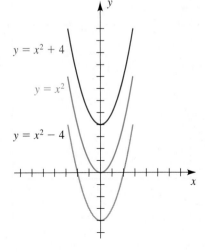

$y = x^2 + 4$

$y = x^2$

$y = x^2 - 4$

Figure 2 (repeated)

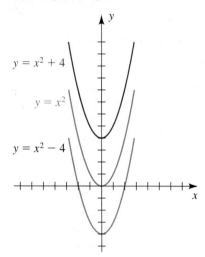

(b) To sketch the graph of $y = x^2 + 4$, we add 4 to the y-coordinate of each point on the graph of $y = x^2$; that is, we shift the graph in part (a) upward 4 units, as shown in the figure.

(c) To sketch the graph of $y = x^2 - 4$, we decrease the y-coordinates of $y = x^2$ by 4; that is, we shift the graph in part (a) downward 4 units.

We can also consider **horizontal shifts** of graphs. Specifically, if $c > 0$, consider the graphs of $y = f(x)$ and $y = g(x) = f(x - c)$ sketched on the same coordinate plane, as illustrated in the next chart. Since

$$g(a + c) = f([a + c] - c) = f(a),$$

we see that the point with x-coordinate a on the graph of $y = f(x)$ has the same y-coordinate as the point with x-coordinate $a + c$ on the graph of $y = g(x) = f(x - c)$. This implies that the graph of $y = g(x) = f(x - c)$ can be obtained by shifting the graph of $y = f(x)$ *to the right* a distance c. Similarly, the graph of $y = h(x) = f(x + c)$ can be obtained by shifting the graph of f *to the left* a distance c, as shown in the chart.

Horizontally Shifting the Graph of $y = f(x)$

Equation	Effect on graph	Graphical interpretation
$y = g(x)$ $= f(x - c)$ with $c > 0$	The graph of f is shifted horizontally to the *right* a distance c.	
$y = h(x)$ $= f(x + c)$ with $c > 0$	The graph of f is shifted horizontally to the *left* a distance c.	

Horizontal and vertical shifts are also referred to as *translations.*

Figure 3

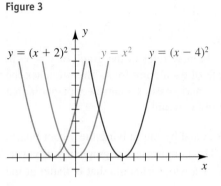

$y = (x + 2)^2$ $y = x^2$ $y = (x - 4)^2$

EXAMPLE 4   Horizontally shifting a graph

Sketch the graph of f:

(a) $f(x) = (x - 4)^2$ **(b)** $f(x) = (x + 2)^2$

SOLUTION   The graph of $y = x^2$ is sketched in Figure 3.

(a) Shifting the graph of $y = x^2$ to the right 4 units gives us the graph of $y = (x - 4)^2$, shown in the figure.

(b) Shifting the graph of $y = x^2$ to the left 2 units leads to the graph of $y = (x + 2)^2$, shown in the figure.

To obtain the graph of $y = cf(x)$ for some real number c, we may *multiply* the y-coordinates of points on the graph of $y = f(x)$ by c. For example, if $y = 2f(x)$, we double the y-coordinates; or if $y = \frac{1}{2}f(x)$, we multiply each y-coordinate by $\frac{1}{2}$. This procedure is referred to as **vertically stretching** the graph of f (if $c > 1$) or **vertically compressing** the graph (if $0 < c < 1$) and is summarized in the following chart.

Vertically Stretching or Compressing the Graph of $y = f(x)$

Equation	$y = cf(x)$ with $c > 1$	$y = cf(x)$ with $0 < c < 1$
Effect on graph	The graph of f is stretched vertically by a factor c.	The graph of f is compressed vertically by a factor $1/c$.
Graphical interpretation		

EXAMPLE 5 Vertically stretching or compressing a graph

Sketch the graph of the equation:

(a) $y = 4x^2$ **(b)** $y = \frac{1}{4}x^2$

Figure 4

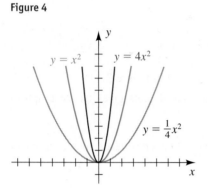

SOLUTION

(a) To sketch the graph of $y = 4x^2$, we may refer to the graph of $y = x^2$ in Figure 4 and multiply the y-coordinate of each point by 4. This stretches the graph of $y = x^2$ vertically by a factor 4 and gives us a narrower parabola that is sharper at the vertex, as illustrated in the figure.

(b) The graph of $y = \frac{1}{4}x^2$ may be sketched by multiplying the y-coordinates of points on the graph of $y = x^2$ by $\frac{1}{4}$. This compresses the graph of $y = x^2$ vertically by a factor $1/\frac{1}{4} = 4$ and gives us a wider parabola that is flatter at the vertex, as shown in Figure 4.

Replacing y with $-y$ reflects the graph of $y = f(x)$ through the x-axis.

We may obtain the graph of $y = -f(x)$ by multiplying the y-coordinate of each point on the graph of $y = f(x)$ by -1. Thus, every point (a, b) on the graph of $y = f(x)$ that lies above the x-axis determines a point $(a, -b)$ on the graph of $y = -f(x)$ that lies below the x-axis. Similarly, if (c, d) lies below the x-axis (that is, $d < 0$), then $(c, -d)$ lies above the x-axis. The graph of $y = -f(x)$ is a **reflection** of the graph of $y = f(x)$ through the x-axis.

Figure 5

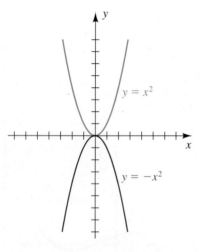

EXAMPLE 6 Reflecting a graph through the x-axis

Sketch the graph of $y = -x^2$.

SOLUTION The graph may be found by plotting points; however, since the graph of $y = x^2$ is familiar to us, we sketch it as in Figure 5 and then multiply the y-coordinates of points by -1. This procedure gives us the reflection through the x-axis indicated in the figure.

Sometimes it is useful to compare the graphs of $y = f(x)$ and $y = f(cx)$ if $c \neq 0$. In this case the function values $f(x)$ for

$$a \leq x \leq b$$

are the same as the function values $f(cx)$ for

$$a \leq cx \leq b \quad \text{or, equivalently,} \quad \frac{a}{c} \leq x \leq \frac{b}{c}.$$

This implies that the graph of f is **horizontally compressed** (if $c > 1$) or **horizontally stretched** (if $0 < c < 1$), as summarized in the following chart.

Horizontally Compressing or Stretching the Graph of $y = f(x)$

Equation	Effect on graph	Graphical interpretation
$y = f(cx)$ with $c > 1$	The graph of f is compressed horizontally by a factor c.	
$y = f(cx)$ with $0 < c < 1$	The graph of f is stretched horizontally by a factor $1/c$.	

If $c < 0$, then the graph of $y = f(cx)$ may be obtained by reflecting the graph of $y = f(|c|x)$ through the y-axis. For example, to sketch the graph of $y = f(-2x)$, we reflect the graph of $y = f(2x)$ through the y-axis. As a special case, the graph of $y = f(-x)$ is a **reflection** of the graph of $y = f(x)$ through the y-axis.

Functions are sometimes described by more than one expression, as in the next examples. We call such functions **piecewise-defined functions.**

EXAMPLE 7 Sketching the graph of a piecewise-defined function

Sketch the graph of the function f if

$$f(x) = \begin{cases} 2x + 5 & \text{if } x \le -1 \\ x^2 & \text{if } |x| < 1 \\ 2 & \text{if } x \ge 1 \end{cases}$$

SOLUTION If $x \le -1$, then $f(x) = 2x + 5$ and the graph of f coincides with the line $y = 2x + 5$ and is represented by the portion of the graph to the left of the line $x = -1$ in Figure 6. The small dot indicates that the point $(-1, 3)$ is on the graph.

(continued)

Figure 6

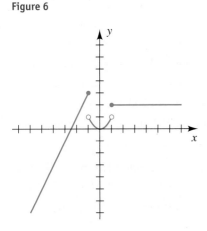

Figure 6 (repeated)

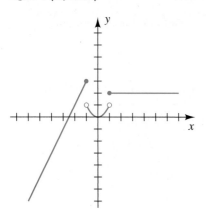

If $|x| < 1$ (or, equivalently, $-1 < x < 1$), we use x^2 to find values of f, and therefore this part of the graph of f coincides with the parabola $y = x^2$, as indicated in the figure. Note that the points $(-1, 1)$ and $(1, 1)$ are *not* on the graph.

Finally, if $x \geq 1$, the values of f are always 2. Thus, the graph of f for $x \geq 1$ is the horizontal half-line in Figure 6.

Note: When you finish sketching the graph of a piecewise-defined function, check that it passes the vertical line test.

It is a common misconception to think that if you move up to a higher tax bracket, *all* your income is taxed at the higher rate. The following example of a graph of a piecewise-defined function helps dispel that notion.

EXAMPLE 8   Application using a piecewise-defined function

Sketch a graph of the 2006 Tax Rate Schedule X, shown in Figure 7. Let x represent the taxable income and T represent the amount of tax. (Assume the domain is the set of nonnegative real numbers.)

Figure 7

2006 Federal Tax Rate Schedules

Schedule X –Use if your Filing status is **single**

If taxable income is over–	But not over–	The tax is:	of the amount over–
$0	$7,550	- - - - - - - 10%	$0
7,550	30,650	$755.00 + 15%	7,550
30,650	74,200	$4,220.00 + 25%	30,650
74,200	154,800	15,107.50 + 28%	74,200
154,800	336,550	37,675.50 + 33%	154,800
336,550	- - - - - - -	97,653.00 + 35%	336,550

SOLUTION   The tax table can be represented by a piecewise-defined function as follows:

$$T(x) = \begin{cases} 0 & \text{if} & x \leq 0 \\ 0.10x & \text{if} & 0 < x \leq 7550 \\ 755.00 + 0.15(x - 7550) & \text{if} & 7550 < x \leq 30{,}650 \\ 4220.00 + 0.25(x - 30{,}650) & \text{if} & 30{,}650 < x \leq 74{,}200 \\ 15{,}107.50 + 0.28(x - 74{,}200) & \text{if} & 74{,}200 < x \leq 154{,}800 \\ 37{,}675.50 + 0.33(x - 154{,}800) & \text{if} & 154{,}800 < x \leq 336{,}550 \\ 97{,}653.00 + 0.35(x - 336{,}550) & \text{if} & x > 336{,}550 \end{cases}$$

Note that the assignment for the 15% tax bracket is *not* $0.15x$, but 10% of the first \$7550 in taxable income plus 15% of the amount *over* \$7550; that is,

$$0.10(7550) + 0.15(x - 7550) = 755.00 + 0.15(x - 7550).$$

The other pieces can be established in a similar fashion. The graph of T is shown in Figure 8; note that the slope of each piece represents the tax rate.

Figure 8

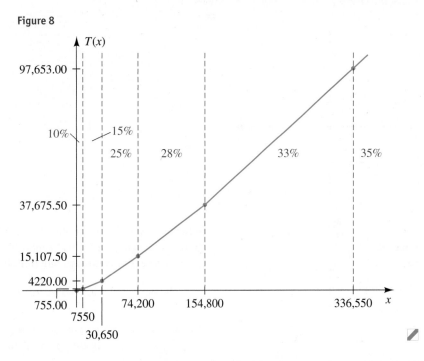

If x is a real number, we define the symbol $[\![x]\!]$ as follows:

$$[\![x]\!] = n, \qquad \text{where } n \text{ is the greatest integer such that } n \leq x$$

If we identify $\mathbb{R}$ with points on a coordinate line, then n is the first integer to the *left* of (or *equal* to) x.

ILLUSTRATION The Symbol $[\![x]\!]$

- $[\![0.5]\!] = 0$
- $[\![1.8]\!] = 1$
- $\big[\!\big[\sqrt{5}\,\big]\!\big] = 2$
- $[\![3]\!] = 3$
- $[\![-3]\!] = -3$
- $[\![-2.7]\!] = -3$
- $\big[\!\big[-\sqrt{3}\,\big]\!\big] = -2$
- $[\![-0.5]\!] = -1$

The **greatest integer function** f is defined by $f(x) = [\![x]\!]$.

EXAMPLE 9 Sketching the graph of the greatest integer function

Sketch the graph of the greatest integer function.

Figure 9

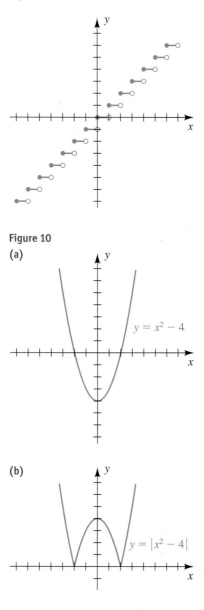

Figure 10

(a)

(b)

Graphing $y = f(|x|)$

SOLUTION The x- and y-coordinates of some points on the graph may be listed as follows:

Values of x	$f(x) = [\![x]\!]$
$\vdots$	$\vdots$
$-2 \le x < -1$	-2
$-1 \le x < 0$	-1
$0 \le x < 1$	0
$1 \le x < 2$	1
$2 \le x < 3$	2
$\vdots$	$\vdots$

Whenever x is between successive integers, the corresponding part of the graph is a segment of a horizontal line. Part of the graph is sketched in Figure 9. The graph continues indefinitely to the right and to the left.

The next example involves absolute values.

EXAMPLE 10 Sketching the graph of an equation containing an absolute value

Sketch the graph of $y = |x^2 - 4|$.

SOLUTION The graph of $y = x^2 - 4$ was sketched in Figure 2 and is re-sketched in Figure 10(a). We note the following facts:

(1) If $x \le -2$ or $x \ge 2$, then $x^2 - 4 \ge 0$, and hence $|x^2 - 4| = x^2 - 4$.

(2) If $-2 < x < 2$, then $x^2 - 4 < 0$, and hence $|x^2 - 4| = -(x^2 - 4)$.

It follows from (1) that the graphs of $y = |x^2 - 4|$ and $y = x^2 - 4$ coincide for $|x| \ge 2$. We see from (2) that if $|x| < 2$, then the graph of $y = |x^2 - 4|$ is the reflection of the graph of $y = x^2 - 4$ through the x-axis. This gives us the sketch in Figure 10(b).

In general, if the graph of $y = f(x)$ contains a point $P(c, -d)$ with d positive, then the graph of $y = |f(x)|$ contains the point $Q(c, d)$—that is, Q is the reflection of P through the x-axis. Points with nonnegative y-values are the same for the graphs of $y = f(x)$ and $y = |f(x)|$.

Later in this text and in calculus, you will encounter functions such as

$$g(x) = \ln |x| \quad \text{and} \quad h(x) = \sin |x|.$$

Both functions are of the form $y = f(|x|)$. The effect of substituting $|x|$ for x can be described as follows: If the graph of $y = f(x)$ contains a point $P(c, d)$

with c positive, then the graph of $y = f(|x|)$ contains the point $Q(-c, d)$—that is, Q is the reflection of P through the y-axis. Points on the y-axis ($x = 0$) are the same for the graphs of $y = f(x)$ and $y = f(|x|)$. Points with negative x-values on the graph of $y = f(x)$ are not on the graph of $y = f(|x|)$, since the result of the absolute value is always nonnegative.

The processes of shifting, stretching, compressing, and reflecting a graph may be collectively termed *transforming* a graph, and the resulting graph is called a **transformation** of the original graph. A graphical summary of the types of transformations encountered in this section appears in Appendix II.

3.5 Exercises

Exer. 1–2: Suppose f is an even function and g is an odd function. Complete the table, if possible.

1

x	-2	2
$f(x)$		7
$g(x)$		-6

2

x	-3	3
$f(x)$		-5
$g(x)$		15

Exer. 3–12: Determine whether f is even, odd, or neither even nor odd.

3 $f(x) = 5x^3 + 2x$

4 $f(x) = |x| - 3$

5 $f(x) = 3x^4 + 2x^2 - 5$

6 $f(x) = 7x^5 - 4x^3$

7 $f(x) = 8x^3 - 3x^2$

8 $f(x) = 12$

9 $f(x) = \sqrt{x^2 + 4}$

10 $f(x) = 3x^2 - 5x + 1$

11 $f(x) = \sqrt[3]{x^3 - x}$

12 $f(x) = x^3 - \dfrac{1}{x}$

Exer. 13–26: Sketch, on the same coordinate plane, the graphs of f for the given values of c. (Make use of symmetry, shifting, stretching, compressing, or reflecting.)

13 $f(x) = |x| + c$; $c = -3, 1, 3$

14 $f(x) = |x - c|$; $c = -3, 1, 3$

15 $f(x) = -x^2 + c$; $c = -4, 2, 4$

16 $f(x) = 2x^2 - c$; $c = -4, 2, 4$

17 $f(x) = 2\sqrt{x} + c$; $c = -3, 0, 2$

18 $f(x) = \sqrt{9 - x^2} + c$; $c = -3, 0, 2$

19 $f(x) = \frac{1}{2}\sqrt{x - c}$; $c = -2, 0, 3$

20 $f(x) = -\frac{1}{2}(x - c)^2$; $c = -2, 0, 3$

21 $f(x) = c\sqrt{4 - x^2}$; $c = -2, 1, 3$

22 $f(x) = (x + c)^3$; $c = -2, 1, 2$

23 $f(x) = cx^3$; $c = -\frac{1}{3}, 1, 2$

24 $f(x) = (cx)^3 + 1$; $c = -1, 1, 4$

25 $f(x) = \sqrt{cx} - 1$; $c = -1, \frac{1}{9}, 4$

26 $f(x) = -\sqrt{16 - (cx)^2}$; $c = 1, \frac{1}{2}, 4$

Exer. 27–32: If the point P is on the graph of a function f, find the corresponding point on the graph of the given function.

27 $P(0, 5)$; $y = f(x + 2) - 1$

28 $P(3, -1)$; $y = 2f(x) + 4$

29 $P(3, -2)$; $y = 2f(x - 4) + 1$

30 $P(-2, 4)$; $y = \frac{1}{2}f(x - 3) + 3$

31 $P(3, 9)$; $y = \frac{1}{3}f(\frac{1}{2}x) - 1$

32 $P(-2, 1)$; $y = -3f(2x) - 5$

Exer. 33–40: Explain how the graph of the function compares to the graph of $y = f(x)$. For example, for the equation $y = 2f(x + 3)$, the graph of f is shifted 3 units to the left and stretched vertically by a factor of 2.

33 $y = f(x - 2) + 3$

34 $y = 3f(x - 1)$

35 $y = f(-x) - 2$

36 $y = -f(x + 4)$

37 $y = -\frac{1}{2}f(x)$

38 $y = f\left(\frac{1}{2}x\right) - 3$

39 $y = -2f\left(\frac{1}{3}x\right)$

40 $y = \frac{1}{3}|f(x)|$

Exer. 41–42: The graph of a function f with domain [0, 4] is shown in the figure. Sketch the graph of the given equation.

41

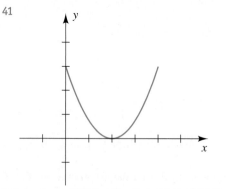

(a) $y = f(x + 3)$ (b) $y = f(x - 3)$

(c) $y = f(x) + 3$ (d) $y = f(x) - 3$

(e) $y = -3f(x)$ (f) $y = -\frac{1}{3}f(x)$

(g) $y = f\left(-\frac{1}{2}x\right)$ (h) $y = f(2x)$

(i) $y = -f(x + 2) - 3$ (j) $y = f(x - 2) + 3$

(k) $y = |f(x)|$ (l) $y = f(|x|)$

42

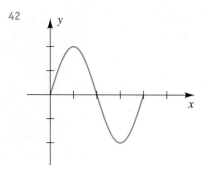

(a) $y = f(x - 2)$ (b) $y = f(x + 2)$

(c) $y = f(x) - 2$ (d) $y = f(x) + 2$

(e) $y = -2f(x)$ (f) $y = -\frac{1}{2}f(x)$

(g) $y = f(-2x)$ (h) $y = f\left(\frac{1}{2}x\right)$

(i) $y = -f(x + 4) - 2$ (j) $y = f(x - 4) + 2$

(k) $y = |f(x)|$ (l) $y = f(|x|)$

Exer. 43–46: The graph of a function f is shown, together with graphs of three other functions (a), (b), and (c). Use properties of symmetry, shifts, and reflecting to find equations for graphs (a), (b), and (c) in terms of f.

43

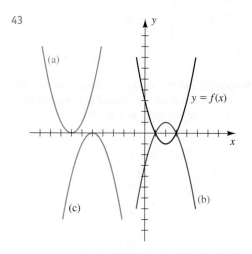

44

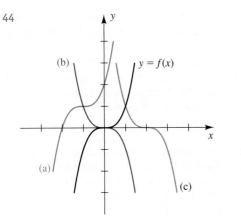

45

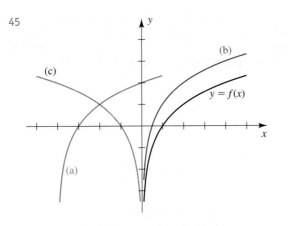

46

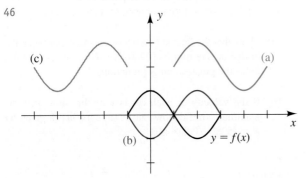

Exer. 47–52: Sketch the graph of f.

47 $f(x) = \begin{cases} 3 & \text{if } x \le -1 \\ -2 & \text{if } x > -1 \end{cases}$

48 $f(x) = \begin{cases} -1 & \text{if } x \text{ is an integer} \\ -2 & \text{if } x \text{ is not an integer} \end{cases}$

49 $f(x) = \begin{cases} 3 & \text{if } x < -2 \\ -x + 1 & \text{if } |x| \le 2 \\ -3 & \text{if } x > 2 \end{cases}$

50 $f(x) = \begin{cases} -2x & \text{if } x < -1 \\ x^2 & \text{if } -1 \le x < 1 \\ -2 & \text{if } x \ge 1 \end{cases}$

51 $f(x) = \begin{cases} x + 2 & \text{if } x \le -1 \\ x^3 & \text{if } |x| < 1 \\ -x + 3 & \text{if } x \ge 1 \end{cases}$

52 $f(x) = \begin{cases} x - 3 & \text{if } x \le -2 \\ -x^2 & \text{if } -2 < x < 1 \\ -x + 4 & \text{if } x \ge 1 \end{cases}$

Exer. 53–54: The symbol $[\![x]\!]$ denotes values of the greatest integer function. Sketch the graph of f.

53 (a) $f(x) = [\![x - 3]\!]$ (b) $f(x) = [\![x]\!] - 3$

    (c) $f(x) = 2[\![x]\!]$ (d) $f(x) = [\![2x]\!]$

    (e) $f(x) = [\![-x]\!]$

54 (a) $f(x) = [\![x + 2]\!]$ (b) $f(x) = [\![x]\!] + 2$

    (c) $f(x) = \frac{1}{2}[\![x]\!]$ (d) $f(x) = [\![\frac{1}{2}x]\!]$

    (e) $f(x) = -[\![-x]\!]$

Exer. 55–56: Explain why the graph of the equation is not the graph of a function.

55 $x = y^2$ 56 $x = -|y|$

Exer. 57–58: For the graph of $y = f(x)$ shown in the figure, sketch the graph of $y = |f(x)|$.

57

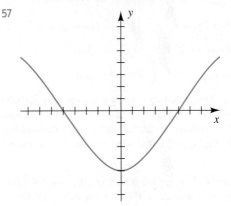

58

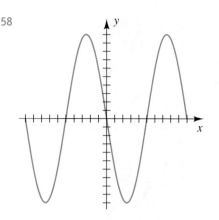

Exer. 59–62: Sketch the graph of the equation.

59 $y = |9 - x^2|$

60 $y = |x^3 - 1|$

61 $y = |\sqrt{x} - 1|$

62 $y = ||x| - 1|$

63 Let $y = f(x)$ be a function with domain $D = [-2, 6]$ and range $R = [-4, 8]$. Find the domain D and range R for each function. Assume $f(2) = 8$ and $f(6) = -4$.

(a) $y = -2f(x)$

(b) $y = f(\frac{1}{2}x)$

(c) $y = f(x - 3) + 1$

(d) $y = f(x + 2) - 3$

(e) $y = f(-x)$

(f) $y = -f(x)$

(g) $y = f(|x|)$

(h) $y = |f(x)|$

64 Let $y = f(x)$ be a function with domain $D = [-6, -2]$ and range $R = [-10, -4]$. Find the domain D and range R for each function.

(a) $y = \frac{1}{2}f(x)$

(b) $y = f(2x)$

(c) $y = f(x - 2) + 5$

(d) $y = f(x + 4) - 1$

(e) $y = f(-x)$

(f) $y = -f(x)$

(g) $y = f(|x|)$

(h) $y = |f(x)|$

65 Income tax rates A certain country taxes the first $20,000 of an individual's income at a rate of 15%, and all income over $20,000 is taxed at 20%. Find a piecewise-defined function T that specifies the total tax on an income of x dollars.

66 Property tax rates A certain state taxes the first $500,000 in property value at a rate of 1%; all value over $500,000 is

taxed at 1.25%. Find a piecewise-defined function T that specifies the total tax on a property valued at x dollars.

67 Royalty rates A certain paperback sells for $12. The author is paid royalties of 10% on the first 10,000 copies sold, 12.5% on the next 5000 copies, and 15% on any additional copies. Find a piecewise-defined function R that specifies the total royalties if x copies are sold.

68 Electricity rates An electric company charges its customers $0.0577 per kilowatt-hour (kWh) for the first 1000 kWh used, $0.0532 for the next 4000 kWh, and $0.0511 for any kWh over 5000. Find a piecewise-defined function C for a customer's bill of x kWh.

69 Car rental charges There are two car rental options available for a four-day trip. Option I is $45 per day, with 200 free miles and $0.40 per mile for each additional mile. Option II is $58.75 per day, with a charge of $0.25 per mile.

(a) Determine the cost of a 500-mile trip for both options.

(b) Model the data with a cost function for each four-day option.

(c) Determine the mileages at which each option is preferable.

70 Traffic flow Cars are crossing a bridge that is 1 mile long. Each car is 12 feet long and is required to stay a distance of at least d feet from the car in front of it (see figure).

(a) Show that the largest number of cars that can be on the bridge at one time is $[\![5280/(12 + d)]\!]$, where $[\![\ ]\!]$ denotes the greatest integer function.

(b) If the velocity of each car is v mi/hr, show that the maximum traffic flow rate F (in cars/hr) is given by $F = [\![5280v/(12 + d)]\!]$.

Exercise 70

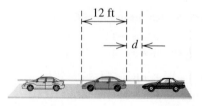

12 ft

d

3.6

Quadratic Functions

If $a \neq 0$, then the graph of $y = ax^2$ is a parabola with vertex at the origin $(0, 0)$, a vertical axis, opening upward if $a > 0$ or downward if $a < 0$ (see, for example, Figures 4 and 5 in Section 3.5). In this section we show that the graph of an equation of the form

$$y = ax^2 + bx + c$$

can be obtained by vertical and/or horizontal shifts of the graph of $y = ax^2$ and hence is also a parabola. An important application of such equations is to describe the trajectory, or path, of an object near the surface of the earth when the only force acting on the object is gravitational attraction. To illustrate, if an outfielder on a baseball team throws a ball into the infield, as illustrated in Figure 1, and if air resistance and other outside forces are negligible, then the path of the ball is a parabola. If suitable coordinate axes are introduced, then the path coincides with the graph of the equation $y = ax^2 + bx + c$ for some a, b, and c. We call the function determined by this equation a *quadratic function*.

Figure 1

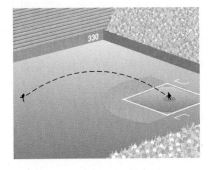

Definition of Quadratic Function	A function f is a **quadratic function** if $$f(x) = ax^2 + bx + c,$$ where a, b, and c are real numbers with $a \neq 0$.

Figure 2

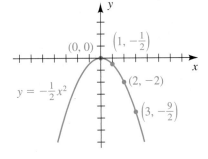

If $b = c = 0$ in the preceding definition, then $f(x) = ax^2$, and the graph is a parabola with vertex at the origin. If $b = 0$ and $c \neq 0$, then

$$f(x) = ax^2 + c,$$

and, from our discussion of vertical shifts in Section 3.5, the graph is a parabola with vertex at the point $(0, c)$ on the y-axis. The following example contains specific illustrations.

EXAMPLE 1 Sketching the graph of a quadratic function

Sketch the graph of f if

(a) $f(x) = -\frac{1}{2}x^2$ **(b)** $f(x) = -\frac{1}{2}x^2 + 4$

SOLUTION

(a) Since f is even, the graph of f (that is, of $y = -\frac{1}{2}x^2$) is symmetric with respect to the y-axis. It is similar in shape to but wider than the parabola $y = -x^2$, sketched in Figure 5 of Section 3.5. Several points on the graph are $(0, 0)$, $\left(1, -\frac{1}{2}\right)$, $(2, -2)$, and $\left(3, -\frac{9}{2}\right)$. Plotting and using symmetry, we obtain the sketch in Figure 2.

Figure 3

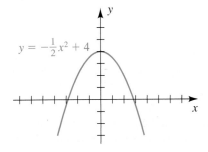

(b) To find the graph of $y = -\frac{1}{2}x^2 + 4$, we shift the graph of $y = -\frac{1}{2}x^2$ upward a distance 4, obtaining the sketch in Figure 3.

If $f(x) = ax^2 + bx + c$ and $b \neq 0$, then, by completing the square, we can change the form to

$$f(x) = a(x - h)^2 + k$$

for some real numbers h and k. This technique is illustrated in the next example.

EXAMPLE 2   Expressing a quadratic function as $f(x) = a(x - h)^2 + k$

If $f(x) = 3x^2 + 24x + 50$, express $f(x)$ in the form $a(x - h)^2 + k$.

SOLUTION 1   Before completing the square, *it is essential that we factor out the coefficient of x^2 from the first two terms of $f(x)$,* as follows:

$$f(x) = 3x^2 + 24x + 50 \qquad \text{given}$$
$$= 3(x^2 + 8x + \quad) + 50 \quad \text{factor out 3 from } 3x^2 + 24x$$

We now complete the square for the expression $x^2 + 8x$ within the parentheses by adding the square of half the coefficient of x—that is, $\left(\frac{8}{2}\right)^2$, or 16. However, if we add 16 to the expression within parentheses, then, because of the factor 3, we are actually adding 48 to $f(x)$. Hence, we must compensate by subtracting 48:

$$f(x) = 3(x^2 + 8x + \quad) + 50 \qquad \text{given}$$
$$= 3(x^2 + 8x + 16) + (50 - 48) \quad \text{complete the square for } x^2 + 8x$$
$$= 3(x + 4)^2 + 2 \qquad \text{equivalent equation}$$

The last expression has the form $a(x - h)^2 + k$ with $a = 3$, $h = -4$, and $k = 2$.

SOLUTION 2   We begin by dividing both sides by the coefficient of x^2.

$$f(x) = 3x^2 + 24x + 50 \qquad \text{given}$$
$$\frac{f(x)}{3} = x^2 + 8x + \frac{50}{3} \qquad \text{divide by 3}$$

$$\left[\frac{1}{2}(8)\right]^2 = 16 \rightarrow$$

$$= x^2 + 8x + \underline{16} + \frac{50}{3} \underline{-16} \quad \begin{array}{l}\text{add and subtract 16, the number that} \\ \text{completes the square for } x^2 + 8x\end{array}$$
$$= (x + 4)^2 + \frac{2}{3} \qquad \text{equivalent equation}$$
$$f(x) = 3(x + 4)^2 + 2 \qquad \text{multiply by 3}$$

If $f(x) = ax^2 + bx + c$, then, by completing the square as in Example 2, we see that the graph of f is the same as the graph of an equation of the form

$$y = a(x - h)^2 + k.$$

The graph of this equation can be obtained from the graph of $y = ax^2$ shown in Figure 4(a) by means of a horizontal and a vertical shift, as follows. First, as in Figure 4(b), we obtain the graph of $y = a(x - h)^2$ by shifting the graph of $y = ax^2$ either to the left or to the right, depending on the sign of h (the figure illustrates the case with $h > 0$). Next, as in Figure 4(c), we shift the graph in (b) vertically a distance $|k|$ (the figure illustrates the case with $k > 0$). It follows that *the graph of a quadratic function is a parabola with a vertical axis.*

Figure 4

(a)   **(b)**   **(c)**

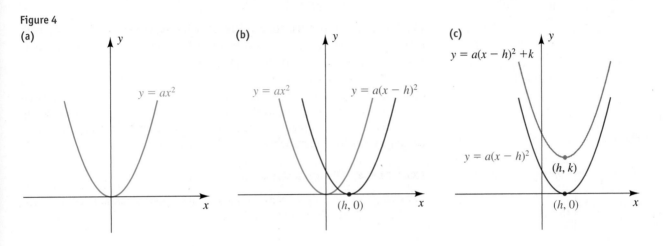

The sketch in Figure 4(c) illustrates one possible graph of the equation $y = ax^2 + bx + c$. If $a > 0$, the point (h, k) is the lowest point on the parabola, and the function f has a **minimum value** $f(h) = k$. If $a < 0$, the parabola opens downward, and the point (h, k) is the highest point on the parabola. In this case, the function f has a **maximum value** $f(h) = k$.

We have obtained the following result.

Standard Equation of a Parabola with Vertical Axis	The graph of the equation $$y = a(x - h)^2 + k$$ for $a \neq 0$ is a parabola that has vertex $V(h, k)$ and a vertical axis. The parabola opens upward if $a > 0$ or downward if $a < 0$.

For convenience, we often refer to the *parabola* $y = ax^2 + bx + c$ when considering the graph of this equation.

EXAMPLE 3   Finding a standard equation of a parabola

Express $y = 2x^2 - 6x + 4$ as a standard equation of a parabola with a vertical axis. Find the vertex and sketch the graph.

Figure 5

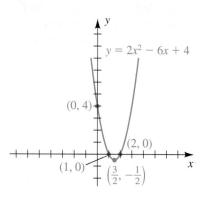

Figure 6

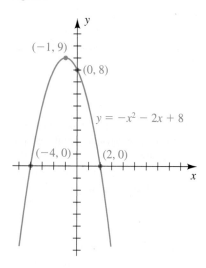

Figure 7

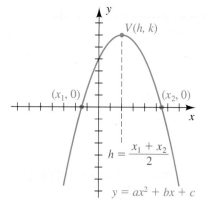

SOLUTION

$$\begin{aligned}
y &= 2x^2 - 6x + 4 && \text{given} \\
&= 2(x^2 - 3x + \phantom{\tfrac{9}{4}}) + 4 && \text{factor out 2 from } 2x^2 - 6x \\
&= 2\left(x^2 - 3x + \tfrac{9}{4}\right) + \left(4 - \tfrac{9}{2}\right) && \text{complete the square for } x^2 - 3x \\
&= 2\left(x - \tfrac{3}{2}\right)^2 - \tfrac{1}{2} && \text{equivalent equation}
\end{aligned}$$

The last equation has the form of the standard equation of a parabola with $a = 2$, $h = \tfrac{3}{2}$, and $k = -\tfrac{1}{2}$. Hence, the vertex $V(h, k)$ of the parabola is $V\!\left(\tfrac{3}{2}, -\tfrac{1}{2}\right)$. Since $a = 2 > 0$, the parabola opens upward.

To find the y-intercept of the graph of $y = 2x^2 - 6x + 4$, we let $x = 0$, obtaining $y = 4$. To find the x-intercepts, we let $y = 0$ and solve the equation $2x^2 - 6x + 4 = 0$ or the equivalent equation $2(x - 1)(x - 2) = 0$, obtaining $x = 1$ and $x = 2$. Plotting the vertex and using the x- and y-intercepts provides enough points for a reasonably accurate sketch (see Figure 5).

EXAMPLE 4 Finding a standard equation of a parabola

Express $y = -x^2 - 2x + 8$ as a standard equation of a parabola with a vertical axis. Find the vertex and sketch the graph.

SOLUTION

$$\begin{aligned}
y &= -x^2 - 2x + 8 && \text{given} \\
&= -(x^2 + 2x +) + 8 && \text{factor out } -1 \text{ from } -x^2 - 2x \\
&= -(x^2 + 2x + 1) + (8 + 1) && \text{complete the square for } x^2 + 2x \\
&= -(x + 1)^2 + 9 && \text{equivalent equation}
\end{aligned}$$

This is the standard equation of a parabola with $h = -1$, $k = 9$, and hence the vertex is $(-1, 9)$. Since $a = -1 < 0$, the parabola opens downward.

The y-intercept of the graph of $y = -x^2 - 2x + 8$ is the constant term, 8. To find the x-intercepts, we solve $-x^2 - 2x + 8 = 0$ or, equivalently, $x^2 + 2x - 8 = 0$. Factoring gives us $(x + 4)(x - 2) = 0$, and hence the intercepts are $x = -4$ and $x = 2$. Using this information gives us the sketch in Figure 6.

If a parabola $y = ax^2 + bx + c$ has x-intercepts x_1 and x_2, as illustrated in Figure 7 for the case $a < 0$, then the axis of the parabola is the vertical line $x = (x_1 + x_2)/2$ through the midpoint of $(x_1, 0)$ and $(x_2, 0)$. Therefore, the x-coordinate h of the vertex (h, k) is $h = (x_1 + x_2)/2$. Some special cases are illustrated in Figures 5 and 6.

In the following example we find an equation of a parabola from given data.

EXAMPLE 5 Finding an equation of a parabola with a given vertex

Find an equation of a parabola that has vertex $V(2, 3)$ and a vertical axis and passes through the point $(5, 1)$.

Figure 8

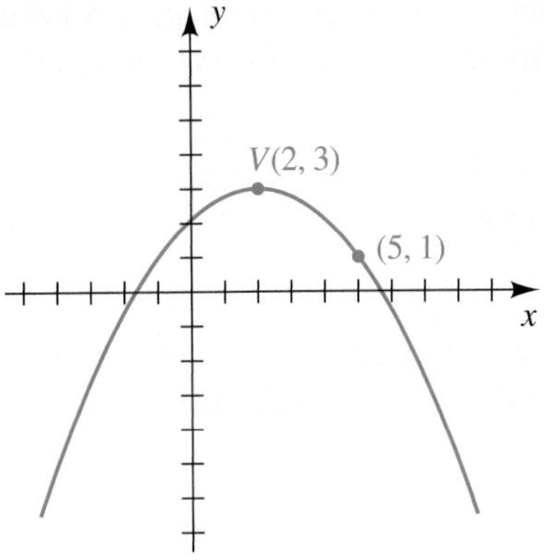

V(2, 3)

(5, 1)

SOLUTION   Figure 8 shows the vertex V, the point $(5, 1)$, and a possible position of the parabola. Using the standard equation

$$y = a(x - h)^2 + k$$

with $h = 2$ and $k = 3$ gives us

$$y = a(x - 2)^2 + 3.$$

To find a, we use the fact that $(5, 1)$ is on the parabola and so is a solution of the last equation. Thus,

$$1 = a(5 - 2)^2 + 3, \qquad \text{or} \qquad a = -\tfrac{2}{9}.$$

Hence, an equation for the parabola is

$$y = -\tfrac{2}{9}(x - 2)^2 + 3.$$

The next theorem gives us a simple formula for locating the vertex of a parabola.

Theorem for Locating the Vertex of a Parabola	The vertex of the parabola $y = ax^2 + bx + c$ has x-coordinate $$-\frac{b}{2a}.$$

PROOF   Let us begin by writing $y = ax^2 + bx + c$ as

$$y = a\left(x^2 + \frac{b}{a}x + \right) + c.$$

Next we complete the square by adding $\left(\dfrac{1}{2}\dfrac{b}{a}\right)^2$ to the expression within parentheses:

$$y = a\left(x^2 + \frac{b}{a}x + \frac{b^2}{4a^2}\right) + \left(c - \frac{b^2}{4a}\right)$$

Note that if $b^2/(4a^2)$ is added *inside* the parentheses, then, because of the factor a on the *outside*, we have actually added $b^2/(4a)$ to y. Therefore, we must compensate by subtracting $b^2/(4a)$. The last equation may be written

$$y = a\left(x + \frac{b}{2a}\right)^2 + \left(c - \frac{b^2}{4a}\right).$$

This is the equation of a parabola that has vertex (h, k) with $h = -b/(2a)$ and $k = c - b^2/(4a)$.

It is unnecessary to remember the formula for the y-coordinate of the vertex of the parabola in the preceding result. Once the x-coordinate has been found, we can calculate the y-coordinate by substituting $-b/(2a)$ for x in the equation of the parabola.

EXAMPLE 6 Finding the vertex of a parabola

Find the vertex of the parabola $y = 2x^2 - 6x + 4$.

SOLUTION   We considered this parabola in Example 3 and found the vertex by completing the square. We shall use the vertex formula with $a = 2$ and $b = -6$, obtaining the x-coordinate

$$\frac{-b}{2a} = \frac{-(-6)}{2(2)} = \frac{6}{4} = \frac{3}{2}.$$

We next find the y-coordinate by substituting $\frac{3}{2}$ for x in the given equation:

$$y = 2\left(\tfrac{3}{2}\right)^2 - 6\left(\tfrac{3}{2}\right) + 4 = -\tfrac{1}{2}$$

Thus, the vertex is $\left(\tfrac{3}{2}, -\tfrac{1}{2}\right)$ (see Figure 5).

Since the graph of $f(x) = ax^2 + bx + c$ for $a \neq 0$ is a parabola, we can use the vertex formula to help find the maximum or minimum value of a quadratic function. Specifically, since the x-coordinate of the vertex V is $-b/(2a)$, the y-coordinate of V is the function value $f(-b/(2a))$. Moreover, since the parabola opens downward if $a < 0$ and upward if $a > 0$, this function value is the maximum or minimum value, respectively, of f. We may summarize these facts as follows.

Theorem on the Maximum or Minimum Value of a Quadratic Function	If $f(x) = ax^2 + bx + c$, where $a \neq 0$, then $f\left(-\dfrac{b}{2a}\right)$ is **(1)** the maximum value of f if $a < 0$ **(2)** the minimum value of f if $a > 0$

We shall use this theorem in the next example.

EXAMPLE 7 Finding the maximum value of a quadratic function

A long rectangular sheet of metal, 12 inches wide, is to be made into a rain gutter by turning up two sides so that they are perpendicular to the sheet. How many inches should be turned up to give the gutter its greatest capacity?

Figure 9

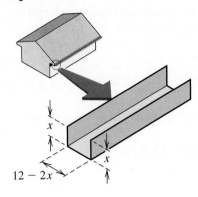

x

x

$12 - 2x$

SOLUTION   The gutter is illustrated in Figure 9. If x denotes the number of inches turned up on each side, the width of the base of the gutter is $12 - 2x$ inches. The capacity will be greatest when the cross-sectional area of the rectangle with sides of lengths x and $12 - 2x$ has its greatest value. Letting $f(x)$ denote this area, we have

$$f(x) = x(12 - 2x)$$
$$= 12x - 2x^2$$
$$= -2x^2 + 12x,$$

which has the form $f(x) = ax^2 + bx + c$ with $a = -2$, $b = 12$, and $c = 0$. Since f is a quadratic function and $a = -2 < 0$, it follows from the preceding theorem that the maximum value of f occurs at

$$x = -\frac{b}{2a} = -\frac{12}{2(-2)} = 3.$$

Thus, 3 inches should be turned up on each side to achieve maximum capacity.

As an alternative solution, we may note that the graph of the function $f(x) = x(12 - 2x)$ has x-intercepts at $x = 0$ and $x = 6$. Hence, the average of the intercepts,

$$x = \frac{0 + 6}{2} = 3,$$

is the x-coordinate of the vertex of the parabola and the value that yields the maximum capacity.

When working with quadratic functions, we are often most interested in finding the vertex and the x-intercepts. Typically, a given quadratic function closely resembles one of the three forms listed in the following chart.

Relationship Between Quadratic Function Forms and Their Vertex and x-intercepts

Form	Vertex (h, k)	x-intercepts (if there are any)
(1) $y = f(x) = a(x - h)^2 + k$	h and k as in the form	$x = h \pm \sqrt{-k/a}$ (see below)
(2) $y = f(x) = a(x - x_1)(x - x_2)$	$h = \dfrac{x_1 + x_2}{2}, \quad k = f(h)$	$x = x_1, x_2$
(3) $y = f(x) = ax^2 + bx + c$	$h = -\dfrac{b}{2a}, \quad k = f(h)$	$x = -\dfrac{b}{2a} \pm \dfrac{\sqrt{b^2 - 4ac}}{2a}$ (see below)

If the radicands in (1) or (3) are negative, then there are no x-intercepts. To find the x-intercepts with form (1), use the special quadratic equation on page 75. If you have a quadratic function in form (3) and want to find the vertex and the x-intercepts, it may be best to first find the x-intercepts by using the quadratic formula. Then you can easily obtain the x-coordinate of the vertex, h, since

$$-\frac{b}{2a} \pm \frac{\sqrt{b^2 - 4ac}}{2a} = h \pm \frac{\sqrt{b^2 - 4ac}}{2a}.$$

Of course, if the function in form (3) is easily factorable, it is not necessary to use the quadratic formula.

We will discuss parabolas further in a later chapter.

3.6   *Exercises*

Exer. 1–4: Find the standard equation of any parabola that has vertex V.

1 $V(-3, 1)$ 2 $V(4, -2)$

3 $V(0, -3)$ 4 $V(-2, 0)$

Exer. 5–12: Express $f(x)$ in the form $a(x - h)^2 + k$.

5 $f(x) = -x^2 - 4x - 8$ 6 $f(x) = x^2 - 6x + 11$

7 $f(x) = 2x^2 - 12x + 22$ 8 $f(x) = 5x^2 + 20x + 17$

9 $f(x) = -3x^2 - 6x - 5$

10 $f(x) = -4x^2 + 16x - 13$

11 $f(x) = -\frac{3}{4}x^2 + 9x - 34$ 12 $f(x) = \frac{2}{5}x^2 - \frac{12}{5}x + \frac{23}{5}$

Exer. 13–22: (a) Use the quadratic formula to find the zeros of f. (b) Find the maximum or minimum value of $f(x)$. (c) Sketch the graph of f.

13 $f(x) = x^2 - 4x$ 14 $f(x) = -x^2 - 6x$

15 $f(x) = -12x^2 + 11x + 15$

16 $f(x) = 6x^2 + 7x - 24$

17 $f(x) = 9x^2 + 24x + 16$ 18 $f(x) = -4x^2 + 4x - 1$

19 $f(x) = x^2 + 4x + 9$ 20 $f(x) = -3x^2 - 6x - 6$

21 $f(x) = -2x^2 + 20x - 43$

22 $f(x) = 2x^2 - 4x - 11$

Exer. 23–26: Find the standard equation of the parabola shown in the figure.

23

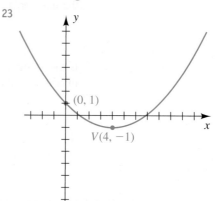

24

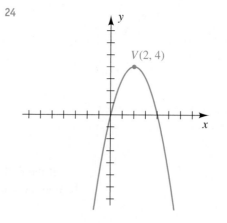

25

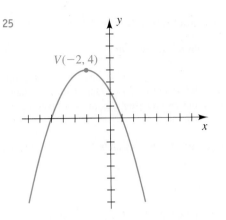

$V(-2, 4)$

26

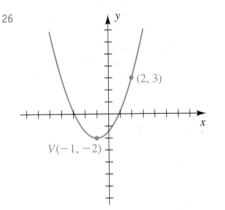

$(2, 3)$

$V(-1, -2)$

Exer. 27–28: Find an equation of the form

$$y = a(x - x_1)(x - x_2)$$

of the parabola shown in the figure. See the chart on page 191.

27

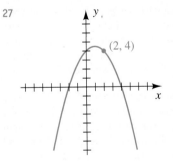

$(2, 4)$

28

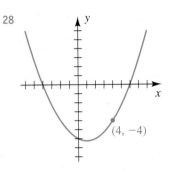

$(4, -4)$

Exer. 29–34: Find the standard equation of a parabola that has a vertical axis and satisfies the given conditions.

29 Vertex $(0, -2)$, passing through $(3, 25)$

30 Vertex $(0, 5)$, passing through $(2, -3)$

31 Vertex $(3, 5)$, x-intercept 0

32 Vertex $(4, -7)$, x-intercept -4

33 x-intercepts -3 and 5, highest point has y-coordinate 4

34 x-intercepts 8 and 0, lowest point has y-coordinate -48

Exer. 35–36: Find the maximum vertical distance d between the parabola and the line for the green region.

35

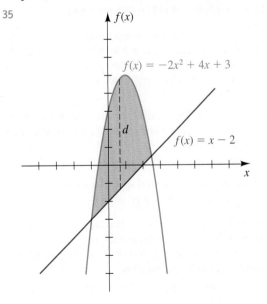

$f(x) = -2x^2 + 4x + 3$

d

$f(x) = x - 2$

36

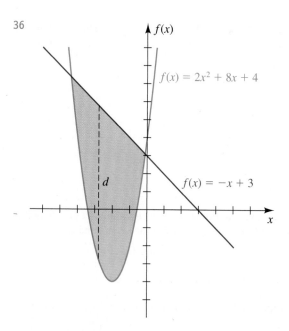

$f(x)$

$f(x) = 2x^2 + 8x + 4$

$f(x) = -x + 3$

d

x

Exer. 37–38: Ozone occurs at all levels of Earth's atmosphere. The density of ozone varies both seasonally and latitudinally. At Edmonton, Canada, the density $D(h)$ of ozone (in 10^{-3} cm/km) for altitudes h between 20 kilometers and 35 kilometers was determined experimentally. For each $D(h)$ and season, approximate the altitude at which the density of ozone is greatest.

37 $D(h) = -0.058h^2 + 2.867h - 24.239$ (autumn)

38 $D(h) = -0.078h^2 + 3.811h - 32.433$ (spring)

39 Infant growth rate The growth rate y (in pounds per month) of an infant is related to present weight x (in pounds) by the formula $y = cx(21 - x)$, where c is a positive constant and $0 < x < 21$. At what weight does the maximum growth rate occur?

40 Gasoline mileage The number of miles M that a certain automobile can travel on one gallon of gasoline at a speed of v mi/hr is given by

$$M = -\tfrac{1}{30}v^2 + \tfrac{5}{2}v \qquad \text{for } 0 < v < 70.$$

(a) Find the most economical speed for a trip.

(b) Find the largest value of M.

41 Height of a projectile An object is projected vertically upward from the top of a building with an initial velocity of 144 ft/sec. Its distance $s(t)$ in feet above the ground after t seconds is given by the equation

$$s(t) = -16t^2 + 144t + 100.$$

(a) Find its maximum distance above the ground.

(b) Find the height of the building.

42 Flight of a projectile An object is projected vertically upward with an initial velocity of v_0 ft/sec, and its distance $s(t)$ in feet above the ground after t seconds is given by the formula $s(t) = -16t^2 + v_0 t$.

(a) If the object hits the ground after 12 seconds, find its initial velocity v_0.

(b) Find its maximum distance above the ground.

43 Find two positive real numbers whose sum is 40 and whose product is a maximum.

44 Find two real numbers whose difference is 40 and whose product is a minimum.

45 Constructing cages One thousand feet of chain-link fence is to be used to construct six animal cages, as shown in the figure.

(a) Express the width y as a function of the length x.

(b) Express the total enclosed area A of the cages as a function of x.

(c) Find the dimensions that maximize the enclosed area.

Exercise 45

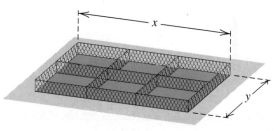

46 Fencing a field A farmer wishes to put a fence around a rectangular field and then divide the field into three rectangular plots by placing two fences parallel to one of the sides. If the farmer can afford only 1000 yards of fencing, what dimensions will give the maximum rectangular area?

47 Leaping animals Flights of leaping animals typically have parabolic paths. The figure on the next page illustrates a frog jump superimposed on a coordinate plane. The length of the leap is 9 feet, and the maximum height off the ground is 3 feet. Find a standard equation for the path of the frog.

Exercise 47

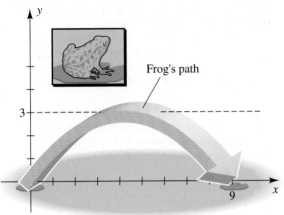

Frog's path

48 **The human cannonball** In the 1940s, the human cannonball stunt was performed regularly by Emmanuel Zacchini for The Ringling Brothers and Barnum & Bailey Circus. The tip of the cannon rose 15 feet off the ground, and the total horizontal distance traveled was 175 feet. When the cannon is aimed at an angle of 45°, an equation of the parabolic flight (see the figure) has the form $y = ax^2 + x + c$.

(a) Use the given information to find an equation of the flight.

(b) Find the maximum height attained by the human cannonball.

Exercise 48

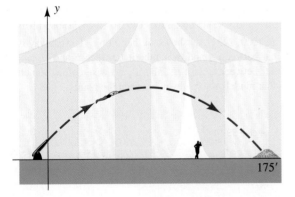

49 **Shape of a suspension bridge** One section of a suspension bridge has its weight uniformly distributed between twin towers that are 400 feet apart and rise 90 feet above the horizontal roadway (see the figure). A cable strung between the tops of the towers has the shape of a parabola, and its center point is 10 feet above the roadway. Suppose coordinate axes are introduced, as shown in the figure.

Exercise 49

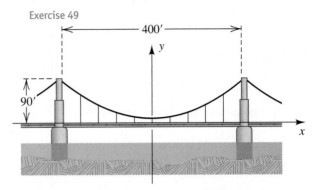

(a) Find an equation for the parabola.

(b) Nine equally spaced vertical cables are used to support the bridge (see the figure). Find the total length of these supports.

50 **Designing a highway** Traffic engineers are designing a stretch of highway that will connect a horizontal highway with one having a 20% grade (that is, slope $\frac{1}{5}$), as illustrated in the figure. The smooth transition is to take place over a horizontal distance of 800 feet, with a parabolic piece of highway used to connect points A and B. If the equation of the parabolic segment is of the form $y = ax^2 + bx + c$, it can be shown that the slope of the tangent line at the point $P(x, y)$ on the parabola is given by $m = 2ax + b$.

(a) Find an equation of the parabola that has a tangent line of slope 0 at A and $\frac{1}{5}$ at B.

(b) Find the coordinates of B.

Exercise 50

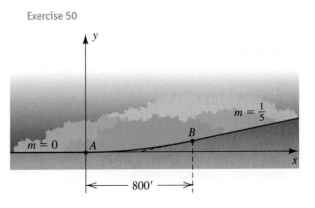

51 **Parabolic doorway** A doorway has the shape of a parabolic arch and is 9 feet high at the center and 6 feet wide at the base. If a rectangular box 8 feet high must fit through the doorway, what is the maximum width the box can have?

52 **Path of a baseball** Assume a baseball hit at home plate follows a parabolic path having equation $y = -\dfrac{3}{4000}x^2 + \dfrac{3}{10}x + 3$, where x and y are both measured in feet.

(a) Find the maximum height of the baseball.

(b) Does the baseball clear an 8-foot fence that is 385 feet from home plate?

53 **Quantity discount** A company sells running shoes to dealers at a rate of $40 per pair if fewer than 50 pairs are ordered. If a dealer orders 50 or more pairs (up to 600), the price per pair is reduced at a rate of 4 cents times the number ordered. What size order will produce the maximum amount of money for the company?

54 **Group discount** A travel agency offers group tours at a rate of $60 per person for the first 30 participants. For larger groups—up to 90—each person receives a $0.50 discount for every participant in excess of 30. For example, if 31 people participate, then the cost per person is $59.50. Determine the size of the group that will produce the maximum amount of money for the agency.

55 **Cable TV fee** A cable television firm presently serves 8000 households and charges $50 per month. A marketing survey indicates that each decrease of $5 in the monthly charge will result in 1000 new customers. Let $R(x)$ denote the total monthly revenue when the monthly charge is x dollars.

(a) Determine the revenue function R.

(b) Sketch the graph of R and find the value of x that results in maximum monthly revenue.

56 **Apartment rentals** A real estate company owns 218 efficiency apartments, which are fully occupied when the rent is $940 per month. The company estimates that for each $25 increase in rent, 5 apartments will become unoccupied. What rent should be charged so that the company will receive the maximum monthly income?

57 **Crest vertical curves** When engineers plan highways, they must design hills so as to ensure proper vision for drivers. Hills are referred to as *crest vertical curves*. Crest vertical curves change the slope of a highway. Engineers use a parabolic shape for a highway hill, with the vertex located at the top of the crest. Two roadways with different slopes are to be connected with a parabolic crest curve. The highway passes through the points $A(-800, -48)$, $B(-500, 0)$, $C(0, 40)$, $D(500, 0)$, and $E(800, -48)$, as shown in the figure. The roadway is linear between A and B, parabolic between B and D, and then linear between D and E. Find a piecewise-defined function f that models the roadway between the points A and E.

Exercise 57

58 **Sag vertical curves** Refer to Exercise 57. Valleys or dips in highways are referred to as *sag vertical curves*. Sag vertical curves are also modeled using parabolas. Two roadways with different grades meeting at a sag curve need to be connected. The highway passes through the points $A\left(-500, 243\frac{1}{3}\right)$, $B(0, 110)$, $C(750, 10)$, $D(1500, 110)$, and $E\left(2000, 243\frac{1}{3}\right)$, as shown in the figure. The roadway is linear between A and B, parabolic between B and D, and linear between D and E. Find a piecewise-defined function f that models the roadway between the points A and E.

Exercise 58

3.7

Operations on Functions

Functions are often defined using sums, differences, products, and quotients of various expressions. For example, if

$$h(x) = x^2 + \sqrt{5x + 1},$$

we may regard $h(x)$ as a sum of values of the functions f and g given by

$$f(x) = x^2 \qquad \text{and} \qquad g(x) = \sqrt{5x + 1}.$$

We call h the *sum* of f and g and denote it by $f + g$. Thus,

$$h(x) = (f + g)(x) = x^2 + \sqrt{5x + 1}.$$

In general, if f and g are *any* functions, we use the terminology and notation given in the following chart.

While it is true that

$$(f + g)(x) = f(x) + g(x),$$

remember that, in general,

$$f(a + b) \quad \neq \quad f(a) + f(b).$$

Sum, Difference, Product, and Quotient of Functions

Terminology	Function value
sum $f + g$	$(f + g)(x) = f(x) + g(x)$
difference $f - g$	$(f - g)(x) = f(x) - g(x)$
product fg	$(fg)(x) = f(x)g(x)$
quotient $\dfrac{f}{g}$	$\left(\dfrac{f}{g}\right)(x) = \dfrac{f(x)}{g(x)}, \; g(x) \neq 0$

The domains of $f + g$, $f - g$, and fg are the intersection I of the domains of f and g—that is, the numbers that are *common* to both domains. The domain of f/g is the subset of I consisting of all x in I such that $g(x) \neq 0$.

EXAMPLE 1 Finding function values of $f + g$, $f - g$, fg, and f/g

If $f(x) = 3x - 2$ and $g(x) = x^3$, find $(f + g)(2)$, $(f - g)(2)$, $(fg)(2)$, and $(f/g)(2)$.

SOLUTION   Since $f(2) = 3(2) - 2 = 4$ and $g(2) = 2^3 = 8$, we have

$$(f + g)(2) = f(2) + g(2) = 4 + 8 = 12$$
$$(f - g)(2) = f(2) - g(2) = 4 - 8 = -4$$
$$(fg)(2) = f(2)g(2) = (4)(8) = 32$$
$$\left(\frac{f}{g}\right)(2) = \frac{f(2)}{g(2)} = \frac{4}{8} = \frac{1}{2}.$$

EXAMPLE 2 Finding $(f + g)(x)$, $(f - g)(x)$, $(fg)(x)$, and $(f/g)(x)$

If $f(x) = \sqrt{4 - x^2}$ and $g(x) = 3x + 1$, find $(f + g)(x)$, $(f - g)(x)$, $(fg)(x)$, and $(f/g)(x)$, and state the domains of the respective functions.

SOLUTION   The domain of f is the closed interval $[-2, 2]$, and the domain of g is $\mathbb{R}$. The intersection of these domains is $[-2, 2]$, which is the domain of $f + g, f - g$, and fg. For the domain of f/g, we exclude each number x in $[-2, 2]$ such that $g(x) = 3x + 1 = 0$ $\left(\text{namely, } x = -\frac{1}{3}\right)$. Thus, we have the following:

$$(f + g)(x) = \sqrt{4 - x^2} + (3x + 1), \qquad -2 \le x \le 2$$

$$(f - g)(x) = \sqrt{4 - x^2} - (3x + 1), \qquad -2 \le x \le 2$$

$$(fg)(x) = \sqrt{4 - x^2}\,(3x + 1), \qquad\qquad -2 \le x \le 2$$

$$\left(\frac{f}{g}\right)(x) = \frac{\sqrt{4 - x^2}}{3x + 1}, \qquad\qquad -2 \le x \le 2 \text{ and } x \ne -\frac{1}{3}$$

A function f is a **polynomial function** if $f(x)$ is a polynomial—that is, if

$$f(x) = a_n x^n + a_{n-1} x^{n-1} + \cdots + a_1 x + a_0,$$

where the coefficients $a_0, a_1, \ldots, a_n$ are real numbers and the exponents are nonnegative integers. A polynomial function may be regarded as a sum of functions whose values are of the form cx^k, where c is a real number and k is a nonnegative integer. Note that the quadratic functions considered in the previous section are polynomial functions.

An **algebraic function** is a function that can be expressed in terms of finite sums, differences, products, quotients, or roots of polynomial functions.

ILLUSTRATION   **Algebraic Function**

■ $f(x) = 5x^4 - 2\sqrt[3]{x} + \dfrac{x(x^2 + 5)}{\sqrt{x^3 + \sqrt{x}}}$

Functions that are not algebraic are **transcendental.** The exponential and logarithmic functions considered in Chapter 5 are examples of transcendental functions.

In the remainder of this section we shall discuss how two functions f and g may be used to obtain the *composite functions* $f \circ g$ and $g \circ f$ (read "f circle g" and "g circle f," respectively). Functions of this type are very important in calculus. The function $f \circ g$ is defined as follows.

Definition of Composite Function	The **composite function** $f \circ g$ of two functions f and g is defined by $$(f \circ g)(x) = f(g(x)).$$ The domain of $f \circ g$ is the set of all x in the domain of g such that $g(x)$ is in the domain of f.

*A number x is in the domain of $(f \circ g)(x)$ if and only if **both** g(x) **and** f(g(x)) are defined.*

Figure 1

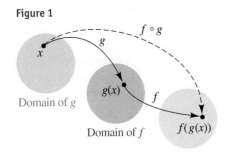

Domain of g

$g(x)$

Domain of f

$f(g(x))$

$f \circ g$

g

x

f

Figure 1 is a schematic diagram that illustrates relationships among f, g, and $f \circ g$. Note that for x in the domain of g, *first we find* $g(x)$ (which must be in the domain of f) and then, *second, we find* $f(g(x))$.

For the composite function $g \circ f$, we reverse this order, first finding $f(x)$ and second finding $g(f(x))$. The domain of $g \circ f$ is the set of all x in the domain of f such that $f(x)$ is in the domain of g.

Since the notation $g(x)$ is read "g of x," we sometimes say that g *is a function of x.* For the composite function $f \circ g$, the notation $f(g(x))$ is read "f of g of x," and we could regard f as a function of $g(x)$. In this sense, *a composite function is a function of a function* or, more precisely, a function of another function's values.

EXAMPLE 3 Finding composite functions

Let $f(x) = x^2 - 1$ and $g(x) = 3x + 5$.

(a) Find $(f \circ g)(x)$ and the domain of $f \circ g$.

(b) Find $(g \circ f)(x)$ and the domain of $g \circ f$.

(c) Find $f(g(2))$ in two different ways: first using the functions f and g separately and second using the composite function $f \circ g$.

SOLUTION

(a) $(f \circ g)(x) = f(g(x))$ definition of $f \circ g$

$\qquad\qquad\quad = f(3x + 5)$ definition of g

$\qquad\qquad\quad = (3x + 5)^2 - 1$ definition of f

$\qquad\qquad\quad = 9x^2 + 30x + 24$ simplify

The domain of both f and g is $\mathbb{R}$. Since for each x in $\mathbb{R}$ (the domain of g), the function value $g(x)$ is in $\mathbb{R}$ (the domain of f), the domain of $f \circ g$ is also $\mathbb{R}$. Note that *both* $g(x)$ *and* $f(g(x))$ are defined for all real numbers.

(b) $(g \circ f)(x) = g(f(x))$ definition of $g \circ f$

$\qquad\qquad\quad = g(x^2 - 1)$ definition of f

$\qquad\qquad\quad = 3(x^2 - 1) + 5$ definition of g

$\qquad\qquad\quad = 3x^2 + 2$ simplify

Since for each x in $\mathbb{R}$ (the domain of f), the function value $f(x)$ is in $\mathbb{R}$ (the domain of g), the domain of $g \circ f$ is $\mathbb{R}$. Note that *both* $f(x)$ *and* $g(f(x))$ are defined for all real numbers.

(c) To find $f(g(2))$ using $f(x) = x^2 - 1$ and $g(x) = 3x + 5$ separately, we may proceed as follows:

$$g(2) = 3(2) + 5 = 11$$
$$f(g(2)) = f(11) = 11^2 - 1 = 120$$

To find $f(g(2))$ using $f \circ g$, we refer to part (a), where we found

$$(f \circ g)(x) = f(g(x)) = 9x^2 + 30x + 24.$$

(continued)

Hence,

$$f(g(2)) = 9(2)^2 + 30(2) + 24$$
$$= 36 + 60 + 24 = 120.$$

Note that in Example 3, $f(g(x))$ and $g(f(x))$ are not always the same; that is, $f \circ g \neq g \circ f$.

If two functions f and g both have domain $\mathbb{R}$, then the domain of $f \circ g$ and $g \circ f$ is also $\mathbb{R}$. This was illustrated in Example 3. The next example shows that the domain of a composite function may differ from those of the two given functions.

EXAMPLE 4 Finding composite functions

Let $f(x) = x^2 - 16$ and $g(x) = \sqrt{x}$.

(a) Find $(f \circ g)(x)$ and the domain of $f \circ g$.

(b) Find $(g \circ f)(x)$ and the domain of $g \circ f$.

SOLUTION We first note that the domain of f is $\mathbb{R}$ and the domain of g is the set of all nonnegative real numbers—that is, the interval $[0, \infty)$. We may proceed as follows.

(a)
$$
\begin{aligned}
(f \circ g)(x) &= f(g(x)) &&\text{definition of } f \circ g\\
&= f\left(\sqrt{x}\right) &&\text{definition of } g\\
&= \left(\sqrt{x}\right)^2 - 16 &&\text{definition of } f\\
&= x - 16 &&\text{simplify}
\end{aligned}
$$

If we consider only the final expression, $x - 16$, we might be led to believe that the domain of $f \circ g$ is $\mathbb{R}$, since $x - 16$ is defined for every real number x. However, this is not the case. By definition, the domain of $f \circ g$ is the set of all x in $[0, \infty)$ (the domain of g) such that $g(x)$ is in $\mathbb{R}$ (the domain of f). Since $g(x) = \sqrt{x}$ is in $\mathbb{R}$ for every x in $[0, \infty)$, it follows that the domain of $f \circ g$ is $[0, \infty)$. Note that *both $g(x)$ and $f(g(x))$* are defined for x in $[0, \infty)$.

(b)
$$
\begin{aligned}
(g \circ f)(x) &= g(f(x)) &&\text{definition of } g \circ f\\
&= g(x^2 - 16) &&\text{definition of } f\\
&= \sqrt{x^2 - 16} &&\text{definition of } g
\end{aligned}
$$

By definition, the domain of $g \circ f$ is the set of all x in $\mathbb{R}$ (the domain of f) such that $f(x) = x^2 - 16$ is in $[0, \infty)$ (the domain of g). The statement "$x^2 - 16$ is in $[0, \infty)$" is equivalent to each of the inequalities

$$x^2 - 16 \geq 0, \qquad x^2 \geq 16, \qquad |x| \geq 4.$$

Thus, the domain of $g \circ f$ is the union $(-\infty, -4] \cup [4, \infty)$. Note that *both $f(x)$ and $g(f(x))$* are defined for x in $(-\infty, -4] \cup [4, \infty)$. Also note that this domain is different from the domains of both f and g.

The next example illustrates how special values of composite functions may sometimes be obtained from tables.

EXAMPLE 5 Finding composite function values from tables

Several values of two functions f and g are listed in the following tables.

x	1	2	3	4
$f(x)$	3	4	2	1

x	1	2	3	4
$g(x)$	4	1	3	2

Find $(f \circ g)(2)$, $(g \circ f)(2)$, $(f \circ f)(2)$, and $(g \circ g)(2)$.

SOLUTION Using the definition of composite function and referring to the tables above, we obtain

$$(f \circ g)(2) = f(g(2)) = f(1) = 3$$
$$(g \circ f)(2) = g(f(2)) = g(4) = 2$$
$$(f \circ f)(2) = f(f(2)) = f(4) = 1$$
$$(g \circ g)(2) = g(g(2)) = g(1) = 4.$$

In some applied problems it is necessary to express a quantity y as a function of time t. The following example illustrates that it is often easier to introduce a third variable x, express x as a function of t (that is, $x = g(t)$), express y as a function of x (that is, $y = f(x)$), and finally form the composite function given by $y = f(x) = f(g(t))$.

EXAMPLE 6 Using a composite function
to find the volume of a balloon

A meteorologist is inflating a spherical balloon with helium gas. If the radius of the balloon is changing at a rate of 1.5 cm/sec, express the volume V of the balloon as a function of time t (in seconds).

SOLUTION Let x denote the radius of the balloon. If we assume that the radius is 0 initially, then after t seconds

$$x = 1.5t. \quad \text{radius of balloon after } t \text{ seconds}$$

To illustrate, after 1 second, the radius is 1.5 centimeters; after 2 seconds, it is 3.0 centimeters; after 3 seconds, it is 4.5 centimeters; and so on.

Next we write

$$V = \tfrac{4}{3}\pi x^3. \quad \text{volume of a sphere of radius } x$$

This gives us a composite function relationship in which V is a function of x, and x is a function of t. By substitution, we obtain

$$V = \tfrac{4}{3}\pi x^3 = \tfrac{4}{3}\pi(1.5t)^3 = \tfrac{4}{3}\pi\left(\tfrac{3}{2}t\right)^3 = \tfrac{4}{3}\pi\left(\tfrac{27}{8}t^3\right).$$

Simplifying, we obtain the following formula for V as a function of t:

$$V(t) = \tfrac{9}{2}\pi t^3$$

If f and g are functions such that

$$y = f(u) \qquad \text{and} \qquad u = g(x),$$

then substituting for u in $y = f(u)$ yields

$$y = f(g(x)).$$

For certain problems in calculus we *reverse* this procedure; that is, given $y = h(x)$ for some function h, we find a *composite function form* $y = f(u)$ and $u = g(x)$ such that $h(x) = f(g(x))$.

EXAMPLE 7 Finding a composite function form

Express $y = (2x + 5)^8$ as a composite function form.

SOLUTION Suppose, for a real number x, we wanted to evaluate the expression $(2x + 5)^8$ by using a calculator. We would first calculate the value of $2x + 5$ and then raise the result to the eighth power. This suggests that we let

$$u = 2x + 5 \qquad \text{and} \qquad y = u^8,$$

which is a composite function form for $y = (2x + 5)^8$.

The method used in the preceding example can be extended to other functions. In general, suppose we are given $y = h(x)$. To choose the *inside* expression $u = g(x)$ in a composite function form, ask the following question: If a calculator were being used, which part of the expression $h(x)$ would be evaluated first? This often leads to a suitable choice for $u = g(x)$. After choosing u, refer to $h(x)$ to determine $y = f(u)$. The following illustration contains typical problems.

ILLUSTRATION Composite Function Forms

Function value	**Choice for** $u = g(x)$	**Choice for** $y = f(u)$
■ $\quad y = (x^3 - 5x + 1)^4$	$u = x^3 - 5x + 1$	$y = u^4$
■ $\quad y = \sqrt{x^2 - 4}$	$u = x^2 - 4$	$y = \sqrt{u}$
■ $\quad y = \dfrac{2}{3x + 7}$	$u = 3x + 7$	$y = \dfrac{2}{u}$

The composite function form is never unique. For example, consider the first expression in the preceding illustration:

$$y = (x^3 - 5x + 1)^4$$

If n is any nonzero integer, we could choose

$$u = (x^3 - 5x + 1)^n \qquad \text{and} \qquad y = u^{4/n}.$$

Thus, there are an *unlimited* number of composite function forms. Generally, our goal is to choose a form such that the expression for y is simple, as we did in the illustration.

3.7 Exercises

Exer. 1–2: Find
(a) $(f + g)(3)$ (b) $(f - g)(3)$
(c) $(fg)(3)$ (d) $(f/g)(3)$

1 $f(x) = x + 3$, $g(x) = x^2$

2 $f(x) = -x^2$, $g(x) = 2x - 1$

Exer. 3–8: Find
(a) $(f + g)(x)$, $(f - g)(x)$, $(fg)(x)$, and $(f/g)(x)$
(b) the domain of $f + g$, $f - g$, and fg
(c) the domain of f/g

3 $f(x) = x^2 + 2$, $g(x) = 2x^2 - 1$

4 $f(x) = x^2 + x$, $g(x) = x^2 - 3$

5 $f(x) = \sqrt{x + 5}$, $g(x) = \sqrt{x + 5}$

6 $f(x) = \sqrt{3 - 2x}$, $g(x) = \sqrt{x + 4}$

7 $f(x) = \dfrac{2x}{x - 4}$, $g(x) = \dfrac{x}{x + 5}$

8 $f(x) = \dfrac{x}{x - 2}$, $g(x) = \dfrac{3x}{x + 4}$

Exer. 9–10: Find
(a) $(f \circ g)(x)$ (b) $(g \circ f)(x)$
(c) $(f \circ f)(x)$ (d) $(g \circ g)(x)$

9 $f(x) = 2x - 1$, $g(x) = -x^2$

10 $f(x) = 3x^2$, $g(x) = x - 1$

Exer. 11–20: Find
(a) $(f \circ g)(x)$ (b) $(g \circ f)(x)$
(c) $f(g(-2))$ (d) $g(f(3))$

11 $f(x) = 2x - 5$, $g(x) = 3x + 7$

12 $f(x) = 5x + 2$, $g(x) = 6x - 1$

13 $f(x) = 3x^2 + 4$, $g(x) = 5x$

14 $f(x) = 3x - 1$, $g(x) = 4x^2$

15 $f(x) = 2x^2 + 3x - 4$, $g(x) = 2x - 1$

16 $f(x) = 5x - 7$, $g(x) = 3x^2 - x + 2$

17 $f(x) = 4x$, $g(x) = 2x^3 - 5x$

18 $f(x) = x^3 + 2x^2$, $g(x) = 3x$

19 $f(x) = |x|$, $g(x) = -7$

20 $f(x) = 5$, $g(x) = x^2$

Exer. 21–34: Find (a) $(f \circ g)(x)$ and the domain of $f \circ g$ and (b) $(g \circ f)(x)$ and the domain of $g \circ f$.

21 $f(x) = x^2 - 3x$, $g(x) = \sqrt{x + 2}$

22 $f(x) = \sqrt{x - 15}$, $g(x) = x^2 + 2x$

23 $f(x) = x^2 - 4$, $g(x) = \sqrt{3x}$

24 $f(x) = -x^2 + 1$, $g(x) = \sqrt{x}$

25 $f(x) = \sqrt{x - 2}$, $g(x) = \sqrt{x + 5}$

26 $f(x) = \sqrt{3 - x}$, $g(x) = \sqrt{x + 2}$

27 $f(x) = \sqrt{3 - x}$, $g(x) = \sqrt{x^2 - 16}$

28 $f(x) = x^3 + 5$, $g(x) = \sqrt[3]{x - 5}$

29 $f(x) = \dfrac{3x + 5}{2}$, $g(x) = \dfrac{2x - 5}{3}$

30 $f(x) = \dfrac{1}{x - 1}$, $g(x) = x - 1$

31 $f(x) = x^2$, $g(x) = \dfrac{1}{x^3}$

32 $f(x) = \dfrac{x}{x - 2}$, $g(x) = \dfrac{3}{x}$

33 $f(x) = \dfrac{x - 1}{x - 2}$, $g(x) = \dfrac{x - 3}{x - 4}$

34 $f(x) = \dfrac{x + 2}{x - 1}$, $g(x) = \dfrac{x - 5}{x + 4}$

Exer. 35–36: Solve the equation $(f \circ g)(x) = 0$.

35 $f(x) = x^2 - 2$, $g(x) = x + 3$

36 $f(x) = x^2 - x - 2$, $g(x) = 2x - 1$

37 Several values of two functions f and g are listed in the following tables:

x	5	6	7	8	9
$f(x)$	8	7	6	5	4

x	5	6	7	8	9
$g(x)$	7	8	6	5	4

If possible, find

(a) $(f \circ g)(6)$ (b) $(g \circ f)(6)$ (c) $(f \circ f)(6)$

(d) $(g \circ g)(6)$ (e) $(f \circ g)(9)$

38 Several values of two functions T and S are listed in the following tables:

t	0	1	2	3	4
$T(t)$	2	3	1	0	5

x	0	1	2	3	4
$S(x)$	1	0	3	2	5

If possible, find

(a) $(T \circ S)(1)$ (b) $(S \circ T)(1)$ (c) $(T \circ T)(1)$

(d) $(S \circ S)(1)$ (e) $(T \circ S)(4)$

39 If $D(t) = \sqrt{400 + t^2}$ and $R(x) = 20x$, find $(D \circ R)(x)$.

40 If $S(r) = 4\pi r^2$ and $D(t) = 2t + 5$, find $(S \circ D)(t)$.

41 If f is an odd function and g is an even function, is fg even, odd, or neither even nor odd?

42 There is one function with domain $\mathbb{R}$ that is both even and odd. Find that function.

43 Payroll functions Let the social security tax function SSTAX be defined as SSTAX$(x) = 0.0765x$, where $x \geq 0$ is the weekly income. Let ROUND2 be the function that rounds a number to two decimal places. Find the value of (ROUND2 $\circ$ SSTAX)(525).

44 Computer science functions Let the function CHR be defined by CHR(65) = "A", CHR(66) = "B", ..., CHR(90) = "Z". Then let the function ORD be defined by ORD("A") = 65, ORD("B") = 66, ..., ORD("Z") = 90. Find

(a) (CHR $\circ$ ORD)("C")   (b) CHR(ORD("A") + 3)

45 Spreading fire A fire has started in a dry open field and is spreading in the form of a circle. If the radius of this circle increases at the rate of 6 ft/min, express the total fire area A as a function of time t (in minutes).

46 Dimensions of a balloon A spherical balloon is being inflated at a rate of $\frac{9}{2}\pi$ ft^3/min. Express its radius r as a function of time t (in minutes), assuming that $r = 0$ when $t = 0$.

47 Dimensions of a sand pile The volume of a conical pile of sand is increasing at a rate of 243π ft^3/min, and the height of the pile always equals the radius r of the base. Express r as a function of time t (in minutes), assuming that $r = 0$ when $t = 0$.

48 Diagonal of a cube The diagonal d of a cube is the distance between two opposite vertices. Express d as a function of the edge x of the cube. (*Hint:* First express the diagonal y of a face as a function of x.)

49 Altitude of a balloon A hot-air balloon rises vertically from ground level as a rope attached to the base of the balloon is released at the rate of 5 ft/sec (see the figure). The pulley that releases the rope is 20 feet from a platform where passengers board the balloon. Express the altitude h of the balloon as a function of time t.

Exercise 49

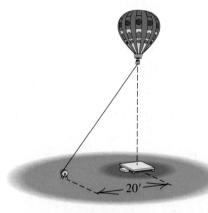

50 Tightrope walker Refer to Exercise 76 of Section 3.4. Starting at the lowest point, the tightrope walker moves up the rope at a steady rate of 2 ft/sec. If the rope is attached 30 feet up the pole, express the height h of the walker above the ground as a function of time t. (*Hint:* Let d denote the total distance traveled along the wire. First express d as a function of t, and then h as a function of d.)

51 **Airplane take-off** Refer to Exercise 77 of Section 3.4. When the airplane is 500 feet down the runway, it has reached a speed of 150 ft/sec (or about 102 mi/hr), which it will maintain until take-off. Express the distance d of the plane from the control tower as a function of time t (in seconds). (*Hint:* In the figure, first write x as a function of t.)

52 **Cable corrosion** A 100-foot-long cable of diameter 4 inches is submerged in seawater. Because of corrosion, the surface area of the cable decreases at the rate of 750 in^2 per year. Express the diameter d of the cable as a function of time t (in years). (Disregard corrosion at the ends of the cable.)

Exer. 53–60: Find a composite function form for y.

53 $y = (x^2 + 3x)^{1/3}$

54 $y = \sqrt[4]{x^4 - 16}$

55 $y = \dfrac{1}{(x - 3)^4}$

56 $y = 4 + \sqrt{x^2 + 1}$

57 $y = (x^4 - 2x^2 + 5)^5$

58 $y = \dfrac{1}{(x^2 + 3x - 5)^3}$

59 $y = \dfrac{\sqrt{x + 4} - 2}{\sqrt{x + 4} + 2}$

60 $y = \dfrac{\sqrt[3]{x}}{1 + \sqrt[3]{x}}$

61 If $f(x) = \sqrt{x} - 1$ and $g(x) = x^3 + 1$, approximate $(f \circ g)(0.0001)$. In order to avoid calculating a zero value for $(f \circ g)(0.0001)$, rewrite the formula for $f \circ g$ as

$$\frac{x^3}{\sqrt{x^3 + 1} + 1}.$$

62 If $f(x) = \dfrac{x^3}{x^2 + x + 2}$ and $g(x) = \left(\sqrt{3x} - x^3\right)^{3/2}$, approximate

$$\frac{(f + g)(1.12) - (f/g)(1.12)}{[(f \circ f)(5.2)]^2}.$$

CHAPTER 3 REVIEW EXERCISES

1 Describe the set of all points (x, y) in a coordinate plane such that $y/x < 0$.

2 Show that the triangle with vertices $A(3, 1)$, $B(-5, -3)$, and $C(4, -1)$ is a right triangle, and find its area.

3 Given $P(-5, 9)$ and $Q(-8, -7)$, find

(a) the distance $d(P, Q)$

(b) the midpoint of the segment PQ

(c) a point R such that Q is the midpoint of PR

4 Find all points on the y-axis that are a distance 13 from $P(12, 6)$.

5 For what values of a is the distance between $P(a, 1)$ and $Q(-2, a)$ less than 3?

6 Find an equation of the circle that has center $C(7, -4)$ and passes through $P(-3, 3)$.

7 Find an equation of the circle that has endpoints of a diameter $A(8, 10)$ and $B(-2, -14)$.

8 Find an equation for the left half of the circle given by $(x + 2)^2 + y^2 = 9$.

9 Find the slope of the line through $C(11, -5)$ and $D(-8, 6)$.

10 Show that $A(-3, 1)$, $B(1, -1)$, $C(4, 1)$, and $D(3, 5)$ are vertices of a trapezoid.

11 Find an equation of the line through $A\left(\frac{1}{2}, -\frac{1}{3}\right)$ that is

(a) parallel to the line $6x + 2y + 5 = 0$

(b) perpendicular to the line $6x + 2y + 5 = 0$

12 Express $8x + 3y - 24 = 0$ in slope-intercept form.

13 Find an equation of the circle that has center $C(-5, -1)$ and is tangent to the line $x = 4$.

14 Find an equation of the line that has x-intercept -3 and passes through the center of the circle that has equation $x^2 + y^2 - 4x + 10y + 26 = 0$.

15 Find a general form of an equation of the line through $P(4, -3)$ with slope 5.

16 Given $A(-1, 2)$ and $B(3, -4)$, find a general form of an equation for the perpendicular bisector of segment AB.

Exer. 17–18: Find the center and radius of the circle with the given equation.

17 $x^2 + y^2 - 12y + 31 = 0$

18 $4x^2 + 4y^2 + 24x - 16y + 39 = 0$

19 If $f(x) = \dfrac{x}{\sqrt{x+3}}$, find

    (a) $f(1)$ (b) $f(-1)$ (c) $f(0)$ (d) $f(-x)$

    (e) $-f(x)$ (f) $f(x^2)$ (g) $[f(x)]^2$

Exer. 20–21: Find *the sign* of $f(4)$ without actually finding $f(4)$.

20 $f(x) = \dfrac{-32(x^2 - 4)}{(9 - x^2)^{5/3}}$

21 $f(x) = \dfrac{-2(x^2 - 20)(5 - x)}{(6 - x^2)^{4/3}}$

22 Find the domain and range of f if

    (a) $f(x) = \sqrt{3x - 4}$ (b) $f(x) = \dfrac{1}{(x + 3)^2}$

Exer. 23–24: Find $\dfrac{f(a + h) - f(a)}{h}$ if $h \neq 0$.

23 $f(x) = -x^2 + x + 5$

24 $f(x) = \dfrac{1}{x + 2}$

25 Find a linear function f such that $f(1) = 2$ and $f(3) = 7$.

26 Determine whether f is even, odd, or neither even nor odd.

    (a) $f(x) = \sqrt[3]{x^3 + 4x}$ (b) $f(x) = \sqrt[3]{3x^2 - x^3}$

    (c) $f(x) = \sqrt[3]{x^4 + 3x^2 + 5}$

Exer. 27–40: Sketch the graph of the equation, and label the x- and y-intercepts.

27 $x + 5 = 0$ **28** $2y - 7 = 0$

29 $2y + 5x - 8 = 0$ **30** $x = 3y + 4$

31 $9y + 2x^2 = 0$ **32** $3x - 7y^2 = 0$

33 $y = \sqrt{1 - x}$ **34** $y = (x - 1)^3$

35 $y^2 = 16 - x^2$

36 $x^2 + y^2 + 4x - 16y + 64 = 0$

37 $x^2 + y^2 - 8x = 0$ **38** $x = -\sqrt{9 - y^2}$

39 $y = (x - 3)^2 - 2$ **40** $y = -x^2 - 2x + 3$

41 Find the center of the small circle.

Exercise 41

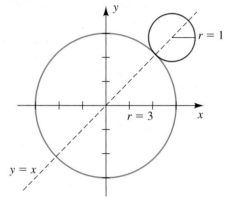

42 Explain how the graph of $y = -f(x - 2)$ compares to the graph of $y = f(x)$.

Exer. 43–52: (a) Sketch the graph of f. (b) Find the domain D and range R of f. (c) Find the intervals on which f is increasing, is decreasing, or is constant.

43 $f(x) = \dfrac{1 - 3x}{2}$ **44** $f(x) = 1000$

45 $f(x) = |x + 3|$ **46** $f(x) = -\sqrt{10 - x^2}$

47 $f(x) = 1 - \sqrt{x + 1}$ **48** $f(x) = \sqrt{2 - x}$

49 $f(x) = 9 - x^2$ **50** $f(x) = x^2 + 6x + 16$

51 $f(x) = \begin{cases} x^2 & \text{if } x < 0 \\ 3x & \text{if } 0 \leq x < 2 \\ 6 & \text{if } x \geq 2 \end{cases}$ **52** $f(x) = 1 + 2[\![x]\!]$

53 Sketch the graphs of the following equations, making use of shifting, stretching, or reflecting:

    (a) $y = \sqrt{x}$ (b) $y = \sqrt{x + 4}$

    (c) $y = \sqrt{x} + 4$ (d) $y = 4\sqrt{x}$

    (e) $y = \frac{1}{4}\sqrt{x}$ (f) $y = -\sqrt{x}$

54 The graph of a function f with domain $[-3, 3]$ is shown in the figure. Sketch the graph of the given equation.

(a) $y = f(x - 2)$ (b) $y = f(x) - 2$

(c) $y = f(-x)$ (d) $y = f(2x)$

(e) $y = f(\frac{1}{2}x)$ (f) $y = |f(x)|$

(g) $y = f(|x|)$

Exercise 54

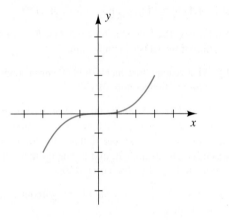

56

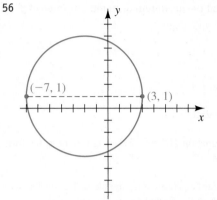

57

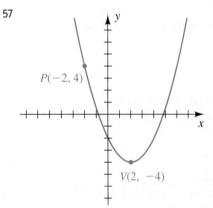

Exer. 55–58: Find an equation for the graph shown in the figure.

55

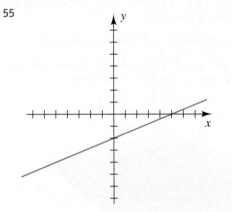

58

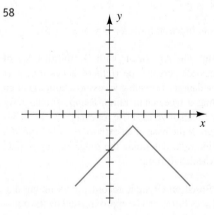

Exer. 59–62: Find the maximum or minimum value of $f(x)$.

59 $f(x) = 5x^2 + 30x + 49$

60 $f(x) = -3x^2 + 30x - 82$

61 $f(x) = -12(x + 1)^2 - 37$

62 $f(x) = 3(x + 2)(x - 10)$

63 Express the function $f(x) = -2x^2 + 12x - 14$ in the form $a(x - h)^2 + k$.

64 Find the standard equation of a parabola with a vertical axis that has vertex $V(3, -2)$ and passes through $(5, 4)$.

65 If $f(x) = \sqrt{4 - x^2}$ and $g(x) = \sqrt{x}$, find the domain of

 (a) fg (b) f/g

66 If $f(x) = 8x - 1$ and $g(x) = \sqrt{x - 2}$, find

 (a) $(f \circ g)(2)$ (b) $(g \circ f)(2)$

Exer. 67–68: Find (a) $(f \circ g)(x)$ and (b) $(g \circ f)(x)$.

67 $f(x) = 2x^2 - 5x + 1,\quad g(x) = 3x + 2$

68 $f(x) = \sqrt{3x + 2},\qquad g(x) = 1/x^2$

Exer. 69–70: Find (a) $(f \circ g)(x)$ and the domain of $f \circ g$ and (b) $(g \circ f)(x)$ and the domain of $g \circ f$.

69 $f(x) = \sqrt{25 - x^2},\quad g(x) = \sqrt{x - 3}$

70 $f(x) = \dfrac{x}{3x + 2},\qquad g(x) = \dfrac{2}{x}$

71 Find a composite function form for $y = \sqrt[3]{x^2 - 5x}$.

72 **Wheelchair ramp** The Americans with Disabilities Act of 1990 guarantees all persons the right of accessibility of public accommodations. Providing access to a building often involves building a wheelchair ramp. Ramps should have approximately 1 inch of vertical rise for every 12–20 inches of horizontal run. If the base of an exterior door is located 3 feet above a sidewalk, determine the range of appropriate lengths for a wheelchair ramp.

73 **Discus throw** Based on Olympic records, the winning distance for the discus throw can be approximated by the equation $d = 181 + 1.065t$, where d is in feet and $t = 0$ corresponds to the year 1948.

 (a) Predict the winning distance for the Summer Olympics in the year 2016.

 (b) Estimate the Olympic year in which the winning distance will be 265 feet.

74 **House appreciation** Six years ago a house was purchased for $179,000. This year it was appraised at $215,000. Assume that the value V of the house after its purchase is a linear function of time t (in years).

 (a) Express V in terms of t.

 (b) How many years after the purchase date was the house worth $193,000?

75 **Temperature scales** The freezing point of water is 0°C, or 32°F, and the boiling point is 100°C, or 212°F.

 (a) Express the Fahrenheit temperature F as a linear function of the Celsius temperature C.

 (b) What temperature increase in °F corresponds to an increase in temperature of 1°C?

76 **Gasoline mileage** Suppose the cost of driving an automobile is a linear function of the number x of miles driven and that gasoline costs $3 per gallon. A certain automobile presently gets 20 mi/gal, and a tune-up that will improve gasoline mileage by 10% costs $120.

 (a) Express the cost C_1 of driving without a tune-up in terms of x.

 (b) Express the cost C_2 of driving with a tune-up in terms of x.

 (c) How many miles must the automobile be driven after a tune-up to make the cost of the tune-up worthwhile?

77 **Dimensions of a pen** A pen consists of five congruent rectangles, as shown in the figure.

 (a) Express the length y as a function of the length x.

 (b) If the sides cost $10 per running foot, express the cost C of the pen as a function of the length x.

Exercise 77

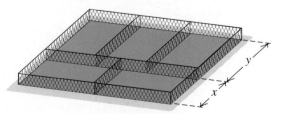

78 **Distance between cars** At noon, car A is 10 feet to the right and 20 feet ahead of car B, as shown in the figure. If car A continues at 88 ft/sec (or 60 mi/hr) while car B continues at 66 ft/sec (or 45 mi/hr), express the distance d between the cars as a function of t, where t denotes the number of seconds after noon.

Exercise 78

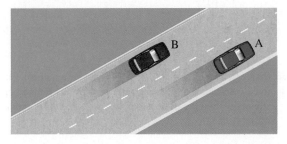

79 **Constructing a storage shelter** An open rectangular storage shelter, consisting of two 4-foot-wide vertical sides and a flat roof, is to be attached to an existing structure, as illustrated in the figure. The flat roof is made of tin and costs $5 per square foot, and the two sides are made of plywood costing $2 per square foot.

(a) If $400 is available for construction, express the length y as a function of the height x.

(b) Express the volume V inside the shelter as a function of x.

Exercise 79

80 **Constructing a cylindrical container** A company plans to manufacture a container having the shape of a right circular cylinder, open at the top, and having a capacity of 24π in³. If the cost of the material for the bottom is $0.30/in² and that for the curved sides is $0.10/in², express the total cost

C of the material as a function of the radius r of the base of the container.

81 **Filling a pool** A cross section of a rectangular pool of dimensions 80 feet by 40 feet is shown in the figure. The pool is being filled with water at a rate of 10 ft³/min.

Exercise 81

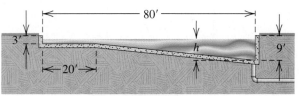

(a) Express the volume V of the water in the pool as a function of time t.

(b) Express V as a function of the depth h at the deep end for $0 \le h \le 6$ and then for $6 < h \le 9$.

(c) Express h as a function of t for $0 \le h \le 6$ and then for $6 < h \le 9$.

82 **Filtering water** Suppose 5 in³ of water is poured into a conical filter and subsequently drips into a cup, as shown in the figure. Let x denote the height of the water in the filter, and let y denote the height of the water in the cup.

(a) Express the radius r shown in the figure as a function of x. (*Hint:* Use similar triangles.)

(b) Express the height y of the water in the cup as a function of x. (*Hint:* What is the sum of the two volumes shown in the figure?)

Exercise 82

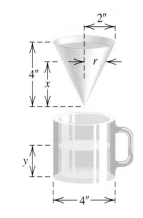

83 Frustum of a cone The shape of the first spacecraft in the Apollo program was a frustum of a right circular cone—a solid formed by truncating a cone by a plane parallel to its base. For the frustum shown in the figure, the radii a and b have already been determined.

Exercise 83

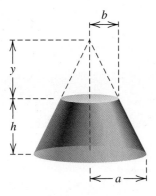

(a) Use similar triangles to express y as a function of h.

(b) Derive a formula for the volume of the frustum as a function of h.

(c) If $a = 6$ ft and $b = 3$ ft, for what value of h is the volume of the frustum 600 ft³?

84 Water usage rates A certain city charges $3.61 per 1000 gallons of water used up to 5000 gallons and $4.17 per 1000 gallons of water used for more than 5000 gallons. Find a piecewise-defined function B that specifies the total bill for water usage of x gallons.

85 Long jump record In 1991, Mike Powell of the United States set the world long jump record of 8.95 meters. Assume that the path of his flight was parabolic and that the highest point cleared was 1 meter. Find an equation for his path.

86 Wire rectangle A piece of wire 24 inches long is bent into the shape of a rectangle having width x and length y.

(a) Express y as a function of x.

(b) Express the area A of the rectangle as a function of x.

(c) Show that the area A is greatest if the rectangle is a square.

87 Distance between ships At 1:00 P.M. ship A is 30 miles due south of ship B and is sailing north at a rate of 15 mi/hr. If ship B is sailing west at a rate of 10 mi/hr, find the time at which the distance d between the ships is minimal (see the figure).

Exercise 87

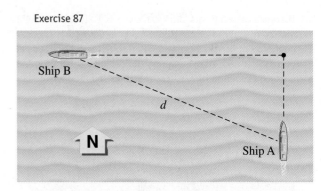

88 Dimensions of a race track The interior of a half-mile race track consists of a rectangle with semicircles at two opposite ends. Find the dimensions that will maximize the area of the rectangle.

89 Vertical leaps When a particular basketball player leaps straight up for a dunk, the player's distance $f(t)$ (in feet) off the floor after t seconds is given by the formula $f(t) = -\frac{1}{2}gt^2 + 16t$, where g is a gravitational constant.

(a) If $g = 32$, find the player's hang time—that is, the total number of seconds that the player is in the air.

(b) Find the player's vertical leap—that is, the maximum distance of the player's feet from the floor.

(c) On the moon, $g = \frac{32}{6}$. Rework parts (a) and (b) for the player on the moon.

90 Trajectory of a rocket A rocket is fired up a hillside, following a path given by $y = -0.016x^2 + 1.6x$. The hillside has slope $\frac{1}{5}$, as illustrated in the figure.

(a) Where does the rocket land?

(b) Find the maximum height of the rocket *above the ground.*

Exercise 90

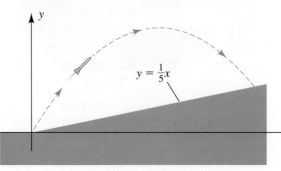

CHAPTER 3 DISCUSSION EXERCISES

1 Compare the graphs of $y = \sqrt[3]{x}$, $y = \sqrt{x}$, $y = x$, $y = x^2$, and $y = x^3$ on the interval $0 \leq x \leq 2$. Write a generalization based on what you find out about graphs of equations of the form $y = x^{p/q}$, where $x \geq 0$ and p and q are positive integers.

2 Write an expression for $g(x)$ if the graph of g is obtained from the graph of $f(x) = \frac{1}{2}x - 3$ by reflecting f about the

(a) x-axis   (b) y-axis

(c) line $y = 2$ (d) line $x = 3$

3 Consider the graph of $g(x) = \sqrt{f(x)}$, where f is given by $f(x) = ax^2 + bx + c$. Discuss the general shape of g, including its domain and range. Discuss the advantages and disadvantages of graphing g as a composition of the functions $h(x) = \sqrt{x}$ and $f(x)$. (*Hint:* You may want to use the following expressions for f: $x^2 - 2x - 8$, $-x^2 + 2x + 8$, $x^2 - 2x + 2$, $-x^2 + 2x - 2$.)

4 Simplify the difference quotient in Exercises 49 and 50 of Section 3.4 for an arbitrary quadratic function of the form $f(x) = ax^2 + bx + c$.

5 Refer to Example 5 in Section 3.4. Geometrically, what does the expression $2x + h + 6$ represent on the graph of f? What do you think it represents if $h = 0$?

6 The midpoint formula could be considered to be the "halfway" formula since it gives us the point that is $\frac{1}{2}$ of the distance from the point $P(x_1, y_1)$ to the point $Q(x_2, y_2)$. Develop an "m-nth way" formula that gives the point $R(x_3, y_3)$ that is m/n of the distance from P to Q (assume m and n are positive integers with $m < n$).

7 Consider the graphs of equations of the quadratic form $y = ax^2 + bx + c$ that have two x-intercepts. Let d denote the distance from the axis of the parabola to either of the x-intercepts, and let h denote the value of the y-coordinate of the vertex. Explore the relationship between d and h for several specific equations, and then develop a formula for this relationship.

8 Billing for service A common method of billing for service calls is to charge a flat fee plus an additional fee for each quarter-hour spent on the call. Create a function for a washer repair company that charges $40 plus $20 for each quarter-hour or portion thereof—for example, a 30-minute repair call would cost $80, while a 31-minute repair call would cost $100. The input to your function is any positive integer. (*Hint:* See Exercise 54(e) of Section 3.5.)

9 Density of the ozone layer The density D (in 10^{-3} cm/km) of the ozone layer at altitudes x between 3 and 15 kilometers during winter at Edmonton, Canada, was determined experimentally to be

$$D = 0.0833x^2 - 0.4996x + 3.5491.$$

Express x as a function of D.

10 Precipitation in Minneapolis The average monthly precipitation in inches in Minneapolis is listed in the table. Model these data with a piecewise function f that is first quadratic and then linear.

Month	Precipitation
Jan.	0.7
Feb.	0.8
Mar.	1.5
Apr.	1.9
May	3.2
June	4.0
July	3.3
Aug.	3.2
Sept.	2.4
Oct.	1.6
Nov.	1.4
Dec.	0.9

4

Polynomial and Rational Functions

Polynomial functions are the most basic functions in mathematics, because they are defined only in terms of addition, subtraction, and multiplication. In applications it is often necessary to sketch their graphs and to find (or approximate) their zeros. In the first part of this chapter we discuss results that are useful in obtaining this information. We then turn our attention to quotients of polynomial functions—that is, rational functions.

4.1

Polynomial Functions of Degree Greater Than 2

If f is a polynomial function with real coefficients of degree n, then

$$f(x) = a_n x^n + a_{n-1} x^{n-1} + \cdots + a_1 x + a_0,$$

with $a_n \neq 0$. The special cases listed in the following chart were previously discussed.

Degree of f	Form of $f(x)$	Graph of f (with y-intercept a_0)
0	$f(x) = a_0$	A horizontal line
1	$f(x) = a_1 x + a_0$	A line with slope a_1
2	$f(x) = a_2 x^2 + a_1 x + a_0$	A parabola with a vertical axis

Figure 1

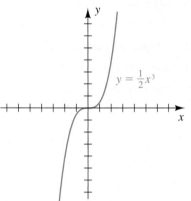

$y = \frac{1}{2} x^3$

In this section we shall discuss graphs of polynomial functions of degree greater than 2. All polynomial functions are **continuous functions**—that is, their graphs can be drawn without any breaks.

If f has degree n *and all the coefficients except a_n are zero,* then

$$f(x) = ax^n \quad \text{for some} \quad a = a_n \neq 0.$$

In this case, if $n = 1$, the graph of f is a line through the origin. If $n = 2$, the graph is a parabola with vertex at the origin. Two illustrations with $n = 3$ (**cubic polynomials**) are given in the next example.

EXAMPLE 1 Sketching graphs of $y = ax^3$

Sketch the graph of f if

(a) $f(x) = \frac{1}{2} x^3$ (b) $f(x) = -\frac{1}{2} x^3$

SOLUTION

(a) The following table lists several points on the graph of $y = \frac{1}{2} x^3$.

Figure 2

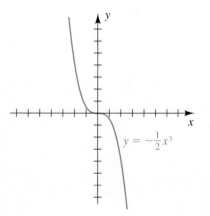

$y = -\frac{1}{2} x^3$

x	0	$\frac{1}{2}$	1	$\frac{3}{2}$	2	$\frac{5}{2}$
y	0	$\frac{1}{16} \approx 0.06$	$\frac{1}{2}$	$\frac{27}{16} \approx 1.7$	4	$\frac{125}{16} \approx 7.8$

Since f is an odd function, the graph of f is symmetric with respect to the origin, and hence points such as $\left(-\frac{1}{2}, -\frac{1}{16}\right)$ and $\left(-1, -\frac{1}{2}\right)$ are also on the graph. The graph is sketched in Figure 1.

(b) If $y = -\frac{1}{2} x^3$, the graph can be obtained from that in part (a) by multiplying all y-coordinates by -1 (that is, by reflecting the graph in part (a) through the x-axis). This gives us the sketch in Figure 2. ◢

If $f(x) = ax^n$ and n is an *odd* positive integer, then f is an odd function and the graph of f is symmetric with respect to the origin, as illustrated in Figures 1 and 2. For $a > 0$, the graph is similar in shape to that in Figure 1; however, as either n or a increases, the graph rises more rapidly for $x > 1$. If $a < 0$, we reflect the graph through the x-axis, as in Figure 2.

If $f(x) = ax^n$ and n is an *even* positive integer, then f is an even function and the graph of f is symmetric with respect to the y-axis, as illustrated in Figure 3 for the case $a = 1$ and $n = 4$. Note that as the exponent increases, the graph becomes flatter at the origin. It also rises more rapidly for $x > 1$. If $a < 0$, we reflect the graph through the x-axis. Also note that the graph *intersects* the x-axis at the origin, but it does not *cross* the x-axis (change sign).

Figure 3

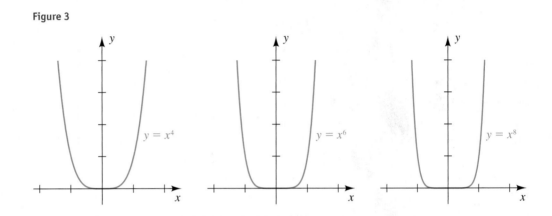

A complete analysis of graphs of polynomial functions of degree greater than 2 requires methods that are used in calculus. As the degree increases, the graphs usually become more complicated. They always have a smooth appearance, however, with a number of high points and low points, such as P, Q, R, and S in Figure 4. Such points are sometimes called **turning points** for the graph. It should be noted that an n-degree polynomial has at most $n - 1$ turning points. Each function value (y-coordinate) corresponding to a high or low point is called an **extremum** of the function f. At an extremum, f changes from an increasing function to a decreasing function, or vice versa.

The intermediate value theorem specifies another important property of polynomial functions.

Figure 4

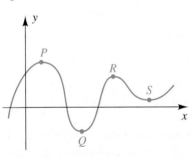

Intermediate Value Theorem for Polynomial Functions	If f is a polynomial function and $f(a) \neq f(b)$ for $a < b$, then f takes on every value between $f(a)$ and $f(b)$ in the interval $[a, b]$.

The intermediate value theorem for polynomial functions states that if w is any number between $f(a)$ and $f(b)$, there is at least one number c between a and b such that $f(c) = w$. If we regard the graph of f as extending continuously

Figure 5

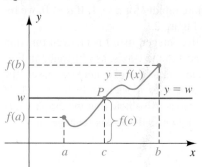

from the point $(a, f(a))$ to the point $(b, f(b))$, as illustrated in Figure 5, then for any number w between $f(a)$ and $f(b)$, the horizontal line $y = w$ intersects the graph in at least one point P. The x-coordinate c of P is a number such that $f(c) = w$.

A consequence of the intermediate value theorem is that if $f(a)$ and $f(b)$ have opposite signs (one positive and one negative), there is at least one number c between a and b such that $f(c) = 0$; that is, f *has a* **zero** *at c*. Thus, if the point $(a, f(a))$ lies below the x-axis and the point $(b, f(b))$ lies above the x-axis, or vice versa, the graph crosses the x-axis at least once between $x = a$ and $x = b$, as illustrated in Figure 6.

Figure 6

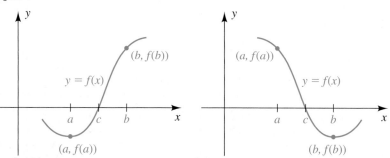

EXAMPLE 2   **Using the intermediate value theorem**

Show that $f(x) = x^5 + 2x^4 - 6x^3 + 2x - 3$ has a zero between 1 and 2.

SOLUTION Substituting 1 and 2 for x gives us the following function values:

$$f(1) = 1 + 2 - 6 + 2 - 3 = -4$$
$$f(2) = 32 + 32 - 48 + 4 - 3 = 17$$

Since $f(1)$ and $f(2)$ have opposite signs ($f(1) = -4 < 0$ and $f(2) = 17 > 0$), we see that $f(c) = 0$ for at least one real number c between 1 and 2.

Example 2 illustrates a method for locating real zeros of polynomials. By using *successive approximations,* we can approximate each zero at any degree of accuracy by locating it in smaller and smaller intervals.

If c and d are *successive* at real zeros of $f(x)$—that is, there are no other zeros between c and d—then $f(x)$ *does not change sign on the interval* (c, d). Thus, if we choose any number k such that $c < k < d$ and if $f(k)$ is positive, then $f(x)$ is positive throughout (c, d). Similarly, if $f(k)$ is negative, then $f(x)$ is negative throughout (c, d). We shall call $f(k)$ a **test value** for $f(x)$ on the interval (c, d). Test values may also be used on infinite intervals of the form $(-\infty, a)$ or (a, ∞), provided that $f(x)$ has no zeros on these intervals. The use of test values in graphing is similar to the technique used for inequalities in Section 2.7.

EXAMPLE 3   Sketching the graph of a polynomial function of degree 3

Let $f(x) = x^3 + x^2 - 4x - 4$. Find all values of x such that $f(x) > 0$ and all x such that $f(x) < 0$, and then sketch the graph of f.

SOLUTION   We may factor $f(x)$ as follows:

$$
\begin{aligned}
f(x) &= x^3 + x^2 - 4x - 4 && \text{given} \\
&= (x^3 + x^2) + (-4x - 4) && \text{group terms} \\
&= x^2(x + 1) - 4(x + 1) && \text{factor out } x^2 \text{ and } -4 \\
&= (x^2 - 4)(x + 1) && \text{factor out } (x + 1) \\
&= (x + 2)(x - 2)(x + 1) && \text{difference of squares}
\end{aligned}
$$

Figure 7

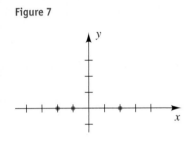

We see from the last equation that the zeros of $f(x)$ (the x-intercepts of the graph) are -2, -1, and 2. The corresponding points on the graph (see Figure 7) divide the x-axis into four parts, and we consider the open intervals

$$(-\infty, -2), \quad (-2, -1), \quad (-1, 2), \quad (2, \infty).$$

As in our work with inequalities in Section 2.7, the sign of $f(x)$ in each of these intervals can be determined by using a sign chart. The graph of f lies above the x-axis for values of x such that $f(x) > 0$, and it lies below the x-axis for all x such that $f(x) < 0$.

Interval	$(-\infty, -2)$	$(-2, -1)$	$(-1, 2)$	$(2, \infty)$
Sign of $x + 2$	−	+	+	+
Sign of $x + 1$	−	−	+	+
Sign of $x - 2$	−	−	−	+
Sign of $f(x)$	−	+	−	+
Position of graph	Below x-axis	Above x-axis	Below x-axis	Above x-axis

Figure 8

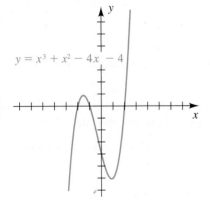

$y = x^3 + x^2 - 4x - 4$

Referring to the sign of $f(x)$ in the chart, we conclude that

$$f(x) > 0 \quad \text{if } x \text{ is in } (-2, -1) \cup (2, \infty)$$

and

$$f(x) < 0 \quad \text{if } x \text{ is in } (-\infty, -2) \cup (-1, 2).$$

Using this information leads to the sketch in Figure 8. To find the turning points on the graph, it would be necessary to use a computational device or methods developed in calculus.

The graph of every polynomial function of degree 3 has an appearance similar to that of Figure 8, or it has an inverted version of that graph if the coefficient of x^3 is negative. Sometimes, however, the graph may have only one x-intercept or the shape may be elongated, as in Figures 1 and 2.

EXAMPLE 4 Sketching the graph of a polynomial function of degree 4

Let $f(x) = x^4 - 4x^3 + 3x^2$. Find all values of x such that $f(x) > 0$ and all x such that $f(x) < 0$, and then sketch the graph of f.

SOLUTION   We begin by factoring $f(x)$:

$$
\begin{aligned}
f(x) &= x^4 - 4x^3 + 3x^2 && \text{given} \\
&= x^2(x^2 - 4x + 3) && \text{factor out } x^2 \\
&= x^2(x - 1)(x - 3) && \text{factor } x^2 - 4x + 3
\end{aligned}
$$

Next, we construct the sign diagram in Figure 9, where the vertical lines indicate the zeros 0, 1, and 3 of the factors. Since the factor x^2 is always positive if $x \neq 0$, it has no effect on the sign of the product and hence may be omitted from the diagram.

Figure 10

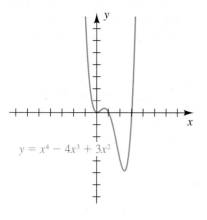

$y = x^4 - 4x^3 + 3x^2$

Figure 9

Referring to the sign of $f(x)$ in the diagram, we see that

$$f(x) > 0 \quad \text{if } x \text{ is in } (-\infty, 0) \cup (0, 1) \cup (3, \infty)$$

and $\qquad f(x) < 0 \quad \text{if } x \text{ is in } (1, 3)$.

Note that the sign of $f(x)$ does not change at $x = 0$. Making use of these facts leads to the sketch in Figure 10.

In the next example we construct a graph of a polynomial knowing only its sign.

EXAMPLE 5 Sketch the graph of a polynomial knowing its sign

Given the sign diagram in Figure 11, sketch a possible graph of the polynomial f.

Figure 11

Figure 12

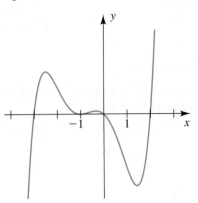

SOLUTION   Since the sign of $f(x)$ is *negative* in the interval $(-\infty, -3)$, the graph of f must be *below* the x-axis, as shown in Figure 12. In the interval $(-3, -1)$, the sign of $f(x)$ is *positive,* so the graph of f is *above* the x-axis.

The sign of $f(x)$ is also *positive* in the next interval, $(-1, 0)$. Thus, the graph of f must touch the x-axis at the x-intercept -1 and then remain *above* the x-axis. (The graph of f is *tangent* to the x-axis at $x = -1$.)

In the interval $(0, 2)$, the sign of $f(x)$ is *negative,* so the graph of f is *below* the x-axis. Lastly, the sign of $f(x)$ is *positive* in the interval $(2, \infty)$, and the graph of f is *above* the x-axis.

In the last example we used the function

$$f(x) = (x + 3)(x + 1)^2(x)(x - 2).$$

Note how the graph of f relates to the solutions of the following inequalities.

Inequality	Solution	Position of graph in relation to the x-axis
(1) $f(x) > 0$	$(-3, -1) \cup (-1, 0) \cup (2, \infty)$	Above
(2) $f(x) \geq 0$	$[-3, 0] \cup [2, \infty)$	Above or on
(3) $f(x) < 0$	$(-\infty, -3) \cup (0, 2)$	Below
(4) $f(x) \leq 0$	$(-\infty, -3] \cup \{-1\} \cup [0, 2]$	Below or on

Notice that every real number must be in the solution to either inequality (1) or inequality (4)—the same can be said for inequalities (2) and (3).

4.1   *Exercises*

Exer. 1–4: Sketch the graph of f for the indicated value of c or a.

1 $f(x) = 2x^3 + c$

  (a) $c = 3$ (b) $c = -3$

2 $f(x) = -2x^3 + c$

  (a) $c = -2$ (b) $c = 2$

3 $f(x) = ax^3 + 2$

  (a) $a = 2$ (b) $a = -\frac{1}{3}$

4 $f(x) = ax^3 - 3$

  (a) $a = -2$ (b) $a = \frac{1}{4}$

Exer. 5–10: Use the intermediate value theorem to show that f has a zero between a and b.

5 $f(x) = x^3 - 4x^2 + 3x - 2;$ $a = 3,$ $b = 4$

6 $f(x) = 2x^3 + 5x^2 - 3;$ $a = -3,$ $b = -2$

7 $f(x) = -x^4 + 3x^3 - 2x + 1;$ $a = 2,$ $b = 3$

8 $f(x) = 2x^4 + 3x - 2;$ $a = \frac{1}{2},$ $b = \frac{3}{4}$

9 $f(x) = x^5 + x^3 + x^2 + x + 1;$ $a = -\frac{1}{2},$ $b = -1$

10 $f(x) = x^5 - 3x^4 - 2x^3 + 3x^2 - 9x - 6;$
$a = 3,$ $b = 4$

Exer. 11–12: Match each graph with an equation.

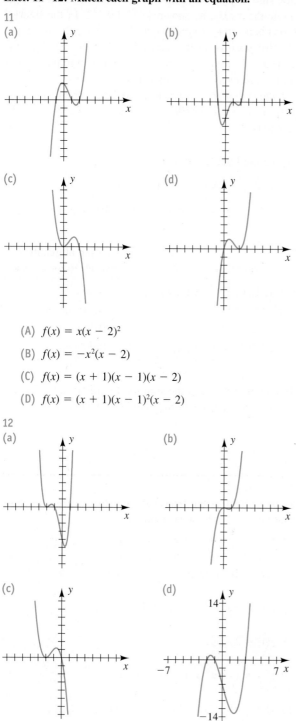

11
(a)

(b)

(c)

(d)

(A) $f(x) = x(x - 2)^2$

(B) $f(x) = -x^2(x - 2)$

(C) $f(x) = (x + 1)(x - 1)(x - 2)$

(D) $f(x) = (x + 1)(x - 1)^2(x - 2)$

12
(a)

(b)

(c)

(d)

(A) $f(x) = x^2(x - 1)$

(B) $f(x) = -x(x + 2)^2$

(C) $f(x) = (x + 2)(x + 1)(x - 3)$

(D) $f(x) = (x + 2)^2(x + 1)(x - 1)$

Exer. 13–28: Find all values of x such that $f(x) > 0$ and all x such that $f(x) < 0$, and sketch the graph of f.

13 $f(x) = \frac{1}{4}x^3 - 2$

14 $f(x) = -\frac{1}{9}x^3 - 3$

15 $f(x) = -\frac{1}{16}x^4 + 1$

16 $f(x) = x^5 + 1$

17 $f(x) = x^4 - 4x^2$

18 $f(x) = 9x - x^3$

19 $f(x) = -x^3 + 3x^2 + 10x$

20 $f(x) = x^4 + 3x^3 - 4x^2$

21 $f(x) = \frac{1}{6}(x + 2)(x - 3)(x - 4)$

22 $f(x) = -\frac{1}{8}(x + 4)(x - 2)(x - 6)$

23 $f(x) = x^3 + 2x^2 - 4x - 8$

24 $f(x) = x^3 - 3x^2 - 9x + 27$

25 $f(x) = x^4 - 6x^2 + 8$

26 $f(x) = -x^4 + 12x^2 - 27$

27 $f(x) = x^2(x + 2)(x - 1)^2(x - 2)$

28 $f(x) = x^3(x + 1)^2(x - 2)(x - 4)$

Exer. 29–30: Sketch the graph of a polynomial given the sign diagram.

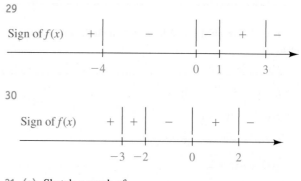

29

30

31 (a) Sketch a graph of
$$f(x) = (x - a)(x - b)(x - c),$$
where $a < 0 < b < c$.

(b) What is the y-intercept?   *(continued)*

(c) What is the solution to $f(x) < 0$?

(d) What is the solution to $f(x) \geq 0$?

32 (a) Sketch a graph of

$$f(x) = (x - a)^2(x - b)(x - c),$$

where $a < b < 0 < c$.

(b) What is the y-intercept?

(c) What is the solution to $f(x) > 0$?

(d) What is the solution to $f(x) \leq 0$?

33 Let $f(x)$ be a polynomial such that the coefficient of every odd power of x is 0. Show that f is an even function.

34 Let $f(x)$ be a polynomial such that the coefficient of every even power of x is 0. Show that f is an odd function.

35 If $f(x) = 3x^3 - kx^2 + x - 5k$, find a number k such that the graph of f contains the point $(-1, 4)$.

36 If $f(x) = kx^3 + x^2 - kx + 2$, find a number k such that the graph of f contains the point $(2, 12)$.

37 If one zero of $f(x) = x^3 - 2x^2 - 16x + 16k$ is 2, find two other zeros.

38 If one zero of $f(x) = x^3 - 3x^2 - kx + 12$ is -2, find two other zeros.

39 A Legendre polynomial The third-degree Legendre polynomial $P(x) = \frac{1}{2}(5x^3 - 3x)$ occurs in the solution of heat transfer problems in physics and engineering. Find all values of x such that $P(x) > 0$ and all x such that $P(x) < 0$, and sketch the graph of P.

40 A Chebyshev polynomial The fourth-degree Chebyshev polynomial $f(x) = 8x^4 - 8x^2 + 1$ occurs in statistical studies. Find all values of x such that $f(x) > 0$. (*Hint:* Let $z = x^2$, and use the quadratic formula.)

41 Constructing a box From a rectangular piece of cardboard having dimensions 20 inches × 30 inches, an open box is to be made by cutting out identical squares of area x^2 from each corner and turning up the sides (see Exercise 65 of Section 3.4).

(a) Show that the volume of the box is given by the function $V(x) = x(20 - 2x)(30 - 2x)$.

(b) Find all positive values of x such that $V(x) > 0$, and sketch the graph of V for $x > 0$.

42 Constructing a crate The frame for a shipping crate is to be constructed from 24 feet of 2 × 2 lumber (see the figure).

(a) If the crate is to have square ends of side x feet, express the outer volume V of the crate as a function of x (disregard the thickness of the lumber).

(b) Sketch the graph of V for $x > 0$.

Exercise 42

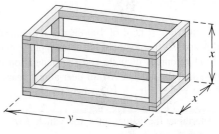

43 Determining temperatures A meteorologist determines that the temperature T (in °F) for a certain 24-hour period in winter was given by the formula $T = \frac{1}{20}t(t - 12)(t - 24)$ for $0 \leq t \leq 24$, where t is time in hours and $t = 0$ corresponds to 6 A.M.

(a) When was $T > 0$, and when was $T < 0$?

(b) Sketch the graph of T.

(c) Show that the temperature was 32°F sometime between 12 noon and 1 P.M. (*Hint:* Use the intermediate value theorem.)

44 Deflections of diving boards A diver stands at the very end of a diving board before beginning a dive (see the figure).

Exercise 44

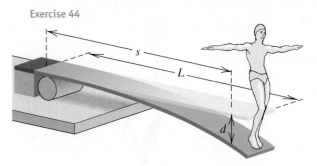

The deflection d of the board at a position s feet from the stationary end is given by $d = cs^2(3L - s)$ for $0 \le s \le L$, where L is the length of the board and c is a positive constant that depends on the weight of the diver and on the physical properties of the board. Suppose the board is 10 feet long.

(a) If the deflection at the end of the board is 1 foot, find c.

(b) Show that the deflection is $\frac{1}{2}$ foot somewhere between $s = 6.5$ and $s = 6.6$.

45 Deer population A herd of 100 deer is introduced onto a small island. At first the herd increases rapidly, but eventually food resources dwindle and the population declines. Suppose that the number $N(t)$ of deer after t years is given by $N(t) = -t^4 + 21t^2 + 100$, where $t > 0$.

(a) Determine the values of t for which $N(t) > 0$, and sketch the graph of N.

(b) Does the population become extinct? If so, when?

46 Deer population Refer to Exercise 45. It can be shown by means of calculus that the rate R (in deer per year) at which the deer population changes at time t is given by $R = -4t^3 + 42t$.

(a) When does the population cease to grow?

(b) Determine the positive values of t for which $R > 0$.

47 (a) Construct a table containing the values of the fourth-degree polynomials

$$f(x) = 2x^4,$$
$$g(x) = 2x^4 - 5x^2 + 1,$$
$$h(x) = 2x^4 + 5x^2 - 1,$$

and

$$k(x) = 2x^4 - x^3 + 2x,$$

when $x = \pm 20, \pm 40,$ and ± 60.

(b) As $|x|$ becomes large, how do the values for each function compare?

(c) Which term has the greatest influence on each function's value when $|x|$ is large?

4.2

Properties of Division

In this section we use $f(x)$, $g(x)$, and so on, to denote polynomials in x. If $g(x)$ is a factor of $f(x)$, then $f(x)$ is **divisible** by $g(x)$. For example, $x^4 - 16$ is divisible by $x^2 - 4$, by $x^2 + 4$, by $x + 2$, and by $x - 2$.

The polynomial $x^4 - 16$ is not divisible by $x^2 + 3x + 1$; however, we can use the process called **long division** to find a *quotient* and a *remainder*, as in the following illustration, where we have inserted terms with zero coefficients.

ILLUSTRATION Long Division of Polynomials

$$
\begin{array}{r}
\overbrace{x^2 - 3x + 8}^{\text{quotient}} \\
x^2 + 3x + 1 \overline{\smash{\big)}\, x^4 + 0x^3 + 0x^2 + 0x - 16} \\
\underline{x^4 + 3x^3 + x^2} \qquad\quad x^2(x^2 + 3x + 1) \\
-3x^3 - x^2 \qquad\qquad \text{subtract} \\
\underline{-3x^3 - 9x^2 - 3x} \qquad -3x(x^2 + 3x + 1) \\
8x^2 + 3x - 16 \quad \text{subtract} \\
\underline{8x^2 + 24x + 8} \quad 8(x^2 + 3x + 1) \\
-21x - 24 \quad \text{subtract} \\
\underbrace{}_{\text{remainder}}
\end{array}
$$

The long division process ends when we arrive at a polynomial (the remainder) that either is 0 or has smaller degree than the divisor. The result of the long division in the preceding illustration can be written

$$\frac{x^4 - 16}{x^2 + 3x + 1} = (x^2 - 3x + 8) + \left(\frac{-21x - 24}{x^2 + 3x + 1}\right).$$

Multiplying both sides of this equation by $x^2 + 3x + 1$, we obtain

$$x^4 - 16 = (x^2 + 3x + 1)(x^2 - 3x + 8) + (-21x - 24).$$

This example illustrates the following theorem.

Division Algorithm for Polynomials	If $f(x)$ and $p(x)$ are polynomials and if $p(x) \neq 0$, then there exist unique polynomials $q(x)$ and $r(x)$ such that $$f(x) = p(x) \cdot q(x) + r(x),$$ where either $r(x) = 0$ or the degree of $r(x)$ is less than the degree of $p(x)$. The polynomial $q(x)$ is the **quotient,** and $r(x)$ is the **remainder** in the division of $f(x)$ by $p(x)$.

A useful special case of the division algorithm for polynomials occurs if $f(x)$ is divided by $x - c$, where c is a real number. If $x - c$ is a factor of $f(x)$, then

$$f(x) = (x - c)q(x)$$

for some quotient $q(x)$, and the remainder $r(x)$ is 0. If $x - c$ is not a factor of $f(x)$, then the degree of the remainder $r(x)$ is less than the degree of $x - c$, and hence $r(x)$ must have degree 0. This means that the remainder is a nonzero number. Consequently, for every $x - c$ we have

$$f(x) = (x - c)q(x) + d,$$

where the remainder d is a real number (possibly $d = 0$). If we substitute c for x, we obtain

$$f(c) = (c - c)q(c) + d$$
$$= 0 \cdot q(c) + d$$
$$= 0 + d = d.$$

This proves the following theorem.

Remainder Theorem	If a polynomial $f(x)$ is divided by $x - c$, then the remainder is $f(c)$.

EXAMPLE 1 Using the remainder theorem

If $f(x) = x^3 - 3x^2 + x + 5$, use the remainder theorem to find $f(2)$.

SOLUTION According to the remainder theorem, $f(2)$ is the remainder when $f(x)$ is divided by $x - 2$. By long division,

$$
\begin{array}{r}
x^2 - x - 1 \\
x - 2\overline{\smash{\big)}\,x^3 - 3x^2 + x + 5} \\
\underline{x^3 - 2x^2} \qquad \qquad x^2(x-2) \\
-x^2 + x \qquad \qquad \text{subtract} \\
\underline{-x^2 + 2x} \qquad \qquad -x(x-2) \\
-x + 5 \qquad \text{subtract} \\
\underline{-x + 2} \qquad (-1)(x-2) \\
3 \qquad \text{subtract}
\end{array}
$$

Hence, $f(2) = 3$. We may check this fact by direct substitution:

$$f(2) = 2^3 - 3(2)^2 + 2 + 5 = 3$$

We shall use the remainder theorem to prove the following important result.

Factor Theorem	A polynomial $f(x)$ has a factor $x - c$ if and only if $f(c) = 0$.

PROOF By the remainder theorem,

$$f(x) = (x - c)q(x) + f(c)$$

for some quotient $q(x)$.

If $f(c) = 0$, then $f(x) = (x - c)q(x)$; that is, $x - c$ is a factor of $f(x)$. Conversely, if $x - c$ is a factor of $f(x)$, then the remainder upon division of $f(x)$ by $x - c$ must be 0, and hence, by the remainder theorem, $f(c) = 0$.

The factor theorem is useful for finding factors of polynomials, as illustrated in the next example.

EXAMPLE 2 Using the factor theorem

Show that $x - 2$ is a factor of $f(x) = x^3 - 4x^2 + 3x + 2$.

SOLUTION Since $f(2) = 8 - 16 + 6 + 2 = 0$, we see from the factor theorem that $x - 2$ is a factor of $f(x)$. Another method of solution would be to divide $f(x)$ by $x - 2$ and show that the remainder is 0. The quotient in the division would be another factor of $f(x)$.

EXAMPLE 3 Finding a polynomial with prescribed zeros

Find a polynomial $f(x)$ of degree 3 that has zeros 2, -1, and 3.

SOLUTION By the factor theorem, $f(x)$ has factors $x - 2$, $x + 1$, and $x - 3$. Thus,

$$f(x) = a(x - 2)(x + 1)(x - 3),$$

where any nonzero value may be assigned to a. If we let $a = 1$ and multiply, we obtain

$$f(x) = x^3 - 4x^2 + x + 6.$$

To apply the remainder theorem it is necessary to divide a polynomial $f(x)$ by $x - c$. The method of **synthetic division** may be used to simplify this work. The following guidelines state how to proceed. The method can be justified by a careful (and lengthy) comparison with the method of long division.

Guidelines for Synthetic Division of $a_n x^n + a_{n-1} x^{n-1} + \cdots + a_1 x + a_0$ **by** $x - c$	1 Begin with the following display, supplying zeros for any missing coefficients in the given polynomial.

$$\underline{c}\ |\ a_n \quad a_{n-1} \quad a_{n-2} \quad \ldots \quad a_1 \quad a_0$$

$$\overline{a_n}$$

2 Multiply a_n by c, and place the product ca_n underneath a_{n-1}, as indicated by the arrow in the following display. (This arrow, and others, is used only to clarify these guidelines and will not appear in *specific* synthetic divisions.) Next find the sum $b_1 = a_{n-1} + ca_n$, and place it below the line as shown.

$$\underline{c}\ |\ a_n \quad a_{n-1} \quad a_{n-2} \quad \ldots \qquad\qquad a_1 \quad a_0$$
$$\quad\quad ca_n \quad cb_1 \quad cb_2 \quad \ldots \qquad cb_{n-2} \quad cb_{n-1}$$
$$\overline{a_n \quad b_1 \quad\quad b_2 \quad \ldots \qquad\quad b_{n-2} \quad b_{n-1} \quad r}$$

3 Multiply b_1 by c, and place the product cb_1 underneath a_{n-2}, as indicated by the second arrow. Proceeding, we next find the sum $b_2 = a_{n-2} + cb_1$ and place it below the line as shown.

4 Continue this process, as indicated by the arrows, until the final sum $r = a_0 + cb_{n-1}$ is obtained. The numbers

$$a_n, \quad b_1, \quad b_2, \quad \ldots, \quad b_{n-2}, \quad b_{n-1}$$

are the coefficients of the quotient $q(x)$; that is,

$$q(x) = a_n x^{n-1} + b_1 x^{n-2} + \cdots + b_{n-2} x + b_{n-1},$$

and r is the remainder.

Synthetic division does not replace long division; it is merely a faster method and is applicable only when the divisor is of the form $x - c$.

The following examples illustrate synthetic division for some special cases.

EXAMPLE 4   Using synthetic division to find a quotient and remainder

Use synthetic division to find the quotient $q(x)$ and remainder r if the polynomial $2x^4 + 5x^3 - 2x - 8$ is divided by $x + 3$.

SOLUTION   Since the divisor is $x + 3 = x - (-3)$, the value of c in the expression $x - c$ is -3. Hence, the synthetic division takes this form:

$$
\begin{array}{r|rrrrr}
-3 & 2 & 5 & 0 & -2 & -8 \\
   &   & -6 & 3 & -9 & 33 \\
\hline
   & 2 & -1 & 3 & -11 & 25
\end{array}
$$

$\underbrace{\qquad\qquad\qquad}_{\text{coefficients of quotient}}$ $\underbrace{\quad}_{\text{remainder}}$

As we have indicated, the first four numbers in the third row are the coefficients of the quotient $q(x)$, and the last number is the remainder r. Thus,

$$q(x) = 2x^3 - x^2 + 3x - 11 \qquad \text{and} \qquad r = 25.$$
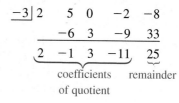

Synthetic division can be used to find values of polynomial functions, as illustrated in the next example.

EXAMPLE 5   Using synthetic division to find values of a polynomial

If $f(x) = 3x^5 - 38x^3 + 5x^2 - 1$, use synthetic division to find $f(4)$.

SOLUTION   By the remainder theorem, $f(4)$ is the remainder when $f(x)$ is divided by $x - 4$. Dividing synthetically, we obtain

$$
\begin{array}{r|rrrrrr}
4 & 3 & 0 & -38 & 5 & 0 & -1 \\
  &   & 12 & 48 & 40 & 180 & 720 \\
\hline
  & 3 & 12 & 10 & 45 & 180 & 719
\end{array}
$$

$\underbrace{\qquad\qquad\qquad\qquad}_{\text{coefficients of quotient}}$ $\underbrace{\quad}_{\text{remainder}}$

Consequently, $f(4) = 719$.

Synthetic division may be used to help find zeros of polynomials. By the method illustrated in the preceding example, $f(c) = 0$ if and only if the remainder in the synthetic division by $x - c$ is 0.

EXAMPLE 6   Using synthetic division to find zeros of a polynomial

Show that -11 is a zero of the polynomial

$$f(x) = x^3 + 8x^2 - 29x + 44.$$

SOLUTION   Dividing synthetically by $x - (-11) = x + 11$ gives us

*The quotient gives us the **depressed equation**,*

$$x^2 - 3x + 4 = 0, \rightarrow$$

which can be used to find the remaining zeros of f.

$$\begin{array}{r|rrrr}
-11 & 1 & 8 & -29 & 44 \\
    &   & -11 & 33 & -44 \\
\hline
    & 1 & -3 & 4 & 0
\end{array}$$

$$\underbrace{}_{\substack{\text{coefficients} \\ \text{of quotient}}} \quad \underbrace{}_{\text{remainder}}$$

Thus, $f(-11) = 0$, and -11 is a zero of f.

Example 6 shows that the number -11 is a solution of the equation $x^3 + 8x^2 - 29x + 44 = 0$. In Section 4.4 we shall use synthetic division to find rational solutions of equations.

At this stage you should recognize that the following three statements are equivalent for a polynomial function f whose graph is the graph of the equation $y = f(x)$.

equivalent statements for $f(a) = b$

(1) The point (a, b) is on the graph of f.

(2) The value of f at $x = a$ equals b; that is, $f(a) = b$.

(3) If $f(x)$ is divided by $x - a$, then the remainder is b.

Furthermore, if b is equal to 0, then the next four statements are also equivalent.

additional equivalent statements for $f(a) = 0$

(1) The number a is a zero of the function f.

(2) The point $(a, 0)$ is on the graph of f; that is, a is an x-intercept.

(3) The number a is a solution of the equation $f(x) = 0$.

(4) The binomial $x - a$ is a factor of the polynomial $f(x)$.

You should become familiar with these statements—so familiar that if you know one of them is true, you can easily recall and apply any appropriate equivalent statement.

4.2 Exercises

Exer. 1–8: Find the quotient and remainder if $f(x)$ is divided by $p(x)$.

1 $f(x) = 2x^4 - x^3 - 3x^2 + 7x - 12;$ $p(x) = x^2 - 3$

2 $f(x) = 3x^4 + 2x^3 - x^2 - x - 6;$ $p(x) = x^2 + 1$

3 $f(x) = 3x^3 + 2x - 4;$ $p(x) = 2x^2 + 1$

4 $f(x) = 3x^3 - 5x^2 - 4x - 8;$ $p(x) = 2x^2 + x$

5 $f(x) = 7x + 2;$ $p(x) = 2x^2 - x - 4$

6 $f(x) = -5x^2 + 3;$ $p(x) = x^3 - 3x + 9$

7 $f(x) = 9x + 4;$ $p(x) = 2x - 5$

8 $f(x) = 7x^2 + 3x - 10;$ $p(x) = x^2 - x + 10$

Exer. 9–12: Use the remainder theorem to find $f(c)$.

9 $f(x) = 3x^3 - x^2 + 5x - 4;$ $c = 2$

10 $f(x) = 2x^3 + 4x^2 - 3x - 1;$ $c = 3$

11 $f(x) = x^4 - 6x^2 + 4x - 8;$ $c = -3$

12 $f(x) = x^4 + 3x^2 - 12;$ $c = -2$

Exer. 13–16: Use the factor theorem to show that $x - c$ is a factor of $f(x)$.

13 $f(x) = x^3 + x^2 - 2x + 12;$ $\qquad c = -3$

14 $f(x) = x^3 + x^2 - 11x + 10;$ $\qquad c = 2$

15 $f(x) = x^{12} - 4096;$ $\qquad c = -2$

16 $f(x) = x^4 - 3x^3 - 2x^2 + 5x + 6;$ $\quad c = 2$

Exer. 17–20: Find a polynomial $f(x)$ with leading coefficient 1 and having the given degree and zeros.

17 degree 3; zeros $-2, 0, 5$

18 degree 3; zeros $\pm 2, 3$

19 degree 4; zeros $-2, \pm 1, 4$

20 degree 4; zeros $-3, 0, 1, 5$

Exer. 21–28: Use synthetic division to find the quotient and remainder if the first polynomial is divided by the second.

21 $2x^3 - 3x^2 + 4x - 5;$ $\quad x - 2$

22 $3x^3 - 4x^2 - x + 8;$ $\quad x + 4$

23 $x^3 - 8x - 5;$ $\qquad x + 3$

24 $5x^3 - 6x^2 + 15;$ $\qquad x - 4$

25 $3x^5 + 6x^2 + 7;$ $\qquad x + 2$

26 $-2x^4 + 10x - 3;$ $\qquad x - 3$

27 $4x^4 - 5x^2 + 1;$ $\qquad x - \frac{1}{2}$

28 $9x^3 - 6x^2 + 3x - 4;$ $\quad x - \frac{1}{3}$

Exer. 29–34: Use synthetic division to find $f(c)$.

29 $f(x) = 2x^3 + 3x^2 - 4x + 4;$ $\quad c = 3$

30 $f(x) = -x^3 + 4x^2 + x;$ $\qquad c = -2$

31 $f(x) = 0.3x^3 + 0.04x - 0.034;$ $\; c = -0.2$

32 $f(x) = 8x^5 - 3x^2 + 7;$ $\qquad c = \frac{1}{2}$

33 $f(x) = x^2 + 3x - 5;$ $\qquad c = 2 + \sqrt{3}$

34 $f(x) = x^3 - 3x^2 - 8;$ $\qquad c = 1 + \sqrt{2}$

Exer. 35–38: Use synthetic division to show that c is a zero of $f(x)$.

35 $f(x) = 3x^4 + 8x^3 - 2x^2 - 10x + 4;$ $\quad c = -2$

36 $f(x) = 4x^3 - 9x^2 - 8x - 3;$ $\qquad c = 3$

37 $f(x) = 4x^3 - 6x^2 + 8x - 3;$ $\qquad c = \frac{1}{2}$

38 $f(x) = 27x^4 - 9x^3 + 3x^2 + 6x + 1;$ $\; c = -\frac{1}{3}$

Exer. 39–40: Find all values of k such that $f(x)$ is divisible by the given linear polynomial.

39 $f(x) = kx^3 + x^2 + k^2x + 3k^2 + 11;$ $\quad x + 2$

40 $f(x) = k^2x^3 - 4kx + 3;$ $\qquad x - 1$

Exer. 41–42: Show that $x - c$ is not a factor of $f(x)$ for any real number c.

41 $f(x) = 3x^4 + x^2 + 5$ $\qquad$ 42 $f(x) = -x^4 - 3x^2 - 2$

43 Find the remainder if the polynomial

$$3x^{100} + 5x^{85} - 4x^{38} + 2x^{17} - 6$$

is divided by $x + 1$.

Exer. 44–46: Use the factor theorem to verify the statement.

44 $x - y$ is a factor of $x^n - y^n$ for every positive integer n.

45 $x + y$ is a factor of $x^n - y^n$ for every positive even integer n.

46 $x + y$ is a factor of $x^n + y^n$ for every positive odd integer n.

47 Let $P(x, y)$ be a first-quadrant point on $y = 6 - x$, and consider the vertical line segment PQ shown in the figure.

(a) If PQ is rotated about the y-axis, determine the volume V of the resulting cylinder.

(b) For what point $P(x, y)$ with $x \neq 1$ is the volume V in part (a) the same as the volume of the cylinder of radius 1 and altitude 5 shown in the figure?

Exercise 47

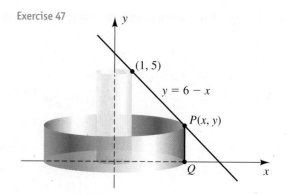

48 **Strength of a beam** The strength of a rectangular beam is directly proportional to the product of its width and the square of the depth of a cross section (see the figure). A beam of width 1.5 feet has been cut from a cylindrical log of radius 1 foot. Find the width of a second rectangular beam of equal strength that could have been cut from the log.

Exercise 48

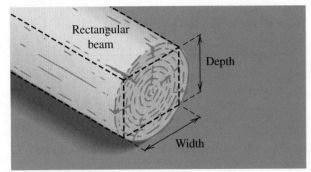

49 **Parabolic arch** An arch has the shape of the parabola $y = 4 - x^2$. A rectangle is fit under the arch by selecting a point (x, y) on the parabola (see the figure).

Exercise 49

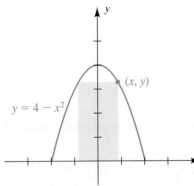

(a) Express the area A of the rectangle in terms of x.

(b) If $x = 1$, the rectangle has base 2 and height 3. Find the base of a second rectangle that has the same area.

50 **Dimensions of a capsule** An aspirin tablet in the shape of a right circular cylinder has height $\frac{1}{3}$ centimeter and radius $\frac{1}{2}$ centimeter. The manufacturer also wishes to market the aspirin in capsule form. The capsule is to be $\frac{3}{2}$ centimeters long, in the shape of a right circular cylinder with hemispheres attached at both ends (see the figure).

(a) If r denotes the radius of a hemisphere, find a formula for the volume of the capsule.

(b) Find the radius of the capsule so that its volume is equal to that of the tablet.

Exercise 50

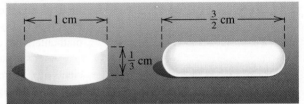

4.3

Zeros of Polynomials

The **zeros of a polynomial** $f(x)$ are the solutions of the equation $f(x) = 0$. Each real zero is an x-intercept of the graph of f. In applied fields, calculators and computers are usually used to find or approximate zeros. Before using a calculator, however, it is worth knowing what type of zeros to expect. Some questions we could ask are

(1) How many zeros of $f(x)$ are real? imaginary?

(2) How many real zeros of $f(x)$ are positive? negative?

(3) How many real zeros of $f(x)$ are rational? irrational?

(4) Are the real zeros of $f(x)$ large or small in value?

In this and the following section we shall discuss results that help answer some of these questions. These results form the basis of the *theory of equations*.

The factor and remainder theorems can be extended to the system of complex numbers. Thus, a complex number $c = a + bi$ is a zero of a polynomial $f(x)$ if and only if $x - c$ is a factor of $f(x)$. Except in special cases, zeros of polynomials are very difficult to find. For example, there are no obvious zeros of $f(x) = x^5 - 3x^4 + 4x^3 - 4x - 10$. Although we have no formula that can be used to find the zeros, the next theorem states that there is at *least* one zero c, and hence, by the factor theorem, $f(x)$ has a factor of the form $x - c$.

Fundamental Theorem of Algebra	If a polynomial $f(x)$ has positive degree and complex coefficients, then $f(x)$ has at least one complex zero.

The standard proof of this theorem requires results from an advanced field of mathematics called *functions of a complex variable*. A prerequisite for studying this field is a strong background in calculus. The first proof of the fundamental theorem of algebra was given by the German mathematician Carl Friedrich Gauss (1777–1855), who is considered by many to be the greatest mathematician of all time.

As a special case of the fundamental theorem of algebra, if all the coefficients of $f(x)$ are real, then $f(x)$ has at least one complex zero. If $a + bi$ is a complex zero, it may happen that $b = 0$, in which case the number a is a real zero.

The fundamental theorem of algebra enables us, at least in theory, to express every polynomial $f(x)$ of positive degree as a product of polynomials of degree 1, as in the next theorem.

Complete Factorization Theorem for Polynomials	If $f(x)$ is a polynomial of degree $n > 0$, then there exist n complex numbers $c_1, c_2, \ldots, c_n$ such that $$f(x) = a(x - c_1)(x - c_2) \cdots (x - c_n),$$ where a is the leading coefficient of $f(x)$. Each number c_k is a zero of $f(x)$.

PROOF   If $f(x)$ has degree $n > 0$, then, by the fundamental theorem of algebra, $f(x)$ has a complex zero c_1. Hence, by the factor theorem, $f(x)$ has a factor $x - c_1$; that is,

$$f(x) = (x - c_1)f_1(x),$$

where $f_1(x)$ is a polynomial of degree $n - 1$. If $n - 1 > 0$, then, by the same argument, $f_1(x)$ has a complex zero c_2 and therefore a factor $x - c_2$. Thus,

$$f_1(x) = (x - c_2)f_2(x),$$

where $f_2(x)$ is a polynomial of degree $n - 2$. Hence,

$$f(x) = (x - c_1)(x - c_2)f_2(x).$$

Continuing this process, after n steps we arrive at a polynomial $f_n(x)$ of degree 0. Thus, $f_n(x) = a$ for some nonzero number a, and we may write

$$f(x) = a(x - c_1)(x - c_2) \cdots (x - c_n),$$

where each complex number c_k is a zero of $f(x)$. The leading coefficient of the polynomial on the right-hand side in the last equation is a, and therefore a is the leading coefficient of $f(x)$. ◢

ILLUSTRATION   **Complete Factorization Theorem for Polynomials**

A Polynomial $f(x)$	A Factored Form of $f(x)$	Zeros of $f(x)$
■ $3x^2 - (12 + 6i)x + 24i$	$3(x - 4)(x - 2i)$	$4, 2i$
■ $-6x^3 - 2x^2 - 6x - 2$	$-6\left(x + \frac{1}{3}\right)(x + i)(x - i)$	$-\frac{1}{3}, \pm i$
■ $5x^3 - 30x^2 + 65x$	$5(x - 0)[x - (3 + 2i)][x - (3 - 2i)]$	$0, 3 \pm 2i$
■ $\frac{2}{3}x^3 + 8x^2 - \frac{2}{3}x - 8$	$\frac{2}{3}(x + 12)(x + 1)(x - 1)$	$-12, \pm 1$

We may now prove the following.

Theorem on the Maximum Number of Zeros of a Polynomial	A polynomial of degree $n > 0$ has at most n different complex zeros.

PROOF   We will give an indirect proof; that is, we will suppose $f(x)$ has *more* than n different complex zeros and show that this supposition leads to a contradiction. Let us choose $n + 1$ of the zeros and label them $c_1, c_2, \ldots, c_n$, and c. We may use the c_k to obtain the factorization indicated in the statement of the complete factorization theorem for polynomials. Substituting c for x and using the fact that $f(c) = 0$, we obtain

$$0 = a(c - c_1)(c - c_2) \cdots (c - c_n).$$

However, each factor on the right-hand side is different from zero because $c \neq c_k$ for every k. Since the product of nonzero numbers cannot equal zero, we have a contradiction. ◢

EXAMPLE 1 Finding a polynomial with prescribed zeros

Find a polynomial $f(x)$ in factored form that has degree 3; has zeros 2, -1, and 3; and satisfies $f(1) = 5$.

SOLUTION By the factor theorem, $f(x)$ has factors $x - 2$, $x + 1$, and $x - 3$. No other factors of degree 1 exist, since, by the factor theorem, another linear factor $x - c$ would produce a fourth zero of $f(x)$, contrary to the preceding theorem. Hence, $f(x)$ has the form

$$f(x) = a(x - 2)(x + 1)(x - 3)$$

for some number a. Since $f(1) = 5$, we can find a as follows:

$$5 = a(1 - 2)(1 + 1)(1 - 3) \quad \text{let } x = 1 \text{ in } f(x)$$
$$5 = a(-1)(2)(-2) \quad \text{simplify}$$
$$a = \tfrac{5}{4} \quad \text{solve for } a$$

Consequently,

$$f(x) = \tfrac{5}{4}(x - 2)(x + 1)(x - 3).$$

If we multiply the factors, we obtain the polynomial

$$f(x) = \tfrac{5}{4}x^3 - 5x^2 + \tfrac{5}{4}x + \tfrac{15}{2}.$$

The numbers $c_1, c_2, \ldots, c_n$ in the complete factorization theorem are not necessarily all different. To illustrate, $f(x) = x^3 + x^2 - 5x + 3$ has the factorization

$$f(x) = (x + 3)(x - 1)(x - 1).$$

If a factor $x - c$ occurs m times in the factorization, then c is a **zero of multiplicity** m of the polynomial $f(x)$, or a **root of multiplicity** m of the equation $f(x) = 0$. In the preceding display, 1 is a zero of multiplicity 2, and -3 is a zero of multiplicity 1.

If c is a real zero of $f(x)$ of multiplicity m, then $f(x)$ has the factor $(x - c)^m$ and the graph of f has an x-intercept c. The general shape of the graph at $(c, 0)$ depends on whether m is an odd integer or an even integer. If m is odd, then $(x - c)^m$ changes sign as x increases through c, and hence the graph of f crosses the x-axis at $(c, 0)$, as indicated in the first row of the following chart. The figures in the chart do not show the complete graph of f, but only its general shape near $(c, 0)$. If m is even, then $(x - c)^m$ does not change sign at c and the graph of f near $(c, 0)$ has the appearance of one of the two figures in the second row.

Factor of $f(x)$	General shape of the graph of f near $(c, 0)$
$(x - c)^m$, with m odd and $m \neq 1$	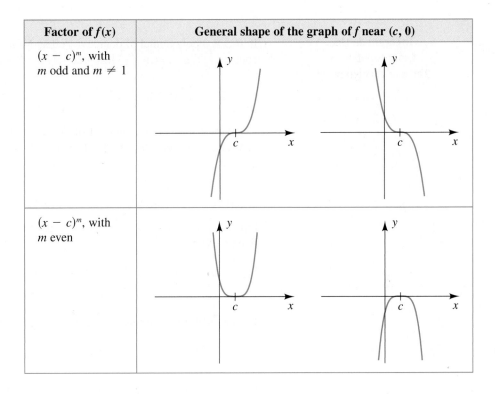
$(x - c)^m$, with m even	

Figure 1

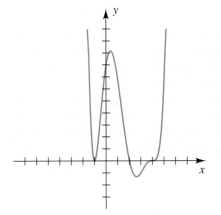

EXAMPLE 2 Finding multiplicities of zeros

Find the zeros of the polynomial $f(x) = \frac{1}{16}(x - 2)(x - 4)^3(x + 1)^2$, state the multiplicity of each, and then sketch the graph of f.

SOLUTION We see from the factored form that $f(x)$ has three distinct zeros, 2, 4, and -1. The zero 2 has multiplicity 1, the zero 4 has multiplicity 3, and the zero -1 has multiplicity 2. Note that $f(x)$ has degree 6.

The x-intercepts of the graph of f are the real zeros -1, 2, and 4. Since the multiplicity of -1 is an even integer, the graph intersects, but does not cross, the x-axis at $(-1, 0)$. Since the multiplicities of 2 and 4 are odd, the graph crosses the x-axis at $(2, 0)$ and $(4, 0)$. (Note that the graph is "flatter" at 4 than at 2.) The y-intercept is $f(0) = \frac{1}{16}(-2)(-4)^3(1)^2 = 8$. The graph is shown in Figure 1.

If $f(x) = a(x - c_1)(x - c_2) \cdots (x - c_n)$ is a polynomial of degree n, then the n complex numbers $c_1, c_2, \ldots, c_n$ are zeros of $f(x)$. Counting a zero of multiplicity m as m zeros tells us that $f(x)$ has at least n zeros (not necessarily all different). Combining this fact with the fact that $f(x)$ has at most n zeros gives us the next result.

Theorem on the Exact Number of Zeros of a Polynomial	If $f(x)$ is a polynomial of degree $n > 0$ and if a zero of multiplicity m is counted m times, then $f(x)$ has precisely n zeros.

Notice how the polynomial of degree 6 in Example 2 relates to the last theorem. The multiplicities are 1, 3, and 2, so f has precisely $1 + 3 + 2 = 6$ zeros.

EXAMPLE 3   Finding the zeros of a polynomial

Express $f(x) = x^5 - 4x^4 + 13x^3$ as a product of linear factors, and find the five zeros of $f(x)$.

SOLUTION   We begin by factoring out x^3:

$$f(x) = x^3(x^2 - 4x + 13)$$

By the quadratic formula, the zeros of the polynomial $x^2 - 4x + 13$ are

$$\frac{-(-4) \pm \sqrt{(-4)^2 - 4(1)(13)}}{2(1)} = \frac{4 \pm \sqrt{-36}}{2} = \frac{4 \pm 6i}{2} = 2 \pm 3i.$$

Hence, by the factor theorem, $x^2 - 4x + 13$ has factors $x - (2 + 3i)$ and $x - (2 - 3i)$, and we obtain the factorization

$$f(x) = x \cdot x \cdot x \cdot (x - 2 - 3i)(x - 2 + 3i).$$

Since $x - 0$ occurs as a factor three times, the number 0 is a zero of multiplicity 3, and the five zeros of $f(x)$ are 0, 0, 0, $2 + 3i$, and $2 - 3i$.   ◢

We next show how to use *Descartes' rule of signs* to obtain information about the zeros of a polynomial $f(x)$ with real coefficients. In the statement of the rule we assume that the terms of $f(x)$ are arranged in order of decreasing powers of x and that terms with zero coefficients are deleted. We also assume that the **constant term**—that is, the term that does not contain x—is different from 0. We say there is a **variation of sign** in $f(x)$ if two consecutive coefficients have opposite signs. To illustrate, the polynomial $f(x)$ in the following illustration has *three* variations of sign, as indicated by the braces—one variation from $2x^5$ to $-7x^4$, a second from $-7x^4$ to $3x^2$, and a third from $6x$ to -5.

ILLUSTRATION   Variations of Sign in $f(x) = 2x^5 - 7x^4 + 3x^2 + 6x - 5$

$$\underbrace{\quad}_{+\text{ to }-} \qquad \underbrace{\quad}_{-\text{ to }+} \qquad \underbrace{\quad}_{\text{no variation}} \qquad \underbrace{\quad}_{+\text{ to }-}$$

■ $\quad f(x) = 2x^5 \quad - 7x^4 \quad + 3x^2 \quad + 6x \quad - 5$

Descartes' rule also refers to the variations of sign in $f(-x)$. Using the previous illustration, note that

$$f(-x) = 2(-x)^5 - 7(-x)^4 + 3(-x)^2 + 6(-x) - 5$$
$$= -2x^5 - 7x^4 + 3x^2 - 6x - 5.$$

Hence, as indicated in the next illustration, there are *two* variations of sign in $f(-x)$—one from $-7x^4$ to $3x^2$ and a second from $3x^2$ to $-6x$.

ILLUSTRATION   Variations of Sign in $f(-x)$ if $f(x) = 2x^5 - 7x^4 + 3x^2 + 6x - 5$

	no variation	− to +	+ to −	no variation	
$f(-x) = -2x^5$		$- 7x^4$	$+ 3x^2$	$- 6x$	$- 5$

We may state Descartes' rule as follows.

Descartes' Rule of Signs	Let $f(x)$ be a polynomial with real coefficients and a nonzero constant term.
	(1) The number of *positive* real zeros of $f(x)$ either is equal to the number of variations of sign in $f(x)$ or is less than that number by an even integer.
	(2) The number of *negative* real zeros of $f(x)$ either is equal to the number of variations of sign in $f(-x)$ or is less than that number by an even integer.

A proof of Descartes' rule will not be given.

EXAMPLE 4   Using Descartes' rule of signs

Discuss the number of possible positive and negative real solutions and imaginary solutions of the equation $f(x) = 0$, where

$$f(x) = 2x^5 - 7x^4 + 3x^2 + 6x - 5.$$

SOLUTION   The polynomial $f(x)$ is the one given in the two previous illustrations. Since there are three variations of sign in $f(x)$, the equation has either three positive real solutions or one positive real solution.

Since $f(-x)$ has two variations of sign, the equation has either two negative solutions or no negative solution. Because $f(x)$ has degree 5, there are a total of 5 solutions. The solutions that are not positive or negative real numbers are imaginary numbers. The following table summarizes the various possibilities that can occur for solutions of the equation.

(continued)

Number of positive real solutions	3	3	1	1
Number of negative real solutions	2	0	2	0
Number of imaginary solutions	0	2	2	4
Total number of solutions	5	5	5	5

Descartes' rule stipulates that the constant term of the polynomial $f(x)$ is different from 0. If the constant term is 0, as in the equation

$$x^4 - 3x^3 + 2x^2 - 5x = 0,$$

we factor out the lowest power of x, obtaining

$$x(x^3 - 3x^2 + 2x - 5) = 0.$$

Thus, one solution is $x = 0$, and we apply Descartes' rule to the polynomial $x^3 - 3x^2 + 2x - 5$ to determine the nature of the remaining three solutions.

When applying Descartes' rule, we count roots of multiplicity k as k roots. For example, given $x^2 - 2x + 1 = 0$, the polynomial $x^2 - 2x + 1$ has two variations of sign, and hence the equation has either two positive real roots or none. The factored form of the equation is $(x - 1)^2 = 0$, and hence 1 is a root of multiplicity 2.

We next discuss the *bounds* for the real zeros of a polynomial $f(x)$ that has real coefficients. By definition, a real number b is an **upper bound** for the zeros if no zero is greater than b. A real number a is a **lower bound** for the zeros if no zero is less than a. Thus, if r is any real zero of $f(x)$, then $a \le r \le b$; that is, r is in the closed interval $[a, b]$, as illustrated in Figure 2. Note that upper and lower bounds are not unique, since any number greater than b is also an upper bound and any number less than a is also a lower bound.

Figure 2

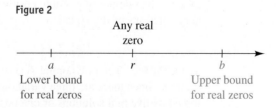

Any real zero

a r b

Lower bound for real zeros   Upper bound for real zeros

We may use synthetic division to find upper and lower bounds for the zeros of $f(x)$. Recall that if we divide $f(x)$ synthetically by $x - c$, the third row in the division process contains the coefficients of the quotient $q(x)$ together with the remainder $f(c)$. The following theorem indicates how this third row may be used to find upper and lower bounds for the real solutions.

Theorem on Bounds for Real Zeros of Polynomials	Suppose that $f(x)$ is a polynomial with real coefficients and a positive leading coefficient and that $f(x)$ is divided synthetically by $x - c$.
	(1) If $c > 0$ and if all numbers in the third row of the division process are either positive or zero, then c is an upper bound for the real zeros of $f(x)$.
	(2) If $c < 0$ and if the numbers in the third row of the division process are alternately positive and negative (and a 0 in the third row is considered to be either positive or negative), then c is a lower bound for the real zeros of $f(x)$.

EXAMPLE 5 Finding bounds for the solutions of an equation

Find upper and lower bounds for the real solutions of the equation $f(x) = 0$, where $f(x) = 2x^3 + 5x^2 - 8x - 7$.

SOLUTION   We divide $f(x)$ synthetically by $x - 1$ and $x - 2$.

$$
\begin{array}{r|rrrr}
1 & 2 & 5 & -8 & -7 \\
  &   & 2 & 7 & -1 \\
\hline
  & 2 & 7 & -1 & -8
\end{array}
\qquad
\begin{array}{r|rrrr}
2 & 2 & 5 & -8 & -7 \\
  &   & 4 & 18 & 20 \\
\hline
  & 2 & 9 & 10 & 13
\end{array}
$$

The third row of the synthetic division by $x - 1$ contains negative numbers, and hence part (1) of the theorem on bounds for real zeros of polynomials does not apply. However, since all numbers in the third row of the synthetic division by $x - 2$ are positive, it follows from part (1) that 2 is an upper bound for the real solutions of the equation. This fact is also evident if we express the division by $x - 2$ in the division algorithm form

$$2x^3 + 5x^2 - 8x - 7 = (x - 2)(2x^2 + 9x + 10) + 13,$$

for if $x > 2$, then the right-hand side of the equation is positive (why?), and hence $f(x)$ is not zero.

We now find a lower bound. After some trial-and-error attempts using $x - (-1)$, $x - (-2)$, and $x - (-3)$, we see that synthetic division of f by $x - (-4)$ gives us

$$
\begin{array}{r|rrrr}
-4 & 2 & 5 & -8 & -7 \\
   &   & -8 & 12 & -16 \\
\hline
   & 2 & -3 & 4 & -23
\end{array}
$$

Since the numbers in the third row are alternately positive and negative, it follows from part (2) of the preceding theorem that -4 is a lower bound for the
(continued)

Figure 3

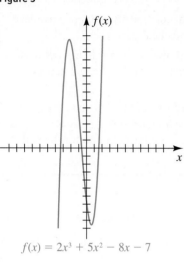

$f(x) = 2x^3 + 5x^2 - 8x - 7$

real solutions. This can also be proved by expressing the division by $x + 4$ in the form

$$2x^3 + 5x^2 - 8x - 7 = (x + 4)(2x^2 - 3x + 4) - 23,$$

for if $x < -4$, then the right-hand side of this equation is negative (why?), and hence $f(x)$ is not zero.

Since lower and upper bounds for the real solutions are -4 and 2, respectively, it follows that all real solutions are in the closed interval $[-4, 2]$.

The graph of f in Figure 3 shows that the three zeros of f are in the intervals $[-4, -3]$, $[-1, 0]$, and $[1, 2]$, respectively.

EXAMPLE 6 Finding a polynomial from a graph

Shown in Figure 4 are all the zeros of a polynomial function f.

(a) Find a factored form for f that has minimal degree.

(b) Assuming the leading coefficient of f is 1, find the y-intercept.

SOLUTION

(a) The zero at $x = -2$ must have a multiplicity that is an even number, since f does not change sign at $x = -2$. The zero at $x = 1$ must have an odd multiplicity of 3 or greater, since f changes sign at $x = 1$ and levels off. The zero at $x = 3$ is of multiplicity 1, since f changes sign and does not level off. Thus, a factored form of f is

$$f(x) = a(x + 2)^m(x - 1)^n(x - 3)^1.$$

Because we desire the function having minimal degree, we let $m = 2$ and $n = 3$, obtaining

$$f(x) = a(x + 2)^2(x - 1)^3(x - 3),$$

which is a sixth-degree polynomial.

(b) If the leading coefficient of f is to be 1, then, from the complete factorization theorem for polynomials, we know that the value of a is 1. To find the y-intercept, we let $x = 0$ and compute $f(0)$:

$$f(0) = 1(0 + 2)^2(0 - 1)^3(0 - 3) = 1(4)(-1)(-3) = 12$$

Hence, the y-intercept is 12.

Figure 4

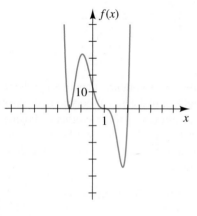

4.3 Exercises

Exer. 1–6: Find a polynomial $f(x)$ of degree 3 that has the indicated zeros and satisfies the given condition.

1 $-1, 2, 3;$ $f(-2) = 80$

2 $-5, 2, 4;$ $f(3) = -24$

3 $-4, 3, 0;$ $f(2) = -36$

4 $-3, -2, 0;$ $f(-4) = 16$

5 $-2i, 2i, 3;$ $f(1) = 20$

6 $-3i, 3i, 4; \quad f(-1) = 50$

7 Find a polynomial $f(x)$ of degree 4 with leading coefficient 1 such that both -4 and 3 are zeros of multiplicity 2, and sketch the graph of f.

8 Find a polynomial $f(x)$ of degree 4 with leading coefficient 1 such that both -5 and 2 are zeros of multiplicity 2, and sketch the graph of f.

9 Find a polynomial $f(x)$ of degree 6 such that 0 and 3 are both zeros of multiplicity 3 and $f(2) = -24$. Sketch the graph of f.

10 Find a polynomial $f(x)$ of degree 7 such that -2 and 2 are both zeros of multiplicity 2, 0 is a zero of multiplicity 3, and $f(-1) = 27$. Sketch the graph of f.

11 Find the third-degree polynomial function whose graph is shown in the figure.

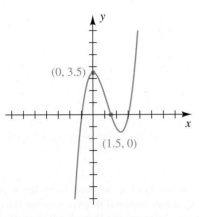

12 Find the fourth-degree polynomial function whose graph is shown in the figure.

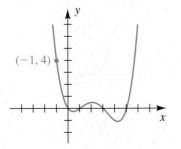

Exer. 13–14: Find the polynomial function of degree 3 whose graph is shown in the figure.

13

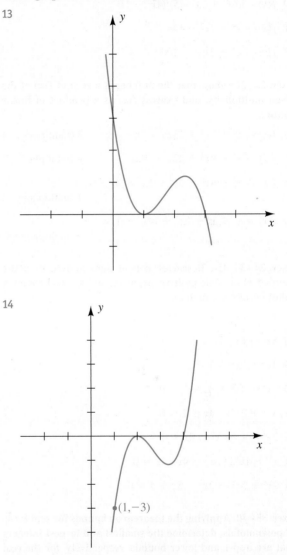

14

Exer. 15–22: Find the zeros of $f(x)$, and state the multiplicity of each zero.

15 $f(x) = x^2(3x + 2)(2x - 5)^3$

16 $f(x) = x(x + 1)^4(3x - 7)^2$

17 $f(x) = 4x^5 + 12x^4 + 9x^3$

18 $f(x) = (4x^2 - 5)^2$

19 $f(x) = (x^2 + x - 12)^3(x^2 - 9)^2$

20 $f(x) = (6x^2 + 7x - 5)^4(4x^2 - 1)^2$

21 $f(x) = x^4 + 7x^2 - 144$

22 $f(x) = x^4 + 21x^2 - 100$

Exer. 23–26: Show that the number is a zero of $f(x)$ of the given multiplicity, and express $f(x)$ as a product of linear factors.

23 $f(x) = x^4 + 7x^3 + 13x^2 - 3x - 18$; -3 (multiplicity 2)

24 $f(x) = x^4 - 9x^3 + 22x^2 - 32$;   4 (multiplicity 2)

25 $f(x) = x^6 - 4x^5 + 5x^4 - 5x^2 + 4x - 1$;
                      1 (multiplicity 5)

26 $f(x) = x^5 + x^4 - 6x^3 - 14x^2 - 11x - 3$;
                      -1 (multiplicity 4)

Exer. 27–34: Use Descartes' rule of signs to determine the number of possible positive, negative, and nonreal complex solutions of the equation.

27 $4x^3 - 6x^2 + x - 3 = 0$

28 $5x^3 - 6x - 4 = 0$

29 $4x^3 + 2x^2 + 1 = 0$

30 $3x^3 - 4x^2 + 3x + 7 = 0$

31 $3x^4 + 2x^3 - 4x + 2 = 0$

32 $2x^4 - x^3 + x^2 - 3x + 4 = 0$

33 $x^5 + 4x^4 + 3x^3 - 4x + 2 = 0$

34 $2x^6 + 5x^5 + 2x^2 - 3x + 4 = 0$

Exer. 35–40: Applying the theorem on bounds for real zeros of polynomials, determine the smallest and largest integers that are upper and lower bounds, respectively, for the real solutions of the equation.

35 $x^3 - 4x^2 - 5x + 7 = 0$

36 $2x^3 - 5x^2 + 4x - 8 = 0$

37 $x^4 - x^3 - 2x^2 + 3x + 6 = 0$

38 $2x^4 - 9x^3 - 8x - 10 = 0$

39 $2x^5 - 13x^3 + 2x - 5 = 0$

40 $3x^5 + 2x^4 - x^3 - 8x^2 - 7 = 0$

Exer. 41–42: Find a factored form for a polynomial function f that has a minimal degree. Assume that the intercept values are integers.

41

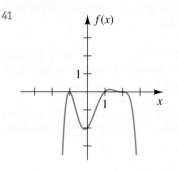

42

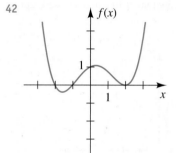

Exer. 43–44: (a) Find a factored form for a polynomial function f that has minimal degree. Assume that the intercept values are integers. (b) If the leading coefficient of f is a, find the y-intercept.

43 $a = 1$

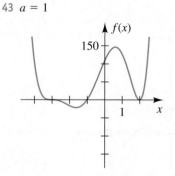

44 $a = -1$

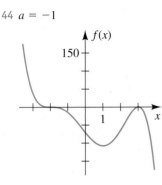

Exer. 45–48: Is there a polynomial of the given degree n whose graph contains the indicated points?

45 $n = 4$;
$(-2, 0), (0, -24), (1, 0), (3, 0), (2, 0), (-1, -52)$

46 $n = 5$;
$(0, 0), (-3, 0), (-1, 0), (2, 0), (3, 0), (-2, 5), (1, 2)$

47 $n = 3$;
$(1.1, -49.815), (2, 0), (3.5, 25.245), (5.2, 0),$
$(6.4, -29.304), (10.1, 0)$

48 $n = 4$;
$(1.25, 0), (2, 0), (2.5, 56.25), (3, 128.625), (6.5, 0),$
$(9, -307.75), (10, 0)$

49 Using limited data A scientist has limited data on the temperature T (in °C) during a 24-hour period. If t denotes time in hours and $t = 0$ corresponds to midnight, find the fourth-degree polynomial that fits the information in the following table.

t (hours)	0	5	12	19	24
T (°C)	0	0	10	0	0

50 Lagrange interpolation polynomial A polynomial $f(x)$ of degree 3 with zeros at c_1, c_2, and c_3 and with $f(c) = 1$ for $c_2 < c < c_3$ is a third-degree *Lagrange interpolation polynomial*. Find an explicit formula for $f(x)$ in terms of c_1, c_2, c_3, and c.

4.4

Complex and Rational Zeros of Polynomials

Example 3 of the preceding section illustrates an important fact about polynomials with real coefficients: The two complex zeros $2 + 3i$ and $2 - 3i$ of $x^5 - 4x^4 + 13x^3$ are conjugates of each other. The relationship is not accidental, since the following general result is true.

Theorem on Conjugate Pair Zeros of a Polynomial	If a polynomial $f(x)$ of degree $n > 1$ has real coefficients and if $z = a + bi$ with $b \neq 0$ is a complex zero of $f(x)$, then the conjugate $\bar{z} = a - bi$ is also a zero of $f(x)$.

A proof is left as a discussion exercise at the end of the chapter.

EXAMPLE 1 Finding a polynomial with prescribed zeros

Find a polynomial $f(x)$ of degree 4 that has real coefficients and zeros $2 + i$ and $-3i$.

SOLUTION By the theorem on conjugate pair zeros of a polynomial, $f(x)$ must also have zeros $2 - i$ and $3i$. Applying the factor theorem, we find that $f(x)$ has the following factors:

$$x - (2 + i), \quad x - (2 - i), \quad x - (-3i), \quad x - (3i)$$

(continued)

Multiplying these four factors gives us

$$\begin{aligned} f(x) &= [x - (2 + i)][x - (2 - i)](x + 3i)(x - 3i) \\ &= (x^2 - 4x + 5)(x^2 + 9) \qquad\qquad (*)\\ &= x^4 - 4x^3 + 14x^2 - 36x + 45. \end{aligned}$$

Note that in $(*)$ the symbol i does not appear. This is not a coincidence, since if $a + bi$ is a zero of a polynomial with real coefficients, then $a - bi$ is also a zero and we can multiply the associated factors as follows:

$$[x - (a + bi)][x - (a - bi)] = x^2 - 2ax + a^2 + b^2$$

In Example 1 we have $a = 2$ and $b = 1$, so $-2a = -4$ and $a^2 + b^2 = 5$ and the associated quadratic factor is $x^2 - 4x + 5$. This resulting quadratic factor will always have real coefficients, as stated in the next theorem.

Theorem on Expressing a Polynomial as a Product of Linear and Quadratic Factors	Every polynomial with real coefficients and positive degree n can be expressed as a product of linear and quadratic polynomials with real coefficients such that the quadratic factors are irreducible over $\mathbb{R}$.

PROOF   Since $f(x)$ has precisely n complex zeros $c_1, c_2, \ldots, c_n$, we may write

$$f(x) = a(x - c_1)(x - c_2) \cdots (x - c_n),$$

where a is the leading coefficient of $f(x)$. Of course, some of the zeros may be real. In such cases we obtain the linear factors referred to in the statement of the theorem.

If a zero c_k is not real, then, by the theorem on conjugate pair zeros of a polynomial, the conjugate $\overline{c_k}$ is also a zero of $f(x)$ and hence must be one of the numbers $c_1, c_2, \ldots, c_n$. This implies that both $x - c_k$ and $x - \overline{c_k}$ appear in the factorization of $f(x)$. If those factors are multiplied, we obtain

$$(x - c_k)(x - \overline{c_k}) = x^2 - (c_k + \overline{c_k})x + c_k\overline{c_k},$$

which has *real* coefficients, since $c_k + \overline{c_k}$ and $c_k\overline{c_k}$ are real numbers. Thus, if c_k is a complex zero, then the product $(x - c_k)(x - \overline{c_k})$ is a quadratic polynomial that is irreducible over $\mathbb{R}$. This completes the proof.

EXAMPLE 2   Expressing a polynomial as a product
of linear and quadratic factors

Express $x^5 - 4x^3 + x^2 - 4$ as a product of

(a) linear and quadratic polynomials with real coefficients that are irreducible over $\mathbb{R}$

(b) linear polynomials

SOLUTION

(a) $x^5 - 4x^3 + x^2 - 4$

$$\begin{aligned}
&= (x^5 - 4x^3) + (x^2 - 4) && \text{group terms} \\
&= x^3(x^2 - 4) + 1(x^2 - 4) && \text{factor out } x^3 \\
&= (x^3 + 1)(x^2 - 4) && \text{factor out } (x^2 - 4) \\
&= (x + 1)(x^2 - x + 1)(x + 2)(x - 2) && \text{factor as the sum of cubes}
\end{aligned}$$

and the difference of squares

Using the quadratic formula, we see that the polynomial $x^2 - x + 1$ has the complex zeros

$$\frac{-(-1) \pm \sqrt{(-1)^2 - 4(1)(1)}}{2(1)} = \frac{1 \pm \sqrt{3}i}{2} = \frac{1}{2} \pm \frac{\sqrt{3}}{2}i$$

and hence is irreducible over $\mathbb{R}$. Thus, the desired factorization is

$$(x + 1)(x^2 - x + 1)(x + 2)(x - 2).$$

(b) Since the polynomial $x^2 - x + 1$ in part (a) has zeros $\frac{1}{2} \pm (\sqrt{3}/2)i$, it follows from the factor theorem that the polynomial has factors

$$x - \left(\frac{1}{2} + \frac{\sqrt{3}}{2}i\right) \quad \text{and} \quad x - \left(\frac{1}{2} - \frac{\sqrt{3}}{2}i\right).$$

Substituting in the factorization found in part (a), we obtain the following complete factorization into linear polynomials:

$$(x + 1)\left(x - \frac{1}{2} - \frac{\sqrt{3}}{2}i\right)\left(x - \frac{1}{2} + \frac{\sqrt{3}}{2}i\right)(x + 2)(x - 2)$$

We previously pointed out that it is generally very difficult to find the zeros of a polynomial of high degree. If all the coefficients are integers, however, there is a method for finding the *rational* zeros, if they exist. The method is a consequence of the following result.

Theorem on Rational Zeros of a Polynomial	If the polynomial $$f(x) = a_n x^n + a_{n-1}x^{n-1} + \cdots + a_1 x + a_0$$ has *integer* coefficients and if c/d is a rational zero of $f(x)$ such that c and d have no common prime factor, then **(1)** the numerator c of the zero is a factor of the constant term a_0 **(2)** the denominator d of the zero is a factor of the leading coefficient a_n

PROOF Assume that $c > 0$. (The proof for $c < 0$ is similar.) Let us show that c is a factor of a_0. The case $c = 1$ is trivial, since 1 is a factor of *any*

(continued)

number. Thus, suppose $c \neq 1$. In this case $c/d \neq 1$, for if $c/d = 1$, we obtain $c = d$, and since c and d have no prime factor in common, this implies that $c = d = 1$, a contradiction. Hence, in the following discussion we have $c \neq 1$ and $c \neq d$.

Since $f(c/d) = 0$,

$$a_n \frac{c^n}{d^n} + a_{n-1} \frac{c^{n-1}}{d^{n-1}} + \cdots + a_1 \frac{c}{d} + a_0 = 0.$$

We multiply by d^n and then add $-a_0 d^n$ to both sides:

$$a_n c^n + a_{n-1} c^{n-1} d + \cdots + a_1 c d^{n-1} = -a_0 d^n$$
$$c(a_n c^{n-1} + a_{n-1} c^{n-2} d + \cdots + a_1 d^{n-1}) = -a_0 d^n$$

The last equation shows that c is a factor of the integer $a_0 d^n$. Since c and d have no common factor, c is a factor of a_0. A similar argument may be used to prove that d is a factor of a_n.   ◢

As an aid in listing the possible rational zeros, remember the following quotient:

$$\text{Possible rational zeros} = \frac{\text{factors of the constant term } a_0}{\text{factors of the leading coefficient } a_n}$$

The theorem on rational zeros of a polynomial may be applied to equations with rational coefficients by merely multiplying both sides of the equation by the lcd of all the coefficients to obtain an equation with integral coefficients.

EXAMPLE 3   Showing a polynomial has no rational zeros

Show that $f(x) = x^3 - 4x - 2$ has no rational zeros.

SOLUTION   If $f(x)$ has a rational zero c/d such that c and d have no common prime factor, then, by the theorem on rational zeros of a polynomial, c is a factor of the constant term -2 and hence is either 2 or -2 (which we write as ± 2) or ± 1. The denominator d is a factor of the leading coefficient 1 and hence is ± 1. Thus, the only possibilities for c/d are

$$\frac{\pm 1}{\pm 1} \quad \text{and} \quad \frac{\pm 2}{\pm 1} \qquad \text{or, equivalently,} \qquad \pm 1 \quad \text{and} \quad \pm 2.$$

Substituting each of these numbers for x, we obtain

$$f(1) = -5, \quad f(-1) = 1, \quad f(2) = -2, \quad \text{and} \quad f(-2) = -2.$$

Since $f(\pm 1) \neq 0$ and $f(\pm 2) \neq 0$, it follows that $f(x)$ has no rational zeros.   ◢

EXAMPLE 4 Finding the rational solutions of an equation

Find all rational solutions of the equation

$$3x^4 + 14x^3 + 14x^2 - 8x - 8 = 0.$$

SOLUTION   The problem is equivalent to finding the rational zeros of the polynomial on the left-hand side of the equation. If c/d is a rational zero and c and d have no common factor, then c is a factor of the constant term -8 and d is a factor of the leading coefficient 3. All possible choices are listed in the following table.

Choices for the numerator c	$\pm 1, \pm 2, \pm 4, \pm 8$
Choices for the denominator d	$\pm 1, \pm 3$
Choices for c/d	$\pm 1, \pm 2, \pm 4, \pm 8, \pm\frac{1}{3}, \pm\frac{2}{3}, \pm\frac{4}{3}, \pm\frac{8}{3}$

We can reduce the number of choices by finding upper and lower bounds for the real solutions; however, we shall not do so here. It is necessary to determine which of the choices for c/d, if any, are zeros. We see by substitution that neither 1 nor -1 is a solution. If we divide synthetically by $x + 2$, we obtain

$$
\begin{array}{r|rrrr}
-2 & 3 & 14 & 14 & -8 & -8 \\
   &   & -6 & -16 & 4 & 8 \\
\hline
   & 3 & 8 & -2 & -4 & 0
\end{array}
$$

This result shows that -2 is a zero. Moreover, the synthetic division provides the coefficients of the quotient in the division of the polynomial by $x + 2$. Hence, we have the following factorization of the given polynomial:

$$(x + 2)(3x^3 + 8x^2 - 2x - 4)$$

The remaining solutions of the equation must be zeros of the second factor, so we use that polynomial to check for solutions. *Do not* use the polynomial in the original equation. (Note that $\pm\frac{8}{3}$ are no longer candidates, since the numerator must be a factor of 4.) Again proceeding by trial and error, we ultimately find that synthetic division by $x + \frac{2}{3}$ gives us the following result:

$$
\begin{array}{r|rrrr}
-\frac{2}{3} & 3 & 8 & -2 & -4 \\
             &   & -2 & -4 & 4 \\
\hline
             & 3 & 6 & -6 & 0
\end{array}
$$

Therefore, $-\frac{2}{3}$ is also a zero.

Using the coefficients of the quotient, we know that the remaining zeros are solutions of the equation $3x^2 + 6x - 6 = 0$. Dividing both sides by 3

(continued)

gives us the equivalent equation $x^2 + 2x - 2 = 0$. By the quadratic formula, this equation has solutions

$$\frac{-2 \pm \sqrt{2^2 - 4(1)(-2)}}{2(1)} = \frac{-2 \pm \sqrt{12}}{2} = \frac{-2 \pm 2\sqrt{3}}{2} = -1 \pm \sqrt{3}.$$

Hence, the given polynomial has two rational roots, -2 and $-\frac{2}{3}$, and two irrational roots, $-1 + \sqrt{3} \approx 0.732$ and $-1 - \sqrt{3} \approx -2.732$. ◢

EXAMPLE 5 Finding the radius of a grain silo

A grain silo has the shape of a right circular cylinder with a hemisphere attached to the top. If the total height of the structure is 30 feet, find the radius of the cylinder that results in a total volume of 1008π ft^3.

SOLUTION Let x denote the radius of the cylinder as shown in Figure 1. The volume of the cylinder is $\pi r^2 h = \pi x^2(30 - x)$, and the volume of the hemisphere is $\frac{2}{3}\pi r^3 = \frac{2}{3}\pi x^3$, so we solve for x as follows:

$$\pi x^2(30 - x) + \tfrac{2}{3}\pi x^3 = 1008\pi \qquad \text{total volume is } 1008\pi$$

$$3x^2(30 - x) + 2x^3 = 3024 \qquad \text{multiply by } \frac{3}{\pi}$$

$$90x^2 - x^3 = 3024 \qquad \text{simplify}$$

$$x^3 - 90x^2 + 3024 = 0 \qquad \text{equivalent equation}$$

Since the leading coefficient of the polynomial on the left-hand side of the last equation is 1, any rational root has the form $c/1 = c$, where c is a factor of 3024. If we factor 3024 into primes, we find that $3024 = 2^4 \cdot 3^3 \cdot 7$. It follows that some of the positive factors of 3024 are

$$1, \quad 2, \quad 3, \quad 4, \quad 6, \quad 7, \quad 8, \quad 9, \quad 12, \quad \dots.$$

To help us decide which of these numbers to test first, let us make a rough estimate of the radius by assuming that the silo has the shape of a right circular cylinder of height 30 feet. In that case, the volume would be $\pi r^2 h = 30\pi r^2$. Since this volume should be close to 1008π, we see that

$$30r^2 = 1008, \qquad \text{or} \qquad r^2 = 1008/30 = 33.6.$$

This suggests that we use 6 in our first synthetic division, as follows:

$$\begin{array}{r|rrrr} 6 & 1 & -90 & 0 & 3024 \\ & & 6 & -504 & -3024 \\ \hline & 1 & -84 & -504 & 0 \end{array}$$

Thus, 6 is a solution of the equation $x^3 - 90x^2 + 3024 = 0$.

The remaining two solutions of the equation can be found by solving the depressed equation $x^2 - 84x - 504 = 0$. These zeros are approximately -5.62 and 89.62—neither of which satisfies the conditions of the problem. Hence, the desired radius is 6 feet. ◢

Figure 1

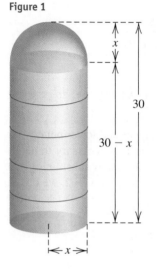

4.4 Exercises

Exer. 1–10: A polynomial $f(x)$ with real coefficients and leading coefficient 1 has the given zero(s) and degree. Express $f(x)$ as a product of linear and quadratic polynomials with real coefficients that are irreducible over $\mathbb{R}$.

1 $3 + 2i$; degree 2

2 $-4 + 3i$; degree 2

3 $2, -2 - 5i$; degree 3

4 $-3, 1 - 7i$; degree 3

5 $-1, 0, 3 + i$; degree 4

6 $0, 2, -2 - i$; degree 4

7 $4 + 3i, -2 + i$; degree 4

8 $3 + 5i, -1 - i$; degree 4

9 $0, -2i, 1 - i$; degree 5

10 $0, 3i, 4 + i$; degree 5

Exer. 11–14: Show that the equation has no rational root.

11 $x^3 + 3x^2 - 4x + 6 = 0$

12 $3x^3 - 4x^2 + 7x + 5 = 0$

13 $x^5 - 3x^3 + 4x^2 + x - 2 = 0$

14 $2x^5 + 3x^3 + 7 = 0$

Exer. 15–24: Find all solutions of the equation.

15 $x^3 - x^2 - 10x - 8 = 0$

16 $x^3 + x^2 - 14x - 24 = 0$

17 $2x^3 - 3x^2 - 17x + 30 = 0$

18 $12x^3 + 8x^2 - 3x - 2 = 0$

19 $x^4 + 3x^3 - 30x^2 - 6x + 56 = 0$

20 $3x^5 - 10x^4 - 6x^3 + 24x^2 + 11x - 6 = 0$

21 $6x^5 + 19x^4 + x^3 - 6x^2 = 0$

22 $6x^4 + 5x^3 - 17x^2 - 6x = 0$

23 $8x^3 + 18x^2 + 45x + 27 = 0$

24 $3x^3 - x^2 + 11x - 20 = 0$

Exer. 25–26: Find a factored form with integer coefficients of the polynomial f shown in the figure.

25 $f(x) = 6x^5 - 23x^4 + 24x^3 + x^2 - 12x + 4$

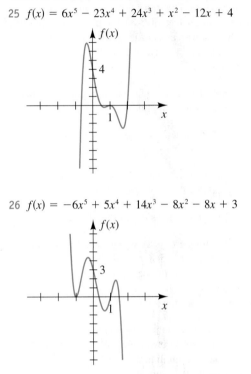

26 $f(x) = -6x^5 + 5x^4 + 14x^3 - 8x^2 - 8x + 3$

27 Does there exist a polynomial of degree 3 with real coefficients that has zeros 1, -1, and i? Justify your answer.

28 The polynomial $f(x) = x^3 - ix^2 + 2ix + 2$ has the complex number i as a zero; however, the conjugate $-i$ of i is not a zero. Why doesn't this result contradict the theorem on conjugate pair zeros of a polynomial?

29 If n is an odd positive integer, prove that a polynomial of degree n with real coefficients has at least one real zero.

30 If a polynomial of the form

$$x^n + a_{n-1}x^{n-1} + \cdots + a_1x + a_0,$$

where each a_k is an integer, has a rational root r, show that r is an integer and is a factor of a_0.

31 Constructing a box From a rectangular piece of cardboard having dimensions 20 inches $\times$ 30 inches, an open box is to be made by removing squares of area x^2 from each corner and turning up the sides. (See Exercise 41 of Section 4.1.)

(a) Show that there are two boxes that have a volume of 1000 in³.

(b) Which box has the smaller surface area?

32 **Constructing a crate** The frame for a shipping crate is to be constructed from 24 feet of 2 × 2 lumber. Assuming the crate is to have square ends of length x feet, determine the value(s) of x that result(s) in a volume of 4 ft³. (See Exercise 42 of Section 4.1.)

33 A right triangle has area 30 ft² and a hypotenuse that is 1 foot longer than one of its sides.

(a) If x denotes the length of this side, then show that $2x^3 + x^2 - 3600 = 0$.

(b) Show that there is a positive root of the equation in part (a) and that this root is less than 13.

(c) Find the lengths of the sides of the triangle.

34 **Constructing a storage tank** A storage tank for propane gas is to be constructed in the shape of a right circular cylinder of altitude 10 feet with a hemisphere attached to each end. Determine the radius x so that the resulting volume is 27π ft³. (See Example 8 of Section 3.4.)

35 **Constructing a storage shelter** A storage shelter is to be constructed in the shape of a cube with a triangular prism forming the roof (see the figure). The length x of a side of the cube is yet to be determined.

(a) If the total height of the structure is 6 feet, show that its volume V is given by $V = x^3 + \frac{1}{2}x^2(6 - x)$.

(b) Determine x so that the volume is 80 ft³.

Exercise 35

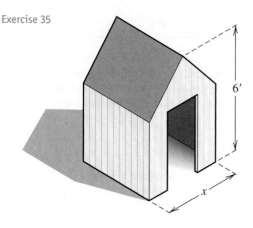

36 **Designing a tent** A canvas camping tent is to be constructed in the shape of a pyramid with a square base. An 8-foot pole will form the center support, as illustrated in the figure. Find the length x of a side of the base so that the total amount of canvas needed for the sides and bottom is 384 ft².

Exercise 36

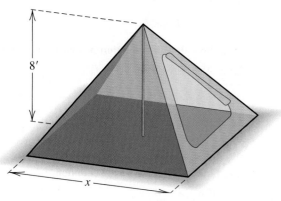

4.5

Rational Functions

A function f is a **rational function** if

$$f(x) = \frac{g(x)}{h(x)},$$

where $g(x)$ and $h(x)$ are polynomials. The domain of f consists of all real numbers *except* the zeros of the denominator $h(x)$.

ILLUSTRATION **Rational Functions and Their Domains**

■ $f(x) = \dfrac{1}{x-2};$ *domain:* all x *except* $x = 2$

■ $f(x) = \dfrac{5x}{x^2-9};$ *domain:* all x *except* $x = \pm 3$

■ $f(x) = \dfrac{x^3-8}{x^2+4};$ *domain:* all real numbers x

Previously we simplified rational expressions as follows:

Figure 1

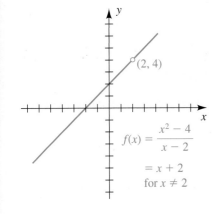

$$\frac{x^2-4}{x-2} = \frac{(x+2)(x-2)}{x-2} \overset{\text{if } x \neq 2}{=} \frac{x+2}{1} = x+2$$

If we let $f(x) = \dfrac{x^2-4}{x-2}$ and $g(x) = x+2$, then the domain of f is all x except $x = 2$ and the domain of g is all real numbers. These domains and the above simplification suggest that the graphs of f and g are the same except for $x = 2$. What happens to the graph of f at $x = 2$? There is a *hole* in the graph—that is, a single point is missing. To find the y-value of the hole, we can substitute 2 for x in the reduced function, which is simply $g(2) = 4$. A graph of f is shown in Figure 1.

We now turn our attention to rational functions that do not have a common factor in the numerator and the denominator.

When sketching the graph of a rational function f, it is important to answer the following two questions.

Question 1 What can be said of the function values $f(x)$ when x is close to (but not equal to) a zero of the denominator?

Question 2 What can be said of the function values $f(x)$ when x is large positive or when x is large negative?

As we shall see, if a is a zero of the denominator, one of several situations often occurs. These are shown in Figure 2, where we have used notations from the following chart.

Notation	Terminology
$x \to a^-$	x approaches a from the left (through values *less* than a).
$x \to a^+$	x approaches a from the right (through values *greater* than a).
$f(x) \to \infty$	$f(x)$ increases without bound (can be made as large positive as desired).
$f(x) \to -\infty$	$f(x)$ decreases without bound (can be made as large negative as desired).

Figure 2

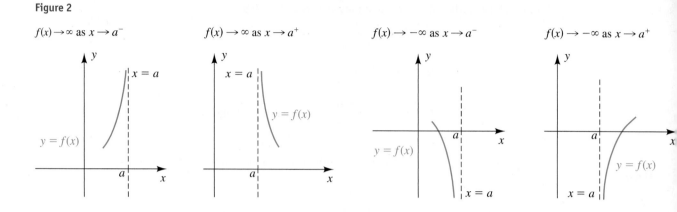

$f(x) \to \infty$ as $x \to a^-$ $f(x) \to \infty$ as $x \to a^+$ $f(x) \to -\infty$ as $x \to a^-$ $f(x) \to -\infty$ as $x \to a^+$

The symbols ∞ (read "infinity") and $-\infty$ (read "minus infinity") do not represent real numbers; they simply specify certain types of behavior of functions and variables.

The dashed line $x = a$ in Figure 2 is called a *vertical asymptote,* as in the following definition.

Definition of Vertical Asymptote	The line $x = a$ is a **vertical asymptote** for the graph of a function f if $$f(x) \to \infty \qquad \text{or} \qquad f(x) \to -\infty$$ as x approaches a from either the left or the right.

Thus, the answer to Question 1 is that if a is a zero of the denominator of a rational function f, then the graph of f *may* have a vertical asymptote $x = a$. There are rational functions where this is *not* the case (as in Figure 1 of this section). If the numerator and denominator have no common factor, then f *must* have a vertical asymptote $x = a$.

Let us next consider Question 2. For x *large positive* or *large negative,* the graph of a rational function may look like one of those in Figure 3, where the notation

$$f(x) \to c \quad \text{as} \quad x \to \infty$$

is read "$f(x)$ approaches c as x increases without bound" or "$f(x)$ approaches c as x approaches infinity," and the notation

$$f(x) \to c \quad \text{as} \quad x \to -\infty$$

is read "$f(x)$ approaches c as x decreases without bound."

Figure 3 $\quad f(x) \to c \text{ as } x \to \infty$ $\qquad\qquad\qquad\qquad f(x) \to c \text{ as } x \to -\infty$

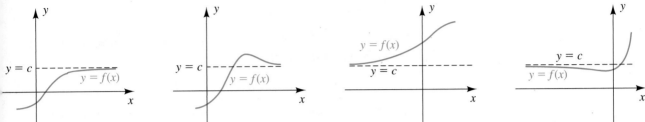

We call the dashed line in Figure 3 a *horizontal asymptote,* as in the next definition.

Definition of Horizontal Asymptote	The line $y = c$ is a **horizontal asymptote** for the graph of a function f if $$f(x) \to c \quad \text{as} \quad x \to \infty \quad \text{or as} \quad x \to -\infty.$$

Thus, the answer to Question 2 is that $f(x)$ *may* be very close to some number c when x is large positive or large negative; that is, the graph of f may have a horizontal asymptote $y = c$. There are rational functions where this is *not* the case (as in Examples 2(c) and 9).

Note that, as in the second and fourth sketches in Figure 3, the graph of f may cross a horizontal asymptote.

In the next example we find the asymptotes for the graph of a simple rational function.

EXAMPLE 1   Sketching the graph of a rational function

Sketch the graph of f if

$$f(x) = \frac{1}{x - 2}.$$

SOLUTION   Let us begin by considering Question 1, stated at the beginning of this section. The denominator $x - 2$ is zero at $x = 2$. If x is close to 2 and $x > 2$, then $f(x)$ is large positive, as indicated in the following table.

x	2.1	2.01	2.001	2.0001	2.00001
$\dfrac{1}{x - 2}$	10	100	1000	10,000	100,000

(continued)

Since we can make $1/(x - 2)$ as large as desired by taking x close to 2 (and $x > 2$), we see that

$$f(x) \to \infty \quad \text{as} \quad x \to 2^{+}.$$

If $f(x)$ is close to 2 and $x < 2$, then $f(x)$ is large negative; for example, $f(1.9999) = -10{,}000$ and $f(1.99999) = -100{,}000$. Thus,

$$f(x) \to -\infty \quad \text{as} \quad x \to 2^{-}.$$

The line $x = 2$ is a vertical asymptote for the graph of f, as illustrated in Figure 4.

We next consider Question 2. The following table lists some approximate values for $f(x)$ when x is large and positive.

Figure 4

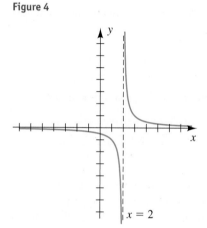

x	100	1000	10,000	100,000	1,000,000
$\dfrac{1}{x - 2}$ **(approx.)**	0.01	0.001	0.0001	0.00001	0.000001

We may describe this behavior of $f(x)$ by writing

$$f(x) \to 0 \quad \text{as} \quad x \to \infty.$$

Similarly, $f(x)$ is close to 0 when x is large negative; for example, $f(-100{,}000) \approx -0.00001$. Thus,

$$f(x) \to 0 \quad \text{as} \quad x \to -\infty.$$

The line $y = 0$ (the x-axis) is a horizontal asymptote, as shown in Figure 4.

Plotting the points $(1, -1)$ and $(3, 1)$ helps give us a rough sketch of the graph.

The function considered in Example 1, $f(x) = 1/(x - 2)$, closely resembles one of the simplest rational functions, the **reciprocal function.** The reciprocal function has equation $f(x) = 1/x$, vertical asymptote $x = 0$ (the y-axis), and horizontal asymptote $y = 0$ (the x-axis). The graph of the reciprocal function (shown in Appendix I) is the graph of a *hyperbola* (discussed later in the text). Note that we can obtain the graph of $y = 1/(x - 2)$ by shifting the graph of $y = 1/x$ to the right 2 units.

The following theorem is useful for finding the horizontal asymptote for the graph of a rational function.

Theorem on Horizontal Asymptotes	Let $f(x) = \dfrac{a_n x^n + a_{n-1} x^{n-1} + \cdots + a_1 x + a_0}{b_k x^k + b_{k-1} x^{k-1} + \cdots + b_1 x + b_0}$, where $a_n \neq 0$ and $b_k \neq 0$.

(1) If $n < k$, then the x-axis (the line $y = 0$) is the horizontal asymptote for the graph of f.

(2) If $n = k$, then the line $y = a_n/b_k$ (the ratio of leading coefficients) is the horizontal asymptote for the graph of f.

(3) If $n > k$, the graph of f has no horizontal asymptote. Instead, either $f(x) \to \infty$ or $f(x) \to -\infty$ as $x \to \infty$ or as $x \to -\infty$.

Proofs for each part of this theorem may be patterned after the solutions in the next example. Concerning part (3), if $q(x)$ is the quotient obtained by dividing the numerator by the denominator, then $f(x) \to \infty$ if $q(x) \to \infty$ or $f(x) \to -\infty$ if $q(x) \to -\infty$.

EXAMPLE 2 Finding horizontal asymptotes

Find the horizontal asymptote for the graph of f, if it exists.

(a) $f(x) = \dfrac{3x - 1}{x^2 - x - 6}$ **(b)** $f(x) = \dfrac{5x^2 + 1}{3x^2 - 4}$

(c) $f(x) = \dfrac{2x^4 - 3x^2 + 5}{x^2 + 1}$

SOLUTION

(a) The degree of the numerator, 1, is less than the degree of the denominator, 2, so, by part (1) of the theorem on horizontal asymptotes, the x-axis is a horizontal asymptote. To verify this directly, we divide the numerator and denominator of the quotient by x^2 (since 2 is the highest power on x in the denominator), obtaining

$$f(x) = \frac{\dfrac{3x - 1}{x^2}}{\dfrac{x^2 - x - 6}{x^2}} = \frac{\dfrac{3}{x} - \dfrac{1}{x^2}}{1 - \dfrac{1}{x} - \dfrac{6}{x^2}} \quad \text{for} \quad x \neq 0.$$

If x is large positive or large negative, then $3/x$, $1/x^2$, $1/x$, and $6/x^2$ are close to 0, and hence

$$f(x) \approx \frac{0 - 0}{1 - 0 - 0} = \frac{0}{1} = 0.$$

Thus,

$$f(x) \to 0 \quad \text{as} \quad x \to \infty \quad \text{or as} \quad x \to -\infty.$$

Since $f(x)$ is the y-coordinate of a point on the graph, the last statement means that the line $y = 0$ (that is, the x-axis) is a horizontal asymptote.

(continued)

(b) If $f(x) = (5x^2 + 1)/(3x^2 - 4)$, then the numerator and denominator have the same degree, 2, and the leading coefficients are 5 and 3, respectively. Hence, by part (2) of the theorem on horizontal asymptotes, the line $y = \frac{5}{3}$ is the horizontal asymptote. We could also show that $y = \frac{5}{3}$ is the horizontal asymptote by dividing the numerator and denominator of $f(x)$ by x^2, as in part (a).

(c) The degree of the numerator, 4, is greater than the degree of the denominator, 2, so, by part (3) of the theorem on horizontal asymptotes, the graph has no horizontal asymptote. If we use long division, we obtain

$$f(x) = 2x^2 - 5 + \frac{10}{x^2 + 1}.$$

As either $x \to \infty$ or $x \to -\infty$, the quotient $2x^2 - 5$ increases without bound and $10/(x^2 + 1) \to 0$. Hence, $f(x) \to \infty$ as $x \to \infty$ or as $x \to -\infty$.

We next list some guidelines for sketching the graph of a rational function. Their use will be illustrated in Examples 3, 6, and 7.

Guidelines for Sketching the Graph of a Rational Function	Assume that $f(x) = \dfrac{g(x)}{h(x)}$, where $g(x)$ and $h(x)$ are polynomials that have no common factor.

1 Find the x-intercepts—that is, the real zeros of the numerator $g(x)$—and plot the corresponding points on the x-axis.

2 Find the real zeros of the denominator $h(x)$. For each real zero a, sketch the vertical asymptote $x = a$ with dashes.

3 Find the y-intercept $f(0)$, if it exists, and plot the point $(0, f(0))$ on the y-axis.

4 Apply the theorem on horizontal asymptotes. If there is a horizontal asymptote $y = c$, sketch it with dashes.

5 If there is a horizontal asymptote $y = c$, determine whether it intersects the graph. The x-coordinates of the points of intersection are the solutions of the equation $f(x) = c$. Plot these points, if they exist.

6 Sketch the graph of f in each of the regions in the xy-plane determined by the vertical asymptotes in guideline 2. If necessary, use the sign of specific function values to tell whether the graph is above or below the x-axis or the horizontal asymptote. Use guideline 5 to decide whether the graph approaches the horizontal asymptote from above or below.

In the following examples our main objective is to determine the general shape of the graph, paying particular attention to how the graph approaches the asymptotes. We will plot only a few points, such as those corresponding to the *x*-intercepts and *y*-intercept or the intersection of the graph with a horizontal asymptote.

EXAMPLE 3 Sketching the graph of a rational function

Sketch the graph of *f* if

$$f(x) = \frac{3x + 4}{2x - 5}.$$

SOLUTION   We follow the guidelines.

Guideline 1   To find the *x*-intercepts we find the zeros of the numerator. Solving $3x + 4 = 0$ gives us $x = -\frac{4}{3}$, and we plot the point $\left(-\frac{4}{3}, 0\right)$ on the *x*-axis, as shown in Figure 5.

Guideline 2   The denominator has zero $\frac{5}{2}$, so the line $x = \frac{5}{2}$ is a vertical asymptote. We sketch this line with dashes, as in Figure 5.

Guideline 3   The *y*-intercept is $f(0) = -\frac{4}{5}$, and we plot the point $\left(0, -\frac{4}{5}\right)$ in Figure 5.

Guideline 4   The numerator and denominator of $f(x)$ have the same degree, 1. The leading coefficients are 3 and 2, so by part (2) of the theorem on horizontal asymptotes, the line $y = \frac{3}{2}$ is a horizontal asymptote. We sketch the line with dashes in Figure 5.

Guideline 5   The *x*-coordinates of the points where the graph intersects the horizontal asymptote $y = \frac{3}{2}$ are solutions of the equation $f(x) = \frac{3}{2}$. We solve this equation as follows:

$$\frac{3x + 4}{2x - 5} = \frac{3}{2} \qquad \text{let } f(x) = \frac{3}{2}$$

$$2(3x + 4) = 3(2x - 5) \qquad \text{multiply by } 2(2x - 5)$$

$$6x + 8 = 6x - 15 \qquad \text{multiply}$$

$$8 = -15 \qquad \text{subtract } 6x$$

Since $8 \neq -15$ for any value of *x*, this result indicates that the graph of *f* does *not* intersect the horizontal asymptote. As an aid in sketching, we can now think of the horizontal asymptote as a boundary that cannot be crossed.

Guideline 6   The vertical asymptote in Figure 5 divides the *xy*-plane into two regions:

$$R_1: \quad \text{the region to the left of } x = \frac{5}{2}$$

$$R_2: \quad \text{the region to the right of } x = \frac{5}{2}$$

For R_1, we have the two points $\left(-\frac{4}{3}, 0\right)$ and $\left(0, -\frac{4}{5}\right)$ that the graph of *f* must pass through, as well as the two asymptotes that the graph must approach. This portion of *f* is shown in Figure 6.

(continued)

Figure 5

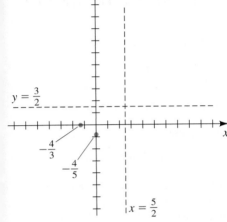

Figure 6

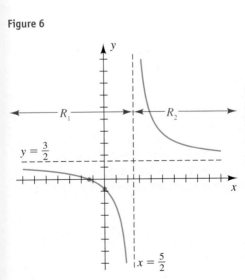

Figure 7

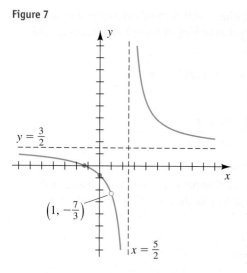

$y = \frac{3}{2}$

$\left(1, -\frac{7}{3}\right)$

$x = \frac{5}{2}$

For R_2, the graph must again approach the two asymptotes. Since the graph cannot cross the x-axis (there is no x-intercept in R_2), it must be above the horizontal asymptote, as shown in Figure 6.

EXAMPLE 4   Sketching a graph that has a hole

Sketch the graph of g if

$$g(x) = \frac{(3x + 4)(x - 1)}{(2x - 5)(x - 1)}.$$

SOLUTION   The domain of g is all real numbers except $\frac{5}{2}$ and 1. If g is reduced, we obtain the function f in the previous example. The only difference between the graphs of f and g is that g has a hole at $x = 1$. Since $f(1) = -\frac{7}{3}$, we need only make a hole on the graph in Figure 6 to obtain the graph of g in Figure 7.

EXAMPLE 5   Finding an equation of a rational function
satisfying prescribed conditions

Find an equation of a rational function f that satisfies the following conditions:

$$x\text{-intercept: 4, vertical asymptote: } x = -2,$$

$$\text{horizontal asymptote: } y = -\tfrac{3}{5}, \text{ and a hole at } x = 1$$

SOLUTION   An x-intercept of 4 implies that $x - 4$ must be a factor in the numerator, and a vertical asymptote of $x = -2$ implies that $x + 2$ is a factor in the denominator. So we can start with the form

$$\frac{x - 4}{x + 2}.$$

The horizontal asymptote is $y = -\frac{3}{5}$. We can multiply the numerator by -3 and the denominator by 5 to get the form

$$\frac{-3(x - 4)}{5(x + 2)}.$$

(Do *not* write $(-3x - 4)/(5x + 2)$, since that would change the x-intercept and the vertical asymptote.) Lastly, since there is a hole at $x = 1$, we must have a factor of $x - 1$ in both the numerator and the denominator. Thus, an equation for f is

$$f(x) = \frac{-3(x - 4)(x - 1)}{5(x + 2)(x - 1)} \quad \text{or, equivalently,} \quad f(x) = \frac{-3x^2 + 15x - 12}{5x^2 + 5x - 10}.$$

EXAMPLE 6 Sketching the graph of a rational function

Sketch the graph of f if

$$f(x) = \frac{x - 1}{x^2 - x - 6}.$$

SOLUTION   It is useful to express both numerator and denominator in factored form. Thus, we begin by writing

$$f(x) = \frac{x - 1}{x^2 - x - 6} = \frac{x - 1}{(x + 2)(x - 3)}.$$

Figure 8

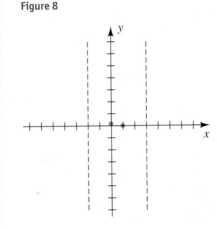

Guideline 1   To find the x-intercepts we find the zeros of the numerator. Solving $x - 1 = 0$ gives us $x = 1$, and we plot the point $(1, 0)$ on the x-axis, as
shown in Figure 8.

Guideline 2   The denominator has zeros -2 and 3. Hence, the lines $x = -2$
and $x = 3$ are vertical asymptotes; we sketch them with dashes, as in Figure 8.

Guideline 3   The y-intercept is $f(0) = \frac{1}{6}$, and we plot the point $\left(0, \frac{1}{6}\right)$, shown
in Figure 8.

Guideline 4   The degree of the numerator of $f(x)$ is less than the degree of the
denominator, so, by part (1) of the theorem on horizontal asymptotes, the
x-axis is the horizontal asymptote.

Guideline 5   The points where the graph intersects the horizontal asymptote
(the x-axis) found in guideline 4 correspond to the x-intercepts. We already
plotted the point $(1, 0)$ in guideline 1.

Guideline 6   The vertical asymptotes in Figure 8 divide the xy-plane into three
regions:

R_1:   the region to the left of $x = -2$
R_2:   the region between $x = -2$ and $x = 3$
R_3:   the region to the right of $x = 3$

For R_1, we have $x < -2$. There are only two choices for the shape of the
graph of f in R_1: as $x \rightarrow -\infty$, the graph approaches the x-axis either from
above or from below. To determine which choice is correct, we will examine
the *sign* of a typical function value in R_1. Choosing -10 for x, we use the factored form of $f(x)$ to find the sign of $f(-10)$ (this process is similar to the one
used in Section 2.7):

$$f(-10) = \frac{(-)}{(-)(-)} = -$$

The negative value of $f(-10)$ indicates that the graph approaches the hori-
zontal asymptote from *below* as $x \rightarrow -\infty$. Moreover, as $x \rightarrow -2^-$, the graph

(continued)

extends *downward;* that is, $f(x) \to -\infty$. A sketch of f on R_1 is shown in Figure 9(a).

Figure 9

(a)

(b)

(c)

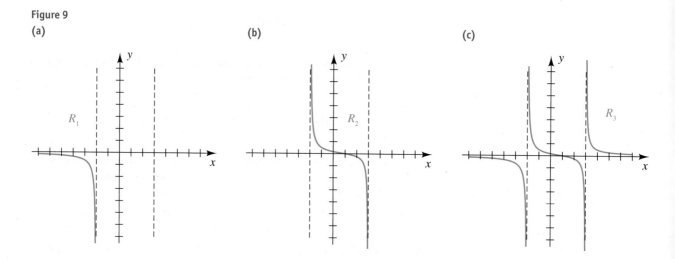

In R_2, we have $-2 < x < 3$, and the graph crosses the x-axis at $x = 1$. Since, for example, $f(0)$ is positive, it follows that the graph lies *above* the x-axis if $-2 < x < 1$. Thus, as $x \to -2^+$, the graph extends *upward;* that is, $f(x) \to \infty$. Since $f(2)$ can be shown to be negative, the graph lies *below* the x-axis if $1 < x < 3$. Hence, as $x \to 3^-$, the graph extends *downward;* that is, $f(x) \to -\infty$. A sketch of f on R_2 is shown in Figure 9(b).

Finally, in R_3, $x > 3$, and the graph does not cross the x-axis. Since, for example, $f(10)$ can be shown to be positive, the graph lies *above* the x-axis. It follows that $f(x) \to \infty$ as $x \to 3^+$ and that the graph approaches the horizontal asymptote from *above* as $x \to \infty$. The graph of f is sketched in Figure 9(c).

EXAMPLE 7   Sketching the graph of a rational function

Sketch the graph of f if

$$f(x) = \frac{x^2}{x^2 - x - 2}.$$

SOLUTION   Factoring the denominator gives us

$$f(x) = \frac{x^2}{x^2 - x - 2} = \frac{x^2}{(x + 1)(x - 2)}.$$

We again follow the guidelines.

Figure 10

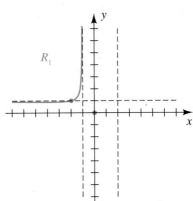

Guideline 1   To find the *x*-intercepts we find the zeros of the numerator. Solving $x^2 = 0$ gives us $x = 0$, and we plot the point $(0, 0)$ on the *x*-axis, as shown in Figure 10.

Guideline 2   The denominator has zeros -1 and 2. Hence, the lines $x = -1$ and $x = 2$ are vertical asymptotes, and we sketch them with dashes, as in Figure 10.

Guideline 3   The *y*-intercept is $f(0) = 0$. This gives us the same point $(0, 0)$ found in guideline 1.

Guideline 4   The numerator and denominator of $f(x)$ have the same degree, and the leading coefficients are both 1. Hence, by part (2) of the theorem on horizontal asymptotes, the line $y = \frac{1}{1} = 1$ is a horizontal asymptote. We sketch the line with dashes, as in Figure 10.

Guideline 5   The *x*-coordinates of the points where the graph intersects the horizontal asymptote $y = 1$ are solutions of the equation $f(x) = 1$. We solve this equation as follows:

$$\frac{x^2}{x^2 - x - 2} = 1 \qquad\qquad \text{let } f(x) = 1$$

$$x^2 = x^2 - x - 2 \qquad \text{multiply by } x^2 - x - 2$$

$$x = -2 \qquad\qquad \text{subtract } x^2 \text{ and add } x$$

This result indicates that the graph intersects the horizontal asymptote $y = 1$ *only* at $x = -2$; hence, we plot the point $(-2, 1)$ shown in Figure 10.

Guideline 6   The vertical asymptotes in Figure 10 divide the *xy*-plane into three regions:

R_1:   the region to the left of $x = -1$

R_2:   the region between $x = -1$ and $x = 2$

R_3:   the region to the right of $x = 2$

For R_1, let us first consider the portion of the graph that corresponds to $-2 < x < -1$. From the point $(-2, 1)$ on the horizontal asymptote, the graph must extend *upward* as $x \to -1^-$ (it cannot extend downward, since there is no *x*-intercept between $x = -2$ and $x = -1$). As $x \to -\infty$, there will be a low point on the graph between $y = 0$ and $y = 1$, and then the graph will approach the horizontal asymptote $y = 1$ from *below*. It is difficult to see where the low point occurs in Figure 10 because the function values are very close to one another. Using calculus, it can be shown that the low point is $\left(-4, \frac{8}{9}\right)$.

In R_2, we have $-1 < x < 2$, and the graph intersects the *x*-axis at $x = 0$. Since the function does not cross the horizontal asymptote in this region, we know that the graph extends *downward* as $x \to -1^+$ and as $x \to 2^-$, as shown in Figure 11(a).

(continued)

Figure 11

(a)

(b)

(c)

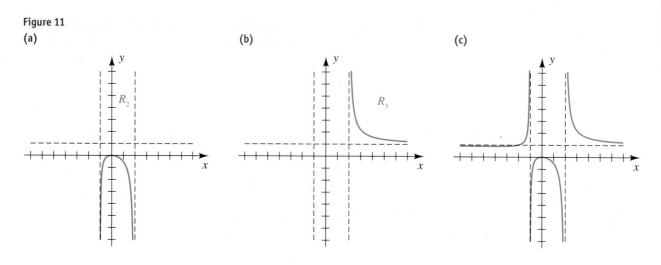

In R_3, the graph approaches the horizontal asymptote $y = 1$ (from either above or below) as $x \to \infty$. Furthermore, the graph must extend *upward* as $x \to 2^+$ because there are no x-intercepts in R_3. This implies that as $x \to \infty$, the graph approaches the horizontal asymptote from *above,* as in Figure 11(b).

The graph of f is sketched in Figure 11(c).

In the remaining solutions we will not formally write down each guideline.

EXAMPLE 8 Sketching the graph of a rational function

Sketch the graph of f if

$$f(x) = \frac{2x^4}{x^4 + 1}.$$

Figure 12

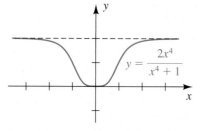

$$y = \frac{2x^4}{x^4 + 1}$$

SOLUTION Note that since $f(-x) = f(x)$, the function is even, and hence the graph is symmetric with respect to the y-axis.

The graph intersects the x-axis at $(0, 0)$. Since the denominator of $f(x)$ has no real zero, the graph has no vertical asymptote.

The numerator and denominator of $f(x)$ have the same degree. Since the leading coefficients are 2 and 1, respectively, the line $y = \frac{2}{1} = 2$ is the horizontal asymptote. The graph does not cross the horizontal asymptote $y = 2$, since the equation $f(x) = 2$ has no real solution.

Plotting the points $(1, 1)$ and $\left(2, \frac{32}{17}\right)$ and making use of symmetry leads to the sketch in Figure 12.

An **oblique asymptote** for a graph is a line $y = ax + b$, with $a \neq 0$, such that the graph approaches this line as $x \to \infty$ or as $x \to -\infty$. (If the graph is a line, we consider it to be its own asymptote.) If the rational function

$f(x) = g(x)/h(x)$ for polynomials $g(x)$ and $h(x)$ and *if the degree of $g(x)$ is one greater than the degree of $h(x)$*, then the graph of f has an oblique asymptote. To find this oblique asymptote we may use long division to express $f(x)$ in the form

$$f(x) = \frac{g(x)}{h(x)} = (ax + b) + \frac{r(x)}{h(x)},$$

where either $r(x) = 0$ or the degree of $r(x)$ is less than the degree of $h(x)$. From part (1) of the theorem on horizontal asymptotes,

$$\frac{r(x)}{h(x)} \to 0 \quad \text{as} \quad x \to \infty \quad \text{or as} \quad x \to -\infty.$$

Consequently, $f(x)$ approaches the line $y = ax + b$ as x increases or decreases without bound; that is, $y = ax + b$ is an oblique asymptote.

EXAMPLE 9 Finding an oblique asymptote

Find all the asymptotes and sketch the graph of f if

$$f(x) = \frac{x^2 - 9}{2x - 4}.$$

SOLUTION A vertical asymptote occurs if $2x - 4 = 0$ (that is, if $x = 2$).
The degree of the numerator of $f(x)$ is greater than the degree of the denominator. Hence, by part (3) of the theorem on horizontal asymptotes, there is no *horizontal* asymptote; but since the degree of the numerator, 2, is *one* greater than the degree of the denominator, 1, the graph has an *oblique* asymptote. By long division we obtain

$$
\begin{array}{r}
\frac{1}{2}x + 1 \\
2x - 4 \overline{\smash{\big)}\ x^2 \qquad\ - 9} \\
\underline{x^2 - 2x} \qquad \left(\frac{1}{2}x\right)(2x - 4) \\
2x - 9 \qquad \text{subtract} \\
\underline{2x - 4} \qquad (1)(2x - 4) \\
-5 \qquad \text{subtract}
\end{array}
$$

Therefore,

$$\frac{x^2 - 9}{2x - 4} = \left(\frac{1}{2}x + 1\right) - \frac{5}{2x - 4}.$$

As we indicated in the discussion preceding this example, the line $y = \frac{1}{2}x + 1$ is an oblique asymptote. This line and the vertical asymptote $x = 2$ are sketched with dashes in Figure 13.
The x-intercepts of the graph are the solutions of $x^2 - 9 = 0$ and hence are 3 and -3. The y-intercept is $f(0) = \frac{9}{4}$. The corresponding points are plotted in Figure 13. We may now show that the graph has the shape indicated in Figure 14.

Figure 13

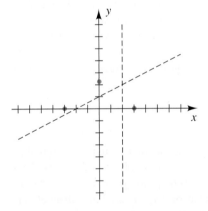

Figure 14

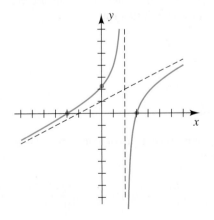

In Example 9, the graph of f approaches the line $y = \frac{1}{2}x + 1$ *asymptotically* as $x \to \infty$ or as $x \to -\infty$. Graphs of rational functions may approach different types of curves asymptotically. For example, if

$$f(x) = \frac{x^4 - x}{x^2} = x^2 - \frac{1}{x},$$

then for large values of $|x|$, $1/x \approx 0$ and hence $f(x) \approx x^2$. Thus, the graph of f approaches the parabola $y = x^2$ asymptotically as $x \to \infty$ or as $x \to -\infty$. In general, if $f(x) = g(x)/h(x)$ and if $q(x)$ is the quotient obtained by dividing $g(x)$ by $h(x)$, then the graph of f approaches the graph of $y = q(x)$ asymptotically as $x \to \infty$ or as $x \to -\infty$.

Graphs of rational functions may become increasingly complicated as the degrees of the polynomials in the numerator and denominator increase. Techniques developed in calculus are very helpful in achieving a more thorough treatment of such graphs.

Formulas that represent physical quantities may determine rational functions. For example, consider Ohm's law in electrical theory, which states that $I = V/R$, where R is the resistance (in ohms) of a conductor, V is the potential difference (in volts) across the conductor, and I is the current (in amperes) that flows through the conductor. The resistance of certain alloys approaches zero as the temperature approaches absolute zero (approximately $-273°C$), and the alloy becomes a *superconductor* of electricity. If the voltage V is fixed, then, for such a superconductor,

$$I = \frac{V}{R} \to \infty \quad \text{as} \quad R \to 0^+;$$

that is, as R approaches 0, the current increases without bound. Superconductors allow very large currents to be used in generating plants and motors. They also have applications in experimental high-speed ground transportation, where the strong magnetic fields produced by superconducting magnets enable trains to levitate so that there is essentially no friction between the wheels and the track. Perhaps the most important use for superconductors is in circuits for computers, because such circuits produce very little heat.

4.5 Exercises

Exer. 1–2: (a) Sketch the graph of f. (b) Find the domain D and range R of f. (c) Find the intervals on which f is increasing or is decreasing.

1 $f(x) = \dfrac{4}{x}$

2 $f(x) = \dfrac{1}{x^2}$

Exer. 3–4: Identify any vertical asymptotes, horizontal asymptotes, and holes.

3 $f(x) = \dfrac{-2(x + 5)(x - 6)}{(x - 3)(x - 6)}$

4 $f(x) = \dfrac{2(x + 4)(x + 2)}{5(x + 2)(x - 1)}$

Exer. 5–6: All asymptotes, intercepts, and holes of a rational function f are labeled in the figure. Sketch a graph of f and find a formula for f.

5

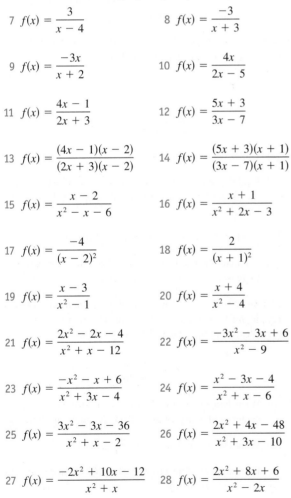

6

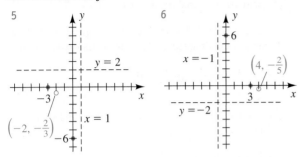

Exer. 7–32: Sketch the graph of f.

7 $f(x) = \dfrac{3}{x - 4}$

8 $f(x) = \dfrac{-3}{x + 3}$

9 $f(x) = \dfrac{-3x}{x + 2}$

10 $f(x) = \dfrac{4x}{2x - 5}$

11 $f(x) = \dfrac{4x - 1}{2x + 3}$

12 $f(x) = \dfrac{5x + 3}{3x - 7}$

13 $f(x) = \dfrac{(4x - 1)(x - 2)}{(2x + 3)(x - 2)}$

14 $f(x) = \dfrac{(5x + 3)(x + 1)}{(3x - 7)(x + 1)}$

15 $f(x) = \dfrac{x - 2}{x^2 - x - 6}$

16 $f(x) = \dfrac{x + 1}{x^2 + 2x - 3}$

17 $f(x) = \dfrac{-4}{(x - 2)^2}$

18 $f(x) = \dfrac{2}{(x + 1)^2}$

19 $f(x) = \dfrac{x - 3}{x^2 - 1}$

20 $f(x) = \dfrac{x + 4}{x^2 - 4}$

21 $f(x) = \dfrac{2x^2 - 2x - 4}{x^2 + x - 12}$

22 $f(x) = \dfrac{-3x^2 - 3x + 6}{x^2 - 9}$

23 $f(x) = \dfrac{-x^2 - x + 6}{x^2 + 3x - 4}$

24 $f(x) = \dfrac{x^2 - 3x - 4}{x^2 + x - 6}$

25 $f(x) = \dfrac{3x^2 - 3x - 36}{x^2 + x - 2}$

26 $f(x) = \dfrac{2x^2 + 4x - 48}{x^2 + 3x - 10}$

27 $f(x) = \dfrac{-2x^2 + 10x - 12}{x^2 + x}$

28 $f(x) = \dfrac{2x^2 + 8x + 6}{x^2 - 2x}$

29 $f(x) = \dfrac{x - 1}{x^3 - 4x}$

30 $f(x) = \dfrac{x^2 - 2x + 1}{x^3 - 9x}$

31 $f(x) = \dfrac{-3x^2}{x^2 + 1}$

32 $f(x) = \dfrac{x^2 - 4}{x^2 + 1}$

Exer. 33–36: Find the oblique asymptote, and sketch the graph of f.

33 $f(x) = \dfrac{x^2 - x - 6}{x + 1}$

34 $f(x) = \dfrac{2x^2 - x - 3}{x - 2}$

35 $f(x) = \dfrac{8 - x^3}{2x^2}$

36 $f(x) = \dfrac{x^3 + 1}{x^2 - 9}$

Exer. 37–44: Simplify $f(x)$, and sketch the graph of f.

37 $f(x) = \dfrac{2x^2 + x - 6}{x^2 + 3x + 2}$

38 $f(x) = \dfrac{x^2 - x - 6}{x^2 - 2x - 3}$

39 $f(x) = \dfrac{x - 1}{1 - x^2}$

40 $f(x) = \dfrac{x + 2}{x^2 - 4}$

41 $f(x) = \dfrac{x^2 + x - 2}{x + 2}$

42 $f(x) = \dfrac{x^3 - 2x^2 - 4x + 8}{x - 2}$

43 $f(x) = \dfrac{x^2 + 4x + 4}{x^2 + 3x + 2}$

44 $f(x) = \dfrac{(x^2 + x)(2x - 1)}{(x^2 - 3x + 2)(2x - 1)}$

Exer. 45–48: Find an equation of a rational function f that satisfies the given conditions.

45 vertical asymptote: $x = 4$
horizontal asymptote: $y = -1$
x-intercept: 3

46 vertical asymptotes: $x = -2, x = 0$
horizontal asymptote: $y = 0$
x-intercept: 2; $f(3) = 1$

47 vertical asymptotes: $x = -3, x = 1$
horizontal asymptote: $y = 0$
x-intercept: -1; $f(0) = -2$
hole at $x = 2$

48 vertical asymptotes: $x = -1, x = 3$
horizontal asymptote: $y = 2$
x-intercepts: $-2, 1$; hole at $x = 0$

49 **A container for radioactive waste** A cylindrical container for storing radioactive waste is to be constructed from lead. This container must be 6 inches thick. The volume of the outside cylinder shown in the figure is to be 16π ft^3.

(a) Express the height h of the inside cylinder as a function of the inside radius r.

(b) Show that the inside volume $V(r)$ is given by

$$V(r) = \pi r^2 \left[\frac{16}{(r + 0.5)^2} - 1 \right].$$

(c) What values of r must be excluded in part (b)?

Exercise 49

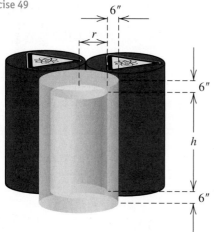

50 **Drug dosage** Young's rule is a formula that is used to modify adult drug dosage levels for young children. If a denotes the adult dosage (in milligrams) and if t is the age of the child (in years), then the child's dose y is given by the equation $y = ta/(t + 12)$. Sketch the graph of this equation for $t > 0$ and $a = 100$.

51 **Salt concentration** Salt water of concentration 0.1 pound of salt per gallon flows into a large tank that initially contains 50 gallons of pure water.

(a) If the flow rate of salt water into the tank is 5 gal/min, find the volume $V(t)$ of water and the amount $A(t)$ of salt in the tank after t minutes.

(b) Find a formula for the salt concentration $c(t)$ (in lb/gal) after t minutes.

(c) Discuss the variation of $c(t)$ as $t \to \infty$.

52 **Amount of rainfall** The total number of inches $R(t)$ of rain during a storm of length t hours can be approximated by

$$R(t) = \frac{at}{t + b},$$

where a and b are positive constants that depend on the geographical locale.

(a) Discuss the variation of $R(t)$ as $t \to \infty$.

(b) The intensity I of the rainfall (in in./hr) is defined by $I = R(t)/t$. If $a = 2$ and $b = 8$, sketch the graph of R and I on the same coordinate plane for $t > 0$.

53 **Salmon propagation** For a particular salmon population, the relationship between the number S of spawners and the number R of offspring that survive to maturity is given by the formula

$$R = \frac{4500S}{S + 500}.$$

(a) Under what conditions is $R > S$?

(b) Find the number of spawners that would yield 90% of the greatest possible number of offspring that survive to maturity.

(c) Work part (b) with 80% replacing 90%.

(d) Compare the results for S and R (in terms of percentage increases) from parts (b) and (c).

54 **Population density** The population density D (in people/mi^2) in a large city is related to the distance x (in miles) from the center of the city by

$$D = \frac{5000x}{x^2 + 36}.$$

(a) What happens to the density as the distance from the center of the city changes from 20 miles to 25 miles?

(b) What eventually happens to the density?

(c) In what areas of the city does the population density exceed 400 people/mi^2?

55 Let $f(x)$ be the polynomial

$$(x + 3)(x + 2)(x + 1)(x)(x - 1)(x - 2)(x - 3).$$

(a) Describe the graph of $g(x) = f(x)/f(x)$.

(b) Describe the graph of $h(x) = g(x)p(x)$, where $p(x)$ is a polynomial function.

56 Refer to Exercise 55.

(a) Describe the graph of $y = f(x)$.

(b) Describe the graph of $k(x) = 1/f(x)$.

57 Grade point average (GPA)

(a) A student has finished 48 credit hours with a GPA of 2.75. How many additional credit hours y at 4.0 will raise the student's GPA to some desired value x? (Determine y as a function of x.)

(b) Create a table of values for x and y, starting with $x = 2.8$ and using increments of 0.2.

(c) Graph the function in part (a).

(d) What is the vertical asymptote of the graph in part (c)?

(e) Explain the practical significance of the value $x = 4$.

4.6
Variation

In some scientific investigations, the terminology of *variation* or *proportion* is used to describe relationships between variable quantities. In the following chart, k is a nonzero real number called a **constant of variation** or a **constant of proportionality**.

Terminology	General formula	Illustration
y **varies directly** as x, or y is **directly proportional** to x	$y = kx$	$C = 2\pi r$, where C is the circumference of a circle, r is the radius, and $k = 2\pi$
y **varies inversely** as x, or y is **inversely proportional** to x	$y = \dfrac{k}{x}$	$I = \dfrac{110}{R}$, where I is the current in an electrical circuit, R is the resistance, and $k = 110$ is the voltage

The variable x in the chart can also represent a power. For example, the formula $A = \pi r^2$ states that the area A of a circle varies directly as the *square* of the radius r, where π is the constant of variation. Similarly, the formula $V = \frac{4}{3}\pi r^3$ states that the volume V of a sphere is directly proportional to the *cube* of the radius. In this case the constant of proportionality is $\frac{4}{3}\pi$.

In general, graphs of variables related by *direct variation* resemble graphs of **power functions** of the form $y = x^n$ with $n > 0$ (such as $y = \sqrt{x}$ or $y = x^2$ for nonnegative x-values, as shown in Figure 1). With direct variation, as one variable increases, so does the other variable. An example of two quantities that are directly related is the number of miles run and the number of calories burned.

Figure 1

As x increases, y increases,
or as x decreases, y decreases

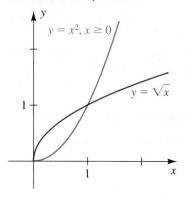

Graphs of variables related by *inverse variation* resemble graphs of power functions of the form $y = x^n$ with $n < 0$ (such as $y = 1/\sqrt{x}$ or $y = 1/x^2$ for positive x-values, as shown in Figure 2). In this case, as one variable increases, the other variable decreases. An example of two quantities that are inversely related is the number of inches of rainfall and the number of grass fires.

EXAMPLE 1   **Directly proportional variables**

Suppose a variable q is directly proportional to a variable z.

(a) If $q = 12$ when $z = 5$, determine the constant of proportionality.

(b) Find the value of q when $z = 7$ and sketch a graph of this relationship.

Figure 2

As x increases, y decreases,
or as x decreases, y increases

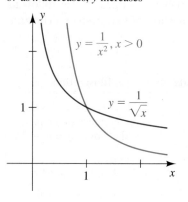

SOLUTION   Since q is directly proportional to z,

$$q = kz,$$

where k is a constant of proportionality.

(a) Substituting $q = 12$ and $z = 5$ gives us

$$12 = k \cdot 5, \qquad \text{or} \qquad k = \tfrac{12}{5}.$$

(b) Since $k = \tfrac{12}{5}$, the formula $q = kz$ has the specific form

$$q = \tfrac{12}{5}z.$$

Thus, when $z = 7$,

$$q = \tfrac{12}{5} \cdot 7 = \tfrac{84}{5} = 16.8.$$

Figure 3 illustrates the relationship of the variables q and z—a simple linear relationship.

Figure 3

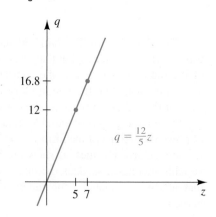

The following guidelines may be used to solve applied problems that involve variation or proportion.

Guidelines for Solving Variation Problems	*1* Write a *general* formula that involves the variables and a constant of variation (or proportion) k.
	2 Find the value of k in guideline 1 by using the initial data given in the statement of the problem.
	3 Substitute the value of k found in guideline 2 into the formula of guideline 1, obtaining a *specific* formula that involves the variables.
	4 Use the new data to solve the problem.

We shall follow these guidelines in the solution of the next example.

EXAMPLE 2   Pressure and volume as inversely proportional quantities

If the temperature remains constant, the pressure of an enclosed gas is inversely proportional to the volume. The pressure of a certain gas within a spherical balloon of radius 9 inches is 20 lb/in². If the radius of the balloon increases to 12 inches, approximate the new pressure of the gas. Sketch a graph of the relationship between the pressure and the volume.

SOLUTION

Guideline 1   If we denote the pressure by P (in lb/in²) and the volume by V (in in³), then since P is inversely proportional to V,

$$P = \frac{k}{V}$$

for some constant of proportionality k.

Guideline 2   We find the constant of proportionality k in guideline 1. Since the volume V of a sphere of radius r is $V = \frac{4}{3}\pi r^3$, the initial volume of the balloon is $V = \frac{4}{3}\pi(9)^3 = 972\pi$ in³. This leads to the following:

$$20 = \frac{k}{972\pi} \qquad \qquad P = 20 \text{ when } V = 972\pi$$

$$k = 20(972\pi) = 19{,}440\pi \quad \text{solve for } k$$

Guideline 3   Substituting $k = 19{,}440\pi$ into $P = k/V$, we find that the pressure corresponding to any volume V is given by

$$P = \frac{19{,}440\pi}{V}.$$

(continued)

Guideline 4 If the new radius of the balloon is 12 inches, then

$$V = \tfrac{4}{3}\pi(12)^3 = 2304\pi \text{ in}^3.$$

Substituting this number for V in the formula obtained in guideline 3 gives us

$$P = \frac{19{,}440\pi}{2304\pi} = \frac{135}{16} = 8.4375.$$

Thus, the pressure decreases to approximately 8.4 lb/in² when the radius increases to 12 inches.

Figure 4 illustrates the relationship of the variables P and V for $V > 0$. Since $P = 19{,}440\pi/V$ and $V = \tfrac{4}{3}\pi r^3$, we can show that $(P \circ V)(r) = 14{,}580/r^3$, so we could also say that P is inversely proportional to r^3. Note that this is a graph of a simple rational function.

Figure 4

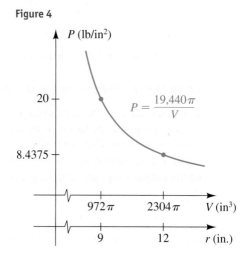

There are other types of variation. If x, y, and z are variables and $y = kxz$ for some real number k, we say that y *varies directly as the product of x and z* or **y varies jointly as x and z.** If $y = k(x/z)$, then y *varies directly as x and inversely as z.* As a final illustration, if a variable w varies directly as the product of x and the cube of y and inversely as the square of z, then

$$w = k\frac{xy^3}{z^2},$$

where k is a constant of proportionality. Graphs of equations for these types of variation will not be considered in this text.

EXAMPLE 3 Combining several types of variation

A variable w varies directly as the product of u and v and inversely as the square of s.

(a) If $w = 20$ when $u = 3$, $v = 5$, and $s = 2$, find the constant of variation.

(b) Find the value of w when $u = 7$, $v = 4$, and $s = 3$.

SOLUTION   A general formula for w is

$$w = k\frac{uv}{s^2},$$

where k is a constant of variation.

(a) Substituting $w = 20$, $u = 3$, $v = 5$, and $s = 2$ gives us

$$20 = k\frac{3 \cdot 5}{2^2}, \qquad \text{or} \qquad k = \frac{80}{15} = \frac{16}{3}.$$

(b) Since $k = \frac{16}{3}$, the specific formula for w is

$$w = \frac{16}{3}\frac{uv}{s^2}.$$

Thus, when $u = 7$, $v = 4$, and $s = 3$,

$$w = \frac{16}{3}\frac{7 \cdot 4}{3^2} = \frac{448}{27} \approx 16.6.$$

In the next example we again follow the guidelines stated in this section.

EXAMPLE 4   Finding the support load of a rectangular beam

The weight that can be safely supported by a beam with a rectangular cross section varies directly as the product of the width and square of the depth of the cross section and inversely as the length of the beam. If a 2-inch by 4-inch beam that is 8 feet long safely supports a load of 500 pounds, what weight can be safely supported by a 2-inch by 8-inch beam that is 10 feet long? (Assume that the width is the *shorter* dimension of the cross section.)

SOLUTION

Guideline 1   If the width, depth, length, and weight are denoted by w, d, l, and W, respectively, then a general formula for W is

$$W = k\frac{wd^2}{l},$$

where k is a constant of variation.

Guideline 2   To find the value of k in guideline 1, we see from the given data that

$$500 = k\frac{2(4^2)}{8}, \qquad \text{or} \qquad k = 125.$$

Guideline 3   Substituting $k = 125$ into the formula of guideline 1 gives us the specific formula

$$W = 125\frac{wd^2}{l}.$$

Guideline 4   To answer the question, we substitute $w = 2$, $d = 8$, and $l = 10$ into the formula found in guideline 3, obtaining

$$W = 125 \cdot \frac{2 \cdot 8^2}{10} = 1600 \text{ lb.}$$

4.6 Exercises

Exer. 1–12: Express the statement as a formula that involves the given variables and a constant of proportionality k, and then determine the value of k from the given conditions.

1 u is directly proportional to v. If $v = 30$, then $u = 12$.

2 s varies directly as t. If $t = 10$, then $s = 18$.

3 r varies directly as s and inversely as t. If $s = -2$ and $t = 4$, then $r = 7$.

4 w varies directly as z and inversely as the square root of u. If $z = 2$ and $u = 9$, then $w = 6$.

5 y is directly proportional to the square of x and inversely proportional to the cube of z. If $x = 5$ and $z = 3$, then $y = 25$.

6 q is inversely proportional to the sum of x and y. If $x = 0.5$ and $y = 0.7$, then $q = 1.4$.

7 z is directly proportional to the product of the square of x and the cube of y. If $x = 7$ and $y = -2$, then $z = 16$.

8 r is directly proportional to the product of s and v and inversely proportional to the cube of p. If $s = 2$, $v = 3$, and $p = 5$, then $r = 40$.

9 y is directly proportional to x and inversely proportional to the square of z. If $x = 4$ and $z = 3$, then $y = 16$.

10 y is directly proportional to x and inversely proportional to the sum of r and s. If $x = 3$, $r = 5$, and $s = 7$, then $y = 2$.

11 y is directly proportional to the square root of x and inversely proportional to the cube of z. If $x = 9$ and $z = 2$, then $y = 5$.

12 y is directly proportional to the square of x and inversely proportional to the square root of z. If $x = 5$ and $z = 16$, then $y = 10$.

13 Liquid pressure The pressure P acting at a point in a liquid is directly proportional to the distance d from the surface of the liquid to the point.

(a) Express P as a function of d by means of a formula that involves a constant of proportionality k.

(b) In a certain oil tank, the pressure at a depth of 2 feet is 118 lb/ft². Find the value of k in part (a).

(continued)

(c) Find the pressure at a depth of 5 feet for the oil tank in part (b).

(d) Sketch a graph of the relationship between P and d for $d \geq 0$.

14 Hooke's law Hooke's law states that the force F required to stretch a spring x units beyond its natural length is directly proportional to x.

(a) Express F as a function of x by means of a formula that involves a constant of proportionality k.

(b) A weight of 4 pounds stretches a certain spring from its natural length of 10 inches to a length of 10.3 inches. Find the value of k in part (a).

(c) What weight will stretch the spring in part (b) to a length of 11.5 inches?

(d) Sketch a graph of the relationship between F and x for $x \geq 0$.

15 Electrical resistance The electrical resistance R of a wire varies directly as its length l and inversely as the square of its diameter d.

(a) Express R in terms of l, d, and a constant of variation k.

(b) A wire 100 feet long of diameter 0.01 inch has a resistance of 25 ohms. Find the value of k in part (a).

(c) Sketch a graph of the relationship between R and d for $l = 100$ and $d > 0$.

(d) Find the resistance of a wire made of the same material that has a diameter of 0.015 inch and is 50 feet long.

16 Intensity of illumination The intensity of illumination I from a source of light varies inversely as the square of the distance d from the source.

(a) Express I in terms of d and a constant of variation k.

(b) A searchlight has an intensity of 1,000,000 candlepower at a distance of 50 feet. Find the value of k in part (a).

(c) Sketch a graph of the relationship between I and d for $d > 0$.

(d) Approximate the intensity of the searchlight in part (b) at a distance of 1 mile.

17 **Period of a pendulum** The period P of a simple pendulum—that is, the time required for one complete oscillation—is directly proportional to the square root of its length l.

(a) Express P in terms of l and a constant of proportionality k.

(b) If a pendulum 2 feet long has a period of 1.5 seconds, find the value of k in part (a).

(c) Find the period of a pendulum 6 feet long.

18 **Dimensions of a human limb** A circular cylinder is sometimes used in physiology as a simple representation of a human limb.

(a) Express the volume V of a cylinder in terms of its length L and the square of its circumference C.

(b) The formula obtained in part (a) can be used to approximate the volume of a limb from length and circumference measurements. Suppose the (average) circumference of a human forearm is 22 centimeters and the average length is 27 centimeters. Approximate the volume of the forearm to the nearest cm^3.

19 **Period of a planet** Kepler's third law states that the period T of a planet (the time needed to make one complete revolution about the sun) is directly proportional to the $\frac{3}{2}$ power of its average distance d from the sun.

(a) Express T as a function of d by means of a formula that involves a constant of proportionality k.

(b) For the planet Earth, $T = 365$ days and $d = 93$ million miles. Find the value of k in part (a).

(c) Estimate the period of Venus if its average distance from the sun is 67 million miles.

20 **Range of a projectile** It is known from physics that the range R of a projectile is directly proportional to the square of its velocity v.

(a) Express R as a function of v by means of a formula that involves a constant of proportionality k.

(b) A motorcycle daredevil has made a jump of 150 feet. If the speed coming off the ramp was 70 mi/hr, find the value of k in part (a).

(c) If the daredevil can reach a speed of 80 mi/hr coming off the ramp and maintain proper balance, estimate the possible length of the jump.

21 **Automobile skid marks** The speed V at which an automobile was traveling before the brakes were applied can sometimes be estimated from the length L of the skid marks. Assume that V is directly proportional to the square root of L.

(a) Express V as a function of L by means of a formula that involves a constant of proportionality k.

(b) For a certain automobile on a dry surface, $L = 50$ ft when $V = 35$ mi/hr. Find the value of k in part (a).

(c) Estimate the initial speed of the automobile in part (b) if the skid marks are 150 feet long.

22 **Coulomb's law** Coulomb's law in electrical theory states that the force F of attraction between two oppositely charged particles varies directly as the product of the magnitudes Q_1 and Q_2 of the charges and inversely as the square of the distance d between the particles.

(a) Find a formula for F in terms of Q_1, Q_2, d, and a constant of variation k.

(b) What is the effect of reducing the distance between the particles by a factor of one-fourth?

23 **Threshold weight** Threshold weight W is defined to be that weight beyond which risk of death increases significantly. For middle-aged males, W is directly proportional to the third power of the height h.

(a) Express W as a function of h by means of a formula that involves a constant of proportionality k.

(b) For a 6-foot male, W is about 200 pounds. Find the value of k in part (a).

(c) Estimate, to the nearest pound, the threshold weight for an individual who is 5 feet 6 inches tall.

24 **The ideal gas law** The ideal gas law states that the volume V that a gas occupies is directly proportional to the product of the number n of moles of gas and the temperature T (in K) and is inversely proportional to the pressure P (in atmospheres).

(a) Express V in terms of n, T, P, and a constant of proportionality k.

(b) What is the effect on the volume if the number of moles is doubled and both the temperature and the pressure are reduced by a factor of one-half?

25 **Poiseuille's law** Poiseuille's law states that the blood flow rate F (in L/min) through a major artery is directly proportional to the product of the fourth power of the radius r of the artery and the blood pressure P.

(a) Express F in terms of P, r, and a constant of proportionality k.

(b) During heavy exercise, normal blood flow rates sometimes triple. If the radius of a major artery increases by 10%, approximately how much harder must the heart pump?

26 **Trout population** Suppose 200 trout are caught, tagged, and released in a lake's general population. Let T denote the number of tagged fish that are recaptured when a sample of n trout are caught at a later date. The validity of the mark-recapture method for estimating the lake's total trout population is based on the assumption that T is directly proportional to n. If 10 tagged trout are recovered from a sample of 300, estimate the total trout population of the lake.

27 **Radioactive decay of radon gas** When uranium disintegrates into lead, one step in the process is the radioactive decay of radium into radon gas. Radon enters through the soil into home basements, where it presents a health hazard if inhaled. In the simplest case of radon detection, a sample of air with volume V is taken. After equilibrium has been established, the radioactive decay D of the radon gas is counted with efficiency E over time t. The radon concentration C present in the sample of air varies directly as the product of D and E and inversely as the product of V and t.

For a fixed radon concentration C and time t, find the change in the radioactive decay count D if V is doubled and E is reduced by 20%.

28 **Radon concentration** Refer to Exercise 27. Find the change in the radon concentration C if D increases by 30%, t increases by 60%, V decreases by 10%, and E remains constant.

29 **Density at a point** A thin flat plate is situated in an xy-plane such that the density d (in lb/ft^2) at the point $P(x, y)$ is inversely proportional to the square of the distance from the origin. What is the effect on the density at P if the x- and y-coordinates are each multiplied by $\frac{1}{3}$?

30 **Temperature at a point** A flat metal plate is positioned in an xy-plane such that the temperature T (in °C) at the point (x, y) is inversely proportional to the distance from the origin. If the temperature at the point $P(3, 4)$ is 20°C, find the temperature at the point $Q(24, 7)$.

Exer. 31–34: Examine the expression for the given set of data points of the form (x, y). Find the constant of variation and a formula that describes how y varies with respect to x.

31 y/x; $\{(0.6, 0.72), (1.2, 1.44), (4.2, 5.04), (7.1, 8.52), (9.3, 11.16)\}$

32 xy; $\{(0.2, -26.5), (0.4, -13.25), (0.8, -6.625), (1.6, -3.3125), (3.2, -1.65625)\}$

33 x^2y; $\{(0.16, -394.53125), (0.8, -15.78125), (1.6, -3.9453125), (3.2, -0.986328125)\}$

34 y/x^3; $\{(0.11, 0.00355377), (0.56, 0.46889472), (1.2, 4.61376), (2.4, 36.91008)\}$

CHAPTER 4 REVIEW EXERCISES

Exer. 1–6: Find all values of x such that $f(x) > 0$ and all x such that $f(x) < 0$, and sketch the graph of f.

1 $f(x) = (x + 2)^3$

2 $f(x) = x^6 - 32$

3 $f(x) = -\frac{1}{4}(x + 2)(x - 1)^2(x - 3)$

4 $f(x) = 2x^2 + x^3 - x^4$

5 $f(x) = x^3 + 2x^2 - 8x$

6 $f(x) = \frac{1}{15}(x^5 - 20x^3 + 64x)$

7 If $f(x) = x^3 - 5x^2 + 7x - 9$, use the intermediate value theorem for polynomial functions to prove that there is a real number a such that $f(a) = 100$.

8 Prove that the equation $x^5 - 3x^4 - 2x^3 - x + 1 = 0$ has a solution between 0 and 1.

Exer. 9–10: Find the quotient and remainder if $f(x)$ is divided by $p(x)$.

9 $f(x) = 3x^5 - 4x^3 + x + 5$; $p(x) = x^3 - 2x + 7$

10 $f(x) = 4x^3 - x^2 + 2x - 1$; $p(x) = x^2$

11 If $f(x) = -4x^4 + 3x^3 - 5x^2 + 7x - 10$, use the remainder theorem to find $f(-2)$.

12 Use the factor theorem to show that $x - 3$ is a factor of $f(x) = 2x^4 - 5x^3 - 4x^2 + 9$.

Exer. 13–14: Use synthetic division to find the quotient and remainder if $f(x)$ is divided by $p(x)$.

13 $f(x) = 6x^5 - 4x^2 + 8;$ $\qquad p(x) = x + 2$

14 $f(x) = 2x^3 + 5x^2 - 2x + 1;$ $\ p(x) = x - \sqrt{2}$

Exer. 15–16: A polynomial $f(x)$ with real coefficients has the indicated zero(s) and degree and satisfies the given condition. Express $f(x)$ as a product of linear and quadratic polynomials with real coefficients that are irreducible over $\mathbb{R}$.

15 $-3 + 5i, -1;$ degree 3; $f(1) = 4$

16 $1 - i, 3, 0;$ degree 4; $f(2) = -1$

17 Find a polynomial $f(x)$ of degree 7 with leading coefficient 1 such that -3 is a zero of multiplicity 2 and 0 is a zero of multiplicity 5, and sketch the graph of f.

18 Show that 2 is a zero of multiplicity 3 of the polynomial $f(x) = x^5 - 4x^4 - 3x^3 + 34x^2 - 52x + 24$, and express $f(x)$ as a product of linear factors.

Exer. 19–20: Find the zeros of $f(x)$, and state the multiplicity of each zero.

19 $f(x) = (x^2 - 2x + 1)^2(x^2 + 2x - 3)$

20 $f(x) = x^6 + 2x^4 + x^2$

Exer. 21–22: (a) Use Descartes' rule of signs to determine the number of possible positive, negative, and nonreal complex solutions of the equation. (b) Find the smallest and largest integers that are upper and lower bounds, respectively, for the real solutions of the equation.

21 $2x^4 - 4x^3 + 2x^2 - 5x - 7 = 0$

22 $x^5 - 4x^3 + 6x^2 + x + 4 = 0$

23 Show that $7x^6 + 2x^4 + 3x^2 + 10$ has no real zero.

Exer. 24–26: Find all solutions of the equation.

24 $x^4 + 9x^3 + 31x^2 + 49x + 30 = 0$

25 $16x^3 - 20x^2 - 8x + 3 = 0$

26 $x^4 - 7x^2 + 6 = 0$

Exer. 27–28: Find an equation for the sixth-degree polynomial f shown in the figure.

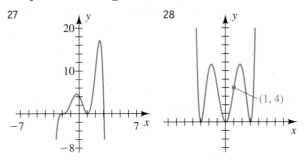

29 Identify any vertical asymptotes, horizontal asymptotes, intercepts, and holes for $f(x) = \dfrac{4(x + 2)(x - 1)}{3(x + 2)(x - 5)}$.

Exer. 30–39: Sketch the graph of f.

30 $f(x) = \dfrac{-2}{(x + 1)^2}$

31 $f(x) = \dfrac{1}{(x - 1)^3}$

32 $f(x) = \dfrac{3x^2}{16 - x^2}$

33 $f(x) = \dfrac{x}{(x + 5)(x^2 - 5x + 4)}$

34 $f(x) = \dfrac{x^3 - 2x^2 - 8x}{-x^2 + 2x}$

35 $f(x) = \dfrac{x^2 - 2x + 1}{x^3 - x^2 + x - 1}$

36 $f(x) = \dfrac{3x^2 + x - 10}{x^2 + 2x}$

37 $f(x) = \dfrac{-2x^2 - 8x - 6}{x^2 - 6x + 8}$

38 $f(x) = \dfrac{x^2 + 2x - 8}{x + 3}$

39 $f(x) = \dfrac{x^4 - 16}{x^3}$

40 Find an equation of a rational function f that satisfies the given conditions.

  vertical asymptote: $x = -3$
  horizontal asymptote: $y = \frac{3}{2}$
  x-intercept: 5
  hole at $x = 2$

41 Suppose y is directly proportional to the cube root of x and inversely proportional to the square of z. Find the constant of proportionality if $y = 6$ when $x = 8$ and $z = 3$.

42 Suppose y is inversely proportional to the square of x. Sketch a graph of this relationship for $x > 0$, given that $y = 18$ when $x = 4$. Include a point for $x = 12$.

43 **Deflection of a beam** A horizontal beam l feet long is supported at one end and unsupported at the other end (see the figure). If the beam is subjected to a uniform load and if y denotes the deflection of the beam at a position x feet from the supported end, then it can be shown that

$$y = cx^2(x^2 - 4lx + 6l^2),$$

where c is a positive constant that depends on the weight of the load and the physical properties of the beam.

(a) If the beam is 10 feet long and the deflection at the unsupported end of the beam is 2 feet, find c.

(b) Show that the deflection is 1 foot somewhere between $x = 6.1$ and $x = 6.2$.

Exercise 43

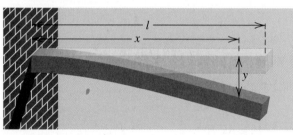

44 **Elastic cylinder** A rectangle made of elastic material is to be made into a cylinder by joining edge AD to edge BC, as shown in the figure. A wire of fixed length l is placed along the diagonal of the rectangle to support the structure. Let x denote the height of the cylinder.

(a) Express the volume V of the cylinder in terms of x.

(b) For what positive values of x is $V > 0$?

Exercise 44

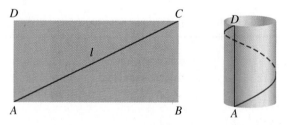

45 **Determining temperatures** A meteorologist determines that the temperature T (in °F) for a certain 24-hour period in winter was given by the formula $T = \frac{1}{20}t(t - 12)(t - 24)$ for $0 \le t \le 24$, where t is time in hours and $t = 0$ corresponds to 6 A.M. At what time(s) was the temperature 32°F?

46 **Deer propagation** A herd of 100 deer is introduced onto a small island. Assuming the number $N(t)$ of deer after t years is given by $N(t) = -t^4 + 21t^2 + 100$ (for $t > 0$), determine when the herd size exceeds 180.

47 **Threshold response curve** In biochemistry, the general threshold response curve is the graph of an equation

$$R = \frac{kS^n}{S^n + a^n},$$

where R is the chemical response when the level of the substance being acted on is S and a, k, and n are positive constants. An example is the removal rate R of alcohol from the bloodstream by the liver when the blood alcohol concentration is S.

(a) Find an equation of the horizontal asymptote for the graph.

(b) In the case of alcohol removal, $n = 1$ and a typical value of k is 0.22 gram per liter per minute. What is the interpretation of k in this setting?

48 **Oil spill clean-up** The cost $C(x)$ of cleaning up x percent of an oil spill that has washed ashore increases greatly as x approaches 100. Suppose that

$$C(x) = \frac{0.3x}{101 - x} \text{ (million dollars)}.$$

(a) Compare $C(100)$ to $C(90)$.

(b) Sketch the graph of C for $0 < x < 100$.

49 **Telephone calls** In a certain county, the average number of telephone calls per day between any two cities is directly proportional to the product of their populations and inversely proportional to the square of the distance between them. Cities A and B are 25 miles apart and have populations of 10,000 and 5000, respectively. Telephone records indicate an average of 2000 calls per day between the two cities. Estimate the average number of calls per day between city A and another city of 15,000 people that is 100 miles from A.

50 **Power of a wind rotor** The power P generated by a wind rotor is directly proportional to the product of the square of the area A swept out by the blades and the third power of the wind velocity v. Suppose the diameter of the circular area swept out by the blades is 10 feet, and $P = 3000$ watts when $v = 20$ mi/hr. Find the power generated when the wind velocity is 30 mi/hr.

CHAPTER 4 DISCUSSION EXERCISES

1 Compare the domain, range, number of x-intercepts, and general shape of even-degreed polynomials and odd-degreed polynomials.

2 When using synthetic division, could you use a complex number c rather than a real number in $x - c$?

3 Discuss how synthetic division can be used to help find the quotient and remainder when $4x^3 - 8x^2 - 11x + 9$ is divided by $2x + 3$. Discuss how synthetic division can be used with any linear factor of the form $ax + b$.

4 Draw (by hand) a graph of a polynomial function of degree 3 that has x-intercepts 1, 2, and 3, has a y-intercept of 6, and passes through the point $(-1, 25)$. Can you actually have the graph you just drew?

5 How many different points do you need to specify a polynomial of degree n?

6 Prove the theorem on conjugate pair zeros of a polynomial. (*Hint:* For an arbitrary polynomial f, examine the conjugates of both sides of the equation $f(z) = 0$.)

7 Give an example of a rational function that has a common factor in the numerator and denominator, but does *not* have a hole in its graph. Discuss, in general, how this can happen.

8 (a) Can the graph of $f(x) = \dfrac{ax + b}{cx + d}$ (where $ax + b \neq cx + d$) cross its horizontal asymptote? If yes, then where?

   (b) Can the graph of $f(x) = \dfrac{ax^2 + bx + c}{dx^2 + ex + f}$ (assume there are no like factors) cross its horizontal asymptote? If yes, then where?

9 Gambling survival formula An empirical formula for the bankroll B (in dollars) that is needed to survive a gambling session with confidence C (a percent expressed as a decimal) is given by the formula

$$B = \frac{GW}{29.3 + 53.1E - 22.7C},$$

where G is the number of games played in the session, W is the wager per game, and E is the player's edge on the game (expressed as a decimal).

(a) Approximate the bankroll needed for a player who plays 500 games per hour for 3 hours at $5 per game with a -5% edge, provided the player wants a 95% chance of surviving the 3-hour session.

(b) Discuss the validity of the formula; a table and graph may help.

10 Multiply three consecutive integers together and then add the second integer to that product. Use synthetic division to help prove that the sum is the cube of an integer, and determine which integer.

11 Personal tax rate Assume the total amount of state tax paid consists of an amount P for personal property and S percent of income I.

(a) Find a function that calculates an individual's state tax rate R—that is, the percentage of the individual's income that is paid in taxes. (It is helpful to consider specific values to create the function.)

(b) What happens to R as I gets very large?

(c) Discuss the statement "Rich people pay a lower percentage of their income in state taxes than any other group."

12 NFL passer rating The National Football League ranks its passers by assigning a passer rating R based on the numbers of completions C, attempts A, yards Y, touchdowns T, and interceptions I. In a normal situation, it can be shown that the passer rating can be calculated using the formula

$$R = \frac{25(A + 40C + 2Y + 160T - 200I)}{12A}.$$

(a) In 1994, Steve Young completed 324 of 461 passes for 3969 yards and had 35 touchdown passes as well as 10 interceptions. Calculate his record-setting rating.

(b) How many more yards would he have needed to obtain a passer rating of at least 113?

(c) If he could make one more touchdown pass, how long would it have to be for him to obtain a passer rating of at least 114?

5

Inverse, Exponential, and Logarithmic Functions

Exponential and logarithmic functions are transcendental functions, since they cannot be defined in terms of only addition, subtraction, multiplication, division, and rational powers of a variable x, as is the case for the algebraic functions considered in previous chapters. Such functions are of major importance in mathematics and have applications in almost every field of human endeavor. They are especially useful in the fields of chemistry, biology, physics, and engineering, where they help describe the manner in which quantities in nature grow or decay. As we shall see in this chapter, there is a close relationship between specific exponential and logarithmic functions—they are inverse functions of each other.

5.1

Inverse Functions

A function *f* may have the same value for different numbers in its domain. For example, if $f(x) = x^2$, then $f(2) = 4$ and $f(-2) = 4$, but $2 \neq -2$. For *the inverse of a function* to be defined, it is essential that different numbers in the domain *always* give different values of *f*. Such functions are called *one-to-one functions*.

Definition of One-to-One Function	A function *f* with domain *D* and range *R* is a **one-to-one function** if either of the following equivalent conditions is satisfied: **(1)** Whenever $a \neq b$ in *D*, then $f(a) \neq f(b)$ in *R*. **(2)** Whenever $f(a) = f(b)$ in *R*, then $a = b$ in *D*.

Figure 1

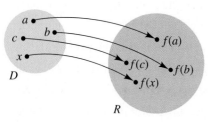

The arrow diagram in Figure 1 illustrates a one-to-one function. Note that each function value in the range *R* corresponds to *exactly one* element in the domain *D*. The function illustrated in Figure 2 of Section 3.4 is not one-to-one, since $f(w) = f(z)$, but $w \neq z$.

EXAMPLE 1   Determining whether a function is one-to-one

(a) If $f(x) = 3x + 2$, prove that *f* is one-to-one.

(b) If $g(x) = x^2 - 3$, prove that *g* is not one-to-one.

SOLUTION

(a) We shall use condition 2 of the preceding definition. Thus, suppose that $f(a) = f(b)$ for some numbers *a* and *b* in the domain of *f*. This gives us the following:

$$3a + 2 = 3b + 2 \quad \text{definition of } f(x)$$
$$3a = 3b \quad \text{subtract 2}$$
$$a = b \quad \text{divide by 3}$$

Since we have concluded that *a* must equal *b*, *f* is one-to-one.

(b) Showing that a function *is* one-to-one requires a *general* proof, as in part (a). To show that *g* is *not* one-to-one we need only find two distinct real numbers in the domain that produce the same function value. For example, $-1 \neq 1$, but $g(-1) = g(1)$. In fact, since *g* is an even function, $g(-a) = g(a)$ for every real number *a*.

Figure 2

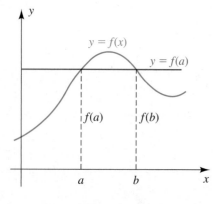

If we know the graph of a function *f*, it is easy to determine whether *f* is one-to-one. For example, the function whose graph is sketched in Figure 2 is not one-to-one, since $a \neq b$, but $f(a) = f(b)$. Note that the horizontal line $y = f(a)$ (or $y = f(b)$) intersects the graph in more than one point. In general, we may use the following graphical test to determine whether a function is one-to-one.

Horizontal Line Test	A function f is one-to-one if and only if every horizontal line intersects the graph of f in at most one point.

Let's apply the horizontal line test to the functions in Example 1.

EXAMPLE 2   Using the horizontal line test

Use the horizontal line test to determine if the function is one-to-one.

(a) $f(x) = 3x + 2$

(b) $g(x) = x^2 - 3$

SOLUTION

(a) The graph of $f(x) = 3x + 2$ is a line with y-intercept 2 and slope 3, as shown in Figure 3. We see that any horizontal line intersects the graph of f in at most one point. Thus, f is one-to-one.

Figure 3   Figure 4

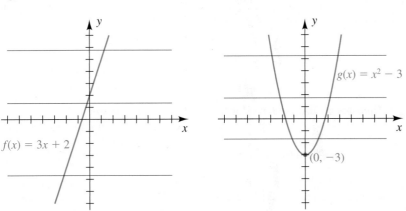

(b) The graph of $g(x) = x^2 - 3$ is a parabola opening upward with vertex $(0, -3)$, as shown in Figure 4. In this case, any horizontal line with equation $y = k$, where $k > -3$, will intersect the graph of g in two points. Thus, g is *not* one-to-one.

We may surmise from Example 2 that every increasing function or decreasing function passes the horizontal line test. Hence, we obtain the following result.

Theorem: Increasing or Decreasing Functions Are One-to-One	**(1)** A function that is increasing throughout its domain is one-to-one. **(2)** A function that is decreasing throughout its domain is one-to-one.

Let f be a one-to-one function with domain D and range R. Thus, for each number y in R, there is *exactly one* number x in D such that $y = f(x)$, as illustrated by the arrow in Figure 5(a). We may, therefore, define a function g from R to D by means of the following rule:

$$x = g(y)$$

As in Figure 5(b), g *reverses the correspondence given by f.* We call g the *inverse function* of f, as in the next definition.

Figure 5
(a) $y = f(x)$ **(b)** $x = g(y)$

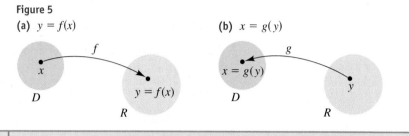

Definition of Inverse Function	Let f be a one-to-one function with domain D and range R. A function g with domain R and range D is the **inverse function** of f, provided the following condition is true for every x in D and every y in R:
	$$y = f(x) \quad \text{if and only if} \quad x = g(y)$$

Remember that for the inverse of a function f to be defined, *it is absolutely essential that f be one-to-one.* The following theorem, stated without proof, is useful to verify that a function g is the inverse of f.

Theorem on Inverse Functions	Let f be a one-to-one function with domain D and range R. If g is a function with domain R and range D, then g is the inverse function of f if and only if both of the following conditions are true:
	(1) $g(f(x)) = x$ for every x in D
	(2) $f(g(y)) = y$ for every y in R

Conditions 1 and 2 of the preceding theorem are illustrated in Figure 6(a) and (b), respectively, where the blue arrow indicates that f is a function from D to R and the red arrow indicates that g is a function from R to D.

Figure 6
(a) First f, then g **(b)** First g, then f

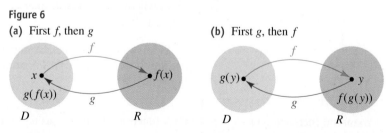

Note that in Figure 6(a) we first apply f to the number x in D, obtaining the function value $f(x)$ in R, and then apply g to $f(x)$, obtaining the number $g(f(x))$ in D. Condition 1 of the theorem states that $g(f(x)) = x$ for every x; that is, g *reverses the correspondence given by f.*

In Figure 6(b) we use the opposite order for the functions. We first apply g to the number y in R, obtaining the function value $g(y)$ in D, and then apply

f to $g(y)$, obtaining the number $f(g(y))$ in R. Condition 2 of the theorem states that $f(g(y)) = y$ for every y; that is, f *reverses* the correspondence given by g.

If a function f has an inverse function g, we often denote g by f^{-1}. The -1 used in this notation should not be mistaken for an exponent; that is,

$$f^{-1}(y) \text{ does not mean } 1/[f(y)].$$

The reciprocal $1/[f(y)]$ may be denoted by $[f(y)]^{-1}$. It is important to remember the following facts about the domain and range of f and f^{-1}.

Domain and Range of f and f^{-1}	$\begin{aligned} \text{domain of } f^{-1} &= \text{range of } f \\ \text{range of } f^{-1} &= \text{domain of } f \end{aligned}$

When we discuss functions, we often let x denote an arbitrary number in the domain. Thus, for the inverse function f^{-1}, we may wish to consider $f^{-1}(x)$, *where x is in the domain R of f^{-1}*. In this event, the two conditions in the theorem on inverse functions are written as follows:

(1) $f^{-1}(f(x)) = x$ for every x in the domain of f
(2) $f(f^{-1}(x)) = x$ for every x in the domain of f^{-1}

Figure 6 contains a hint for finding the inverse of a one-to-one function in certain cases: If possible, *we solve the equation $y = f(x)$ for x in terms of y,* obtaining an equation of the form $x = g(y)$. If the two conditions $g(f(x)) = x$ and $f(g(x)) = x$ are true for every x in the domains of f and g, respectively, then g is the required inverse function f^{-1}. The following guidelines summarize this procedure; in guideline 2, in anticipation of finding f^{-1}, we write $x = f^{-1}(y)$ instead of $x = g(y)$.

Guidelines for Finding f^{-1} in Simple Cases	*1* Verify that f is a one-to-one function throughout its domain.
	2 Solve the equation $y = f(x)$ for x in terms of y, obtaining an equation of the form $x = f^{-1}(y)$.
	3 Verify the following two conditions:
	(a) $f^{-1}(f(x)) = x$ for every x in the domain of f
	(b) $f(f^{-1}(x)) = x$ for every x in the domain of f^{-1}

The success of this method depends on the nature of the equation $y = f(x)$, since we must be able to solve for x in terms of y. For this reason, we include the phrase *in simple cases* in the title of the guidelines. We shall follow these guidelines in the next four examples.

EXAMPLE 3   Finding the inverse of a function

Let $f(x) = 3x - 5$. Find the inverse function of f.

SOLUTION

Guideline 1   The graph of the linear function f is a line of slope 3, and hence f is increasing throughout $\mathbb{R}$. Thus, f is one-to-one and the inverse function f^{-1} exists. Moreover, since the domain and range of f are $\mathbb{R}$, the same is true for f^{-1}.

Guideline 2   Solve the equation $y = f(x)$ for x:

$$y = 3x - 5 \quad \text{let } y = f(x)$$

$$x = \frac{y + 5}{3} \quad \text{solve for } x \text{ in terms of } y$$

We now formally let $x = f^{-1}(y)$; that is,

$$f^{-1}(y) = \frac{y + 5}{3}.$$

Since the symbol used for the variable is immaterial, we may also write

$$f^{-1}(x) = \frac{x + 5}{3},$$

where x is in the domain of f^{-1}.

Guideline 3   Since the domain and range of both f and f^{-1} are $\mathbb{R}$, we must verify conditions (a) and (b) for every real number x. We proceed as follows:

(a) $f^{-1}(f(x)) = f^{-1}(3x - 5)$ definition of f

$$= \frac{(3x - 5) + 5}{3} \quad \text{definition of } f^{-1}$$

$$= x \quad \text{simplify}$$

(b) $f(f^{-1}(x)) = f\left(\dfrac{x + 5}{3}\right)$ definition of f^{-1}

$$= 3\left(\frac{x + 5}{3}\right) - 5 \quad \text{definition of } f$$

$$= x \quad \text{simplify}$$

These verifications prove that the inverse function of f is given by

$$f^{-1}(x) = \frac{x + 5}{3}.$$

EXAMPLE 4   Finding the inverse of a function

Let $f(x) = \dfrac{3x + 4}{2x - 5}$. Find the inverse function of f.

SOLUTION

Guideline 1   A graph of the rational function f is shown in Figure 7 (refer to Example 3 of Section 4.5). It is decreasing throughout its domain, $\left(-\infty, \frac{5}{2}\right) \cup \left(\frac{5}{2}, \infty\right)$. Thus, f is one-to-one and the inverse function f^{-1} exists. We also know that the aforementioned domain is the range of f^{-1} and that the range of f, $\left(-\infty, \frac{3}{2}\right) \cup \left(\frac{3}{2}, \infty\right)$, is the domain of f^{-1}.

Guideline 2   Solve the equation $y = f(x)$ for x.

$$y = \frac{3x + 4}{2x - 5} \quad \text{let } y = f(x)$$

$$y(2x - 5) = 3x + 4 \quad \text{multiply by } 2x - 5$$

$$2xy - 5y = 3x + 4 \quad \text{multiply}$$

$$2xy - 3x = 5y + 4 \quad \text{put all } x\text{-terms on one side}$$

$$x(2y - 3) = 5y + 4 \quad \text{factor out } x$$

$$x = \frac{5y + 4}{2y - 3} \quad \text{divide by } 2y - 3$$

Figure 7

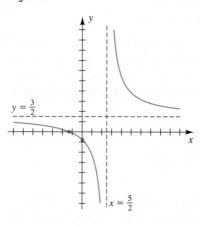

$y = \frac{3}{2}$

$x = \frac{5}{2}$

Thus,

$$f^{-1}(y) = \frac{5y + 4}{2y - 3}, \quad \text{or, equivalently,} \quad f^{-1}(x) = \frac{5x + 4}{2x - 3}.$$

Guideline 3   We verify conditions (a) and (b) for x in the domains of f and f^{-1}, respectively.

For a specific example of guideline 3, if $x = 3$, then $f(3) = \frac{13}{1} = 13$ and $f^{-1}(13) = \frac{69}{23} = 3$. Thus, $f^{-1}(f(3)) = f^{-1}(13) = 3$ and $f(f^{-1}(13)) = f(3) = 13$. **Suggestion:** *After finding an inverse function f^{-1}, pick an arbitrary number in the domain of f (such as 3 above), and verify conditions (a) and (b) in guideline 3. It is highly likely that if these conditions "check," then the correct inverse has been found.*

(a) $f^{-1}(f(x)) = f^{-1}\left(\dfrac{3x + 4}{2x - 5}\right) = \dfrac{5\left(\dfrac{3x + 4}{2x - 5}\right) + 4}{2\left(\dfrac{3x + 4}{2x - 5}\right) - 3} = \dfrac{\dfrac{5(3x + 4) + 4(2x - 5)}{2x - 5}}{\dfrac{2(3x + 4) - 3(2x - 5)}{2x - 5}}$

$$= \frac{15x + 20 + 8x - 20}{6x + 8 - 6x + 15} = \frac{23x}{23} = x$$

(b) $f(f^{-1}(x)) = f\left(\dfrac{5x + 4}{2x - 3}\right) = \dfrac{3\left(\dfrac{5x + 4}{2x - 3}\right) + 4}{2\left(\dfrac{5x + 4}{2x - 3}\right) - 5} = \dfrac{\dfrac{3(5x + 4) + 4(2x - 3)}{2x - 3}}{\dfrac{2(5x + 4) - 5(2x - 3)}{2x - 3}}$

$$= \frac{15x + 12 + 8x - 12}{10x + 8 - 10x + 15} = \frac{23x}{23} = x$$

Thus, the inverse function is given by

$$f^{-1}(x) = \frac{5x + 4}{2x - 3}.$$

EXAMPLE 5   Finding the inverse of a function

Let $f(x) = x^2 - 3$ for $x \geq 0$. Find the inverse function of f.

SOLUTION

Guideline 1   The graph of f is sketched in Figure 8. The domain of f is $[0, \infty)$, and the range is $[-3, \infty)$. Since f is increasing, it is one-to-one and hence has an inverse function f^{-1} with domain $[-3, \infty)$ and range $[0, \infty)$.

Guideline 2   We consider the equation

$$y = x^2 - 3$$

and solve for x, obtaining

$$x = \pm\sqrt{y + 3}.$$

Since x is nonnegative, we reject $x = -\sqrt{y + 3}$ and let

$$f^{-1}(y) = \sqrt{y + 3} \quad \text{or, equivalently,} \quad f^{-1}(x) = \sqrt{x + 3}.$$

(Note that if the function f had domain $x \leq 0$, we would choose the function $f^{-1}(x) = -\sqrt{x + 3}$.)

Guideline 3   We verify conditions (a) and (b) for x in the domains of f and f^{-1}, respectively.

(a) $f^{-1}(f(x)) = f^{-1}(x^2 - 3)$

$$= \sqrt{(x^2 - 3) + 3} = \sqrt{x^2} = x \text{ for } x \geq 0$$

(b) $f(f^{-1}(x)) = f\left(\sqrt{x + 3}\right)$

$$= \left(\sqrt{x + 3}\right)^2 - 3 = (x + 3) - 3 = x \text{ for } x \geq -3$$

Figure 8

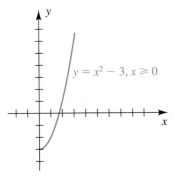

$y = x^2 - 3, x \geq 0$

Figure 9

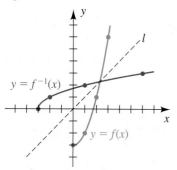

$y = f^{-1}(x)$

$y = f(x)$

Note that the graphs of f and f⁻¹ intersect on the line y = x.

Figure 10

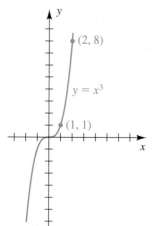

(2, 8)

$y = x^3$

(1, 1)

Figure 11

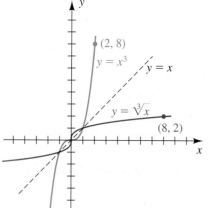

(2, 8)

$y = x^3$ / $y = x$

$y = \sqrt[3]{x}$

(8, 2)

Thus, the inverse function is given by

$$f^{-1}(x) = \sqrt{x + 3} \quad \text{for } x \geq -3.$$

There is an interesting relationship between the graph of a function f and the graph of its inverse function f^{-1}. We first note that $b = f(a)$ is equivalent to $a = f^{-1}(b)$. These equations imply that *the point (a, b) is on the graph of f if and only if the point (b, a) is on the graph of f^{-1}.*

As an illustration, in Example 5 we found that the functions f and f^{-1} given by

$$f(x) = x^2 - 3 \quad \text{and} \quad f^{-1}(x) = \sqrt{x + 3}$$

are inverse functions of each other, provided that x is suitably restricted. Some points on the graph of f are $(0, -3)$, $(1, -2)$, $(2, 1)$, and $(3, 6)$. Corresponding points on the graph of f^{-1} are $(-3, 0)$, $(-2, 1)$, $(1, 2)$, and $(6, 3)$. The graphs of f and f^{-1} are sketched on the same coordinate plane in Figure 9. If the page is folded along the line $y = x$ that bisects quadrants I and III (as indicated by the dashes in the figure), then the graphs of f and f^{-1} coincide. The two graphs are *reflections* of each other through the line $y = x$, or are *symmetric* with respect to this line. This is typical of the graph of every function f that has an inverse function f^{-1} (see Exercise 50).

EXAMPLE 6 The relationship between the graphs of f and f^{-1}

Let $f(x) = x^3$. Find the inverse function f^{-1} of f, and sketch the graphs of f and f^{-1} on the same coordinate plane.

SOLUTION The graph of f is sketched in Figure 10. Note that f is an odd function, and hence the graph is symmetric with respect to the origin.

Guideline 1 Since f is increasing throughout its domain $\mathbb{R}$, it is one-to-one and hence has an inverse function f^{-1}.

Guideline 2 We consider the equation

$$y = x^3$$

and solve for x by taking the cube root of each side, obtaining

$$x = y^{1/3} = \sqrt[3]{y}.$$

We now let

$$f^{-1}(y) = \sqrt[3]{y} \quad \text{or, equivalently,} \quad f^{-1}(x) = \sqrt[3]{x}.$$

Guideline 3 We verify conditions (a) and (b):

(a) $f^{-1}(f(x)) = f^{-1}(x^3) = \sqrt[3]{x^3} = x$ for every x in $\mathbb{R}$

(b) $f(f^{-1}(x)) = f(\sqrt[3]{x}) = (\sqrt[3]{x})^3 = x$ for every x in $\mathbb{R}$

The graph of f^{-1} (that is, the graph of the equation $y = \sqrt[3]{x}$) may be obtained by reflecting the graph in Figure 10 through the line $y = x$, as shown in Figure 11. Three points on the graph of f^{-1} are $(0, 0)$, $(1, 1)$, and $(8, 2)$.

5.1 Exercises

Exer. 1–2: If possible, find (a) $f^{-1}(5)$ and (b) $g^{-1}(6)$.

1

x	2	4	6
$f(x)$	3	5	9

2

t	0	3	5
$f(t)$	2	5	6

x	1	3	5
$g(x)$	6	2	6

t	1	2	4
$g(t)$	3	6	6

Exer. 3–4: Determine if the graph is a graph of a one-to-one function.

3 (a)   (b)   (c)

4 (a)   (b)   (c)

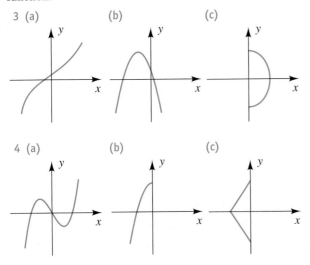

Exer. 5–16: Determine whether the function f is one-to-one.

5 $f(x) = 3x - 7$

6 $f(x) = \dfrac{1}{x - 2}$

7 $f(x) = x^2 - 9$

8 $f(x) = x^2 + 4$

9 $f(x) = \sqrt{x}$

10 $f(x) = \sqrt[3]{x}$

11 $f(x) = |x|$

12 $f(x) = 3$

13 $f(x) = \sqrt{4 - x^2}$

14 $f(x) = 2x^3 - 4$

15 $f(x) = \dfrac{1}{x}$

16 $f(x) = \dfrac{1}{x^2}$

Exer. 17–20: Use the theorem on inverse functions to prove that f and g are inverse functions of each other, and sketch the graphs of f and g on the same coordinate plane.

17 $f(x) = 3x - 2$; $g(x) = \dfrac{x + 2}{3}$

18 $f(x) = x^2 + 5, x \le 0$; $g(x) = -\sqrt{x - 5}, x \ge 5$

19 $f(x) = -x^2 + 3, x \ge 0$; $g(x) = \sqrt{3 - x}, x \le 3$

20 $f(x) = x^3 - 4$; $g(x) = \sqrt[3]{x + 4}$

Exer. 21–24: Determine the domain and range of f^{-1} for the given function without actually finding f^{-1}. Hint: First find the domain and range of f.

21 $f(x) = -\dfrac{2}{x - 1}$

22 $f(x) = \dfrac{5}{x + 3}$

23 $f(x) = \dfrac{4x + 5}{3x - 8}$

24 $f(x) = \dfrac{2x - 7}{9x + 1}$

Exer. 25–42: Find the inverse function of f.

25 $f(x) = 3x + 5$

26 $f(x) = 7 - 2x$

27 $f(x) = \dfrac{1}{3x - 2}$

28 $f(x) = \dfrac{1}{x + 3}$

29 $f(x) = \dfrac{3x + 2}{2x - 5}$

30 $f(x) = \dfrac{4x}{x - 2}$

31 $f(x) = 2 - 3x^2, x \le 0$

32 $f(x) = 5x^2 + 2, x \ge 0$

33 $f(x) = 2x^3 - 5$

34 $f(x) = -x^3 + 2$

35 $f(x) = \sqrt{3 - x}$

36 $f(x) = \sqrt{4 - x^2}, 0 \le x \le 2$

37 $f(x) = \sqrt[3]{x} + 1$

38 $f(x) = (x^3 + 1)^5$

39 $f(x) = x$

40 $f(x) = -x$

41 $f(x) = x^2 - 6x, x \ge 3$

42 $f(x) = x^2 - 4x + 3, x \le 2$

Exer. 43–44: Let $h(x) = 4 - x$. Use h, the table, and the graph to evaluate the expression.

x	2	3	4	5	6
$f(x)$	-1	0	1	2	3

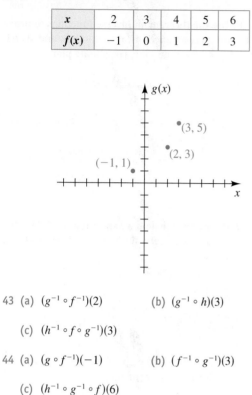

43 (a) $(g^{-1} \circ f^{-1})(2)$ (b) $(g^{-1} \circ h)(3)$

   (c) $(h^{-1} \circ f \circ g^{-1})(3)$

44 (a) $(g \circ f^{-1})(-1)$ (b) $(f^{-1} \circ g^{-1})(3)$

   (c) $(h^{-1} \circ g^{-1} \circ f)(6)$

Exer. 45–48: The graph of a one-to-one function f is shown. **(a)** Use the reflection property to sketch the graph of f^{-1}. **(b)** Find the domain D and range R of the function f. **(c)** Find the domain D_1 and range R_1 of the inverse function f^{-1}.

45
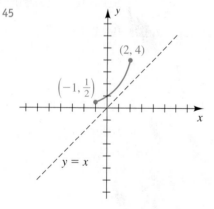

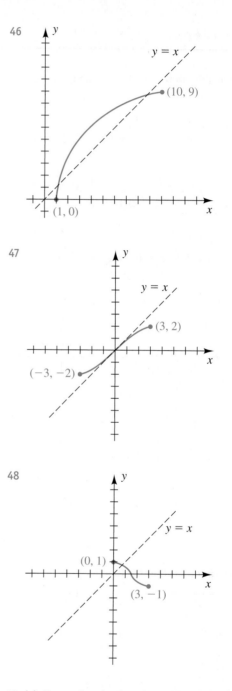

49 (a) Prove that the function defined by $f(x) = ax + b$ (a linear function) for $a \neq 0$ has an inverse function, and find $f^{-1}(x)$.

   (b) Does a constant function have an inverse? Explain.

50 Show that the graph of f^{-1} is the reflection of the graph of f through the line $y = x$ by verifying the following conditions:

(1) If $P(a, b)$ is on the graph of f, then $Q(b, a)$ is on the graph of f^{-1}.

(2) The midpoint of line segment PQ is on the line $y = x$.

(3) The line PQ is perpendicular to the line $y = x$.

51 Verify that $f(x) = f^{-1}(x)$ if

(a) $f(x) = -x + b$ (b) $f(x) = \dfrac{ax + b}{cx - a}$ for $c \neq 0$

(c) $f(x)$ has the following graph:

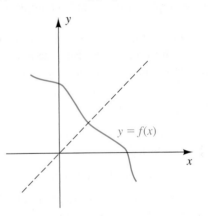

52 Let n be any positive integer. Find the inverse function of f if

(a) $f(x) = x^n$ for $x \geq 0$

(b) $f(x) = x^{m/n}$ for $x \geq 0$ and m any positive integer

53 **Ventilation requirements** Ventilation is an effective way to improve indoor air quality. In nonsmoking restaurants, air circulation requirements (in ft³/min) are given by the function $V(x) = 35x$, where x is the number of people in the dining area.

(a) Determine the ventilation requirements for 23 people.

(b) Find $V^{-1}(x)$. Explain the significance of V^{-1}.

(c) Use V^{-1} to determine the maximum number of people that should be in a restaurant having a ventilation capability of 2350 ft³/min.

54 **Radio stations** The table lists the total numbers of radio stations in the United States for certain years.

Year	Number
1950	2773
1960	4133
1970	6760
1980	8566
1990	10,770
2000	12,717

(a) Determine a linear function $f(x) = ax + b$ that models these data, where x is the year.

(b) Find $f^{-1}(x)$. Explain the significance of f^{-1}.

(c) Use f^{-1} to predict the year in which there were 11,987 radio stations. Compare it with the true value, which is 1995.

5.2
Exponential Functions

Previously, we considered functions having terms of the form

$$\text{variable base}^{\text{constant power}},$$

such as x^2, $0.2x^{1.3}$, and $8x^{2/3}$. We now turn our attention to functions having terms of the form

$$\text{constant base}^{\text{variable power}},$$

such as 2^x, $(1.04)^{4x}$, and 3^{-x}. Let us begin by considering the function f defined by

$$f(x) = 2^x,$$

Figure 1

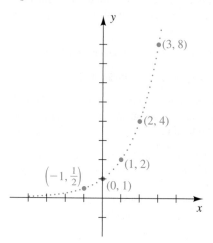

where x is restricted to *rational* numbers. $\left(\text{Recall that if } x = m/n \text{ for integers}\right.$ m and n with $n > 0$, then $2^x = 2^{m/n} = \left(\sqrt[n]{2}\right)^m$.$\left.\right)$ Coordinates of several points on the graph of $y = 2^x$ are listed in the following table.

x	-10	-3	-2	-1	0	1	2	3	10
$y = 2^x$	$\frac{1}{1024}$	$\frac{1}{8}$	$\frac{1}{4}$	$\frac{1}{2}$	1	2	4	8	1024

Other values of y for x rational, such as $2^{1/3}$, $2^{-9/7}$, and $2^{5.143}$, can be approximated with a calculator. We can show algebraically that if x_1 and x_2 are rational numbers such that $x_1 < x_2$, then $2^{x_1} < 2^{x_2}$. Thus, f is an increasing function, and its graph rises. Plotting points leads to the sketch in Figure 1, where the small dots indicate that only the points with *rational* x-coordinates are on the graph. There is a *hole* in the graph whenever the x-coordinate of a point is irrational.

To extend the domain of f to all real numbers, it is necessary to define 2^x for every *irrational* exponent x. To illustrate, if we wish to define 2^π, we could use the nonterminating decimal representing $3.1415926\ldots$ for π and consider the following *rational* powers of 2:

$$2^3, \quad 2^{3.1}, \quad 2^{3.14}, \quad 2^{3.141}, \quad 2^{3.1415}, \quad 2^{3.14159}, \quad \ldots$$

It can be shown, using calculus, that each successive power gets closer to a unique real number, denoted by 2^π. Thus,

$$2^x \to 2^\pi \quad \text{as} \quad x \to \pi, \quad \text{with } x \text{ rational.}$$

The same technique can be used for any other irrational power of 2. To sketch the graph of $y = 2^x$ with x *real,* we replace the holes in the graph in Figure 1 with points, and we obtain the graph in Figure 2. The function f defined by $f(x) = 2^x$ for every real number x is called the **exponential function** *with base 2.*

Let us next consider *any* base a, where a is a positive real number different from 1. As in the preceding discussion, to each real number x there corresponds exactly one positive number a^x such that the laws of exponents are true. Thus, as in the following chart, we may define a function f whose domain is $\mathbb{R}$ and range is the set of positive real numbers.

Figure 2

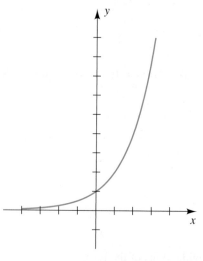

Terminology	Definition	Graph of f for $a > 1$	Graph of f for $0 < a < 1$
Exponential function f with base a	$f(x) = a^x$ for every x in $\mathbb{R}$, where $a > 0$ and $a \neq 1$		

The graphs in the chart show that if $a > 1$, then f is increasing on $\mathbb{R}$, and if $0 < a < 1$, then f is decreasing on $\mathbb{R}$. (These facts can be proved using calculus.) The graphs merely indicate the *general* appearance—the *exact* shape depends on the value of a. Note, however, that since $a^0 = 1$, the y-intercept is 1 for every a.

Note that if $a > 1$, then $a = 1 + d$ ($d > 0$) and the base a in $y = a^x$ can be thought of as representing multiplication by more than 100% as x increases by 1, so the function is increasing. For example, if $a = 1.15$, then $y = (1.15)^x$ can be considered to be a 15% per year growth function. More details on this concept appear later.

If $a > 1$, then as x *decreases* through negative values, the graph of f approaches the x-axis (see the third column in the chart). Thus, the x-axis is a *horizontal asymptote*. As x increases through positive values, the graph rises rapidly. This type of variation is characteristic of the **exponential law of growth,** and f is sometimes called a **growth function.**

If $0 < a < 1$, then as x *increases,* the graph of f approaches the x-axis asymptotically (see the last column in the chart). This type of variation is known as **exponential decay.**

When considering a^x we exclude the cases $a \leq 0$ and $a = 1$. Note that if $a < 0$, then a^x is not a real number for many values of x such as $\frac{1}{2}, \frac{3}{4}$, and $\frac{11}{6}$. If $a = 0$, then $a^0 = 0^0$ is undefined. Finally, if $a = 1$, then $a^x = 1$ for every x, and the graph of $y = a^x$ is a horizontal line.

The graph of an exponential function f is either increasing throughout its domain or decreasing throughout its domain. Thus, f is one-to-one by the theorem on page 279. Combining this result with the definition of a one-to-one function (see page 278) gives us parts (1) and (2) of the following theorem.

Theorem: Exponential Functions Are One-to-One	The exponential function f given by $$f(x) = a^x \quad \text{for} \quad 0 < a < 1 \quad \text{or} \quad a > 1$$ is one-to-one. Thus, the following equivalent conditions are satisfied for real numbers x_1 and x_2. (1) If $x_1 \neq x_2$, then $a^{x_1} \neq a^{x_2}$. (2) If $a^{x_1} = a^{x_2}$, then $x_1 = x_2$.

When using this theorem as a reason for a step in the solution to an example, we will state that *exponential functions are one-to-one.*

ILLUSTRATION   **Exponential Functions Are One-to-One**

■   If $7^{3x} = 7^{2x+5}$, then $3x = 2x + 5$, or $x = 5$.

In the following example we solve a simple *exponential equation*—that is, an equation in which the variable appears in an exponent.

EXAMPLE 1 Solving an exponential equation

Solve the equation $3^{5x-8} = 9^{x+2}$.

SOLUTION

$$3^{5x-8} = 9^{x+2} \qquad \text{given}$$
$$3^{5x-8} = (3^2)^{x+2} \qquad \text{express both sides with the same base}$$
$$3^{5x-8} = 3^{2x+4} \qquad \text{law of exponents}$$
$$5x - 8 = 2x + 4 \qquad \text{exponential functions are one-to-one}$$
$$3x = 12 \qquad \text{subtract } 2x \text{ and add } 8$$
$$x = 4 \qquad \text{divide by } 3$$

Note that the solution in Example 1 depended on the fact that the base 9 could be written as 3 to some power. We will consider only exponential equations of this type for now, but we will solve more general exponential equations later in the chapter.

In the next two examples we sketch the graphs of several different exponential functions.

EXAMPLE 2 Sketching graphs of exponential functions

If $f(x) = \left(\frac{3}{2}\right)^x$ and $g(x) = 3^x$, sketch the graphs of f and g on the same coordinate plane.

SOLUTION Since $\frac{3}{2} > 1$ and $3 > 1$, each graph *rises* as x increases. The following table displays coordinates for several points on the graphs.

Figure 3

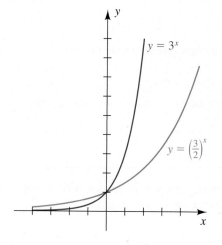

x	-2	-1	0	1	2	3	4
$y = \left(\frac{3}{2}\right)^x$	$\frac{4}{9} \approx 0.4$	$\frac{2}{3} \approx 0.7$	1	$\frac{3}{2}$	$\frac{9}{4} \approx 2.3$	$\frac{27}{8} \approx 3.4$	$\frac{81}{16} \approx 5.1$
$y = 3^x$	$\frac{1}{9} \approx 0.1$	$\frac{1}{3} \approx 0.3$	1	3	9	27	81

Plotting points and being familiar with the general graph of $y = a^x$ leads to the graphs in Figure 3.

Example 2 illustrates the fact that if $1 < a < b$, then $a^x < b^x$ for positive values of x and $b^x < a^x$ for negative values of x. In particular, since $\frac{3}{2} < 2 < 3$, the graph of $y = 2^x$ in Figure 2 lies between the graphs of f and g in Figure 3.

Figure 4

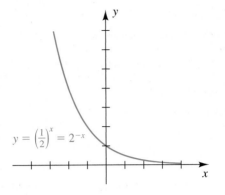

$$y = \left(\tfrac{1}{2}\right)^x = 2^{-x}$$

Figure 5

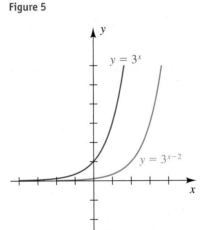

Figure 6

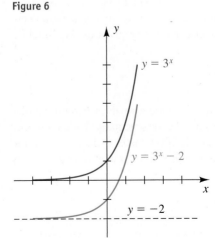

EXAMPLE 3 Sketching the graph of an exponential function

Sketch the graph of the equation $y = \left(\tfrac{1}{2}\right)^x$.

SOLUTION   Since $0 < \tfrac{1}{2} < 1$, the graph *falls* as x increases. Coordinates of some points on the graph are listed in the following table.

x	-3	-2	-1	0	1	2	3
$y = \left(\tfrac{1}{2}\right)^x$	8	4	2	1	$\tfrac{1}{2}$	$\tfrac{1}{4}$	$\tfrac{1}{8}$

The graph is sketched in Figure 4. Since $\left(\tfrac{1}{2}\right)^x = (2^{-1})^x = 2^{-x}$, the graph is the same as the graph of the equation $y = 2^{-x}$. Note that the graph is a reflection through the y-axis of the graph of $y = 2^x$ in Figure 2.

Equations of the form $y = a^u$, where u is some expression in x, occur in applications. The next two examples illustrate equations of this form.

EXAMPLE 4 Shifting graphs of exponential functions

Sketch the graph of the equation:

(a) $y = 3^{x-2}$ **(b)** $y = 3^x - 2$

SOLUTION

(a) The graph of $y = 3^x$, sketched in Figure 3, is resketched in Figure 5. From the discussion of horizontal shifts in Section 3.5, we can obtain the graph of $y = 3^{x-2}$ by shifting the graph of $y = 3^x$ two units to the right, as shown in Figure 5.

The graph of $y = 3^{x-2}$ can also be obtained by plotting several points and using them as a guide to sketch an exponential-type curve.

(b) From the discussion of vertical shifts in Section 3.5, we can obtain the graph of $y = 3^x - 2$ by shifting the graph of $y = 3^x$ two units downward, as shown in Figure 6. Note that the y-intercept is -1 and the line $y = -2$ is a horizontal asymptote for the graph.

EXAMPLE 5 Finding an equation of an exponential function satisfying prescribed conditions

Find an exponential function of the form $f(x) = ba^{-x} + c$ that has horizontal asymptote $y = -2$, y-intercept 16, and x-intercept 2.

SOLUTION   The horizontal asymptote of the graph of an exponential function of the form $f(x) = ba^{-x}$ is the x-axis—that is, $y = 0$. Since the desired horizontal asymptote is $y = -2$, we must have $c = -2$, so $f(x) = ba^{-x} - 2$.

Because the y-intercept is 16, $f(0)$ must equal 16. But $f(0) = ba^{-0} - 2 = b - 2$, so $b - 2 = 16$ and $b = 18$. Thus, $f(x) = 18a^{-x} - 2$.

(continued)

Figure 7

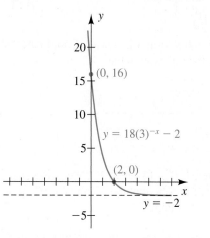

Lastly, we find the value of a:

$$f(x) = 18a^{-x} - 2 \qquad \text{given form of } f$$

$$0 = 18(a)^{-2} - 2 \qquad f(2) = 0 \text{ since 2 is the } x\text{-intercept}$$

$$2 = 18 \cdot \frac{1}{a^2} \qquad \text{add 2; definition of negative exponent}$$

$$a^2 = 9 \qquad \text{multiply by } a^2/2$$

$$a = \pm 3 \qquad \text{take square root}$$

Since a must be positive, we have

$$f(x) = 18(3)^{-x} - 2.$$

Figure 7 shows a graph of f that satisfies all of the conditions in the problem statement. Note that $f(x)$ could be written in the equivalent form

$$f(x) = 18\left(\tfrac{1}{3}\right)^x - 2.$$

The bell-shaped graph of the function in the next example is similar to a *normal probability curve* used in statistical studies.

EXAMPLE 6   Sketching a bell-shaped graph

If $f(x) = 2^{-x^2}$, sketch the graph of f.

Figure 8

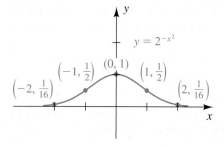

SOLUTION   If we rewrite $f(x)$ as

$$f(x) = \frac{1}{2^{(x^2)}},$$

we see that as x increases through positive values, $f(x)$ decreases rapidly; hence the graph approaches the x-axis asymptotically. Since x^2 is smallest when $x = 0$, the maximum value of f is $f(0) = 1$. Since f is an even function, the graph is symmetric with respect to the y-axis. Some points on the graph are $(0, 1)$, $\left(1, \tfrac{1}{2}\right)$, and $\left(2, \tfrac{1}{16}\right)$. Plotting and using symmetry gives us the sketch in Figure 8.

APPLICATION   Bacterial Growth

Exponential functions may be used to describe the growth of certain populations. As an illustration, suppose it is observed experimentally that the number of bacteria in a culture doubles every day. If 1000 bacteria are present at the start, then we obtain the following table, where t is the time in days and $f(t)$ is the bacteria count at time t.

t (time in days)	0	1	2	3	4
$f(t)$ (bacteria count)	1000	2000	4000	8000	16,000

Figure 9

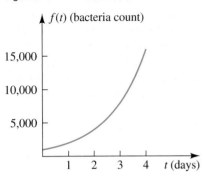

It appears that $f(t) = (1000)2^t$. With this formula we can predict the number of bacteria present at any time t. For example, at $t = 1.5 = \frac{3}{2}$,

$$f(t) = (1000)2^{3/2} \approx 2828.$$

The graph of f is sketched in Figure 9.

APPLICATION   Radioactive Decay

Certain physical quantities *decrease* exponentially. In such cases, if a is the base of the exponential function, then $0 < a < 1$. One of the most common examples of exponential decrease is the decay of a radioactive substance, or isotope. The **half-life** of an isotope is the time it takes for one-half the original amount in a given sample to decay. The half-life is the principal characteristic used to distinguish one radioactive substance from another. The polonium isotope ^{210}Po has a half-life of approximately 140 days; that is, given any amount, one-half of it will disintegrate in 140 days. If 20 milligrams of ^{210}Po is present initially, then the following table indicates the amount remaining after various intervals of time.

Figure 10

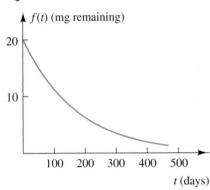

t (time in days)	0	140	280	420	560
$f(t)$ (mg remaining)	20	10	5	2.5	1.25

The sketch in Figure 10 illustrates the exponential nature of the disintegration.

Other radioactive substances have much longer half-lives. In particular, a by-product of nuclear reactors is the radioactive plutonium isotope ^{239}Pu, which has a half-life of approximately 24,000 years. It is for this reason that the disposal of radioactive waste is a major problem in modern society.

APPLICATION   Compound Interest

Compound interest provides a good illustration of exponential growth. If a sum of money P, the *principal,* is invested at a *simple* interest rate r, then the interest at the end of one interest period is the product Pr when r is expressed as a decimal. For example, if $P = \$1000$ and the interest rate is 9% per year, then $r = 0.09$, and the interest at the end of one year is $\$1000(0.09)$, or $\$90$.

If the interest is reinvested with the principal at the end of the interest period, then the new principal is

$$P + Pr \quad \text{or, equivalently,} \quad P(1 + r).$$

Note that to find the new principal we may multiply the original principal by $(1 + r)$. In the preceding example, the new principal is $\$1000(1.09)$, or $\$1090$.

After another interest period has elapsed, the new principal may be found by multiplying $P(1 + r)$ by $(1 + r)$. Thus, the principal after two interest periods is $P(1 + r)^2$. If we continue to reinvest, the principal after three periods is $P(1 + r)^3$; after four it is $P(1 + r)^4$; and, in general, the amount A accumulated after k interest periods is

$$A = P(1 + r)^k.$$

Interest accumulated by means of this formula is **compound interest.** Note that A is expressed in terms of an exponential function with base $1 + r$. The interest period may be measured in years, months, weeks, days, or any other suitable unit of time. When applying the formula for A, remember that *r is the interest rate per interest period expressed as a decimal.* For example, if the rate is stated as 6% *per year compounded monthly,* then the rate per month is $\frac{6}{12}\%$ or, equivalently, 0.5%. Thus, $r = 0.005$ and k is the number of months. If $100 is invested at this rate, then the formula for A is

$$A = 100(1 + 0.005)^k = 100(1.005)^k.$$

In general, we have the following formula.

Compound Interest Formula

$$A = P\left(1 + \frac{r}{n}\right)^{nt},$$

where P = principal
r = annual interest rate expressed as a decimal
n = number of interest periods per year
t = number of years P is invested
A = amount after t years.

The next example illustrates a special case of the compound interest formula.

EXAMPLE 7   Using the compound interest formula

Suppose that $1000 is invested at an interest rate of 9% compounded monthly. Find the new amount of principal after 5 years, after 10 years, and after 15 years. Illustrate graphically the growth of the investment.

SOLUTION   Applying the compound interest formula with $r = 9\% = 0.09$, $n = 12$, and $P = \$1000$, we find that the amount after t years is

$$A = 1000\left(1 + \frac{0.09}{12}\right)^{12t} = 1000(1.0075)^{12t}.$$

Substituting $t = 5$, 10, and 15 and using a calculator, we obtain the following table.

Note that when working with monetary values, we use $=$ instead of $\approx$ and round to two decimal places.

Number of years	Amount
5	$A = \$1000(1.0075)^{60} = \$1565.68$
10	$A = \$1000(1.0075)^{120} = \$2451.36$
15	$A = \$1000(1.0075)^{180} = \$3838.04$

Figure 11
Compound interest: $A = 1000(1.0075)^{12t}$

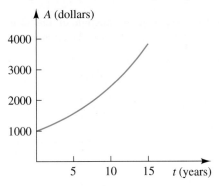

The exponential nature of the increase is indicated by the fact that during the first five years, the growth in the investment is $565.68; during the second five-year period, the growth is $885.68; and during the last five-year period, it is $1386.68.

The sketch in Figure 11 illustrates the growth of $1000 invested over a period of 15 years.

EXAMPLE 8   Finding an exponential model

In 1938, a federal law establishing a minimum wage was enacted, and the wage was set at $0.25 per hour; the wage had risen to $5.15 per hour by 1997. Find a simple exponential function of the form $y = ab^t$ that models the federal minimum wage for 1938–1997.

SOLUTION

$$y = ab^t \qquad \text{given}$$
$$0.25 = ab^0 \qquad \text{let } t = 0 \text{ for 1938}$$
$$0.25 = a \qquad b^0 = 1$$
$$y = 0.25b^t \qquad \text{replace } a \text{ with } 0.25$$
$$5.15 = 0.25b^{59} \qquad t = 1997 - 1938 = 59$$
$$b^{59} = \frac{5.15}{0.25} = 20.6 \qquad \text{divide by } 0.25$$
$$b = \sqrt[59]{20.6} \qquad \text{take 59th root}$$
$$b \approx 1.0526 \qquad \text{approximate}$$

We obtain the model $y = 0.25(1.0526)^t$, which indicates that the federal minimum wage rose about 5.26% per year from 1938 to 1997. A graph of the model is shown in Figure 12. Do you think this model will hold true through the year 2016?

Figure 12

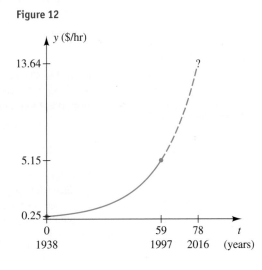

5.2   Exercises

Exer. 1–10: Solve the equation.

1 $7^{x+6} = 7^{3x-4}$

2 $6^{7-x} = 6^{2x+1}$

3 $3^{2x+3} = 3^{(x^2)}$

4 $9^{(x^2)} = 3^{3x+2}$

5 $2^{-100x} = (0.5)^{x-4}$

6 $\left(\frac{1}{2}\right)^{6-x} = 2$

7 $4^{x-3} = 8^{4-x}$

8 $27^{x-1} = 9^{2x-3}$

9 $4^x \cdot \left(\frac{1}{2}\right)^{3-2x} = 8 \cdot (2^x)^2$

10 $9^{2x} \cdot \left(\frac{1}{3}\right)^{x+2} = 27 \cdot (3^x)^{-2}$

11 Sketch the graph of f if $a = 2$.

   (a) $f(x) = a^x$

   (b) $f(x) = -a^x$

   (c) $f(x) = 3a^x$

   (d) $f(x) = a^{x+3}$

   (e) $f(x) = a^x + 3$

   (f) $f(x) = a^{x-3}$

   (g) $f(x) = a^x - 3$

   (h) $f(x) = a^{-x}$

   (i) $f(x) = \left(\dfrac{1}{a}\right)^x$

   (j) $f(x) = a^{3-x}$

12 Work Exercise 11 if $a = \frac{1}{2}$.

Exer. 13–24: Sketch the graph of f.

13 $f(x) = \left(\frac{2}{5}\right)^{-x}$

14 $f(x) = \left(\frac{2}{5}\right)^{x}$

15 $f(x) = 5\left(\frac{1}{2}\right)^x + 3$

16 $f(x) = 8(4)^{-x} - 2$

17 $f(x) = -\left(\frac{1}{2}\right)^x + 4$

18 $f(x) = -3^x + 9$

19 $f(x) = 2^{|x|}$

20 $f(x) = 2^{-|x|}$

21 $f(x) = 3^{1-x^2}$

22 $f(x) = 2^{-(x+1)^2}$

23 $f(x) = 3^x + 3^{-x}$

24 $f(x) = 3^x - 3^{-x}$

Exer. 25–28: Find an exponential function of the form $f(x) = ba^x$ or $f(x) = ba^x + c$ that has the given graph.

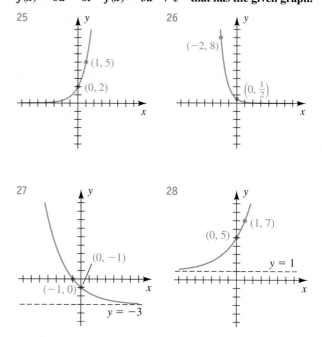

25

26

27

28

Exer. 29–30: Find an exponential function of the form $f(x) = ba^x$ that has the given y-intercept and passes through the point P.

29 y-intercept 8; $P(3, 1)$

30 y-intercept 6; $P\left(2, \frac{3}{32}\right)$

Exer. 31–32: Find an exponential function of the form $f(x) = ba^{-x} + c$ that has the given horizontal asymptote and y-intercept and passes through point P.

31 $y = 32$; y-intercept 212; $P(2, 112)$

32 $y = 72$; y-intercept 425; $P(1, 248.5)$

33 Elk population One hundred elk, each 1 year old, are introduced into a game preserve. The number $N(t)$ alive after t years is predicted to be $N(t) = 100(0.9)^t$. Estimate the number alive after

   (a) 1 year   (b) 5 years   (c) 10 years

34 Drug dosage A drug is eliminated from the body through urine. Suppose that for an initial dose of 10 milligrams, the amount $A(t)$ in the body t hours later is given by $A(t) = 10(0.8)^t$.

(a) Estimate the amount of the drug in the body 8 hours after the initial dose.

(b) What percentage of the drug still in the body is eliminated each hour?

35 Bacterial growth The number of bacteria in a certain culture increased from 600 to 1800 between 7:00 A.M. and 9:00 A.M. Assuming growth is exponential, the number $f(t)$ of bacteria t hours after 7:00 A.M. is given by $f(t) = 600(3)^{t/2}$.

(a) Estimate the number of bacteria in the culture at 8:00 A.M., 10:00 A.M., and 11:00 A.M.

(b) Sketch the graph of f for $0 \le t \le 4$.

36 Newton's law of cooling According to Newton's law of cooling, the rate at which an object cools is directly proportional to the difference in temperature between the object and the surrounding medium. The face of a household iron cools from 125° to 100° in 30 minutes in a room that remains at a constant temperature of 75°. From calculus, the temperature $f(t)$ of the face after t hours of cooling is given by $f(t) = 50(2)^{-2t} + 75$.

(a) Assuming $t = 0$ corresponds to 1:00 P.M., approximate to the nearest tenth of a degree the temperature of the face at 2:00 P.M., 3:30 P.M., and 4:00 P.M.

(b) Sketch the graph of f for $0 \le t \le 4$.

37 Radioactive decay The radioactive bismuth isotope ^{210}Bi has a half-life of 5 days. If there is 100 milligrams of ^{210}Bi present at $t = 0$, then the amount $f(t)$ remaining after t days is given by $f(t) = 100(2)^{-t/5}$.

(a) How much ^{210}Bi remains after 5 days? 10 days? 12.5 days?

(b) Sketch the graph of f for $0 \le t \le 30$.

38 Light penetration in an ocean An important problem in oceanography is to determine the amount of light that can penetrate to various ocean depths. The Beer-Lambert law asserts that the exponential function given by $I(x) = I_0 c^x$ is a model for this phenomenon (see the figure). For a certain location, $I(x) = 10(0.4)^x$ is the amount of light (in calories/cm^2/sec) reaching a depth of x meters.

(a) Find the amount of light at a depth of 2 meters.

(b) Sketch the graph of I for $0 \le x \le 5$.

Exercise 38

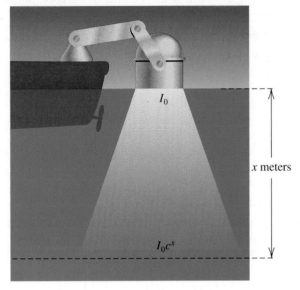

39 Decay of radium The half-life of radium is 1600 years. If the initial amount is q_0 milligrams, then the quantity $q(t)$ remaining after t years is given by $q(t) = q_0 2^{kt}$. Find k.

40 Dissolving salt in water If 10 grams of salt is added to a quantity of water, then the amount $q(t)$ that is undissolved after t minutes is given by $q(t) = 10(\frac{4}{5})^t$. Sketch a graph that shows the value $q(t)$ at any time from $t = 0$ to $t = 10$.

41 Compound interest If $1000 is invested at a rate of 7% per year compounded monthly, find the principal after

(a) 1 month   (b) 6 months

(c) 1 year   (d) 20 years

42 Compound interest If a savings fund pays interest at a rate of 6% per year compounded semiannually, how much money invested now will amount to $5000 after 1 year?

43 Automobile trade-in value If a certain make of automobile is purchased for C dollars, its trade-in value $V(t)$ at the end of t years is given by $V(t) = 0.78C(0.85)^{t-1}$. If the original cost is $25,000, calculate, to the nearest dollar, the value after

(a) 1 year   (b) 4 years   (c) 7 years

44 Real estate appreciation If the value of real estate increases at a rate of 5% per year, after t years the value V of a house purchased for P dollars is $V = P(1.05)^t$. A graph for the value of a house purchased for $80,000 in 1986 is shown in the figure. Approximate the value of the house, to the nearest $1000, in the year 2010.

Exercise 44

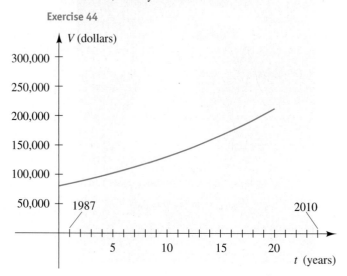

45 Manhattan Island The Island of Manhattan was sold for $24 in 1626. How much would this amount have grown to by 2006 if it had been invested at 6% per year compounded quarterly?

46 Credit-card interest A certain department store requires its credit-card customers to pay interest on unpaid bills at the rate of 18% per year compounded monthly. If a customer buys a television set for $500 on credit and makes no payments for one year, how much is owed at the end of the year?

47 Depreciation The declining balance method is an accounting method in which the amount of depreciation taken each year is a fixed percentage of the present value of the item. If y is the value of the item in a given year, the depreciation taken is ay for some depreciation rate a with $0 < a < 1$, and the new value is $(1 - a)y$.

(a) If the initial value of the item is y_0, show that the value after n years of depreciation is $(1 - a)^n y_0$.

(b) At the end of T years, the item has a salvage value of s dollars. The taxpayer wishes to choose a depreciation rate such that the value of the item after T years will equal the salvage value (see the figure). Show that $a = 1 - \sqrt[T]{s/y_0}$.

Exercise 47

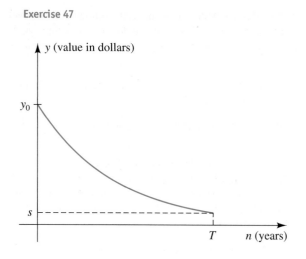

48 Language dating Glottochronology is a method of dating a language at a particular stage, based on the theory that over a long period of time linguistic changes take place at a fairly constant rate. Suppose that a language originally had N_0 basic words and that at time t, measured in millennia (1 millennium = 1000 years), the number $N(t)$ of basic words that remain in common use is given by $N(t) = N_0(0.805)^t$.

(a) Approximate the percentage of basic words lost every 100 years.

(b) If $N_0 = 200$, sketch the graph of N for $0 \le t \le 5$.

Exer. 49–52: Some lending institutions calculate the monthly payment M on a loan of L dollars at an interest rate r (expressed as a decimal) by using the formula

$$M = \frac{Lrk}{12(k - 1)},$$

where $k = [1 + (r/12)]^{12t}$ and t is the number of years that the loan is in effect.

49 Home mortgage

(a) Find the monthly payment on a 30-year $250,000 home mortgage if the interest rate is 8%.

(b) Find the total interest paid on the loan in part (a).

50 Home mortgage Find the largest 25-year home mortgage that can be obtained at an interest rate of 7% if the monthly payment is to be $1500.

51 Car loan An automobile dealer offers customers no-down-payment 3-year loans at an interest rate of 10%. If a customer can afford to pay $500 per month, find the price of the most expensive car that can be purchased.

52 Business loan The owner of a small business decides to finance a new computer by borrowing $3000 for 2 years at an interest rate of 7.5%.

   (a) Find the monthly payment.

   (b) Find the total interest paid on the loan.

Exer. 53–54: Approximate the function at the value of x to four decimal places.

53 (a) $f(x) = 13^{\sqrt{x+1.1}}$, $x = 3$

   (b) $g(x) = \left(\frac{5}{42}\right)^{-x}$, $x = 1.43$

   (c) $h(x) = (2^x + 2^{-x})^{2x}$, $x = 1.06$

54 (a) $f(x) = 2^{\sqrt[3]{1-x}}$, $x = 2.5$

   (b) $g(x) = \left(\frac{2}{25} + x\right)^{-3x}$, $x = 2.1$

   (c) $h(x) = \dfrac{3^{-x} + 5}{3^x - 16}$, $x = \sqrt{2}$

55 Cost of a stamp The price of a first-class stamp was 3¢ in 1958 and 39¢ in 2006 (it was 2¢ in 1885). Find a simple ex-ponential function of the form $y = ab^t$ that models the cost of a first-class stamp for 1958–2006, and predict its value for 2010.

56 Consumer Price Index The CPI is the most widely used measure of inflation. In 1970, the CPI was 37.8, and in 2000, the CPI was 168.8. This means that an urban consumer who paid $37.80 for a market basket of consumer goods and services in 1970 would have needed $168.80 for similar goods and services in 2000. Find a simple exponential function of the form $y = ab^t$ that models the CPI for 1970–2000, and predict its value for 2010.

57 Inflation comparisons In 1974, Johnny Miller won 8 tournaments on the PGA tour and accumulated $353,022 in official season earnings. In 1999, Tiger Woods accumulated $6,616,585 with a similar record.

   (a) Suppose the monthly inflation rate from 1974 to 1999 was 0.0025 (3%/yr). Use the compound interest formula to estimate the equivalent value of Miller's winnings in the year 1999. Compare your answer with that from an inflation calculation on the web (e.g., bls.gov/cpi/home.htm).

   (b) Find the annual interest rate needed for Miller's winnings to be equivalent in value to Woods's winnings.

   (c) What type of function did you use in part (a)? part (b)?

5.3
The Natural Exponential Function

The *compound interest formula* discussed in the preceding section is

$$A = P\left(1 + \frac{r}{n}\right)^{nt},$$

where P is the principal invested, r is the annual interest rate (expressed as a decimal), n is the number of interest periods per year, and t is the number of years that the principal is invested. The next example illustrates what happens if the rate and total time invested are fixed, but the *interest period* is varied.

EXAMPLE 1 Using the compound interest formula

Suppose $1000 is invested at a compound interest rate of 9%. Find the new amount of principal after one year if the interest is compounded quarterly, monthly, weekly, daily, hourly, and each minute.

SOLUTION   If we let $P = \$1000$, $t = 1$, and $r = 0.09$ in the compound interest formula, then

$$A = \$1000\left(1 + \frac{0.09}{n}\right)^n$$

(continued)

for n interest periods per year. The values of n we wish to consider are listed in the following table, where we have assumed that there are 365 days in a year and hence $(365)(24) = 8760$ hours and $(8760)(60) = 525,600$ minutes. (In many business transactions an investment year is considered to be only 360 days.)

Interest period	Quarter	Month	Week	Day	Hour	Minute
n	4	12	52	365	8760	525,600

Using the compound interest formula (and a calculator), we obtain the amounts given in the following table.

Interest period	Amount after one year
Quarter	$\$1000\left(1 + \dfrac{0.09}{4}\right)^{4} = \$1093.08$
Month	$\$1000\left(1 + \dfrac{0.09}{12}\right)^{12} = \$1093.81$
Week	$\$1000\left(1 + \dfrac{0.09}{52}\right)^{52} = \$1094.09$
Day	$\$1000\left(1 + \dfrac{0.09}{365}\right)^{365} = \$1094.16$
Hour	$\$1000\left(1 + \dfrac{0.09}{8760}\right)^{8760} = \$1094.17$
Minute	$\$1000\left(1 + \dfrac{0.09}{525,600}\right)^{525,600} = \$1094.17$

Note that, in the preceding example, after we reach an interest period of one hour, the number of interest periods per year has no effect on the final amount. If interest had been compounded each *second*, the result would still be $1094.17. (Some decimal places *beyond* the first two *do* change.) Thus, the amount approaches a fixed value as n increases. Interest is said to be **compounded continuously** if the number n of time periods per year increases without bound.

If we let $P = 1$, $r = 1$, and $t = 1$ in the compound interest formula, we obtain

$$A = \left(1 + \frac{1}{n}\right)^{n}.$$

The expression on the right-hand side of the equation is important in calculus. In Example 1 we considered a similar situation: as n increased, A approached a limiting value. The same phenomenon occurs for this formula, as illustrated by the following table.

n	Approximation to $\left(1 + \dfrac{1}{n}\right)^n$
1	2.00000000
10	2.59374246
100	2.70481383
1000	2.71692393
10,000	2.71814593
100,000	2.71826824
1,000,000	2.71828047
10,000,000	2.71828169
100,000,000	2.71828181
1,000,000,000	2.71828183

In calculus it is shown that as n increases without bound, the value of the expression $[1 + (1/n)]^n$ approaches a certain irrational number, denoted by e. The number e arises in the investigation of many physical phenomena. An approximation is $e \approx 2.71828$. Using the notation we developed for rational functions in Section 4.5, we denote this fact as follows.

The Number e	If n is a positive integer, then $$\left(1 + \frac{1}{n}\right)^n \to e \approx 2.71828 \quad \text{as} \quad n \to \infty.$$

In the following definition we use e as a base for an important exponential function.

Definition of the Natural Exponential Function	The **natural exponential function** f is defined by $$f(x) = e^x$$ for every real number x.

The natural exponential function is one of the most useful functions in advanced mathematics and applications. Since $2 < e < 3$, the graph of $y = e^x$

Figure 1

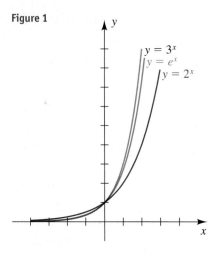

$y = 3^x$
$y = e^x$
$y = 2^x$

The $\boxed{e^x}$ key can be accessed by pressing $\boxed{\text{2nd}}$ $\boxed{\text{LN}}$.

lies between the graphs of $y = 2^x$ and $y = 3^x$, as shown in Figure 1. Scientific calculators have an $\boxed{e^x}$ key for approximating values of the natural exponential function.

APPLICATION   Continuously Compounded Interest

The compound interest formula is

$$A = P\left(1 + \frac{r}{n}\right)^{nt}.$$

If we let $1/k = r/n$, then $k = n/r$, $n = kr$, and $nt = krt$, and we may rewrite the formula as

$$A = P\left(1 + \frac{1}{k}\right)^{krt} = P\left[\left(1 + \frac{1}{k}\right)^{k}\right]^{rt}.$$

For continuously compounded interest we let n (the number of interest periods per year) increase without bound, denoted by $n \to \infty$ or, equivalently, by $k \to \infty$. Using the fact that $[1 + (1/k)]^k \to e$ as $k \to \infty$, we see that

$$P\left[\left(1 + \frac{1}{k}\right)^{k}\right]^{rt} \to P[e]^{rt} = Pe^{rt} \quad \text{as} \quad k \to \infty.$$

This result gives us the following formula.

Continuously Compounded Interest Formula	$A = Pe^{rt},$

where P = principal
r = annual interest rate expressed as a decimal
t = number of years P is invested
A = amount after t years.

The next example illustrates the use of this formula.

EXAMPLE 2 Using the continuously compounded interest formula

Suppose $20,000 is deposited in a money market account that pays interest at a rate of 6% per year compounded continuously. Determine the balance in the account after 5 years.

SOLUTION Applying the formula for continuously compounded interest with $P = 20,000$, $r = 0.06$, and $t = 5$, we have

$$A = Pe^{rt} = 20,000e^{0.06(5)} = 20,000e^{0.3}.$$

Using a calculator, we find that $A = \$26,997.18$.

The continuously compounded interest formula is just one specific case of the following law.

Law of Growth (or Decay) Formula	Let q_0 be the value of a quantity q at time $t = 0$ (that is, q_0 is the initial amount of q). If q changes instantaneously at a rate proportional to its current value, then $$q = q(t) = q_0e^{rt},$$ where $r > 0$ is the rate of growth (or $r < 0$ is the rate of decay) of q.

EXAMPLE 3 Predicting the population of a city

The population of a city in 1970 was 153,800. Assuming that the population increases continuously at a rate of 5% per year, predict the population of the city in the year 2010.

SOLUTION We apply the growth formula $q = q_0e^{rt}$ with initial population $q_0 = 153,800$, rate of growth $r = 0.05$, and time $t = 2010 - 1970 = 40$ years. Thus, a prediction for the population of the city in the year 2010 is

$$153,800e^{(0.05)(40)} = 153,800e^2 \approx 1,136,437.$$

The function f in the next example is important in advanced applications of mathematics.

EXAMPLE 4 Sketching a graph involving two exponential functions

Sketch the graph of f if

$$f(x) = \frac{e^x + e^{-x}}{2}.$$

SOLUTION Note that f is an even function, because

$$f(-x) = \frac{e^{-x} + e^{-(-x)}}{2} = \frac{e^{-x} + e^x}{2} = f(x).$$

Thus, the graph is symmetric with respect to the y-axis. Using a calculator, we obtain the following approximations of $f(x)$.

x	0	0.5	1.0	1.5	2.0
$f(x)$ (approx.)	1	1.13	1.54	2.35	3.76

Plotting points and using symmetry with respect to the y-axis gives us the sketch in Figure 2. The graph *appears* to be a parabola; however, this is not actually the case.

Figure 2

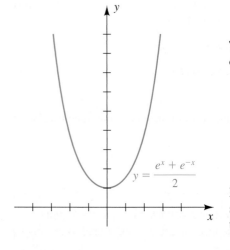

$$y = \frac{e^x + e^{-x}}{2}$$

APPLICATION Flexible Cables

Figure 3

The function f of Example 4 occurs in applied mathematics and engineering, where it is called the **hyperbolic cosine function.** This function can be used to describe the shape of a uniform flexible cable or chain whose ends are supported from the same height, such as a telephone or power line cable (see Figure 3). If we introduce a coordinate system, as indicated in the figure, then it can be shown that an equation that corresponds to the shape of the cable is

$$y = \frac{a}{2}(e^{x/a} + e^{-x/a}),$$

where a is a real number. The graph is called a **catenary,** after the Latin word for *chain.* The function in Example 4 is the special case in which $a = 1$.

APPLICATION Radiotherapy

Exponential functions play an important role in the field of *radiotherapy,* the treatment of tumors by radiation. The fraction of cells in a tumor that survive a treatment, called the *surviving fraction,* depends not only on the energy and nature of the radiation, but also on the depth, size, and characteristics of the tumor itself. The exposure to radiation may be thought of as a number of potentially damaging events, where at least one *hit* is required to kill a tumor cell. For instance, suppose that each cell has exactly one *target* that must be hit. If k denotes the average target size of a tumor cell and if x is the number of damaging events (the *dose*), then the surviving fraction $f(x)$ is given by

$$f(x) = e^{-kx}.$$

This is called the *one target–one hit surviving fraction.*

Suppose next that each cell has n targets and that each target must be hit once for the cell to die. In this case, the *n target–one hit surviving fraction* is given by

$$f(x) = 1 - (1 - e^{-kx})^n.$$

The graph of f may be analyzed to determine what effect increasing the dosage x will have on decreasing the surviving fraction of tumor cells. Note that $f(0) = 1$; that is, if there is no dose, then all cells survive. As an example, if $k = 1$ and $n = 2$, then

$$
\begin{aligned}
f(x) &= 1 - (1 - e^{-x})^2 \\
&= 1 - (1 - 2e^{-x} + e^{-2x}) \\
&= 2e^{-x} - e^{-2x}.
\end{aligned}
$$

Figure 4

Surviving fraction of tumor cells after a radiation treatment

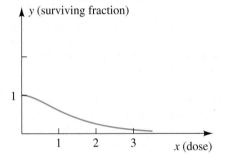

A complete analysis of the graph of f requires calculus. The graph is sketched in Figure 4. The *shoulder* on the curve near the point $(0, 1)$ represents the threshold nature of the treatment—that is, a small dose results in very little tumor cell elimination. Note that for a large x, an increase in dosage has little effect on the surviving fraction. To determine the ideal dose to administer to a patient, specialists in radiation therapy must also take into account the number of healthy cells that are killed during a treatment.

Problems of the type illustrated in the next example occur in the study of calculus.

EXAMPLE 5   Finding zeros of a function involving exponentials

If $f(x) = x^2(-2e^{-2x}) + 2xe^{-2x}$, find the zeros of f.

SOLUTION   We may factor $f(x)$ as follows:

$$
\begin{aligned}
f(x) &= 2xe^{-2x} - 2x^2e^{-2x} & \text{given} \\
&= 2xe^{-2x}(1 - x) & \text{factor out } 2xe^{-2x}
\end{aligned}
$$

To find the zeros of f, we solve the equation $f(x) = 0$. Since $e^{-2x} > 0$ for every x, we see that $f(x) = 0$ if and only if $x = 0$ or $1 - x = 0$. Thus, the zeros of f are 0 and 1.

5.3 Exercises

Exer. 1–4: Use the graph of $y = e^x$ to help sketch the graph of f.

1 (a) $f(x) = e^{-x}$ (b) $f(x) = -e^x$

2 (a) $f(x) = e^{2x}$ (b) $f(x) = 2e^x$

3 (a) $f(x) = e^{x+4}$ (b) $f(x) = e^x + 4$

4 (a) $f(x) = e^{-2x}$ (b) $f(x) = -2e^x$

Exer. 5–6: If P dollars is deposited in a savings account that pays interest at a rate of $r\%$ per year compounded continuously, find the balance after t years.

5 $P = 1000, \quad r = 8\frac{1}{4} \quad t = 5$

6 $P = 100, \quad r = 6\frac{1}{2}, \quad t = 10$

Exer. 7–8: How much money, invested at an interest rate of $r\%$ per year compounded continuously, will amount to A dollars after t years?

7 $A = 100{,}000, \quad r = 6.4, \quad t = 18$

8 $A = 15{,}000, \quad r = 5.5, \quad t = 4$

Exer. 9–10: An investment of P dollars increased to A dollars in t years. If interest was compounded continuously, find the interest rate. (*Hint:* Use trial and error.)

9 $A = 13{,}464, \quad P = 1000, \quad t = 20$

10 $A = 890.20, \quad P = 400, \quad t = 16$

Exer. 11–12: Solve the equation.

11 $e^{(x^2)} = e^{7x-12}$ 12 $e^{3x} = e^{2x-1}$

Exer. 13–16: Find the zeros of f.

13 $f(x) = xe^x + e^x$

14 $f(x) = -x^2e^{-x} + 2xe^{-x}$

15 $f(x) = x^3(4e^{4x}) + 3x^2e^{4x}$

16 $f(x) = x^2(2e^{2x}) + 2xe^{2x} + e^{2x} + 2xe^{2x}$

Exer. 17–18: Simplify the expression.

17 $\dfrac{(e^x + e^{-x})(e^x + e^{-x}) - (e^x - e^{-x})(e^x - e^{-x})}{(e^x + e^{-x})^2}$

18 $\dfrac{(e^x - e^{-x})^2 - (e^x + e^{-x})^2}{(e^x + e^{-x})^2}$

19 **Crop growth** An exponential function W such that $W(t) = W_0e^{kt}$ for $k > 0$ describes the first month of growth for crops such as maize, cotton, and soybeans. The function value $W(t)$ is the total weight in milligrams, W_0 is the weight on the day of emergence, and t is the time in days. If, for a species of soybean, $k = 0.2$ and $W_0 = 68$ mg, predict the weight at the end of 30 days.

20 **Crop growth** Refer to Exercise 19. It is often difficult to measure the weight W_0 of a plant from when it first emerges from the soil. If, for a species of cotton, $k = 0.21$ and the weight after 10 days is 575 milligrams, estimate W_0.

21 **U.S. population growth** The 1980 population of the United States was approximately 231 million, and the population has been growing continuously at a rate of 1.03% per year. Predict the population $N(t)$ in the year 2020 if this growth trend continues.

22 **Population growth in India** The 1985 population estimate for India was 766 million, and the population has been growing continuously at a rate of about 1.82% per year. Assuming that this rapid growth rate continues, estimate the population $N(t)$ of India in the year 2015.

23 **Longevity of halibut** In fishery science, a cohort is the collection of fish that results from one annual reproduction. It is usually assumed that the number of fish $N(t)$ still alive after t years is given by an exponential function. For Pacific halibut, $N(t) = N_0e^{-0.2t}$, where N_0 is the initial size of the cohort. Approximate the percentage of the original number still alive after 10 years.

24 **Radioactive tracer** The radioactive tracer ^{51}Cr can be used to locate the position of the placenta in a pregnant woman. Often the tracer must be ordered from a medical laboratory. If A_0 units (microcuries) are shipped, then because of the radioactive decay, the number of units $A(t)$ present after t days is given by $A(t) = A_0e^{-0.0249t}$.

(a) If 35 units are shipped and it takes 2 days for the tracer to arrive, approximately how many units will be available for the test?

(b) If 35 units are needed for the test, approximately how many units should be shipped?

25 **Blue whale population growth** In 1980, the population of blue whales in the southern hemisphere was thought to number 4500. The population $N(t)$ has been decreasing according to the formula $N(t) = 4500e^{-0.1345t}$, where t is in years and $t = 0$ corresponds to 1980. If this trend continues, predict the population in the year 2015.

26 **Halibut growth** The length (in centimeters) of many common commercial fish t years old can be approximated by a von Bertalanffy growth function having an equation of the form $f(t) = a(1 - be^{-kt})$, where a, b, and k are constants.

(a) For Pacific halibut, $a = 200$, $b = 0.956$, and $k = 0.18$. Estimate the length of a 10-year-old halibut.

(b) Use the graph of f to estimate the maximum attainable length of the Pacific halibut.

27 **Atmospheric pressure** Under certain conditions the atmospheric pressure p (in inches) at altitude h feet is given by $p = 29e^{-0.000034h}$. What is the pressure at an altitude of 40,000 feet?

28 **Polonium isotope decay** If we start with c milligrams of the polonium isotope ^{210}Po, the amount remaining after t days may be approximated by $A = ce^{-0.00495t}$. If the initial amount is 50 milligrams, approximate, to the nearest hundredth, the amount remaining after

(a) 30 days   (b) 180 days   (c) 365 days

29 **Growth of children** The Jenss model is generally regarded as the most accurate formula for predicting the height of preschool children. If y is height (in centimeters) and x is age (in years), then

$$y = 79.041 + 6.39x - e^{3.261 - 0.993x}$$

for $\frac{1}{4} \le x \le 6$. From calculus, the rate of growth R (in cm/year) is given by $R = 6.39 + 0.993e^{3.261 - 0.993x}$. Find the height and rate of growth of a typical 1-year-old child.

30 **Particle velocity** A very small spherical particle (on the order of 5 microns in diameter) is projected into still air with an initial velocity of v_0 m/sec, but its velocity decreases because of drag forces. Its velocity t seconds later is given by $v(t) = v_0 e^{-at}$ for some $a > 0$, and the distance $s(t)$ the particle travels is given by

$$s(t) = \frac{v_0}{a}(1 - e^{-at}).$$

The stopping distance is the total distance traveled by the particle.

(a) Find a formula that approximates the stopping distance in terms of v_0 and a.

(b) Use the formula in part (a) to estimate the stopping distance if $v_0 = 10$ m/sec and $a = 8 \times 10^5$.

31 **Minimum wage** In 1971 the minimum wage in the United States was \$1.60 per hour. Assuming that the rate of inflation is 5% per year, find the equivalent minimum wage in the year 2010.

32 **Land value** In 1867 the United States purchased Alaska from Russia for \$7,200,000. There is 586,400 square miles of land in Alaska. Assuming that the value of the land increases continuously at 3% per year and that land can be purchased at an equivalent price, determine the price of 1 acre in the year 2010. (One square mile is equivalent to 640 acres.)

Exer. 33–34: The *effective yield* (or effective annual interest rate) for an investment is the simple interest rate that would yield at the end of one year the same amount as is yielded by the compounded rate that is actually applied. Approximate, to the nearest 0.01%, the effective yield corresponding to an interest rate of $r\%$ per year compounded (a) quarterly and (b) continuously.

33 $r = 7$ 34 $r = 12$

35 **Probability density function** In statistics, the probability density function for the normal distribution is defined by

$$f(x) = \frac{1}{\sigma\sqrt{2\pi}} e^{-z^2/2} \quad \text{with} \quad z = \frac{x - \mu}{\sigma},$$

where μ and σ are real numbers (μ is the *mean* and σ^2 is the *variance* of the distribution). Sketch the graph of f for the case $\sigma = 1$ and $\mu = 0$.

5.4

Logarithmic Functions

In Section 5.2 we observed that the exponential function given by $f(x) = a^x$ for $0 < a < 1$ or $a > 1$ is one-to-one. Hence, f has an inverse function f^{-1} (see Section 5.1). This inverse of the exponential function with base a is called the **logarithmic function with base a** and is denoted by $\log_a$. Its values are written $\log_a (x)$ or $\log_a x$, read "the logarithm of x with base a." Since, by the definition of an inverse function f^{-1},

$$y = f^{-1}(x) \qquad \text{if and only if} \qquad x = f(y),$$

the definition of $\log_a$ may be expressed as follows.

Definition of $\log_a$	Let a be a positive real number different from 1. The **logarithm of x with base a** is defined by
	$$y = \log_a x \qquad \text{if and only if} \qquad x = a^y$$
	for every $x > 0$ and every real number y.

Note that the two equations in the definition are equivalent. We call the first equation the **logarithmic form** and the second the **exponential form.** You should strive to become an expert in changing each form into the other. The following diagram may help you achieve this goal.

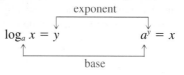

$$\text{Logarithmic form} \qquad \text{Exponential form}$$

Observe that when forms are changed, *the bases of the logarithmic and exponential forms are the same.* The number y (that is, $\log_a x$) corresponds to the exponent in the exponential form. In words, $\log_a x$ is *the exponent to which the base a must be raised to obtain x.* This is what people are referring to when they say "Logarithms are exponents."

The following illustration contains examples of equivalent forms.

ILLUSTRATION   **Equivalent Forms**

Logarithmic form	Exponential form
■ $\log_5 u = 2$	$5^2 = u$
■ $\log_b 8 = 3$	$b^3 = 8$
■ $r = \log_p q$	$p^r = q$
■ $w = \log_4 (2t + 3)$	$4^w = 2t + 3$
■ $\log_3 x = 5 + 2z$	$3^{5+2z} = x$

The next example contains an application that involves changing from an exponential form to a logarithmic form.

EXAMPLE 1 Changing exponential form to logarithmic form

The number N of bacteria in a certain culture after t hours is given by $N = (1000)2^t$. Express t as a logarithmic function of N with base 2.

SOLUTION

$$N = (1000)2^t \qquad \text{given}$$

$$\frac{N}{1000} = 2^t \qquad \text{isolate the exponential expression}$$

$$t = \log_2 \frac{N}{1000} \qquad \text{change to logarithmic form}$$

Some special cases of logarithms are given in the next example.

EXAMPLE 2 Finding logarithms

Find the number, if possible.

(a) $\log_{10} 100$ (b) $\log_2 \frac{1}{32}$ (c) $\log_9 3$ (d) $\log_7 1$ (e) $\log_3 (-2)$

SOLUTION   In each case we are given $\log_a x$ and must find the exponent y such that $a^y = x$. We obtain the following.

(a) $\log_{10} 100 = 2$ because $10^2 = 100$.

(b) $\log_2 \frac{1}{32} = -5$ because $2^{-5} = \frac{1}{32}$.

(c) $\log_9 3 = \frac{1}{2}$ because $9^{1/2} = 3$.

(d) $\log_7 1 = 0$ because $7^0 = 1$.

(e) $\log_3 (-2)$ is not possible because $3^y \neq -2$ for any real number y.

The following general properties follow from the interpretation of $\log_a x$ as an exponent.

Property of $\log_a x$	Reason	Illustration
(1) $\log_a 1 = 0$	$a^0 = 1$	$\log_3 1 = 0$
(2) $\log_a a = 1$	$a^1 = a$	$\log_{10} 10 = 1$
(3) $\log_a a^x = x$	$a^x = a^x$	$\log_2 8 = \log_2 2^3 = 3$
(4) $a^{\log_a x} = x$	as follows	$5^{\log_5 7} = 7$

The reason for property 4 follows directly from the definition of $\log_a$, since

$$\text{if} \quad y = \log_a x, \quad \text{then} \quad x = a^y, \quad \text{or} \quad x = a^{\log_a x}.$$

The logarithmic function with base a is the inverse of the exponential function with base a, so the graph of $y = \log_a x$ can be obtained by reflecting the graph of $y = a^x$ through the line $y = x$ (see Section 5.1). This procedure is illustrated in Figure 1 for the case $a > 1$. Note that the x-intercept of the graph is 1, the domain is the set of positive real numbers, the range is $\mathbb{R}$, and the

Figure 1

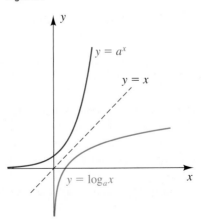

y-axis is a vertical asymptote. Logarithms with base $0 < a < 1$ are seldom used, so we will not emphasize their graphs.

We see from Figure 1 that if $a > 1$, then $\log_a x$ is increasing on $(0, \infty)$ and hence is one-to-one by the theorem on page 279. Combining this result with parts (1) and (2) of the definition of one-to-one function on page 278 gives us the following theorem, which can also be proved if $0 < a < 1$.

Theorem: Logarithmic Functions Are One-to-One	The logarithmic function with base a is one-to-one. Thus, the following equivalent conditions are satisfied for positive real numbers x_1 and x_2. **(1)** If $x_1 \neq x_2$, then $\log_a x_1 \neq \log_a x_2$. **(2)** If $\log_a x_1 = \log_a x_2$, then $x_1 = x_2$.

When using this theorem as a reason for a step in the solution to an example, we will state that *logarithmic functions are one-to-one.*

In the following example we solve a simple *logarithmic equation*—that is, an equation involving a logarithm of an expression that contains a variable. Extraneous solutions may be introduced when logarithmic equations are solved. Hence, we must check solutions of logarithmic equations to make sure that we are taking logarithms of *only positive real numbers;* otherwise, a logarithmic function is not defined.

EXAMPLE 3 Solving a logarithmic equation

Solve the equation $\log_6 (4x - 5) = \log_6 (2x + 1)$.

SOLUTION

$$\log_6 (4x - 5) = \log_6 (2x + 1) \quad \text{given}$$
$$4x - 5 = 2x + 1 \quad \text{logarithmic functions are one-to-one}$$
$$2x = 6 \quad \text{subtract } 2x; \text{ add } 5$$
$$x = 3 \quad \text{divide by } 2$$

Check $x = 3$ LS: $\log_6 (4 \cdot 3 - 5) = \log_6 7$
RS: $\log_6 (2 \cdot 3 + 1) = \log_6 7$

Since $\log_6 7 = \log_6 7$ is a true statement, $x = 3$ is a solution.

When we check the solution $x = 3$ in Example 3, it is not required that the solution be positive. But it is required that the two expressions, $4x - 5$ and $2x + 1$, be positive after we substitute 3 for x. If we extend our idea of *argument* from variables to expressions, then when checking solutions, we can simply remember that *arguments must be positive.*

In the next example we use the definition of logarithm to solve a logarithmic equation.

EXAMPLE 4   Solving a logarithmic equation

Solve the equation $\log_4 (5 + x) = 3$.

SOLUTION

$$\log_4 (5 + x) = 3 \qquad \text{given}$$
$$5 + x = 4^3 \qquad \text{change to exponential form}$$
$$x = 59 \qquad \text{solve for } x$$

Check $x = 59$ LS: $\log_4 (5 + 59) = \log_4 64 = \log_4 4^3 = 3$

RS: 3

Since $3 = 3$ is a true statement, $x = 59$ is a solution.

We next sketch the graph of a specific logarithmic function.

EXAMPLE 5   Sketching the graph of a logarithmic function

Sketch the graph of f if $f(x) = \log_3 x$.

SOLUTION   We will describe three methods for sketching the graph.

Method 1   Since the functions given by $\log_3 x$ and 3^x are inverses of each other, we proceed as we did for $y = \log_a x$ in Figure 1; that is, we first sketch the graph of $y = 3^x$ and then reflect it through the line $y = x$. This gives us the sketch in Figure 2. Note that the points $(-1, 3^{-1})$, $(0, 1)$, $(1, 3)$, and $(2, 9)$ on the graph of $y = 3^x$ reflect into the points $(3^{-1}, -1)$, $(1, 0)$, $(3, 1)$, and $(9, 2)$ on the graph of $y = \log_3 x$.

Figure 2

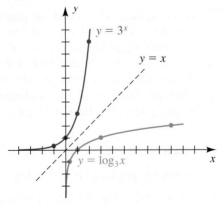

Method 2   We can find points on the graph of $y = \log_3 x$ by letting $x = 3^k$, where k is a real number, and then applying property 3 of logarithms on page 309, as follows:

$$y = \log_3 x = \log_3 3^k = k$$

(continued)

Using this formula, we obtain the points on the graph listed in the following table.

$x = 3^k$	3^{-3}	3^{-2}	3^{-1}	3^0	3^1	3^2	3^3
$y = \log_3 x = k$	-3	-2	-1	0	1	2	3

Figure 3

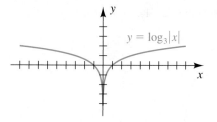

This gives us the same points obtained using the first method.

Method 3   We can sketch the graph of $y = \log_3 x$ by sketching the graph of the equivalent exponential form $x = 3^y$.

Before proceeding, let's plot one more point on $y = \log_3 x$ in Figure 2. If we let $x = 5$, then $y = \log_3 5$ (see Figure 3). (We see that $\log_3 5$ is a number between 1 and 2; we'll be able to better approximate $\log_3 5$ in Section 5.6.) Now on the graph of $y = 3^x$ we have the point $(x, y) = (\log_3 5, 5)$, so $5 = 3^{\log_3 5}$, which illustrates property 4 of logarithms on page 309 and reinforces the claim that *logarithms are exponents*.

As in the following examples, we often wish to sketch the graph of $f(x) = \log_a u$, where u is some expression involving x.

Figure 4

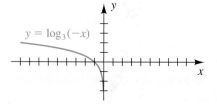

EXAMPLE 6   Sketching the graph of a logarithmic function

Sketch the graph of f if $f(x) = \log_3 |x|$ for $x \neq 0$.

SOLUTION   The graph is symmetric with respect to the y-axis, since

$$f(-x) = \log_3 |-x| = \log_3 |x| = f(x).$$

If $x > 0$, then $|x| = x$ and the graph coincides with the graph of $y = \log_3 x$ sketched in Figure 2. Using symmetry, we reflect that part of the graph through the y-axis, obtaining the sketch in Figure 4.

Alternatively, we may think of this function as $g(x) = \log_3 x$ with $|x|$ substituted for x (refer to the discussion on page 180). Since all points on the graph of g have positive x-coordinates, we can obtain the graph of f by combining g with the reflection of g through the y-axis.

Figure 5

EXAMPLE 7   Reflecting the graph of a logarithmic function

Sketch the graph of f if $f(x) = \log_3 (-x)$.

SOLUTION   The domain of f is the set of negative real numbers, since $\log_3 (-x)$ exists only if $-x > 0$ or, equivalently, $x < 0$. We can obtain the graph of f from the graph of $y = \log_3 x$ by replacing each point (x, y) in Figure 2 by $(-x, y)$. This is equivalent to reflecting the graph of $y = \log_3 x$ through the y-axis. The graph is sketched in Figure 5.

Another method is to change $y = \log_3 (-x)$ to the exponential form $3^y = -x$ and then sketch the graph of $x = -3^y$.

EXAMPLE 8 Shifting graphs of logarithmic equations

Sketch the graph of the equation:

(a) $y = \log_3 (x - 2)$ (b) $y = \log_3 x - 2$

Figure 6

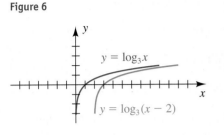

SOLUTION

(a) The graph of $y = \log_3 x$ was sketched in Figure 2 and is resketched in Figure 6. From the discussion of horizontal shifts in Section 3.5, we can obtain the graph of $y = \log_3 (x - 2)$ by shifting the graph of $y = \log_3 x$ two units to the right, as shown in Figure 6.

(b) From the discussion of vertical shifts in Section 3.5, the graph of the equation $y = \log_3 x - 2$ can be obtained by shifting the graph of $y = \log_3 x$ two units downward, as shown in Figure 7. Note that the x-intercept is given by $\log_3 x = 2$, or $x = 3^2 = 9$.

Figure 7

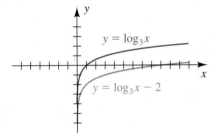

EXAMPLE 9 Reflecting the graph of a logarithmic function

Sketch the graph of f if $f(x) = \log_3 (2 - x)$.

SOLUTION   If we write

$$f(x) = \log_3 (2 - x) = \log_3 [-(x - 2)],$$

then, by applying the same technique used to obtain the graph of the equation $y = \log_3 (-x)$ in Example 7 (with x replaced by $x - 2$), we see that the graph of f is the reflection of the graph of $y = \log_3 (x - 2)$ through the vertical line $x = 2$. This gives us the sketch in Figure 8.

Another method is to change $y = \log_3 (2 - x)$ to the exponential form $3^y = 2 - x$ and then sketch the graph of $x = 2 - 3^y$.

Figure 8

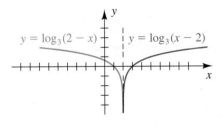

Before electronic calculators were invented, logarithms with base 10 were used for complicated numerical computations involving products, quotients, and powers of real numbers. Base 10 was used because it is well suited for numbers that are expressed in scientific form. Logarithms with base 10 are called **common logarithms.** The symbol **log x** is used as an abbreviation for $\log_{10} x$, just as $\sqrt{}$ is used as an abbreviation for $\sqrt[2]{}$.

Definition of Common Logarithm	$\log x = \log_{10} x$ for every $x > 0$

Since inexpensive calculators are now available, there is no need for common logarithms as a tool for computational work. Base 10 does occur in applications, however, and hence many calculators have a LOG key, which can be used to approximate common logarithms.

The natural exponential function is given by $f(x) = e^x$. The logarithmic function with base e is called the **natural logarithmic function.** The symbol **ln x** (read "ell-en of x") is an abbreviation for $\log_e x$, and we refer to it as the **natural logarithm of x.** Thus, *the natural logarithmic function and the natural exponential function are inverse functions of each other.*

Definition of Natural Logarithm	$\ln x = \log_e x \qquad$ for every $\qquad x > 0$

Most calculators have a key labeled $\boxed{\text{LN}}$, which can be used to approximate natural logarithms. The next illustration gives several examples of equivalent forms involving common and natural logarithms.

ILLUSTRATION   **Equivalent Forms**

Logarithmic form	**Exponential form**
■ $\log x = 2$	$10^2 = x$
■ $\log z = y + 3$	$10^{y+3} = z$
■ $\ln x = 2$	$e^2 = x$
■ $\ln z = y + 3$	$e^{y+3} = z$

To find x when given $\log x$ or $\ln x$, we may use the $\boxed{10^x}$ key or the $\boxed{e^x}$ key, respectively, on a calculator, as in the next example. If your calculator has an $\boxed{\text{INV}}$ key (for inverse), you may enter x and successively press $\boxed{\text{INV}}\ \boxed{\text{LOG}}$ or $\boxed{\text{INV}}\ \boxed{\text{LN}}$.

EXAMPLE 10   Solving a simple logarithmic equation

Find x if

(a) $\log x = 1.7959$ **(b)** $\ln x = 4.7$

SOLUTION

(a) Changing $\log x = 1.7959$ to its equivalent exponential form gives us

$$x = 10^{1.7959}.$$

Evaluating the last expression to three-decimal-place accuracy yields

$$x \approx 62.503.$$

(b) Changing $\ln x = 4.7$ to its equivalent exponential form gives us

$$x = e^{4.7} \approx 109.95.$$

The following chart lists common and natural logarithmic forms for the properties on page 309.

Logarithms with base a	Common logarithms	Natural logarithms
(1) $\log_a 1 = 0$	$\log 1 = 0$	$\ln 1 = 0$
(2) $\log_a a = 1$	$\log 10 = 1$	$\ln e = 1$
(3) $\log_a a^x = x$	$\log 10^x = x$	$\ln e^x = x$
(4) $a^{\log_a x} = x$	$10^{\log x} = x$	$e^{\ln x} = x$

The last property for natural logarithms allows us to write the number a as $e^{\ln a}$, so the exponential function $f(x) = a^x$ can be written as $f(x) = (e^{\ln a})^x$ or as $f(x) = e^{x \ln a}$. Many calculators compute an exponential regression model of the form $y = ab^x$. If an exponential model with base e is desired, we can write the model

$$y = ab^x \quad \text{as} \quad y = ae^{x \ln b}.$$

ILLUSTRATION **Converting to Base e Expressions**

- ■ 3^x is equivalent to $e^{x \ln 3}$
- ■ x^3 is equivalent to $e^{3 \ln x}$
- ■ $4 \cdot 2^x$ is equivalent to $4 \cdot e^{x \ln 2}$

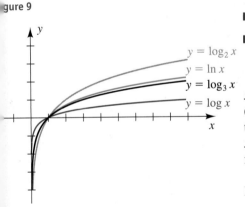

Figure 9

Figure 9 shows four logarithm graphs with base $a > 1$. Note that for $x > 1$, as the base of the logarithm increases, the graphs increase more slowly (they are more horizontal). This makes sense when we consider the graphs of the inverses of these functions: $y = 2^x$, $y = e^x$, $y = 3^x$, and $y = 10^x$. Here, for $x > 0$, as the base of the exponential expression increases, the graphs increase faster (they are more vertical).

The next four examples illustrate applications of common and natural logarithms.

EXAMPLE 11   The Richter scale

On the Richter scale, the magnitude R of an earthquake of intensity I is given by

$$R = \log \frac{I}{I_0},$$

where I_0 is a certain minimum intensity.

(a) If the intensity of an earthquake is $1000 I_0$, find R.

(b) Express I in terms of R and I_0.

SOLUTION

(a) $R = \log \dfrac{I}{I_0}$ given

$ = \log \dfrac{1000I_0}{I_0}$ let $I = 1000I_0$

$ = \log 1000$ cancel I_0

$ = \log 10^3$ $1000 = 10^3$

$ = 3$ $\log 10^x = x$ for every x

From this result we see that a tenfold increase in intensity results in an increase of 1 in magnitude (if 1000 were changed to 10,000, then 3 would change to 4).

(b) $R = \log \dfrac{I}{I_0}$ given

$\dfrac{I}{I_0} = 10^R$ change to exponential form

$I = I_0 \cdot 10^R$ multiply by I_0

EXAMPLE 12   Newton's law of cooling

Newton's law of cooling states that the rate at which an object cools is directly proportional to the difference in temperature between the object and its surrounding medium. Newton's law can be used to show that under certain conditions the temperature T (in °C) of an object at time t (in hours) is given by $T = 75e^{-2t}$. Express t as a function of T.

SOLUTION $T = 75e^{-2t}$ given

$e^{-2t} = \dfrac{T}{75}$ isolate the exponential expression

$-2t = \ln \dfrac{T}{75}$ change to logarithmic form

$t = -\dfrac{1}{2} \ln \dfrac{T}{75}$ divide by -2

EXAMPLE 13   Approximating a doubling time

Assume that a population is growing continuously at a rate of 4% per year. Approximate the amount of time it takes for the population to double its size — that is, its **doubling time.**

SOLUTION   Note that an initial population size is not given. Not knowing the initial size does not present a problem, however, since we wish only to determine the time needed to obtain a population size *relative* to the initial population size. Using the growth formula $q = q_0 e^{rt}$ with $r = 0.04$ gives us

$2q_0 = q_0 e^{0.04t}$ let $q = 2q_0$

$2 = e^{0.04t}$ divide by q_0 $(q_0 \neq 0)$

$$0.04t = \ln 2 \qquad \text{change to logarithmic form}$$
$$t = 25 \ln 2 \approx 17.3 \text{ yr.} \quad \text{multiply by } \frac{1}{0.04} = 25$$

The fact that q_0 did not have any effect on the answer indicates that the doubling time for a population of 1000 is the same as the doubling time for a population of 1,000,000 or any other reasonable initial population.

From the last example we may obtain a general formula for the doubling time of a population—namely,

$$rt = \ln 2 \qquad \text{or, equivalently,} \qquad t = \frac{\ln 2}{r}.$$

Since $\ln 2 \approx 0.69$, we see that the doubling time t for a growth of this type is approximately $0.69/r$. Because the numbers 70 and 72 are close to 69 but have more divisors, some resources refer to this doubling relationship as the **rule of 70** or the **rule of 72.** As an illustration of the rule of 72, if the growth rate of a population is 8%, then it takes about $72/8 = 9$ years for the population to double. More precisely, this value is

$$\frac{\ln 2}{8} \cdot 100 \approx 8.7 \text{ yr.}$$

EXAMPLE 14 Determining the half-life of a radioactive substance

A physicist finds that an unknown radioactive substance registers 2000 counts per minute on a Geiger counter. Ten days later the substance registers 1500 counts per minute. Using calculus, it can be shown that after t days the amount of radioactive material, and hence the number of counts per minute $N(t)$, is directly proportional to e^{ct} for some constant c. Determine the half-life of the substance.

SOLUTION   Since $N(t)$ is directly proportional to e^{ct},

$$N(t) = ke^{ct},$$

where k is a constant. Letting $t = 0$ and using $N(0) = 2000$, we obtain

$$2000 = ke^{c \cdot 0} = k \cdot 1 = k.$$

Hence, the formula for $N(t)$ may be written

$$N(t) = 2000e^{ct}.$$

Since $N(10) = 1500$, we may determine c as follows:

$$1500 = 2000e^{c \cdot 10} \quad \text{let } t = 10 \text{ in } N(t)$$
$$\tfrac{3}{4} = e^{10c} \qquad\quad \text{isolate the exponential expression}$$
$$10c = \ln \tfrac{3}{4} \qquad \text{change to logarithmic form}$$
$$c = \tfrac{1}{10} \ln \tfrac{3}{4} \qquad \text{divide by 10}$$

(continued)

Finally, since the half-life corresponds to the time t at which $N(t)$ is equal to 1000, we have the following:

$$1000 = 2000e^{ct} \qquad \text{let } N(t) = 1000$$

$$\tfrac{1}{2} = e^{ct} \qquad \text{isolate the exponential expression}$$

$$ct = \ln \tfrac{1}{2} \qquad \text{change to logarithmic form}$$

$$t = \frac{1}{c} \ln \frac{1}{2} \qquad \text{divide by } c$$

$$= \frac{1}{\frac{1}{10} \ln \frac{3}{4}} \ln \frac{1}{2} \qquad c = \tfrac{1}{10} \ln \tfrac{3}{4}$$

$$\approx 24 \text{ days} \qquad \text{approximate}$$

5.4 Exercises

Exer. 1–2: Change to logarithmic form.

1 (a) $4^3 = 64$ (b) $4^{-3} = \frac{1}{64}$ (c) $t^r = s$

(d) $3^x = 4 - t$ (e) $5^{7t} = \dfrac{a + b}{a}$ (f) $(0.7)^t = 5.3$

2 (a) $3^5 = 243$ (b) $3^{-4} = \frac{1}{81}$ (c) $c^p = d$

(d) $7^x = 100p$ (e) $3^{-2x} = \dfrac{P}{F}$ (f) $(0.9)^t = \frac{1}{2}$

Exer. 3–4: Change to exponential form.

3 (a) $\log_2 32 = 5$ (b) $\log_3 \frac{1}{243} = -5$

(c) $\log_t r = p$ (d) $\log_3 (x + 2) = 5$

(e) $\log_2 m = 3x + 4$ (f) $\log_b 512 = \frac{3}{2}$

4 (a) $\log_3 81 = 4$ (b) $\log_4 \frac{1}{256} = -4$

(c) $\log_v w = q$ (d) $\log_6 (2x - 1) = 3$

(e) $\log_4 p = 5 - x$ (f) $\log_a 343 = \frac{3}{4}$

Exer. 5–10: Solve for t using logarithms with base a.

5 $2a^{t/3} = 5$ 6 $3a^{4t} = 10$

7 $K = H - Ca^t$ 8 $F = D + Ba^t$

9 $A = Ba^{Ct} + D$ 10 $L = Ma^{t/N} - P$

Exer. 11–12: Change to logarithmic form.

11 (a) $10^5 = 100,000$ (b) $10^{-3} = 0.001$

(c) $10^x = y + 1$ (d) $e^7 = p$

(e) $e^{2t} = 3 - x$

12 (a) $10^4 = 10,000$ (b) $10^{-2} = 0.01$

(c) $10^x = 38z$ (d) $e^4 = D$

(e) $e^{0.1t} = x + 2$

Exer. 13–14: Change to exponential form.

13 (a) $\log x = 50$ (b) $\log x = 20t$

(c) $\ln x = 0.1$ (d) $\ln w = 4 + 3x$

(e) $\ln (z - 2) = \frac{1}{6}$

14 (a) $\log x = -8$ (b) $\log x = y - 2$

(c) $\ln x = \frac{1}{2}$ (d) $\ln z = 7 + x$

(e) $\ln (t - 5) = 1.2$

Exer. 15–16: Find the number, if possible.

15 (a) $\log_5 1$ (b) $\log_3 3$ (c) $\log_4 (-2)$

    (d) $\log_7 7^2$ (e) $3^{\log_3 8}$ (f) $\log_5 125$

    (g) $\log_4 \frac{1}{16}$

16 (a) $\log_8 1$ (b) $\log_9 9$ (c) $\log_5 0$

    (d) $\log_6 6^7$ (e) $5^{\log_5 4}$ (f) $\log_3 243$

    (g) $\log_2 128$

Exer. 17–18: Find the number.

17 (a) $10^{\log 3}$ (b) $\log 10^5$ (c) $\log 100$

    (d) $\log 0.0001$ (e) $e^{\ln 2}$ (f) $\ln e^{-3}$

    (g) $e^{2+\ln 3}$

18 (a) $10^{\log 7}$ (b) $\log 10^{-6}$ (c) $\log 100{,}000$

    (d) $\log 0.001$ (e) $e^{\ln 8}$ (f) $\ln e^{2/3}$

    (g) $e^{1+\ln 5}$

Exer. 19–34: Solve the equation.

19 $\log_4 x = \log_4 (8 - x)$

20 $\log_3 (x + 4) = \log_3 (1 - x)$

21 $\log_5 (x - 2) = \log_5 (3x + 7)$

22 $\log_7 (x - 5) = \log_7 (6x)$

23 $\log x^2 = \log (-3x - 2)$

24 $\ln x^2 = \ln (12 - x)$

25 $\log_3 (x - 4) = 2$

26 $\log_2 (x - 5) = 4$

27 $\log_9 x = \frac{3}{2}$ 28 $\log_4 x = -\frac{3}{2}$

29 $\ln x^2 = -2$ 30 $\log x^2 = -4$

31 $e^{2 \ln x} = 9$ 32 $e^{-\ln x} = 0.2$

33 $e^{x \ln 3} = 27$ 34 $e^{x \ln 2} = 0.25$

35 Sketch the graph of f if $a = 4$:

    (a) $f(x) = \log_a x$ (b) $f(x) = -\log_a x$

    (c) $f(x) = 2 \log_a x$ (d) $f(x) = \log_a (x + 2)$

    (e) $f(x) = (\log_a x) + 2$ (f) $f(x) = \log_a (x - 2)$

    (g) $f(x) = (\log_a x) - 2$ (h) $f(x) = \log_a |x|$

    (i) $f(x) = \log_a (-x)$ (j) $f(x) = \log_a (3 - x)$

    (k) $f(x) = |\log_a x|$ (l) $f(x) = \log_{1/a} x$

36 Work Exercise 35 if $a = 5$.

Exer. 37–42: Sketch the graph of f.

37 $f(x) = \log (x + 10)$ 38 $f(x) = \log (x + 100)$

39 $f(x) = \ln |x|$ 40 $f(x) = \ln |x - 1|$

41 $f(x) = \ln e + x$ 42 $f(x) = \ln (e + x)$

Exer. 43–44: Find a logarithmic function of the form $f(x) = \log_a x$ for the given graph.

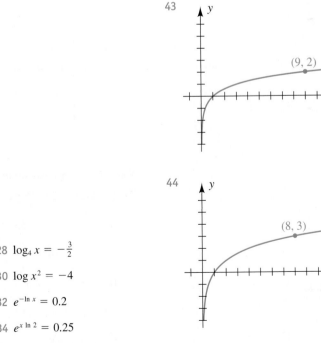

43

44

Exer. 45–50: Shown in the figure is the graph of a function f. Express $f(x)$ in terms of F.

$\boxed{F(x) = \log_a x}$

$(a^2, 2)$

$(1, 0)$ $(a, 1)$

$\left(\dfrac{1}{a}, -1\right)$

45

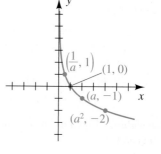

$\left(\dfrac{1}{a}, 1\right)$

$(1, 0)$

$(a, -1)$

$(a^2, -2)$

46

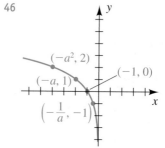

$(-a^2, 2)$

$(-1, 0)$

$(-a, 1)$

$\left(-\dfrac{1}{a}, -1\right)$

47

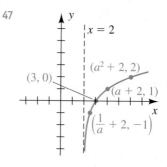

$x = 2$

$(a^2 + 2, 2)$

$(3, 0)$

$(a + 2, 1)$

$\left(\dfrac{1}{a} + 2, -1\right)$

48

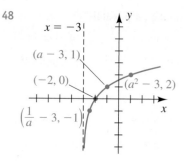

$x = -3$

$(a - 3, 1)$

$(-2, 0)$

$(a^2 - 3, 2)$

$\left(\dfrac{1}{a} - 3, -1\right)$

49

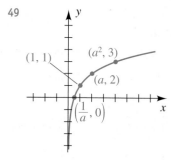

$(1, 1)$ $(a^2, 3)$

$(a, 2)$

$\left(\dfrac{1}{a}, 0\right)$

50

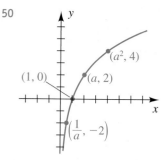

$(a^2, 4)$

$(1, 0)$ $(a, 2)$

$\left(\dfrac{1}{a}, -2\right)$

Exer. 51–52: Approximate x to three significant figures.

51   (a) $\log x = 3.6274$ (b) $\log x = 0.9469$

     (c) $\log x = -1.6253$ (d) $\ln x = 2.3$

     (e) $\ln x = 0.05$ (f) $\ln x = -1.6$

52   (a) $\log x = 1.8965$ (b) $\log x = 4.9680$

     (c) $\log x = -2.2118$ (d) $\ln x = 3.7$

     (e) $\ln x = 0.95$ (f) $\ln x = -5$

53 **Finding a growth rate** Change $f(x) = 1000(1.05)^x$ to an exponential function with base e and approximate the growth rate of f.

54 **Finding a decay rate** Change $f(x) = 100(\frac{1}{2})^x$ to an exponential function with base e and approximate the decay rate of f.

55 **Radium decay** If we start with q_0 milligrams of radium, the amount q remaining after t years is given by the formula $q = q_0(2)^{-t/1600}$. Express t in terms of q and q_0.

56 **Bismuth isotope decay** The radioactive bismuth isotope ^{210}Bi disintegrates according to $Q = k(2)^{-t/5}$, where k is a constant and t is the time in days. Express t in terms of Q and k.

57 **Electrical circuit** A schematic of a simple electrical circuit consisting of a resistor and an inductor is shown in the figure. The current I at time t is given by the formula $I = 20e^{-Rt/L}$, where R is the resistance and L is the inductance. Solve this equation for t.

Exercise 57

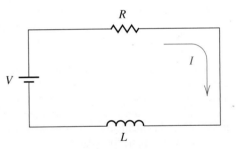

58 **Electrical condenser** An electrical condenser with initial charge Q_0 is allowed to discharge. After t seconds the charge Q is $Q = Q_0e^{kt}$, where k is a constant. Solve this equation for t.

59 **Richter scale** Use the Richter scale formula $R = \log(I/I_0)$ to find the magnitude of an earthquake that has an intensity

(a) 100 times that of I_0

(b) 10,000 times that of I_0

(c) 100,000 times that of I_0

60 **Richter scale** Refer to Exercise 59. The largest recorded magnitudes of earthquakes have been between 8 and 9 on the Richter scale. Find the corresponding intensities in terms of I_0.

61 **Sound intensity** The loudness of a sound, as experienced by the human ear, is based on its intensity level. A formula used for finding the intensity level α (in decibels) that corresponds to a sound intensity I is $\alpha = 10 \log(I/I_0)$, where I_0 is a special value of I agreed to be the weakest sound that can be detected by the ear under certain conditions. Find α if

(a) I is 10 times as great as I_0

(b) I is 1000 times as great as I_0

(c) I is 10,000 times as great as I_0 (This is the intensity level of the average voice.)

62 **Sound intensity** Refer to Exercise 61. A sound intensity level of 140 decibels produces pain in the average human ear. Approximately how many times greater than I_0 must I be in order for α to reach this level?

63 **U.S. population growth** The population $N(t)$ (in millions) of the United States t years after 1980 may be approximated by the formula $N(t) = 231e^{0.0103t}$. When will the population be twice what it was in 1980?

64 **Population growth in India** The population $N(t)$ (in millions) of India t years after 1985 may be approximated by the formula $N(t) = 766e^{0.0182t}$. When will the population reach 1.5 billion?

65 **Children's weight** The Ehrenberg relation

$$\ln W = \ln 2.4 + (1.84)h$$

is an empirically based formula relating the height h (in meters) to the average weight W (in kilograms) for children 5 through 13 years old.

(a) Express W as a function of h that does not contain ln.

(b) Estimate the average weight of an 8-year-old child who is 1.5 meters tall.

66 **Continuously compounded interest** If interest is compounded continuously at the rate of 6% per year, approximate the number of years it will take an initial deposit of $6000 to grow to $25,000.

67 **Air pressure** The air pressure $p(h)$ (in lb/in^2) at an altitude of h feet above sea level may be approximated by the formula $p(h) = 14.7e^{-0.0000385h}$. At approximately what altitude h is the air pressure

(a) 10 lb/in^2?

(b) one-half its value at sea level?

68 Vapor pressure A liquid's vapor pressure P (in lb/in²), a measure of its volatility, is related to its temperature T (in °F) by the Antoine equation

$$\log P = a + \frac{b}{c + T},$$

where a, b, and c are constants. Vapor pressure increases rapidly with an increase in temperature. Express P as a function of T.

69 Elephant growth The weight W (in kilograms) of a female African elephant at age t (in years) may be approximated by

$$W = 2600(1 - 0.51e^{-0.075t})^3.$$

(a) Approximate the weight at birth.

(b) Estimate the age of a female African elephant weighing 1800 kilograms by using (1) the accompanying graph and (2) the formula for W.

Exercise 69

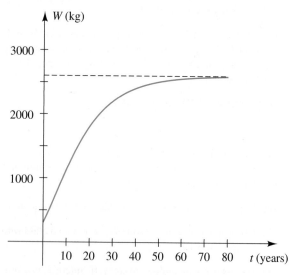

70 Coal consumption A country presently has coal reserves of 50 million tons. Last year 6.5 million tons of coal was consumed. Past years' data and population projections suggest that the rate of consumption R (in million tons/year) will increase according to the formula $R = 6.5e^{0.02t}$, and the total amount T (in million tons) of coal that will be used in t years is given by the formula $T = 325(e^{0.02t} - 1)$. If the country uses only its own resources, when will the coal reserves be depleted?

71 Urban population density An urban density model is a formula that relates the population density D (in thousands/mi²) to the distance x (in miles) from the center of the city. The formula $D = ae^{-bx}$ for the central density a and coefficient of decay b has been found to be appropriate for many large U.S. cities. For the city of Atlanta in 1970, $a = 5.5$ and $b = 0.10$. At approximately what distance was the population density 2000 per square mile?

72 Brightness of stars Stars are classified into categories of brightness called magnitudes. The faintest stars, with light flux L_0, are assigned a magnitude of 6. Brighter stars of light flux L are assigned a magnitude m by means of the formula

$$m = 6 - 2.5 \log \frac{L}{L_0}.$$

(a) Find m if $L = 10^{0.4}L_0$.

(b) Solve the formula for L in terms of m and L_0.

73 Radioactive iodine decay Radioactive iodine ^{131}I is frequently used in tracer studies involving the thyroid gland. The substance decays according to the formula $A(t) = A_0 a^{-t}$, where A_0 is the initial dose and t is the time in days. Find a, assuming the half-life of ^{131}I is 8 days.

74 Radioactive contamination Radioactive strontium ^{90}Sr has been deposited in a large field by acid rain. If sufficient amounts make their way through the food chain to humans, bone cancer can result. It has been determined that the radioactivity level in the field is 2.5 times the safe level S. ^{90}Sr decays according to the formula

$$A(t) = A_0 e^{-0.0239t},$$

where A_0 is the amount currently in the field and t is the time in years. For how many years will the field be contaminated?

75 Walking speed In a survey of 15 cities ranging in population P from 300 to 3,000,000, it was found that the average walking speed S (in ft/sec) of a pedestrian could be approximated by $S = 0.05 + 0.86 \log P$.

(a) How does the population affect the average walking speed?

(b) For what population is the average walking speed 5 ft/sec?

76 Computer chips For manufacturers of computer chips, it is important to consider the fraction F of chips that will fail after t years of service. This fraction can sometimes be approximated by the formula $F = 1 - e^{-ct}$, where c is a positive constant.

(a) How does the value of c affect the reliability of a chip?

(b) If $c = 0.125$, after how many years will 35% of the chips have failed?

Exer. 77–78: Approximate the function at the value of x to four decimal places.

77 (a) $f(x) = \ln(x + 1) + e^x, \quad x = 2$

(b) $g(x) = \dfrac{(\log x)^2 - \log x}{4}, \quad x = 3.97$

78 (a) $f(x) = \log(2x^2 + 1) - 10^{-x}, \quad x = 1.95$

(b) $g(x) = \dfrac{x - 3.4}{\ln x + 4}, \quad x = 0.55$

79 Cholesterol level in women Studies relating serum cholesterol level to coronary heart disease suggest that a risk factor is the ratio x of the total amount C of cholesterol in the blood to the amount H of high-density lipoprotein cholesterol in the blood. For a female, the lifetime risk R of having a heart attack can be approximated by the formula

$$R = 2.07 \ln x - 2.04 \quad \text{provided} \quad 0 \le R \le 1.$$

For example, if $R = 0.65$, then there is a 65% chance that a woman will have a heart attack over an average lifetime. Calculate R for a female with $C = 242$ and $H = 78$.

80 Cholesterol level in men Refer to Exercise 79. For a male, the risk can be approximated by the formula $R = 1.36 \ln x - 1.19$. Calculate R for a male with $C = 287$ and $H = 65$.

5.5

Properties of Logarithms

In the preceding section we observed that $\log_a x$ can be interpreted as an exponent. Thus, it seems reasonable to expect that the laws of exponents can be used to obtain corresponding laws of logarithms. This is demonstrated in the proofs of the following laws, which are fundamental for all work with logarithms.

Laws of Logarithms	If u and w denote positive real numbers, then
	(1) $\log_a(uw) = \log_a u + \log_a w$
	(2) $\log_a\left(\dfrac{u}{w}\right) = \log_a u - \log_a w$
	(3) $\log_a(u^c) = c \log_a u \quad$ for every real number c

PROOFS   For all three proofs, let

$$r = \log_a u \quad \text{and} \quad s = \log_a w.$$

The equivalent exponential forms are

$$u = a^r \quad \text{and} \quad w = a^s.$$

We now proceed as follows:

(1) $uw = a^r a^s$ definition of u and w

   $uw = a^{r+s}$ law 1 of exponents

   $\log_a (uw) = r + s$ change to logarithmic form

   $\log_a (uw) = \log_a u + \log_a w$ definition of r and s

(2) $\dfrac{u}{w} = \dfrac{a^r}{a^s}$ definition of u and w

   $\dfrac{u}{w} = a^{r-s}$ law 5(a) of exponents

   $\log_a \left(\dfrac{u}{w} \right) = r - s$ change to logarithmic form

   $\log_a \left(\dfrac{u}{w} \right) = \log_a u - \log_a w$ definition of r and s

(3) $u^c = (a^r)^c$ definition of u

   $u^c = a^{cr}$ law 2 of exponents

   $\log_a (u^c) = cr$ change to logarithmic form

   $\log_a (u^c) = c \log_a u$ definition of r

The laws of logarithms for the special cases $a = 10$ (common logs) and $a = e$ (natural logs) are written as shown in the following chart.

Common logarithms	Natural logarithms
(1) $\log (uw) = \log u + \log w$	**(1)** $\ln (uw) = \ln u + \ln w$
(2) $\log \left(\dfrac{u}{w} \right) = \log u - \log w$	**(2)** $\ln \left(\dfrac{u}{w} \right) = \ln u - \ln w$
(3) $\log (u^c) = c \log u$	**(3)** $\ln (u^c) = c \ln u$

As indicated by the following warning, there are no laws for expressing $\log_a (u + w)$ or $\log_a (u - w)$ in terms of simpler logarithms.

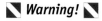 *Warning!*

$$\log_a (u + w) \neq \log_a u + \log_a w$$
$$\log_a (u - w) \neq \log_a u - \log_a w$$

The following examples illustrate uses of the laws of logarithms.

EXAMPLE 1 Using laws of logarithms

Express $\log_a \dfrac{x^3 \sqrt{y}}{z^2}$ in terms of logarithms of x, y, and z.

SOLUTION   We write $\sqrt{y}$ as $y^{1/2}$ and use laws of logarithms:

$$\log_a \frac{x^3 \sqrt{y}}{z^2} = \log_a (x^3 y^{1/2}) - \log_a z^2 \qquad \text{law 2}$$

$$= \log_a x^3 + \log_a y^{1/2} - \log_a z^2 \qquad \text{law 1}$$

$$= 3 \log_a x + \tfrac{1}{2} \log_a y - 2 \log_a z \qquad \text{law 3}$$

Note that if a term with a positive exponent (such as x^3) is in the numerator of the original expression, it will have a positive coefficient in the expanded form, and if it is in the denominator (such as z^2), it will have a negative coefficient in the expanded form.

EXAMPLE 2 Using laws of logarithms

Express as one logarithm:

$$\tfrac{1}{3} \log_a (x^2 - 1) - \log_a y - 4 \log_a z$$

SOLUTION   We apply the laws of logarithms as follows:

$$\tfrac{1}{3} \log_a (x^2 - 1) - \log_a y - 4 \log_a z$$

$$= \log_a (x^2 - 1)^{1/3} - \log_a y - \log_a z^4 \qquad \text{law 3}$$

$$= \log_a \sqrt[3]{x^2 - 1} - (\log_a y + \log_a z^4) \qquad \text{algebra}$$

$$= \log_a \sqrt[3]{x^2 - 1} - \log_a (yz^4) \qquad \text{law 1}$$

$$= \log_a \frac{\sqrt[3]{x^2 - 1}}{yz^4} \qquad \text{law 2}$$

EXAMPLE 3 Solving a logarithmic equation

Solve the equation $\log_5 (2x + 3) = \log_5 11 + \log_5 3$.

SOLUTION

$$\log_5 (2x + 3) = \log_5 11 + \log_5 3 \qquad \text{given}$$

$$\log_5 (2x + 3) = \log_5 (11 \cdot 3) \qquad \text{law 1 of logarithms}$$

$$2x + 3 = 33 \qquad \text{logarithmic functions are one-to-one}$$

$$x = 15 \qquad \text{solve for } x$$

Check $x = 15$ LS: $\log_5 (2 \cdot 15 + 3) = \log_5 33$

RS: $\log_5 11 + \log_5 3 = \log_5 (11 \cdot 3) = \log_5 33$

Since $\log_5 33 = \log_5 33$ is a true statement, $x = 15$ is a solution.

The laws of logarithms were proved for logarithms of *positive* real numbers u and w. If we apply these laws to equations in which u and w are expressions involving a variable, then extraneous solutions may occur. Answers should therefore be substituted for the variable in u and w to determine whether these expressions are defined.

EXAMPLE 4   Solving a logarithmic equation

Solve the equation $\log_2 x + \log_2 (x + 2) = 3$.

SOLUTION

$$
\begin{array}{ll}
\log_2 x + \log_2 (x + 2) = 3 & \text{given} \\
\log_2 [x(x + 2)] = 3 & \text{law 1 of logarithms} \\
x(x + 2) = 2^3 & \text{change to exponential form} \\
x^2 + 2x - 8 = 0 & \text{multiply and set equal to 0} \\
(x - 2)(x + 4) = 0 & \text{factor} \\
x - 2 = 0, \quad x + 4 = 0 & \text{zero factor theorem} \\
x = 2, \qquad x = -4 & \text{solve for } x
\end{array}
$$

✔ Check $x = 2$ LS: $\log_2 2 + \log_2 (2 + 2) = 1 + \log_2 4$
$$= 1 + \log_2 2^2 = 1 + 2 = 3$$

RS: 3

Since $3 = 3$ is a true statement, $x = 2$ is a solution.

✔ Check $x = -4$ LS: $\log_2 (-4) + \log_2 (-4 + 2)$

Since logarithms of negative numbers are undefined, $x = -4$ is not a solution.

EXAMPLE 5   Solving a logarithmic equation

Solve the equation $\ln (x + 6) - \ln 10 = \ln (x - 1) - \ln 2$.

SOLUTION

$$
\begin{array}{ll}
\ln (x + 6) - \ln (x - 1) = \ln 10 - \ln 2 & \text{rearrange terms} \\[2mm]
\ln \left(\dfrac{x + 6}{x - 1} \right) = \ln \dfrac{10}{2} & \text{law 2 of logarithms} \\[3mm]
\dfrac{x + 6}{x - 1} = 5 & \text{ln is one-to-one} \\[3mm]
x + 6 = 5x - 5 & \text{multiply by } x - 1 \\[2mm]
x = \tfrac{11}{4} & \text{solve for } x
\end{array}
$$

✔ Check   Since both $\ln (x + 6)$ and $\ln (x - 1)$ are defined at $x = \frac{11}{4}$ (they are logarithms of positive real numbers) and since our algebraic steps are correct, it follows that $\frac{11}{4}$ is a solution of the given equation.

EXAMPLE 6 Shifting the graph of a logarithmic equation

Sketch the graph of $y = \log_3 (81x)$.

SOLUTION   We may rewrite the equation as follows:

$$
\begin{aligned}
y &= \log_3 (81x) && \text{given} \\
&= \log_3 81 + \log_3 x && \text{law 1 of logarithms} \\
&= \log_3 3^4 + \log_3 x && 81 = 3^4 \\
&= 4 + \log_3 x && \log_a a^x = x
\end{aligned}
$$

Thus, we can obtain the graph of $y = \log_3 (81x)$ by vertically shifting the graph of $y = \log_3 x$ in Figure 2 in Section 5.4 upward four units. This gives us the sketch in Figure 1.

Figure 1

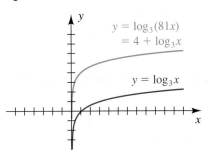

$y = \log_3(81x)$
$= 4 + \log_3 x$

$y = \log_3 x$

EXAMPLE 7 Sketching graphs of logarithmic equations

Sketch the graph of the equation:

(a) $y = \log_3 (x^2)$ **(b)** $y = 2 \log_3 x$

SOLUTION

(a) Since $x^2 = |x|^2$, we may rewrite the given equation as

$$y = \log_3 |x|^2.$$

Using law 3 of logarithms, we have

$$y = 2 \log_3 |x|.$$

We can obtain the graph of $y = 2 \log_3 |x|$ by multiplying the y-coordinates of points on the graph of $y = \log_3 |x|$ in Figure 4 of Section 5.4 by 2. This gives us the graph in Figure 2(a).

Figure 2
(a)   **(b)**

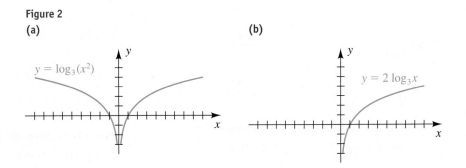

$y = \log_3(x^2)$

$y = 2 \log_3 x$

(b) If $y = 2 \log_3 x$, then x must be positive. Hence, the graph is identical to that part of the graph of $y = 2 \log_3 |x|$ in Figure 2(a) that lies to the right of the y-axis. This gives us Figure 2(b).

EXAMPLE 8 A relationship between selling price and demand

In the study of economics, the demand D for a product is often related to its selling price p by an equation of the form

$$\log_a D = \log_a c - k \log_a p,$$

where a, c, and k are positive constants.

(a) Solve the equation for D.

(b) How does increasing or decreasing the selling price affect the demand?

SOLUTION

(a) $\log_a D = \log_a c - k \log_a p$ given

$\log_a D = \log_a c - \log_a p^k$ law 3 of logarithms

$\log_a D = \log_a \dfrac{c}{p^k}$ law 2 of logarithms

$D = \dfrac{c}{p^k}$ $\log_a$ is one-to-one

(b) If the price p is increased, the denominator p^k in $D = c/p^k$ will also increase and hence the demand D for the product will decrease. If the price is decreased, then p^k will decrease and the demand D will increase.

5.5 Exercises

Exer. 1–8: Express in terms of logarithms of x, y, z, or w.

1 (a) $\log_4 (xz)$ (b) $\log_4 (y/x)$ (c) $\log_4 \sqrt[3]{z}$

2 (a) $\log_3 (xyz)$ (b) $\log_3 (xz/y)$ (c) $\log_3 \sqrt[5]{y}$

3 $\log_a \dfrac{x^3 w}{y^2 z^4}$

4 $\log_a \dfrac{y^5 w^2}{x^4 z^3}$

5 $\log \dfrac{\sqrt[3]{z}}{x\sqrt{y}}$

6 $\log \dfrac{\sqrt{y}}{x^4 \sqrt[3]{z}}$

7 $\ln \sqrt[4]{\dfrac{x^7}{y^5 z}}$

8 $\ln x \sqrt[3]{\dfrac{y^4}{z^5}}$

Exer. 9–16: Write the expression as one logarithm.

9 (a) $\log_3 x + \log_3 (5y)$ (b) $\log_3 (2z) - \log_3 x$

(c) $5 \log_3 y$

10 (a) $\log_4 (3z) + \log_4 x$ (b) $\log_4 x - \log_4 (7y)$

(c) $\frac{1}{3} \log_4 w$

11 $2 \log_a x + \frac{1}{3} \log_a (x - 2) - 5 \log_a (2x + 3)$

12 $5 \log_a x - \frac{1}{2} \log_a (3x - 4) - 3 \log_a (5x + 1)$

13 $\log (x^3 y^2) - 2 \log x \sqrt[3]{y} - 3 \log \left(\dfrac{x}{y}\right)$

14 $2 \log \dfrac{y^3}{x} - 3 \log y + \dfrac{1}{2} \log x^4 y^2$

15 $\ln y^3 + \frac{1}{3} \ln (x^3 y^6) - 5 \ln y$

16 $2 \ln x - 4 \ln (1/y) - 3 \ln (xy)$

Exer. 17–34: Solve the equation.

17 $\log_6 (2x - 3) = \log_6 12 - \log_6 3$

18 $\log_4 (3x + 2) = \log_4 5 + \log_4 3$

19 $2 \log_3 x = 3 \log_3 5$

20 $3 \log_2 x = 2 \log_2 3$

21 $\log x - \log (x + 1) = 3 \log 4$

22 $\log (x + 2) - \log x = 2 \log 4$

23 $\ln (-4 - x) + \ln 3 = \ln (2 - x)$

24 $\ln x + \ln (x + 6) = \frac{1}{2} \ln 9$

25 $\log_2 (x + 7) + \log_2 x = 3$

26 $\log_6 (x + 5) + \log_6 x = 2$

27 $\log_3 (x + 3) + \log_3 (x + 5) = 1$

28 $\log_3 (x - 2) + \log_3 (x - 4) = 2$

29 $\log (x + 3) = 1 - \log (x - 2)$

30 $\log (57x) = 2 + \log (x - 2)$

31 $\ln x = 1 - \ln (x + 2)$

32 $\ln x = 1 + \ln (x + 1)$

33 $\log_3 (x - 2) = \log_3 27 - \log_3 (x - 4) - 5^{\log_5 1}$

34 $\log_2 (x + 3) = \log_2 (x - 3) + \log_3 9 + 4^{\log_4 3}$

Exer. 35–46: Sketch the graph of f.

35 $f(x) = \log_3 (3x)$

36 $f(x) = \log_4 (16x)$

37 $f(x) = 3 \log_3 x$

38 $f(x) = \frac{1}{3} \log_3 x$

39 $f(x) = \log_3 (x^2)$

40 $f(x) = \log_2 (x^2)$

41 $f(x) = \log_2 (x^3)$

42 $f(x) = \log_3 (x^3)$

43 $f(x) = \log_2 \sqrt{x}$

44 $f(x) = \log_2 \sqrt[3]{x}$

45 $f(x) = \log_3 \left(\dfrac{1}{x} \right)$

46 $f(x) = \log_2 \left(\dfrac{1}{x} \right)$

Exer. 47–50: Shown in the figure is the graph of a function f. Express f(x) as one logarithm with base 2.

47

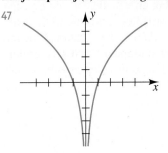

48

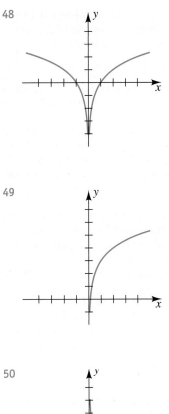

49

50

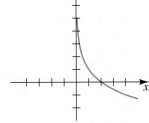

51 **Volume and decibels** When the volume control on a stereo system is increased, the voltage across a loudspeaker changes from V_1 to V_2, and the decibel increase in gain is given by

$$\text{db} = 20 \log \frac{V_2}{V_1}.$$

Find the decibel increase if the voltage changes from 2 volts to 4.5 volts.

52 **Volume and decibels** Refer to Exercise 51. What voltage ratio k is needed for a +20 decibel gain? for a +40 decibel gain?

53 Pareto's law Pareto's law for capitalist countries states that the relationship between annual income x and the number y of individuals whose income exceeds x is

$$\log y = \log b - k \log x,$$

where b and k are positive constants. Solve this equation for y.

54 Price and demand If p denotes the selling price (in dollars) of a commodity and x is the corresponding demand (in number sold per day), then the relationship between p and x is sometimes given by $p = p_0 e^{-ax}$, where p_0 and a are positive constants. Express x as a function of p.

55 Wind velocity If v denotes the wind velocity (in m/sec) at a height of z meters above the ground, then under certain conditions $v = c \ln(z/z_0)$, where c is a positive constant and z_0 is the height at which the velocity is zero. Sketch the graph of this equation on a zv-plane for $c = 0.5$ and $z_0 = 0.1$ m.

56 Eliminating pollution If the pollution of Lake Erie were stopped suddenly, it has been estimated that the level y of pollutants would decrease according to the formula $y = y_0 e^{-0.3821t}$, where t is the time in years and y_0 is the pollutant level at which further pollution ceased. How many years would it take to clear 50% of the pollutants?

57 Reaction to a stimulus Let R denote the reaction of a subject to a stimulus of strength x. There are many possibilities for R and x. If the stimulus x is saltiness (in grams of salt per liter), R may be the subject's estimate of how salty the solution tasted, based on a scale from 0 to 10. One relationship between R and x is given by the Weber-Fechner formula, $R(x) = a \log(x/x_0)$, where a is a positive constant and x_0 is called the threshold stimulus.

(a) Find $R(x_0)$.

(b) Find a relationship between $R(x)$ and $R(2x)$.

58 Electron energy The energy $E(x)$ of an electron after passing through material of thickness x is given by the equation $E(x) = E_0 e^{-x/x_0}$, where E_0 is the initial energy and x_0 is the radiation length.

(a) Express, in terms of E_0, the energy of an electron after it passes through material of thickness x_0.

(b) Express, in terms of x_0, the thickness at which the electron loses 99% of its initial energy.

59 Ozone layer One method of estimating the thickness of the ozone layer is to use the formula

$$\ln I_0 - \ln I = kx,$$

where I_0 is the intensity of a particular wavelength of light from the sun before it reaches the atmosphere, I is the intensity of the same wavelength after passing through a layer of ozone x centimeters thick, and k is the absorption constant of ozone for that wavelength. Suppose for a wavelength of 3176×10^{-8} cm with $k \approx 0.39$, I_0/I is measured as 1.12. Approximate the thickness of the ozone layer to the nearest 0.01 centimeter.

60 Ozone layer Refer to Exercise 59. Approximate the percentage decrease in the intensity of light with a wavelength of 3176×10^{-8} centimeter if the ozone layer is 0.24 centimeter thick.

5.6

Exponential and Logarithmic Equations

In this section we shall consider various types of exponential and logarithmic equations and their applications. When solving an equation involving exponential expressions with constant bases and variables appearing in the exponent(s), we often *equate the logarithms of both sides* of the equation. When we do so, the variables in the exponent become multipliers, and the resulting equation is usually easier to solve. We will refer to this step as simply "take log of both sides."

EXAMPLE 1   Solving an exponential equation

Solve the equation $3^x = 21$.

SOLUTION

$$3^x = 21 \qquad \text{given}$$

$$\log(3^x) = \log 21 \qquad \text{take log of both sides}$$

$$x \log 3 = \log 21 \qquad \text{law 3 of logarithms}$$

$$x = \frac{\log 21}{\log 3} \qquad \text{divide by log 3}$$

We could also have used natural logarithms to obtain

$$x = \frac{\ln 21}{\ln 3}.$$

Using a calculator gives us the approximate solution $x \approx 2.77$. A partial check is to note that since $3^2 = 9$ and $3^3 = 27$, the number x such that $3^x = 21$ must be between 2 and 3, somewhat closer to 3 than to 2. ◢

We could also have solved the equation in Example 1 by changing the exponential form $3^x = 21$ to logarithmic form, as we did in Section 5.4, obtaining

$$x = \log_3 21.$$

This is, in fact, the solution of the equation; however, since calculators typically have keys only for log and ln, we cannot approximate $\log_3 21$ directly. The next theorem gives us a simple *change of base formula* for finding $\log_b u$ if $u > 0$ and b is *any* logarithmic base.

Theorem: Change of Base Formula	If $u > 0$ and if a and b are positive real numbers different from 1, then $$\log_b u = \frac{\log_a u}{\log_a b}.$$

PROOF   We begin with the equivalent equations

$$w = \log_b u \qquad \text{and} \qquad b^w = u$$

and proceed as follows:

$$b^w = u \qquad \text{given}$$

$$\log_a b^w = \log_a u \qquad \text{take } \log_a \text{ of both sides}$$

$$w \log_a b = \log_a u \qquad \text{law 3 of logarithms}$$

$$w = \frac{\log_a u}{\log_a b} \qquad \text{divide by } \log_a b$$

Since $w = \log_b u$, we obtain the formula. ◢

The following special case of the change of base formula is obtained by letting $u = a$ and using the fact that $\log_a a = 1$:

$$\log_b a = \frac{1}{\log_a b}$$

The change of base formula is sometimes confused with law 2 of logarithms. The first of the following warnings could be remembered with the phrase "a quotient of logs is *not* the log of the quotient."

◥ **Warning!** ◥

$$\frac{\log_a u}{\log_a b} \neq \log_a \frac{u}{b}; \qquad \frac{\log_a u}{\log_a b} \neq \log_a (u - b)$$

The most frequently used special cases of the change of base formula are those for $a = 10$ (common logarithms) and $a = e$ (natural logarithms), as stated in the next box.

Special Change of Base Formulas	$\textbf{(1)} \quad \log_b u = \dfrac{\log_{10} u}{\log_{10} b} = \dfrac{\log u}{\log b}$ $\qquad$ $\textbf{(2)} \quad \log_b u = \dfrac{\log_e u}{\log_e b} = \dfrac{\ln u}{\ln b}$

Next, we will rework Example 1 using a change of base formula.

EXAMPLE 2 Using a change of base formula

Solve the equation $3^x = 21$.

SOLUTION We proceed as follows:

$$3^x = 21 \qquad \text{given}$$
$$x = \log_3 21 \qquad \text{change to logarithmic form}$$
$$= \frac{\log 21}{\log 3} \qquad \text{special change of base formula 1}$$

Another method is to use special change of base formula 2, obtaining

$$x = \frac{\ln 21}{\ln 3}.$$

◪

Logarithms with base 2 are used in computer science. The next example indicates how to approximate logarithms with base 2 using change of base formulas.

EXAMPLE 3 Approximating a logarithm with base 2

Approximate $\log_2 5$ using

(a) common logarithms   **(b)** natural logarithms

SOLUTION   Using special change of base formulas 1 and 2, we obtain the following:

(a) $\log_2 5 = \dfrac{\log 5}{\log 2} \approx 2.322$

(b) $\log_2 5 = \dfrac{\ln 5}{\ln 2} \approx 2.322$

EXAMPLE 4   Solving an exponential equation

Solve the equation $5^{2x+1} = 6^{x-2}$.

SOLUTION   We can use either common or natural logarithms. Using common logarithms gives us the following:

$$5^{2x+1} = 6^{x-2} \qquad \text{given}$$

$$\log(5^{2x+1}) = \log(6^{x-2}) \qquad \text{take log of both sides}$$

$$(2x + 1)\log 5 = (x - 2)\log 6 \qquad \text{law 3 of logarithms}$$

$$2x \log 5 + \log 5 = x \log 6 - 2 \log 6 \qquad \text{multiply}$$

$$2x \log 5 - x \log 6 = -\log 5 - 2 \log 6 \qquad \text{get all terms with } x \text{ on one side}$$

$$x(\log 5^2 - \log 6) = -(\log 5 + \log 6^2) \qquad \text{factor, and use law 3 of logarithms}$$

$$x = -\frac{\log(5 \cdot 36)}{\log \frac{25}{6}} \qquad \begin{array}{l}\text{solve for } x\text{, and use laws of}\\ \text{logarithms}\end{array}$$

Substituting $-\log 180/\log \frac{25}{6} \approx -3.64$ for x in both 5^{2x+1} and 6^{x-2} gives us the approximate value 0.00004. We deduce from this that the graphs of $y = 5^{2x+1}$ and $y = 6^{x-2}$ intersect at approximately $(-3.64, 0.00004)$.

EXAMPLE 5   Solving an exponential equation

Solve the equation $\dfrac{5^x - 5^{-x}}{2} = 3$.

SOLUTION

$$\frac{5^x - 5^{-x}}{2} = 3 \qquad \text{given}$$

$$5^x - 5^{-x} = 6 \qquad \text{multiply by 2}$$

$$5^x - \frac{1}{5^x} = 6 \qquad \text{definition of negative exponent}$$

$$5^x(5^x) - \frac{1}{5^x}(5^x) = 6(5^x) \qquad \text{multiply by the lcd, } 5^x$$

$$(5^x)^2 - 6(5^x) - 1 = 0 \qquad \text{simplify and subtract } 6(5^x)$$

(continued)

Note that $(5^x)^2$ can be written as 5^{2x}.

We recognize this form of the equation as a quadratic in 5^x and proceed as follows:

$$(5^x)^2 - 6(5^x) - 1 = 0 \qquad \text{law of exponents}$$

$$5^x = \frac{6 \pm \sqrt{36 + 4}}{2} \qquad \text{quadratic formula}$$

$$5^x = 3 \pm \sqrt{10} \qquad \text{simplify}$$

$$5^x = 3 + \sqrt{10} \qquad 5^x > 0, \text{ but } 3 - \sqrt{10} < 0$$

$$\log 5^x = \log\left(3 + \sqrt{10}\right) \qquad \text{take log of both sides}$$

$$x \log 5 = \log\left(3 + \sqrt{10}\right) \qquad \text{law 3 of logarithms}$$

$$x = \frac{\log\left(3 + \sqrt{10}\right)}{\log 5} \qquad \text{divide by } \log 5$$

An approximation is $x \approx 1.13$.

EXAMPLE 6 Solving an equation involving logarithms

Solve the equation $\log \sqrt[3]{x} = \sqrt{\log x}$ for x.

SOLUTION

$$\log x^{1/3} = \sqrt{\log x} \qquad \sqrt[n]{x} = x^{1/n}$$

$$\tfrac{1}{3} \log x = \sqrt{\log x} \qquad \log x^r = r \log x$$

$$\tfrac{1}{9}(\log x)^2 = \log x \qquad \text{square both sides}$$

$$(\log x)^2 = 9 \log x \qquad \text{multiply by 9}$$

$$(\log x)^2 - 9 \log x = 0 \qquad \text{make one side 0}$$

$$(\log x)(\log x - 9) = 0 \qquad \text{factor out } \log x$$

$$\log x = 0, \quad \log x - 9 = 0 \qquad \text{set each factor equal to 0}$$

$$\log x = 9 \qquad \text{add 9}$$

$$x = 10^0 = 1 \quad \text{or} \quad x = 10^9 \qquad \log_{10} x = a \Longleftrightarrow x = 10^a$$

✔ Check $x = 1$ LS: $\log \sqrt[3]{1} = \log 1 = 0$
RS: $\sqrt{\log 1} = \sqrt{0} = 0$

✔ Check $x = 10^9$ LS: $\log \sqrt[3]{10^9} = \log 10^3 = 3$
RS: $\sqrt{\log 10^9} = \sqrt{9} = 3$

The equation has two solutions, 1 and 1 billion.

The function $y = 2/(e^x + e^{-x})$ is called the **hyperbolic secant function.** In the next example we solve this equation for x in terms of y. Under suitable restrictions, this gives us the inverse function.

EXAMPLE 7 Finding an inverse hyperbolic function

Solve $y = 2/(e^x + e^{-x})$ for x in terms of y.

SOLUTION
$$y = \frac{2}{e^x + e^{-x}} \qquad \text{given}$$

$$ye^x + ye^{-x} = 2 \qquad \text{multiply by } e^x + e^{-x}$$

$$ye^x + \frac{y}{e^x} = 2 \qquad \text{definition of negative exponent}$$

$$ye^x(e^x) + \frac{y}{e^x}(e^x) = 2(e^x) \qquad \text{multiply by the lcd, } e^x$$

$$y(e^x)^2 - 2e^x + y = 0 \qquad \text{simplify and subtract } 2e^x$$

We recognize this form of the equation as a quadratic in e^x with coefficients $a = y$, $b = -2$, and $c = y$. Note that we are solving for e^x, not x.

$$e^x = \frac{-(-2) \pm \sqrt{(-2)^2 - 4(y)(y)}}{2(y)} \qquad \text{quadratic formula}$$

$$= \frac{2 \pm \sqrt{4 - 4y^2}}{2y} \qquad \text{simplify}$$

$$= \frac{2 \pm \sqrt{4}\sqrt{1 - y^2}}{2y} \qquad \text{factor out } \sqrt{4}$$

$$e^x = \frac{1 \pm \sqrt{1 - y^2}}{y} \qquad \text{cancel a factor of 2}$$

$$x = \ln \frac{1 \pm \sqrt{1 - y^2}}{y} \qquad \text{take ln of both sides}$$

For the blue curve $y = f(x)$ in Figure 1, the inverse function is

$$y = f^{-1}(x) = \ln \frac{1 + \sqrt{1 - x^2}}{x},$$

shown in blue in Figure 2. Notice the domain and range relationships. For the red curve $y = g(x)$ in Figure 1, the inverse function is

$$y = g^{-1}(x) = \ln \frac{1 - \sqrt{1 - x^2}}{x},$$

shown in red in Figure 2. Since the hyperbolic secant is not one-to-one, it cannot have one simple equation for its inverse.

Figure 1

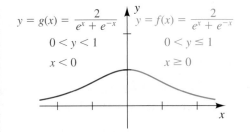

$$y = g(x) = \frac{2}{e^x + e^{-x}} \qquad y = f(x) = \frac{2}{e^x + e^{-x}}$$
$$0 < y < 1 \qquad\qquad 0 < y \leq 1$$
$$x < 0 \qquad\qquad\qquad x \geq 0$$

Figure 2

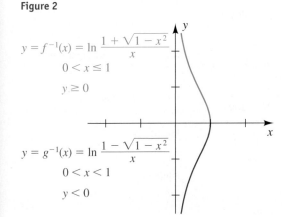

$$y = f^{-1}(x) = \ln \frac{1 + \sqrt{1 - x^2}}{x}$$
$$0 < x \leq 1$$
$$y \geq 0$$

$$y = g^{-1}(x) = \ln \frac{1 - \sqrt{1 - x^2}}{x}$$
$$0 < x < 1$$
$$y < 0$$

The inverse hyperbolic secant is part of the equation of the curve called a **tractrix.** The curve is associated with Gottfried Wilhelm von Leibniz's (1646–1716) solution to the question "What is the path of an object dragged along a horizontal plane by a string of constant length when the end of the string not joined to the object moves along a straight line in the plane?"

EXAMPLE 8 Approximating light penetration in an ocean

The Beer-Lambert law states that the amount of light I that penetrates to a depth of x meters in an ocean is given by $I = I_0 c^x$, where $0 < c < 1$ and I_0 is the amount of light at the surface.

(a) Solve for x in terms of common logarithms.

(b) If $c = \frac{1}{4}$, approximate the depth at which $I = 0.01I_0$. (This determines the photic zone where photosynthesis can take place.)

SOLUTION

(a) $I = I_0 c^x$ given

$\dfrac{I}{I_0} = c^x$ isolate the exponential expression

$x = \log_c \dfrac{I}{I_0}$ change to logarithmic form

$= \dfrac{\log (I/I_0)}{\log c}$ special change of base formula 1

(b) Letting $I = 0.01I_0$ and $c = \frac{1}{4}$ in the formula for x obtained in part (a), we have

$$x = \dfrac{\log (0.01I_0/I_0)}{\log \frac{1}{4}} \qquad \text{substitute for } I \text{ and } c$$

$$= \dfrac{\log (0.01)}{\log 1 - \log 4} \qquad \text{cancel } I_0; \text{ law 2 of logarithms}$$

$$= \dfrac{\log 10^{-2}}{0 - \log 4} \qquad \text{property of logarithms}$$

$$= \dfrac{-2}{-\log 4} \qquad \log 10^x = x$$

$$= \dfrac{2}{\log 4}. \qquad \text{simplify}$$

An approximation is $x \approx 3.32$ m.

EXAMPLE 9 Comparing light intensities

If a beam of light that has intensity I_0 is projected vertically downward into water, then its intensity $I(x)$ at a depth of x meters is $I(x) = I_0 e^{-1.4x}$ (see Figure 3). At what depth is the intensity one-half its value at the surface?

SOLUTION   At the surface, $x = 0$, and the intensity is

$$I(0) = I_0 e^0$$
$$= I_0.$$

Figure 3

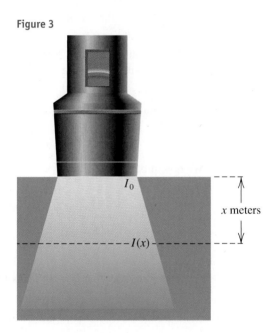

I_0

x meters

$I(x)$

We wish to find the value of x such that $I(x) = \frac{1}{2}I_0$. This leads to the following:

$$I(x) = \tfrac{1}{2}I_0 \qquad \text{desired intensity}$$
$$I_0 e^{-1.4x} = \tfrac{1}{2}I_0 \qquad \text{formula for } I(x)$$
$$e^{-1.4x} = \tfrac{1}{2} \qquad \text{divide by } I_0 \,(I_0 \neq 0)$$
$$-1.4x = \ln \tfrac{1}{2} \qquad \text{change to logarithmic form}$$
$$x = \frac{\ln \frac{1}{2}}{-1.4} \qquad \text{divide by } -1.4$$

An approximation is $x \approx 0.495$ m.

EXAMPLE 10   A logistic curve

A **logistic curve** is the graph of an equation of the form

$$y = \frac{k}{1 + be^{-cx}},$$

where k, b, and c are positive constants. Such curves are useful for describing a population y that grows rapidly initially, but whose growth rate decreases after x reaches a certain value. In a famous study of the growth of protozoa by Gause, a population of *Paramecium caudata* was found to be described by a logistic equation with $c = 1.1244$, $k = 105$, and x the time in days.

(a) Find b if the initial population was 3 protozoa.

(b) In the study, the maximum growth rate took place at $y = 52$. At what time x did this occur?

(c) Show that after a long period of time, the population described by any logistic curve approaches the constant k.

SOLUTION

(a) Letting $c = 1.1244$ and $k = 105$ in the logistic equation, we obtain

$$y = \frac{105}{1 + be^{-1.1244x}}.$$

We now proceed as follows:

$$3 = \frac{105}{1 + be^{0}} = \frac{105}{1 + b} \qquad y = 3 \text{ when } x = 0$$

$$1 + b = 35 \qquad \text{multiply by } \frac{1 + b}{3}$$

$$b = 34 \qquad \text{solve for } b$$

(b) Using the fact that $b = 34$ leads to the following:

$$52 = \frac{105}{1 + 34e^{-1.1244x}} \qquad \text{let } y = 52 \text{ in part (a)}$$

$$1 + 34e^{-1.1244x} = \frac{105}{52} \qquad \text{multiply by } \frac{1 + 34e^{-1.1244x}}{52}$$

$$e^{-1.1244x} = \left(\tfrac{105}{52} - 1\right) \cdot \tfrac{1}{34} = \tfrac{53}{1768} \qquad \text{isolate } e^{-1.1244x}$$

$$-1.1244x = \ln \tfrac{53}{1768} \qquad \text{change to logarithmic form}$$

$$x = \frac{\ln \tfrac{53}{1768}}{-1.1244} \approx 3.12 \text{ days} \qquad \text{divide by } -1.1244$$

(c) As $x \to \infty$, $e^{-cx} \to 0$. Hence,

$$y = \frac{k}{1 + be^{-cx}} \to \frac{k}{1 + b \cdot 0} = k.$$

A sketch of the logistic curve that has equation $y = 105/(1 + 34e^{-1.1244x})$ is shown in Figure 4. ◢

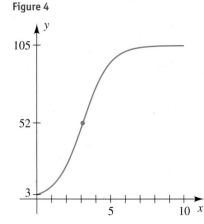

Figure 4

5.6 Exercises

Exer. 1–4: Find the exact solution and a two-decimal-place approximation for it by using (a) the method of Example 1 and (b) the method of Example 2.

1 $5^x = 8$

2 $4^x = 3$

3 $3^{4-x} = 5$

4 $\left(\frac{1}{3}\right)^x = 100$

Exer. 5–8: Estimate using the change of base formula.

5 $\log_5 6$

6 $\log_2 20$

7 $\log_9 0.2$

8 $\log_6 \frac{1}{2}$

Exer. 9–10: Evaluate using the change of base formula (without a calculator).

9 $\dfrac{\log_5 16}{\log_5 4}$

10 $\dfrac{\log_7 243}{\log_7 3}$

Exer. 11–24: Find the exact solution, using common logarithms, and a two-decimal-place approximation of each solution, when appropriate.

11 $3^{x+4} = 2^{1-3x}$

12 $4^{2x+3} = 5^{x-2}$

13 $2^{2x-3} = 5^{x-2}$

14 $3^{2-3x} = 4^{2x+1}$

15 $2^{-x} = 8$

16 $2^{-x^2} = 5$

17 $\log x = 1 - \log (x - 3)$

18 $\log (5x + 1) = 2 + \log (2x - 3)$

19 $\log (x^2 + 4) - \log (x + 2) = 2 + \log (x - 2)$

20 $\log (x - 4) - \log (3x - 10) = \log (1/x)$

21 $5^x + 125(5^{-x}) = 30$

22 $3(3^x) + 9(3^{-x}) = 28$

23 $4^x - 3(4^{-x}) = 8$

24 $2^x - 6(2^{-x}) = 6$

Exer. 25–32: Solve the equation without using a calculator.

25 $\log (x^2) = (\log x)^2$

26 $\log \sqrt{x} = \sqrt{\log x}$

27 $\log (\log x) = 2$

28 $\log \sqrt{x^3 - 9} = 2$

29 $x^{\sqrt{\log x}} = 10^8$

30 $\log (x^3) = (\log x)^3$

31 $e^{2x} + 2e^x - 15 = 0$

32 $e^x + 4e^{-x} = 5$

Exer. 33–34: Solve the equation.

33 $\log_3 x - \log_9 (x + 42) = 0$

34 $\log_4 x + \log_8 x = 1$

Exer. 35–38: Use common logarithms to solve for x in terms of y.

35 $y = \dfrac{10^x + 10^{-x}}{2}$

36 $y = \dfrac{10^x - 10^{-x}}{2}$

37 $y = \dfrac{10^x - 10^{-x}}{10^x + 10^{-x}}$

38 $y = \dfrac{10^x + 10^{-x}}{10^x - 10^{-x}}$

Exer. 39–42: Use natural logarithms to solve for x in terms of y.

39 $y = \dfrac{e^x - e^{-x}}{2}$

40 $y = \dfrac{e^x + e^{-x}}{2}$

41 $y = \dfrac{e^x + e^{-x}}{e^x - e^{-x}}$

42 $y = \dfrac{e^x - e^{-x}}{e^x + e^{-x}}$

Exer. 43–44: Sketch the graph of f, and use the change of base formula to approximate the y-intercept.

43 $f(x) = \log_2 (x + 3)$

44 $f(x) = \log_3 (x + 5)$

Exer. 45–46: Sketch the graph of f, and use the change of base formula to approximate the x-intercept.

45 $f(x) = 4^x - 3$

46 $f(x) = 3^x - 6$

Exer. 47–50: Chemists use a number denoted by pH to describe quantitatively the acidity or basicity of solutions. By definition, pH $= -\log [H^+]$, where $[H^+]$ is the hydrogen ion concentration in moles per liter.

47 Approximate the pH of each substance.

   (a) vinegar: $[H^+] \approx 6.3 \times 10^{-3}$

   (b) carrots: $[H^+] \approx 1.0 \times 10^{-5}$

   (c) sea water: $[H^+] \approx 5.0 \times 10^{-9}$

48 Approximate the hydrogen ion concentration $[H^+]$ of each substance.

   (a) apples: pH ≈ 3.0

   (b) beer: pH ≈ 4.2

   (c) milk: pH ≈ 6.6

49 A solution is considered basic if $[H^+] < 10^{-7}$ or acidic if $[H^+] > 10^{-7}$. Find the corresponding inequalities involving pH.

50 Many solutions have a pH between 1 and 14. Find the corresponding range of $[H^+]$.

51 Compound interest Use the compound interest formula to determine how long it will take for a sum of money to double if it is invested at a rate of 6% per year compounded monthly.

52 Compound interest Solve the compound interest formula

$$A = P\left(1 + \frac{r}{n}\right)^{nt}$$

for t by using natural logarithms.

53 Photic zone Refer to Example 8. The most important zone in the sea from the viewpoint of marine biology is the photic zone, in which photosynthesis takes place. The photic zone ends at the depth where about 1% of the surface light penetrates. In very clear waters in the Caribbean, 50% of the light at the surface reaches a depth of about 13 meters. Estimate the depth of the photic zone.

54 Photic zone In contrast to the situation described in the previous exercise, in parts of New York harbor, 50% of the surface light does not reach a depth of 10 centimeters. Estimate the depth of the photic zone.

55 Drug absorption If a 100-milligram tablet of an asthma drug is taken orally and if none of the drug is present in the body when the tablet is first taken, the total amount A in the bloodstream after t minutes is predicted to be

$$A = 100[1 - (0.9)^t] \quad \text{for} \quad 0 \le t \le 10.$$

(a) Sketch the graph of the equation.

(b) Determine the number of minutes needed for 50 milligrams of the drug to have entered the bloodstream.

56 Drug dosage A drug is eliminated from the body through urine. Suppose that for a dose of 10 milligrams, the amount $A(t)$ remaining in the body t hours later is given by $A(t) = 10(0.8)^t$ and that in order for the drug to be effective, at least 2 milligrams must be in the body.

(a) Determine when 2 milligrams is left in the body.

(b) What is the half-life of the drug?

57 Genetic mutation The basic source of genetic diversity is mutation, or changes in the chemical structure of genes. If a gene mutates at a constant rate m and if other evolutionary forces are negligible, then the frequency F of the original gene after t generations is given by $F = F_0(1 - m)^t$, where F_0 is the frequency at $t = 0$.

(a) Solve the equation for t using common logarithms.

(b) If $m = 5 \times 10^{-5}$, after how many generations does $F = \frac{1}{2}F_0$?

58 Employee productivity Certain learning processes may be illustrated by the graph of an equation of the form $f(x) = a + b(1 - e^{-cx})$, where a, b, and c are positive constants. Suppose a manufacturer estimates that a new employee can produce five items the first day on the job. As the employee becomes more proficient, the daily production increases until a certain maximum production is reached. Suppose that on the nth day on the job, the number $f(n)$ of items produced is approximated by

$$f(n) = 3 + 20(1 - e^{-0.1n}).$$

(a) Estimate the number of items produced on the fifth day, the ninth day, the twenty-fourth day, and the thirtieth day.

(b) Sketch the graph of f from $n = 0$ to $n = 30$. (Graphs of this type are called *learning curves* and are used frequently in education and psychology.)

(c) What happens as n increases without bound?

59 Height of trees The growth in height of trees is frequently described by a logistic equation. Suppose the height h (in feet) of a tree at age t (in years) is

$$h = \frac{120}{1 + 200e^{-0.2t}},$$

as illustrated by the graph in the figure.

(a) What is the height of the tree at age 10?

(b) At what age is the height 50 feet?

Exercise 59

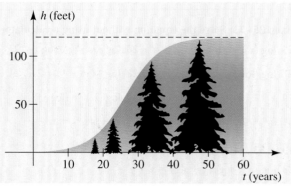

60 Employee productivity Manufacturers sometimes use empirically based formulas to predict the time required to produce the nth item on an assembly line for an integer n. If $T(n)$ denotes the time required to assemble the nth item and T_1 denotes the time required for the first, or prototype, item, then typically $T(n) = T_1 n^{-k}$ for some positive constant k.

(a) For many airplanes, the time required to assemble the second airplane, $T(2)$, is equal to $(0.80)T_1$. Find the value of k.

(b) Express, in terms of T_1, the time required to assemble the fourth airplane.

(c) Express, in terms of $T(n)$, the time $T(2n)$ required to assemble the $(2n)$th airplane.

61 Vertical wind shear Refer to Exercises 67–68 in Section 3.3. If v_0 is the wind speed at height h_0 and if v_1 is the wind speed at height h_1, then the vertical wind shear can be described by the equation

$$\frac{v_0}{v_1} = \left(\frac{h_0}{h_1}\right)^P,$$

where P is a constant. During a one-year period in Montreal, the maximum vertical wind shear occurred when the winds at the 200-foot level were 25 mi/hr while the winds at the 35-foot level were 6 mi/hr. Find P for these conditions.

62 Vertical wind shear Refer to Exercise 61. The average vertical wind shear is given by the equation

$$s = \frac{v_1 - v_0}{h_1 - h_0}.$$

Suppose that the velocity of the wind increases with increasing altitude and that all values for wind speeds taken at the 35-foot and 200-foot altitudes are greater than 1 mi/hr. Does increasing the value of P produce larger or smaller values of s?

Exer. 63–64: An economist suspects that the following data points lie on the graph of $y = c2^{kx}$, where c and k are constants. If the data points have three-decimal-place accuracy, is this suspicion correct?

63 (0, 4), (1, 3.249), (2, 2.639), (3, 2.144)

64 (0, −0.3), (0.5, −0.345), (1, −0.397), (1.5, −0.551), (2, −0.727)

Exer. 65–66: It is suspected that the following data points lie on the graph of $y = c \log (kx + 10)$, where c and k are constants. If the data points have three-decimal-place accuracy, is this suspicion correct?

65 (0, 1.5), (1, 1.619), (2, 1.720), (3, 1.997)

66 (0, 0.7), (1, 0.782), (2, 0.847), (3, 0.900), (4, 0.945)

Exer. 67–68: Approximate the function at the value of x to four decimal places.

67 $h(x) = \log_4 x - 2 \log_8 1.2x;$ $\qquad\qquad x = 5.3$

68 $h(x) = 3 \log_3 (2x - 1) + 7 \log_2 (x + 0.2);$ $\quad x = 52.6$

69 Human memory A group of elementary students were taught long division over a one-week period. Afterward, they were given a test. The average score was 85. Each week thereafter, they were given an equivalent test, without any review. Let $n(t)$ represent the average score after $t \geq 0$ weeks. Determine which function best models the situation.

(1) $n(t) = 85e^{t/3}$

(2) $n(t) = 70 + 10 \ln (t + 1)$

(3) $n(t) = 86 - e^t$

(4) $n(t) = 85 - 15 \ln (t + 1)$

70 Cooling A jar of boiling water at 212°F is set on a table in a room with a temperature of 72°F. If $T(t)$ represents the temperature of the water after t hours, determine which function best models the situation.

(1) $T(t) = 212 - 50t$

(2) $T(t) = 140e^{-t} + 72$

(3) $T(t) = 212e^{-t}$

(4) $T(t) = 72 + 10 \ln (140t + 1)$

CHAPTER 5 REVIEW EXERCISES

1 Is $f(x) = 2x^3 - 5$ a one-to-one function?

2 The graph of a function f with domain $[-3, 3]$ is shown in the figure. Sketch the graph of $y = f^{-1}(x)$.

Exercise 2

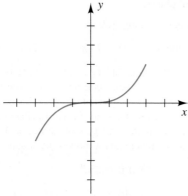

Exer. 3–4: (a) Find $f^{-1}(x)$. (b) Sketch the graphs of f and f^{-1} on the same coordinate plane.

3 $f(x) = 10 - 15x$ **4** $f(x) = 9 - 2x^2, x \le 0$

5 Refer to the figure to determine each of the following:

Exercise 5

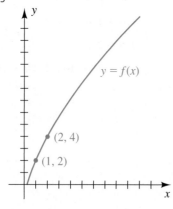

(a) $f(1)$ (b) $(f \circ f)(1)$ (c) $f^{-1}(4)$

(d) all x such that $f(x) = 4$

(e) all x such that $f(x) > 4$

6 Suppose f and g are one-to-one functions such that $f(2) = 7$, $f(4) = 2$, and $g(2) = 5$. Find the value, if possible.

(a) $(g \circ f^{-1})(7)$ (b) $(f \circ g^{-1})(5)$

(c) $(f^{-1} \circ g^{-1})(5)$ (d) $(g^{-1} \circ f^{-1})(2)$

Exer. 7–22: Sketch the graph of f.

7 $f(x) = 3^{x+2}$ **8** $f(x) = \left(\frac{3}{5}\right)^x$

9 $f(x) = \left(\frac{3}{2}\right)^{-x}$ **10** $f(x) = 3^{-2x}$

11 $f(x) = 3^{-x^2}$ **12** $f(x) = 1 - 3^{-x}$

13 $f(x) = e^{x/2}$ **14** $f(x) = \frac{1}{2}e^x$

15 $f(x) = e^{x-2}$ **16** $f(x) = e^{2-x}$

17 $f(x) = \log_6 x$ **18** $f(x) = \log_6 (36x)$

19 $f(x) = \log_4 (x^2)$ **20** $f(x) = \log_4 \sqrt[3]{x}$

21 $f(x) = \log_2 (x + 4)$ **22** $f(x) = \log_2 (4 - x)$

Exer. 23–24: Evaluate without using a calculator.

23 (a) $\log_2 \frac{1}{16}$ (b) $\log_\pi 1$ (c) $\ln e$

     (d) $6^{\log_6 4}$ (e) $\log 1{,}000{,}000$ (f) $10^{3 \log 2}$

     (g) $\log_4 2$

24 (a) $\log_5 \sqrt[3]{5}$ (b) $\log_5 1$ (c) $\log 10$

     (d) $e^{\ln 5}$ (e) $\log \log 10^{10}$ (f) $e^{2 \ln 5}$

     (g) $\log_{27} 3$

Exer. 25–44: Solve the equation without using a calculator.

25 $2^{3x-1} = \frac{1}{2}$ **26** $8^{2x} \cdot \left(\frac{1}{4}\right)^{x-2} = 4^{-x} \cdot \left(\frac{1}{2}\right)^{2-x}$

27 $\log \sqrt{x} = \log (x - 6)$ **28** $\log_8 (x - 5) = \frac{2}{3}$

29 $\log_4 (x + 1) = 2 + \log_4 (3x - 2)$

30 $2 \ln (x + 3) - \ln (x + 1) = 3 \ln 2$

31 $\ln (x + 2) = \ln e^{\ln 2} - \ln x$ **32** $\log \sqrt[4]{x + 1} = \frac{1}{2}$

33 $2^{5-x} = 6$ **34** $3^{(x^2)} = 7$

35 $2^{5x+3} = 3^{2x+1}$

36 $\log_3 (3x) = \log_3 x + \log_3 (4 - x)$

37 $\log_4 x = \sqrt[3]{\log_4 x}$ **38** $e^{x+\ln 4} = 3e^x$

39 $10^{2 \log x} = 5$ **40** $e^{\ln (x+1)} = 3$

41 $x^2(-2xe^{-x^2}) + 2xe^{-x^2} = 0$ 42 $e^x + 2 = 8e^{-x}$

43 (a) $\log x^2 = \log (6 - x)$ (b) $2 \log x = \log (6 - x)$

44 (a) $\ln (e^x)^2 = 16$ (b) $\ln e^{(x^2)} = 16$

45 Express $\log x^4 \sqrt[3]{y^2/z}$ in terms of logarithms of x, y, and z.

46 Express $\log (x^2/y^3) + 4 \log y - 6 \log \sqrt{xy}$ as   one logarithm.

47 Find an exponential function that has y-intercept 6 and passes through the point $(1, 8)$.

48 Sketch the graph of $f(x) = \log_3(x + 2)$.

Exer. 49–50: Use common logarithms to solve the equation for x in terms of y.

49 $y = \dfrac{1}{10^x + 10^{-x}}$ 50 $y = \dfrac{1}{10^x - 10^{-x}}$

Exer. 51–52: Approximate x to three significant figures.

51 (a) $x = \ln 6.6$ (b) $\log x = 1.8938$

(c) $\ln x = -0.75$

52 (a) $x = \log 8.4$ (b) $\log x = -2.4260$

(c) $\ln x = 1.8$

Exer. 53–54: (a) Find the domain and range of the function. (b) Find the inverse of the function and its domain and range.

53 $y = \log_2 (x + 1)$ 54 $y = 2^{3-x} - 2$

55 Bacteria growth The number of bacteria in a certain culture at time t (in hours) is given by $Q(t) = 2(3^t)$, where $Q(t)$ is measured in thousands.

(a) What is the number of bacteria at $t = 0$?

(b) Find the number of bacteria after 10 minutes, 30 minutes, and 1 hour.

56 Compound interest If \$1000 is invested at a rate of 8% per year compounded quarterly, what is the principal after one year?

57 Radioactive iodine decay Radioactive iodine ^{131}I, which is frequently used in tracer studies involving the thyroid gland, decays according to $N = N_0(0.5)^{t/8}$, where N_0 is the initial dose and t is the time in days.

(a) Sketch the graph of the equation if $N_0 = 64$.

(b) Find the half-life of ^{131}I.

58 Trout population A pond is stocked with 1000 trout. Three months later, it is estimated that 600 remain. Find a formula of the form $N = N_0 a^{ct}$ that can be used to estimate the number of trout remaining after t months.

59 Continuously compounded interest Ten thousand dollars is invested in a savings fund in which interest is compounded continuously at the rate of 7% per year.

(a) When will the account contain \$35,000?

(b) How long does it take for money to double in the account?

60 Ben Franklin's will In 1790, Ben Franklin left \$4000 with instructions that it go to the city of Philadelphia in 200 years. It was worth about \$2 million at that time. Approximate the annual interest rate for the growth.

61 Electrical current The current $I(t)$ in a certain electrical circuit at time t is given by $I(t) = I_0 e^{-Rt/L}$, where R is the resistance, L is the inductance, and I_0 is the initial current at $t = 0$. Find the value of t, in terms of L and R, for which $I(t)$ is 1% of I_0.

62 Sound intensity The sound intensity level formula is $\alpha = 10 \log (I/I_0)$.

(a) Solve for I in terms of α and I_0.

(b) Show that a one-decibel rise in the intensity level α corresponds to a 26% increase in the intensity I.

63 Fish growth The length L of a fish is related to its age by means of the von Bertalanffy growth formula

$$L = a(1 - be^{-kt}),$$

where a, b, and k are positive constants that depend on the type of fish. Solve this equation for t to obtain a formula that can be used to estimate the age of a fish from a length measurement.

64 Earthquake area in the West In the western United States, the area A (in mi^2) affected by an earthquake is related to the magnitude R of the quake by the formula

$$R = 2.3 \log (A + 3000) - 5.1.$$

Solve for A in terms of R.

65 Earthquake area in the East Refer to Exercise 64. For the eastern United States, the area-magnitude formula has the form

$$R = 2.3 \log (A + 34,000) - 7.5.$$

If A_1 is the area affected by an earthquake of magnitude R in the West and A_2 is the area affected by a similar quake in the East, find a formula for A_1/A_2 in terms of R.

66 Earthquake area in the Central states Refer to Exercise 64. For the Rocky Mountain and Central states, the area-magnitude formula has the form

$$R = 2.3 \log (A + 14{,}000) - 6.6.$$

If an earthquake has magnitude 4 on the Richter scale, estimate the area A of the region that will feel the quake.

67 Atmospheric pressure Under certain conditions, the atmospheric pressure p at altitude h is given by the formula $p = 29e^{-0.000034h}$. Express h as a function of p.

68 Rocket velocity A rocket of mass m_1 is filled with fuel of initial mass m_2. If frictional forces are disregarded, the total mass m of the rocket at time t after ignition is related to its upward velocity v by $v = -a \ln m + b$, where a and b are constants. At ignition time $t = 0$, $v = 0$ and $m = m_1 + m_2$. At burnout, $m = m_1$. Use this information to find a formula, in terms of one logarithm, for the velocity of the rocket at burnout.

69 Earthquake frequency Let n be the average number of earthquakes per year that have magnitudes between R and $R + 1$ on the Richter scale. A formula that approximates the relationship between n and R is

$$\log n = 7.7 - (0.9)R.$$

(a) Solve the equation for n in terms of R.

(b) Find n if $R = 4, 5,$ and 6.

70 Earthquake energy The energy E (in ergs) released during an earthquake of magnitude R may be approximated by using the formula

$$\log E = 11.4 + (1.5)R.$$

(a) Solve for E in terms of R.

(b) Find the energy released during the earthquake off the coast of Sumatra in 2004, which measured 9.0 on the Richter scale.

71 Radioactive decay A certain radioactive substance decays according to the formula $q(t) = q_0 e^{-0.0063t}$, where q_0 is the initial amount of the substance and t is the time in days. Approximate the half-life of the substance.

72 Children's growth The Count Model is a formula that can be used to predict the height of preschool children. If h is height (in centimeters) and t is age (in years), then

$$h = 70.228 + 5.104t + 9.222 \ln t$$

for $\frac{1}{4} \le t \le 6$. From calculus, the rate of growth R (in cm/year) is given by $R = 5.104 + (9.222/t)$. Predict the height and rate of growth of a typical 2-year-old.

73 Electrical circuit The current I in a certain electrical circuit at time t is given by

$$I = \frac{V}{R}(1 - e^{-Rt/L}),$$

where V is the electromotive force, R is the resistance, and L is the inductance. Solve the equation for t.

74 Carbon 14 dating The technique of carbon 14 (^{14}C) dating is used to determine the age of archaeological and geological specimens. The formula $T = -8310 \ln x$ is sometimes used to predict the age T (in years) of a bone fossil, where x is the percentage (expressed as a decimal) of ^{14}C still present in the fossil.

(a) Estimate the age of a bone fossil that contains 4% of the ^{14}C found in an equal amount of carbon in present-day bone.

(b) Approximate the percentage of ^{14}C present in a fossil that is 10,000 years old.

75 Population of Kenya Based on present birth and death rates, the population of Kenya is expected to increase according to the formula $N = 30.7e^{0.022t}$, with N in millions and $t = 0$ corresponding to 2000. How many years will it take for the population to double?

76 Language history Refer to Exercise 48 of Section 5.2. If a language originally had N_0 basic words of which $N(t)$ are still in use, then $N(t) = N_0(0.805)^t$, where time t is measured in millennia. After how many years are one-half the basic words still in use?

CHAPTER 5 DISCUSSION EXERCISES

1 (a) Sketch the graph of $f(x) = -(x - 1)^3 + 1$ along with the graph of $y = f^{-1}(x)$.

(b) Discuss what happens to the graph of $y = f^{-1}(x)$ (in general) as the graph of $y = f(x)$ is increasing or is decreasing.

(c) What can you conclude about the intersection points of the graphs of a function and its inverse?

2 Find the inverse function of $f(x) = \dfrac{9x}{\sqrt{x^2 + 1}}$ and identify any asymptotes of the graph of f^{-1}. How do they relate to the asymptotes of the graph of f?

3 Shown in the figure is a graph of $f(x) = (\ln x)/x$ for $x > 0$. The maximum value of $f(x)$ occurs at $x = e$.

(a) The integers 2 and 4 have the unusual property that $2^4 = 4^2$. Show that if $x^y = y^x$ for positive real numbers x and y, then $(\ln x)/x = (\ln y)/y$.

(b) Use the graph of f to explain why many pairs of real numbers satisfy the equation $x^y = y^x$.

Exercise 3

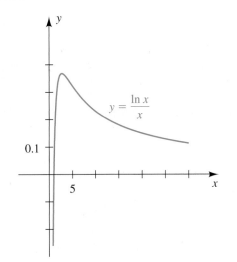

$y = \dfrac{\ln x}{x}$

4 Refer to Exercise 70 of Section 5.4. Discuss how to solve this exercise *without* the use of the formula for the total amount T. Proceed with your solution, and compare your answer to the answer arrived at using the formula for T.

5 Since $y = \log_3 (x^2)$ is equivalent to $y = 2 \log_3 x$ by law 3 of logarithms, why aren't the graphs in Figure 2(a) and (b) of Section 5.5 the same?

6 (a) Compare the growth of the functions $f(x) = (1.085)^x$ and $g(x) = e^{0.085x}$, discuss what they could represent, and explain the difference between the two functions.

(b) Now suppose you are investing money at 8.5% per year compounded monthly. How would a graph of this growth compare with the two graphs in part (a)?

7 **Salary increases** Suppose you started a job at $40,000 per year. In 5 years, you are scheduled to be making $60,000 per year. Determine the annual exponential rate of increase that describes this situation. Assume that the same exponential rate of increase will continue for 40 years. Using the rule of 70 (page 317), mentally estimate your annual salary in 40 years, and compare the estimate to an actual computation.

8 **Energy release** Consider these three events:

(1) On May 18, 1980, the volcanic eruption of Mount St. Helens in Washington released approximately 1.7×10^{18} joules of energy.

(2) When a 1-megaton nuclear bomb detonates, it releases about 4×10^{15} joules of energy.

(3) The 1989 San Francisco earthquake registered 7.1 on the Richter scale.

(a) Make some comparisons (i.e., how many of one event is equivalent to another) in terms of energy released. (*Hint:* Refer to Exercise 70 in Chapter 5 Review Exercises.) *Note:* The atomic bombs dropped in World War II were 1-kiloton bombs (1000 1-kiloton bombs = 1 1-megaton bomb).

(b) What reading on the Richter scale would be equivalent to the Mount St. Helens eruption? Has there ever been a reading that high?

9 Discuss how many solutions the equation

$$\log_5 x + \log_7 x = 11$$

has. Solve the equation using the change of base formula.

9

Systems of Equations and Inequalities

Applications of mathematics sometimes require working simultaneously with more than one equation in several variables—that is, with a system of equations. In this chapter we develop methods for finding solutions that are common to all the equations in a system. Of particular importance are the techniques involving matrices, because they are well suited for computer programs and can be readily applied to systems containing any number of linear equations in any number of variables. We shall also consider systems of inequalities and linear programming—topics that are of major importance in business applications and statistics. The last part of the chapter provides an introduction to the algebra of matrices and determinants.

9.1

Systems of Equations

Figure 1

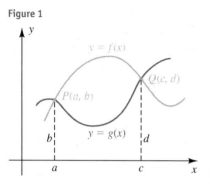

Figure 2

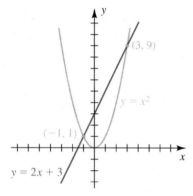

Consider the graphs of the two functions f and g, illustrated in Figure 1. In applications it is often necessary to find points such as $P(a, b)$ and $Q(c, d)$ at which the graphs intersect. Since $P(a, b)$ is on each graph, the pair (a, b) is a **solution** of *both* of the equations $y = f(x)$ and $y = g(x)$; that is,

$$b = f(a) \quad \text{and} \quad b = g(a).$$

We say that (a, b) is a solution of the **system of equations** (or simply **system**)

$$\begin{cases} y = f(x) \\ y = g(x) \end{cases}$$

where the brace is used to indicate that the equations are to be treated simultaneously. Similarly, the pair (c, d) is a solution of the system. To **solve** a system of equations means to find all the solutions.

As a special case, consider the system

$$\begin{cases} y = x^2 \\ y = 2x + 3 \end{cases}$$

The graphs of the equations are the parabola and line sketched in Figure 2. The following table shows that the points $(-1, 1)$ and $(3, 9)$ are on both graphs.

(x, y)	$y = x^2$	$y = 2x + 3$
$(-1, 1)$	$1 = (-1)^2$, or $1 = 1$	$1 = 2(-1) + 3$, or $1 = 1$
$(3, 9)$	$9 = 3^2$, or $9 = 9$	$9 = 2(3) + 3$, or $9 = 9$

Hence, $(-1, 1)$ and $(3, 9)$ are solutions of the system.

The preceding discussion does not give us a strategy for actually finding the solutions. The next two examples illustrate how to find the solutions of the system using only algebraic methods.

EXAMPLE 1 Solving a system of two equations

Solve the system

$$\begin{cases} y = x^2 \\ y = 2x + 3 \end{cases}$$

SOLUTION   If (x, y) is a solution of the system, then the variable y in the equation $y = 2x + 3$ must satisfy the condition $y = x^2$. Hence, we *substitute* x^2 for y in $y = 2x + 3$:

$$\begin{aligned}
x^2 &= 2x + 3 &&\text{substitute } y = x^2 \text{ in } y = 2x + 3 \\
x^2 - 2x - 3 &= 0 &&\text{subtract } 2x + 3 \\
(x + 1)(x - 3) &= 0 &&\text{factor} \\
x + 1 = 0, \quad x - 3 &= 0 &&\text{zero factor theorem} \\
x = -1, \quad x &= 3 &&\text{solve for } x
\end{aligned}$$

This gives us the x-values for the solutions (x, y) of the system. To find the corresponding y-values, we may use either $y = x^2$ or $y = 2x + 3$. Using $y = x^2$, we find that

$$\text{if } \quad x = -1, \quad \text{then} \quad y = (-1)^2 = 1$$

and $\qquad\qquad\qquad\qquad$ if $\quad x = 3, \qquad$ then $\quad y = 3^2 = 9.$

Hence, the solutions of the system are $(-1, 1)$ and $(3, 9)$.

We could also have found the solutions by substituting $y = 2x + 3$ in the *first* equation, $y = x^2$, obtaining

$$2x + 3 = x^2.$$

The remainder of the solution is the same.

Given the system in Example 1, we *could* have solved one of the equations for x in terms of y and then substituted in the other equation, obtaining an equation in y alone. Solving the latter equation would give us the y-values for the solutions of the system. The x-values could then be found using one of the given equations. In general, we may use the following guidelines, where u and v denote any two variables (*possibly* x and y). This technique is called the **method of substitution.**

Guidelines for the Method of Substitution for Two Equations in Two Variables	
	1 Solve one of the equations for one variable u in terms of the other variable v.
	2 Substitute the expression for u found in guideline 1 in the other equation, obtaining an equation in v alone.
	3 Find the solutions of the equation in v obtained in guideline 2.
	4 Substitute the v-values found in guideline 3 in the equation of guideline 1 to find the corresponding u-values.
	5 Check each pair (u, v) found in guideline 4 in the given system.

EXAMPLE 2 Using the method of substitution

Solve the following system and then sketch the graph of each equation, showing the points of intersection:

$$\begin{cases} x + y^2 = 6 \\ x + 2y = 3 \end{cases}$$

SOLUTION We must first decide which equation to solve and which variable to solve for. Let's examine the possibilities.

Solve the first equation for y: $\quad y = \pm\sqrt{6 - x}$

Solve the first equation for x: $\quad x = 6 - y^2$

Solve the second equation for y: $\quad y = (3 - x)/2$

Solve the second equation for x: $x = 3 - 2y$

(continued)

Guideline 1 Looking ahead to guideline 2, we note that solving either equation for x will result in a simple substitution. Thus, we will use $x = 3 - 2y$ and follow the guidelines with $u = x$ and $v = y$.

Guideline 2 Substitute the expression for x found in guideline 1 in the first equation of the system:

$$(3 - 2y) + y^2 = 6 \quad \text{substitute } x = 3 - 2y \text{ in } x + y^2 = 6$$
$$y^2 - 2y - 3 = 0 \quad \text{simplify}$$

Guideline 3 Solve the equation in guideline 2 for y:

$$(y - 3)(y + 1) = 0 \quad \text{factor } y^2 - 2y - 3$$
$$y - 3 = 0, \quad y + 1 = 0 \quad \text{zero factor theorem}$$
$$y = 3, \qquad y = -1 \quad \text{solve for } y$$

These are the only possible y-values for the solutions of the system.

Guideline 4 Use the equation $x = 3 - 2y$ from guideline 1 to find the corresponding x-values:

$$\text{if} \quad y = 3, \quad \text{then} \quad x = 3 - 2(3) = 3 - 6 = -3$$
$$\text{if} \quad y = -1, \quad \text{then} \quad x = 3 - 2(-1) = 3 + 2 = 5$$

Thus, possible solutions are $(-3, 3)$ and $(5, -1)$.

Guideline 5 Substituting $x = -3$ and $y = 3$ in $x + y^2 = 6$, the first equation of the system, yields $-3 + 9 = 6$, a true statement. Substituting $x = -3$ and $y = 3$ in $x + 2y = 3$, the second equation of the system, yields $-3 + 6 = 3$, also a true statement. Hence, $(-3, 3)$ is a solution of the system. In a similar manner, we may check that $(5, -1)$ is also a solution.

The graphs of the two equations (a parabola and a line, respectively) are sketched in Figure 3, showing the two points of intersection.

Figure 3

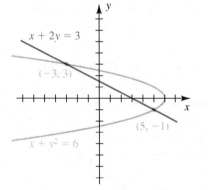

In future examples we will not list the specific guidelines that are used in finding solutions of systems.

In solving certain systems using the method of substitution, it is convenient to let u or v in the guidelines denote an *expression* involving another variable. This technique is illustrated in the next example with $u = x^2$.

EXAMPLE 3 Using the method of substitution

Solve the following system and then sketch the graph of each equation, showing the points of intersection:

$$\begin{cases} x^2 + y^2 = 25 \\ x^2 + y = 19 \end{cases}$$

SOLUTION   We proceed as follows:

$$x^2 = 19 - y \quad \text{solve } x^2 + y = 19 \text{ for } x^2$$

$$(19 - y) + y^2 = 25 \quad \text{substitute } x^2 = 19 - y \text{ in } x^2 + y^2 = 25$$

$$y^2 - y - 6 = 0 \quad \text{simplify}$$

$$(y - 3)(y + 2) = 0 \quad \text{factor}$$

$$y - 3 = 0, \quad y + 2 = 0 \quad \text{zero factor theorem}$$

$$y = 3, \qquad y = -2 \quad \text{solve for } y$$

These are the only possible y-values for the solutions of the system. To find the corresponding x-values, we use $x^2 = 19 - y$:

If $\quad y = 3, \quad$ then $\quad x^2 = 19 - 3 = 16 \quad$ and $\quad x = \pm 4$

If $\quad y = -2, \quad$ then $\quad x^2 = 19 - (-2) = 21 \quad$ and $\quad x = \pm\sqrt{21}$

Thus, the only possible solutions of the system are

$$(4, 3), \quad (-4, 3), \quad \left(\sqrt{21}, -2\right), \quad \text{and} \quad \left(-\sqrt{21}, -2\right).$$

We can check by substitution in the given equations that all four pairs are solutions.

The graph of $x^2 + y^2 = 25$ is a circle of radius 5 with center at the origin, and the graph of $y = 19 - x^2$ is a parabola with a vertical axis. The graphs are sketched in Figure 4. The points of intersection correspond to the solutions of the system.

There are, of course, other ways to find the solutions. We could solve the first equation for x^2, $x^2 = 25 - y^2$, and then substitute in the second, obtaining $25 - y^2 + y = 19$. Another method is to solve the second equation for y, $y = 19 - x^2$, and substitute in the first.

We can also consider equations in three variables x, y, and z, such as

$$x^2y + xz + 3^y = 4z^3.$$

Such an equation has a **solution** (a, b, c) if substitution of a, b, and c, for x, y, and z, respectively, yields a true statement. We refer to (a, b, c) as an **ordered triple** of real numbers. Systems of equations are **equivalent systems** provided they have the same solutions. A system of equations in three variables and the solutions of the system are defined as in the two-variable case. Similarly, we can consider systems of *any* number of equations in *any* number of variables.

The method of substitution can be extended to these more complicated systems. For example, given three equations in three variables, suppose that it is possible to solve one of the equations for one variable in terms of the remaining two variables. By substituting that expression in each of the other equations, we obtain a system of two equations in two variables. The solutions of the two-variable system can then be used to find the solutions of the original system.

Figure 4

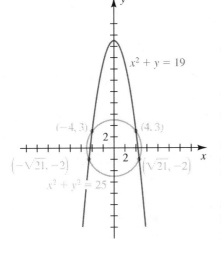

EXAMPLE 4 Solving a system of three equations

Solve the system

$$\begin{cases} x - y + z = 2 \\ xyz = 0 \\ 2y + z = 1 \end{cases}$$

SOLUTION   We proceed as follows:

$$z = 1 - 2y \quad \text{solve } 2y + z = 1 \text{ for } z$$

$$\begin{cases} x - y + (1 - 2y) = 2 \\ xy(1 - 2y) = 0 \end{cases} \quad \begin{array}{l} \text{substitute } z = 1 - 2y \text{ in the} \\ \text{first two equations} \end{array}$$

$$\begin{cases} x - 3y - 1 = 0 \\ xy(1 - 2y) = 0 \end{cases} \quad \text{equivalent system}$$

We now find the solutions of the last system:

$$x = 3y + 1 \quad \text{solve } x - 3y - 1 = 0 \text{ for } x$$

$$(3y + 1)y(1 - 2y) = 0 \quad \begin{array}{l} \text{substitute } x = 3y + 1 \text{ in} \\ xy(1 - 2y) = 0 \end{array}$$

$$3y + 1 = 0, \quad y = 0, \quad 1 - 2y = 0 \quad \text{zero factor theorem}$$

$$y = -\tfrac{1}{3}, \quad y = 0, \quad y = \tfrac{1}{2} \quad \text{solve for } y$$

These are the only possible y-values for the solutions of the system.

To obtain the corresponding x-values, we substitute for y in the equation $x = 3y + 1$, obtaining

$$x = 0, \quad x = 1, \quad \text{and} \quad x = \tfrac{5}{2}.$$

Using $z = 1 - 2y$ gives us the corresponding z-values

$$z = \tfrac{5}{3}, \quad z = 1, \quad \text{and} \quad z = 0.$$

Thus, the solutions (x, y, z) of the original system must be among the ordered triples

$$\left(0, -\tfrac{1}{3}, \tfrac{5}{3}\right), \quad (1, 0, 1), \quad \text{and} \quad \left(\tfrac{5}{2}, \tfrac{1}{2}, 0\right).$$

Checking each shows that the three ordered triples are solutions of the system.

EXAMPLE 5 An application of a system of equations

Is it possible to construct an aquarium with a glass top and two square ends that holds 16 ft³ of water and requires 40 ft² of glass? (Disregard the thickness of the glass.)

SOLUTION   We begin by sketching a typical aquarium and labeling it as in Figure 5, with x and y in feet. Referring to the figure and using formulas for volume and area, we see that

$$\text{volume of the aquarium} = x^2y \qquad \text{length} \times \text{width} \times \text{height}$$
$$\text{square feet of glass required} = 2x^2 + 4xy. \qquad \text{2 ends, 2 sides, top, and bottom}$$

Figure 5

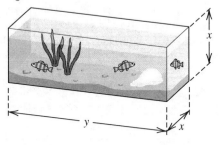

Since the volume is to be 16 ft³ and the area of the glass required is 40 ft², we obtain the following system of equations:

$$\begin{cases} x^2y = 16 \\ 2x^2 + 4xy = 40 \end{cases}$$

We find the solutions as follows:

$$y = \frac{16}{x^2} \qquad \text{solve } x^2y = 16 \text{ for } y$$

$$2x^2 + 4x\left(\frac{16}{x^2}\right) = 40 \qquad \text{substitute } y = \frac{16}{x^2} \text{ in } 2x^2 + 4xy = 40$$

$$x^2 + \frac{32}{x} = 20 \qquad \text{cancel } x, \text{ and divide by 2}$$

$$x^3 + 32 = 20x \qquad \text{multiply by } x\ (x \neq 0)$$

$$x^3 - 20x + 32 = 0 \qquad \text{subtract } 20x$$

We next look for rational solutions of the last equation. Dividing the polynomial $x^3 - 20x + 32$ synthetically by $x - 2$ gives us

$$\begin{array}{r|rrrr} 2 & 1 & 0 & -20 & 32 \\ & & 2 & 4 & -32 \\ \hline & 1 & 2 & -16 & 0 \end{array}$$

Thus, one solution of $x^3 - 20x + 32 = 0$ is 2, and the remaining two solutions are zeros of the quotient $x^2 + 2x - 16$—that is, roots of the depressed equation

$$x^2 + 2x - 16 = 0.$$

(continued)

By the quadratic formula,

$$x = \frac{-2 \pm \sqrt{2^2 - 4(1)(-16)}}{2(1)} = \frac{-2 \pm 2\sqrt{17}}{2} = -1 \pm \sqrt{17}.$$

Since x is positive, we may discard $x = -1 - \sqrt{17}$. Hence, the only possible values of x are

$$x = 2 \quad \text{and} \quad x = -1 + \sqrt{17} \approx 3.12.$$

The corresponding y-values can be found by substituting for x in the equation $y = 16/x^2$. Letting $x = 2$ gives us $y = \frac{16}{4} = 4$. Using these values, we obtain the dimensions 2 feet by 2 feet by 4 feet for the aquarium.

Letting $x = -1 + \sqrt{17}$, we obtain $y = 16/\left(-1 + \sqrt{17}\right)^2$, which simplifies to $y = \frac{1}{8}\left(9 + \sqrt{17}\right) \approx 1.64$. Thus, approximate dimensions for another aquarium are 3.12 feet by 3.12 feet by 1.64 feet.

9.1 Exercises

Exer. 1–30: Use the method of substitution to solve the system.

1 $\begin{cases} y = x^2 - 4 \\ y = 2x - 1 \end{cases}$

2 $\begin{cases} y = x^2 + 1 \\ x + y = 3 \end{cases}$

3 $\begin{cases} y^2 = 1 - x \\ x + 2y = 1 \end{cases}$

4 $\begin{cases} y^2 = x \\ x + 2y + 3 = 0 \end{cases}$

5 $\begin{cases} 2y = x^2 \\ y = 4x^3 \end{cases}$

6 $\begin{cases} x - y^3 = 1 \\ 2x = 9y^2 + 2 \end{cases}$

7 $\begin{cases} x + 2y = -1 \\ 2x - 3y = 12 \end{cases}$

8 $\begin{cases} 3x - 4y + 20 = 0 \\ 3x + 2y + 8 = 0 \end{cases}$

9 $\begin{cases} 2x - 3y = 1 \\ -6x + 9y = 4 \end{cases}$

10 $\begin{cases} 4x - 5y = 2 \\ 8x - 10y = -5 \end{cases}$

11 $\begin{cases} x + 3y = 5 \\ x^2 + y^2 = 25 \end{cases}$

12 $\begin{cases} 3x - 4y = 25 \\ x^2 + y^2 = 25 \end{cases}$

13 $\begin{cases} x^2 + y^2 = 8 \\ y - x = 4 \end{cases}$

14 $\begin{cases} x^2 + y^2 = 25 \\ 3x + 4y = -25 \end{cases}$

15 $\begin{cases} x^2 + y^2 = 9 \\ y - 3x = 2 \end{cases}$

16 $\begin{cases} x^2 + y^2 = 16 \\ y + 2x = -1 \end{cases}$

17 $\begin{cases} x^2 + y^2 = 16 \\ 2y - x = 4 \end{cases}$

18 $\begin{cases} x^2 + y^2 = 1 \\ y + 2x = -3 \end{cases}$

19 $\begin{cases} (x - 1)^2 + (y + 2)^2 = 10 \\ x + y = 1 \end{cases}$

20 $\begin{cases} xy = 2 \\ 3x - y + 5 = 0 \end{cases}$

21 $\begin{cases} y = \dfrac{4}{x + 2} \\ y = x + 5 \end{cases}$

22 $\begin{cases} y = \dfrac{10}{x + 3} \\ y = -x + 8 \end{cases}$

23 $\begin{cases} y = 20/x^2 \\ y = 9 - x^2 \end{cases}$

24 $\begin{cases} x = y^2 - 4y + 5 \\ x - y = 1 \end{cases}$

25 $\begin{cases} y^2 - 4x^2 = 4 \\ 9y^2 + 16x^2 = 140 \end{cases}$

26 $\begin{cases} 25y^2 - 16x^2 = 400 \\ 9y^2 - 4x^2 = 36 \end{cases}$

27 $\begin{cases} x^2 - y^2 = 4 \\ x^2 + y^2 = 12 \end{cases}$

28 $\begin{cases} 6x^3 - y^3 = 1 \\ 3x^3 + 4y^3 = 5 \end{cases}$

29 $\begin{cases} x + 2y - z = -1 \\ 2x - y + z = 9 \\ x + 3y + 3z = 6 \end{cases}$

30 $\begin{cases} 2x - 3y - z^2 = 0 \\ x - y - z^2 = -1 \\ x^2 - xy = 0 \end{cases}$

31 $\begin{cases} x^2 + z^2 = 5 \\ 2x + y = 1 \\ y + z = 1 \end{cases}$

32 $\begin{cases} x + 2z = 1 \\ 2y - z = 4 \\ xyz = 0 \end{cases}$

33 Find the values of b such that the system represented in the graph on the next page has
(a) one solution   (b) two solutions   (c) no solution

Exercise 33

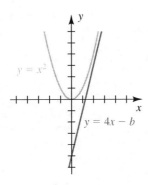

Interpret (a)–(c) graphically.

34 Find the values of b such that the system

$$\begin{cases} x^2 + y^2 = 4 \\ \quad\quad y = x + b \end{cases}$$

has

(a) one solution   (b) two solutions

(c) no solution

Interpret (a)–(c) graphically.

35 Is there a real number x such that $x = 2^{-x}$? Decide by displaying graphically the system

$$\begin{cases} y = x \\ y = 2^{-x} \end{cases}$$

36 Is there a real number x such that $x = \log x$? Decide by displaying graphically the system

$$\begin{cases} y = x \\ y = \log x \end{cases}$$

37 Shown in the figure is the graph of $x = y^2$ and a line of slope m that passes through the point $(4, 2)$. Find the value of m such that the line intersects the graph only at $(4, 2)$ and interpret graphically.

Exercise 37

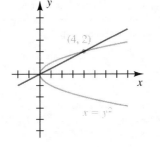

38 Shown in the figure is the graph of $y = x^2$ and a line of slope m that passes through the point $(1, 1)$. Find the value of m such that the line intersects the graph only at $(1, 1)$, and interpret graphically.

Exercise 38

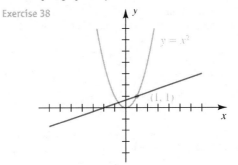

Exer. 39–40: Find an exponential function of the form $f(x) = ba^x + c$ for the graph.

39   40

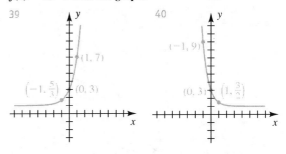

41 The perimeter of a rectangle is 40 inches, and its area is 96 in². Find its length and width.

42 Constructing tubing Sections of cylindrical tubing are to be made from thin rectangular sheets that have an area of 200 in² (see the figure). Is it possible to construct a tube that has a volume of 200 in³? If so, find r and h.

Exercise 42

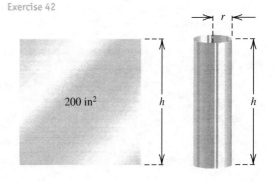

43 Fish population In fishery science, spawner-recruit functions are used to predict the number of adult fish R in next year's breeding population from an estimate S of the number of fish presently spawning.

(a) For a certain species of fish, $R = aS/(S + b)$. Estimate a and b from the data in the following table.

Year	2007	2008	2009
Number spawning	40,000	60,000	72,000

(b) Predict the breeding population for the year 2010.

44 Fish population Refer to Exercise 43. Ricker's spawner-recruit function is given by

$$R = aSe^{-bS}$$

for positive constants a and b. This relationship predicts low recruitment from very high stocks and has been found to be appropriate for many species, such as arctic cod. Rework Exercise 43 using Ricker's spawner-recruit function.

45 Competition for food A *competition model* is a collection of equations that specifies how two or more species interact in competition for the food resources of an ecosystem. Let x and y denote the numbers (in hundreds) of two competing species, and suppose that the respective rates of growth R_1 and R_2 are given by

$$R_1 = 0.01x(50 - x - y),$$
$$R_2 = 0.02y(100 - y - 0.5x).$$

Determine the population levels (x, y) at which both rates of growth are zero. (Such population levels are called *stationary points*.)

46 Fencing a region A rancher has 2420 feet of fence to enclose a rectangular region that lies along a straight river. If no fence is used along the river (see the figure), is it possible to enclose 10 acres of land? Recall that 1 acre $= 43,560$ ft².

Exercise 46

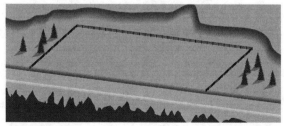

47 Constructing an aquarium Refer to Example 5. Is it possible to construct a small aquarium with an *open* top and two square ends that holds 2 ft³ of water and requires 8 ft² of glass? If so, approximate the dimensions. (Disregard the thickness of the glass.)

48 Isoperimetric problem The isoperimetric problem is to prove that of all plane geometric figures with the same perimeter (isoperimetric figures), the circle has the greatest area. Show that no rectangle has both the same area and the same perimeter as any circle.

49 Moiré pattern A moiré pattern is formed when two geometrically regular patterns are superimposed. Shown in the figure is a pattern obtained from the family of circles $x^2 + y^2 = n^2$ and the family of horizontal lines $y = m$ for integers m and n.

(a) Show that the points of intersection of the circle $x^2 + y^2 = n^2$ and the line $y = n - 1$ lie on a parabola.

(b) Work part (a) using the line $y = n - 2$.

Exercise 49

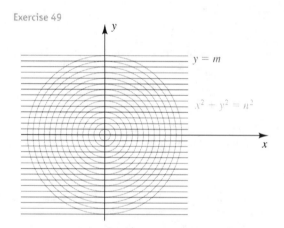

50 Dimensions of a pill A spherical pill has diameter 1 centimeter. A second pill in the shape of a right circular cylinder is to be manufactured with the same volume and twice the surface area of the spherical pill.

(a) If r is the radius and h is the height of the cylindrical pill, show that $6r^2h = 1$ and $r^2 + rh = 1$. Conclude that $6r^3 - 6r + 1 = 0$.

(b) The positive solutions of $6r^3 - 6r + 1 = 0$ are approximately 0.172 and 0.903. Find the corresponding heights, and interpret these results.

51 Hammer throw A hammer thrower is working on his form in a small practice area. The hammer spins, generating a circle with a radius of 5 feet, and when released, it hits a tall screen that is 50 feet from the center of the throwing area. Let coordinate axes be introduced as shown in the figure (not to scale).

(a) If the hammer is released at $(-4, -3)$ and travels in the tangent direction, where will it hit the screen?

(b) If the hammer is to hit at $(0, -50)$, where on the circle should it be released?

Exercise 51

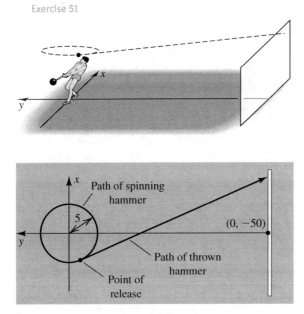

52 Path of a tossed ball A person throws a ball from the edge of a hill, at an angle of $45°$ with the horizontal, as illustrated in the figure. The ball lands 50 feet down the hill, which has slope $-\frac{3}{4}$. Using calculus, it can be shown that the path of the ball is given by $y = ax^2 + x + c$ for some constants a and c.

(a) Disregarding the height of the person, find an equation for the path.

(b) What is the maximum height of the ball *off the ground*?

Exercise 52

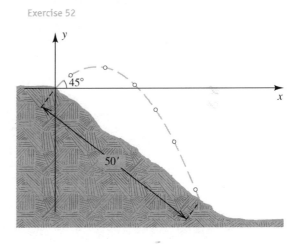

9.2

Systems of Linear Equations in Two Variables

An equation $ax + by = c$ (or, equivalently, $ax + by - c = 0$), with a and b not both zero, is a linear equation in two variables x and y. Similarly, the equation $ax + by + cz = d$ is a linear equation in three variables x, y, and z. We may also consider linear equations in four, five, or *any* number of variables. The most common systems of equations are those in which every equation is linear. In this section we shall consider only systems of two linear equations in two variables. Systems involving more than two variables are discussed in a later section.

Two systems of equations are equivalent if they have the same solutions. To find the solutions of a system, we may manipulate the equations until we obtain an equivalent system of simple equations for which the solutions can be found readily. Some manipulations (or *transformations*) that lead to equivalent systems are stated in the next theorem.

Theorem on Equivalent Systems	Given a system of equations, an equivalent system results if **(1)** two equations are interchanged. **(2)** an equation is multiplied or divided by a nonzero constant. **(3)** a constant multiple of one equation is added to another equation.

A *constant multiple* of an equation is obtained by multiplying *each* term of the equation by the same nonzero constant k. When applying part (3) of the theorem, we often use the phrase *add to one equation k times any other equation*. To *add* two equations means to add corresponding sides of the equations.

The next example illustrates how the theorem on equivalent systems may be used to solve a system of linear equations.

EXAMPLE 1 Using the theorem on equivalent systems

Solve the system

$$\begin{cases} x + 3y = -1 \\ 2x - y = 5 \end{cases}$$

SOLUTION We often multiply one of the equations by a constant that will give us the additive inverse of the coefficient of one of the variables in the other equation. Doing so enables us to add the two equations and obtain an equation in only one variable, as follows:

$$\begin{cases} x + 3y = -1 \\ 6x - 3y = 15 \end{cases} \quad \text{multiply the second equation by 3}$$

$$\begin{cases} x + 3y = -1 \\ 7x = 14 \end{cases} \quad \text{add the first equation to the second}$$

We see from the last system that $7x = 14$, and hence $x = \frac{14}{7} = 2$. To find the corresponding y-value, we substitute 2 for x in $x + 3y = -1$, obtaining $y = -1$. Thus, $(2, -1)$ is the only solution of the system.

There are many other ways to use the theorem on equivalent systems to find the solution. Another approach is to proceed as follows:

Figure 1

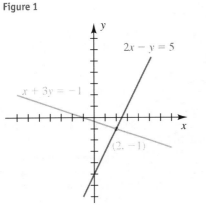

$$\begin{cases} x + 3y = -1 \\ 2x - y = 5 \end{cases} \quad \text{given}$$

$$\begin{cases} -2x - 6y = 2 \\ 2x - y = 5 \end{cases} \quad \text{multiply the first equation by } -2$$

$$\begin{cases} -2x - 6y = 2 \\ - 7y = 7 \end{cases} \quad \text{add the first equation to the second}$$

We see from the last system that $-7y = 7$, or $y = -1$. To find the corresponding x-value, we could substitute -1 for y in $x + 3y = -1$, obtaining $x = 2$. Hence, $(2, -1)$ is the solution.

The graphs of the two equations are lines that intersect at the point $(2, -1)$, as shown in Figure 1.

The technique used in Example 1 is called the **method of elimination**, since it involves the elimination of a variable from one of the equations. The method of elimination usually leads to solutions in fewer steps than does the method of substitution discussed in the preceding section.

EXAMPLE 2 A system of linear equations with an infinite number of solutions

Solve the system

$$\begin{cases} 3x + y = 6 \\ 6x + 2y = 12 \end{cases}$$

Figure 2

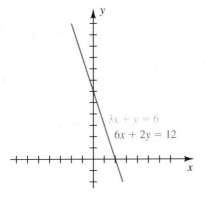

SOLUTION Multiplying the second equation by $\frac{1}{2}$ gives us

$$\begin{cases} 3x + y = 6 \\ 3x + y = 6 \end{cases}$$

Thus, (a, b) is a solution if and only if $3a + b = 6$—that is, $b = 6 - 3a$. It follows that the solutions consist of ordered pairs of the form $(a, 6 - 3a)$, where a is any real number. If we wish to find particular solutions, we may substitute various values for a. A few solutions are $(0, 6)$, $(1, 3)$, $(3, -3)$, $(-2, 12)$, and $\left(\sqrt{2}, 6 - 3\sqrt{2}\right)$.

It is incorrect to say that the solution is "all reals." It is correct to say that the solution is the set of all ordered pairs such that $3x + y = 6$, which can be written

$$\{(x, y) \mid 3x + y = 6\}.$$

The graph of each equation is the same line, as shown in Figure 2.

EXAMPLE 3 A system of linear equations with no solutions

Solve the system

$$\begin{cases} 3x + y = 6 \\ 6x + 2y = 20 \end{cases}$$

Figure 3

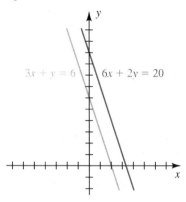

SOLUTION   If we add to the second equation -2 times the first equation, $-6x - 2y = -12$, we obtain the equivalent system

$$\begin{cases} 3x + y = 6 \\ 0 = 8 \end{cases}$$

The last equation can be written $0x + 0y = 8$, which is false for every ordered pair (x, y). Thus, the system has no solution.

The graphs of the two equations in the given system are lines that have the same slope and hence are parallel (see Figure 3). The conclusion that the system has no solution corresponds to the fact that these lines do not intersect.

The preceding three examples illustrate typical outcomes of solving a system of two linear equations in two variables: there is either exactly one solution, an infinite number of solutions, or no solution. A system is **consistent** if it has at least one solution. A system with an infinite number of solutions is **dependent and consistent**. A system is **inconsistent** if it has no solution.

Since the graph of any linear equation $ax + by = c$ is a line, *exactly one* of the three cases listed in the following table holds for any system of two such equations.

Characteristics of a System of Two Linear Equations in Two Variables

Graphs	Number of solutions	Classification
Nonparallel lines	One solution	Consistent system
Identical lines	Infinite number of solutions	Dependent and consistent system
Parallel lines	No solution	Inconsistent system

In practice, there should be little difficulty determining which of the three cases occurs. The case of the unique solution will become apparent when suitable transformations are applied to the system, as illustrated in Example 1. The case of an infinite number of solutions is similar to that of Example 2, where one of the equations can be transformed into the other. The case of no solution is indicated by a contradiction, such as the statement $0 = 8$, which appeared in Example 3.

In the process of solving a system, suppose we obtain for x a rational number such as $-\frac{41}{29}$. Substituting $-\frac{41}{29}$ for x to find the value of y is cumbersome. It is easier to select a different multiplier for each of the original equations that will enable us to eliminate x and solve for y. This technique is illustrated in the next example.

EXAMPLE 4 Solving a system

Solve the system

$$\begin{cases} 4x + 7y = 11 \\ 3x - 2y = -9 \end{cases}$$

SOLUTION We select multipliers to eliminate y. (The least common multiple of 7 and 2 is 14.)

$$\begin{cases} 8x + 14y = 22 & \text{multiply the first equation by 2} \\ 21x - 14y = -63 & \text{multiply the second equation by 7} \end{cases}$$

Adding the first equation to the second gives us

$$29x = -41, \quad \text{so} \quad x = -\tfrac{41}{29}.$$

Next, we return to the original system and select multipliers to eliminate x. (The least common multiple of 4 and 3 is 12.)

$$\begin{cases} 4x + 7y = 11 \\ 3x - 2y = -9 \end{cases} \quad \text{original system}$$

$$\begin{cases} 12x + 21y = 33 & \text{multiply the first equation by 3} \\ -12x + 8y = 36 & \text{multiply the second equation by } -4 \end{cases}$$

Adding the equations gives us

$$29y = 69, \quad \text{so} \quad y = \tfrac{69}{29}.$$

Hence, the solution is $\left(-\tfrac{41}{29}, \tfrac{69}{29}\right)$.

Check $(x, y) = \left(-\tfrac{41}{29}, \tfrac{69}{29}\right)$

We substitute the values of x and y into the original equations.

$$4x + 7y = 4\left(-\tfrac{41}{29}\right) + 7\left(\tfrac{69}{29}\right) = -\tfrac{164}{29} + \tfrac{483}{29} = \tfrac{319}{29} = 11 \qquad \text{first equation checks}$$

$$3x - 2y = 3\left(-\tfrac{41}{29}\right) - 2\left(\tfrac{69}{29}\right) = -\tfrac{123}{29} - \tfrac{138}{29} = -\tfrac{261}{29} = -9 \qquad \text{so does the second}$$

Certain applied problems can be solved by introducing systems of two linear equations, as illustrated in the next two examples.

EXAMPLE 5 An application of a system of linear equations

A produce company has a 100-acre farm on which it grows lettuce and cabbage. Each acre of cabbage requires 600 hours of labor, and each acre of lettuce needs 400 hours of labor. If 45,000 hours are available and if all land and labor resources are to be used, find the number of acres of each crop that should be planted.

SOLUTION   Let us introduce variables to denote the unknown quantities as follows:

$$x = \text{number of acres of cabbage}$$
$$y = \text{number of acres of lettuce}$$

Thus, the number of hours of labor required for each crop can be expressed as follows:

$$600x = \text{number of hours required for cabbage}$$
$$400y = \text{number of hours required for lettuce}$$

Using the facts that the total number of acres is 100 and the total number of hours available is 45,000 leads to the following system:

$$\begin{cases} x + y = 100 \\ 600x + 400y = 45{,}000 \end{cases}$$

We next use the method of elimination:

$$\begin{cases} x + y = 100 \\ 6x + 4y = 450 \end{cases} \qquad \text{divide the second equation by 100}$$

$$\begin{cases} -6x - 6y = -600 \\ 6x + 4y = 450 \end{cases} \qquad \text{multiply the first equation by } -6$$

$$\begin{cases} -6x - 6y = -600 \\ -2y = -150 \end{cases} \qquad \text{add the first equation to the second}$$

We see from the last equation that $-2y = -150$, or $y = 75$. Substituting 75 for y in $x + y = 100$ gives us $x = 25$. Hence, the company should plant 25 acres of cabbage and 75 acres of lettuce.

Check   Planting 25 acres of cabbage and 75 acres of lettuce requires $(25)(600) + (75)(400) = 45{,}000$ hours of labor. Thus, all 100 acres of land and 45,000 hours of labor are used.

EXAMPLE 6   Finding the speed of the current in a river

A motorboat, operating at full throttle, made a trip 4 miles upstream (against a constant current) in 15 minutes. The return trip (with the same current and at full throttle) took 12 minutes. Find the speed of the current and the equivalent speed of the boat in still water.

SOLUTION   We begin by introducing variables to denote the unknown quantities. Thus, let

$$x = \text{speed of boat (in mi/hr)}$$
$$y = \text{speed of current (in mi/hr)}.$$

We plan to use the formula $d = rt$, where d denotes the distance traveled, r the rate, and t the time. Since the current slows the boat as it travels upstream but adds to its speed as it travels downstream, we obtain

$$\text{upstream rate} = x - y \quad (\text{in mi/hr})$$
$$\text{downstream rate} = x + y \quad (\text{in mi/hr}).$$

The time (in hours) traveled in each direction is

$$\text{upstream time} = \tfrac{15}{60} = \tfrac{1}{4} \text{ hr}$$
$$\text{downstream time} = \tfrac{12}{60} = \tfrac{1}{5} \text{ hr}.$$

The distance is 4 miles for each trip. Substituting in $d = rt$ gives us the system

$$\begin{cases} 4 = (x - y)\left(\tfrac{1}{4}\right) \\ 4 = (x + y)\left(\tfrac{1}{5}\right) \end{cases}$$

Applying the theorem on equivalent systems, we obtain

$$\begin{cases} x - y = 16 \\ x + y = 20 \end{cases} \quad \text{multiply the first equation by 4 and the second by 5}$$

$$\begin{cases} x - y = 16 \\ 2x = 36 \end{cases} \quad \text{add the first equation to the second}$$

We see from the last equation that $2x = 36$, or $x = 18$. Substituting 18 for x in $x + y = 20$ gives us $y = 2$. Hence, the speed of the boat in still water is 18 mi/hr, and the speed of the current is 2 **mi/hr**.

Check   The upstream rate is $18 - 2 = 16 \text{ mi/hr}$, and the downstream rate is $18 + 2 = 20 \text{ mi/hr}$. An upstream 4-mile trip would take $\tfrac{4}{16} = \tfrac{1}{4}$ hr $= 15$ min, and a downstream 4-mile trip would take $\tfrac{4}{20} = \tfrac{1}{5}$ hr $= 12$ min.

9.2   *Exercises*

Exer. 1–22: Solve the system.

1 $\begin{cases} 2x + 3y = 2 \\ x - 2y = 8 \end{cases}$

2 $\begin{cases} 4x + 5y = 13 \\ 3x + y = -4 \end{cases}$

3 $\begin{cases} 2x + 5y = 16 \\ 3x - 7y = 24 \end{cases}$

4 $\begin{cases} 7x - 8y = 9 \\ 4x + 3y = -10 \end{cases}$

5 $\begin{cases} 3r + 4s = 3 \\ r - 2s = -4 \end{cases}$

6 $\begin{cases} 9u + 2v = 0 \\ 3u - 5v = 17 \end{cases}$

7 $\begin{cases} 5x - 6y = 4 \\ 3x + 7y = 8 \end{cases}$

8 $\begin{cases} 2x + 8y = 7 \\ 3x - 5y = 4 \end{cases}$

9 $\begin{cases} \tfrac{1}{3}c + \tfrac{1}{2}d = 5 \\ c - \tfrac{2}{3}d = -1 \end{cases}$

10 $\begin{cases} \tfrac{1}{2}t - \tfrac{1}{5}v = \tfrac{3}{2} \\ \tfrac{2}{3}t + \tfrac{1}{4}v = \tfrac{5}{12} \end{cases}$

11 $\begin{cases} \sqrt{3}x - \sqrt{2}y = 2\sqrt{3} \\ 2\sqrt{2}x + \sqrt{3}y = \sqrt{2} \end{cases}$

12 $\begin{cases} \sqrt{5}x + \sqrt{3}y = 14\sqrt{3} \\ \sqrt{3}x - 2\sqrt{5}y = -2\sqrt{5} \end{cases}$

13 $\begin{cases} -0.03x + 0.07y = 0.23 \\ 0.04x - 0.05y = 0.15 \end{cases}$

14 $\begin{cases} 0.11x - 0.03y = 0.25 \\ 0.12x + 0.05y = 0.70 \end{cases}$

15 $\begin{cases} 2x - 3y = 5 \\ -6x + 9y = 12 \end{cases}$

16 $\begin{cases} 3p - q = 7 \\ -12p + 4q = 3 \end{cases}$

17 $\begin{cases} 3m - 4n = 2 \\ -6m + 8n = -4 \end{cases}$ 18 $\begin{cases} x - 5y = 2 \\ 3x - 15y = 6 \end{cases}$

19 $\begin{cases} 2y - 5x = 0 \\ 3y + 4x = 0 \end{cases}$ 20 $\begin{cases} 3x + 7y = 9 \\ y = 5 \end{cases}$

21 $\begin{cases} \dfrac{2}{x} + \dfrac{3}{y} = -2 \\ \dfrac{4}{x} - \dfrac{5}{y} = 1 \end{cases}$ $\left(Hint\text{: Let } u = \dfrac{1}{x} \text{ and } v = \dfrac{1}{y}. \right)$

22 $\begin{cases} \dfrac{3}{x-1} + \dfrac{4}{y+2} = 2 \\ \dfrac{6}{x-1} - \dfrac{7}{y+2} = -3 \end{cases}$

23 Ticket sales The price of admission to a high school play was $3.00 for students and $4.50 for nonstudents. If 450 tickets were sold for a total of $1555.50, how many of each kind were purchased?

24 Air travel An airline that flies from Los Angeles to Albuquerque with a stopover in Phoenix charges a fare of $90 to Phoenix and a fare of $120 from Los Angeles to Albuquerque. A total of 185 passengers boarded the plane in Los Angeles, and fares totaled $21,000. How many passengers got off the plane in Phoenix?

25 Crayon dimensions A crayon 8 centimeters in length and 1 centimeter in diameter will be made from 5 cm³ of colored wax. The crayon is to have the shape of a cylinder surmounted by a small conical tip (see the figure). Find the length x of the cylinder and the height y of the cone.

Exercise 25

26 Rowing a boat A man rows a boat 500 feet upstream against a constant current in 10 minutes. He then rows 300 feet downstream (with the same current) in 5 minutes. Find the speed of the current and the equivalent rate at which he can row in still water.

27 Table top dimensions A large table for a conference room is to be constructed in the shape of a rectangle with two semicircles at the ends (see the figure). The table is to have a perimeter of 40 feet, and the area of the rectangular portion is to be twice the sum of the areas of the two ends. Find the length l and the width w of the rectangular portion.

Exercise 27

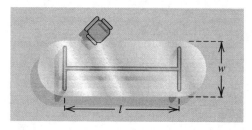

28 Investment income A woman has $19,000 to invest in two funds that pay simple interest at the rates of 4% and 6% per year. Interest on the 4% fund is tax-exempt; however, income tax must be paid on interest on the 6% fund. Being in a high tax bracket, the woman does not wish to invest the entire sum in the 6% account. Is there a way of investing the money so that she will receive $1000 in interest at the end of one year?

29 Bobcat population A bobcat population is classified by age into kittens (less than 1 year old) and adults (at least 1 year old). All adult females, including those born the prior year, have a litter each June, with an average litter size of 3 kittens. The springtime population of bobcats in a certain area is estimated to be 6000, and the male-female ratio is one. Estimate the number of adults and kittens in the population.

30 Flow rates A 300-gallon water storage tank is filled by a single inlet pipe, and two identical outlet pipes can be used to supply water to the surrounding fields (see the figure). It takes 5 hours to fill an empty tank when both outlet pipes are open. When one outlet pipe is closed, it takes 3 hours to fill the tank. Find the flow rates (in gallons per hour) in and out of the pipes.

Exercise 30

31 Mixing a silver alloy A silversmith has two alloys, one containing 35% silver and the other 60% silver. How much of each should be melted and combined to obtain 100 grams of an alloy containing 50% silver?

32 Mixing nuts A merchant wishes to mix peanuts costing $3 per pound with cashews costing $8 per pound to obtain 60 pounds of a mixture costing $5 per pound. How many pounds of each variety should be mixed?

33 Air travel An airplane, flying with a tail wind, travels 1200 miles in 2 hours. The return trip, against the wind, takes $2\frac{1}{2}$ hours. Find the cruising speed of the plane and the speed of the wind (assume that both rates are constant).

34 Filling orders A stationery company sells two types of notepads to college bookstores, the first wholesaling for 50¢ and the second for 70¢. The company receives an order for 500 notepads, together with a check for $286. If the order fails to specify the number of each type, how should the company fill the order?

35 Acceleration As a ball rolls down an inclined plane, its velocity $v(t)$ (in cm/sec) at time t (in seconds) is given by $v(t) = v_0 + at$ for initial velocity v_0 and acceleration a (in cm/sec^2). If $v(2) = 16$ and $v(5) = 25$, find v_0 and a.

36 Vertical projection If an object is projected vertically upward from an altitude of s_0 feet with an initial velocity of v_0 ft/sec, then its distance $s(t)$ above the ground after t seconds is

$$s(t) = -16t^2 + v_0 t + s_0.$$

If $s(1) = 84$ and $s(2) = 116$, what are v_0 and s_0?

37 Planning production A small furniture company manufactures sofas and recliners. Each sofa requires 8 hours of labor and $180 in materials, while a recliner can be built for $105 in 6 hours. The company has 340 hours of labor available each week and can afford to buy $6750 worth of materials. How many recliners and sofas can be produced if all labor hours and all materials must be used?

38 Livestock diet A rancher is preparing an oat-cornmeal mixture for livestock. Each ounce of oats provides 4 grams of protein and 18 grams of carbohydrates, and an ounce of cornmeal provides 3 grams of protein and 24 grams of carbohydrates. How many ounces of each can be used to meet the nutritional goals of 200 grams of protein and 1320 grams of carbohydrates per feeding?

39 Services swap A plumber and an electrician are each doing repairs on their offices and agree to swap services. The number of hours spent on each of the projects is shown in the following table.

	Plumber's office	Electrician's office
Plumber's hours	6	4
Electrician's hours	5	6

They would prefer to call the matter even, but because of tax laws, they must charge for all work performed. They agree to select hourly wage rates so that the bill on each project will match the income that each person would ordinarily receive for a comparable job.

(a) If x and y denote the hourly wages of the plumber and electrician, respectively, show that

$$6x + 5y = 10x \quad \text{and} \quad 4x + 6y = 11y.$$

Describe the solutions to this system.

(b) If the plumber ordinarily makes $35 per hour, what should the electrician charge?

40 Find equations for the altitudes of the triangle with vertices $A(-3, 2)$, $B(5, 4)$, and $C(3, -8)$, and find the point at which the altitudes intersect.

41 Warming trend in Paris As a result of urbanization, the temperatures in Paris have increased. In 1891 the average daily minimum and maximum temperatures were 5.8°C and 15.1°C, respectively. Between 1891 and 1968, these average temperatures rose 0.019°C/yr and 0.011°C/yr, respectively. Assuming the increases were linear, find the year when the difference between the minimum and maximum temperatures was 9°C, and determine the corresponding average maximum temperature.

42 Long distance telephone rates A telephone company charges customers a certain amount for the first minute of a long distance call and another amount for each additional minute. A customer makes two calls to the same city—a 36-minute call for $2.93 and a 13-minute call for $1.09.

(a) Determine the cost for the first minute and the cost for each additional minute.

(b) If there is a federal tax rate of 3.2% and a state tax rate of 7.2% on all long distance calls, find, to the nearest minute, the longest call to the same city whose cost will not exceed $5.00.

43 VCR taping An avid tennis watcher wants to record 6 hours of a major tournament on a single tape. Her tape can hold 5 hours and 20 minutes at the LP speed and 8 hours at the slower SLP speed. The LP speed produces a better quality picture, so she wishes to maximize the time recorded at the LP speed. Find the amount of time to be recorded at each speed.

44 Price and demand Suppose consumers will buy 1,000,000 T-shirts if the selling price is \$15, but for each \$1 increase in price, they will buy 100,000 fewer T-shirts. Moreover, suppose vendors will order 2,000,000 T-shirts if the selling price is \$20, and for every \$1 increase in price, they will order an additional 150,000.

(a) Express the number Q of T-shirts consumers will buy if the selling price is p dollars.

(b) Express the number K of T-shirts vendors will order if the selling price is p dollars.

(c) Determine the market price—that is, the price when $Q = K$.

Exer. 45–48: Solve the system for a and b. (*Hint:* Treat terms such as e^{3x}, $\cos x$, and $\sin x$ as "constant coefficients.")

45 $\begin{cases} ae^{3x} + be^{-3x} = 0 \\ a(3e^{3x}) + b(-3e^{-3x}) = e^{3x} \end{cases}$

46 $\begin{cases} ae^{-x} + be^{4x} = 0 \\ -ae^{-x} + b(4e^{4x}) = 2 \end{cases}$

47 $\begin{cases} a\cos x + b\sin x = 0 \\ -a\sin x + b\cos x = \tan x \end{cases}$

48 $\begin{cases} a\cos x + b\sin x = 0 \\ -a\sin x + b\cos x = \sin x \end{cases}$

9.5

Systems of Linear Equations in More Than Two Variables

For systems of linear equations containing more than two variables, we can use either the method of substitution explained in Section 9.1 or the method of elimination developed in Section 9.2. The method of elimination is the shorter and more straightforward technique for finding solutions. In addition, it leads to the matrix technique, discussed in this section.

EXAMPLE 1 Using the method of elimination to solve a system of linear equations

Solve the system

$$\begin{cases} x - 2y + 3z = 4 \\ 2x + y - 4z = 3 \\ -3x + 4y - z = -2 \end{cases}$$

SOLUTION

$$\begin{cases} x - 2y + 3z = 4 \\ 5y - 10z = -5 \\ -3x + 4y - z = -2 \end{cases}$$ add -2 times the first equation to the second equation

$$\begin{cases} x - 2y + 3z = 4 \\ 5y - 10z = -5 \\ -2y + 8z = 10 \end{cases}$$ add 3 times the first equation to the third equation

$$\begin{cases} x - 2y + 3z = 4 \\ y - 2z = -1 \\ y - 4z = -5 \end{cases}$$ multiply the second equation by $\frac{1}{5}$ and the third equation by $-\frac{1}{2}$

$$\begin{cases} x - 2y + 3z = 4 \\ y - 2z = -1 \\ -2z = -4 \end{cases}$$ add -1 times the second equation to the third equation

$$\begin{cases} x - 2y + 3z = 4 \\ y - 2z = -1 \\ z = 2 \end{cases}$$ multiply the third equation by $-\frac{1}{2}$

The solutions of the last system are easy to find by **back substitution.** From the third equation, we see that $z = 2$. Substituting 2 for z in the second equation, $y - 2z = -1$, we get $y = 3$. Finally, we find the x-value by substituting $y = 3$ and $z = 2$ in the first equation, $x - 2y + 3z = 4$, obtaining $x = 4$. Thus, there is one solution, $(4, 3, 2)$.

Any system of three linear equations in three variables has either a *unique solution,* an *infinite number of solutions,* or *no solution.* As for two equations in two variables, the terminology used to describe these systems is *consistent, dependent and consistent,* or *inconsistent,* respectively.

If we analyze the method of solution in Example 1, we see that the symbols used for the variables are immaterial. The *coefficients* of the variables are what we must consider. Thus, if different symbols such as r, s, and t are used for the variables, we obtain the system

$$\begin{cases} r - 2s + 3t = 4 \\ 2r + s - 4t = 3 \\ -3r + 4s - t = -2 \end{cases}$$

The method of elimination can then proceed exactly as in the example. Since this is true, it is possible to simplify the process. Specifically, we introduce a scheme for keeping track of the coefficients in such a way that we do not have to write down the variables. Referring to the preceding system, we first check that variables appear in the same order in each equation and that terms not involving variables are to the right of the equal signs. We then list the numbers that are involved in the equations as follows:

$$\begin{bmatrix} 1 & -2 & 3 & 4 \\ 2 & 1 & -4 & 3 \\ -3 & 4 & -1 & -2 \end{bmatrix}$$

An array of numbers of this type is called a **matrix.** The **rows** of the matrix are the numbers that appear next to each other *horizontally:*

$$\begin{array}{rrrrl} 1 & -2 & 3 & 4 & \text{first row, } R_1 \\ 2 & 1 & -4 & 3 & \text{second row, } R_2 \\ -3 & 4 & -1 & -2 & \text{third row, } R_3 \end{array}$$

The **columns** of the matrix are the numbers that appear next to each other *vertically:*

first column, C_1	second column, C_2	third column, C_3	fourth column, C_4
1	-2	3	4
2	1	-4	3
-3	4	-1	-2

The matrix obtained from a system of linear equations in the preceding manner is the **matrix of the system.** If we delete the last column of this matrix, the remaining array of numbers is the **coefficient matrix.** Since the matrix of the system can be obtained from the coefficient matrix by adjoining one column, we call it the **augmented coefficient matrix** or simply the **augmented matrix.** Later, when we use matrices to find the solutions of a system of linear equations, we shall introduce a vertical line segment in the augmented matrix to indicate where the equal signs would appear in the corresponding system of equations, as in the next illustration.

ILLUSTRATION Coefficient Matrix and Augmented Matrix

system

$$\begin{cases} x - 2y + 3z = 4 \\ 2x + y - 4z = 3 \\ -3x + 4y - z = -2 \end{cases}$$

coefficient matrix

$$\begin{bmatrix} 1 & -2 & 3 \\ 2 & 1 & -4 \\ -3 & 4 & -1 \end{bmatrix}$$

augmented matrix

$$\begin{bmatrix} 1 & -2 & 3 & 4 \\ 2 & 1 & -4 & 3 \\ -3 & 4 & -1 & -2 \end{bmatrix}$$

Before discussing a matrix method of solving a system of linear equations, let us state a general definition of a matrix. We shall use a **double subscript notation,** denoting the number that appears in row i and column j by a_{ij}. The **row subscript** of a_{ij} is i, and the **column subscript** is j.

Definition of a Matrix	Let m and n be positive integers. An $m \times n$ **matrix** is an array of the following form, where each a_{ij} is a real number:

$$\begin{bmatrix} a_{11} & a_{12} & a_{13} & \cdots & a_{1n} \\ a_{21} & a_{22} & a_{23} & \cdots & a_{2n} \\ a_{31} & a_{32} & a_{33} & \cdots & a_{3n} \\ \cdot & \cdot & \cdot & & \cdot \\ \cdot & \cdot & \cdot & & \cdot \\ \cdot & \cdot & \cdot & & \cdot \\ a_{m1} & a_{m2} & a_{m3} & \cdots & a_{mn} \end{bmatrix}$$

The notation $m \times n$ in the definition is read "m by n." We often say that the matrix *is* $m \times n$ and call $m \times n$ the **size** of the matrix. It is possible to consider matrices in which the symbols a_{ij} represent complex numbers, polynomials, or other mathematical objects. The rows and columns of a matrix are defined as before. Thus, the matrix in the definition has m rows and n columns. Note that a_{23} is in row 2 and column 3 and a_{32} is in row 3 and column 2. Each a_{ij} is an **element of the matrix.** If $m = n$, the matrix is a **square matrix of order n** and the elements $a_{11}, a_{22}, a_{33}, \ldots, a_{nn}$ are the **main diagonal elements.**

ILLUSTRATION $m \times n$ Matrices

2×3

$\blacksquare$ $\begin{bmatrix} -5 & 3 & 1 \\ 7 & 0 & -2 \end{bmatrix}$

2×2

$\blacksquare$ $\begin{bmatrix} 5 & -1 \\ 2 & 3 \end{bmatrix}$

1×3

$\blacksquare$ $\begin{bmatrix} 3 & 1 & -2 \end{bmatrix}$

3×2

$\blacksquare$ $\begin{bmatrix} 2 & -1 \\ 0 & 1 \\ 8 & 3 \end{bmatrix}$

3×1

$\blacksquare$ $\begin{bmatrix} -4 \\ 0 \\ 5 \end{bmatrix}$

To find the solutions of a system of linear equations, we begin with the augmented matrix. If a variable does not appear in an equation, we assume that the coefficient is zero. We then work with the rows of the matrix *just as though they were equations*. The only items missing are the symbols for the variables, the addition or subtraction signs used between terms, and the equal signs. We simply keep in mind that the numbers in the first column are the coefficients of the first variable, the numbers in the second column are the coefficients of the second variable, and so on. The rules for transforming a matrix are formulated so that they always produce a matrix of an equivalent system of equations.

The next theorem is a restatement, in terms of matrices, of the theorem on equivalent systems in Section 9.2. In part (2) of the theorem, the terminology *a row is multiplied by a nonzero constant* means that each element in the row is multiplied by the constant. To *add* two rows of a matrix, as in part (3), we add corresponding elements in each row.

Theorem on Matrix Row Transformations	Given a matrix of a system of linear equations, a matrix of an equivalent system results if
	(1) two rows are interchanged.
	(2) a row is multiplied or divided by a nonzero constant.
	(3) a constant multiple of one row is added to another row.

We refer to 1–3 as the **elementary row transformations** of a matrix. If a matrix is obtained from another matrix by one or more elementary row transformations, the two matrices are said to be **equivalent** or, more precisely, **row equivalent.** We shall use the symbols in the following chart to denote elementary row transformations of a matrix, where the arrow $\rightarrow$ may be read "replaces." Thus, for the transformation $k\mathrm{R}_i \rightarrow \mathrm{R}_i$, the constant multiple $k\mathrm{R}_i$ *replaces* R_i. Similarly, for $k\mathrm{R}_i + \mathrm{R}_j \rightarrow \mathrm{R}_j$, the sum $k\mathrm{R}_i + \mathrm{R}_j$ *replaces* R_j. For convenience, we shall write $(-1)\mathrm{R}_i$ as $-\mathrm{R}_i$.

Elementary Row Transformations of a Matrix

Symbol	**Meaning**
$\mathrm{R}_i \leftrightarrow \mathrm{R}_j$	Interchange rows i and j
$k\mathrm{R}_i \rightarrow \mathrm{R}_i$	Multiply row i by k
$k\mathrm{R}_i + \mathrm{R}_j \rightarrow \mathrm{R}_j$	Add k times row i to row j

We shall next rework Example 1 using matrices. You should compare the two solutions, since analogous steps are used in each case.

EXAMPLE 2 Using matrices to solve a system of linear equations

Solve the system

$$\begin{cases} x - 2y + 3z = 4 \\ 2x + y - 4z = 3 \\ -3x + 4y - z = -2 \end{cases}$$

SOLUTION We begin with the matrix of the system—that is, with the augmented matrix:

$$\begin{bmatrix} 1 & -2 & 3 & 4 \\ 2 & 1 & -4 & 3 \\ -3 & 4 & -1 & -2 \end{bmatrix}$$

We next apply elementary row transformations to obtain another (simpler) matrix of an equivalent system of equations. These transformations correspond to the manipulations used for equations in Example 1. We will place appropriate symbols between equivalent matrices.

$$\begin{bmatrix} 1 & -2 & 3 & | & 4 \\ 2 & 1 & -4 & | & 3 \\ -3 & 4 & -1 & | & -2 \end{bmatrix} \begin{matrix} \\ -2R_1 + R_2 \to R_2 \\ 3R_1 + R_3 \to R_3 \end{matrix} \begin{bmatrix} 1 & -2 & 3 & | & 4 \\ 0 & 5 & -10 & | & -5 \\ 0 & -2 & 8 & | & 10 \end{bmatrix} \begin{matrix} \\ \text{add } -2R_1 \text{ to } R_2 \\ \text{add } 3R_1 \text{ to } R_3 \end{matrix}$$

$$\begin{matrix} \tfrac{1}{5}R_2 \to R_2 \\ -\tfrac{1}{2}R_3 \to R_3 \end{matrix} \begin{bmatrix} 1 & -2 & 3 & | & 4 \\ 0 & 1 & -2 & | & -1 \\ 0 & 1 & -4 & | & -5 \end{bmatrix} \begin{matrix} \text{multiply } R_2 \text{ by } \tfrac{1}{5} \\ \text{multiply } R_3 \text{ by } -\tfrac{1}{2} \end{matrix}$$

$$-R_2 + R_3 \to R_3 \begin{bmatrix} 1 & -2 & 3 & | & 4 \\ 0 & 1 & -2 & | & -1 \\ 0 & 0 & -2 & | & -4 \end{bmatrix} \text{add } -R_2 \text{ to } R_3$$

$$-\tfrac{1}{2}R_3 \to R_3 \begin{bmatrix} 1 & -2 & 3 & | & 4 \\ 0 & 1 & -2 & | & -1 \\ 0 & 0 & 1 & | & 2 \end{bmatrix} \text{multiply } R_3 \text{ by } -\tfrac{1}{2}$$

We use the last matrix to return to the system of equations

$$\begin{bmatrix} 1 & -2 & 3 & | & 4 \\ 0 & 1 & -2 & | & -1 \\ 0 & 0 & 1 & | & 2 \end{bmatrix} \iff \begin{cases} x - 2y + 3z = 4 \\ y - 2z = -1 \\ z = 2 \end{cases}$$

which is equivalent to the original system. The solution $x = 4$, $y = 3$, $z = 2$ may now be found by back substitution, as in Example 1.

The final matrix in the solution of Example 2 is in **echelon form.** In general, a matrix is in echelon form if it satisfies the following conditions.

Echelon Form of a Matrix	
	(1) The first nonzero number in each row, reading from left to right, is 1.
	(2) The column containing the first nonzero number in any row is to the left of the column containing the first nonzero number in the row below.
	(3) Rows consisting entirely of zeros may appear at the bottom of the matrix.

The following is an illustration of matrices in echelon form. The symbols a_{ij} represent real numbers.

ILLUSTRATION Echelon Form

$$\blacksquare \begin{bmatrix} 1 & a_{12} & a_{13} & a_{14} \\ 0 & 1 & a_{23} & a_{24} \\ 0 & 0 & 1 & a_{34} \end{bmatrix}$$

$$\blacksquare \begin{bmatrix} 1 & a_{12} & a_{13} & a_{14} & a_{15} & a_{16} & a_{17} \\ 0 & 1 & a_{23} & a_{24} & a_{25} & a_{26} & a_{27} \\ 0 & 0 & 0 & 1 & a_{35} & a_{36} & a_{37} \\ 0 & 0 & 0 & 0 & 0 & 1 & a_{47} \\ 0 & 0 & 0 & 0 & 0 & 0 & 0 \\ 0 & 0 & 0 & 0 & 0 & 0 & 0 \end{bmatrix}$$

The following guidelines may be used to find echelon forms.

Guidelines for Finding the Echelon Form of a Matrix	1 Locate the *first* column that contains nonzero elements, and apply elementary row transformations to get the number 1 into the first row of that column.
	2 Apply elementary row transformations of the type $kR_1 + R_j \rightarrow R_j$ for $j > 1$ to get 0 underneath the number 1 obtained in guideline 1 in each of the remaining rows.
	3 *Disregard the first row.* Locate the next column that contains nonzero elements, and apply elementary row transformations to get the number 1 into the *second* row of that column.
	4 Apply elementary row transformations of the type $kR_2 + R_j \rightarrow R_j$ for $j > 2$ to get 0 underneath the number 1 obtained in guideline 3 in each of the remaining rows.
	5 *Disregard the first and second rows.* Locate the next column that contains nonzero elements, and repeat the procedure.
	6 Continue the process until the echelon form is reached.

Not all echelon forms contain rows consisting of only zeros (see Example 2).

We can use elementary row operations to transform the matrix of any system of linear equations to echelon form. The echelon form can then be used to produce a system of equations that is equivalent to the original system. The solutions of the given system may be found by back substitution. The next example illustrates this technique for a system of four linear equations.

EXAMPLE 3 Using an echelon form to solve a system of linear equations

Solve the system

$$\begin{cases} -2x + 3y + 4z = -1 \\ x - 2z + 2w = 1 \\ y + z - w = 0 \\ 3x + y - 2z - w = 3 \end{cases}$$

SOLUTION We have arranged the equations so that the same variables appear in vertical columns. We begin with the augmented matrix and then obtain an echelon form as described in the guidelines.

$$\begin{bmatrix} -2 & 3 & 4 & 0 & | & -1 \\ 1 & 0 & -2 & 2 & | & 1 \\ 0 & 1 & 1 & -1 & | & 0 \\ 3 & 1 & -2 & -1 & | & 3 \end{bmatrix} \overset{R_1 \leftrightarrow R_2}{\Longrightarrow} \begin{bmatrix} 1 & 0 & -2 & 2 & | & 1 \\ -2 & 3 & 4 & 0 & | & -1 \\ 0 & 1 & 1 & -1 & | & 0 \\ 3 & 1 & -2 & -1 & | & 3 \end{bmatrix}$$

$$\overset{\substack{2R_1 + R_2 \to R_2 \\ \\ -3R_1 + R_4 \to R_4}}{\Longrightarrow} \begin{bmatrix} 1 & 0 & -2 & 2 & | & 1 \\ 0 & 3 & 0 & 4 & | & 1 \\ 0 & 1 & 1 & -1 & | & 0 \\ 0 & 1 & 4 & -7 & | & 0 \end{bmatrix}$$

$$\overset{R_2 \leftrightarrow R_3}{\Longrightarrow} \begin{bmatrix} 1 & 0 & -2 & 2 & | & 1 \\ 0 & 1 & 1 & -1 & | & 0 \\ 0 & 3 & 0 & 4 & | & 1 \\ 0 & 1 & 4 & -7 & | & 0 \end{bmatrix}$$

$$\overset{\substack{-3R_2 + R_3 \to R_3 \\ -R_2 + R_4 \to R_4}}{\Longrightarrow} \begin{bmatrix} 1 & 0 & -2 & 2 & | & 1 \\ 0 & 1 & 1 & -1 & | & 0 \\ 0 & 0 & -3 & 7 & | & 1 \\ 0 & 0 & 3 & -6 & | & 0 \end{bmatrix}$$

$$\overset{R_3 + R_4 \to R_4}{\Longrightarrow} \begin{bmatrix} 1 & 0 & -2 & 2 & | & 1 \\ 0 & 1 & 1 & -1 & | & 0 \\ 0 & 0 & -3 & 7 & | & 1 \\ 0 & 0 & 0 & 1 & | & 1 \end{bmatrix}$$

$$\overset{-\frac{1}{3}R_3 \to R_3}{\Longrightarrow} \begin{bmatrix} 1 & 0 & -2 & 2 & | & 1 \\ 0 & 1 & 1 & -1 & | & 0 \\ 0 & 0 & 1 & -\frac{7}{3} & | & -\frac{1}{3} \\ 0 & 0 & 0 & 1 & | & 1 \end{bmatrix}$$

The final matrix is in echelon form and corresponds to the following system of equations:

$$\begin{cases} x & - 2z + 2w = 1 \\ y + z - w = 0 \\ z - \frac{7}{3}w = -\frac{1}{3} \\ w = 1 \end{cases}$$

We now use back substitution to find the solution. From the last equation we see that $w = 1$. Substituting in the third equation, $z - \frac{7}{3}w = -\frac{1}{3}$, we get

$$z - \frac{7}{3}(1) = -\frac{1}{3}, \quad \text{or} \quad z = \frac{6}{3} = 2.$$

(continued)

Substituting $w = 1$ and $z = 2$ in the second equation, $y + z - w = 0$, we obtain

$$y + 2 - 1 = 0, \quad \text{or} \quad y = -1.$$

Finally, from the first equation, $x - 2z + 2w = 1$, we have

$$x - 2(2) + 2(1) = 1, \quad \text{or} \quad x = 3.$$

Hence, the system has one solution, $x = 3$, $y = -1$, $z = 2$, and $w = 1$. ⟋

After obtaining an echelon form, it is often convenient to apply additional elementary row operations of the type $k\mathbf{R}_i + \mathbf{R}_j \rightarrow \mathbf{R}_j$ so that 0 also appears *above* the first 1 in each row. We refer to the resulting matrix as being in **reduced echelon form.** The following is an illustration of matrices in reduced echelon form. (Compare them with the echelon forms on page 603.)

ILLUSTRATION Reduced Echelon Form

■ $\begin{bmatrix} 1 & 0 & 0 & a_{14} \\ 0 & 1 & 0 & a_{24} \\ 0 & 0 & 1 & a_{34} \end{bmatrix}$ ■ $\begin{bmatrix} 1 & 0 & a_{13} & 0 & a_{15} & 0 & a_{17} \\ 0 & 1 & a_{23} & 0 & a_{25} & 0 & a_{27} \\ 0 & 0 & 0 & 1 & a_{35} & 0 & a_{37} \\ 0 & 0 & 0 & 0 & 0 & 1 & a_{47} \\ 0 & 0 & 0 & 0 & 0 & 0 & 0 \\ 0 & 0 & 0 & 0 & 0 & 0 & 0 \end{bmatrix}$

EXAMPLE 4 Using a reduced echelon form to solve a system of linear equations

Solve the system in Example 3 using reduced echelon form.

SOLUTION   We begin with the echelon form obtained in Example 3 and apply additional row operations as follows:

$$\begin{bmatrix} 1 & 0 & -2 & 2 & | & 1 \\ 0 & 1 & 1 & -1 & | & 0 \\ 0 & 0 & 1 & -\frac{7}{3} & | & -\frac{1}{3} \\ 0 & 0 & 0 & 1 & | & 1 \end{bmatrix} \begin{array}{c} -2\mathbf{R}_4 + \mathbf{R}_1 \rightarrow \mathbf{R}_1 \\ \mathbf{R}_4 + \mathbf{R}_2 \rightarrow \mathbf{R}_2 \\ \frac{7}{3}\mathbf{R}_4 + \mathbf{R}_3 \rightarrow \mathbf{R}_3 \end{array} \begin{bmatrix} 1 & 0 & -2 & 0 & | & -1 \\ 0 & 1 & 1 & 0 & | & 1 \\ 0 & 0 & 1 & 0 & | & 2 \\ 0 & 0 & 0 & 1 & | & 1 \end{bmatrix}$$

$$\begin{array}{c} 2\mathbf{R}_3 + \mathbf{R}_1 \rightarrow \mathbf{R}_1 \\ -\mathbf{R}_3 + \mathbf{R}_2 \rightarrow \mathbf{R}_2 \end{array} \begin{bmatrix} 1 & 0 & 0 & 0 & | & 3 \\ 0 & 1 & 0 & 0 & | & -1 \\ 0 & 0 & 1 & 0 & | & 2 \\ 0 & 0 & 0 & 1 & | & 1 \end{bmatrix}$$

The system of equations corresponding to the reduced echelon form gives us the solution *without* using back substitution:

$$x = 3, \quad y = -1, \quad z = 2, \quad w = 1$$

⟋

Sometimes it is necessary to consider systems in which the number of equations is not the same as the number of variables. The same matrix techniques are applicable, as illustrated in the next example.

EXAMPLE 5 Solving a system of two linear equations in three variables

Solve the system

$$\begin{cases} 2x + 3y + 4z = 1 \\ 3x + 4y + 5z = 3 \end{cases}$$

SOLUTION We shall begin with the augmented matrix and then find a reduced echelon form. There are many different ways of getting the number 1 into the first position of the first row. For example, the elementary row transformation $\frac{1}{2}R_1 \rightarrow R_1$ or $-\frac{1}{3}R_2 + R_1 \rightarrow R_1$ would accomplish this in one step. Another way, which does not involve fractions, is demonstrated in the following steps:

$$\begin{bmatrix} 2 & 3 & 4 & | & 1 \\ 3 & 4 & 5 & | & 3 \end{bmatrix} \xrightarrow{R_1 \leftrightarrow R_2} \begin{bmatrix} 3 & 4 & 5 & | & 3 \\ 2 & 3 & 4 & | & 1 \end{bmatrix}$$

$$\xrightarrow{-R_2 + R_1 \rightarrow R_1} \begin{bmatrix} 1 & 1 & 1 & | & 2 \\ 2 & 3 & 4 & | & 1 \end{bmatrix}$$

$$\xrightarrow{-2R_1 + R_2 \rightarrow R_2} \begin{bmatrix} 1 & 1 & 1 & | & 2 \\ 0 & 1 & 2 & | & -3 \end{bmatrix}$$

$$\xrightarrow{-R_2 + R_1 \rightarrow R_1} \begin{bmatrix} 1 & 0 & -1 & | & 5 \\ 0 & 1 & 2 & | & -3 \end{bmatrix}$$

The reduced echelon form is the matrix of the system

$$\begin{cases} x \quad - \quad z = \quad 5 \\ \quad y + 2z = -3 \end{cases}$$

or, equivalently,

$$\begin{cases} x = \quad z + 5 \\ y = -2z - 3 \end{cases}$$

There are an infinite number of solutions to this system; they can be found by assigning z any value c and then using the last two equations to express x and y in terms of c. This gives us

$$x = c + 5, \qquad y = -2c - 3, \qquad z = c.$$

Thus, the solutions of the system consist of all ordered triples of the form

$$(c + 5, -2c - 3, c)$$

for any real number c. The solutions may be checked by substituting $c + 5$ for x, $-2c - 3$ for y, and c for z in the two original equations.

We can obtain any number of solutions for the system by substituting specific real numbers for c. For example, if $c = 0$, we obtain $(5, -3, 0)$; if $c = 2$, we have $(7, -7, 2)$; and so on.

(continued)

There are other ways to specify the general solution. For example, starting with $x = z + 5$ and $y = -2z - 3$, we could let $z = d - 5$ for any real number d. In this case,

$$x = z + 5 = (d - 5) + 5 = d$$
$$y = -2z - 3 = -2(d - 5) - 3 = -2d + 7,$$

and the solutions of the system have the form

$$(d, -2d + 7, d - 5).$$

These triples produce the same solutions as $(c + 5, -2c - 3, c)$. For example, if $d = 5$, we get $(5, -3, 0)$; if $d = 7$, we obtain $(7, -7, 2)$; and so on.

A system of linear equations is **homogeneous** if all the terms that do not contain variables—that is, the *constant terms*—are zero. A system of homogeneous equations always has the **trivial solution** obtained by substituting zero for each variable. Nontrivial solutions sometimes exist. The procedure for finding solutions is the same as that used for nonhomogeneous systems.

EXAMPLE 6 Solving a homogeneous system of linear equations

Solve the homogeneous system

$$\begin{cases} x - y + 4z = 0 \\ 2x + y - z = 0 \\ -x - y + 2z = 0 \end{cases}$$

SOLUTION   We begin with the augmented matrix and find a reduced echelon form:

$$\begin{bmatrix} 1 & -1 & 4 & | & 0 \\ 2 & 1 & -1 & | & 0 \\ -1 & -1 & 2 & | & 0 \end{bmatrix} \begin{matrix} \\ -2R_1 + R_2 \rightarrow R_2 \\ R_1 + R_3 \rightarrow R_3 \end{matrix} \begin{bmatrix} 1 & -1 & 4 & | & 0 \\ 0 & 3 & -9 & | & 0 \\ 0 & -2 & 6 & | & 0 \end{bmatrix}$$

$$\begin{matrix} \\ \frac{1}{3}R_2 \rightarrow R_2 \\ -\frac{1}{2}R_3 \rightarrow R_3 \end{matrix} \begin{bmatrix} 1 & -1 & 4 & | & 0 \\ 0 & 1 & -3 & | & 0 \\ 0 & 1 & -3 & | & 0 \end{bmatrix}$$

$$\begin{matrix} R_2 + R_1 \rightarrow R_1 \\ \\ -R_2 + R_3 \rightarrow R_3 \end{matrix} \begin{bmatrix} 1 & 0 & 1 & | & 0 \\ 0 & 1 & -3 & | & 0 \\ 0 & 0 & 0 & | & 0 \end{bmatrix}$$

The reduced echelon form corresponds to the system

$$\begin{cases} x \quad + z = 0 \\ \quad y - 3z = 0 \end{cases}$$

or, equivalently,

$$\begin{cases} x = -z \\ y = 3z \end{cases}$$

Assigning any value c to z, we obtain $x = -c$ and $y = 3c$. The solutions consist of all ordered triples of the form $(-c, 3c, c)$ for any real number c.

EXAMPLE 7 A homogeneous system with only the trivial solution

Solve the system

$$\begin{cases} x + y + z = 0 \\ x - y + z = 0 \\ x - y - z = 0 \end{cases}$$

SOLUTION We begin with the augmented matrix and find a reduced echelon form:

$$\begin{bmatrix} 1 & 1 & 1 & | & 0 \\ 1 & -1 & 1 & | & 0 \\ 1 & -1 & -1 & | & 0 \end{bmatrix} \begin{matrix} \\ -R_1 + R_2 \rightarrow R_2 \\ -R_1 + R_3 \rightarrow R_3 \end{matrix} \begin{bmatrix} 1 & 1 & 1 & | & 0 \\ 0 & -2 & 0 & | & 0 \\ 0 & -2 & -2 & | & 0 \end{bmatrix}$$

$$\begin{matrix} -\frac{1}{2}R_2 \rightarrow R_2 \\ -\frac{1}{2}R_3 \rightarrow R_3 \end{matrix} \begin{bmatrix} 1 & 1 & 1 & | & 0 \\ 0 & 1 & 0 & | & 0 \\ 0 & 1 & 1 & | & 0 \end{bmatrix}$$

$$\begin{matrix} -R_2 + R_1 \rightarrow R_1 \\ \\ -R_2 + R_3 \rightarrow R_3 \end{matrix} \begin{bmatrix} 1 & 0 & 1 & | & 0 \\ 0 & 1 & 0 & | & 0 \\ 0 & 0 & 1 & | & 0 \end{bmatrix}$$

$$\begin{matrix} -R_3 + R_1 \rightarrow R_1 \\ \\ \\ \end{matrix} \begin{bmatrix} 1 & 0 & 0 & | & 0 \\ 0 & 1 & 0 & | & 0 \\ 0 & 0 & 1 & | & 0 \end{bmatrix}$$

The reduced echelon form is the matrix of the system

$$x = 0, \qquad y = 0, \qquad z = 0.$$

Thus, the only solution for the given system is the trivial one, $(0, 0, 0)$.

The next two examples illustrate applied problems.

EXAMPLE 8 Using a system of equations to determine maximum profit

A manufacturer of electrical equipment has the following information about the weekly profit from the production and sale of an electric motor.

Production level x	25	50	100
Profit $P(x)$ (dollars)	5250	7500	4500

(a) Determine a, b, and c so that the graph of $P(x) = ax^2 + bx + c$ fits this information.

(b) According to the quadratic function P in part (a), how many motors should be produced each week for maximum profit? What is the maximum weekly profit?

SOLUTION

(a) We see from the table that the graph of $P(x) = ax^2 + bx + c$ contains the points $(25, 5250)$, $(50, 7500)$, and $(100, 4500)$. This gives us the system of equations

$$\begin{cases} 5250 = 625a + 25b + c \\ 7500 = 2500a + 50b + c \\ 4500 = 10{,}000a + 100b + c \end{cases}$$

It is easy to solve any of the equations for c, so we'll start solving the system by solving the first equation for c,

$$c = 5250 - 625a - 25b,$$

and then substituting that expression for c in the other two equations:

$$\begin{cases} 7500 = 2500a + 50b + (5250 - 625a - 25b) \\ 4500 = 10{,}000a + 100b + (5250 - 625a - 25b) \end{cases}$$

Note that we have reduced the system of three equations and three variables to two equations and two variables. Simplifying the system gives us

$$\begin{cases} 1875a + 25b = 2250 \\ 9375a + 75b = -750 \end{cases}$$

At this point we could divide the equations by 25, but we see that 75 is just 3 times 25, so we'll use the method of elimination to eliminate b:

$$\begin{cases} -5625a - 75b = -6750 \quad \text{multiply the first} \\ 9375a + 75b = -750 \quad \text{equation by } -3 \end{cases}$$

*Note that we have used **both** the method of substitution and the method of elimination in solving this system of equations.*

Adding the equations gives us $3750a = -7500$, so $a = -2$. We can verify that the solution is $a = -2$, $b = 240$, $c = 500$.

(b) From part (a),

$$P(x) = -2x^2 + 240x + 500.$$

Since $a = -2 < 0$, the graph of the quadratic function P is a parabola that opens downward. By the formula on page 189, the x-coordinate of the vertex (the highest point on the parabola) is

$$x = \frac{-b}{2a} = \frac{-240}{2(-2)} = \frac{-240}{-4} = 60.$$

Hence, for the maximum profit, the manufacturer should produce and sell 60 motors per week. The maximum weekly profit is

$$P(60) = -2(60)^2 + 240(60) + 500 = \$7700.$$

EXAMPLE 9   Solving a mixture problem

A merchant wishes to mix two grades of peanuts costing \$3 and \$4 per pound, respectively, with cashews costing \$8 per pound, to obtain 140 pounds of a mixture costing \$6 per pound. If the merchant also wants the amount of lower-grade peanuts to be twice that of the higher-grade peanuts, how many pounds of each variety should be mixed?

SOLUTION   Let us introduce three variables, as follows:

$$x = \text{number of pounds of peanuts at \$3 per pound}$$
$$y = \text{number of pounds of peanuts at \$4 per pound}$$
$$z = \text{number of pounds of cashews at \$8 per pound}$$

We refer to the statement of the problem and obtain the following system:

$$\begin{cases} x + y + z = 140 & \text{weight equation} \\ 3x + 4y + 8z = 6(140) & \text{value equation} \\ x = 2y & \text{constraint} \end{cases}$$

You may verify that the solution of this system is $x = 40$, $y = 20$, $z = 80$. Thus, the merchant should use 40 pounds of the \$3/lb peanuts, 20 pounds of the \$4/lb peanuts, and 80 pounds of cashews.

Sometimes we can combine row transformations to simplify our work. For example, consider the augmented matrix

$$\begin{bmatrix} 11 & 3 & 8 & 9 \\ 7 & -2 & 2 & 1 \\ 0 & 87 & 80 & 94 \end{bmatrix}.$$

To obtain a 1 in the first column, it appears we have to multiply row 1 by $\frac{1}{11}$ or row 2 by $\frac{1}{7}$. However, we can multiply row 1 by 2 and row 2 by -3 and then add those two rows to obtain

$$2(11) + (-3)(7) = 22 + (-21) = 1$$

in column one, as shown in the next matrix:

$$2\mathbf{R_1} - 3\mathbf{R_2} \rightarrow \mathbf{R_1} \begin{bmatrix} 1 & 12 & 10 & 15 \\ 7 & -2 & 2 & 1 \\ 0 & 87 & 80 & 94 \end{bmatrix}$$

We can then proceed to find the reduced echelon form without the cumbersome use of fractions. This process is called using a **linear combination of rows**.

9.5 *Exercises*

Exer. 1–22: Use matrices to solve the system.

$1 \begin{cases} x - 2y - 3z = -1 \\ 2x + y + z = 6 \\ x + 3y - 2z = 13 \end{cases}$
$\quad$
$2 \begin{cases} x + 3y - z = -3 \\ 3x - y + 2z = 1 \\ 2x - y + z = -1 \end{cases}$

$3 \begin{cases} 5x + 2y - z = -7 \\ x - 2y + 2z = 0 \\ 3y + z = 17 \end{cases}$
$\quad$
$4 \begin{cases} 4x - y + 3z = 6 \\ -8x + 3y - 5z = -6 \\ 5x - 4y = -9 \end{cases}$

$5 \begin{cases} 2x + 6y - 4z = 1 \\ x + 3y - 2z = 4 \\ 2x + y - 3z = -7 \end{cases}$
$\quad$
$6 \begin{cases} x + 3y - 3z = -5 \\ 2x - y + z = -3 \\ -6x + 3y - 3z = 4 \end{cases}$

$7 \begin{cases} 2x - 3y + 2z = -3 \\ -3x + 2y + z = 1 \\ 4x + y - 3z = 4 \end{cases}$
$\quad$
$8 \begin{cases} 2x - 3y + z = 2 \\ 3x + 2y - z = -5 \\ 5x - 2y + z = 0 \end{cases}$

$9 \begin{cases} x + 3y + z = 0 \\ x + y - z = 0 \\ x - 2y - 4z = 0 \end{cases}$
$\quad$
$10 \begin{cases} 2x - y + z = 0 \\ x - y - 2z = 0 \\ 2x - 3y - z = 0 \end{cases}$

$11 \begin{cases} 2x + y + z = 0 \\ x - 2y - 2z = 0 \\ x + y + z = 0 \end{cases}$
$\quad$
$12 \begin{cases} x + y - 2z = 0 \\ x - y - 4z = 0 \\ y + z = 0 \end{cases}$

$13 \begin{cases} 3x - 2y + 5z = 7 \\ x + 4y - z = -2 \end{cases}$
$\quad$
$14 \begin{cases} 2x - y + 4z = 8 \\ -3x + y - 2z = 5 \end{cases}$

$15 \begin{cases} 4x - 2y + z = 5 \\ 3x + y - 4z = 0 \end{cases}$
$\quad$
$16 \begin{cases} 5x + 2y - z = 10 \\ y + z = -3 \end{cases}$

$17 \begin{cases} 5x + 2z = 1 \\ y - 3z = 2 \\ 2x + y = 3 \end{cases}$
$\quad$
$18 \begin{cases} 2x - 3y = 12 \\ 3y + z = -2 \\ 5x - 3z = 3 \end{cases}$

$19 \begin{cases} 4x - 3y = 1 \\ 2x + y = -7 \\ -x + y = -1 \end{cases}$
$\quad$
$20 \begin{cases} 2x + 3y = -2 \\ x + y = 1 \\ x - 2y = 13 \end{cases}$

$21 \begin{cases} 2x + 3y = 5 \\ x - 3y = 4 \\ x + y = -2 \end{cases}$
$\quad$
$22 \begin{cases} 4x - y = 2 \\ 2x + 2y = 1 \\ 4x - 5y = 3 \end{cases}$

23 Mixing acid solutions Three solutions contain a certain acid. The first contains 10% acid, the second 30%, and the third 50%. A chemist wishes to use all three solutions to obtain a 50-liter mixture containing 32% acid. If the chemist wants to use twice as much of the 50% solution as of the 30% solution, how many liters of each solution should be used?

24 Filling a pool A swimming pool can be filled by three pipes, A, B, and C. Pipe A alone can fill the pool in 8 hours. If pipes A and C are used together, the pool can be filled in 6 hours; if B and C are used together, it takes 10 hours. How long does it take to fill the pool if all three pipes are used?

25 Production capability A company has three machines, A, B, and C, that are each capable of producing a certain item. However, because of a lack of skilled operators, only two of the machines can be used simultaneously. The following table indicates production over a three-day period, using various combinations of the machines. How long would it take each machine, if used alone, to produce 1000 items?

Machines used	Hours used	Items produced
A and B	6	4500
A and C	8	3600
B and C	7	4900

26 Electrical resistance In electrical circuits, the formula $1/R = (1/R_1) + (1/R_2)$ is used to find the total resistance R if two resistors R_1 and R_2 are connected in parallel. Given three resistors, A, B, and C, suppose that the total resistance is 48 ohms if A and B are connected in parallel, 80 ohms if B and C are connected in parallel, and 60 ohms if A and C are connected in parallel. Find the resistances of A, B, and C.

27 Mixing fertilizers A supplier of lawn products has three types of grass fertilizer, G_1, G_2, and G_3, having nitrogen contents of 30%, 20%, and 15%, respectively. The supplier plans to mix them, obtaining 600 pounds of fertilizer with a

25% nitrogen content. The mixture is to contain 100 pounds more of type G_3 than of type G_2. How much of each type should be used?

28 Particle acceleration If a particle moves along a coordinate line with a constant acceleration a (in cm/sec^2), then at time t (in seconds) its distance $s(t)$ (in centimeters) from the origin is

$$s(t) = \tfrac{1}{2}at^2 + v_0t + s_0$$

for velocity v_0 and distance s_0 from the origin at $t = 0$. If the distances of the particle from the origin at $t = \tfrac{1}{2}$, $t = 1$, and $t = \tfrac{3}{2}$ are 7, 11, and 17, respectively, find a, v_0, and s_0.

29 Electrical currents Shown in the figure is a schematic of an electrical circuit containing three resistors, a 6-volt battery, and a 12-volt battery. It can be shown, using Kirchhoff's laws, that the three currents I_1, I_2, and I_3 are solutions of the following system of equations:

$$\begin{cases} I_1 - I_2 + I_3 = 0 \\ R_1I_1 + R_2I_2 = 6 \\ R_2I_2 + R_3I_3 = 12 \end{cases}$$

Find the three currents if

(a) $R_1 = R_2 = R_3 = 3$ ohms

(b) $R_1 = 4$ ohms, $R_2 = 1$ ohm, and $R_3 = 4$ ohms

Exercise 29

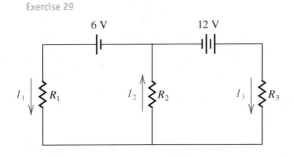

30 Bird population A stable population of 35,000 birds lives on three islands. Each year 10% of the population on island A migrates to island B, 20% of the population on island B migrates to island C, and 5% of the population on island C migrates to island A. Find the number of birds on each island if the population count on each island does not vary from year to year.

31 Blending coffees A shop specializes in preparing blends of gourmet coffees. From Colombian, Costa Rican, and Kenyan coffees, the owner wishes to prepare 1-pound bags that will sell for $12.50. The cost per pound of these coffees is $14, $10, and $12, respectively. The amount of Colombian is to be three times the amount of Costa Rican. Find the amount of each type of coffee in the blend.

32 Weights of chains There are three chains, weighing 450, 610, and 950 ounces, each consisting of links of three different sizes. Each chain has 10 small links. The chains also have 20, 30, and 40 medium links and 30, 40, and 70 large links, respectively. Find the weights of the small, medium, and large links.

33 Traffic flow Shown in the figure is a system of four one-way streets leading into the center of a city. The numbers in the figure denote the average number of vehicles per hour that travel in the directions shown. A total of 300 vehicles enter the area and 300 vehicles leave the area every hour. Signals at intersections A, B, C, and D are to be timed in order to avoid congestion, and this timing will determine traffic flow rates x_1, x_2, x_3, and x_4.

Exercise 33

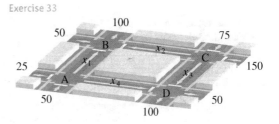

(a) If the number of vehicles entering an intersection per hour must equal the number leaving the intersection per hour, describe the traffic flow rates at each intersection with a system of equations.

(b) If the signal at intersection C is timed so that x_3 is equal to 100, find x_1, x_2, and x_4.

(c) Make use of the system in part (a) to explain why $75 \le x_3 \le 150$.

34 If $f(x) = ax^3 + bx + c$, determine a, b, and c such that the graph of f passes through the points $P(-3, -12)$, $Q(-1, 22)$, and $R(2, 13)$.

Exer. 35–36: Find an equation of the circle of the form $x^2 + y^2 + ax + by + c = 0$ that passes through the given points.

35 $P(2, 1)$, $Q(-1, -4)$, $R(3, 0)$

36 $P(-5, 5)$, $Q(-2, -4)$, $R(2, 4)$

Exer. 37–38: Find an equation of the cubic polynomial $f(x) = ax^3 + bx^2 + cx + d$ that passes through the given points.

37 $P(0, -6)$, $Q(1, -11)$, $R(-1, -5)$, $S(2, -14)$

38 $P(0, 4)$, $Q(1, 2)$, $R(-1, 10)$, $S(2, -2)$

9.6

The Algebra of Matrices

Matrices were introduced in Section 9.5 as an aid to finding solutions of systems of equations. In this section we discuss some of the properties of matrices. These properties are important in advanced fields of mathematics and in applications.

In the following definition, the symbol (a_{ij}) denotes an $m \times n$ matrix A of the type displayed in the definition on page 601. We use similar notations for the matrices B and C.

Definition of Equality and Addition of Matrices	Let $A = (a_{ij})$, $B = (b_{ij})$, and $C = (c_{ij})$ be $m \times n$ matrices. (1) $A = B$ if and only if $a_{ij} = b_{ij}$ for every i and j. (2) $C = A + B$ if and only if $c_{ij} = a_{ij} + b_{ij}$ for every i and j.

Note that two matrices are equal if and only if they have the same size and corresponding elements are equal.

ILLUSTRATION   **Equality of Matrices**

■ $\begin{bmatrix} 1 & 0 & 5 \\ \sqrt[3]{8} & 3^2 & -2 \end{bmatrix} = \begin{bmatrix} (-1)^2 & 0 & \sqrt{25} \\ 2 & 9 & -2 \end{bmatrix}$

Using the parentheses notation for matrices, we may write the definition of addition of two $m \times n$ matrices as

$$(a_{ij}) + (b_{ij}) = (a_{ij} + b_{ij}).$$

Thus, to add two matrices, we add the elements in corresponding positions in each matrix. *Two matrices can be added only if they have the same size.*

ILLUSTRATION Addition of Matrices

- $$\begin{bmatrix} 4 & -5 \\ 0 & 4 \\ -6 & 1 \end{bmatrix} + \begin{bmatrix} 3 & 2 \\ 7 & -4 \\ -2 & 1 \end{bmatrix} = \begin{bmatrix} 4+3 & -5+2 \\ 0+7 & 4+(-4) \\ -6+(-2) & 1+1 \end{bmatrix} = \begin{bmatrix} 7 & -3 \\ 7 & 0 \\ -8 & 2 \end{bmatrix}$$

- $$\begin{bmatrix} 2 & 3 \\ -4 & 1 \end{bmatrix} + \begin{bmatrix} -2 & -3 \\ 4 & -1 \end{bmatrix} = \begin{bmatrix} 0 & 0 \\ 0 & 0 \end{bmatrix}$$

- $$\begin{bmatrix} 1 & 3 & -2 \\ 0 & -5 & 4 \end{bmatrix} + \begin{bmatrix} 0 & 0 & 0 \\ 0 & 0 & 0 \end{bmatrix} = \begin{bmatrix} 1 & 3 & -2 \\ 0 & -5 & 4 \end{bmatrix}$$

The **$m \times n$ zero matrix,** denoted by O, is the matrix with m rows and n columns in which every element is 0.

ILLUSTRATION Zero Matrices

- $$\begin{bmatrix} 0 & 0 \\ 0 & 0 \end{bmatrix}$$
- $$\begin{bmatrix} 0 & 0 \\ 0 & 0 \\ 0 & 0 \end{bmatrix}$$
- $$\begin{bmatrix} 0 & 0 & 0 & 0 \\ 0 & 0 & 0 & 0 \end{bmatrix}$$

The **additive inverse** $-A$ of the matrix $A = (a_{ij})$ is the matrix $(-a_{ij})$ obtained by changing the sign of each nonzero element of A.

ILLUSTRATION Additive Inverse

- $$-\begin{bmatrix} 2 & -3 & 4 \\ -1 & 0 & 5 \end{bmatrix} = \begin{bmatrix} -2 & 3 & -4 \\ 1 & 0 & -5 \end{bmatrix}$$

The proof of the next theorem follows from the definition of addition of matrices.

Theorem on Matrix Properties	If A, B, and C are $m \times n$ matrices and if O is the $m \times n$ zero matrix, then
	(1) $A + B = B + A$
	(2) $A + (B + C) = (A + B) + C$
	(3) $A + O = A$
	(4) $A + (-A) = O$

Subtraction of two $m \times n$ matrices is defined by

$$A - B = A + (-B).$$

Using the parentheses notation, we have

$$(a_{ij}) - (b_{ij}) = (a_{ij}) + (-b_{ij})$$
$$= (a_{ij} - b_{ij}).$$

Thus, to subtract two matrices, we subtract the elements in corresponding positions.

ILLUSTRATION   **Subtraction of Matrices**

$$\begin{bmatrix} 4 & -5 \\ 0 & 4 \\ -6 & 1 \end{bmatrix} - \begin{bmatrix} 3 & 2 \\ 7 & -4 \\ -2 & 1 \end{bmatrix} = \begin{bmatrix} 4-3 & -5-2 \\ 0-7 & 4-(-4) \\ -6-(-2) & 1-1 \end{bmatrix} = \begin{bmatrix} 1 & -7 \\ -7 & 8 \\ -4 & 0 \end{bmatrix}$$

Definition of the Product of a Real Number and a Matrix	The **product** of a real number c and an $m \times n$ matrix $A = (a_{ij})$ is $$cA = (ca_{ij}).$$

Note that to find cA, we multiply each element of A by c.

ILLUSTRATION   **Product of a Real Number and a Matrix**

$$3\begin{bmatrix} 4 & -1 \\ 2 & 3 \end{bmatrix} = \begin{bmatrix} 3 \cdot 4 & 3 \cdot (-1) \\ 3 \cdot 2 & 3 \cdot 3 \end{bmatrix} = \begin{bmatrix} 12 & -3 \\ 6 & 9 \end{bmatrix}$$

We can prove the following.

Theorem on Matrix Properties	If A and B are $m \times n$ matrices and if c and d are real numbers, then **(1)** $c(A + B) = cA + cB$ **(2)** $(c + d)A = cA + dA$ **(3)** $(cd)A = c(dA)$

The next definition, of the product AB of two matrices, may seem unusual, but it has many uses in mathematics and applications. For multiplication, unlike addition, A and B may have different sizes; however, *the number of columns of A must be the same as the number of rows of B.* Thus, if A is $m \times n$, then B must be $n \times p$ for some p. As we shall see, the size of AB is then $m \times p$. If $C = AB$, then a method for finding the element c_{ij} in row i and column j of C is given in the following guidelines.

Guidelines for Finding c_{ij} in the Product $C = AB$ if A is $m \times n$ and B is $n \times p$	*1* Single out the ith row, $\mathbf{R}_i$, of A and the jth column, $\mathbf{C}_j$, of B:

$$\begin{bmatrix} a_{11} & a_{12} & \cdots & a_{1n} \\ \cdot & \cdot & & \cdot \\ \cdot & \cdot & & \cdot \\ a_{i1} & a_{i2} & \cdots & a_{in} \\ \cdot & \cdot & & \cdot \\ \cdot & \cdot & & \cdot \\ a_{m1} & a_{m2} & \cdots & a_{mn} \end{bmatrix} \begin{bmatrix} b_{11} & \cdots & b_{1j} & \cdots & b_{1p} \\ b_{21} & \cdots & b_{2j} & \cdots & b_{2p} \\ \cdot & & \cdot & & \cdot \\ \cdot & & \cdot & & \cdot \\ b_{n1} & \cdots & b_{nj} & \cdots & b_{np} \end{bmatrix}$$

2 *Simultaneously* move to the right along $\mathbf{R}_i$ and down $\mathbf{C}_j$, multiplying pairs of elements, to obtain

$$a_{i1}b_{1j}, \; a_{i2}b_{2j}, \; a_{i3}b_{3j}, \ldots, a_{in}b_{nj}.$$

3 Add the products of the pairs in guideline 2 to obtain c_{ij}:

$$c_{ij} = a_{i1}b_{1j} + a_{i2}b_{2j} + a_{i3}b_{3j} + \cdots + a_{in}b_{nj}$$

Using the guidelines, we see that the element c_{11} in the first row and the first column of $C = AB$ is

$$c_{11} = a_{11}b_{11} + a_{12}b_{21} + a_{13}b_{31} + \cdots + a_{1n}b_{n1}.$$

The element c_{mp} in the last row and the last column of $C = AB$ is

$$c_{mp} = a_{m1}b_{1p} + a_{m2}b_{2p} + a_{m3}b_{3p} + \cdots + a_{mn}b_{np}.$$

The preceding discussion is summarized in the next definition.

Definition of the Product of Two Matrices	Let $A = (a_{ij})$ be an $m \times n$ matrix and let $B = (b_{ij})$ be an $n \times p$ matrix. The **product** AB is the $m \times p$ matrix $C = (c_{ij})$ such that $$c_{ij} = a_{i1}b_{1j} + a_{i2}b_{2j} + a_{i3}b_{3j} + \cdots + a_{in}b_{nj}$$ for $i = 1, 2, 3, \ldots, m$ and $j = 1, 2, 3, \ldots, p$.

The following diagram may help you remember the relationship between sizes of matrices when working with a product AB.

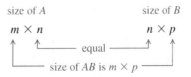

The next illustration contains some special cases.

ILLUSTRATION **Sizes of Matrices in Products**

Size of A	Size of B	Size of AB
■ 2×3	3×5	2×5
■ 4×2	2×3	4×3
■ 3×1	1×3	3×3
■ 1×3	3×1	1×1
■ 5×3	3×5	5×5
■ 5×3	5×3	AB is not defined

In the following example we find the product of two specific matrices.

EXAMPLE 1 Finding the product of two matrices

Find the product AB if

$$A = \begin{bmatrix} 1 & 2 & -3 \\ 4 & 0 & -2 \end{bmatrix} \quad \text{and} \quad B = \begin{bmatrix} 5 & -4 & 2 & 0 \\ -1 & 6 & 3 & 1 \\ 7 & 0 & 5 & 8 \end{bmatrix}.$$

SOLUTION   The matrix A is 2×3, and the matrix B is 3×4. Hence, the product $C = AB$ is defined and is 2×4. We next use the guidelines to find the elements $c_{11}, c_{12}, \ldots, c_{24}$ of the product. For instance, to find the element c_{23} we single out the second row, $\mathbf{R}_2$, of A and the third column, $\mathbf{C}_3$, of B, as illustrated below, and then use guidelines 2 and 3 to obtain

$$c_{23} = 4 \cdot 2 + 0 \cdot 3 + (-2) \cdot 5 = -2.$$

$$\begin{bmatrix} 1 & 2 & -3 \\ 4 & 0 & -2 \end{bmatrix} \begin{bmatrix} 5 & -4 & 2 & 0 \\ -1 & 6 & 3 & 1 \\ 7 & 0 & 5 & 8 \end{bmatrix} = \begin{bmatrix} & & & \\ & & -2 & \end{bmatrix}$$

Similarly, to find the element c_{12} in row 1 and column 2 of the product, we proceed as follows:

$$c_{12} = 1 \cdot (-4) + 2 \cdot 6 + (-3) \cdot 0 = 8$$

$$\begin{bmatrix} 1 & 2 & -3 \\ 4 & 0 & -2 \end{bmatrix} \begin{bmatrix} 5 & -4 & 2 & 0 \\ -1 & 6 & 3 & 1 \\ 7 & 0 & 5 & 8 \end{bmatrix} = \begin{bmatrix} & 8 & & \\ & & -2 & \end{bmatrix}$$

The remaining elements of the product are calculated as follows, where we have indicated the row of A and the column of B that are used when guideline 1 is applied.

Row of A	Column of B	Element of C
R_1	C_1	$c_{11} = 1 \cdot 5 \quad + 2 \cdot (-1) + (-3) \cdot 7 = -18$
R_1	C_3	$c_{13} = 1 \cdot 2 \quad + 2 \cdot 3 \quad + (-3) \cdot 5 = -7$
R_1	C_4	$c_{14} = 1 \cdot 0 \quad + 2 \cdot 1 \quad + (-3) \cdot 8 = -22$
R_2	C_1	$c_{21} = 4 \cdot 5 \quad + 0 \cdot (-1) + (-2) \cdot 7 = 6$
R_2	C_2	$c_{22} = 4 \cdot (-4) + 0 \cdot 6 \quad + (-2) \cdot 0 = -16$
R_2	C_4	$c_{24} = 4 \cdot 0 \quad + 0 \cdot 1 \quad + (-2) \cdot 8 = -16$

Hence,

$$AB = \begin{bmatrix} 1 & 2 & -3 \\ 4 & 0 & -2 \end{bmatrix} \begin{bmatrix} 5 & -4 & 2 & 0 \\ -1 & 6 & 3 & 1 \\ 7 & 0 & 5 & 8 \end{bmatrix}$$

$$= \begin{bmatrix} -18 & 8 & -7 & -22 \\ 6 & -16 & -2 & -16 \end{bmatrix}.$$

A matrix is a **row matrix** if it has only one row. A **column matrix** has only one column. The following illustration contains some products involving row and column matrices. You should check each entry in the products.

ILLUSTRATION **Products Involving Row and Column Matrices**

■ $\begin{bmatrix} -2 & 4 \\ 0 & -1 \\ 5 & 3 \end{bmatrix} \begin{bmatrix} -2 \\ 1 \end{bmatrix} = \begin{bmatrix} 8 \\ -1 \\ -7 \end{bmatrix}$ ■ $\begin{bmatrix} 3 & -1 & 2 \end{bmatrix} \begin{bmatrix} -2 & 4 \\ 0 & -1 \\ 5 & 3 \end{bmatrix} = \begin{bmatrix} 4 & 19 \end{bmatrix}$

■ $\begin{bmatrix} -2 \\ 3 \end{bmatrix} \begin{bmatrix} 1 & 5 \end{bmatrix} = \begin{bmatrix} -2 & -10 \\ 3 & 15 \end{bmatrix}$ ■ $\begin{bmatrix} 1 & 5 \end{bmatrix} \begin{bmatrix} -2 \\ 3 \end{bmatrix} = \begin{bmatrix} 13 \end{bmatrix}$

The product operation for matrices is not commutative. For example, if A is 2×3 and B is 3×4, then AB may be found, since the number of columns of A is the same as the number of rows of B. However, BA is undefined, since the number of columns of B is different from the number of rows of A. Even if AB and BA are both defined, it is often true that these products are different. This is illustrated in the next example, along with the fact that the product of two nonzero matrices may equal a zero matrix.

EXAMPLE 2 Matrix multiplication is not commutative

If $A = \begin{bmatrix} 2 & 2 \\ -1 & -1 \end{bmatrix}$ and $B = \begin{bmatrix} 1 & 2 \\ 1 & 2 \end{bmatrix}$, show that $AB \neq BA$.

SOLUTION   Using the definition of the product of two matrices, we obtain the following:

$$AB = \begin{bmatrix} 2 & 2 \\ -1 & -1 \end{bmatrix}\begin{bmatrix} 1 & 2 \\ 1 & 2 \end{bmatrix} = \begin{bmatrix} 4 & 8 \\ -2 & -4 \end{bmatrix}$$

$$BA = \begin{bmatrix} 1 & 2 \\ 1 & 2 \end{bmatrix}\begin{bmatrix} 2 & 2 \\ -1 & -1 \end{bmatrix} = \begin{bmatrix} 0 & 0 \\ 0 & 0 \end{bmatrix}$$

Hence, $AB \neq BA$. Note that the last equality shows that *the product of two nonzero matrices can equal a zero matrix.*

Although matrix multiplication is not commutative, it is associative. Thus, if A is $m \times n$, B is $n \times p$, and C is $p \times q$, then

$$A(BC) = (AB)C.$$

The distributive properties also hold if the matrices involved have the proper number of rows and columns. If A_1 and A_2 are $m \times n$ matrices and if B_1 and B_2 are $n \times p$ matrices, then

$$A_1(B_1 + B_2) = A_1B_1 + A_1B_2$$
$$(A_1 + A_2)B_1 = A_1B_1 + A_2B_1.$$

As a special case, if all matrices are square, of order n, then both the associative and the distributive property are true.

We conclude this section with an application of the product of two matrices.

EXAMPLE 3   An application of a matrix product

(a) Three investors, I_1, I_2, and I_3, each own a certain number of shares of four stocks, S_1, S_2, S_3, and S_4, according to matrix A. Matrix B contains the present value V of each share of each stock. Find AB, and interpret the meaning of its elements.

number of shares of stock   share value

$$\text{investors} \begin{cases} I_1 \\ I_2 \\ I_3 \end{cases} \begin{array}{cccc} S_1 & S_2 & S_3 & S_4 \end{array} \begin{bmatrix} 50 & 100 & 30 & 25 \\ 100 & 150 & 10 & 30 \\ 100 & 50 & 40 & 100 \end{bmatrix} = A, \qquad \text{stocks} \begin{cases} S_1 \\ S_2 \\ S_3 \\ S_4 \end{cases} \begin{array}{c} V \end{array}\begin{bmatrix} 20.37 \\ 16.21 \\ 90.80 \\ 42.75 \end{bmatrix} = B$$

(b) Matrix C contains the change in the value of each stock for the last week. Find AC, and interpret the meaning of its elements.

$$\text{stocks} \begin{cases} S_1 \\ S_2 \\ S_3 \\ S_4 \end{cases} \begin{bmatrix} +1.03 \\ -0.22 \\ -1.35 \\ +0.15 \end{bmatrix} = C$$

SOLUTION

(a) Since A is a 3×4 matrix and B is a 4×1 matrix, the product AB is a 3×1 matrix:

$$AB = \begin{bmatrix} 50 & 100 & 30 & 25 \\ 100 & 150 & 10 & 30 \\ 100 & 50 & 40 & 100 \end{bmatrix} \begin{bmatrix} 20.37 \\ 16.21 \\ 90.80 \\ 42.75 \end{bmatrix} = \begin{bmatrix} 6432.25 \\ 6659.00 \\ 10{,}754.50 \end{bmatrix}$$

The first element in the product AB, 6432.25, was obtained from the computation

$$50(20.37) + 100(16.21) + 30(90.80) + 25(42.75)$$

and represents the total value that investor I_1 has in all four stocks. Similarly, the second and third elements represent the total value for investors I_2 and I_3, respectively.

(b)

$$AC = \begin{bmatrix} 50 & 100 & 30 & 25 \\ 100 & 150 & 10 & 30 \\ 100 & 50 & 40 & 100 \end{bmatrix} \begin{bmatrix} +1.03 \\ -0.22 \\ -1.35 \\ +0.15 \end{bmatrix} = \begin{bmatrix} -7.25 \\ 61.00 \\ 53.00 \end{bmatrix}$$

The first element in the product AC, -7.25, indicates that the total value that investor I_1 has in all four stocks went down $7.25 in the last week. The second and third elements indicate that the total value that investors I_2 and I_3 have in all four stocks went up $61.00 and $53.00, respectively.

9.6 Exercises

Exer. 1–8: Find, if possible, $A + B$, $A - B$, $2A$, and $-3B$.

1 $A = \begin{bmatrix} 5 & -2 \\ 1 & 3 \end{bmatrix}$, $B = \begin{bmatrix} 4 & 1 \\ -3 & 2 \end{bmatrix}$

2 $A = \begin{bmatrix} 3 & 0 \\ -1 & 2 \end{bmatrix}$, $B = \begin{bmatrix} 3 & -4 \\ 1 & 1 \end{bmatrix}$

3 $A = \begin{bmatrix} 6 & -1 \\ 2 & 0 \\ -3 & 4 \end{bmatrix}$, $B = \begin{bmatrix} 3 & 1 \\ -1 & 5 \\ 6 & 0 \end{bmatrix}$

4 $A = \begin{bmatrix} 0 & -2 & 7 \\ 5 & 4 & -3 \end{bmatrix}$, $B = \begin{bmatrix} 8 & 4 & 0 \\ 0 & 1 & 4 \end{bmatrix}$

5 $A = \begin{bmatrix} 4 & -3 & 2 \end{bmatrix}$, $B = \begin{bmatrix} 7 & 0 & -5 \end{bmatrix}$

6 $A = \begin{bmatrix} 7 \\ -16 \end{bmatrix}$, $B = \begin{bmatrix} -11 \\ 9 \end{bmatrix}$

7 $A = \begin{bmatrix} 3 & -2 & 2 \\ 0 & 1 & -4 \\ -3 & 2 & -1 \end{bmatrix}$, $B = \begin{bmatrix} 4 & 0 \\ 2 & -1 \\ -1 & 3 \end{bmatrix}$

8 $A = \begin{bmatrix} 2 & 1 \end{bmatrix}$, $B = \begin{bmatrix} 3 & -1 & 5 \end{bmatrix}$

Exer. 9–10: Find the given element of the matrix product $C = AB$ in the listed exercise.

9 c_{21}; Exercise 15

10 c_{23}; Exercise 16

Exer. 11–22: Find, if possible, AB and BA.

11 $A = \begin{bmatrix} 2 & 6 \\ 3 & -4 \end{bmatrix}$, $B = \begin{bmatrix} 5 & -2 \\ 1 & 7 \end{bmatrix}$

12 $A = \begin{bmatrix} 4 & -2 \\ -2 & 1 \end{bmatrix}$, $B = \begin{bmatrix} 2 & 1 \\ 4 & 2 \end{bmatrix}$

13 $A = \begin{bmatrix} 3 & 0 & -1 \\ 0 & 4 & 2 \\ 5 & -3 & 1 \end{bmatrix}$, $B = \begin{bmatrix} 1 & -5 & 0 \\ 4 & 1 & -2 \\ 0 & -1 & 3 \end{bmatrix}$

14 $A = \begin{bmatrix} 5 & 0 & 0 \\ 0 & -3 & 0 \\ 0 & 0 & 2 \end{bmatrix}$, $B = \begin{bmatrix} 3 & 0 & 0 \\ 0 & 4 & 0 \\ 0 & 0 & -2 \end{bmatrix}$

15 $A = \begin{bmatrix} 4 & -3 & 1 \\ -5 & 2 & 2 \end{bmatrix}$, $B = \begin{bmatrix} 2 & 1 \\ 0 & 1 \\ -4 & 7 \end{bmatrix}$

16 $A = \begin{bmatrix} 2 & 1 & -1 & 0 \\ 3 & -2 & 0 & 5 \\ -2 & 1 & 4 & 2 \end{bmatrix}$, $B = \begin{bmatrix} 5 & -3 & 1 \\ 1 & 2 & 0 \\ -1 & 0 & 4 \\ 0 & -2 & 3 \end{bmatrix}$

17 $A = \begin{bmatrix} 1 & 2 & 3 \\ 4 & 5 & 6 \\ 7 & 8 & 9 \end{bmatrix}$, $B = \begin{bmatrix} 1 & 0 & 0 \\ 0 & 1 & 0 \\ 0 & 0 & 1 \end{bmatrix}$

18 $A = \begin{bmatrix} 1 & 2 & 3 \\ 2 & 3 & 1 \\ 3 & 1 & 2 \end{bmatrix}$, $B = \begin{bmatrix} 2 & 0 & 0 \\ 0 & 2 & 0 \\ 0 & 0 & 2 \end{bmatrix}$

19 $A = \begin{bmatrix} -3 & 7 & 2 \end{bmatrix}$, $B = \begin{bmatrix} 1 \\ 4 \\ -5 \end{bmatrix}$

20 $A = \begin{bmatrix} 4 & 8 \end{bmatrix}$, $B = \begin{bmatrix} -3 \\ 2 \end{bmatrix}$

21 $A = \begin{bmatrix} 2 & 0 & 1 \\ -1 & 2 & 0 \end{bmatrix}$, $B = \begin{bmatrix} 1 & -1 & 2 \\ 3 & 1 & 0 \\ 0 & 2 & 1 \end{bmatrix}$

22 $A = \begin{bmatrix} 3 & -1 & 4 \end{bmatrix}$, $B = \begin{bmatrix} -2 \\ 5 \end{bmatrix}$

Exer. 23–26: Find AB.

23 $A = \begin{bmatrix} 4 & -2 \\ 0 & 3 \\ -7 & 5 \end{bmatrix}$, $B = \begin{bmatrix} 3 \\ 4 \end{bmatrix}$

24 $A = \begin{bmatrix} 4 \\ -3 \\ 2 \end{bmatrix}$, $B = \begin{bmatrix} 5 & 1 \end{bmatrix}$

25 $A = \begin{bmatrix} 2 & 1 & 0 & -3 \\ -7 & 0 & -2 & 4 \end{bmatrix}$, $B = \begin{bmatrix} 4 & -2 & 0 \\ 1 & 1 & -2 \\ 0 & 0 & 5 \\ -3 & -1 & 0 \end{bmatrix}$

26 $A = \begin{bmatrix} 1 & 2 & -3 \\ 4 & -5 & 6 \end{bmatrix}$, $B = \begin{bmatrix} 1 & -1 & 0 & 2 \\ -2 & 3 & 1 & 0 \\ 0 & 4 & 0 & -3 \end{bmatrix}$

Exer. 27–30: Let

$$A = \begin{bmatrix} 1 & 2 \\ 0 & -3 \end{bmatrix}, \quad B = \begin{bmatrix} 2 & -1 \\ 3 & 1 \end{bmatrix}, \quad C = \begin{bmatrix} 3 & 1 \\ -2 & 0 \end{bmatrix}.$$

Verify the statement.

27 $(A + B)(A - B) \neq A^2 - B^2$, where $A^2 = AA$ and $B^2 = BB$.

28 $(A + B)(A + B) \neq A^2 + 2AB + B^2$

29 $A(B + C) = AB + AC$

30 $A(BC) = (AB)C$

Exer 31–34: Verify the identity for

$$A = \begin{bmatrix} a & b \\ c & d \end{bmatrix}, \quad B = \begin{bmatrix} p & q \\ r & s \end{bmatrix}, \quad C = \begin{bmatrix} w & x \\ y & z \end{bmatrix},$$

and real numbers m and n.

31 $m(A + B) = mA + mB$ 32 $(m + n)A = mA + nA$

33 $A(B + C) = AB + AC$ 34 $A(BC) = (AB)C$

35 Value of inventory A store stocks these sizes of towels, each available in five colors: small, priced at \$8.99 each; medium, priced at \$10.99 each; and large, priced at \$12.99 each. The store's current inventory is as follows:

Towel size	Colors				
	White	Tan	Beige	Pink	Yellow
Small	400	400	300	250	100
Medium	550	450	500	200	100
Large	500	500	600	300	200

(a) Organize these data into an inventory matrix A and a price matrix B so that the product $C = AB$ is defined.

(b) Find C.

(c) Interpret the meaning of element c_{51} in C.

36 Building costs A housing contractor has orders for 4 one-bedroom units, 10 two-bedroom units, and 6 three-bedroom units. The labor and material costs (in thousands of dollars) are given in the following table.

	1-Bedroom	2-Bedroom	3-Bedroom
Labor	70	95	117
Materials	90	105	223

(a) Organize these data into an order matrix A and a cost matrix B so that the product $C = AB$ is defined.

(b) Find C.

(c) Interpret the meaning of each element in C.

Appendixes

APPENDIX I

Common Graphs and Their Equations

(Graphs of conics appear on the back endpaper of this text.)

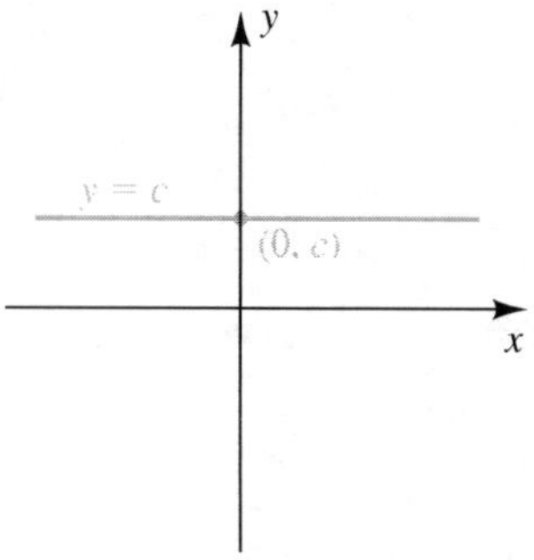

Horizontal line; constant function

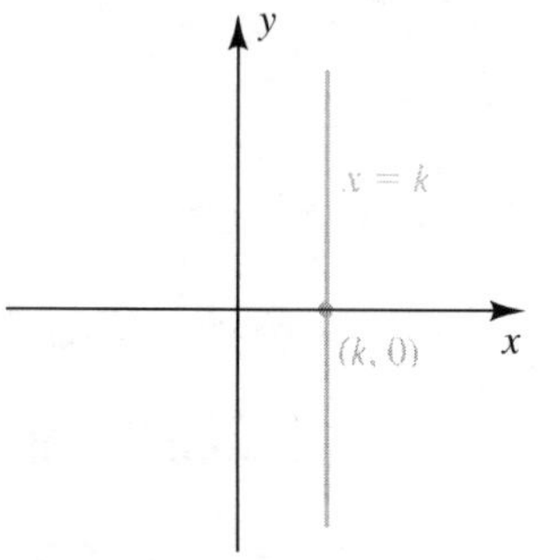

Vertical line

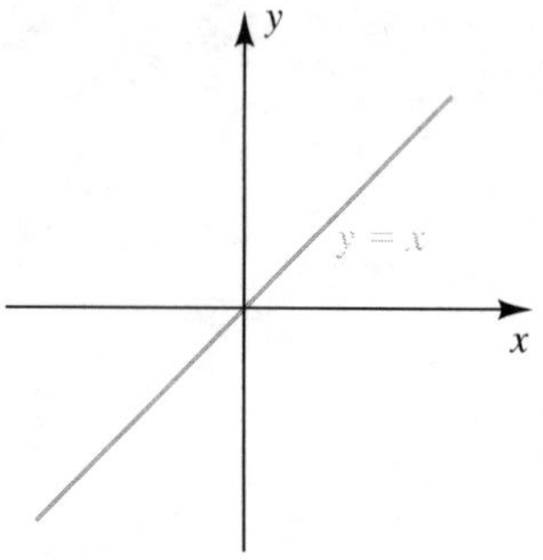

Identity function

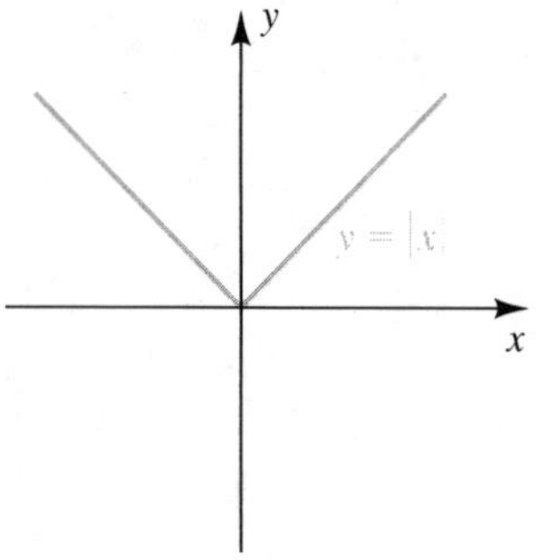

Absolute value function

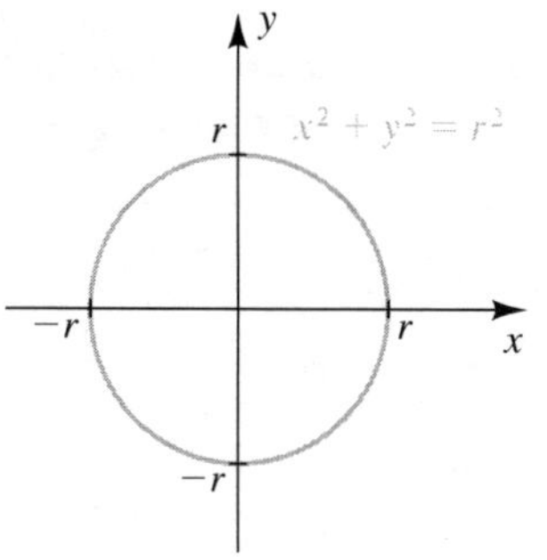

Circle with center (0, 0) and radius r

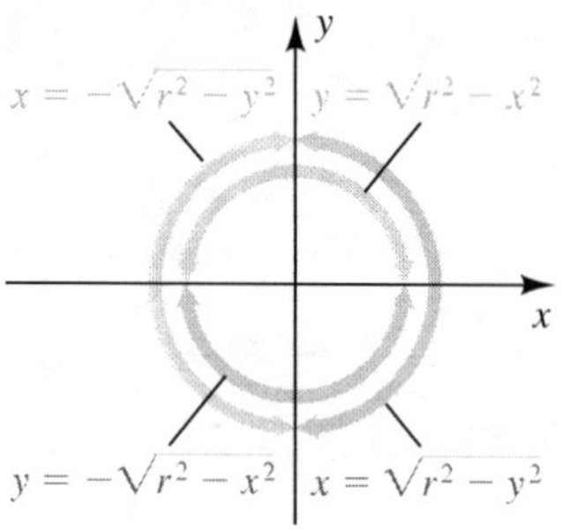

Semicircles

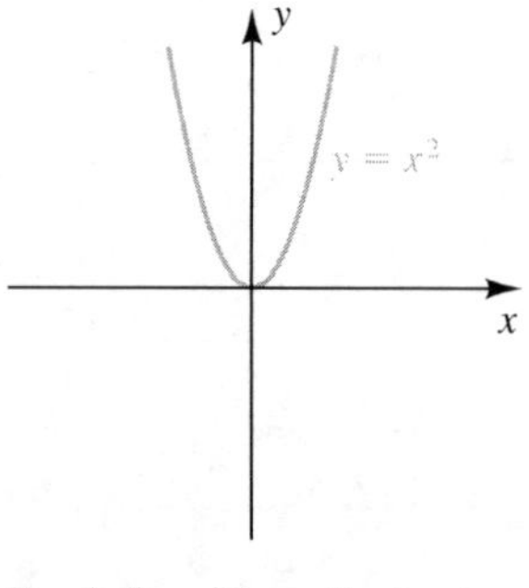

Parabola with vertical axis; squaring function

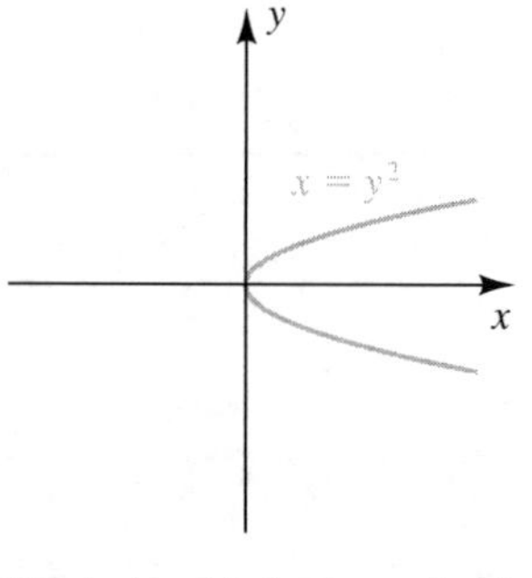

Parabola with horizontal axis

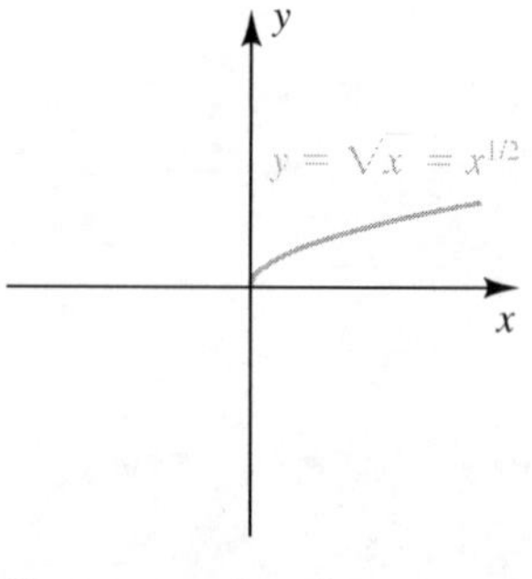

Square root function

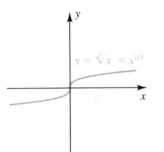

Cube root function

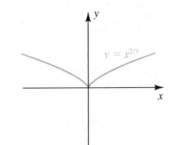

A graph with a cusp at the origin

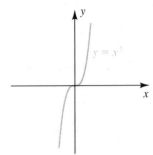

Cubing function

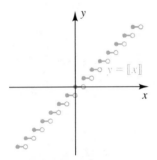

Greatest integer function

Reciprocal function

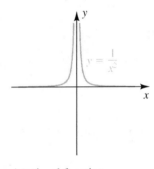

A rational function

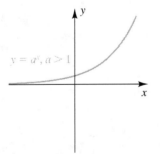

Exponential growth function
(includes natural exponential
function)

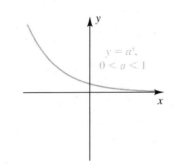

Exponential decay function

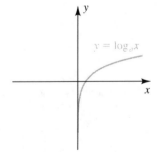

Logarithmic function
(includes common and
natural logarithmic
functions)

APPENDIX II

A Summary of Graph Transformations

The graph of $y = f(x)$ is shown in black in each figure. The domain of f is $[-1, 3]$ and the range of f is $[-4, 3]$.

$y = g(x) = f(x) + 3$

The graph of f is shifted vertically upward 3 units.
Domain of g: $[-1, 3]$ Range of g: $[-1, 6]$

$y = h(x) = f(x) - 4$

The graph of f is shifted vertically downward 4 units.
Domain of h: $[-1, 3]$ Range of h: $[-8, -1]$

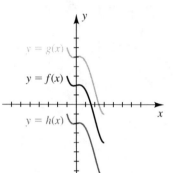

$y = g(x) = f(x - 3)$

The graph of f is shifted horizontally to the right 3 units.
Domain of g: $[2, 6]$ Range of g: $[-4, 3]$

$y = h(x) = f(x + 6)$

The graph of f is shifted horizontally to the left 6 units.
Domain of h: $[-7, -3]$ Range of h: $[-4, 3]$

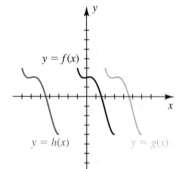

$y = g(x) = 2f(x)$ $[2 > 1]$

The graph of f is stretched vertically by a factor of 2.
Domain of g: $[-1, 3]$ Range of g: $[-8, 6]$

$y = h(x) = \frac{1}{2}f(x)$ $\left[\frac{1}{2} < 1\right]$

The graph of f is compressed vertically by a factor of 2.
Domain of h: $[-1, 3]$ Range of h: $\left[-2, \frac{3}{2}\right]$

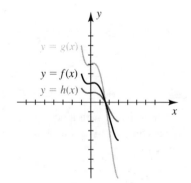

$$y = g(x) = f(2x) \quad [2 > 1]$$

The graph of f is compressed horizontally by a factor of 2.
Domain of g: $\left[-\frac{1}{2}, \frac{3}{2}\right]$ Range of g: $[-4, 3]$

$$y = h(x) = f\left(\tfrac{1}{2}x\right) \quad \left[\tfrac{1}{2} < 1\right]$$

The graph of f is stretched horizontally by a factor of 2.
Domain of h: $[-2, 6]$ Range of h: $[-4, 3]$

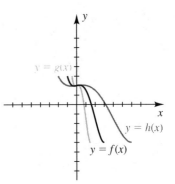

$$y = g(x) = -f(x)$$

The graph of f is reflected through the x-axis.
Domain of g: $[-1, 3]$ Range of g: $[-3, 4]$

$$y = h(x) = f(-x)$$

The graph of f is reflected through the y-axis.
Domain of h: $[-3, 1]$ Range of h: $[-4, 3]$

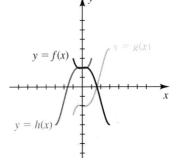

$$y = g(x) = |f(x)|$$

Reflect points on f with negative y-values through the x-axis.
Domain of g: $[-1, 3]$ Range of g: $[0, 4]$

$$y = h(x) = f(|x|)$$

Reflect points on f with positive x-values through the y-axis.
Domain of h: $[-3, 3]$ Range of h: $[-4, 3]$ at most.
In this case, the range is a subset of $[-4, 3]$.

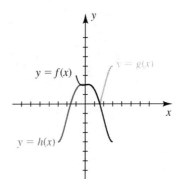

APPENDIX III

Graphs of Trigonometric Functions and Their Inverses

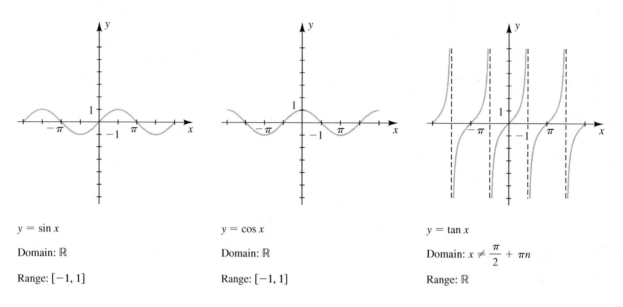

$y = \sin x$

Domain: $\mathbb{R}$

Range: $[-1, 1]$

$y = \cos x$

Domain: $\mathbb{R}$

Range: $[-1, 1]$

$y = \tan x$

Domain: $x \neq \dfrac{\pi}{2} + \pi n$

Range: $\mathbb{R}$

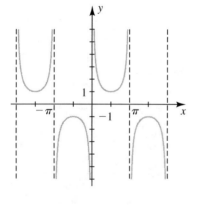

$y = \csc x$

Domain: $x \neq \pi n$

Range: $(-\infty, -1] \cup [1, \infty)$

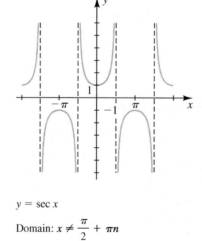

$y = \sec x$

Domain: $x \neq \dfrac{\pi}{2} + \pi n$

Range: $(-\infty, -1] \cup [1, \infty)$

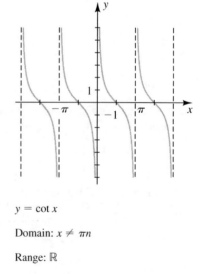

$y = \cot x$

Domain: $x \neq \pi n$

Range: $\mathbb{R}$

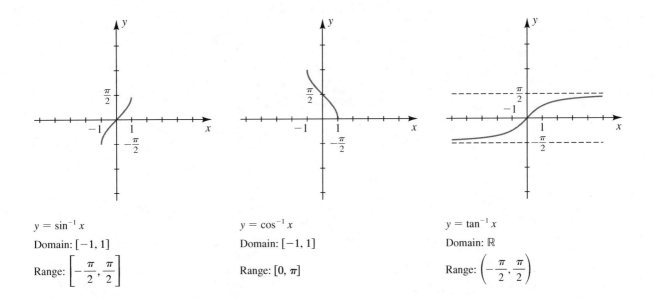

$y = \sin^{-1} x$

Domain: $[-1, 1]$

Range: $\left[-\dfrac{\pi}{2}, \dfrac{\pi}{2} \right]$

$y = \cos^{-1} x$

Domain: $[-1, 1]$

Range: $[0, \pi]$

$y = \tan^{-1} x$

Domain: $\mathbb{R}$

Range: $\left(-\dfrac{\pi}{2}, \dfrac{\pi}{2} \right)$

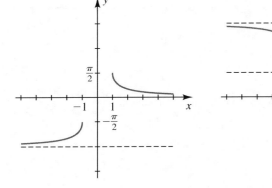

$y = \csc^{-1} x$

Domain: $(-\infty, -1] \cup [1, \infty)$

Range: $\left(-\pi, -\dfrac{\pi}{2} \right] \cup \left(0, \dfrac{\pi}{2} \right]$

$y = \sec^{-1} x$

Domain: $(-\infty, -1] \cup [1, \infty)$

Range: $\left[0, \dfrac{\pi}{2} \right) \cup \left[\pi, \dfrac{3\pi}{2} \right)$

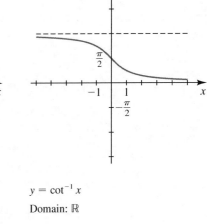

$y = \cot^{-1} x$

Domain: $\mathbb{R}$

Range: $(0, \pi)$

APPENDIX IV

Values of the Trigonometric Functions of Special Angles on a Unit Circle

$$P(x, y) = P(\cos t, \sin t)$$

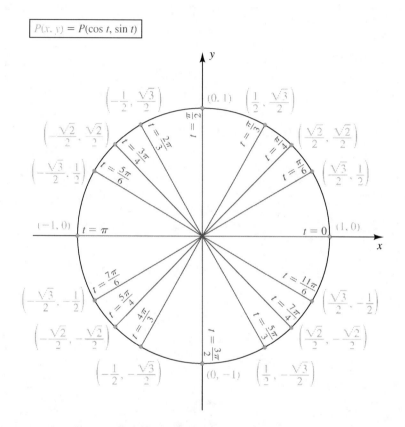

To find the values of the other trigonometric functions, use the following definitions:

$$\tan t = \frac{y}{x} \ (\text{if } x \neq 0) \qquad \cot t = \frac{x}{y} \ (\text{if } y \neq 0)$$

$$\sec t = \frac{1}{x} \ (\text{if } x \neq 0) \qquad \csc t = \frac{1}{y} \ (\text{if } y \neq 0)$$

Answers to Selected Exercises

A *Student's Solutions Manual* to accompany this textbook is available from your college bookstore. The guide contains detailed solutions to approximately one-half of the exercises, as well as strategies for solving other exercises in the text.

Chapter 1

EXERCISES 1.1

1 (a) Negative (b) Positive (c) Negative
   (d) Positive
3 (a) $<$ (b) $>$ (c) $=$
5 (a) $>$ (b) $>$ (c) $>$
7 (a) $x < 0$ (b) $y \geq 0$ (c) $q \leq \pi$ (d) $2 < d < 4$
   (e) $t \geq 5$ (f) $-z \leq 3$ (g) $\dfrac{p}{q} \leq 7$ (h) $\dfrac{1}{w} \geq 9$
   (i) $|x| > 7$ 9 (a) 5 (b) 3 (c) 11
11 (a) -15 (b) -3 (c) 11
13 (a) $4 - \pi$ (b) $4 - \pi$ (c) $1.5 - \sqrt{2}$
15 (a) 4 (b) 12 (c) 12 (d) 8
17 (a) 10 (b) 9 (c) 9 (d) 19 19 $|7 - x| < 5$
21 $|-3 - x| \geq 8$ 23 $|x - 4| \leq 3$ 25 $-x - 3$
27 $2 - x$ 29 $b - a$ 31 $x^2 + 4$ 33 $\neq$ 35 $=$
37 $\neq$ 39 $=$ 41 (a) 8.4652 (b) 14.1428
43 (a) 6.557×10^{-1} (b) 6.708×10^{1}
45 Construct a right triangle with sides of lengths $\sqrt{2}$ and 1. The hypotenuse will have length $\sqrt{3}$. Next, construct a right triangle with sides of lengths $\sqrt{3}$ and $\sqrt{2}$. The hypotenuse will have length $\sqrt{5}$.
47 The large rectangle has area $a(b + c)$. The sum of the areas of the two small rectangles is $ab + ac$.
49 (a) 4.27×10^5 (b) 9.8×10^{-8} (c) 8.1×10^8
51 (a) 830,000 (b) 0.000 000 000 002 9
    (c) 563,000,000
53 1.7×10^{-24} 55 5.87×10^{12} 57 1.678×10^{-24} g
59 4.1472×10^6 frames
61 (a) 201.6 lb (b) 32.256 tons

EXERCISES 1.2

1 $\dfrac{16}{81}$ 3 $\dfrac{9}{8}$ 5 $\dfrac{-47}{3}$ 7 $\dfrac{1}{8}$ 9 $\dfrac{1}{25}$ 11 $8x^9$
13 $\dfrac{6}{x}$ 15 $-2a^{14}$ 17 $\dfrac{9}{2}$ 19 $\dfrac{12u^{11}}{v^2}$ 21 $\dfrac{4}{xy}$
23 $\dfrac{9y^6}{x^8}$ 25 $\dfrac{81}{64}y^6$ 27 $\dfrac{s^6}{4r^8}$ 29 $\dfrac{20y}{x^3}$ 31 $9x^{10}y^{14}$
33 $8a^2$ 35 $24x^{3/2}$ 37 $\dfrac{1}{9a^4}$ 39 $\dfrac{8}{x^{1/2}}$ 41 $4x^2y^4$

43 $\dfrac{3}{x^3y^2}$ 45 1 47 $x^{3/4}$ 49 $(a + b)^{2/3}$
51 $(x^2 + y^2)^{1/2}$ 53 (a) $4x\sqrt{x}$ (b) $8x\sqrt{x}$
55 (a) $8 - \sqrt[3]{y}$ (b) $\sqrt[3]{8 - y}$ 57 9 59 $-2\sqrt[5]{2}$
61 $\dfrac{1}{2}\sqrt[3]{4}$ 63 $\dfrac{3y^3}{x^2}$ 65 $\dfrac{2a^2}{b}$ 67 $\dfrac{1}{2y^2}\sqrt{6xy}$
69 $\dfrac{xy}{3}\sqrt[3]{6y}$ 71 $\dfrac{x}{3}\sqrt[4]{15x^2y^3}$ 73 $\dfrac{1}{2}\sqrt[5]{20x^4y^2}$
75 $\dfrac{3x^5}{y^2}$ 77 $\dfrac{2x}{y^2}\sqrt[5]{x^2y^4}$ 79 $-3tv^2$ 81 $|x^3|y^2$
83 $x^2|y - 1|^3$ 85 $\neq$; $(a^r)^2 = a^{2r} \neq a^{(r^2)}$
87 $\neq$; $(ab)^{xy} = a^{xy}b^{xy} \neq a^xb^y$
89 $=$; $\sqrt[n]{\dfrac{1}{c}} = \left(\dfrac{1}{c}\right)^{1/n} = \dfrac{1^{1/n}}{c^{1/n}} = \dfrac{1}{\sqrt[n]{c}}$
91 (a) 1.5518 (b) 8.5499
93 (a) 2.0351 (b) 3.9670 95 $232,825.78
97 2.82 m 99 The 120-kg lifter

101

Height	Weight	Height	Weight
64	137	72	168
65	141	73	172
66	145	74	176
67	148	75	180
68	152	76	184
69	156	77	188
70	160	78	192
71	164	79	196

EXERCISES 1.3

1 $12x^3 - 13x + 1$ 3 $x^3 - 2x^2 + 4$
5 $6x^2 + x - 35$ 7 $15x^2 + 31xy + 14y^2$
9 $6u^2 - 13u - 12$ 11 $6x^3 + 37x^2 + 30x - 25$
13 $3t^4 + 5t^3 - 15t^2 + 9t - 10$
15 $2x^6 + 2x^5 - 2x^4 + 8x^3 + 10x^2 - 10x - 10$
17 $4y^2 - 5x$ 19 $3v^2 - 2u^2 + uv^2$ 21 $4x^2 - 9y^2$
23 $x^4 - 4y^2$ 25 $x^4 + 5x^2 - 36$
27 $9x^2 + 12xy + 4y^2$ 29 $x^4 - 6x^2y^2 + 9y^4$
31 $x^4 - 8x^2 + 16$ 33 $x - y$ 35 $x - y$
37 $x^3 - 6x^2y + 12xy^2 - 8y^3$
39 $8x^3 + 36x^2y + 54xy^2 + 27y^3$
41 $a^2 + b^2 + c^2 + 2ab - 2ac - 2bc$
43 $4x^2 + y^2 + 9z^2 + 4xy - 12xz - 6yz$

45 $s(r + 4t)$ **47** $3a^2b(b - 2)$ **49** $3x^2y^2(y - 3x)$
51 $5x^3y^2(3y^3 - 5x + 2x^3y^2)$ **53** $(8x + 3)(x - 7)$
55 Irreducible   **57** $(3x - 4)(2x + 5)$
59 $(3x - 5)(4x - 3)$ **61** $(2x - 5)^2$ **63** $(5z + 3)^2$
65 $(5x + 2y)(9x + 4y)$ **67** $(6r + 5t)(6r - 5t)$
69 $(z^2 + 8w)(z^2 - 8w)$ **71** $x^2(x + 2)(x - 2)$
73 Irreducible   **75** $3(5x + 4y)(5x - 4y)$
77 $(4x + 3)(16x^2 - 12x + 9)$
79 $(4x - y^2)(16x^2 + 4xy^2 + y^4)$
81 $(7x + y^3)(49x^2 - 7xy^3 + y^6)$
83 $(5 - 3x)(25 + 15x + 9x^2)$
85 $(2x + y)(a - 3b)$ **87** $3(x + 3)(x - 3)(x + 1)$
89 $(x - 1)(x + 2)(x^2 + x + 1)$ **91** $(a^2 + b^2)(a - b)$
93 $(a + b)(a - b)(a^2 - ab + b^2)(a^2 + ab + b^2)$
95 $(x + 2 + 3y)(x + 2 - 3y)$
97 $(y + 4 + x)(y + 4 - x)$
99 $(y + 2)(y^2 - 2y + 4)(y - 1)(y^2 + y + 1)$
101 $(x^8 + 1)(x^4 + 1)(x^2 + 1)(x + 1)(x - 1)$
103 Area of I is $(x - y)x$, area of II is $(x - y)y$, and
$$A = x^2 - y^2 = (x - y)x + (x - y)y$$
$$= (x - y)(x + y).$$
105 (a) 1525.7; 1454.7
   (b) As people age, they require fewer calories.
   Coefficients of w and h are positive because large
   people require more calories.

EXERCISES 1.4

1 $\dfrac{22}{75}$ **3** $\dfrac{7}{120}$ **5** $\dfrac{x + 3}{x - 4}$ **7** $\dfrac{y + 5}{y^2 + 5y + 25}$

9 $\dfrac{4 - r}{r^2}$ **11** $\dfrac{x}{x - 1}$ **13** $\dfrac{a}{(a^2 + 4)(5a + 2)}$

15 $\dfrac{-3}{x + 2}$ **17** $\dfrac{6s - 7}{(3s + 1)^2}$ **19** $\dfrac{5x^2 + 2}{x^3}$

21 $\dfrac{4(2t + 5)}{t + 2}$ **23** $\dfrac{2(2x + 3)}{3x - 4}$ **25** $\dfrac{2x - 1}{x}$

27 $\dfrac{p^2 + 2p + 4}{p - 3}$ **29** $\dfrac{11u^2 + 18u + 5}{u(3u + 1)}$ **31** $-\dfrac{x + 5}{(x + 2)^2}$

33 $a + b$ **35** $\dfrac{x^2 + xy + y^2}{x + y}$ **37** $x + y$

39 $\dfrac{2x^2 + 7x + 15}{x^2 + 10x + 7}$ **41** $-\dfrac{3}{(x - 1)(a - 1)}$

43 $2x + h - 3$ **45** $-\dfrac{3x^2 + 3xh + h^2}{x^3(x + h)^3}$

47 $\dfrac{-12}{(3x + 3h - 1)(3x - 1)}$ **49** $\dfrac{t + 10\sqrt{t} + 25}{t - 25}$

51 $(9x + 4y)(3\sqrt{x} + 2\sqrt{y})$ **53** $\dfrac{\sqrt[3]{a^2} + \sqrt[3]{ab} + \sqrt[3]{b^2}}{a - b}$

55 $\dfrac{1}{(a + b)(\sqrt{a} + \sqrt{b})}$ **57** $\dfrac{2}{\sqrt{2(x + h) + 1} + \sqrt{2x + 1}}$

59 $\dfrac{-1}{\sqrt{1 - x - h} + \sqrt{1 - x}}$ **61** $4x^{4/3} - x^{1/3} + 5x^{-2/3}$

63 $x^{-1} + 4x^{-3} + 4x^{-5}$ **65** $\dfrac{1 + x^5}{x^3}$ **67** $\dfrac{1 - x^2}{x^{1/2}}$

69 $(3x + 2)^3(36x^2 - 37x + 6)$

71 $\dfrac{(2x + 1)^2(8x^2 + x - 24)}{(x^2 - 4)^{1/2}}$ **73** $\dfrac{(3x + 1)^5(39x - 89)}{(2x - 5)^{1/2}}$

75 $\dfrac{27x^2 - 24x + 2}{(6x + 1)^4}$ **77** $\dfrac{4x(1 - x^2)}{(x^2 + 2)^4}$ **79** $\dfrac{x^2 + 12}{(x^2 + 4)^{4/3}}$

81 $\dfrac{6(3 - 2x)}{(4x^2 + 9)^{3/2}}$

CHAPTER 1 REVIEW EXERCISES

1 (a) $-\dfrac{5}{12}$ **(b)** $\dfrac{39}{20}$ **(c)** $-\dfrac{13}{56}$ **(d)** $\dfrac{5}{8}$

2 (a) $<$ **(b)** $>$ **(c)** $>$

3 (a) $x < 0$ **(b)** $\dfrac{1}{3} < a < \dfrac{1}{2}$ **(c)** $|x| \le 4$

4 (a) 7   **(b)** -1 **(c)** $\dfrac{1}{6}$ **5 (a)** 5   **(b)** 5   **(c)** 7

6 (a) $|-2 - x| \ge 7$ **(b)** $|x - 4| < 4$
7 $-x - 3$ **8** $-(x - 2)(x - 3)$
9 (a) No   **(b)** No   **(c)** Yes
10 (a) 9.37×10^{10} **(b)** 4.02×10^{-6}
11 (a) 68,000,000   **(b)** 0.000 73

12 (a) 286.7639   **(b)** 2.868×10^2 **13** $\dfrac{-71}{9}$

14 $\dfrac{1}{8}$ **15** $18a^5b^5$ **16** $\dfrac{3y}{r^2}$ **17** $\dfrac{xy^5}{9}$ **18** $\dfrac{b^3}{a^8}$

19 $-\dfrac{p^8}{2q}$ **20** $c^{1/3}$ **21** $\dfrac{x^3z}{y^{10}}$ **22** $\dfrac{16x^2}{z^4y^6}$ **23** $\dfrac{b^6}{a^2}$

24 $\dfrac{27u^2v^{27}}{16w^{20}}$ **25** $s + r$ **26** $u + v$ **27** s

28 $\dfrac{y - x^2}{x^2y}$ **29** $\dfrac{x^8}{y^2}$ **30** $2xyz\sqrt[3]{x^2z}$ **31** $\dfrac{1}{2}\sqrt[3]{2}$

32 $\dfrac{ab}{c}\sqrt{bc}$ **33** $2x^2y\sqrt[3]{x}$ **34** $2ab\sqrt{ac}$

35 $\dfrac{1 - \sqrt{t}}{t}$ **36** c^2d^4 **37** $\dfrac{2x}{y^2}$ **38** $a + 2b$

39 $\dfrac{1}{2\pi}\sqrt[3]{4\pi}$ **40** $\dfrac{1}{3y}\sqrt[3]{3x^2y^2}$

41 $\dfrac{1 - 2\sqrt{x} + x}{1 - x}$ **42** $\dfrac{\sqrt{a} - \sqrt{a - 2}}{2}$

43 $(9x + y)(3\sqrt{x} - \sqrt{y})$ **44** $\dfrac{x + 6\sqrt{x} + 9}{9 - x}$
45 $x^4 + x^3 - x^2 + x - 2$
46 $3z^4 - 4z^3 - 3z^2 + 4z + 1$ **47** $-x^2 + 18x + 7$

48 $8x^3 + 2x^2 - 43x + 35$

49 $3y^5 - 2y^4 - 8y^3 + 10y^2 - 3y - 12$

50 $15x^3 - 53x^2 - 102x - 40$ **51** $a^4 - b^4$

52 $3p^2q - 2q^2 + \dfrac{5}{3}p$ **53** $6a^2 + 11ab - 35b^2$

54 $16r^4 - 24r^2s + 9s^2$ **55** $169a^4 - 16b^2$

56 $a^6 - 2a^5 + a^4$ **57** $9y^2 + 6xy + x^2$

58 $c^6 - 3c^4d^2 + 3c^2d^4 - d^6$ **59** $8a^3 + 12a^2b + 6ab^2 + b^3$

60 $x^4 - 4x^3 + 10x^2 - 12x + 9$ **61** $81x^4 - 72x^2y^2 + 16y^4$

62 $a^2 + b^2 + c^2 + d^2 + 2(ab + ac + ad + bc + bd + cd)$

63 $10w(6x + 7)$ **64** $2r^2s^3(r + 2s)(r - 2s)$

65 $(14x + 9)(2x - 1)$ **66** $(4a^2 + 3b^2)^2$

67 $(y - 4z)(2w + 3x)$ **68** $(2c^2 + 3)(c - 6)$

69 $8(x + 2y)(x^2 - 2xy + 4y^2)$

70 $u^3v(v - u)(v^2 + uv + u^2)$

71 $(p^4 + q^4)(p^2 + q^2)(p + q)(p - q)$ **72** $x^2(x - 4)^2$

73 $(w^2 + 1)(w^4 - w^2 + 1)$ **74** $3(x + 2)$

75 Irreducible   **76** $(x - 7 + 7y)(x - 7 - 7y)$

77 $(x - 2)(x + 2)^2(x^2 - 2x + 4)$ **78** $4x^2(x^2 + 3x + 5)$

79 $\dfrac{3x - 5}{2x + 1}$ **80** $\dfrac{r^2 + rt + t^2}{r + t}$ **81** $\dfrac{3x + 2}{x(x - 2)}$

82 $\dfrac{27}{(4x - 5)(10x + 1)}$ **83** $\dfrac{5x^2 - 6x - 20}{x(x + 2)^2}$ **84** $\dfrac{x^3 + 1}{x^2 + 1}$

85 $\dfrac{-2x^2 - x - 3}{x(x + 1)(x + 3)}$ **86** $\dfrac{ab}{a + b}$ **87** $x + 5$

88 $\dfrac{1}{x + 3}$ **89** $(x^2 + 1)^{1/2}(x + 5)^3(7x^2 + 15x + 4)$

90 $\dfrac{2(5x^2 + x + 4)}{(6x + 1)^{2/3}(4 - x^2)^2}$ **91** $x^{3/2} + 10x^{1/2} + 25x^{-1/2}$

92 $\dfrac{x^4 + 1}{x}$ **93** 2.75×10^{13} cells

94 Between 2.94×10^9 and 3.78×10^9 beats

95 0.58 m^2 **96** 0.13 dyne-cm

CHAPTER 1 DISCUSSION EXERCISES

1 0.1% **2** Either $a = 0$ or $b = 0$

3 Add and subtract $10x$; $x + 5 \pm \sqrt{10x}$ are the factors.

4 The first expression can be evaluated at $x = 1$.

5 They get close to the ratio of leading coefficients as x gets larger.

7 If x is the age and y is the height, show that the final value is $100x + y$.

8 $V_{\text{out}} = \frac{1}{3}V_{\text{in}}$ **9 (a)** 109–45   **(b)** 1.88

Chapter 2

EXERCISES 2.1

1 $\dfrac{5}{3}$ **3** 1   **5** $\dfrac{26}{7}$ **7** $\dfrac{35}{17}$ **9** $\dfrac{23}{18}$ **11** $-\dfrac{1}{40}$

13 $\dfrac{49}{4}$ **15** $\dfrac{4}{3}$ **17** $-\dfrac{24}{29}$ **19** $\dfrac{7}{31}$ **21** $-\dfrac{3}{61}$

23 $\dfrac{29}{4}$ **25** $\dfrac{31}{18}$ **27** No solution

29 All real numbers except $\dfrac{1}{2}$ **31** $\dfrac{5}{9}$ **33** $-\dfrac{2}{3}$

35 No solution   **37** 0   **39** All real numbers except ± 2

41 No solution   **43** No solution

45 $(4x - 3)^2 - 16x^2 = (16x^2 - 24x + 9) - 16x^2 = 9 - 24x$

47 $\dfrac{x^2 - 9}{x + 3} = \dfrac{(x + 3)(x - 3)}{x + 3} = x - 3$

49 $\dfrac{3x^2 + 8}{x} = \dfrac{3x^2}{x} + \dfrac{8}{x} = \dfrac{8}{x} + 3x$ **51** $-\dfrac{19}{3}$

53 (a) Yes **(b)** No, 5 is not a solution of the first equation.

55 Choose any a and b such that $b = -\dfrac{5}{3}a$.

57 $x + 1 = x + 2$ **59** $K = \dfrac{D - L}{E + T}$ **61** $Q = \dfrac{1}{M - 1}$

63 $P = \dfrac{I}{rt}$ **65** $h = \dfrac{2A}{b}$ **67** $m = \dfrac{Fd^2}{gM}$

69 $w = \dfrac{P - 2l}{2}$ **71** $b_1 = \dfrac{2A - hb_2}{h}$

73 $q = \dfrac{p(1 - S)}{S(1 - p)}$ **75** $q = \dfrac{fp}{p - f}$

EXERCISES 2.2

1 88   **3** \$820   **5 (a)** 125   **(b)** 21

7 120 mo (or 10 yr)   **9** Not possible   **11** 200 children

13 $\dfrac{14}{3}$ oz of 30% glucose solution and $\dfrac{7}{3}$ oz of water

15 194.6 g of British sterling silver and 5.4 g of copper

17 (a) After 64 sec   **(b)** 96 m and 128 m, respectively

19 6 mi/hr   **21 (a)** $\dfrac{5}{9}$ mi/hr   **(b)** $2\dfrac{2}{9}$ mi

23 1237.5 ft

25 (a) 4050 ft^2 **(b)** 2592 ft^2 **(c)** 3600 ft^2

27 $\dfrac{19}{2} - \dfrac{3\pi}{8} \approx 8.32$ ft   **29** 55 ft   **31** 36 min

33 36 min   **35** 27

37 (a) 40.96°F   **(b)** 6909 ft   **39** 37°F

EXERCISES 2.3

1 $-\dfrac{3}{2}, \dfrac{4}{3}$ **3** $-\dfrac{6}{5}, \dfrac{2}{3}$ **5** $-\dfrac{9}{2}, \dfrac{3}{4}$ **7** $-\dfrac{2}{3}, \dfrac{1}{5}$

9 $-\dfrac{5}{2}$ **11** $-\dfrac{1}{2}$ **13** $-\dfrac{34}{5}$

15 (a) No, -4 is not a solution of $x = 4$.   **(b)** Yes

17 ± 13 **19** $\pm\dfrac{3}{5}$ **21** $3 \pm \sqrt{17}$ **23** $-2 \pm \dfrac{1}{2}\sqrt{11}$

25 (a) $\dfrac{81}{4}$ (b) 16 (c) ± 12 (d) ± 7

27 $-3 \pm \sqrt{2}$ **29** $\dfrac{3}{2} \pm \sqrt{5}$ **31** $-\dfrac{1}{2}, \dfrac{2}{3}$

33 $-2 \pm \sqrt{2}$ **35** $\dfrac{3}{4} \pm \dfrac{1}{4}\sqrt{41}$ **37** $\dfrac{4}{3} \pm \dfrac{1}{3}\sqrt{22}$

39 $\dfrac{5}{2} \pm \dfrac{1}{2}\sqrt{15}$ **41** $\dfrac{9}{2}$ **43** No real solutions

45 $(x + 6)(x - 5)$ **47** $(2x - 3)(6x + 1)$

49 (a) $x = \dfrac{y \pm \sqrt{2y^2 - 1}}{2}$ (b) $y = -2x \pm \sqrt{8x^2 + 1}$

51 $v = \sqrt{\dfrac{2K}{m}}$ **53** $r = \dfrac{-\pi h + \sqrt{\pi^2 h^2 + 2\pi A}}{2\pi}$

55 $r = r_0 \sqrt{1 - (V/V_{\max})}$ **57** $\sqrt{150/\pi} \approx 6.9$ cm
59 (a) After 1 sec and after 3 sec   (b) After 4 sec
61 (a) 4320 m   (b) $96.86°$C   **63** 2 ft
65 12 ft by 12 ft

67 $3 + \dfrac{1}{2}\sqrt{14} \approx 4.9$ mi or $3 - \dfrac{1}{2}\sqrt{14} \approx 1.1$ mi

69 (a) $d = 100\sqrt{20t^2 + 4t + 1}$ (b) 3:30 P.M.
71 14 in. by 27 in.   **73** 7 mi/hr   **75** 300 pairs
77 2 ft   **79** 15.89 sec
81 (a) $0; -4{,}500{,}000$ (b) 2.13×10^{-7}

EXERCISES 2.4

1 $2 + 4i$ **3** $18 - 3i$ **5** $41 - 11i$ **7** $17 - i$
9 $21 - 20i$ **11** $-24 - 7i$ **13** 25
15 (a) $-i$ (b) 1 **17** (a) i (b) -1

19 $\dfrac{3}{10} - \dfrac{3}{5}i$ **21** $\dfrac{1}{2} - i$ **23** $\dfrac{34}{53} + \dfrac{40}{53}i$

25 $\dfrac{2}{5} + \dfrac{4}{5}i$ **27** $-142 - 65i$ **29** $-2 - 14i$

31 $-\dfrac{44}{113} + \dfrac{95}{113}i$ **33** $\dfrac{21}{2}i$ **35** $x = 4, y = -1$

37 $x = 3, y = -4$ **39** $3 \pm 2i$ **41** $-2 \pm 3i$

43 $\dfrac{5}{2} \pm \dfrac{1}{2}\sqrt{55}i$ **45** $-\dfrac{1}{8} \pm \dfrac{1}{8}\sqrt{47}i$

47 $-5, \dfrac{5}{2} \pm \dfrac{5}{2}\sqrt{3}i$ **49** $\dfrac{5}{2}, -\dfrac{25}{26} \pm \dfrac{15}{26}\sqrt{3}i$

51 $\pm 4, \pm 4i$ **53** $\pm 2i, \pm \dfrac{3}{2}i$

55 $0, -\dfrac{3}{2} \pm \dfrac{1}{2}\sqrt{7}i$

57 $\overline{z + w} = \overline{(a + bi) + (c + di)}$
$= \overline{(a + c) + (b + d)i} = (a + c) - (b + d)i$
$= (a - bi) + (c - di) = \overline{z} + \overline{w}$

59 $\overline{z \cdot w} = \overline{(a + bi) \cdot (c + di)}$
$= \overline{(ac - bd) + (ad + bc)i}$
$= (ac - bd) - (ad + bc)i$
$= ac - adi - bd - bci$
$= a(c - di) - bi(c - di)$
$= (a - bi) \cdot (c - di) = \overline{z} \cdot \overline{w}$

61 If $\overline{z} = z$, then $a - bi = a + bi$ and hence $-bi = bi$, or $2bi = 0$. Thus, $b = 0$ and $z = a$ is real. Conversely, if z is real, then $b = 0$ and hence $\overline{z} = \overline{a + 0i} = a - 0i = a + 0i = z$.

EXERCISES 2.5

1 $-15, 7$ **3** $-\dfrac{2}{3}, 2$ **5** No solution   **7** $\pm \dfrac{2}{3}, 2$

9 $\pm \dfrac{1}{2}\sqrt{6}, -\dfrac{5}{2}, 0$ **11** $0, 25$ **13** $-\dfrac{57}{5}$ **15** $\dfrac{9}{5}$

17 $\pm \dfrac{1}{2}\sqrt{62}$ **19** 6 **21** 6 **23** $5, 7$ **25** -3

27 -1 **29** $-\dfrac{5}{4}$ **31** 3 **33** $0, 4$ **35** $\pm 3, \pm 4$

37 $\pm \dfrac{1}{10}\sqrt{70 \pm 10\sqrt{29}}$ **39** $\pm 2, \pm 3$ **41** $\dfrac{8}{27}, -8$

43 $\dfrac{16}{9}$ **45** $-\dfrac{8}{27}, \dfrac{1}{125}$ **47** $-\dfrac{4}{3}, -\dfrac{2}{3}$ **49** $0, 4096$

51 (a) 8 (b) ± 8 (c) No real solutions   (d) 625
(e) No real solutions

53 $l = \dfrac{gT^2}{4\pi^2}$ **55** $h = \dfrac{1}{\pi r}\sqrt{S^2 - \pi^2 r^4}$ **57** $h \approx 97\%$ of L

59 9.16 ft/sec   **61** $\$4.00$ **63** $2\sqrt[3]{\dfrac{432}{\pi}} \approx 10.3$ cm

65 53.4%
67 There are two possible routes, corresponding to $x \approx 0.6743$ mi and $x \approx 2.2887$ mi.

EXERCISES 2.6

1 (a) $-2 < 2$ (b) $-11 < -7$ (c) $-\dfrac{7}{3} < -1$

(d) $1 < \dfrac{7}{3}$

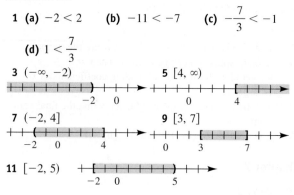

3 $(-\infty, -2)$ **5** $[4, \infty)$

7 $(-2, 4]$ **9** $[3, 7]$

11 $[-2, 5)$

13 $-5 < x \le 8$ **15** $-4 \le x \le -1$ **17** $x \ge 4$

19 $x < -5$ **21** $\left(\dfrac{16}{3}, \infty\right)$ **23** $\left(-\infty, -\dfrac{4}{3}\right]$

25 $(12, \infty)$ **27** $[-6, \infty)$ **29** $(1, 6)$ **31** $[9, 19]$

33 $\left(-\dfrac{26}{3}, \dfrac{16}{3}\right]$ **35** $(6, 12]$ **37** $\left(-\infty, \dfrac{8}{53}\right]$

39 $\left(-\infty, \dfrac{4}{5}\right)$ **41** $\left(-\dfrac{2}{3}, \infty\right)$ **43** $\left(\dfrac{4}{3}, \infty\right)$

45 All real numbers except 1   **47** $(-3, 3)$

49 $(-\infty, -5] \cup [5, \infty)$ **51** $(-3.01, -2.99)$

53 $(-\infty, -2.1] \cup [-1.9, \infty)$ **55** $\left(-\dfrac{9}{2}, -\dfrac{1}{2}\right)$

57 $\left[\dfrac{3}{5}, \dfrac{9}{5}\right]$ **59** $(-\infty, \infty)$ **61** $(-\infty, 3) \cup (3, \infty)$

63 $\left(-\infty, -\dfrac{8}{3}\right] \cup [4, \infty)$ **65** $\left(-\infty, \dfrac{7}{4}\right) \cup \left(\dfrac{13}{4}, \infty\right)$

67 $(-4, 4)$ **69** $(-2, 1) \cup (3, 6)$

71 (a) $-8, -2$ **(b)** $-8 < x < -2$
(c) $(-\infty, -8) \cup (-2, \infty)$

73 $|w - 148| \le 2$ **75** $5 < |T_1 - T_2| < 10$

77 $86 \le F \le 104$ **79** $R \ge 11$ **81** $4 \le p < 6$

83 $6\dfrac{2}{3}$ yr   **85 (a)** 5 ft 8 in.   **(b)** $65.52 \le h \le 66.48$

EXERCISES 2.7

1 $\left(-\dfrac{1}{3}, \dfrac{1}{2}\right)$ **3** $[-2, 1] \cup [4, \infty)$ **5** $(-2, 3)$

7 $(-\infty, -2) \cup (4, \infty)$ **9** $\left(-\infty, -\dfrac{5}{2}\right] \cup [1, \infty)$

11 $(2, 4)$ **13** $(-4, 4)$ **15** $\left(-\dfrac{3}{5}, \dfrac{3}{5}\right)$

17 $(-\infty, 0] \cup \left[\dfrac{9}{16}, \infty\right)$ **19** $(-\infty, -2] \cup [2, \infty)$

21 $\{-2\} \cup [2, \infty)$ **23** $(-\infty, -2) \cup (-2, -1) \cup \{0\}$

25 $(-2, 0) \cup (0, 1]$ **27** $(-2, 2] \cup (5, \infty)$

29 $(-\infty, -3) \cup (0, 3)$ **31** $\left(\dfrac{3}{2}, \dfrac{7}{3}\right)$

33 $(-\infty, -1) \cup \left(2, \dfrac{7}{2}\right]$ **35** $\left(-1, \dfrac{2}{3}\right) \cup [4, \infty)$

37 $\left(1, \dfrac{5}{3}\right) \cup [2, 5]$ **39** $(-1, 0) \cup (1, \infty)$

41 $[0, 2] \cup [3, 5]$ **43** $\dfrac{1}{2}$ sec   **45** $0 \le v < 30$

47 $0 < S < 4000$ **49** height $> 25{,}600$ km
51 $70.5 \le V \le 81.4$

CHAPTER 2 REVIEW EXERCISES

1 $-\dfrac{5}{6}$ **2** 5   **3** -32 **4** No solution

5 Every $x > 0$ **6** $-4, \dfrac{3}{2}$ **7** $-\dfrac{2}{3} \pm \dfrac{1}{3}\sqrt{19}$

8 $\dfrac{5}{2} \pm \dfrac{1}{2}\sqrt{29}$ **9** $\dfrac{1}{2} \pm \dfrac{1}{2}\sqrt{21}$ **10** $\pm\dfrac{5}{2}, \pm\sqrt{2}$

11 $-27, 125$ **12** $\pm\dfrac{1}{2}\sqrt{7}, -\dfrac{2}{5}$ **13** $\dfrac{1}{5} \pm \dfrac{1}{5}\sqrt{14}\,i$

14 $-\dfrac{1}{6} \pm \dfrac{1}{6}\sqrt{71}\,i$ **15** $\pm\dfrac{1}{2}\sqrt{14}\,i, \pm\dfrac{2}{3}\sqrt{3}\,i$

16 $\pm\dfrac{1}{2}\sqrt{6 \pm 2\sqrt{5}}$ **17** $-\dfrac{3}{2}, 2$ **18** $-5, 4$

19 $\dfrac{1}{4}, \dfrac{1}{9}$ **20** $\dfrac{13}{4}$ **21** 2   **22** $-3, 1$ **23** 5

24 ± 8 **25** $2 \pm \sqrt{3}$ **26** $-5 \pm \sqrt{13}\,i$ **27** 3

28 $\left(\dfrac{2}{3}, \infty\right)$ **29** $\left(-\dfrac{11}{4}, \dfrac{9}{4}\right)$ **30** $\left[\dfrac{13}{23}, \infty\right)$

31 $\left(-\infty, -\dfrac{3}{10}\right)$ **32** $\left(-7, \dfrac{7}{2}\right)$

33 $(-\infty, 1) \cup (5, \infty)$ **34** $[0, 6]$

35 $\left(-\infty, \dfrac{11}{3}\right] \cup [7, \infty)$ **36** $(2, 4) \cup (8, 10)$

37 $\left(-\infty, -\dfrac{3}{2}\right) \cup \left(\dfrac{2}{5}, \infty\right)$ **38** $[-2, 5]$

39 $(-\infty, -2) \cup \{0\} \cup [3, \infty)$ **40** $(-3, -1) \cup (-1, 2]$

41 $\left(-\infty, -\dfrac{3}{2}\right) \cup (2, 9)$ **42** $(-\infty, -5) \cup [-1, 5)$

43 $(1, \infty)$ **44** $(0, 1) \cup (2, 3)$ **45** $C = \dfrac{2}{P + N - 1}$

46 $D = \dfrac{CB^3}{(A + E)^3}$ **47** $r = \sqrt[3]{\dfrac{3V}{4\pi}}$

48 $R = \sqrt[4]{\dfrac{8FVL}{\pi P}}$ **49** $h = R \pm \dfrac{1}{2}\sqrt{4R^2 - c^2}$

50 $r = \dfrac{-\pi hR + \sqrt{12\pi hV - 3\pi^2 h^2 R^2}}{2\pi h}$ **51** $15 + 2i$

52 $-28 + 6i$ **53** $-55 + 48i$ **54** $\dfrac{9}{85} + \dfrac{2}{85}i$

55 $-\dfrac{9}{53} - \dfrac{48}{53}i$ **56** $-2 - 5i$ **57** 258   **58** \$79.37

59 56   **60** $R_2 = \dfrac{10}{3}$ ohms   **61** 11.055%

62 $168,000 **63** $\dfrac{6}{11}$ hr **64** 60.3 g

65 6 oz of vegetables and 4 oz of meat

66 315.8 g of ethyl alcohol and 84.2 g of water

67 80 gal of 20% solution and 40 gal of 50% solution

68 260 kg **69** 75 mi **70** 2 **71** 64 mi/hr

72 $\dfrac{640}{11} \approx 58.2$ mi/hr **73** 50 minutes **74** 5 mi/hr

75 1 hr 40 min **76** 165 mi

77 $10 - 5\sqrt{3} \approx 1.34$ mi **78** $3\sqrt{5} - 6 \approx 0.71$ micron

79 (a) $d = \sqrt{2900t^2 - 200t + 4}$

(b) $t = \dfrac{5 + 2\sqrt{19{,}603}}{145} \approx 1.97$, or approximately

11:58 A.M.

80 There are two arrangements: 40 ft $\times$ 25 ft and 50 ft $\times$ 20 ft.

81 (a) $2\sqrt{2}$ ft **(b)** 2 ft **82** 12 ft by 48 ft

83 10 ft by 4 ft **84** After $7\dfrac{2}{3}$ yr **85** $4 \le p \le 8$

86 Over $100,000 **87** $T > 279.57$ K

88 $\dfrac{\pi}{5}\sqrt{10} \le T \le \dfrac{2\pi}{7}\sqrt{5}$

89 $v < \dfrac{626.4}{\sqrt{6472}} \approx 7.786$ km/sec **90** $20 \le w \le 25$

91 36 to 38 trees/acre **92** $990 to $1040

CHAPTER 2 DISCUSSION EXERCISES

1 No **2** $\dfrac{-b}{2a}$

3 (a) $\dfrac{ac + bd}{a^2 + b^2} + \dfrac{ad - bc}{a^2 + b^2}i$ **(b)** Yes

(c) a and b cannot both be 0

5 $a > 0, D \le 0$: $x \in \mathbb{R}$;

$a > 0, D > 0$: $(-\infty, x_1] \cup [x_2, \infty)$;

$a < 0, D < 0$: { };

$a < 0, D = 0$: $x = \dfrac{-b}{2a}$;

$a < 0, D > 0$: $[x_1, x_2]$

6 (a) 11,006 ft **(b)** $h = \dfrac{1}{6}(2497D - 497G - 64{,}000)$

8 $1/10^{1000}$; $cx - 2/c$ must be nonnegative

9 1 gallon ≈ 0.13368 ft^3; 586.85 ft^2

Chapter 3

EXERCISES 3.1

1

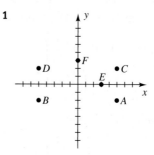

3 The line bisecting quadrants I and III

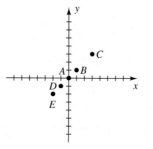

5 $A(3, 3)$, $B(-3, 3)$, $C(-3, -3)$, $D(3, -3)$, $E(3, 0)$, $F(0, 3)$

7 (a) The line parallel to the y-axis that intersects the x-axis at $(-2, 0)$

(b) The line parallel to the x-axis that intersects the y-axis at $(0, 3)$

(c) All points to the right of and on the y-axis

(d) All points in quadrants I and III

(e) All points below the x-axis

(f) All points on the y-axis

9 (a) $\sqrt{29}$ **(b)** $\left(5, -\dfrac{1}{2}\right)$

11 (a) $\sqrt{13}$ **(b)** $\left(-\dfrac{7}{2}, -1\right)$

13 (a) 4 **(b)** $(5, -3)$

15 $d(A, C)^2 = d(A, B)^2 + d(B, C)^2$; area $= 28$

17 $d(A, B) = d(B, C) = d(C, D) = d(D, A)$ and $d(A, C)^2 = d(A, B)^2 + d(B, C)^2$

19 $(13, -28)$ **21** $d(A, C) = d(B, C) = \sqrt{145}$

23 $5x + 2y = 3$

25 $\sqrt{x^2 + y^2} = 5$; a circle of radius 5 with center at the origin

27 $(0, 3 + \sqrt{11}), (0, 3 - \sqrt{11})$ **29** $(-2, -1)$

31 $a < \dfrac{2}{5}$ or $a > 4$

33 Let M be the midpoint of the hypotenuse. Show that
$$d(A, M) = d(B, M) = d(O, M) = \frac{1}{2}\sqrt{a^2 + b^2}.$$

EXERCISES 3.2

Exer. 1–20: x-intercept(s) is listed, followed by y-intercept(s).

1 1.5; -3

3 1; 1

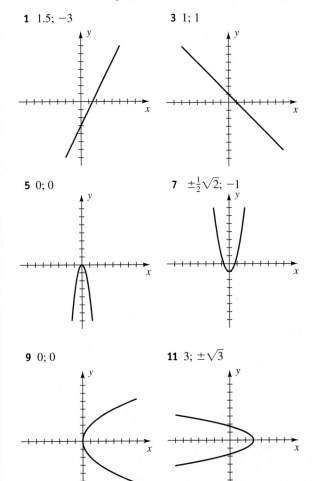

5 0; 0

7 $\pm\frac{1}{2}\sqrt{2}$; -1

9 0; 0

11 3; $\pm\sqrt{3}$

13 0; 0

15 2; -8

17 0; 0

19 16; -4

21 (a) 5, 7 **(b)** 9, 11 **(c)** 13

23

25

27

29

31

33

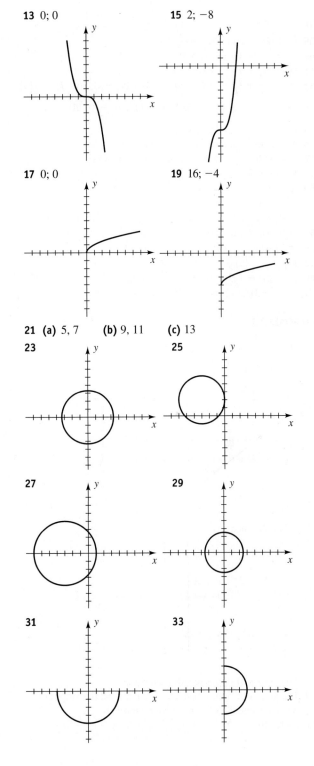

35 $(x - 2)^2 + (y + 3)^2 = 25$ **37** $\left(x - \dfrac{1}{4}\right)^2 + y^2 = 5$

39 $(x + 4)^2 + (y - 6)^2 = 41$

41 $(x + 3)^2 + (y - 6)^2 = 9$

43 $(x + 4)^2 + (y - 4)^2 = 16$

45 $(x - 1)^2 + (y - 2)^2 = 34$ **47** $C(2, -3); r = 7$

49 $C(0, -2); r = 11$ **51** $C(3, -1); r = \dfrac{1}{2}\sqrt{70}$

53 $C(-2, 1); r = 0$ (a point)

55 Not a circle, since r^2 cannot equal -2

57 $y = \sqrt{36 - x^2}; y = -\sqrt{36 - x^2}; x = \sqrt{36 - y^2};$
$x = -\sqrt{36 - y^2}$

59 $y = -1 + \sqrt{49 - (x - 2)^2};$
$y = -1 - \sqrt{49 - (x - 2)^2};$
$x = 2 + \sqrt{49 - (y + 1)^2}; x = 2 - \sqrt{49 - (y + 1)^2}$

61 $(x + 3)^2 + (y - 2)^2 = 4^2$ **63** $y = -\sqrt{4^2 - x^2}$

65 (a) Inside   (b) On   (c) Outside

67 (a) 2   (b) $3 \pm \sqrt{5}$

69 $(x + 2)^2 + (y - 3)^2 = 25$ **71** $\sqrt{5}$

73 $(-\infty, -3) \cup (2, \infty)$ **75** $(-1, 0) \cup (0, 1)$

EXERCISES 3.3

1 $m = -\dfrac{3}{4}$ **3** $m = 0$

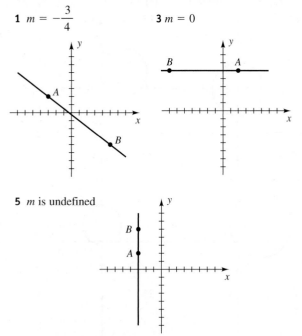

5 m is undefined

7 The slopes of opposite sides are equal.

9 The slopes of opposite sides are equal, and the slopes of two adjacent sides are negative reciprocals.

11 $(-12, 0)$

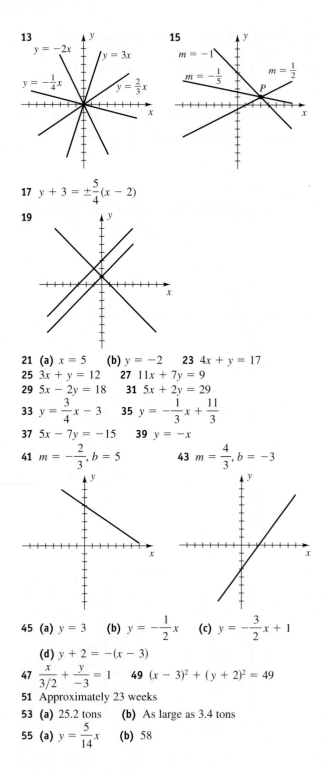

13

15

17 $y + 3 = \pm\dfrac{5}{4}(x - 2)$

19

21 (a) $x = 5$ (b) $y = -2$ **23** $4x + y = 17$

25 $3x + y = 12$ **27** $11x + 7y = 9$

29 $5x - 2y = 18$ **31** $5x + 2y = 29$

33 $y = \dfrac{3}{4}x - 3$ **35** $y = -\dfrac{1}{3}x + \dfrac{11}{3}$

37 $5x - 7y = -15$ **39** $y = -x$

41 $m = -\dfrac{2}{3}, b = 5$ **43** $m = \dfrac{4}{3}, b = -3$

45 (a) $y = 3$ (b) $y = -\dfrac{1}{2}x$ (c) $y = -\dfrac{3}{2}x + 1$

(d) $y + 2 = -(x - 3)$

47 $\dfrac{x}{3/2} + \dfrac{y}{-3} = 1$ **49** $(x - 3)^2 + (y + 2)^2 = 49$

51 Approximately 23 weeks

53 (a) 25.2 tons   (b) As large as 3.4 tons

55 (a) $y = \dfrac{5}{14}x$ (b) 58

57 (a) $W = \dfrac{20}{3}t + 10$ **(b)** 50 lb **(c)** 9 yr

(d)

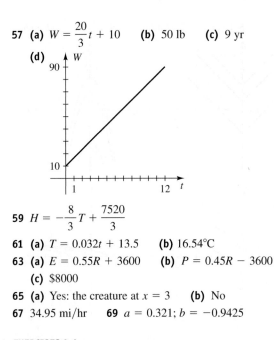

59 $H = -\dfrac{8}{3}T + \dfrac{7520}{3}$

61 (a) $T = 0.032t + 13.5$ **(b)** 16.54°C

63 (a) $E = 0.55R + 3600$ **(b)** $P = 0.45R - 3600$
(c) \$8000

65 (a) Yes: the creature at $x = 3$ **(b)** No

67 34.95 mi/hr **69** $a = 0.321; b = -0.9425$

EXERCISES 3.4

1 $-6, -4, -24$ **3** $-12, -22, -36$

5 (a) $5a - 2$ **(b)** $-5a - 2$ **(c)** $-5a + 2$
(d) $5a + 5h - 2$ **(e)** $5a + 5h - 4$ **(f)** 5

7 (a) $-a^2 + 4$ **(b)** $-a^2 + 4$ **(c)** $a^2 - 4$
(d) $-a^2 - 2ah - h^2 + 4$ **(e)** $-a^2 - h^2 + 8$
(f) $-2a - h$

9 (a) $a^2 - a + 3$ **(b)** $a^2 + a + 3$ **(c)** $-a^2 + a - 3$
(d) $a^2 + 2ah + h^2 - a - h + 3$
(e) $a^2 + h^2 - a - h + 6$ **(f)** $2a + h - 1$

11 (a) $\dfrac{4}{a^2}$ **(b)** $\dfrac{1}{4a^2}$ **(c)** $4a$ **(d)** $2a$

13 (a) $\dfrac{2a}{a^2 + 1}$ **(b)** $\dfrac{a^2 + 1}{2a}$ **(c)** $\dfrac{2\sqrt{a}}{a + 1}$

(d) $\dfrac{\sqrt{2a^3 + 2a}}{a^2 + 1}$

15 The graph is that of a function because it passes the vertical line test.

17 $D = [-4, 1] \cup [2, 4); R = [-3, 3)$

19 (a) $[-3, 4]$ **(b)** $[-2, 2]$ **(c)** 0 **(d)** $-1, \dfrac{1}{2}, 2$

(e) $\left(-1, \dfrac{1}{2}\right) \cup (2, 4]$

21 $\left[-\dfrac{7}{2}, \infty\right)$ **23** $[-3, 3]$

25 All real numbers except $-2, 0,$ and 2

27 $\left[\dfrac{3}{2}, 4\right) \cup (4, \infty)$ **29** $(2, \infty)$ **31** $[-2, 2]$

33 (a) $D = [-5, -3) \cup (-1, 1] \cup (2, 4]$;
$R = \{-3\} \cup [-1, 4]$
(b) Increasing on $[-4, -3) \cup [3, 4]$;
decreasing on $[-5, -4] \cup (2, 3]$;
constant on $(-1, 1]$

35

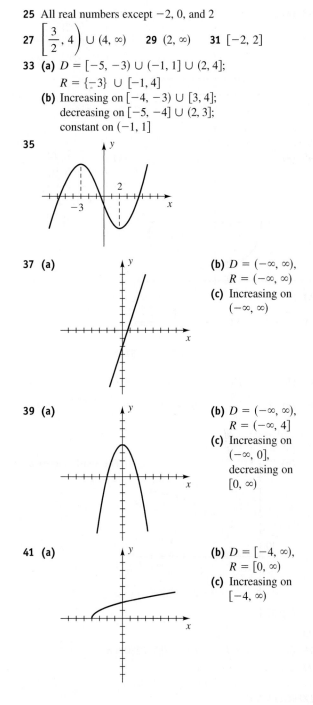

37 (a) **(b)** $D = (-\infty, \infty)$,
$R = (-\infty, \infty)$
(c) Increasing on
$(-\infty, \infty)$

39 (a) **(b)** $D = (-\infty, \infty)$,
$R = (-\infty, 4]$
(c) Increasing on
$(-\infty, 0]$,
decreasing on
$[0, \infty)$

41 (a) **(b)** $D = [-4, \infty)$,
$R = [0, \infty)$
(c) Increasing on
$[-4, \infty)$

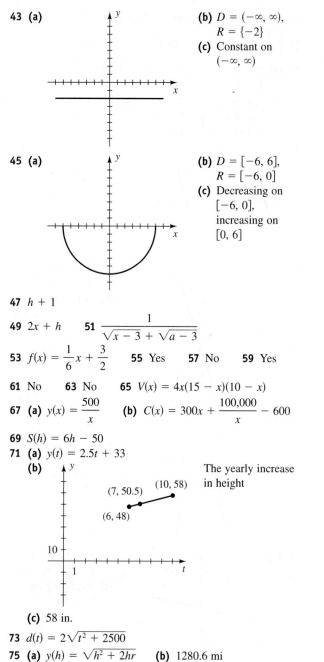

43 (a)

(b) $D = (-\infty, \infty)$,
$R = \{-2\}$
(c) Constant on
$(-\infty, \infty)$

45 (a)

(b) $D = [-6, 6]$,
$R = [-6, 0]$
(c) Decreasing on
$[-6, 0]$,
increasing on
$[0, 6]$

47 $h + 1$

49 $2x + h$ **51** $\dfrac{1}{\sqrt{x - 3} + \sqrt{a - 3}}$

53 $f(x) = \dfrac{1}{6}x + \dfrac{3}{2}$ **55** Yes   **57** No   **59** Yes

61 No   **63** No   **65** $V(x) = 4x(15 - x)(10 - x)$

67 (a) $y(x) = \dfrac{500}{x}$ **(b)** $C(x) = 300x + \dfrac{100{,}000}{x} - 600$

69 $S(h) = 6h - 50$

71 (a) $y(t) = 2.5t + 33$
(b)

The yearly increase
in height

(7, 50.5) (10, 58)
(6, 48)

(c) 58 in.

73 $d(t) = 2\sqrt{t^2 + 2500}$

75 (a) $y(h) = \sqrt{h^2 + 2hr}$ **(b)** 1280.6 mi

77 $d(x) = \sqrt{90{,}400 + x^2}$

EXERCISES 3.5

1 $f(-2) = 7, g(-2) = 6$

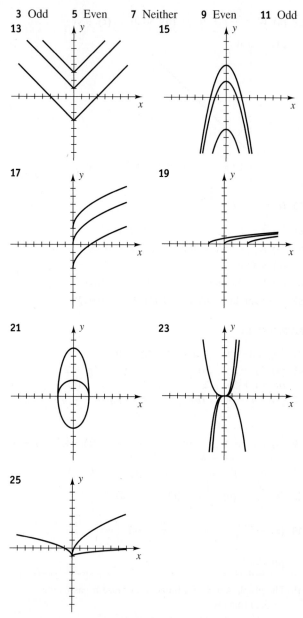

3 Odd   **5** Even   **7** Neither   **9** Even   **11** Odd

13   **15**

17   **19**

21   **23**

25

27 $(-2, 4)$ **29** $(7, -3)$ **31** $(6, 2)$

33 The graph of f is shifted 2 units to the right and 3 units up.

35 The graph of f is reflected about the y-axis and shifted 2 units down.

37 The graph of f is compressed vertically by a factor of 2 and reflected about the x-axis.

39 The graph of f is stretched horizontally by a factor of 3, stretched vertically by a factor of 2, and reflected about the x-axis.

41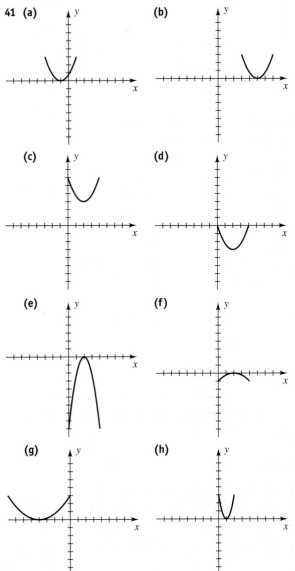

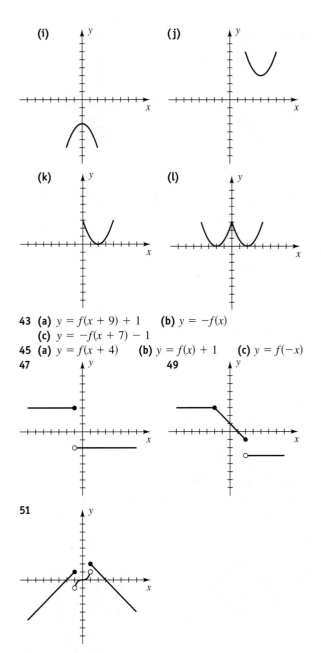

43 (a) $y = f(x + 9) + 1$ (b) $y = -f(x)$
    (c) $y = -f(x + 7) - 1$

45 (a) $y = f(x + 4)$ (b) $y = f(x) + 1$ (c) $y = f(-x)$

47

49

51

53 (a)

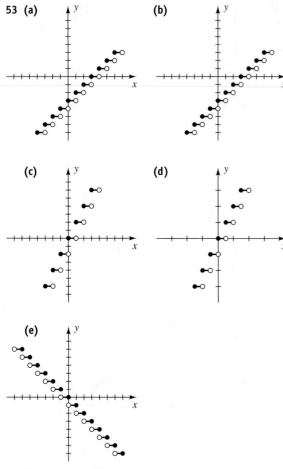

(b)

(c)

(d)

(e)

55 If $x > 0$, two different points on the graph have x-coordinate x.

57

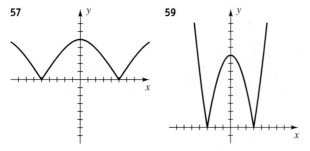

59

61

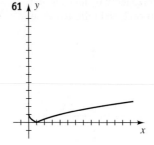

63 (a) $D = [-2, 6]$, $R = [-16, 8]$
    (b) $D = [-4, 12]$, $R = [-4, 8]$
    (c) $D = [1, 9]$, $R = [-3, 9]$
    (d) $D = [-4, 4]$, $R = [-7, 5]$
    (e) $D = [-6, 2]$, $R = [-4, 8]$
    (f) $D = [-2, 6]$, $R = [-8, 4]$
    (g) $D = [-6, 6]$, $R = [-4, 8]$
    (h) $D = [-2, 6]$, $R = [0, 8]$

65 $T(x) = \begin{cases} 0.15x & \text{if } 0 \le x \le 20{,}000 \\ 0.20x - 1000 & \text{if } x > 20{,}000 \end{cases}$

67 $R(x) = \begin{cases} 1.20x & \text{if } 0 \le x \le 10{,}000 \\ 1.50x - 3000 & \text{if } 10{,}000 < x \le 15{,}000 \\ 1.80x - 7500 & \text{if } x > 15{,}000 \end{cases}$

69 (a) $300, $360

   (b) $C_1(x) = \begin{cases} 180 & \text{if } 0 \le x \le 200 \\ 180 + 0.40(x - 200) & \text{if } x > 200 \end{cases}$

   $C_2(x) = 235 + 0.25x$ for $x \ge 0$

   (c) I if $x \in [0, 900)$, II if $x > 900$

EXERCISES 3.6

1 $y = a(x + 3)^2 + 1$ **3** $y = ax^2 - 3$
5 $f(x) = -(x + 2)^2 - 4$ **7** $f(x) = 2(x - 3)^2 + 4$
9 $f(x) = -3(x + 1)^2 - 2$

11 $f(x) = -\dfrac{3}{4}(x - 6)^2 - 7$

13 (a) 0, 4   **(c)**
     (b) Min: $f(2) = -4$

$(2, -4)$

15 (a) $-\dfrac{3}{4}$, $\dfrac{5}{3}$

   (b) Max: $f\left(\dfrac{11}{24}\right) = \dfrac{841}{48}$

   (c)

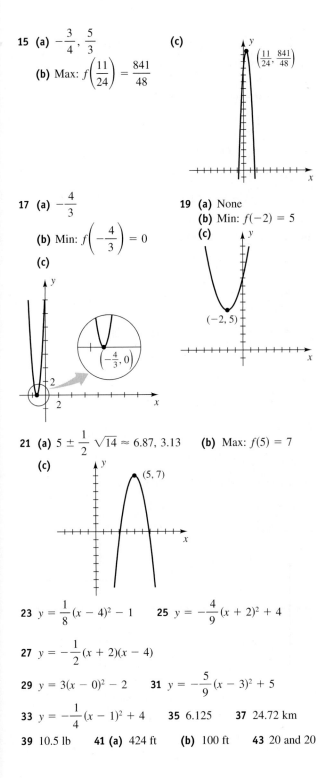

17 (a) $-\dfrac{4}{3}$

   (b) Min: $f\left(-\dfrac{4}{3}\right) = 0$

   (c)

19 (a) None

   (b) Min: $f(-2) = 5$

   (c)

$\left(-2, 5\right)$

21 (a) $5 \pm \dfrac{1}{2} \sqrt{14} \approx 6.87,\ 3.13$ (b) Max: $f(5) = 7$

   (c)

23 $y = \dfrac{1}{8}(x - 4)^2 - 1$ **25** $y = -\dfrac{4}{9}(x + 2)^2 + 4$

27 $y = -\dfrac{1}{2}(x + 2)(x - 4)$

29 $y = 3(x - 0)^2 - 2$ **31** $y = -\dfrac{5}{9}(x - 3)^2 + 5$

33 $y = -\dfrac{1}{4}(x - 1)^2 + 4$ **35** 6.125   **37** 24.72 km

39 10.5 lb   **41** (a) 424 ft   (b) 100 ft   **43** 20 and 20

45 (a) $y(x) = 250 - \dfrac{3}{4}x$ (b) $A(x) = x\left(250 - \dfrac{3}{4}x\right)$

   (c) $166\dfrac{2}{3}$ ft by 125 ft

47 $y = -\dfrac{4}{27}\left(x - \dfrac{9}{2}\right)^2 + 3$

49 (a) $y = \dfrac{1}{500}x^2 + 10$ (b) 282 ft   **51** 2 ft

53 500 pairs

55 (a) $R(x) = 200x(90 - x)$

   (b) \$45

$(45, 405{,}000)$

57 (a) $f(x) = \begin{cases} \dfrac{4}{25}x + 80 & \text{if } -800 \le x < -500 \\[2mm] -\dfrac{1}{6250}x^2 + 40 & \text{if } -500 \le x \le 500 \\[2mm] -\dfrac{4}{25}x + 80 & \text{if } 500 < x \le 800 \end{cases}$

EXERCISES 3.7

1 (a) 15   (b) -3 (c) 54   (d) $\dfrac{2}{3}$

3 (a) $3x^2 + 1$; $3 - x^2$; $2x^4 + 3x^2 - 2$; $\dfrac{x^2 + 2}{2x^2 - 1}$

   (b) $\mathbb{R}$ (c) All real numbers except $\pm\dfrac{1}{2}\sqrt{2}$

5 (a) $2\sqrt{x + 5}$; 0; $x + 5$; 1   (b) $[-5, \infty)$ (c) $(-5, \infty)$

7 (a) $\dfrac{3x^2 + 6x}{(x - 4)(x + 5)}$; $\dfrac{x^2 + 14x}{(x - 4)(x + 5)}$; $\dfrac{2x^2}{(x - 4)(x + 5)}$; $\dfrac{2(x + 5)}{x - 4}$

   (b) All real numbers except -5 and 4

   (c) All real numbers except -5, 0, and 4

9 (a) $-2x^2 - 1$ (b) $-4x^2 + 4x - 1$ (c) $4x - 3$

   (d) $-x^4$

11 (a) $6x + 9$ (b) $6x - 8$ (c) -3 (d) 10

13 (a) $75x^2 + 4$ **(b)** $15x^2 + 20$ **(c)** 304 **(d)** 155

15 (a) $8x^2 - 2x - 5$ **(b)** $4x^2 + 6x - 9$ **(c)** 31

(d) 45

17 (a) $8x^3 - 20x$ **(b)** $128x^3 - 20x$ **(c)** -24

(d) 3396

19 (a) 7 **(b)** -7 **(c)** 7 **(d)** -7

21 (a) $x + 2 - 3\sqrt{x + 2}$; $[-2, \infty)$

(b) $\sqrt{x^2 - 3x + 2}$; $(-\infty, 1] \cup [2, \infty)$

23 (a) $3x - 4$; $[0, \infty)$

(b) $\sqrt{3x^2 - 12}$; $(-\infty, -2] \cup [2, \infty)$

25 (a) $\sqrt{\sqrt{x + 5} - 2}$; $[-1, \infty)$

(b) $\sqrt{\sqrt{x - 2} + 5}$; $[2, \infty)$

27 (a) $\sqrt{3 - \sqrt{x^2 - 16}}$; $[-5, -4] \cup [4, 5]$

(b) $\sqrt{-x - 13}$; $(-\infty, -13]$

29 (a) x; $\mathbb{R}$ **(b)** x; $\mathbb{R}$

31 (a) $\dfrac{1}{x^6}$; all nonzero real numbers

(b) $\dfrac{1}{x^6}$; all nonzero real numbers

33 (a) $\dfrac{1}{5 - x}$; all real numbers except 4 and 5

(b) $\dfrac{-2x + 5}{-3x + 7}$; all real numbers except 2 and $\dfrac{7}{3}$

35 $-3 \pm \sqrt{2}$

37 (a) 5 **(b)** 6 **(c)** 6 **(d)** 5 **(e)** Not possible

39 $20\sqrt{x^2 + 1}$ **41** Odd **43** 40.16

45 $A(t) = 36\pi t^2$ **47** $r(t) = 9\sqrt[3]{t}$

49 $h(t) = 5\sqrt{t^2 + 8t}$

51 $d(t) = \sqrt{90{,}400 + (500 + 150t)^2}$

Exer. 53–60: Answers are not unique.

53 $u = x^2 + 3x$, $y = u^{1/3}$ **55** $u = x - 3$, $y = u^{-4}$

57 $u = x^4 - 2x^2 + 5$, $y = u^5$

59 $u = \sqrt{x + 4}$, $y = \dfrac{u - 2}{u + 2}$ **61** 5×10^{-13}

CHAPTER 3 REVIEW EXERCISES

1 The points in quadrants II and IV

2 $d(A, B)^2 + d(A, C)^2 = d(B, C)^2$; area $= 10$

3 (a) $\sqrt{265}$ **(b)** $\left(-\dfrac{13}{2}, 1\right)$ **(c)** $(-11, -23)$

4 $(0, 1), (0, 11)$ **5** $-2 < a < 1$

6 $(x - 7)^2 + (y + 4)^2 = 149$

7 $(x - 3)^2 + (y + 2)^2 = 169$

8 $x = -2 - \sqrt{9 - y^2}$ **9** $-\dfrac{11}{19}$

10 The slope of AD and BC is $\dfrac{2}{3}$.

11 (a) $18x + 6y = 7$ **(b)** $2x - 6y = 3$

12 $y = -\dfrac{8}{3}x + 8$ **13** $(x + 5)^2 + (y + 1)^2 = 81$

14 $x + y = -3$ **15** $5x - y = 23$

16 $2x - 3y = 5$ **17** $C(0, 6)$; $r = \sqrt{5}$

18 $C(-3, 2)$; $r = \dfrac{1}{2}\sqrt{13}$

19 (a) $\dfrac{1}{2}$ **(b)** $-\dfrac{1}{\sqrt{2}}$ **(c)** 0 **(d)** $-\dfrac{x}{\sqrt{3 - x}}$

(e) $-\dfrac{x}{\sqrt{x + 3}}$ **(f)** $\dfrac{x^2}{\sqrt{x^2 + 3}}$ **(g)** $\dfrac{x^2}{x + 3}$

20 Positive **21** Positive

22 (a) $\left[\dfrac{4}{3}, \infty\right)$; $[0, \infty)$

(b) All real numbers except -3; $(0, \infty)$

23 $-2a - h + 1$ **24** $-\dfrac{1}{(a + h + 2)(a + 2)}$

25 $f(x) = \dfrac{5}{2}x - \dfrac{1}{2}$

26 (a) Odd **(b)** Neither **(c)** Even

Exer. 27–40: x-intercept(s) is listed, followed by y-intercept(s).

27 -5; none **28** None; 3.5

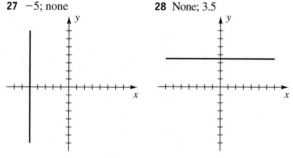

29 1.6; 4

30 4; $-\frac{4}{3}$

37 0, 8; 0

38 -3; ±3

31 0; 0

32 0; 0

39 $3 \pm \sqrt{2}$; 7

40 $-3, 1$; 3

33 1; 1

34 1; -1

41 $\left(\sqrt{8}, \sqrt{8} \right)$

42 The graph of $y = -f(x - 2)$ is the graph of $y = f(x)$ shifted to the right 2 units and reflected about the x-axis.

43 (a)

(b) $D = \mathbb{R}$; $R = \mathbb{R}$
(c) Decreasing on $(-\infty, \infty)$

35 ±4; ±4

36 None; 8

44 (a)

(b) $D = \mathbb{R}$; $R = \{1000\}$
(c) Constant on $(-\infty, \infty)$

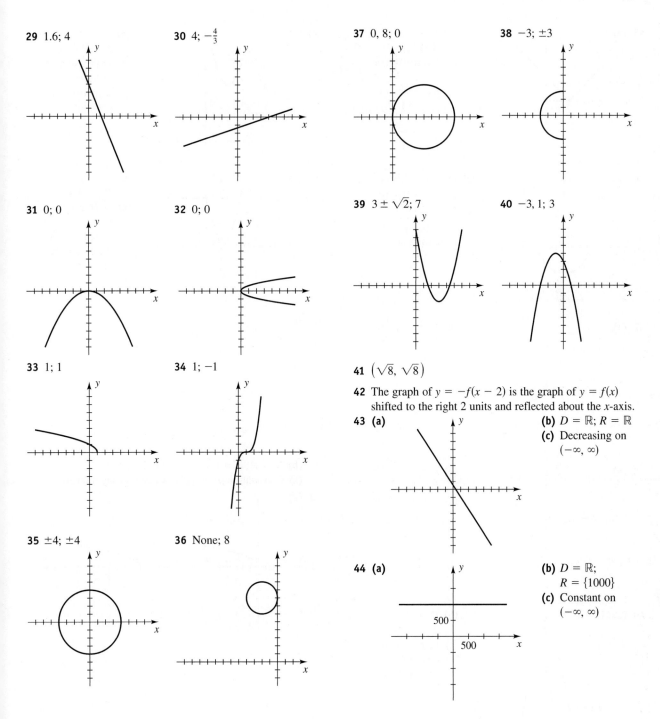

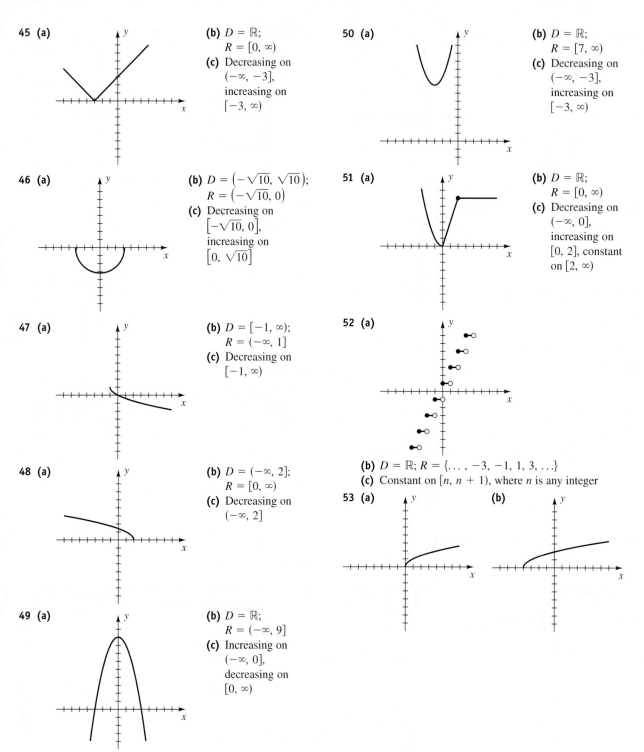

45 (a)

(b) $D = \mathbb{R}$;
$R = [0, \infty)$
(c) Decreasing on
$(-\infty, -3]$,
increasing on
$[-3, \infty)$

50 (a)

(b) $D = \mathbb{R}$;
$R = [7, \infty)$
(c) Decreasing on
$(-\infty, -3]$,
increasing on
$[-3, \infty)$

46 (a)

(b) $D = \left(-\sqrt{10}, \sqrt{10}\right)$;
$R = \left(-\sqrt{10}, 0\right)$
(c) Decreasing on
$\left[-\sqrt{10}, 0\right]$,
increasing on
$\left[0, \sqrt{10}\right]$

51 (a)

(b) $D = \mathbb{R}$;
$R = [0, \infty)$
(c) Decreasing on
$(-\infty, 0]$,
increasing on
$[0, 2]$, constant
on $[2, \infty)$

47 (a)

(b) $D = [-1, \infty)$;
$R = (-\infty, 1]$
(c) Decreasing on
$[-1, \infty)$

52 (a)

(b) $D = \mathbb{R}$; $R = \{\ldots, -3, -1, 1, 3, \ldots\}$
(c) Constant on $[n, n + 1)$, where n is any integer

48 (a)

(b) $D = (-\infty, 2]$;
$R = [0, \infty)$
(c) Decreasing on
$(-\infty, 2]$

53 (a)   **(b)**

49 (a)

(b) $D = \mathbb{R}$;
$R = (-\infty, 9]$
(c) Increasing on
$(-\infty, 0]$,
decreasing on
$[0, \infty)$

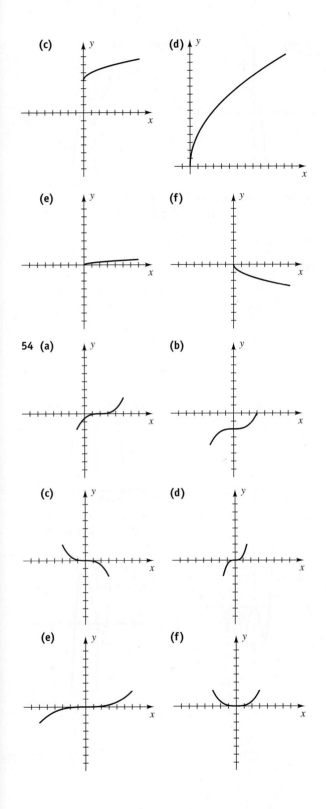

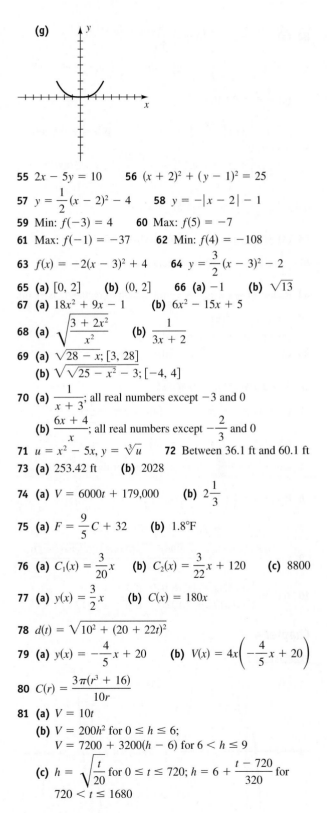

55 $2x - 5y = 10$ **56** $(x + 2)^2 + (y - 1)^2 = 25$

57 $y = \dfrac{1}{2}(x - 2)^2 - 4$ **58** $y = -|x - 2| - 1$

59 Min: $f(-3) = 4$ **60** Max: $f(5) = -7$

61 Max: $f(-1) = -37$ **62** Min: $f(4) = -108$

63 $f(x) = -2(x - 3)^2 + 4$ **64** $y = \dfrac{3}{2}(x - 3)^2 - 2$

65 (a) $[0, 2]$ (b) $(0, 2]$ **66** (a) -1 (b) $\sqrt{13}$

67 (a) $18x^2 + 9x - 1$ (b) $6x^2 - 15x + 5$

68 (a) $\sqrt{\dfrac{3 + 2x^2}{x^2}}$ (b) $\dfrac{1}{3x + 2}$

69 (a) $\sqrt{28 - x}$; $[3, 28]$

    (b) $\sqrt{\sqrt{25 - x^2} - 3}$; $[-4, 4]$

70 (a) $\dfrac{1}{x + 3}$; all real numbers except -3 and 0

    (b) $\dfrac{6x + 4}{x}$; all real numbers except $-\dfrac{2}{3}$ and 0

71 $u = x^2 - 5x, y = \sqrt[3]{u}$ **72** Between 36.1 ft and 60.1 ft

73 (a) 253.42 ft   (b) 2028

74 (a) $V = 6000t + 179{,}000$ (b) $2\dfrac{1}{3}$

75 (a) $F = \dfrac{9}{5}C + 32$ (b) $1.8°F$

76 (a) $C_1(x) = \dfrac{3}{20}x$ (b) $C_2(x) = \dfrac{3}{22}x + 120$ (c) 8800

77 (a) $y(x) = \dfrac{3}{2}x$ (b) $C(x) = 180x$

78 $d(t) = \sqrt{10^2 + (20 + 22t)^2}$

79 (a) $y(x) = -\dfrac{4}{5}x + 20$ (b) $V(x) = 4x\left(-\dfrac{4}{5}x + 20\right)$

80 $C(r) = \dfrac{3\pi(r^3 + 16)}{10r}$

81 (a) $V = 10t$

    (b) $V = 200h^2$ for $0 \le h \le 6$;

        $V = 7200 + 3200(h - 6)$ for $6 < h \le 9$

    (c) $h = \sqrt{\dfrac{t}{20}}$ for $0 \le t \le 720$; $h = 6 + \dfrac{t - 720}{320}$ for

       $720 < t \le 1680$

82 (a) $r = \dfrac{1}{2}x$ **(b)** $y = \dfrac{5}{4\pi} - \dfrac{1}{48}x^3$

83 (a) $y(h) = \dfrac{bh}{a - b}$ **(b)** $V(h) = \dfrac{1}{3}\pi h(a^2 + ab + b^2)$

(c) $\dfrac{200}{7\pi} \approx 9.1$ ft

84 $B(x) = \begin{cases} 3.61\left(\dfrac{x}{1000}\right) & \text{if } 0 \le x \le 5000 \\ 3.61(5) + 4.17\left(\dfrac{x - 5000}{1000}\right) & \text{if } x > 5000 \end{cases}$

85 $y = -\dfrac{1}{4.475^2}(x - 4.475)^2 + 1$

86 (a) $y(x) = 12 - x$ **(b)** $A(x) = x(12 - x)$

87 $\dfrac{18}{13}$ hr after 1:00 P.M., or about 2:23 P.M.

88 Radius of semicircle is $\dfrac{1}{8\pi}$ mi; length of rectangle is $\dfrac{1}{8}$ mi.

89 (a) 1 sec   **(b)** 4 ft
(c) On the moon, 6 sec and 24 ft
90 (a) $(87.5, 17.5)$ **(b)** 30.625 units

CHAPTER 3 DISCUSSION EXERCISES

2 (a) $g(x) = -\dfrac{1}{2}x + 3$ **(b)** $g(x) = -\dfrac{1}{2}x - 3$

(c) $g(x) = -\dfrac{1}{2}x + 7$ **(d)** $g(x) = -\dfrac{1}{2}x$

4 $2ax + ah + b$ **5** m_{PQ}; the slope of the tangent line at P

6 $R(x_3, y_3) = \left(\left(1 - \dfrac{m}{n}\right)x_1 + \dfrac{m}{n}x_2, \left(1 - \dfrac{m}{n}\right)y_1 + \dfrac{m}{n}y_2\right)$

7 $h = -ad^2$ **8** $f(x) = 40 - 20[\![-x/15]\!]$

9 $x = \dfrac{0.4996 + \sqrt{(-0.4996)^2 - 4(0.0833)(3.5491 - D)}}{2(0.0833)}$

10 $f(x) = \begin{cases} 0.132(x - 1)^2 + 0.7 & \text{if } 1 \le x \le 6 \\ -0.517x + 7.102 & \text{if } 6 < x \le 12 \end{cases}$

Chapter 4

EXERCISES 4.1

1 (a)   **(b)**

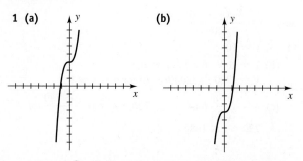

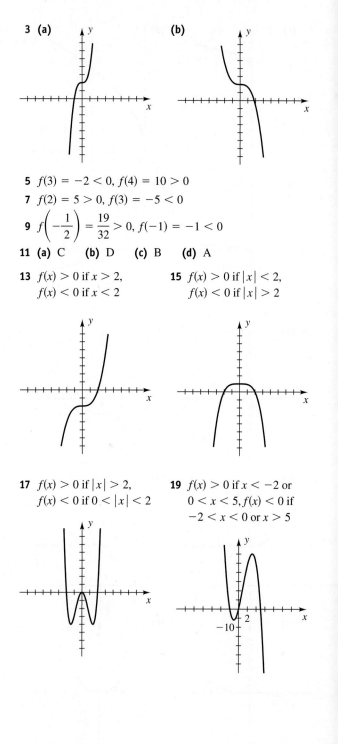

3 (a)   **(b)**

5 $f(3) = -2 < 0$, $f(4) = 10 > 0$
7 $f(2) = 5 > 0$, $f(3) = -5 < 0$
9 $f\left(-\dfrac{1}{2}\right) = \dfrac{19}{32} > 0$, $f(-1) = -1 < 0$
11 (a) C   **(b)** D   **(c)** B   **(d)** A
13 $f(x) > 0$ if $x > 2$,   **15** $f(x) > 0$ if $|x| < 2$,
$f(x) < 0$ if $x < 2$ $f(x) < 0$ if $|x| > 2$

17 $f(x) > 0$ if $|x| > 2$,   **19** $f(x) > 0$ if $x < -2$ or
$f(x) < 0$ if $0 < |x| < 2$ $0 < x < 5$, $f(x) < 0$ if
$-2 < x < 0$ or $x > 5$

21 $f(x) > 0$ if $-2 < x < 3$
or $x > 4$, $f(x) < 0$ if
$x < -2$ or $3 < x < 4$

23 $f(x) > 0$ if $x > 2$,
$f(x) < 0$ if $x < -2$
or $|x| < 2$

33 If n is even, then $(-x)^n = x^n$ and hence $f(-x) = f(x)$.
Thus, f is an even function.

35 $-\dfrac{4}{3}$ **37** ± 4

39 $P(x) > 0$ on $\left(-\frac{1}{5}\sqrt{15}, 0\right)$ and $\left(\frac{1}{5}\sqrt{15}, \infty\right)$;

$P(x) < 0$ on $\left(-\infty, -\frac{1}{5}\sqrt{15}\right)$ and $\left(0, \frac{1}{5}\sqrt{15}\right)$

25 $f(x) > 0$ if $|x| > 2$ or
$|x| < \sqrt{2}$, $f(x) < 0$ if
$\sqrt{2} < |x| < 2$

27 $f(x) > 0$ if $|x| > 2$,
$f(x) < 0$ if $|x| < 2$,
$x \neq 0$, $x \neq 1$

29

31 (a)

(b) $-abc$ **(c)** $(-\infty, a) \cup (b, c)$ **(d)** $[a, b] \cup [c, \infty)$

41 (b) $V(x) > 0$ on $(0, 10)$
and $(15, \infty)$;
allowable values
for x are in $(0, 10)$.

43 (a) $T > 0$ for
$0 < t < 12$;
$T < 0$ for
$12 < t < 24$

(b)

(c) $T(6) = 32.4 > 32$,
$T(7) = 29.75 < 32$

45 (a) $N(t) > 0$ for $0 < t < 5$

(b) The population
becomes extinct after
5 years.

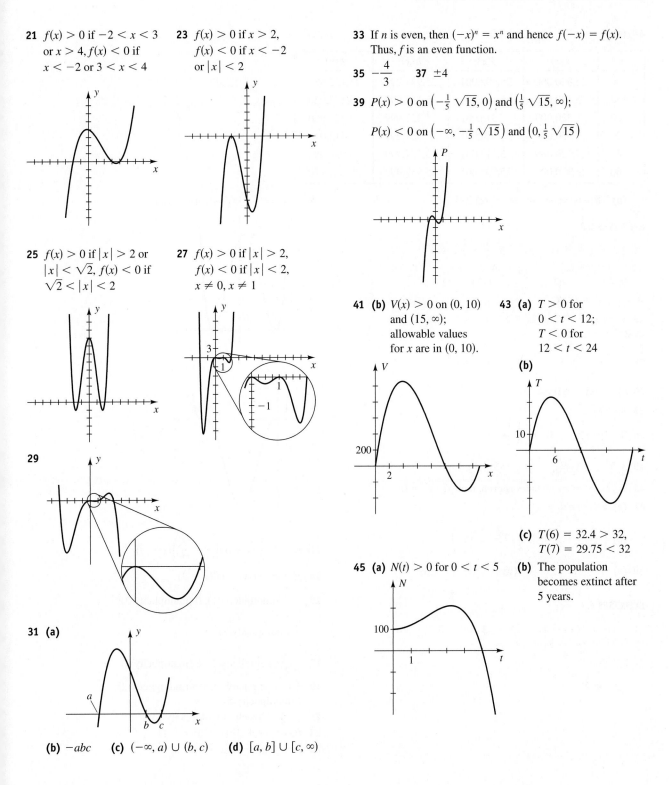

47 (a)

x	$f(x)$	$g(x)$	$h(x)$	$k(x)$
-60	25,920,000	25,902,001	25,937,999	26,135,880
-40	5,120,000	5,112,001	5,127,999	5,183,920
-20	320,000	318,001	321,999	327,960
20	320,000	318,001	321,999	312,040
40	5,120,000	5,112,001	5,127,999	5,056,080
60	25,920,000	25,902,001	25,937,999	25,704,120

(b) They become similar. **(c)** $2x^4$

EXERCISES 4.2

1 $2x^2 - x + 3; 4x - 3$ **3** $\dfrac{3}{2}x; \dfrac{1}{2}x - 4$

5 $0; 7x + 2$ **7** $\dfrac{9}{2}; \dfrac{53}{2}$ **9** 26   **11** 7

13 $f(-3) = 0$ **15** $f(-2) = 0$ **17** $x^3 - 3x^2 - 10x$

19 $x^4 - 2x^3 - 9x^2 + 2x + 8$

21 $2x^2 + x + 6; 7$

23 $x^2 - 3x + 1; -8$

25 $3x^4 - 6x^3 + 12x^2 - 18x + 36; -65$

27 $4x^3 + 2x^2 - 4x - 2; 0$

29 73   **31** -0.0444

33 $8 + 7\sqrt{3}$

35 $f(-2) = 0$ **37** $f\left(\dfrac{1}{2}\right) = 0$

39 3, 5   **41** $f(c) > 0$ **43** -14

45 If $f(x) = x^n - y^n$ and n is even, then $f(-y) = 0$.

47 (a) $V = \pi x^2(6 - x)$

   (b) $\left(\dfrac{1}{2}\left(5 + \sqrt{45}\right), \dfrac{1}{2}\left(7 - \sqrt{45}\right)\right)$

49 (a) $A = 8x - 2x^3$ **(b)** $\sqrt{13} - 1 \approx 2.61$

EXERCISES 4.3

1 $-4x^3 + 16x^2 - 4x - 24$ **3** $3x^3 + 3x^2 - 36x$

5 $-2x^3 + 6x^2 - 8x + 24$

7 $x^4 + 2x^3 - 23x^2 - 24x + 144$

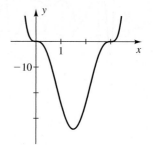

9 $3x^6 - 27x^5 + 81x^4 - 81x^3$

11 $f(x) = \dfrac{7}{9}(x + 1)\left(x - \dfrac{3}{2}\right)(x - 3)$

13 $f(x) = -1(x - 1)^2(x - 3)$

15 $-\dfrac{2}{3}$ (multiplicity 1); 0 (multiplicity 2);

   $\dfrac{5}{2}$ (multiplicity 3)

17 $-\dfrac{3}{2}$ (multiplicity 2); 0 (multiplicity 3)

19 -4 (multiplicity 3); -3 (multiplicity 2); 3 (multiplicity 5)

21 $\pm 4i, \pm 3$ (each of multiplicity 1)

23 $f(x) = (x + 3)^2(x + 2)(x - 1)$

25 $f(x) = (x - 1)^5(x + 1)$

Exer. 27–34: The types of possible solutions are listed in the order positive, negative, nonreal complex.

27 3, 0, 0 or 1, 0, 2   **29** 0, 1, 2

31 2, 2, 0; 2, 0, 2; 0, 2, 2; 0, 0, 4

33 2, 3, 0; 2, 1, 2; 0, 3, 2; 0, 1, 4

35 Upper, 5; lower, -2 **37** Upper, 2; lower, -2

39 Upper, 3; lower, -3

41 $f(x) = -\dfrac{1}{4}(x + 1)^2(x - 1)(x - 2)^3$

43 (a) $f(x) = a(x + 3)^3(x + 1)(x - 2)^2$ **(b)** 108

45 No   **47** Yes: $1.5(x - 2)(x - 5.2)(x - 10.1)$

49 $f(t) = \dfrac{5}{3528}t(t - 5)(t - 19)(t - 24)$

EXERCISES 4.4

1 $x^2 - 6x + 13$ **3** $(x - 2)(x^2 + 4x + 29)$

5 $x(x + 1)(x^2 - 6x + 10)$

7 $(x^2 - 8x + 25)(x^2 + 4x + 5)$

9 $x(x^2 + 4)(x^2 - 2x + 2)$

Exer. 11–14: Show that none of the possible rational roots listed satisfy the equation.

11 $\pm 1, \pm 2, \pm 3, \pm 6$ **13** $\pm 1, \pm 2$ **15** $-2, -1, 4$

17 $-3, 2, \dfrac{5}{2}$ **19** $-7, \pm\sqrt{2}, 4$

21 $-3, -\dfrac{2}{3}, 0$ (multiplicity 2), $\dfrac{1}{2}$

23 $-\dfrac{3}{4}, -\dfrac{3}{4} \pm \dfrac{3}{4}\sqrt{7}i$

25 $f(x) = (3x + 2)(2x - 1)(x - 1)^2(x - 2)$

27 No. If i is a root, then $-i$ is also a root. Hence, the polynomial would have factors $x - 1, x + 1, x - i, x + i$ and therefore would be of degree greater than 3.

29 Since n is odd and nonreal complex zeros occur in conjugate pairs for polynomials with real coefficients, there must be at least one real zero.

31 (a) The two boxes correspond to $x = 5$ and $x = 5(2 - \sqrt{2})$.
   (b) The box corresponding to $x = 5$

33 (c) In feet: 5, 12, and 13   **35 (b)** 4 ft

EXERCISES 4.5

1 (a)   **(b)** $D =$ all nonzero real numbers; $R = D$
   (c) Decreasing on $(-\infty, 0)$ and on $(0, \infty)$

3 VA: $x = 3$;
HA: $y = -2$;
hole: $\left(6, -\dfrac{22}{3}\right)$

5

$f(x) = \dfrac{2(x + 3)(x + 2)}{(x - 1)(x + 2)}$

7   **9**

11   **13**

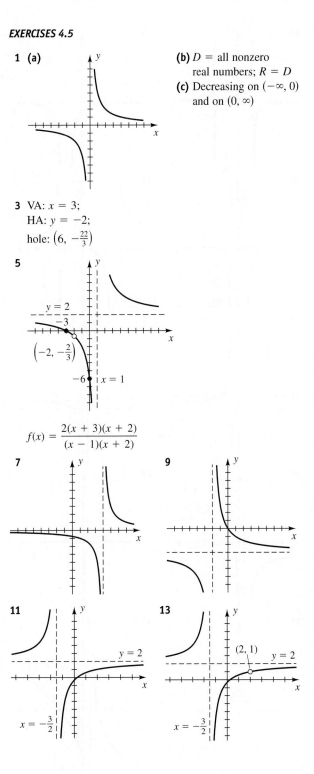

15
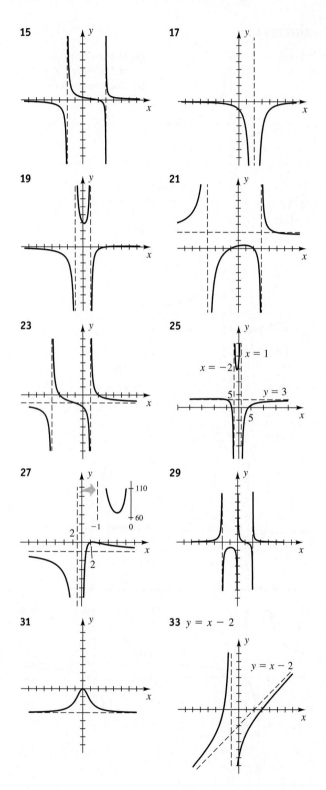

17

19

21

23

25

27

29

31

33 $y = x - 2$

35 $y = -\dfrac{1}{2}x$

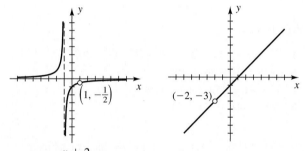

37 $f(x) = \dfrac{2x - 3}{x + 1}$ for $x \neq -2$

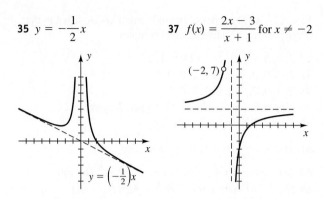

39 $f(x) = \dfrac{-1}{x + 1}$ for $x \neq 1$

41 $f(x) = x - 1$ for $x \neq -2$

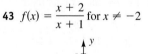

43 $f(x) = \dfrac{x + 2}{x + 1}$ for $x \neq -2$

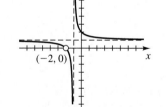

45 $f(x) = \dfrac{3 - x}{x - 4}$

47 $f(x) = \dfrac{6x^2 - 6x - 12}{x^3 - 7x + 6}$

49 **(a)** $h = \dfrac{16}{(r + 0.5)^2} - 1$ **(b)** $V(r) = \pi r^2 h$
  (c) Exclude $r \leq 0$ and $r \geq 3.5$.

51 **(a)** $V(t) = 50 + 5t$, $A(t) = 0.5t$ **(b)** $\dfrac{t}{10t + 100}$
  (c) As $t \to \infty$, $c(t) \to 0.1$ lb of salt per gal.

53 **(a)** $0 < S < 4000$ **(b)** 4500 **(c)** 2000
  (d) A 125% increase in S produces only a 12.5% increase in R.

55 (a) The graph of g is the horizontal line $y = 1$ with holes at $x = 0, \pm1, \pm2, \pm3$.

(b) The graph of h is the graph of p with holes at $x = 0$, $\pm1, \pm2, \pm3$.

57 (a) $y = \dfrac{132 - 48x}{x - 4}$

(b)

x	y
2.8	2
3.0	12
3.2	27
3.4	52
3.6	102
3.8	252
4.0	undefined

(c)

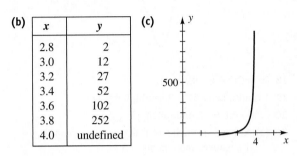

(d) $x = 4$

(e) Regardless of the number of additional credit hours obtained at 4.0, a cumulative GPA of 4.0 is not attainable.

EXERCISES 4.6

1 $u = kv;\ k = \dfrac{2}{5}$ **3** $r = k\dfrac{s}{t};\ k = -14$

5 $y = k\dfrac{x^2}{z^3};\ k = 27$ **7** $z = kx^2y^3;\ k = -\dfrac{2}{49}$

9 $y = k\dfrac{x}{z^2};\ k = 36$ **11** $y = k\dfrac{\sqrt{x}}{z^3};\ k = \dfrac{40}{3}$

13 (a) $P = kd$ **(b)** 59   **(c)** 295 lb/ft^2

(d)

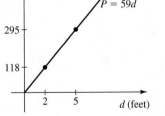

15 (a) $R = k\dfrac{l}{d^2}$ **(b)** $\dfrac{1}{40{,}000}$

(c)

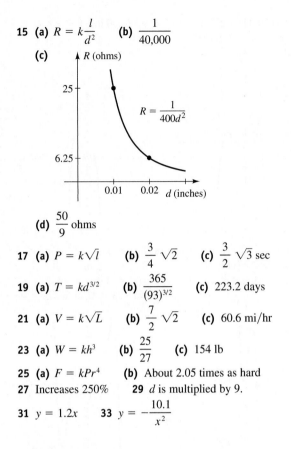

(d) $\dfrac{50}{9}$ ohms

17 (a) $P = k\sqrt{l}$ **(b)** $\dfrac{3}{4}\sqrt{2}$ **(c)** $\dfrac{3}{2}\sqrt{3}$ sec

19 (a) $T = kd^{3/2}$ **(b)** $\dfrac{365}{(93)^{3/2}}$ **(c)** 223.2 days

21 (a) $V = k\sqrt{L}$ **(b)** $\dfrac{7}{2}\sqrt{2}$ **(c)** 60.6 mi/hr

23 (a) $W = kh^3$ **(b)** $\dfrac{25}{27}$ **(c)** 154 lb

25 (a) $F = kPr^4$ **(b)** About 2.05 times as hard

27 Increases 250%   **29** d is multiplied by 9.

31 $y = 1.2x$ **33** $y = -\dfrac{10.1}{x^2}$

CHAPTER 4 REVIEW EXERCISES

1 $f(x) > 0$ if $x > -2$,   **2** $f(x) > 0$ if $x < -\sqrt[6]{32}$
$f(x) < 0$ if $x < -2$ or $x > \sqrt[6]{32},\ f(x) < 0$
if $-\sqrt[6]{32} < x < \sqrt[6]{32}$

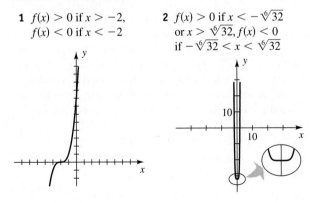

3 $f(x) > 0$ if $-2 < x < 1$
or $1 < x < 3, f(x) < 0$
if $x < -2$ or $x > 3$

4 $f(x) > 0$ if $-1 < x < 0$
or $0 < x < 2$,
$f(x) < 0$ if $x < -1$
or $x > 2$

17 $x^7 + 6x^6 + 9x^5$

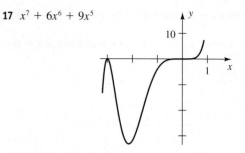

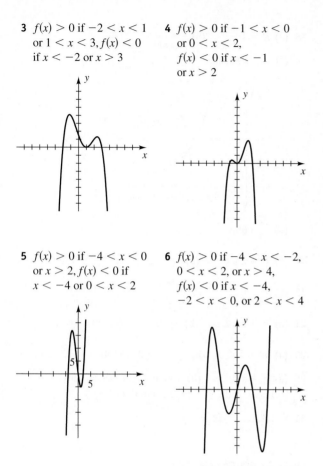

5 $f(x) > 0$ if $-4 < x < 0$
or $x > 2, f(x) < 0$ if
$x < -4$ or $0 < x < 2$

6 $f(x) > 0$ if $-4 < x < -2$,
$0 < x < 2$, or $x > 4$,
$f(x) < 0$ if $x < -4$,
$-2 < x < 0$, or $2 < x < 4$

18 $(x - 2)^3(x + 3)(x - 1)$

19 1 (multiplicity 5); -3 (multiplicity 1)

20 $0, \pm i$ (all have multiplicity 2)

21 (a) Either 3 positive and 1 negative or 1 positive,
1 negative, and 2 nonreal complex

(b) Upper bound, 3; lower bound, -1

22 (a) Either 2 positive and 3 negative; 2 positive, 1 negative,
and 2 nonreal complex; 3 negative and 2 nonreal
complex; or 1 negative and 4 nonreal complex

(b) Upper bound, 2; lower bound, -3

23 Since there are only even powers,
$7x^6 + 2x^4 + 3x^2 + 10 \geq 10$ for every real number x.

24 $-3, -2, -2 \pm i$ **25** $-\dfrac{1}{2}, \dfrac{1}{4}, \dfrac{3}{2}$ **26** $\pm\sqrt{6}, \pm 1$

27 $f(x) = -\dfrac{1}{6}(x + 2)^3(x - 1)^2(x - 3)$

28 $f(x) = \dfrac{1}{16}(x + 3)^2 x^2 (x - 3)^2$

7 $f(0) = -9 < 100$ and $f(10) = 561 > 100$. By the
intermediate value theorem for polynomial functions, f
takes on every value between -9 and 561. Hence, there is
at least one real number a in $[0, 10]$ such that $f(a) = 100$.

8 Let $f(x) = x^5 - 3x^4 - 2x^3 - x + 1$. $f(0) = 1 > 0$ and
$f(1) = -4 < 0$. By the intermediate value theorem for
polynomial functions, f takes on every value between -4
and 1. Hence, there is at least one real number a in $[0, 1]$
such that $f(a) = 0$.

29 VA: $x = 5$; HA: $y = \dfrac{4}{3}$; x-intercept: 1;

y-intercept: $\dfrac{4}{15}$; hole: $\left(-2, \dfrac{4}{7}\right)$

9 $3x^2 + 2; -21x^2 + 5x - 9$ **10** $4x - 1; 2x - 1$

11 -132 **12** $f(3) = 0$

13 $6x^4 - 12x^3 + 24x^2 - 52x + 104; -200$

14 $2x^2 + \left(5 + 2\sqrt{2}\right)x + \left(2 + 5\sqrt{2}\right); 11 + 2\sqrt{2}$

15 $\dfrac{2}{41}(x^2 + 6x + 34)(x + 1)$

16 $\dfrac{1}{4}x(x^2 - 2x + 2)(x - 3)$

30

31

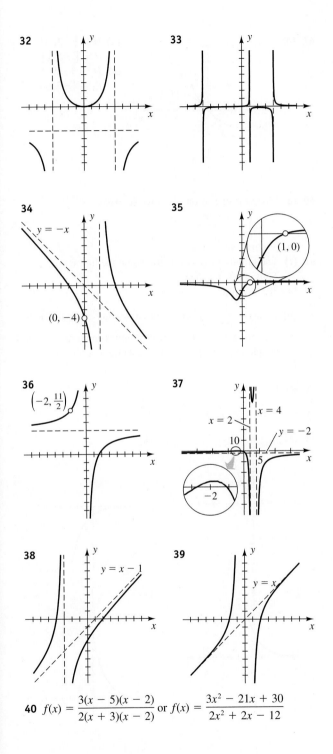

32

33

34
$y = -x$
$(0, -4)$

35
$(1, 0)$

36
$\left(-2, \frac{11}{2}\right)$

37
$x = 2$
$x = 4$
$y = -2$
10
5
-2

38
$y = x - 1$

39
$y = x$

40 $f(x) = \dfrac{3(x - 5)(x - 2)}{2(x + 3)(x - 2)}$ or $f(x) = \dfrac{3x^2 - 21x + 30}{2x^2 + 2x - 12}$

41 27

42

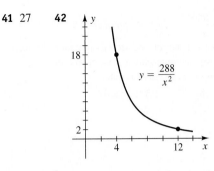

$y = \dfrac{288}{x^2}$

43 (a) $\dfrac{1}{15{,}000}$

(b) $y \approx 0.9754 < 1$ if $x = 6.1$, and
$y \approx 1.0006 > 1$ if $x = 6.2$

44 (a) $V = \dfrac{1}{4\pi} x(l^2 - x^2)$

(b) If $x > 0$, $V > 0$ when $0 < x < l$.

45 $t = 4$ (10:00 A.M.) and $t = 16 - 4\sqrt{6} \approx 6.2020$
(12:12 P.M.)

46 $\sqrt{5} < t < 4$

47 (a) $R = k$
(b) k is the maximum rate at which the liver can remove
alcohol from the bloodstream.

48 (a) $C(100) = \$30$ million and $C(90) \approx \$2.5$ million
(b)

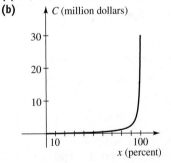

C (million dollars)

30

20

10

10

100

x (percent)

49 375   **50** 10,125 watts

CHAPTER 4 DISCUSSION EXERCISES

2 Yes   **4** No   **5** $n + 1$ **7** $f(x) = \dfrac{(x^2 + 1)(x - 1)}{(x^2 + 1)(x - 2)}$
8 (a) No

(b) Yes, when $x = \dfrac{cd - af}{ae - bd}$, provided the denominator is
not zero

9 (a) $\$1476$
(b) Not valid for high confidence values
10 The second integer

11 (a) $R(I) = \dfrac{P + SI}{I}$ **(b)** R approaches S.

(c) As income gets larger, individuals pay more in taxes, but fixed tax amounts play a smaller role in determining their overall tax rate.

12 (a) 112.8   **(b)** 23   **(c)** 61 yards

Chapter 5

EXERCISES 5.1

1 (a) 4   **(b)** Not possible

3 (a) Yes   **(b)** No   **(c)** Not a function

5 Yes   **7** No   **9** Yes   **11** No   **13** No   **15** Yes

Exer. 17–20: Show that $f(g(x)) = x = g(f(x))$.

17   **19**

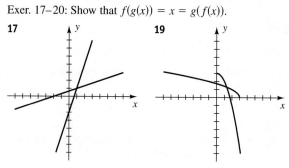

21 $(-\infty, 0) \cup (0, \infty); (-\infty, 1) \cup (1, \infty)$

23 $\left(-\infty, \frac{4}{3}\right) \cup \left(\frac{4}{3}, \infty\right); \left(-\infty, \frac{8}{3}\right) \cup \left(\frac{8}{3}, \infty\right)$

25 $f^{-1}(x) = \dfrac{x - 5}{3}$ **27** $f^{-1}(x) = \dfrac{2x + 1}{3x}$

29 $f^{-1}(x) = \dfrac{5x + 2}{2x - 3}$ **31** $f^{-1}(x) = -\sqrt{\dfrac{2 - x}{3}}$

33 $f^{-1}(x) = \sqrt[3]{\dfrac{x + 5}{2}}$ **35** $f^{-1}(x) = 3 - x^2, x \geq 0$

37 $f^{-1}(x) = (x - 1)^3$ **39** $f^{-1}(x) = x$

41 $f^{-1}(x) = 3 + \sqrt{x + 9}$ **43 (a)** 3   **(b)** −1   **(c)** 5

45 (a)

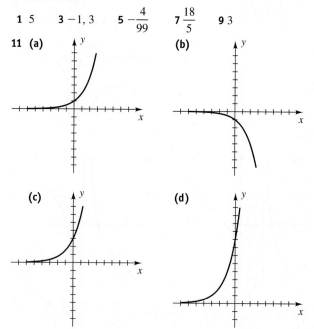

(b) $D = [-1, 2];$
$R = \left[\dfrac{1}{2}, 4\right]$

(c) $D_1 = \left[\dfrac{1}{2}, 4\right];$
$R_1 = [-1, 2]$

47 (a)

(b) $D = [-3, 3];$
$R = [-2, 2]$
(c) $D_1 = [-2, 2];$
$R_1 = [-3, 3]$

49 (a) Since f is one-to-one, an inverse exists;
$$f^{-1}(x) = \dfrac{x - b}{a}$$

(b) No; not one-to-one

51 (c) The graph of f is symmetric about the line $y = x$. Thus, $f(x) = f^{-1}(x)$.

53 (a) 805 ft³/min

(b) $V^{-1}(x) = \dfrac{1}{35}x$. Given an air circulation of x cubic feet per minute, $V^{-1}(x)$ computes the maximum number of people that should be in the restaurant at one time.

(c) 67

EXERCISES 5.2

1 5   **3** −1, 3   **5** $-\dfrac{4}{99}$ **7** $\dfrac{18}{5}$ **9** 3

11 (a)   **(b)**

(c)   **(d)**

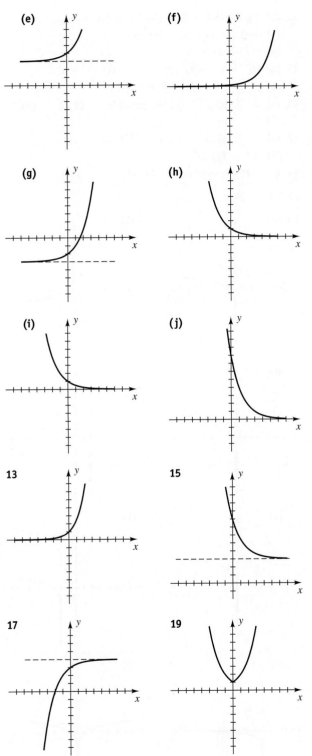

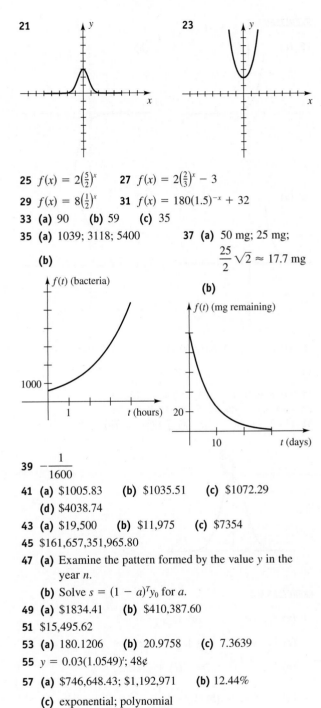

25 $f(x) = 2\left(\frac{5}{2}\right)^x$ **27** $f(x) = 2\left(\frac{2}{3}\right)^x - 3$

29 $f(x) = 8\left(\frac{1}{2}\right)^x$ **31** $f(x) = 180(1.5)^{-x} + 32$

33 (a) 90   **(b)** 59   **(c)** 35

35 (a) 1039; 3118; 5400   **37 (a)** 50 mg; 25 mg;

(b) $\dfrac{25}{2}\sqrt{2} \approx 17.7$ mg

(b)

39 $-\dfrac{1}{1600}$

41 (a) $1005.83   **(b)** $1035.51   **(c)** $1072.29

(d) $4038.74

43 (a) $19,500   **(b)** $11,975   **(c)** $7354

45 $161,657,351,965.80

47 (a) Examine the pattern formed by the value y in the year n.

(b) Solve $s = (1 - a)^T y_0$ for a.

49 (a) $1834.41   **(b)** $410,387.60

51 $15,495.62

53 (a) 180.1206   **(b)** 20.9758   **(c)** 7.3639

55 $y = 0.03(1.0549)^t$; 48¢

57 (a) $746,648.43; $1,192,971   **(b)** 12.44%

(c) exponential; polynomial

EXERCISES 5.3

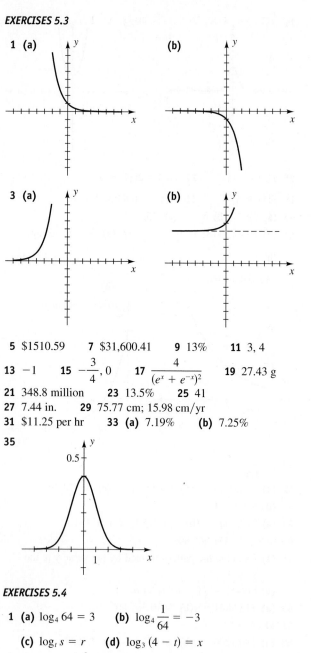

1 (a)   **(b)**

3 (a)   **(b)**

5 $1510.59   **7** $31,600.41   **9** 13%   **11** 3, 4

13 -1 **15** $-\dfrac{3}{4}, 0$ **17** $\dfrac{4}{(e^x + e^{-x})^2}$ **19** 27.43 g

21 348.8 million   **23** 13.5%   **25** 41

27 7.44 in.   **29** 75.77 cm; 15.98 cm/yr

31 $11.25 per hr   **33 (a)** 7.19%   **(b)** 7.25%

35

EXERCISES 5.4

1 (a) $\log_4 64 = 3$ **(b)** $\log_4 \dfrac{1}{64} = -3$

(c) $\log_t s = r$ **(d)** $\log_3 (4 - t) = x$

(e) $\log_5 \dfrac{a + b}{a} = 7t$ **(f)** $\log_{0.7} (5.3) = t$

3 (a) $2^5 = 32$ **(b)** $3^{-5} = \dfrac{1}{243}$ **(c)** $t^p = r$

(d) $3^5 = (x + 2)$ **(e)** $2^{3x+4} = m$ **(f)** $b^{3/2} = 512$

5 $t = 3 \log_a \dfrac{5}{2}$ **7** $t = \log_a \left(\dfrac{H - K}{C}\right)$

9 $t = \dfrac{1}{C} \log_a \left(\dfrac{A - D}{B}\right)$

11 (a) $\log 100{,}000 = 5$ **(b)** $\log 0.001 = -3$

(c) $\log (y + 1) = x$ **(d)** $\ln p = 7$

(e) $\ln (3 - x) = 2t$

13 (a) $10^{50} = x$ **(b)** $10^{20t} = x$ **(c)** $e^{0.1} = x$

(d) $e^{4+3x} = w$ **(e)** $e^{1/6} = z - 2$

15 (a) 0   **(b)** 1   **(c)** Not possible   **(d)** 2   **(e)** 8

(f) 3   **(g)** -2

17 (a) 3   **(b)** 5   **(c)** 2   **(d)** -4 **(e)** 2

(f) -3 **(g)** $3e^2$

19 4   **21** No solution   **23** $-1, -2$ **25** 13

27 27   **29** $\pm \dfrac{1}{e}$ **31** 3   **33** 3

35 (a)   **(b)**

(c)   **(d)**

(e)   **(f)**

(g)   **(h)**

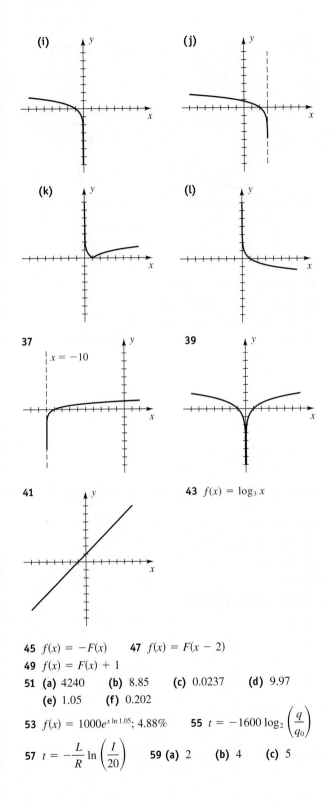

(i)

(j)

(k)

(l)

37

$x = -10$

39

41

43 $f(x) = \log_3 x$

45 $f(x) = -F(x)$ **47** $f(x) = F(x - 2)$

49 $f(x) = F(x) + 1$

51 (a) 4240   **(b)** 8.85   **(c)** 0.0237   **(d)** 9.97

(e) 1.05   **(f)** 0.202

53 $f(x) = 1000e^{x \ln 1.05}$; 4.88%   **55** $t = -1600 \log_2 \left(\dfrac{q}{q_0} \right)$

57 $t = -\dfrac{L}{R} \ln \left(\dfrac{I}{20} \right)$ **59 (a)** 2   **(b)** 4   **(c)** 5

61 (a) 10   **(b)** 30   **(c)** 40   **63** In the year 2047

65 (a) $W = 2.4e^{1.84h}$ **(b)** 37.92 kg

67 (a) 10,007 ft   **(b)** 18,004 ft

69 (a) 305.9 kg   **(b)** (1) 20 yr (2) 19.8 yr

71 10.1 mi   **73** $2^{1/8} \approx 1.09$

75 (a) Pedestrians have faster average walking speeds in large cities.

(b) 570,000

77 (a) 8.4877   **(b)** -0.0601

79 30%

EXERCISES 5.5

1 (a) $\log_4 x + \log_4 z$ **(b)** $\log_4 y - \log_4 x$

(c) $\dfrac{1}{3} \log_4 z$

3 $3 \log_a x + \log_a w - 2 \log_a y - 4 \log_a z$

5 $\dfrac{1}{3} \log z - \log x - \dfrac{1}{2} \log y$

7 $\dfrac{7}{4} \ln x - \dfrac{5}{4} \ln y - \dfrac{1}{4} \ln z$

9 (a) $\log_3 (5xy)$ **(b)** $\log_3 \dfrac{2z}{x}$ **(c)** $\log_3 y^5$

11 $\log_a \dfrac{x^2 \sqrt[3]{x - 2}}{(2x + 3)^5}$ **13** $\log \dfrac{y^{13/3}}{x^2}$ **15** $\ln x$ **17** $\dfrac{7}{2}$

19 $5\sqrt{5}$ **21** No solution   **23** -7 **25** 1

27 -2 **29** $\dfrac{-1 + \sqrt{65}}{2}$ **31** $-1 + \sqrt{1 + e}$

33 $3 + \sqrt{10}$

35

37

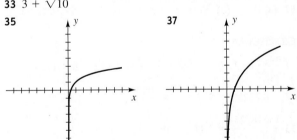

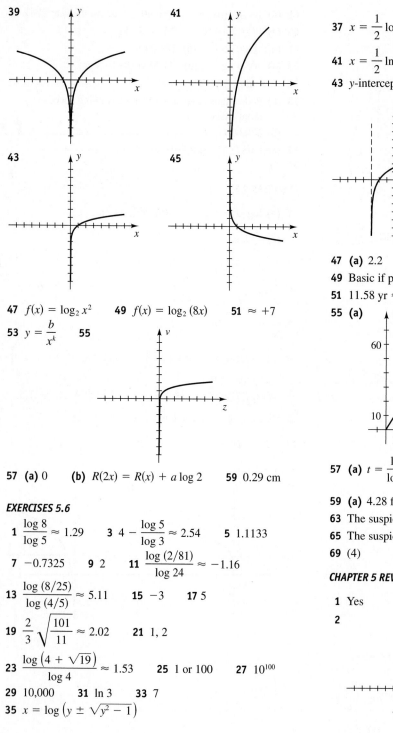

39

41

43

45

47 $f(x) = \log_2 x^2$ **49** $f(x) = \log_2 (8x)$ **51** $\approx +7$

53 $y = \dfrac{b}{x^k}$ **55**

57 (a) 0   (b) $R(2x) = R(x) + a \log 2$ **59** 0.29 cm

EXERCISES 5.6

1 $\dfrac{\log 8}{\log 5} \approx 1.29$ **3** $4 - \dfrac{\log 5}{\log 3} \approx 2.54$ **5** 1.1133

7 -0.7325 **9** 2   **11** $\dfrac{\log (2/81)}{\log 24} \approx -1.16$

13 $\dfrac{\log (8/25)}{\log (4/5)} \approx 5.11$ **15** -3 **17** 5

19 $\dfrac{2}{3}\sqrt{\dfrac{101}{11}} \approx 2.02$ **21** 1, 2

23 $\dfrac{\log (4 + \sqrt{19})}{\log 4} \approx 1.53$ **25** 1 or 100   **27** 10^{100}

29 10,000   **31** $\ln 3$ **33** 7
35 $x = \log\left(y \pm \sqrt{y^2 - 1}\right)$

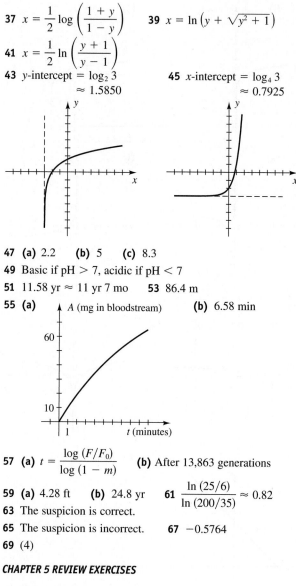

37 $x = \dfrac{1}{2} \log\left(\dfrac{1+y}{1-y}\right)$ **39** $x = \ln\left(y + \sqrt{y^2 + 1}\right)$

41 $x = \dfrac{1}{2} \ln\left(\dfrac{y+1}{y-1}\right)$

43 y-intercept $= \log_2 3$ **45** x-intercept $= \log_4 3$
≈ 1.5850 ≈ 0.7925

47 (a) 2.2   (b) 5   (c) 8.3
49 Basic if pH > 7, acidic if pH < 7
51 11.58 yr $\approx$ 11 yr 7 mo   **53** 86.4 m
55 (a)   (b) 6.58 min

57 (a) $t = \dfrac{\log (F/F_0)}{\log (1 - m)}$ (b) After 13,863 generations

59 (a) 4.28 ft   (b) 24.8 yr   **61** $\dfrac{\ln (25/6)}{\ln (200/35)} \approx 0.82$
63 The suspicion is correct.
65 The suspicion is incorrect.   **67** -0.5764
69 (4)

CHAPTER 5 REVIEW EXERCISES

1 Yes

2

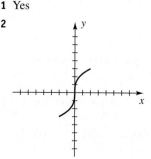

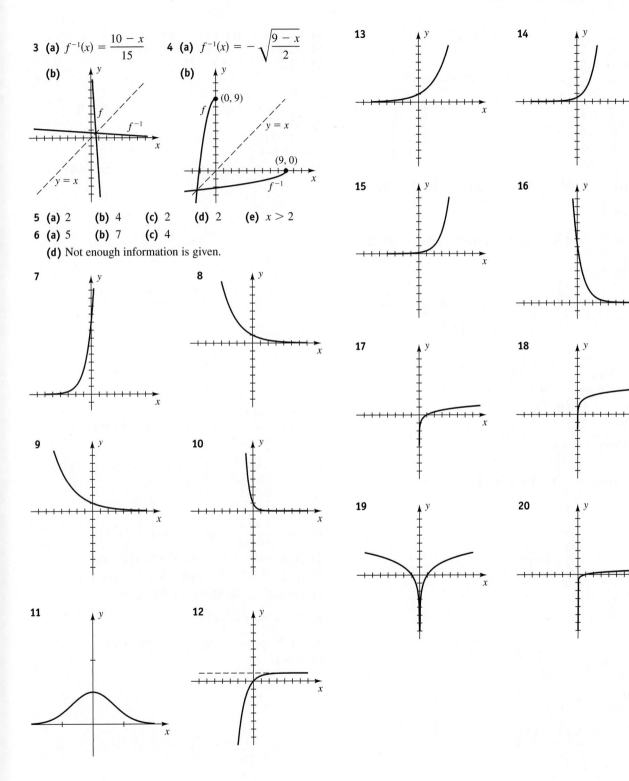

3 (a) $f^{-1}(x) = \dfrac{10 - x}{15}$ **4 (a)** $f^{-1}(x) = -\sqrt{\dfrac{9 - x}{2}}$

(b)   **(b)**

5 (a) 2   **(b)** 4   **(c)** 2   **(d)** 2   **(e)** $x > 2$
6 (a) 5   **(b)** 7   **(c)** 4
    (d) Not enough information is given.

7   **8**

9   **10**

11   **12**

13   **14**

15   **16**

17   **18**

19   **20**

21

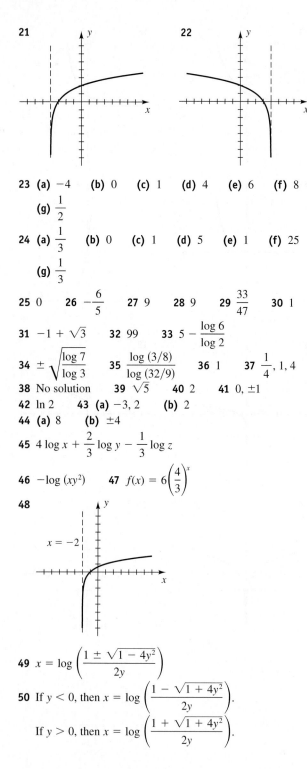

22

23 **(a)** -4 **(b)** 0 **(c)** 1 **(d)** 4 **(e)** 6 **(f)** 8

(g) $\dfrac{1}{2}$

24 **(a)** $\dfrac{1}{3}$ **(b)** 0 **(c)** 1 **(d)** 5 **(e)** 1 **(f)** 25

(g) $\dfrac{1}{3}$

25 0 **26** $-\dfrac{6}{5}$ **27** 9 **28** 9 **29** $\dfrac{33}{47}$ **30** 1

31 $-1 + \sqrt{3}$ **32** 99 **33** $5 - \dfrac{\log 6}{\log 2}$

34 $\pm\sqrt{\dfrac{\log 7}{\log 3}}$ **35** $\dfrac{\log (3/8)}{\log (32/9)}$ **36** 1 **37** $\dfrac{1}{4}, 1, 4$

38 No solution   **39** $\sqrt{5}$ **40** 2 **41** $0, \pm 1$

42 $\ln 2$ **43** **(a)** $-3, 2$ **(b)** 2

44 **(a)** 8 **(b)** ± 4

45 $4 \log x + \dfrac{2}{3} \log y - \dfrac{1}{3} \log z$

46 $-\log (xy^2)$ **47** $f(x) = 6\left(\dfrac{4}{3}\right)^x$

48

$x = -2$

49 $x = \log\left(\dfrac{1 \pm \sqrt{1 - 4y^2}}{2y}\right)$

50 If $y < 0$, then $x = \log\left(\dfrac{1 - \sqrt{1 + 4y^2}}{2y}\right)$.

If $y > 0$, then $x = \log\left(\dfrac{1 + \sqrt{1 + 4y^2}}{2y}\right)$.

51 **(a)** 1.89 **(b)** 78.3 **(c)** 0.472
52 **(a)** 0.924 **(b)** 0.00375 **(c)** 6.05
53 **(a)** $D = (-1, \infty), R = \mathbb{R}$
   (b) $y = 2^x - 1, D = \mathbb{R}, R = (-1, \infty)$
54 **(a)** $D = \mathbb{R}, R = (-2, \infty)$
   (b) $y = 3 - \log_2 (x + 2), D = (-2, \infty), R = \mathbb{R}$
55 **(a)** 2000
   (b) $2000(3^{1/6}) \approx 2401; 2000(3^{1/2}) = 3464; 6000$
56 $\$1082.43$
57 **(a)**

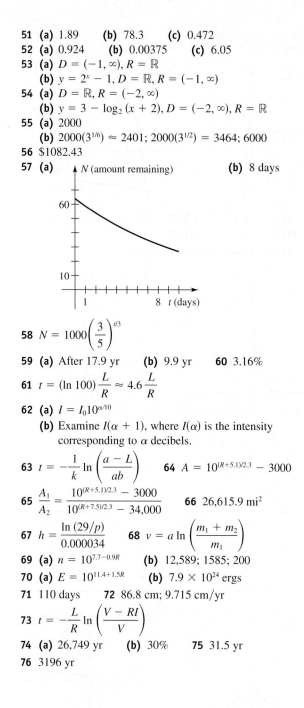

   (b) 8 days

58 $N = 1000\left(\dfrac{3}{5}\right)^{t/3}$

59 **(a)** After 17.9 yr   **(b)** 9.9 yr   **60** 3.16%
61 $t = (\ln 100)\dfrac{L}{R} \approx 4.6 \dfrac{L}{R}$

62 **(a)** $I = I_0 10^{\alpha/10}$
   (b) Examine $I(\alpha + 1)$, where $I(\alpha)$ is the intensity corresponding to α decibels.

63 $t = -\dfrac{1}{k} \ln\left(\dfrac{a - L}{ab}\right)$ **64** $A = 10^{(R+5.1)/2.3} - 3000$

65 $\dfrac{A_1}{A_2} = \dfrac{10^{(R+5.1)/2.3} - 3000}{10^{(R+7.5)/2.3} - 34{,}000}$ **66** $26{,}615.9 \text{ mi}^2$

67 $h = \dfrac{\ln (29/p)}{0.000034}$ **68** $v = a \ln\left(\dfrac{m_1 + m_2}{m_1}\right)$

69 **(a)** $n = 10^{7.7 - 0.9R}$ **(b)** $12{,}589; 1585; 200$
70 **(a)** $E = 10^{11.4 + 1.5R}$ **(b)** 7.9×10^{24} ergs
71 110 days   **72** 86.8 cm; 9.715 cm/yr
73 $t = -\dfrac{L}{R} \ln\left(\dfrac{V - RI}{V}\right)$

74 **(a)** $26{,}749$ yr   **(b)** 30% **75** 31.5 yr
76 3196 yr

CHAPTER 5 DISCUSSION EXERCISES

1 (a) $f^{-1}(x) = \sqrt[3]{1-x} + 1$

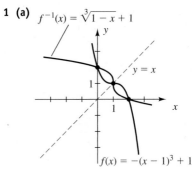

$y = x$

$f(x) = -(x-1)^3 + 1$

2 $f^{-1}(x) = \dfrac{x}{\sqrt{81-x^2}}$. The vertical asymptotes are $x = \pm 9$.
The horizontal asymptotes of f are $y = \pm 9$.

3 (a) *Hint:* Take the natural logarithm of both sides first.

(b) Note that $f(e) = \dfrac{1}{e}$. Any horizontal line $y = k$, with

$0 < k < \dfrac{1}{e}$, will intersect the graph at points

$\left(x_1, \dfrac{\ln x_1}{x_1} \right)$ and $\left(x_2, \dfrac{\ln x_2}{x_2} \right)$, where $1 < x_1 < e$ and
$x_2 > e$.

4 7.16 yr

5 *Hint:* Check the restrictions for the logarithm laws.

6 (a) The difference is in the compounding.

(b) Closer to the graph of the second function

7 8.447177%; $1,025,156.25

8 (a) 3.5 earthquakes = 1 bomb, 425 bombs = 1 eruption

(b) 9.22; yes

9 e^b, with $b = \dfrac{11 \ln 5 \cdot \ln 7}{\ln 35}$

Chapter 6

EXERCISES 6.1

Exer. 1–4: The answers are not unique.

1 (a) $480°, 840°, -240°, -600°$

(b) $495°, 855°, -225°, -585°$

(c) $330°, 690°, -390°, -750°$

3 (a) $260°, 980°, -100°, -460°$

(b) $\dfrac{17\pi}{6}, \dfrac{29\pi}{6}, -\dfrac{7\pi}{6}, -\dfrac{19\pi}{6}$

(c) $\dfrac{7\pi}{4}, \dfrac{15\pi}{4}, -\dfrac{9\pi}{4}, -\dfrac{17\pi}{4}$

5 (a) $84°42'26''$ **(b)** $57.5°$

7 (a) $131°8'23''$ **(b)** $43.58°$

9 (a) $\dfrac{5\pi}{6}$ **(b)** $-\dfrac{\pi}{3}$ **(c)** $\dfrac{5\pi}{4}$

11 (a) $\dfrac{5\pi}{2}$ **(b)** $\dfrac{2\pi}{5}$ **(c)** $\dfrac{5\pi}{9}$

13 (a) $120°$ **(b)** $330°$ **(c)** $135°$

15 (a) $-630°$ **(b)** $1260°$ **(c)** $20°$

17 $114°35'30''$ **19** $286°28'44''$ **21** $37.6833°$

23 $115.4408°$ **25** $63°10'8''$ **27** $310°37'17''$

29 2.5 cm

31 (a) $2\pi \approx 6.28$ cm **(b)** $8\pi \approx 25.13$ cm^2

33 (a) $1.75; \dfrac{315}{\pi} \approx 100.27°$ **(b)** 14 cm^2

35 (a) $\dfrac{20\pi}{9} \approx 6.98$ m **(b)** $\dfrac{80\pi}{9} \approx 27.93$ m^2

37 In miles: **(a)** 4189 **(b)** 3142 **(c)** 2094
(d) 698 **(e)** 70

39 $\dfrac{1}{8}$ radian $\approx 7°10'$ **41** 37.1%

43 7.29×10^{-5} rad/sec

45 (a) 80π rad/min **(b)** $\dfrac{100\pi}{3} \approx 104.72$ ft/min

47 (a) 400π rad/min **(b)** 38π cm/sec **(c)** 380 rpm
(d) $S(r) = \dfrac{1140}{r}$; inversely

49 (a) $\dfrac{21\pi}{8} \approx 8.25$ ft **(b)** $\dfrac{2}{3}d$

51 Large **53** 192.08 rev/min

EXERCISES 6.2

1 (a) B **(b)** D **(c)** A **(d)** C **(e)** E

Note: Answers are in the order *sin, cos, tan, cot, sec, csc* for any exercises that require the values of the six trigonometric functions.

3 $\dfrac{4}{5}, \dfrac{3}{5}, \dfrac{4}{3}, \dfrac{3}{4}, \dfrac{5}{3}, \dfrac{5}{4}$

5 $\dfrac{2}{5}, \dfrac{\sqrt{21}}{5}, \dfrac{2}{\sqrt{21}}, \dfrac{\sqrt{21}}{2}, \dfrac{5}{\sqrt{21}}, \dfrac{5}{2}$

7 $\dfrac{a}{\sqrt{a^2+b^2}}, \dfrac{b}{\sqrt{a^2+b^2}}, \dfrac{a}{b}, \dfrac{b}{a}, \dfrac{\sqrt{a^2+b^2}}{b}, \dfrac{\sqrt{a^2+b^2}}{a}$

9 $\dfrac{b}{c}, \dfrac{\sqrt{c^2-b^2}}{c}, \dfrac{b}{\sqrt{c^2-b^2}}, \dfrac{\sqrt{c^2-b^2}}{b}, \dfrac{c}{\sqrt{c^2-b^2}}, \dfrac{c}{b}$

11 $x = 8; y = 4\sqrt{3}$ **13** $x = 7\sqrt{2}; y = 7$

15 $x = 4\sqrt{3}; y = 4$

17 $\dfrac{3}{5}, \dfrac{4}{5}, \dfrac{3}{4}, \dfrac{4}{3}, \dfrac{5}{4}, \dfrac{5}{3}$ **19** $\dfrac{5}{13}, \dfrac{12}{13}, \dfrac{5}{12}, \dfrac{12}{5}, \dfrac{13}{12}, \dfrac{13}{5}$

21 $\dfrac{\sqrt{11}}{6}, \dfrac{5}{6}, \dfrac{\sqrt{11}}{5}, \dfrac{5}{\sqrt{11}}, \dfrac{6}{5}, \dfrac{6}{\sqrt{11}}$

23 $200\sqrt{3} \approx 346.4$ ft **25** 192 ft **27** 1.02 m

29 (a) 0.6691 (b) 0.2250 (c) 1.1924 (d) -1.0154

31 (a) 4.0572 (b) 1.0323 (c) -0.6335 (d) 4.3813

33 (a) 0.5 (b) -0.9880 (c) 0.9985 (d) -1

35 (a) -1 (b) -4

37 (a) 5 (b) 5

39 $1 - \sin \theta \cos \theta$ **41** $\sin \theta$

43 $\cot \theta = \dfrac{\sqrt{1 - \sin^2 \theta}}{\sin \theta}$ **45** $\sec \theta = \dfrac{1}{\sqrt{1 - \sin^2 \theta}}$

47 $\sin \theta = \dfrac{\sqrt{\sec^2 \theta - 1}}{\sec \theta}$

Exer. 49–70: Typical verifications are given.

49 $\cos \theta \sec \theta = \cos \theta (1/\cos \theta) = 1$

51 $\sin \theta \sec \theta = \sin \theta (1/\cos \theta) = \sin \theta/\cos \theta = \tan \theta$

53 $\dfrac{\csc \theta}{\sec \theta} = \dfrac{1/\sin \theta}{1/\cos \theta} = \dfrac{\cos \theta}{\sin \theta} = \cot \theta$

55 $(1 + \cos 2\theta)(1 - \cos 2\theta) = 1 - \cos^2 2\theta = \sin^2 2\theta$

57 $\cos^2 \theta (\sec^2 \theta - 1) = \cos^2 \theta (\tan^2 \theta)$
$$= \cos^2 \theta \cdot \dfrac{\sin^2 \theta}{\cos^2 \theta} = \sin^2 \theta$$

59 $\dfrac{\sin (\theta/2)}{\csc (\theta/2)} + \dfrac{\cos (\theta/2)}{\sec (\theta/2)} = \dfrac{\sin (\theta/2)}{1/\sin (\theta/2)} + \dfrac{\cos (\theta/2)}{1/\cos (\theta/2)}$
$$= \sin^2 (\theta/2) + \cos^2 (\theta/2) = 1$$

61 $(1 + \sin \theta)(1 - \sin \theta) = 1 - \sin^2 \theta = \cos^2 \theta$
$$= \dfrac{1}{\sec^2 \theta}$$

63 $\sec \theta - \cos \theta = \dfrac{1}{\cos \theta} - \cos \theta = \dfrac{1 - \cos^2 \theta}{\cos \theta} = \dfrac{\sin^2 \theta}{\cos \theta}$
$$= \dfrac{\sin \theta}{\cos \theta} \cdot \sin \theta = \tan \theta \sin \theta$$

65 $(\cot \theta + \csc \theta)(\tan \theta - \sin \theta)$
$= \cot \theta \tan \theta - \cot \theta \sin \theta + \csc \theta \tan \theta$
$\quad - \csc \theta \sin \theta$
$= \dfrac{1}{\tan \theta} \tan \theta - \dfrac{\cos \theta}{\sin \theta} \sin \theta + \dfrac{1}{\sin \theta} \dfrac{\sin \theta}{\cos \theta} - \dfrac{1}{\sin \theta} \sin \theta$
$= 1 - \cos \theta + \dfrac{1}{\cos \theta} - 1 = -\cos \theta + \sec \theta$
$$= \sec \theta - \cos \theta$$

67 $\sec^2 3\theta \csc^2 3\theta = (1 + \tan^2 3\theta)(1 + \cot^2 3\theta)$
$= 1 + \tan^2 3\theta + \cot^2 3\theta + 1$
$= \sec^2 3\theta + \csc^2 3\theta$

69 $\log \csc \theta = \log \left(\dfrac{1}{\sin \theta} \right) = \log 1 - \log \sin \theta$
$= 0 - \log \sin \theta = -\log \sin \theta$

71 $-\dfrac{3}{5}, \dfrac{4}{5}, -\dfrac{3}{4}, -\dfrac{4}{3}, \dfrac{5}{4}, -\dfrac{5}{3}$

73 $-\dfrac{5}{\sqrt{29}}, -\dfrac{2}{\sqrt{29}}, \dfrac{5}{2}, \dfrac{2}{5}, -\dfrac{\sqrt{29}}{2}, -\dfrac{\sqrt{29}}{5}$

75 $\dfrac{4}{\sqrt{17}}, -\dfrac{1}{\sqrt{17}}, -4, -\dfrac{1}{4}, -\sqrt{17}, \dfrac{\sqrt{17}}{4}$

77 $\dfrac{4}{5}, \dfrac{3}{5}, \dfrac{4}{3}, \dfrac{3}{4}, \dfrac{5}{3}, \dfrac{5}{4}$

79 $-\dfrac{7}{\sqrt{53}}, -\dfrac{2}{\sqrt{53}}, \dfrac{7}{2}, \dfrac{2}{7}, -\dfrac{\sqrt{53}}{2}, -\dfrac{\sqrt{53}}{7}$

Note: U denotes *undefined*.

81 (a) 1, 0, U, 0, U, 1 (b) 0, 1, 0, U, 1, U
(c) -1, 0, U, 0, U, -1 (d) 0, -1, 0, U, -1, U

83 (a) IV (b) III (c) II (d) III

85 $\dfrac{3}{5}, -\dfrac{4}{5}, -\dfrac{3}{4}, -\dfrac{4}{3}, -\dfrac{5}{4}, \dfrac{5}{3}$

87 $-\dfrac{5}{13}, \dfrac{12}{13}, -\dfrac{5}{12}, -\dfrac{12}{5}, \dfrac{13}{12}, -\dfrac{13}{5}$

89 $-\dfrac{\sqrt{8}}{3}, -\dfrac{1}{3}, \sqrt{8}, \dfrac{1}{\sqrt{8}}, -3, -\dfrac{3}{\sqrt{8}}$

91 $\dfrac{\sqrt{15}}{4}, -\dfrac{1}{4}, -\sqrt{15}, -\dfrac{1}{\sqrt{15}}, -4, \dfrac{4}{\sqrt{15}}$

93 $-\tan \theta$ **95** $\sec \theta$ **97** $-\sin \dfrac{\theta}{2}$

EXERCISES 6.3

1 $\dfrac{8}{17}, -\dfrac{15}{17}, -\dfrac{8}{15}, -\dfrac{15}{8}, -\dfrac{17}{15}, \dfrac{17}{8}$

3 $-\dfrac{7}{25}, \dfrac{24}{25}, -\dfrac{7}{24}, -\dfrac{24}{7}, \dfrac{25}{24}, -\dfrac{25}{7}$

5 (a) $\left(-\dfrac{3}{5}, -\dfrac{4}{5} \right)$ (b) $\left(-\dfrac{3}{5}, -\dfrac{4}{5} \right)$

(c) $\left(\dfrac{3}{5}, -\dfrac{4}{5} \right)$ (d) $\left(-\dfrac{3}{5}, \dfrac{4}{5} \right)$

7 (a) $\left(\dfrac{12}{13}, \dfrac{5}{13} \right)$ (b) $\left(\dfrac{12}{13}, \dfrac{5}{13} \right)$

(c) $\left(-\dfrac{12}{13}, \dfrac{5}{13} \right)$ (d) $\left(\dfrac{12}{13}, -\dfrac{5}{13} \right)$

Note: U denotes *undefined*.

9 (a) $(1, 0)$; 0, 1, 0, U, 1, U
(b) $(-1, 0)$; 0, -1, 0, U, -1, U

11 (a) $(0, -1)$; -1, 0, U, 0, U, -1
(b) $(0, 1)$; 1, 0, U, 0, U, 1

13 (a) $\left(\dfrac{\sqrt{2}}{2},\dfrac{\sqrt{2}}{2}\right);\dfrac{\sqrt{2}}{2},\dfrac{\sqrt{2}}{2},1,1,\sqrt{2},\sqrt{2}$

(b) $\left(-\dfrac{\sqrt{2}}{2},\dfrac{\sqrt{2}}{2}\right);\dfrac{\sqrt{2}}{2},-\dfrac{\sqrt{2}}{2},-1,-1,-\sqrt{2},\sqrt{2}$

15 (a) $\left(-\dfrac{\sqrt{2}}{2},-\dfrac{\sqrt{2}}{2}\right);-\dfrac{\sqrt{2}}{2},-\dfrac{\sqrt{2}}{2},1,1,-\sqrt{2},-\sqrt{2}$

(b) $\left(\dfrac{\sqrt{2}}{2},-\dfrac{\sqrt{2}}{2}\right);-\dfrac{\sqrt{2}}{2},\dfrac{\sqrt{2}}{2},-1,-1,\sqrt{2},-\sqrt{2}$

17 (a) -1 **(b)** $-\dfrac{\sqrt{2}}{2}$ **(c)** -1

19 (a) 1 **(b)** -1 **(c)** 1

Exer. 21–26: Typical verifications are given.

21 $\sin(-x)\sec(-x)=(-\sin x)\sec x$
$$=(-\sin x)(1/\cos x)$$
$$=-\tan x$$

23 $\dfrac{\cot(-x)}{\csc(-x)}=\dfrac{-\cot x}{-\csc x}=\dfrac{\cos x/\sin x}{1/\sin x}=\cos x$

25 $\dfrac{1}{\cos(-x)}-\tan(-x)\sin(-x)$

$$=\dfrac{1}{\cos x}-(-\tan x)(-\sin x)$$

$$=\dfrac{1}{\cos x}-\dfrac{\sin x}{\cos x}\cdot\sin x$$

$$=\dfrac{1-\sin^2 x}{\cos x}=\dfrac{\cos^2 x}{\cos x}=\cos x$$

27 (a) 0 **(b)** -1 **29 (a)** $\dfrac{\sqrt{2}}{2}$ **(b)** -1

31 (a) 1 **(b)** $-\infty$ **33 (a)** -1 **(b)** ∞

35 (a) ∞ **(b)** $\sqrt{2}$ **37 (a)** $-\infty$ **(b)** 1

39 $\dfrac{3\pi}{2},\dfrac{7\pi}{2}$ **41** $\dfrac{\pi}{6},\dfrac{5\pi}{6},\dfrac{13\pi}{6},\dfrac{17\pi}{6}$ **43** $0,2\pi,4\pi$

45 $\dfrac{\pi}{4},\dfrac{7\pi}{4},\dfrac{9\pi}{4},\dfrac{15\pi}{4}$ **47** $\dfrac{\pi}{4},\dfrac{5\pi}{4}$ **49** $0,\pi$

51 (a) $-\dfrac{11\pi}{6},-\dfrac{7\pi}{6},\dfrac{\pi}{6},\dfrac{5\pi}{6}$

(b) $-\dfrac{11\pi}{6}<x<-\dfrac{7\pi}{6}$ and $\dfrac{\pi}{6}<x<\dfrac{5\pi}{6}$

(c) $-2\pi\le x<-\dfrac{11\pi}{6},-\dfrac{7\pi}{6}<x<\dfrac{\pi}{6}$, and

$\dfrac{5\pi}{6}<x\le 2\pi$

53 (a) $-\dfrac{4\pi}{3},-\dfrac{2\pi}{3},\dfrac{2\pi}{3},\dfrac{4\pi}{3}$

(b) $-2\pi\le x<-\dfrac{4\pi}{3},-\dfrac{2\pi}{3}<x<\dfrac{2\pi}{3}$, and

$\dfrac{4\pi}{3}<x\le 2\pi$

(c) $-\dfrac{4\pi}{3}<x<-\dfrac{2\pi}{3}$ and $\dfrac{2\pi}{3}<x<\dfrac{4\pi}{3}$

55 **57** **59** **61**

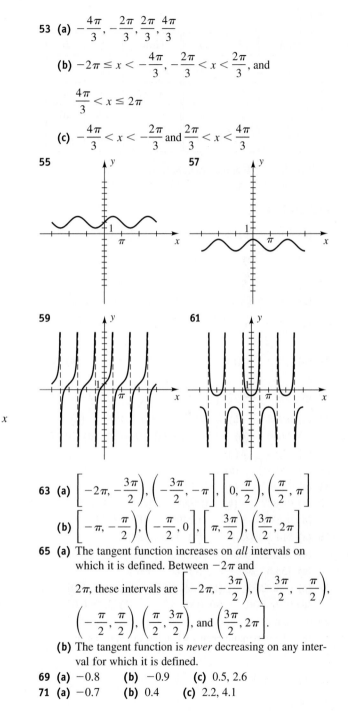

63 (a) $\left[-2\pi,-\dfrac{3\pi}{2}\right),\left(-\dfrac{3\pi}{2},-\pi\right],\left[0,\dfrac{\pi}{2}\right),\left(\dfrac{\pi}{2},\pi\right]$

(b) $\left[-\pi,-\dfrac{\pi}{2}\right),\left(-\dfrac{\pi}{2},0\right],\left[\pi,\dfrac{3\pi}{2}\right),\left(\dfrac{3\pi}{2},2\pi\right]$

65 (a) The tangent function increases on *all* intervals on which it is defined. Between -2π and 2π, these intervals are $\left[-2\pi,-\dfrac{3\pi}{2}\right),\left(-\dfrac{3\pi}{2},-\dfrac{\pi}{2}\right),$
$\left(-\dfrac{\pi}{2},\dfrac{\pi}{2}\right),\left(\dfrac{\pi}{2},\dfrac{3\pi}{2}\right),$ and $\left(\dfrac{3\pi}{2},2\pi\right]$.

(b) The tangent function is *never* decreasing on any interval for which it is defined.

69 (a) -0.8 **(b)** -0.9 **(c)** $0.5, 2.6$

71 (a) -0.7 **(b)** 0.4 **(c)** $2.2, 4.1$

73 (a)

Time	T	H	Time	T	H
12 A.M.	60	60	12 P.M.	60	60
3 A.M.	52	74	3 P.M.	68	46
6 A.M.	48	80	6 P.M.	72	40
9 A.M.	52	74	9 P.M.	68	46

   (b) Max: 72°F at 6:00 P.M., 80% at 6:00 A.M.;
   min: 48°F at 6:00 A.M., 40% at 6:00 P.M.

EXERCISES 6.4

1 (a) 60°   **(b)** 20°   **(c)** 22°   **(d)** 60°

3 (a) $\dfrac{\pi}{4}$ **(b)** $\dfrac{\pi}{3}$ **(c)** $\dfrac{\pi}{6}$ **(d)** $\dfrac{\pi}{4}$

5 (a) $\pi - 3 \approx 8.1°$ **(b)** $\pi - 2 \approx 65.4°$
   (c) $2\pi - 5.5 \approx 44.9°$ **(d)** $32\pi - 100 \approx 30.4°$

7 (a) $\dfrac{\sqrt{3}}{2}$ **(b)** $\dfrac{\sqrt{2}}{2}$ **9 (a)** $-\dfrac{\sqrt{3}}{2}$ **(b)** $\dfrac{1}{2}$

11 (a) $-\dfrac{\sqrt{3}}{3}$ **(b)** $-\sqrt{3}$ **13 (a)** $-\dfrac{\sqrt{3}}{3}$ **(b)** $\sqrt{3}$

15 (a) -2 **(b)** $\dfrac{2}{\sqrt{3}}$ **17 (a)** $-\dfrac{2}{\sqrt{3}}$ **(b)** 2

19 (a) 0.958   **(b)** 0.778   **21 (a)** 0.387   **(b)** 0.472

23 (a) 2.650   **(b)** 3.179   **25 (a)** 30.46°   **(b)** 30°27′

27 (a) 74.88°   **(b)** 74°53′

29 (a) 24.94°   **(b)** 24°57′

31 (a) 76.38°   **(b)** 76°23′

33 (a) 0.9899   **(b)** -0.1097 **(c)** -0.1425
   (d) 0.7907   **(e)** -11.2493 **(f)** 1.3677

35 (a) 214.3°, 325.7°   **(b)** 41.5°, 318.5°
   (c) 70.3°, 250.3°   **(d)** 133.8°, 313.8°
   (e) 153.6°, 206.4°   **(f)** 42.3°, 137.7°

37 (a) 0.43, 2.71   **(b)** 1.69, 4.59   **(c)** 1.87, 5.01
   (d) 0.36, 3.50   **(e)** 0.96, 5.32   **(f)** 3.35, 6.07

39 0.28 cm

41 (a) The maximum occurs when the sun is rising in
   the east.
   (b) $\dfrac{\sqrt{2}}{4} \approx 35\%$

43 $\left(9, 9\sqrt{3}\right)$

EXERCISES 6.5

1 (a) $4, 2\pi$ **(b)** $1, \dfrac{\pi}{2}$

(c) $\dfrac{1}{4}, 2\pi$ **(d)** $1, 8\pi$

(e) $2, 8\pi$ **(f)** $\dfrac{1}{2}, \dfrac{\pi}{2}$

(g) $4, 2\pi$ **(h)** $1, \dfrac{\pi}{2}$

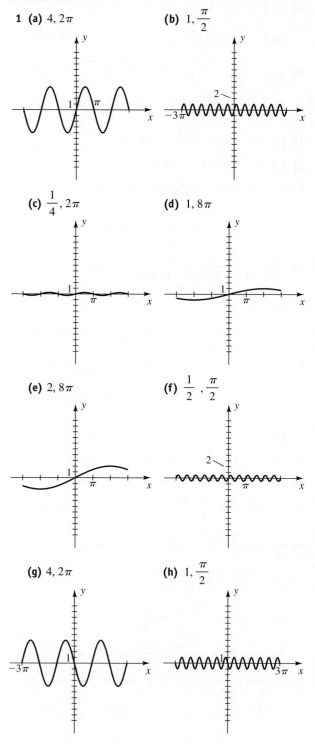

3 (a) $3, 2\pi$

(b) $1, \dfrac{2\pi}{3}$

5 $1, 2\pi, \dfrac{\pi}{2}$

7 $3, 2\pi, -\dfrac{\pi}{6}$

(c) $\dfrac{1}{3}, 2\pi$

(d) $1, 6\pi$

9 $1, 2\pi, -\dfrac{\pi}{2}$

11 $4, 2\pi, \dfrac{\pi}{4}$

(e) $2, 6\pi$

(f) $\dfrac{1}{2}, \dfrac{2\pi}{3}$

13 $1, \pi, \dfrac{\pi}{2}$

15 $1, \dfrac{2\pi}{3}, -\dfrac{\pi}{3}$

(g) $3, 2\pi$

(h) $1, \dfrac{2\pi}{3}$

17 $2, \dfrac{2\pi}{3}, \dfrac{\pi}{3}$

19 $1, 4\pi, \dfrac{2\pi}{3}$

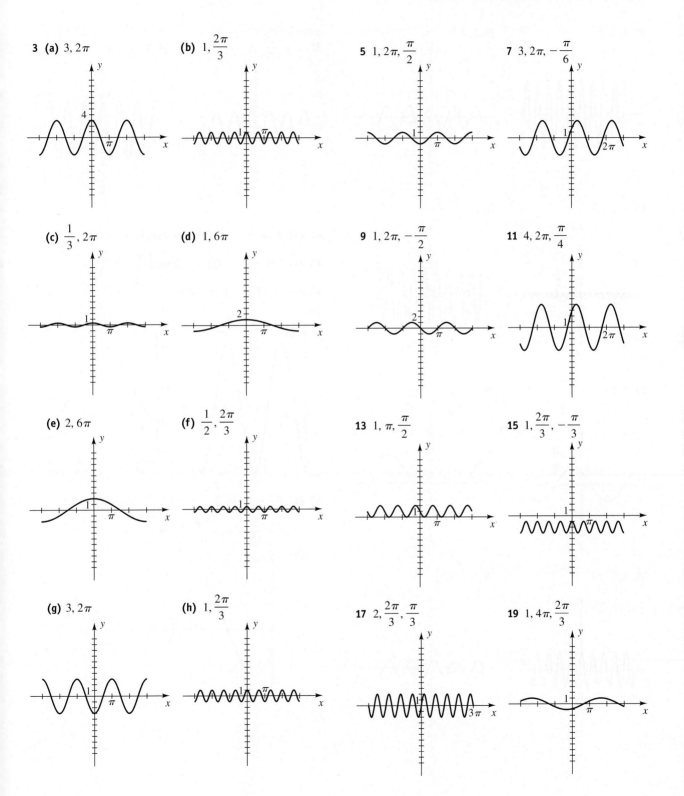

21 6, 2, 0

23 2, 4, 0

37 2, π, $\dfrac{\pi}{2}$

39 5, π, $-\pi$

25 $\dfrac{1}{2}$, 1, 0

27 5, $\dfrac{2\pi}{3}$, $\dfrac{\pi}{6}$

41 **(a)** 4, 2π, $-\pi$ **(b)** $y = 4\sin(x + \pi)$

43 **(a)** 2, 4, -3 **(b)** $y = 2\sin\left(\dfrac{\pi}{2}x + \dfrac{3\pi}{2}\right)$

45 4π **47** $a = 8$, $b = 4\pi$

49

51

29 3, 4π, $\dfrac{\pi}{2}$

31 5, 6π, $-\dfrac{\pi}{2}$

53 **(a)** $f(t) = 10\sin\left[\dfrac{\pi}{12}(t - 10)\right] + 0$, with $a = 10$,

$b = \dfrac{\pi}{12}$, $c = -\dfrac{5\pi}{6}$, $d = 0$

(b)

33 3, 2, -4

35 $\sqrt{2}$, 4, $\dfrac{1}{2}$

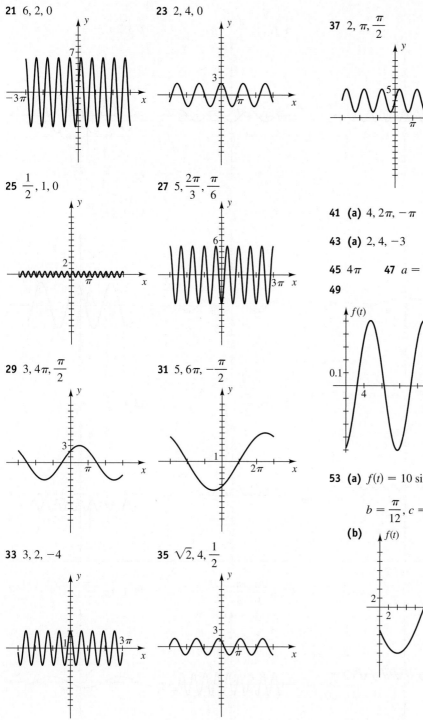
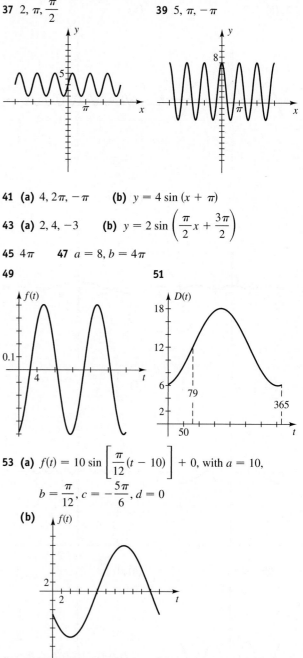

55 (a) $f(t) = 10 \sin\left[\dfrac{\pi}{12}(t - 9)\right] + 20$, with $a = 10$,

$b = \dfrac{\pi}{12}$, $c = -\dfrac{3\pi}{4}$, $d = 20$

(b)

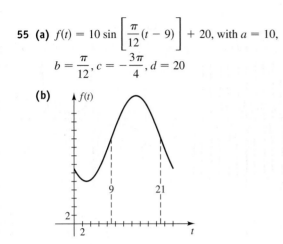

EXERCISES 6.6

1 π

3 π

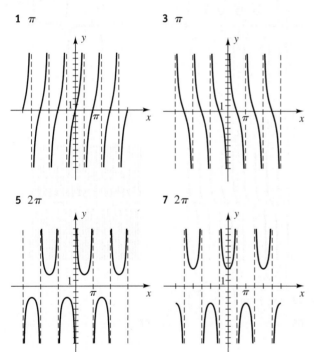

5 2π

7 2π

9 π

11 $\dfrac{\pi}{2}$

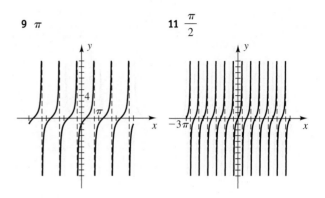

13 4π

15 $\dfrac{\pi}{2}$

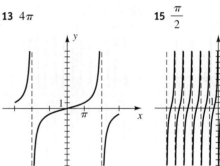

17 2π

19 π

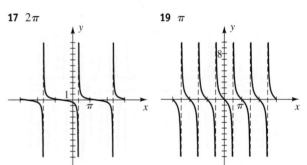

21 $\dfrac{\pi}{2}$

23 3π

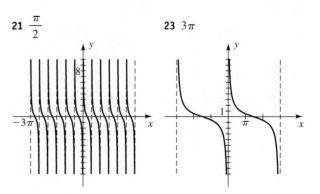

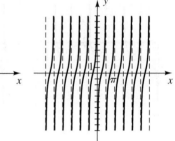

25 $\dfrac{\pi}{2}$

27 2π

41 π

43 6π

29 2π

31 π

45 π

47 4π

33 6π

35 π

49 2

51 1

37 4π

39 2π

53 $y = -\cot\left(x + \dfrac{\pi}{2}\right)$

55

57

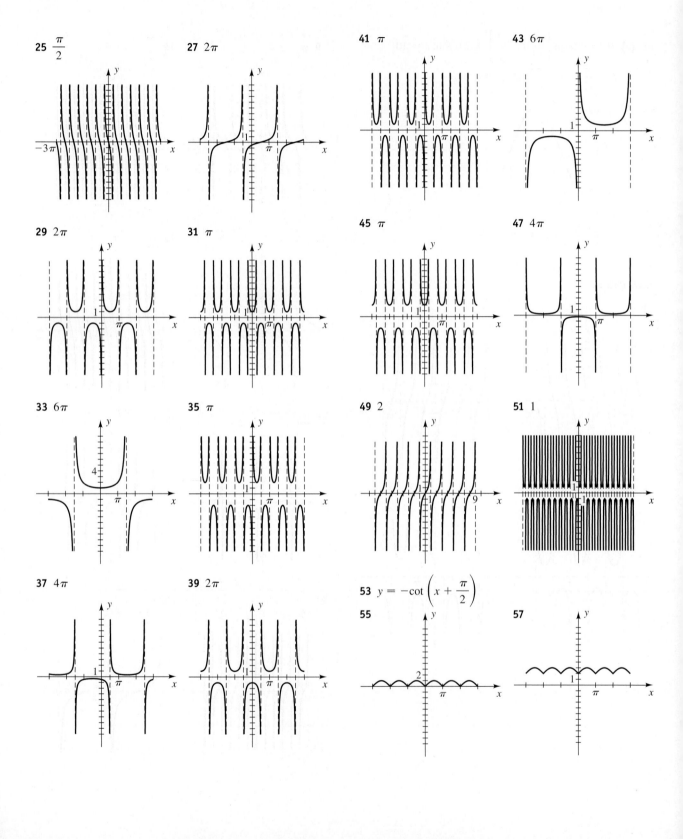

59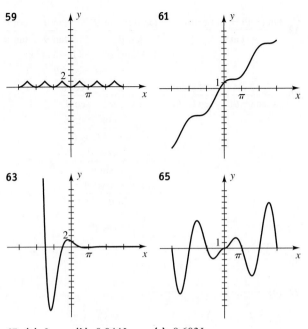

61

63

65

67 (a) I_0 **(b)** $0.044I_0$ **(c)** $0.603I_0$

69 (a) $A_0 e^{-\alpha z}$ **(b)** $\dfrac{\alpha}{k} z_0$ **(c)** $\dfrac{\ln 2}{\alpha}$

EXERCISES 6.7

1 $\beta = 60°, a = \dfrac{20}{3}\sqrt{3}, c = \dfrac{40}{3}\sqrt{3}$

3 $\alpha = 45°, a = b = 15\sqrt{2}$

5 $\alpha = \beta = 45°, c = 5\sqrt{2}$

7 $\alpha = 60°, \beta = 30°, a = 15$

9 $\beta = 53°, a \approx 18, c \approx 30$

11 $\alpha = 18°9', a \approx 78.7, c \approx 252.6$

13 $\alpha \approx 29°, \beta \approx 61°, c \approx 51$

15 $\alpha \approx 69°, \beta \approx 21°, a \approx 5.4$ **17** $b = c \cos \alpha$

19 $a = b \cot \beta$ **21** $c = a \csc \alpha$

23 $b = \sqrt{c^2 - a^2}$

25 $250\sqrt{3} + 4 \approx 437$ ft   **27** 28,800 ft   **29** 160 m

31 9659 ft   **33 (a)** 58 ft   **(b)** 27 ft   **35** 51°20'

37 16.3°   **39** 2063 ft   **41** 1,459,379 ft²

43 21.8°   **45** 20.2 m   **47** 29.7 km   **49** 3944 mi

51 126 mi/hr

53 (a) 45%

(b) Each satellite has a signal range of more than 120°.

55 $h = d \sin \alpha + c$ **57** $h = \dfrac{d}{\cot \alpha - \cot \beta}$

59 $h = d(\tan \beta - \tan \alpha)$

61 N70°E; N40°W; S15°W; S25°E

63 (a) 55 mi   **(b)** S63°E   **65** 324 mi

67 Amplitude, 10 cm; period, $\dfrac{1}{3}$ sec; frequency, 3 osc/sec.

The point is at the origin at $t = 0$. It moves upward with decreasing speed, reaching the point with coordinate 10 at $t = \dfrac{1}{12}$. It then reverses direction and moves downward, gaining speed until it reaches the origin at $t = \dfrac{1}{6}$. It continues downward with decreasing speed, reaching the point with coordinate -10 at $t = \dfrac{1}{4}$. It then reverses direction and moves upward with increasing speed, returning to the origin at $t = \dfrac{1}{3}$.

69 Amplitude, 4 cm; period, $\dfrac{4}{3}$ sec; frequency, $\dfrac{3}{4}$ osc/sec.

The motion is similar to that in Exercise 67; however, the point starts 4 units above the origin and moves downward, reaching the origin at $t = \dfrac{1}{3}$ and the point with coordinate -4 at $t = \dfrac{2}{3}$. It then reverses direction and moves upward, reaching the origin at $t = 1$ and its initial point at $t = \dfrac{4}{3}$.

71 $d = 5 \cos \dfrac{2\pi}{3} t$

73 (a) $y = 25 \cos \dfrac{\pi}{15} t$

(b) 324,000 ft

CHAPTER 6 REVIEW EXERCISES

1 $\dfrac{11\pi}{6}, \dfrac{9\pi}{4}, -\dfrac{5\pi}{6}, \dfrac{4\pi}{3}, \dfrac{\pi}{5}$

2 $810°, -120°, 315°, 900°, 36°$

3 (a) 0.1   **(b)** 0.2 m²

4 (a) $\dfrac{35\pi}{12}$ cm   **(b)** $\dfrac{175\pi}{16}$ cm²

5 $\dfrac{200\pi}{3}, 90\pi$ **6** $\dfrac{100\pi}{3}, \dfrac{105\pi}{4}$

7 $x = 6\sqrt{3}; y = 3\sqrt{3}$ **8** $x = \dfrac{7}{2}\sqrt{2}; y = \dfrac{7}{2}\sqrt{2}$

9 $\tan \theta = \sqrt{\sec^2 \theta - 1}$ **10** $\cot \theta = \sqrt{\csc^2 \theta - 1}$

Exer. 11–20: Typical verifications are given.

11 $\sin \theta \, (\csc \theta - \sin \theta) = \sin \theta \csc \theta - \sin^2 \theta$
$$= 1 - \sin^2 \theta = \cos^2 \theta$$

12 $\cos \theta \, (\tan \theta + \cot \theta) = \cos \theta \cdot \dfrac{\sin \theta}{\cos \theta} + \cos \theta \cdot \dfrac{\cos \theta}{\sin \theta}$
$$= \sin \theta + \frac{\cos^2 \theta}{\sin \theta}$$
$$= \frac{\sin^2 \theta + \cos^2 \theta}{\sin \theta}$$
$$= \frac{1}{\sin \theta} = \csc \theta$$

13 $(\cos^2 \theta - 1)(\tan^2 \theta + 1) = (\cos^2 \theta - 1)(\sec^2 \theta)$
$$= \cos^2 \theta \sec^2 \theta - \sec^2 \theta$$
$$= 1 - \sec^2 \theta$$

14 $\dfrac{\sec \theta - \cos \theta}{\tan \theta} = \dfrac{\dfrac{1}{\cos \theta} - \cos \theta}{\dfrac{\sin \theta}{\cos \theta}} = \dfrac{\dfrac{1 - \cos^2 \theta}{\cos \theta}}{\dfrac{\sin \theta}{\cos \theta}} = \dfrac{\dfrac{\sin^2 \theta}{\cos \theta}}{\dfrac{\sin \theta}{\cos \theta}}$

$$= \frac{\dfrac{\sin \theta}{\cos \theta}}{\dfrac{1}{\cos \theta}} = \frac{\tan \theta}{\sec \theta}$$

15 $\dfrac{1 + \tan^2 \theta}{\tan^2 \theta} = \dfrac{1}{\tan^2 \theta} + \dfrac{\tan^2 \theta}{\tan^2 \theta} = \cot^2 \theta + 1 = \csc^2 \theta$

16 $\dfrac{\sec \theta + \csc \theta}{\sec \theta - \csc \theta} = \dfrac{\dfrac{1}{\cos \theta} + \dfrac{1}{\sin \theta}}{\dfrac{1}{\cos \theta} - \dfrac{1}{\sin \theta}} = \dfrac{\dfrac{\sin \theta + \cos \theta}{\cos \theta \sin \theta}}{\dfrac{\sin \theta - \cos \theta}{\cos \theta \sin \theta}}$

$$= \frac{\sin \theta + \cos \theta}{\sin \theta - \cos \theta}$$

17 $\dfrac{\cot \theta - 1}{1 - \tan \theta} = \dfrac{\dfrac{\cos \theta}{\sin \theta} - 1}{1 - \dfrac{\sin \theta}{\cos \theta}} = \dfrac{\dfrac{\cos \theta - \sin \theta}{\sin \theta}}{\dfrac{\cos \theta - \sin \theta}{\cos \theta}}$

$$= \frac{(\cos \theta - \sin \theta) \cos \theta}{(\cos \theta - \sin \theta) \sin \theta} = \frac{\cos \theta}{\sin \theta} = \cot \theta$$

18 $\dfrac{1 + \sec \theta}{\tan \theta + \sin \theta} = \dfrac{1 + \dfrac{1}{\cos \theta}}{\dfrac{\sin \theta}{\cos \theta} + \dfrac{\sin \theta \cos \theta}{\cos \theta}} = \dfrac{\dfrac{\cos \theta + 1}{\cos \theta}}{\dfrac{\sin \theta \, (1 + \cos \theta)}{\cos \theta}}$

$$= \frac{1}{\sin \theta} = \csc \theta$$

19 $\dfrac{\tan (-\theta) + \cot (-\theta)}{\tan \theta} = \dfrac{-\tan \theta - \cot \theta}{\tan \theta} = -\dfrac{\tan \theta}{\tan \theta} - \dfrac{\cot \theta}{\tan \theta}$
$$= -1 - \cot^2 \theta = -(1 + \cot^2 \theta)$$
$$= -\csc^2 \theta$$

20 $-\dfrac{1}{\csc (-\theta)} - \dfrac{\cot (-\theta)}{\sec (-\theta)} = -\dfrac{1}{-\csc \theta} - \dfrac{-\cot \theta}{\sec \theta}$
$$= \sin \theta + \frac{\cos \theta / \sin \theta}{1 / \cos \theta}$$
$$= \sin \theta + \frac{\cos^2 \theta}{\sin \theta}$$
$$= \frac{\sin^2 \theta + \cos^2 \theta}{\sin \theta}$$
$$= \frac{1}{\sin \theta} = \csc \theta$$

21 $\dfrac{\sqrt{33}}{7}, \dfrac{4}{7}, \dfrac{\sqrt{33}}{4}, \dfrac{4}{\sqrt{33}}, \dfrac{7}{4}, \dfrac{7}{\sqrt{33}}$

22 (a) $-\dfrac{4}{5}, \dfrac{3}{5}, -\dfrac{4}{3}, -\dfrac{3}{4}, \dfrac{5}{3}, -\dfrac{5}{4}$

(b) $\dfrac{2}{\sqrt{13}}, -\dfrac{3}{\sqrt{13}}, -\dfrac{2}{3}, -\dfrac{3}{2}, -\dfrac{\sqrt{13}}{3}, \dfrac{\sqrt{13}}{2}$

(c) $-1, 0, \text{U}, 0, \text{U}, -1$

23 (a) II   **(b)** III   **(c)** IV

24 (a) $-\dfrac{4}{5}, \dfrac{3}{5}, -\dfrac{4}{3}, -\dfrac{3}{4}, \dfrac{5}{3}, -\dfrac{5}{4}$

(b) $\dfrac{2}{\sqrt{13}}, -\dfrac{3}{\sqrt{13}}, -\dfrac{2}{3}, -\dfrac{3}{2}, -\dfrac{\sqrt{13}}{3}, \dfrac{\sqrt{13}}{2}$

25 $(-1, 0); (0, -1); (0, 1);$
$$\left(-\frac{\sqrt{2}}{2}, -\frac{\sqrt{2}}{2} \right); (1, 0); \left(\frac{\sqrt{3}}{2}, \frac{1}{2} \right)$$

26 $\left(\dfrac{3}{5}, \dfrac{4}{5} \right); \left(\dfrac{3}{5}, \dfrac{4}{5} \right); \left(-\dfrac{3}{5}, \dfrac{4}{5} \right); \left(-\dfrac{3}{5}, \dfrac{4}{5} \right)$

27 (a) $\dfrac{\pi}{4}, \dfrac{\pi}{6}, \dfrac{\pi}{8}$ **(b)** $65°, 43°, 8°$

28 (a) $1, 0, \text{U}, 0, \text{U}, 1$

(b) $\dfrac{\sqrt{2}}{2}, -\dfrac{\sqrt{2}}{2}, -1, -1, -\sqrt{2}, \sqrt{2}$

(c) $0, 1, 0, \text{U}, 1, \text{U}$

(d) $-\dfrac{1}{2}, \dfrac{\sqrt{3}}{2}, -\dfrac{\sqrt{3}}{3}, -\sqrt{3}, \dfrac{2}{\sqrt{3}}, -2$

29 (a) $-\dfrac{\sqrt{2}}{2}$ **(b)** $-\dfrac{\sqrt{3}}{3}$ **(c)** $-\dfrac{1}{2}$ **(d)** -2

(e) -1 **(f)** $-\dfrac{2}{\sqrt{3}}$

30 310.5°   **31** 1.2206; 4.3622   **32** 52.44°; 307.56°

33 5, 2π   **34** $\dfrac{2}{3}$, 2π

35 $\dfrac{1}{3}$, $\dfrac{2\pi}{3}$ **36** $\dfrac{1}{2}$, 6π

37 3, 4π   **38** 4, π

39 2, 2   **40** 4, 4

41 (a) 1.43, 2   (b) $y = 1.43 \sin \pi x$

42 (a) 3.27, 3π   (b) $y = -3.27 \sin \dfrac{2}{3} x$

43 (a) 3, $\dfrac{4\pi}{3}$ (b) $y = -3 \cos \dfrac{3}{2} x$

44 (a) 2, 4   (b) $y = 2 \cos \dfrac{\pi}{2} x$

45   **46**

47   **48**

49   **50**

51   **52**

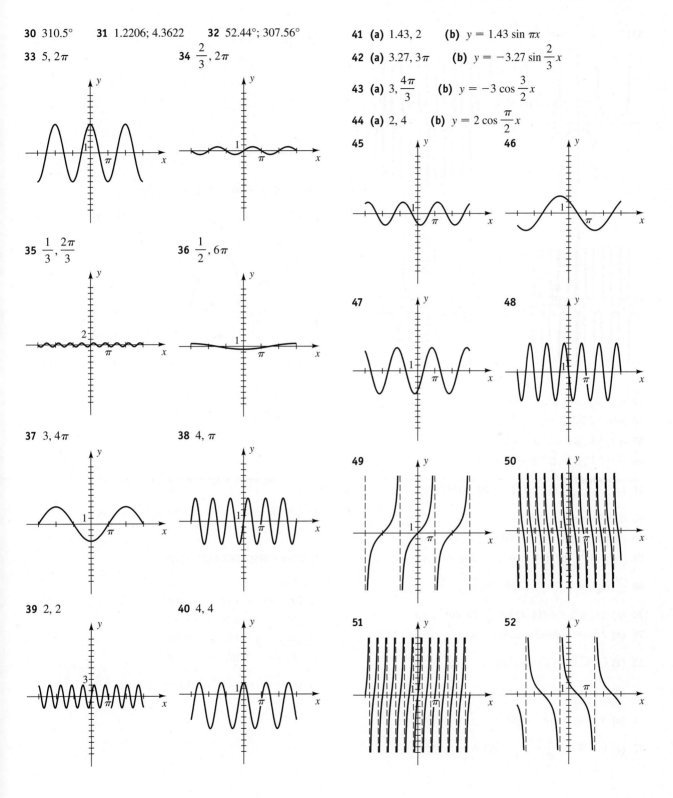

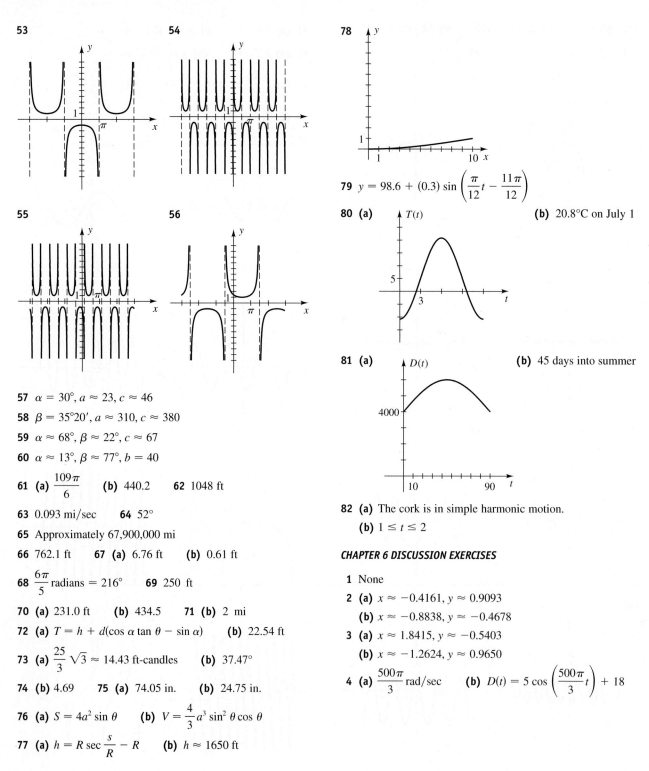

53

54

78

79 $y = 98.6 + (0.3) \sin\left(\dfrac{\pi}{12}t - \dfrac{11\pi}{12}\right)$

80 (a) **(b)** 20.8°C on July 1

55

56

81 (a) **(b)** 45 days into summer

57 $\alpha = 30°, a \approx 23, c \approx 46$

58 $\beta = 35°20', a \approx 310, c \approx 380$

59 $\alpha \approx 68°, \beta \approx 22°, c \approx 67$

60 $\alpha \approx 13°, \beta \approx 77°, b = 40$

61 (a) $\dfrac{109\pi}{6}$ **(b)** 440.2 **62** 1048 ft

63 0.093 mi/sec **64** 52°

65 Approximately 67,900,000 mi

66 762.1 ft **67 (a)** 6.76 ft **(b)** 0.61 ft

68 $\dfrac{6\pi}{5}$ radians = 216° **69** 250 ft

70 (a) 231.0 ft **(b)** 434.5 **71 (b)** 2 mi

72 (a) $T = h + d(\cos\alpha\tan\theta - \sin\alpha)$ **(b)** 22.54 ft

73 (a) $\dfrac{25}{3}\sqrt{3} \approx 14.43$ ft-candles **(b)** 37.47°

74 (b) 4.69 **75 (a)** 74.05 in. **(b)** 24.75 in.

76 (a) $S = 4a^2\sin\theta$ **(b)** $V = \dfrac{4}{3}a^3\sin^2\theta\cos\theta$

77 (a) $h = R\sec\dfrac{s}{R} - R$ **(b)** $h \approx 1650$ ft

82 (a) The cork is in simple harmonic motion.

　　(b) $1 \leq t \leq 2$

CHAPTER 6 DISCUSSION EXERCISES

1 None

2 (a) $x \approx -0.4161, y \approx 0.9093$

　　(b) $x \approx -0.8838, y \approx -0.4678$

3 (a) $x \approx 1.8415, y \approx -0.5403$

　　(b) $x \approx -1.2624, y \approx 0.9650$

4 (a) $\dfrac{500\pi}{3}$ rad/sec **(b)** $D(t) = 5\cos\left(\dfrac{500\pi}{3}t\right) + 18$

Chapter 7

EXERCISES 7.1

Exer. 1–50: Typical verifications are given for Exercises 1, 5, 9,..., 49.

1 $\csc\theta - \sin\theta = \dfrac{1}{\sin\theta} - \sin\theta = \dfrac{1 - \sin^2\theta}{\sin\theta} = \dfrac{\cos^2\theta}{\sin\theta}$

$\qquad = \dfrac{\cos\theta}{\sin\theta}\cos\theta = \cot\theta\cos\theta$

5 $\dfrac{\csc^2\theta}{1 + \tan^2\theta} = \dfrac{\csc^2\theta}{\sec^2\theta} = \dfrac{1/\sin^2\theta}{1/\cos^2\theta} = \dfrac{\cos^2\theta}{\sin^2\theta}$

$\qquad = \left(\dfrac{\cos\theta}{\sin\theta}\right)^2 = \cot^2\theta$

9 $\dfrac{1}{1 - \cos\gamma} + \dfrac{1}{1 + \cos\gamma} = \dfrac{1 + \cos\gamma + 1 - \cos\gamma}{1 - \cos^2\gamma}$

$\qquad = \dfrac{2}{\sin^2\gamma} = 2\csc^2\gamma$

13 $\csc^4 t - \cot^4 t = (\csc^2 t + \cot^2 t)(\csc^2 t - \cot^2 t)$

$\qquad = (\csc^2 t + \cot^2 t)(1)$

$\qquad = \csc^2 t + \cot^2 t$

17 $\dfrac{\tan^2 x}{\sec x + 1} = \dfrac{\sec^2 x - 1}{\sec x + 1} = \dfrac{(\sec x + 1)(\sec x - 1)}{\sec x + 1}$

$\qquad = \sec x - 1 = \dfrac{1}{\cos x} - 1 = \dfrac{1 - \cos x}{\cos x}$

21 $\sin^4 r - \cos^4 r = (\sin^2 r - \cos^2 r)(\sin^2 r + \cos^2 r)$

$\qquad = (\sin^2 r - \cos^2 r)(1)$

$\qquad = \sin^2 r - \cos^2 r$

25 $(\sec t + \tan t)^2 = \left(\dfrac{1}{\cos t} + \dfrac{\sin t}{\cos t}\right)^2 = \left(\dfrac{1 + \sin t}{\cos t}\right)^2$

$\qquad = \dfrac{(1 + \sin t)^2}{\cos^2 t} = \dfrac{(1 + \sin t)^2}{1 - \sin^2 t}$

$\qquad = \dfrac{(1 + \sin t)^2}{(1 + \sin t)(1 - \sin t)} = \dfrac{1 + \sin t}{1 - \sin t}$

29 $\dfrac{1 + \csc\beta}{\cot\beta + \cos\beta} = \dfrac{1 + \dfrac{1}{\sin\beta}}{\dfrac{\cos\beta}{\sin\beta} + \cos\beta} = \dfrac{\dfrac{\sin\beta + 1}{\sin\beta}}{\dfrac{\cos\beta + \cos\beta\sin\beta}{\sin\beta}}$

$\qquad = \dfrac{\sin\beta + 1}{\cos\beta(1 + \sin\beta)} = \dfrac{1}{\cos\beta} = \sec\beta$

33 $\text{RS} = \dfrac{\tan\alpha + \tan\beta}{1 - \tan\alpha\tan\beta} = \dfrac{\dfrac{\sin\alpha}{\cos\alpha} + \dfrac{\sin\beta}{\cos\beta}}{1 - \dfrac{\sin\alpha}{\cos\alpha}\cdot\dfrac{\sin\beta}{\cos\beta}}$

$\qquad = \dfrac{\dfrac{\sin\alpha\cos\beta + \cos\alpha\sin\beta}{\cos\alpha\cos\beta}}{\dfrac{\cos\alpha\cos\beta - \sin\alpha\sin\beta}{\cos\alpha\cos\beta}}$

$\qquad = \dfrac{\sin\alpha\cos\beta + \cos\alpha\sin\beta}{\cos\alpha\cos\beta - \sin\alpha\sin\beta}$

$\qquad = \text{LS}$

37 $\dfrac{1}{\tan\beta + \cot\beta} = \dfrac{1}{\dfrac{\sin\beta}{\cos\beta} + \dfrac{\cos\beta}{\sin\beta}} = \dfrac{1}{\dfrac{\sin^2\beta + \cos^2\beta}{\cos\beta\sin\beta}}$

$\qquad = \sin\beta\cos\beta$

41 $\text{RS} = \sec^4\phi - 4\tan^2\phi = (\sec^2\phi)^2 - 4\tan^2\phi$

$\qquad = (1 + \tan^2\phi)^2 - 4\tan^2\phi$

$\qquad = 1 + 2\tan^2\phi + \tan^4\phi - 4\tan^2\phi$

$\qquad = 1 - 2\tan^2\phi + \tan^4\phi$

$\qquad = (1 - \tan^2\phi)^2 = \text{LS}$

45 $\log 10^{\tan t} = \log_{10} 10^{\tan t} = \tan t$, since $\log_a a^x = x$.

49 $\ln|\sec\theta + \tan\theta| = \ln\left|\dfrac{(\sec\theta + \tan\theta)(\sec\theta - \tan\theta)}{\sec\theta - \tan\theta}\right|$

$\qquad = \ln\left|\dfrac{\sec^2\theta - \tan^2\theta}{\sec\theta - \tan\theta}\right|$

$\qquad = \ln\left|\dfrac{1}{\sec\theta - \tan\theta}\right|$

$\qquad = \ln|1| - \ln|\sec\theta - \tan\theta|$

$\qquad = -\ln|\sec\theta - \tan\theta|$

Exer. 51–62: A typical value of t or θ and the resulting nonequality are given.

51 $\pi, -1 \neq 1$ **53** $\dfrac{3\pi}{2}, 1 \neq -1$ **55** $\dfrac{\pi}{4}, 2 \neq 1$

57 $\pi, -1 \neq 1$ **59** $\dfrac{\pi}{4}, \cos\sqrt{2} \neq 1$

61 Not an identity   **63** Identity

65 $a^3\cos^3\theta$ **67** $a\tan\theta\sin\theta$ **69** $a\sec\theta$

71 $\dfrac{1}{a^2}\cos^2\theta$ **73** $a\tan\theta$ **75** $a^4\sec^3\theta\tan\theta$

EXERCISES 7.2

Exer. 1–34: n denotes any integer.

1 $\dfrac{5\pi}{4} + 2\pi n, \dfrac{7\pi}{4} + 2\pi n$ **3** $\dfrac{\pi}{3} + \pi n$

5 $\dfrac{\pi}{3} + 2\pi n, \dfrac{5\pi}{3} + 2\pi n$

7 No solution, since $\dfrac{\pi}{2} > 1$.

9 All θ except $\theta = \dfrac{\pi}{2} + \pi n$

11 $\dfrac{\pi}{12} + \pi n, \dfrac{11\pi}{12} + \pi n$ **13** $\dfrac{\pi}{2} + 3\pi n$

15 $-\dfrac{\pi}{12} + 2\pi n, \dfrac{7\pi}{12} + 2\pi n$

17 $\dfrac{\pi}{4} + \pi n, \dfrac{7\pi}{12} + \pi n$ **19** $\dfrac{2\pi}{3} + 2\pi n, \dfrac{4\pi}{3} + 2\pi n$

21 $\dfrac{\pi}{4} + \dfrac{\pi}{2}n$ **23** $2\pi n, \dfrac{3\pi}{2} + 2\pi n$

25 $\dfrac{\pi}{3} + \pi n, \dfrac{2\pi}{3} + \pi n$ **27** $\dfrac{4\pi}{3} + 2\pi n, \dfrac{5\pi}{3} + 2\pi n$

29 $\dfrac{\pi}{6} + \pi n, \dfrac{5\pi}{6} + \pi n$ **31** $\dfrac{7\pi}{6} + 2\pi n, \dfrac{11\pi}{6} + 2\pi n$

33 $\dfrac{\pi}{3} + 2\pi n, \dfrac{5\pi}{3} + 2\pi n, \pi + 2\pi n$

35 $\dfrac{\pi}{12} + \pi n, \dfrac{5\pi}{12} + \pi n$ **37** $e^{(\pi/2) + \pi n}$

39 $\dfrac{3\pi}{8}, \dfrac{7\pi}{8}, \dfrac{11\pi}{8}, \dfrac{15\pi}{8}$ **41** $\dfrac{\pi}{3}, \dfrac{2\pi}{3}, \dfrac{4\pi}{3}, \dfrac{5\pi}{3}$

43 $\dfrac{\pi}{6}, \dfrac{5\pi}{6}, \dfrac{3\pi}{2}$ **45** $0, \pi, \dfrac{\pi}{4}, \dfrac{3\pi}{4}, \dfrac{5\pi}{4}, \dfrac{7\pi}{4}$

47 $\dfrac{\pi}{2}, \dfrac{3\pi}{2}, \dfrac{2\pi}{3}, \dfrac{4\pi}{3}$ **49** No solution   **51** $\dfrac{11\pi}{6}, \dfrac{\pi}{2}$

53 $0, \dfrac{\pi}{2}$ **55** $\dfrac{\pi}{4}, \dfrac{5\pi}{4}$

57 All α in $[0, 2\pi)$ except $0, \dfrac{\pi}{2}, \pi,$ and $\dfrac{3\pi}{2}$

59 $\dfrac{\pi}{2}, \dfrac{3\pi}{2}, \dfrac{7\pi}{6}, \dfrac{11\pi}{6}$ **61** $\dfrac{3\pi}{4}, \dfrac{7\pi}{4}$

63 $15°30', 164°30'$ **65** $135°, 315°, 116°30', 296°30'$
67 $41°50', 138°10', 194°30', 345°30'$ **69** 10
71 $t \approx 3.50$ and $t \approx 8.50$ **73 (a)** 3.29   **(b)** 4

75 (a)

(b) $0 \le t < \dfrac{5}{3}$ and $\dfrac{25}{3} < t \le 10$

77 $A\left(-\dfrac{4\pi}{3}, -\dfrac{2\pi}{3} + \dfrac{1}{2}\sqrt{3}\right), B\left(-\dfrac{2\pi}{3}, -\dfrac{\pi}{3} - \dfrac{1}{2}\sqrt{3}\right),$
$C\left(\dfrac{2\pi}{3}, \dfrac{\pi}{3} + \dfrac{1}{2}\sqrt{3}\right), D\left(\dfrac{4\pi}{3}, \dfrac{2\pi}{3} - \dfrac{1}{2}\sqrt{3}\right)$

79 $\dfrac{7}{360}$ **81 (a)** $37.6°$ **(b)** $52.5°$

EXERCISES 7.3

1 (a) $\cos 43°23'$ **(b)** $\sin 16°48'$ **(c)** $\cot \dfrac{\pi}{3}$
(d) $\csc 72.72°$

3 (a) $\sin \dfrac{3\pi}{20}$ **(b)** $\cos\left(\dfrac{2\pi - 1}{4}\right)$ **(c)** $\cot\left(\dfrac{\pi - 2}{2}\right)$
(d) $\sec\left(\dfrac{\pi}{2} - 0.53\right)$

5 (a) $\dfrac{\sqrt{2} + \sqrt{3}}{2}$ **(b)** $\dfrac{\sqrt{6} - \sqrt{2}}{4}$

7 (a) $\sqrt{3} + 1$ **(b)** $-2 - \sqrt{3}$
9 (a) $\dfrac{\sqrt{2} - 1}{2}$ **(b)** $\dfrac{\sqrt{6} + \sqrt{2}}{4}$

11 $\cos 25°$ **13** $\sin(-5°)$ **15** $\sin(-5)$

17 $\dfrac{12\sqrt{3} - 5}{26}$

19 (a) $\dfrac{77}{85}$ **(b)** $\dfrac{36}{85}$ **(c)** I

21 (a) $-\dfrac{24}{25}$ **(b)** $-\dfrac{24}{7}$ **(c)** IV

23 (a) $\dfrac{3\sqrt{21} - 8}{25} \approx 0.23$ **(b)** $\dfrac{4\sqrt{21} + 6}{25} \approx 0.97$ **(c)** I

25 $\sin(\theta + \pi) = \sin \theta \cos \pi + \cos \theta \sin \pi$
$= \sin \theta(-1) + \cos \theta(0) = -\sin \theta$

27 $\sin\left(x - \dfrac{5\pi}{2}\right) = \sin x \cos \dfrac{5\pi}{2} - \cos x \sin \dfrac{5\pi}{2}$
$= -\cos x$

29 $\cos(\theta - \pi) = \cos \theta \cos \pi + \sin \theta \sin \pi = -\cos \theta$

31 $\cos\left(x + \dfrac{3\pi}{2}\right) = \cos x \cos \dfrac{3\pi}{2} - \sin x \sin \dfrac{3\pi}{2}$
$= \sin x$

33 $\tan\left(x - \dfrac{\pi}{2}\right) = \dfrac{\sin\left(x - \dfrac{\pi}{2}\right)}{\cos\left(x - \dfrac{\pi}{2}\right)}$

$$= \dfrac{\sin x \cos\dfrac{\pi}{2} - \cos x \sin\dfrac{\pi}{2}}{\cos x \cos\dfrac{\pi}{2} + \sin x \sin\dfrac{\pi}{2}}$$

$$= \dfrac{-\cos x}{\sin x} = -\cot x$$

35 $\tan\left(\theta + \dfrac{\pi}{2}\right) = \cot\left[\dfrac{\pi}{2} - \left(\theta + \dfrac{\pi}{2}\right)\right]$

$$= \cot(-\theta) = -\cot\theta$$

37 $\sin\left(\theta + \dfrac{\pi}{4}\right) = \sin\theta\cos\dfrac{\pi}{4} + \cos\theta\sin\dfrac{\pi}{4}$

$$= \dfrac{\sqrt{2}}{2}\sin\theta + \dfrac{\sqrt{2}}{2}\cos\theta$$

$$= \dfrac{\sqrt{2}}{2}(\sin\theta + \cos\theta)$$

39 $\tan\left(u + \dfrac{\pi}{4}\right) = \dfrac{\tan u + \tan\dfrac{\pi}{4}}{1 - \tan u \tan\dfrac{\pi}{4}} = \dfrac{1 + \tan u}{1 - \tan u}$

41 $\cos(u + v) + \cos(u - v)$
$= (\cos u \cos v - \sin u \sin v) + (\cos u \cos v + \sin u \sin v)$
$= 2\cos u \cos v$

43 $\sin(u + v) \cdot \sin(u - v)$
$= (\sin u \cos v + \cos u \sin v) \cdot$
$\quad (\sin u \cos v - \cos u \sin v)$
$= \sin^2 u \cos^2 v - \cos^2 u \sin^2 v$
$= \sin^2 u(1 - \sin^2 v) - (1 - \sin^2 u)\sin^2 v$
$= \sin^2 u - \sin^2 u \sin^2 v - \sin^2 v + \sin^2 u \sin^2 v$
$= \sin^2 u - \sin^2 v$

45 $\dfrac{1}{\cot\alpha - \cot\beta} = \dfrac{1}{\dfrac{\cos\alpha}{\sin\alpha} - \dfrac{\cos\beta}{\sin\beta}}$

$$= \dfrac{1}{\dfrac{\cos\alpha\sin\beta - \cos\beta\sin\alpha}{\sin\alpha\sin\beta}}$$

$$= \dfrac{\sin\alpha\sin\beta}{\sin(\beta - \alpha)}$$

47 $\sin u \cos v \cos w + \cos u \sin v \cos w +$
$\cos u \cos v \sin w - \sin u \sin v \sin w$

49 $\cot(u + v) = \dfrac{\cos(u + v)}{\sin(u + v)}$

$$= \dfrac{(\cos u \cos v - \sin u \sin v)(1/\sin u \sin v)}{(\sin u \cos v + \cos u \sin v)(1/\sin u \sin v)}$$

$$= \dfrac{\cot u \cot v - 1}{\cot v + \cot u}$$

51 $\sin(u - v) = \sin[u + (-v)]$
$= \sin u \cos(-v) + \cos u \sin(-v)$
$= \sin u \cos v - \cos u \sin v$

53 $\dfrac{f(x + h) - f(x)}{h} = \dfrac{\cos(x + h) - \cos x}{h}$

$$= \dfrac{\cos x \cos h - \sin x \sin h - \cos x}{h}$$

$$= \dfrac{\cos x \cos h - \cos x}{h} - \dfrac{\sin x \sin h}{h}$$

$$= \cos x\left(\dfrac{\cos h - 1}{h}\right) - \sin x\left(\dfrac{\sin h}{h}\right)$$

55 (a) Each side ≈ 0.0523 **(b)** $\alpha = 60°$
(c) $\alpha = 60°$, $\beta = 3°$

57 $0, \dfrac{\pi}{3}, \dfrac{2\pi}{3}$ **59** $\dfrac{\pi}{6}, \dfrac{\pi}{2}, \dfrac{5\pi}{6}$

61 $\dfrac{\pi}{12}, \dfrac{5\pi}{12}; \dfrac{3\pi}{4}$ is extraneous

63 (a) $f(x) = 2\cos\left(2x - \dfrac{\pi}{6}\right)$ **(b)** $2, \pi, \dfrac{\pi}{12}$

(c)

65 (a) $f(x) = 2\sqrt{2} \cos\left(3x + \dfrac{\pi}{4}\right)$ **(b)** $2\sqrt{2}, \dfrac{2\pi}{3}, -\dfrac{\pi}{12}$

(c)

67 $y = 10\sqrt{41} \cos\left(60\pi t - \tan^{-1}\dfrac{5}{4}\right)$

   $\approx 10\sqrt{41} \cos(60\pi t - 0.8961)$

69 (a) $y = \sqrt{13} \cos(t - C)$ with $\tan C = \dfrac{3}{2}$; $\sqrt{13}, 2\pi$

(b) $t = C + \dfrac{\pi}{2} + \pi n \approx 2.55 + \pi n$ for every nonnegative integer n

71 (a) $p(t) = A \sin \omega t + B \sin(\omega t + \tau)$

   $= A \sin \omega t + B(\sin \omega t \cos \tau + \cos \omega t \sin \tau)$

   $= (B \sin \tau) \cos \omega t + (A + B \cos \tau) \sin \omega t$

   $= a \cos \omega t + b \sin \omega t$

   with $a = B \sin \tau$ and $b = A + B \cos \tau$

(b) $C^2 = (B \sin \tau)^2 + (A + B \cos \tau)^2$

   $= B^2 \sin^2 \tau + A^2 + 2AB \cos \tau + B^2 \cos^2 \tau$

   $= A^2 + B^2(\sin^2 \tau + \cos^2 \tau) + 2AB \cos \tau$

   $= A^2 + B^2 + 2AB \cos \tau$

73 (a) $C^2 = A^2 + B^2 + 2AB \cos \tau \leq A^2 + B^2 + 2AB$,

   since $\cos \tau \leq 1$ and $A > 0, B > 0$. Thus,

   $C^2 \leq (A + B)^2$, and hence $C \leq A + B$.

(b) $0, 2\pi$ **(c)** $\cos \tau > -B/(2A)$

EXERCISES 7.4

1 $\dfrac{24}{25}, -\dfrac{7}{25}, -\dfrac{24}{7}$ **3** $-\dfrac{4}{9}\sqrt{2}, -\dfrac{7}{9}, \dfrac{4}{7}\sqrt{2}$

5 $\dfrac{1}{10}\sqrt{10}, \dfrac{3}{10}\sqrt{10}, \dfrac{1}{3}$

7 $-\dfrac{1}{2}\sqrt{2 + \sqrt{2}}, \dfrac{1}{2}\sqrt{2 - \sqrt{2}}, -\sqrt{2} - 1$

9 (a) $\dfrac{1}{2}\sqrt{2 - \sqrt{2}}$ **(b)** $\dfrac{1}{2}\sqrt{2 - \sqrt{3}}$ **(c)** $\sqrt{2} + 1$

11 $\sin 10\theta = \sin(2 \cdot 5\theta) = 2 \sin 5\theta \cos 5\theta$

13 $4 \sin \dfrac{x}{2} \cos \dfrac{x}{2} = 2 \cdot 2 \sin \dfrac{x}{2} \cos \dfrac{x}{2} = 2 \sin\left(2 \cdot \dfrac{x}{2}\right)$

       $= 2 \sin x$

15 $(\sin t + \cos t)^2 = \sin^2 t + 2 \sin t \cos t + \cos^2 t$

       $= 1 + \sin 2t$

17 $\sin 3u = \sin(2u + u)$

   $= \sin 2u \cos u + \cos 2u \sin u$

   $= (2 \sin u \cos u) \cos u + (1 - 2 \sin^2 u) \sin u$

   $= 2 \sin u \cos^2 u + \sin u - 2 \sin^3 u$

   $= 2 \sin u(1 - \sin^2 u) + \sin u - 2 \sin^3 u$

   $= 2 \sin u - 2 \sin^3 u + \sin u - 2 \sin^3 u$

   $= 3 \sin u - 4 \sin^3 u = \sin u(3 - 4 \sin^2 u)$

19 $\cos 4\theta = \cos(2 \cdot 2\theta) = 2 \cos^2 2\theta - 1$

   $= 2(2 \cos^2 \theta - 1)^2 - 1$

   $= 2(4 \cos^4 \theta - 4 \cos^2 \theta + 1) - 1$

   $= 8 \cos^4 \theta - 8 \cos^2 \theta + 1$

21 $\sin^4 t = (\sin^2 t)^2 = \left(\dfrac{1 - \cos 2t}{2}\right)^2$

   $= \dfrac{1}{4}(1 - 2 \cos 2t + \cos^2 2t)$

   $= \dfrac{1}{4} - \dfrac{1}{2} \cos 2t + \dfrac{1}{4}\left(\dfrac{1 + \cos 4t}{2}\right)$

   $= \dfrac{1}{4} - \dfrac{1}{2} \cos 2t + \dfrac{1}{8} + \dfrac{1}{8} \cos 4t$

   $= \dfrac{3}{8} - \dfrac{1}{2} \cos 2t + \dfrac{1}{8} \cos 4t$

23 $\sec 2\theta = \dfrac{1}{\cos 2\theta} = \dfrac{1}{2 \cos^2 \theta - 1} = \dfrac{1}{2\left(\dfrac{1}{\sec^2 \theta}\right) - 1}$

   $= \dfrac{1}{\dfrac{2 - \sec^2 \theta}{\sec^2 \theta}} = \dfrac{\sec^2 \theta}{2 - \sec^2 \theta}$

25 $2 \sin^2 2t + \cos 4t = 2 \sin^2 2t + \cos(2 \cdot 2t)$

       $= 2 \sin^2 2t + (1 - 2 \sin^2 2t) = 1$

27 $\tan 3u = \tan(2u + u) = \dfrac{\tan 2u + \tan u}{1 - \tan 2u \tan u}$

   $= \dfrac{\dfrac{2 \tan u}{1 - \tan^2 u} + \tan u}{1 - \dfrac{2 \tan u}{1 - \tan^2 u} \cdot \tan u}$

   $= \dfrac{\dfrac{2 \tan u + \tan u - \tan^3 u}{1 - \tan^2 u}}{\dfrac{1 - \tan^2 u - 2 \tan^2 u}{1 - \tan^2 u}}$

   $= \dfrac{3 \tan u - \tan^3 u}{1 - 3 \tan^2 u} = \dfrac{\tan u(3 - \tan^2 u)}{1 - 3 \tan^2 u}$

29 $\tan \dfrac{\theta}{2} = \dfrac{1 - \cos \theta}{\sin \theta} = \dfrac{1}{\sin \theta} - \dfrac{\cos \theta}{\sin \theta} = \csc \theta - \cot \theta$

31 $\dfrac{3}{8} + \dfrac{1}{2} \cos \theta + \dfrac{1}{8} \cos 2\theta$

33 $\dfrac{3}{8} - \dfrac{1}{2} \cos 4x + \dfrac{1}{8} \cos 8x$ **35** $0, \pi, \dfrac{2\pi}{3}, \dfrac{4\pi}{3}$

37 $\dfrac{\pi}{3}, \dfrac{5\pi}{3}, \pi$ **39** $0, \pi$ **41** $0, \dfrac{\pi}{3}, \dfrac{5\pi}{3}$

45 (a) 1.20, 5.09

(b) $P\left(\dfrac{2\pi}{3}, -1.5\right), Q(\pi, -1), R\left(\dfrac{4\pi}{3}, -1.5\right)$

47 (a) $-\dfrac{3\pi}{2}, -\dfrac{\pi}{2}, \dfrac{\pi}{2}, \dfrac{3\pi}{2}$

(b) $0, \pm \pi, \pm 2\pi, \pm \dfrac{\pi}{4}, \pm \dfrac{3\pi}{4}, \pm \dfrac{5\pi}{4}, \pm \dfrac{7\pi}{4}$

49 (b) Yes, point B is 25 miles from A.

51 (a) $V = \dfrac{5}{2} \sin \theta$ **(b)** 53.13° **53 (b)** 12.43 mm

EXERCISES 7.5

1 $\dfrac{1}{2} \cos 4t - \dfrac{1}{2} \cos 10t$ **3** $\dfrac{1}{2} \cos 2u + \dfrac{1}{2} \cos 10u$

5 $\sin 12\theta + \sin 6\theta$ **7** $\dfrac{3}{2} \sin 3x + \dfrac{3}{2} \sin x$

9 $2 \sin 4\theta \cos 2\theta$ **11** $-2 \sin 4x \sin x$

13 $-2 \cos 5t \sin 2t$ **15** $2 \cos \dfrac{3}{2}x \cos \dfrac{1}{2}x$

17 $\dfrac{\sin 4t + \sin 6t}{\cos 4t - \cos 6t} = \dfrac{2 \sin 5t \cos t}{2 \sin 5t \sin t} = \cot t$

19 $\dfrac{\sin u + \sin v}{\cos u + \cos v} = \dfrac{2 \sin \dfrac{1}{2}(u + v) \cos \dfrac{1}{2}(u - v)}{2 \cos \dfrac{1}{2}(u + v) \cos \dfrac{1}{2}(u - v)}$

$= \tan \dfrac{1}{2}(u + v)$

21 $\dfrac{\sin u - \sin v}{\sin u + \sin v} = \dfrac{2 \cos \dfrac{1}{2}(u + v) \sin \dfrac{1}{2}(u - v)}{2 \sin \dfrac{1}{2}(u + v) \cos \dfrac{1}{2}(u - v)}$

$= \cot \dfrac{1}{2}(u + v) \tan \dfrac{1}{2}(u - v)$

$= \dfrac{\tan \dfrac{1}{2}(u - v)}{\tan \dfrac{1}{2}(u + v)}$

23 $4 \cos x \cos 2x \sin 3x = 2 \cos 2x \,(2 \sin 3x \cos x)$
$= 2 \cos 2x \,(\sin 4x + \sin 2x)$
$= (2 \cos 2x \sin 4x) + (2 \cos 2x \sin 2x)$
$= [\sin 6x - \sin (-2x)] + (\sin 4x - \sin 0)$
$= \sin 2x + \sin 4x + \sin 6x$

25 $\dfrac{1}{2} \sin [(a + b)x] + \dfrac{1}{2} \sin [(a - b)x]$ **27** $\dfrac{\pi}{4}n$

29 $\dfrac{\pi}{2}n$ **31** $\dfrac{\pi}{2} + \pi n, \dfrac{\pi}{12} + \dfrac{\pi}{2}n, \dfrac{5\pi}{12} + \dfrac{\pi}{2}n$

33 $\dfrac{\pi}{7} + \dfrac{2\pi}{7}n, \dfrac{2\pi}{3}n$ **35** $\dfrac{\pi}{4}, \dfrac{3\pi}{4}, \dfrac{5\pi}{4}, \dfrac{7\pi}{4}, \dfrac{\pi}{2}, \dfrac{3\pi}{2}$

37 $0, \pm \pi, \pm 2\pi, \pm \dfrac{\pi}{4}, \pm \dfrac{3\pi}{4}, \pm \dfrac{5\pi}{4}, \pm \dfrac{7\pi}{4}$

39 $f(x) = \dfrac{1}{2} \sin \dfrac{\pi n}{l}(x + kt) + \dfrac{1}{2} \sin \dfrac{\pi n}{l}(x - kt)$

EXERCISES 7.6

1 (a) $-\dfrac{\pi}{4}$ **(b)** $\dfrac{2\pi}{3}$ **(c)** $-\dfrac{\pi}{3}$

3 (a) $\dfrac{\pi}{3}$ **(b)** $\dfrac{\pi}{4}$ **(c)** $\dfrac{\pi}{6}$

5 (a) Not defined **(b)** Not defined **(c)** $\dfrac{\pi}{4}$

7 (a) $-\dfrac{3}{10}$ **(b)** $\dfrac{1}{2}$ **(c)** 14

9 (a) $\dfrac{\pi}{3}$ **(b)** $\dfrac{5\pi}{6}$ **(c)** $-\dfrac{\pi}{6}$

11 (a) $-\dfrac{\pi}{4}$ **(b)** $\dfrac{3\pi}{4}$ **(c)** $-\dfrac{\pi}{4}$

13 (a) $\dfrac{\sqrt{3}}{2}$ **(b)** $\dfrac{\sqrt{2}}{2}$ **(c)** Not defined

15 (a) $\dfrac{\sqrt{5}}{2}$ **(b)** $\dfrac{\sqrt{34}}{5}$ **(c)** $\dfrac{4}{\sqrt{15}}$

17 (a) $\dfrac{\sqrt{3}}{2}$ **(b)** 0 **(c)** $-\dfrac{77}{36}$

19 (a) $-\dfrac{24}{25}$ **(b)** $-\dfrac{161}{289}$ **(c)** $\dfrac{24}{7}$

21 (a) $-\dfrac{1}{10}\sqrt{2}$ **(b)** $\dfrac{4}{17}\sqrt{17}$ **(c)** $\dfrac{1}{2}$

23 $\dfrac{x}{\sqrt{x^2 + 1}}$ **25** $\dfrac{\sqrt{x^2 + 4}}{2}$ **27** $2x\sqrt{1 - x^2}$

29 $\sqrt{\dfrac{1 + x}{2}}$ **31 (a)** $-\dfrac{\pi}{2}$ **(b)** 0 **(c)** $\dfrac{\pi}{2}$

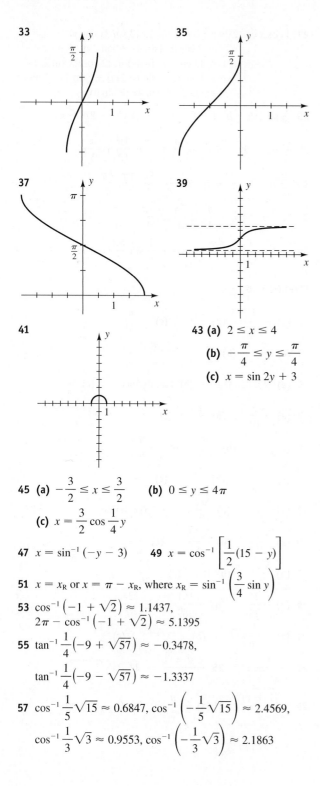

33

35

37

39

41

43 (a) $2 \le x \le 4$

(b) $-\dfrac{\pi}{4} \le y \le \dfrac{\pi}{4}$

(c) $x = \sin 2y + 3$

45 (a) $-\dfrac{3}{2} \le x \le \dfrac{3}{2}$ (b) $0 \le y \le 4\pi$

(c) $x = \dfrac{3}{2} \cos \dfrac{1}{4} y$

47 $x = \sin^{-1}(-y - 3)$ **49** $x = \cos^{-1}\left[\dfrac{1}{2}(15 - y)\right]$

51 $x = x_R$ or $x = \pi - x_R$, where $x_R = \sin^{-1}\left(\dfrac{3}{4}\sin y\right)$

53 $\cos^{-1}\left(-1 + \sqrt{2}\right) \approx 1.1437,$
$2\pi - \cos^{-1}\left(-1 + \sqrt{2}\right) \approx 5.1395$

55 $\tan^{-1}\dfrac{1}{4}\left(-9 + \sqrt{57}\right) \approx -0.3478,$

$\tan^{-1}\dfrac{1}{4}\left(-9 - \sqrt{57}\right) \approx -1.3337$

57 $\cos^{-1}\dfrac{1}{5}\sqrt{15} \approx 0.6847, \cos^{-1}\left(-\dfrac{1}{5}\sqrt{15}\right) \approx 2.4569,$

$\cos^{-1}\dfrac{1}{3}\sqrt{3} \approx 0.9553, \cos^{-1}\left(-\dfrac{1}{3}\sqrt{3}\right) \approx 2.1863$

59 $\sin^{-1}\left(\pm\dfrac{1}{6}\sqrt{30}\right) \approx \pm 1.1503$

61 $\cos^{-1}\left(-\dfrac{3}{5}\right) \approx 2.2143, \cos^{-1}\dfrac{1}{3} \approx 1.2310,$

$2\pi - \cos^{-1}\left(-\dfrac{3}{5}\right) \approx 4.0689, 2\pi - \cos^{-1}\dfrac{1}{3} \approx 5.0522$

63 $\cos^{-1}\dfrac{2}{3} \approx 0.8411, 2\pi - \cos^{-1}\dfrac{2}{3} \approx 5.4421,$

$\dfrac{\pi}{3} \approx 1.0472, \dfrac{5\pi}{3} \approx 5.2360$

65 (a) 1.65 m   (b) 0.92 m   (c) 0.43 m   **67** 3.07°

69 (a) $\alpha = \theta - \sin^{-1}\dfrac{d}{k}$ (b) 40°

71 Let $\alpha = \sin^{-1} x$ and $\beta = \tan^{-1}\dfrac{x}{\sqrt{1 + x^2}}$ with

$-\dfrac{\pi}{2} < \alpha < \dfrac{\pi}{2}$ and $-\dfrac{\pi}{2} < \beta < \dfrac{\pi}{2}$. Thus, $\sin \alpha = x$

and $\sin \beta = x$. Since the sine function is one-to-one on

$\left(-\dfrac{\pi}{2}, \dfrac{\pi}{2}\right)$, we have $\alpha = \beta$.

73 Let $\alpha = \arcsin(-x)$ and $\beta = \arcsin x$ with

$-\dfrac{\pi}{2} \le \alpha \le \dfrac{\pi}{2}$ and $-\dfrac{\pi}{2} \le \beta \le \dfrac{\pi}{2}$. Thus,

$\sin \alpha = -x$ and $\sin \beta = x$. Consequently,
$\sin \alpha = -\sin \beta = \sin(-\beta)$. Since the sine function
is one-to-one on $\left[-\dfrac{\pi}{2}, \dfrac{\pi}{2}\right]$, we have $\alpha = -\beta$.

75 Let $\alpha = \arctan x$ and $\beta = \arctan(1/x)$. Since $x > 0$, we

have $0 < \alpha < \dfrac{\pi}{2}$ and $0 < \beta < \dfrac{\pi}{2}$, and hence

$0 < \alpha + \beta < \pi$. Thus,

$\tan(\alpha + \beta) = \dfrac{\tan \alpha + \tan \beta}{1 - \tan \alpha \tan \beta} = \dfrac{x + (1/x)}{1 - x \cdot (1/x)} = $

$\dfrac{x + (1/x)}{0}$. Since the denominator is 0, $\tan(\alpha + \beta)$ is

undefined and hence $\alpha + \beta = \dfrac{\pi}{2}$.

CHAPTER 7 REVIEW EXERCISES

1 $(\cot^2 x + 1)(1 - \cos^2 x) = (\csc^2 x)(\sin^2 x) = 1$

2 $\cos \theta + \sin \theta \tan \theta = \cos \theta + \sin \theta \cdot \dfrac{\sin \theta}{\cos \theta}$

$= \dfrac{\cos^2 \theta + \sin^2 \theta}{\cos \theta} = \dfrac{1}{\cos \theta} = \sec \theta$

3 $\dfrac{(\sec^2 \theta - 1)\cot \theta}{\tan \theta \sin \theta + \cos \theta} = \dfrac{(\tan^2 \theta)\cot \theta}{\dfrac{\sin \theta}{\cos \theta} \cdot \sin \theta + \cos \theta}$

$= \dfrac{\tan \theta}{\dfrac{\sin^2 \theta + \cos^2 \theta}{\cos \theta}} = \dfrac{\sin \theta/\cos \theta}{1/\cos \theta}$

$= \sin \theta$

4 $(\tan x + \cot x)^2 = \left(\dfrac{\sin x}{\cos x} + \dfrac{\cos x}{\sin x}\right)^2$

$= \left(\dfrac{\sin^2 x + \cos^2 x}{\cos x \sin x}\right)^2$

$= \dfrac{1}{\cos^2 x \sin^2 x} = \sec^2 x \csc^2 x$

5 $\dfrac{1}{1 + \sin t} \cdot \dfrac{1 - \sin t}{1 - \sin t} = \dfrac{1 - \sin t}{1 - \sin^2 t} = \dfrac{1 - \sin t}{\cos^2 t}$

$= \dfrac{1 - \sin t}{\cos t} \cdot \dfrac{1}{\cos t}$

$= \left(\dfrac{1}{\cos t} - \dfrac{\sin t}{\cos t}\right) \cdot \sec t$

$= (\sec t - \tan t)\sec t$

6 $\dfrac{\sin(\alpha - \beta)}{\cos(\alpha + \beta)} = \dfrac{(\sin \alpha \cos \beta - \cos \alpha \sin \beta)/\cos \alpha \cos \beta}{(\cos \alpha \cos \beta - \sin \alpha \sin \beta)/\cos \alpha \cos \beta}$

$= \dfrac{\tan \alpha - \tan \beta}{1 - \tan \alpha \tan \beta}$

7 $\tan 2u = \dfrac{2 \tan u}{1 - \tan^2 u} = \dfrac{2 \cdot \dfrac{1}{\cot u}}{1 - \dfrac{1}{\cot^2 u}} = \dfrac{\dfrac{2}{\cot u}}{\dfrac{\cot^2 u - 1}{\cot^2 u}}$

$= \dfrac{2 \cot u}{\cot^2 u - 1} = \dfrac{2 \cot u}{(\csc^2 u - 1) - 1} = \dfrac{2 \cot u}{\csc^2 u - 2}$

8 $\cos^2 \dfrac{v}{2} = \dfrac{1 + \cos v}{2} = \dfrac{1 + \dfrac{1}{\sec v}}{2} = \dfrac{\dfrac{\sec v + 1}{\sec v}}{2}$

$= \dfrac{1 + \sec v}{2 \sec v}$

9 $\dfrac{\tan^3 \phi - \cot^3 \phi}{\tan^2 \phi + \csc^2 \phi}$

$= \dfrac{(\tan \phi - \cot \phi)[(\tan^2 \phi + \tan \phi \cot \phi + \cot^2 \phi)]}{[\tan^2 \phi + (1 + \cot^2 \phi)]}$

$= \tan \phi - \cot \phi$

10 LS $= \dfrac{\sin u + \sin v}{\csc u + \csc v} = \dfrac{\sin u + \sin v}{\dfrac{1}{\sin u} + \dfrac{1}{\sin v}} = \dfrac{\sin u + \sin v}{\dfrac{\sin v + \sin u}{\sin u \sin v}}$

$= \sin u \sin v$

RS $= \dfrac{1 - \sin u \sin v}{-1 + \csc u \csc v} = \dfrac{1 - \sin u \sin v}{-1 + \dfrac{1}{\sin u \sin v}}$

$= \dfrac{1 - \sin u \sin v}{\dfrac{1 - \sin u \sin v}{\sin u \sin v}}$

$= \sin u \sin v$

Since the LS and RS equal the same expression and the steps are reversible, the identity is verified.

11 $\left(\dfrac{\sin^2 x}{\tan^4 x}\right)^3 \left(\dfrac{\csc^3 x}{\cot^6 x}\right)^2 = \left(\dfrac{\sin^6 x}{\tan^{12} x}\right)\left(\dfrac{\csc^6 x}{\cot^{12} x}\right) = \dfrac{(\sin x \csc x)^6}{(\tan x \cot x)^{12}}$

$= \dfrac{(1)^6}{(1)^{12}} = 1$

12 $\dfrac{\cos \gamma}{1 - \tan \gamma} + \dfrac{\sin \gamma}{1 - \cot \gamma} = \dfrac{\cos \gamma}{\dfrac{\cos \gamma - \sin \gamma}{\cos \gamma}} + \dfrac{\sin \gamma}{\dfrac{\sin \gamma - \cos \gamma}{\sin \gamma}}$

$= \dfrac{\cos^2 \gamma}{\cos \gamma - \sin \gamma} + \dfrac{\sin^2 \gamma}{\sin \gamma - \cos \gamma}$

$= \dfrac{\cos^2 \gamma - \sin^2 \gamma}{\cos \gamma - \sin \gamma}$

$= \dfrac{(\cos \gamma + \sin \gamma)(\cos \gamma - \sin \gamma)}{\cos \gamma - \sin \gamma}$

$= \cos \gamma + \sin \gamma$

13 $\dfrac{\cos(-t)}{\sec(-t) + \tan(-t)} = \dfrac{\cos t}{\sec t - \tan t} = \dfrac{\cos t}{\dfrac{1}{\cos t} - \dfrac{\sin t}{\cos t}}$

$= \dfrac{\cos t}{\dfrac{1 - \sin t}{\cos t}} = \dfrac{\cos^2 t}{1 - \sin t} = \dfrac{1 - \sin^2 t}{1 - \sin t}$

$= \dfrac{(1 - \sin t)(1 + \sin t)}{1 - \sin t} = 1 + \sin t$

14 $\dfrac{\cot(-t) + \csc(-t)}{\sin(-t)} = \dfrac{-\cot t - \csc t}{-\sin t} = \dfrac{\dfrac{\cos t}{\sin t} + \dfrac{1}{\sin t}}{\sin t}$

$= \dfrac{\cos t + 1}{\sin^2 t} = \dfrac{\cos t + 1}{1 - \cos^2 t}$

$= \dfrac{\cos t + 1}{(1 - \cos t)(1 + \cos t)} = \dfrac{1}{1 - \cos t}$

15 $\sqrt{\dfrac{1 - \cos t}{1 + \cos t}} = \sqrt{\dfrac{(1 - \cos t)}{(1 + \cos t)} \cdot \dfrac{(1 - \cos t)}{(1 - \cos t)}}$

$= \sqrt{\dfrac{(1 - \cos t)^2}{1 - \cos^2 t}}$

$= \sqrt{\dfrac{(1 - \cos t)^2}{\sin^2 t}} = \dfrac{|1 - \cos t|}{|\sin t|} = \dfrac{1 - \cos t}{|\sin t|},$

since $(1 - \cos t) \geq 0.$

16 $\sqrt{\dfrac{1-\sin\theta}{1+\sin\theta}}=\sqrt{\dfrac{(1-\sin\theta)}{(1+\sin\theta)}\cdot\dfrac{(1+\sin\theta)}{(1+\sin\theta)}}$

$\qquad=\sqrt{\dfrac{1-\sin^2\theta}{(1+\sin\theta)^2}}$

$\qquad=\sqrt{\dfrac{\cos^2\theta}{(1+\sin\theta)^2}}$

$\qquad=\dfrac{|\cos\theta|}{|1+\sin\theta|}=\dfrac{|\cos\theta|}{1+\sin\theta}$,

since $(1+\sin\theta)\ge0$.

17 $\cos\left(x-\dfrac{5\pi}{2}\right)=\cos x\cos\dfrac{5\pi}{2}+\sin x\sin\dfrac{5\pi}{2}=\sin x$

18 $\tan\left(x+\dfrac{3\pi}{4}\right)=\dfrac{\tan x+\tan\dfrac{3\pi}{4}}{1-\tan x\tan\dfrac{3\pi}{4}}=\dfrac{\tan x-1}{1+\tan x}$

19 $\dfrac14\sin4\beta=\dfrac14\sin(2\cdot2\beta)=\dfrac14(2\sin2\beta\cos2\beta)$

$\qquad=\dfrac12(2\sin\beta\cos\beta)(\cos^2\beta-\sin^2\beta)$

$\qquad=\sin\beta\cos^3\beta-\cos\beta\sin^3\beta$

20 $\tan\dfrac12\theta=\dfrac{1-\cos\theta}{\sin\theta}=\dfrac{1}{\sin\theta}-\dfrac{\cos\theta}{\sin\theta}=\csc\theta-\cot\theta$

21 $\sin8\theta=2\sin4\theta\cos4\theta$

$\qquad=2(2\sin2\theta\cos2\theta)(1-2\sin^22\theta)$

$\qquad=8\sin\theta\cos\theta(1-2\sin^2\theta)[1-2(2\sin\theta\cos\theta)^2]$

$\qquad=8\sin\theta\cos\theta(1-2\sin^2\theta)(1-8\sin^2\theta\cos^2\theta)$

22 Let $\alpha=\arctan x$ and $\beta=\arctan\dfrac{2x}{1-x^2}$. Because

$-1<x<1,\ -\dfrac{\pi}{4}<\alpha<\dfrac{\pi}{4}$. Thus, $\tan\alpha=x$ and

$\tan\beta=\dfrac{2x}{1-x^2}=\dfrac{2\tan\alpha}{1-\tan^2\alpha}=\tan2\alpha$. Since the tangent

function is one-to-one on $\left(-\dfrac{\pi}{2},\dfrac{\pi}{2}\right)$, we have $\beta=2\alpha$ or,

equivalently, $\alpha=\dfrac12\beta$.

23 $\dfrac{\pi}{2},\dfrac{3\pi}{2},\dfrac{\pi}{4},\dfrac{7\pi}{4},\dfrac{3\pi}{4},\dfrac{5\pi}{4}$ **24** $\dfrac{7\pi}{6},\dfrac{11\pi}{6}$ **25** $0,\pi$

26 $\dfrac{\pi}{4},\dfrac{3\pi}{4},\dfrac{5\pi}{4},\dfrac{7\pi}{4}$ **27** $0,\pi,\dfrac{2\pi}{3},\dfrac{4\pi}{3}$

28 $\dfrac{\pi}{2},\dfrac{3\pi}{2},\dfrac{\pi}{4},\dfrac{5\pi}{4},\dfrac{3\pi}{4},\dfrac{7\pi}{4}$ **29** $\dfrac{7\pi}{6},\dfrac{11\pi}{6},\dfrac{\pi}{2}$

30 $\dfrac{2\pi}{3},\dfrac{4\pi}{3},\pi$ **31** $\dfrac{\pi}{6},\dfrac{5\pi}{6},\dfrac{\pi}{3},\dfrac{5\pi}{3}$

32 All x in $[0,2\pi)$ except $\dfrac{\pi}{4},\dfrac{3\pi}{4},\dfrac{5\pi}{4},\dfrac{7\pi}{4}$

33 $\dfrac{\pi}{3},\dfrac{5\pi}{3}$ **34** $0,\dfrac{\pi}{3},\dfrac{2\pi}{3},\pi,\dfrac{4\pi}{3},\dfrac{5\pi}{3}$

35 $\dfrac34,\dfrac74,\dfrac{11}{4},\dfrac{15}{4},\dfrac{19}{4},\dfrac{23}{4}$ **36** $0,\pi,\dfrac{\pi}{3},\dfrac{5\pi}{3}$

37 $\dfrac{\pi}{3},\dfrac{5\pi}{3}$ **38** $\dfrac{\pi}{6},\dfrac{5\pi}{6},\dfrac{7\pi}{6},\dfrac{11\pi}{6}$

39 $0,\dfrac{\pi}{8},\dfrac{3\pi}{8},\dfrac{5\pi}{8},\dfrac{7\pi}{8},\pi,\dfrac{9\pi}{8},\dfrac{11\pi}{8},\dfrac{13\pi}{8},\dfrac{15\pi}{8}$

40 $\dfrac{\pi}{5},\dfrac{3\pi}{5},\pi,\dfrac{7\pi}{5},\dfrac{9\pi}{5}$ **41** $\dfrac{\sqrt6-\sqrt2}{4}$

42 $-2-\sqrt3$ **43** $\dfrac{\sqrt2-\sqrt6}{4}$ **44** $\dfrac{2}{\sqrt{2-\sqrt2}}$

45 $\dfrac{84}{85}$ **46** $-\dfrac{13}{85}$ **47** $-\dfrac{84}{13}$ **48** $-\dfrac{36}{77}$

49 $\dfrac{36}{85}$ **50** $-\dfrac{36}{85}$ **51** $\dfrac{240}{289}$ **52** $-\dfrac{161}{289}$

53 $\dfrac{24}{7}$ **54** $\dfrac{1}{10}\sqrt{10}$ **55** $\dfrac13$ **56** $\dfrac{5}{34}\sqrt{34}$

57 (a) $\dfrac12\cos3t-\dfrac12\cos11t$

(b) $\dfrac12\cos\dfrac{1}{12}u+\dfrac12\cos\dfrac{5}{12}u$

(c) $3\sin8x-3\sin2x$ **(d)** $2\sin10\theta-2\sin4\theta$

58 (a) $2\sin5u\cos3u$ **(b)** $2\sin\dfrac{11}{2}\theta\sin\dfrac52\theta$

(c) $2\cos\dfrac{9}{40}t\sin\dfrac{1}{40}t$ **(d)** $6\cos4x\cos2x$

59 $\dfrac{\pi}{6}$ **60** $\dfrac{\pi}{4}$ **61** $\dfrac{\pi}{3}$ **62** π **63** $-\dfrac{\pi}{4}$

64 $\dfrac{3\pi}{4}$ **65** $\dfrac12$ **66** 2 **67** Not defined **68** $\dfrac{\pi}{2}$

69 $\dfrac{240}{289}$ **70** $-\dfrac{7}{25}$

71

72

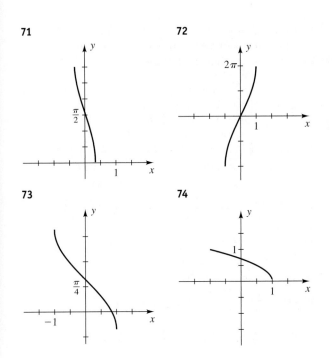

73

74

4 (a) The **inverse sawtooth function,** denoted by saw^{-1}, is defined by $y = \text{saw}^{-1} x$ iff $x = \text{saw } y$ for $-2 \le x \le 2$ and $-1 \le y \le 1$.
(b) 0.85; -0.4
(c) $\text{saw } (\text{saw}^{-1} x) = x$ if $-2 \le x \le 2$;
$\text{saw}^{-1} (\text{saw } y) = y$ if $-1 \le y \le 1$
(d)

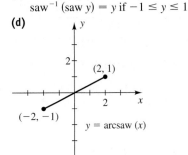

$y = \text{arcsaw } (x)$

5 *Hint:* Write the equation in the form $\dfrac{\pi}{4} + \alpha = 4\theta$, and take the tangent of both sides.

Chapter 8

EXERCISES 8.1

1 $\beta = 62°$, $b \approx 14.1$, $c \approx 15.6$
3 $\gamma = 100°10'$, $b \approx 55.1$, $c \approx 68.7$
5 $\beta = 78°30'$, $a \approx 13.6$, $c \approx 17.8$
7 No triangle exists.
9 $\alpha \approx 77°30'$, $\beta \approx 49°10'$, $b \approx 108$;
$\alpha \approx 102°30'$, $\beta \approx 24°10'$, $b \approx 59$
11 $\alpha \approx 82.54°$, $\beta \approx 49.72°$, $b \approx 100.85$;
$\alpha \approx 97.46°$, $\beta \approx 34.80°$, $b \approx 75.45$
13 $\beta \approx 53°40'$, $\gamma \approx 61°10'$, $c \approx 20.6$
15 $\alpha \approx 25.993°$, $\gamma \approx 32.383°$, $a \approx 0.146$ **17** 219 yd
19 (a) 1.6 mi **(b)** 0.6 mi **21** 2.7 mi **23** 628 m
25 3.7 mi from A and 5.4 mi from B **27** 350 ft
29 (a) 18.7 **(b)** 814 **31** (3949.9, 2994.2)

EXERCISES 8.2

1 (a) B **(b)** F **(c)** D **(d)** E
(e) A **(f)** C
3 (a) α, law of sines **(b)** a, law of cosines
(c) Any angle, law of cosines
(d) Not enough information given
(e) γ, $\alpha + \beta + \gamma = 180°$
(f) c, law of sines; or γ, $\alpha + \beta + \gamma = 180°$
5 $a \approx 26$, $\beta \approx 41°$, $\gamma \approx 79°$
7 $b \approx 180$, $\alpha \approx 25°$, $\gamma \approx 5°$
9 $c \approx 2.75$, $\alpha \approx 21°10'$, $\beta \approx 43°40'$

75 $\cos (\alpha + \beta + \gamma) = \cos [(\alpha + \beta) + \gamma]$
$= \cos (\alpha + \beta) \cos \gamma - \sin (\alpha + \beta) \sin \gamma$
$= (\cos \alpha \cos \beta - \sin \alpha \sin \beta) \cos \gamma -$
$\quad (\sin \alpha \cos \beta + \cos \alpha \sin \beta) \sin \gamma$
$= \cos \alpha \cos \beta \cos \gamma - \sin \alpha \sin \beta \cos \gamma -$
$\quad \sin \alpha \cos \beta \sin \gamma - \cos \alpha \sin \beta \sin \gamma$

76 (b) $t = 0, \pm \dfrac{\pi}{4b}$ **(c)** $\dfrac{2}{3}\sqrt{2}A$

77 $\pm \dfrac{\pi}{4}, \pm \dfrac{3\pi}{4}, \pm \dfrac{5\pi}{4}, \pm \dfrac{7\pi}{4}, \pm \dfrac{\pi}{3}, \pm \dfrac{5\pi}{3}$

78 (a) $x = 2d \tan \dfrac{1}{2}\theta$ **(b)** $d \le 1000$ ft

79 (a) $d = r\left(\sec \dfrac{1}{2}\theta - 1\right)$ **(b)** $43°$

80 (a) $78.7°$ **(b)** $61.4°$

CHAPTER 7 DISCUSSION EXERCISES

1 *Hint:* Factor $\sin^3 x - \cos^3 x$ as the difference of cubes.
2 $\sqrt{a^2 - x^2}$
$$= \begin{cases} a \cos \theta & \text{if } 0 \le \theta \le \pi/2 \text{ or } 3\pi/2 \le \theta < 2\pi \\ -a \cos \theta & \text{if } \pi/2 < \theta < 3\pi/2 \end{cases}$$
3 45; approximately 6.164

11 $\alpha \approx 29°$, $\beta \approx 47°$, $\gamma \approx 104°$

13 $\alpha \approx 12°30'$, $\beta \approx 136°30'$, $\gamma \approx 31°00'$ **15** 196 ft

17 24 mi **19** 39 mi **21** 2.3 mi **23** N55°31'E

25 63.7 ft from first and third base; 66.8 ft from second base

27 37,039 ft $\approx$ 7 mi

29 *Hint:* Use the formula $\sin \dfrac{\theta}{2} = \sqrt{\dfrac{1 - \cos \theta}{2}}$.

31 (a) 72°, 108°, 36° (b) 0.62 (c) 0.59, 0.36

Exer. 33–40: The answer is in square units.

33 260 **35** 11.21 **37** 13.1 **39** 517.0

41 1.62 acres **43** 123.4 ft^2

EXERCISES 8.3

1 $\langle 3, 1 \rangle$, $\langle 1, -7 \rangle$, $\langle 13, 8 \rangle$, $\langle 3, -32 \rangle$, $\sqrt{13}$

3 $\langle -15, 6 \rangle$, $\langle 1, -2 \rangle$, $\langle -68, 28 \rangle$, $\langle 12, -12 \rangle$, $\sqrt{53}$

5 $4\mathbf{i} - 3\mathbf{j}$, $-2\mathbf{i} + 7\mathbf{j}$, $19\mathbf{i} - 17\mathbf{j}$, $-11\mathbf{i} + 33\mathbf{j}$, $\sqrt{5}$

7 Terminal points are (3, 2), (−1, 5), (2, 7), (6, 4), (3, −15).

9 Terminal points are (−4, 6), (−2, 3), (−6, 9), (−8, 12), (6, −9).

11 $-\mathbf{b}$ **13** $\mathbf{f}$ **15** $-\dfrac{1}{2}\mathbf{e}$

17 $\mathbf{a} + (\mathbf{b} + \mathbf{c}) = \langle a_1, a_2 \rangle + (\langle b_1, b_2 \rangle + \langle c_1, c_2 \rangle)$
$= \langle a_1, a_2 \rangle + \langle b_1 + c_1, b_2 + c_2 \rangle$
$= \langle a_1 + b_1 + c_1, a_2 + b_2 + c_2 \rangle$
$= \langle a_1 + b_1, a_2 + b_2 \rangle + \langle c_1, c_2 \rangle$
$= (\langle a_1, a_2 \rangle + \langle b_1, b_2 \rangle) + \langle c_1, c_2 \rangle$
$= (\mathbf{a} + \mathbf{b}) + \mathbf{c}$

19 $\mathbf{a} + (-\mathbf{a}) = \langle a_1, a_2 \rangle + (-\langle a_1, a_2 \rangle)$
$= \langle a_1, a_2 \rangle + \langle -a_1, -a_2 \rangle$
$= \langle a_1 - a_1, a_2 - a_2 \rangle$
$= \langle 0, 0 \rangle = \mathbf{0}$

21 $(mn)\mathbf{a} = (mn)\langle a_1, a_2 \rangle$
$= \langle (mn)a_1, (mn)a_2 \rangle$
$= \langle mna_1, mna_2 \rangle$
$= m\langle na_1, na_2 \rangle$ or $n\langle ma_1, ma_2 \rangle$
$= m(n\langle a_1, a_2 \rangle)$ or $n(m\langle a_1, a_2 \rangle)$
$= m(n\mathbf{a})$ or $n(m\mathbf{a})$

23 $0\mathbf{a} = 0\langle a_1, a_2 \rangle = \langle 0a_1, 0a_2 \rangle = \langle 0, 0 \rangle = \mathbf{0}$.
Also, $m\mathbf{0} = m\langle 0, 0 \rangle = \langle m0, m0 \rangle = \langle 0, 0 \rangle = \mathbf{0}$.

25 $-(\mathbf{a} + \mathbf{b}) = -(\langle a_1, a_2 \rangle + \langle b_1, b_2 \rangle)$
$= -(\langle a_1 + b_1, a_2 + b_2 \rangle)$
$= \langle -(a_1 + b_1), -(a_2 + b_2) \rangle$
$= \langle -a_1 - b_1, -a_2 - b_2 \rangle$
$= \langle -a_1, -a_2 \rangle + \langle -b_1, -b_2 \rangle$
$= -\mathbf{a} + (-\mathbf{b}) = -\mathbf{a} - \mathbf{b}$

27 $\|2\mathbf{v}\| = \|2\langle a, b \rangle\| = \|\langle 2a, 2b \rangle\| = \sqrt{(2a)^2 + (2b)^2}$
$= \sqrt{4a^2 + 4b^2} = 2\sqrt{a^2 + b^2} = 2\|\langle a, b \rangle\|$
$= 2\|\mathbf{v}\|$

29 $3\sqrt{2}; \dfrac{7\pi}{4}$ **31** 5; π **33** $\sqrt{41}$; $\tan^{-1}\left(-\dfrac{5}{4}\right) + \pi$

35 18; $\dfrac{3\pi}{2}$ **37** 102 lb **39** 7.2 lb

41 89 lb; S66°W **43** 5.8 lb; 129°

45 40.96; 28.68 **47** −6.18; 19.02

49 (a) $-\dfrac{8}{17}\mathbf{i} + \dfrac{15}{17}\mathbf{j}$ (b) $\dfrac{8}{17}\mathbf{i} - \dfrac{15}{17}\mathbf{j}$

51 (a) $\left\langle \dfrac{2}{\sqrt{29}}, -\dfrac{5}{\sqrt{29}} \right\rangle$ (b) $\left\langle -\dfrac{2}{\sqrt{29}}, \dfrac{5}{\sqrt{29}} \right\rangle$

53 (a) $\langle -12, 6 \rangle$ (b) $\left\langle -3, \dfrac{3}{2} \right\rangle$

55 $-\dfrac{24}{\sqrt{65}}\mathbf{i} + \dfrac{42}{\sqrt{65}}\mathbf{j}$

57 (a) $\mathbf{F} = \langle 7, 2 \rangle$ (b) $\mathbf{G} = -\mathbf{F} = \langle -7, -2 \rangle$

59 (a) $\mathbf{F} \approx \langle -5.86, 1.13 \rangle$
(b) $\mathbf{G} = -\mathbf{F} \approx \langle 5.86, -1.13 \rangle$

61 $\sin^{-1}(0.4) \approx 23.6°$ **63** 56°; 232 mi/hr

65 420 mi/hr; 244° **67** N22°W

69 $\mathbf{v}_1 \approx 4.1\mathbf{i} - 7.10\mathbf{j}$; $\mathbf{v}_2 \approx 0.98\mathbf{i} - 3.67\mathbf{j}$

71 (a) (24.51, 20.57) (b) (−24.57, 18.10)

73 28.2 lb/person

EXERCISES 8.4

1 (a) 24 (b) $\cos^{-1}\left(\dfrac{24}{\sqrt{29}\sqrt{45}}\right) \approx 48°22'$

3 (a) −14 (b) $\cos^{-1}\left(\dfrac{-14}{\sqrt{17}\sqrt{13}}\right) \approx 160°21'$

5 (a) 45 (b) $\cos^{-1}\left(\dfrac{45}{\sqrt{81}\sqrt{41}}\right) \approx 38°40'$

7 (a) $-\dfrac{149}{5}$ (b) $\cos^{-1}\left(\dfrac{-149/5}{\sqrt{149}\sqrt{149/25}}\right) = 180°$

9 $\langle 4, -1 \rangle \cdot \langle 2, 8 \rangle = 0$ **11** $(-4\mathbf{j}) \cdot (-7\mathbf{i}) = 0$

13 Opposite **15** Same **17** $\dfrac{6}{5}$ **19** $\pm\dfrac{3}{8}$

21 (a) −23 (b) −23 **23** −51

25 $17/\sqrt{26} \approx 3.33$ **27** 2.2 **29** 7

31 28 **33** 12

35 $\mathbf{a} \cdot \mathbf{a} = \langle a_1, a_2 \rangle \cdot \langle a_1, a_2 \rangle = a_1^2 + a_2^2$
$$= \left(\sqrt{a_1^2 + a_2^2} \right)^2 = \|\mathbf{a}\|^2$$

37 $(m\mathbf{a}) \cdot \mathbf{b} = (m\langle a_1, a_2 \rangle) \cdot \langle b_1, b_2 \rangle$
$$= \langle ma_1, ma_2 \rangle \cdot \langle b_1, b_2 \rangle$$
$$= ma_1 b_1 + ma_2 b_2$$
$$= m(a_1 b_1 + a_2 b_2) = m(\mathbf{a} \cdot \mathbf{b})$$

39 $\mathbf{0} \cdot \mathbf{a} = \langle 0, 0 \rangle \cdot \langle a_1, a_2 \rangle = 0(a_1) + 0(a_2)$
$$= 0 + 0 = 0$$

41 $1000\sqrt{3} \approx 1732$ ft-lb

43 (a) $\mathbf{v} = (93 \times 10^6)\mathbf{i} + (0.432 \times 10^6)\mathbf{j}$;
$\mathbf{w} = (93 \times 10^6)\mathbf{i} - (0.432 \times 10^6)\mathbf{j}$

(b) $0.53°$

45 $\left\langle \dfrac{4}{5}, \dfrac{3}{5} \right\rangle$ **47** 2.6 **49** 24.33

51 $16\sqrt{3} \approx 27.7$ horsepower

EXERCISES 8.5

1 5 **3** $\sqrt{85}$ **5** 8 **7** 1 **9** 0

Note: Point P is the point corresponding to the geometric representation.

11 $P(4, 2)$ **13** $P(3, -5)$ **15** $P(-3, 6)$
17 $P(-6, 4)$ **19** $P(0, 2)$

21 $\sqrt{2}$ cis $\dfrac{7\pi}{4}$ **23** 8 cis $\dfrac{5\pi}{6}$ **25** 4 cis $\dfrac{\pi}{6}$

27 $4\sqrt{2}$ cis $\dfrac{5\pi}{4}$ **29** 20 cis $\dfrac{3\pi}{2}$ **31** 12 cis 0

33 7 cis π **35** 6 cis $\dfrac{\pi}{2}$ **37** 10 cis $\dfrac{4\pi}{3}$

39 $\sqrt{5}$ cis $\left(\tan^{-1} \dfrac{1}{2} \right)$

41 $\sqrt{10}$ cis $\left[\tan^{-1}\left(-\dfrac{1}{3} \right) + \pi \right]$

43 $\sqrt{34}$ cis $\left(\tan^{-1} \dfrac{3}{5} + \pi \right)$

45 5 cis $\left[\tan^{-1}\left(-\dfrac{3}{4} \right) + 2\pi \right]$

47 $2\sqrt{2} + 2\sqrt{2}i$ **49** $-3 + 3\sqrt{3}i$ **51** -5

53 $5 + 3i$ **55** $2 - i$ **57** $-2, i$

59 $10\sqrt{3} - 10i, -\dfrac{2}{5}\sqrt{3} + \dfrac{2}{5}i$ **61** $40, \dfrac{5}{2}$

63 $8 - 4i, \dfrac{8}{5} + \dfrac{4}{5}i$ **65** $-15 + 10i, -\dfrac{15}{13} - \dfrac{10}{13}i$

69 $17.21 + 24.57i$ **71** $11.01 + 9.24i$

73 $\sqrt{365}$ ohms **75** 70.43 volts

EXERCISES 8.6

1 $-972 - 972i$ **3** $-32i$ **5** -8

7 $-\dfrac{1}{2}\sqrt{2} - \dfrac{1}{2}\sqrt{2}i$ **9** $-\dfrac{1}{2} - \dfrac{1}{2}\sqrt{3}i$

11 $-64\sqrt{3} - 64i$ **13** $\pm\left(\dfrac{1}{2}\sqrt{6} + \dfrac{1}{2}\sqrt{2}i \right)$

15 $\pm\left(\dfrac{\sqrt[4]{2}}{2} + \dfrac{\sqrt[4]{18}}{2}i \right), \pm\left(\dfrac{\sqrt[4]{18}}{2} - \dfrac{\sqrt[4]{2}}{2}i \right)$

17 $3i, \pm\dfrac{3}{2}\sqrt{3} - \dfrac{3}{2}i$

19 $\pm 1, \dfrac{1}{2} \pm \dfrac{1}{2}\sqrt{3}i,$ **21** $\sqrt[10]{2}$ cis θ with $\theta = 9°$,
$\quad -\dfrac{1}{2} \pm \dfrac{1}{2}\sqrt{3}i$ $\quad 81°, 153°, 225°, 297°$

23 $\pm 2, \pm 2i$ **25** $\pm 2i, \sqrt{3} \pm i, -\sqrt{3} \pm i$

27 $2i, \pm\sqrt{3} - i$

29 3 cis θ with $\theta = 0°, 72°, 144°, 216°, 288°$

31 $[r(\cos\theta + i\sin\theta)]^n = [r(e^{i\theta})]^n$
$$= r^n(e^{i\theta})^n$$
$$= r^n e^{i(n\theta)}$$
$$= r^n(\cos n\theta + i\sin n\theta)$$

CHAPTER 8 REVIEW EXERCISES

1 $a = \sqrt{43}, \beta = \cos^{-1}\left(\dfrac{4}{43}\sqrt{43} \right), \gamma = \cos^{-1}\left(\dfrac{5}{86}\sqrt{43} \right)$

2 $\alpha = 60°, \beta = 90°, b = 4; \alpha = 120°, \beta = 30°, b = 2$

3 $\gamma = 75°, a = 50\sqrt{6}, c = 50\left(1 + \sqrt{3}\right)$

4 $\alpha = \cos^{-1}\left(\dfrac{7}{8}\right), \beta = \cos^{-1}\left(\dfrac{11}{16}\right), \gamma = \cos^{-1}\left(-\dfrac{1}{4}\right)$

5 $\alpha = 38°, a \approx 8.0, c \approx 13$

6 $\gamma \approx 19°10', \beta \approx 137°20', b \approx 258$

7 $\alpha \approx 24°, \gamma \approx 41°, b \approx 10.1$

8 $\alpha \approx 42°, \beta \approx 87°, \gamma \approx 51°$ **9** 290 **10** 10.9

11 Terminal points are $(-2, -3), (-6, 13),$ $(-8, 10), (-1, 4).$

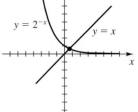

12 **(a)** $12\mathbf{i} + 19\mathbf{j}$ **(b)** $-8\mathbf{i} + 13\mathbf{j}$ **(c)** $\sqrt{40} \approx 6.32$
(d) $\sqrt{29} - \sqrt{17} \approx 1.26$

13 $\langle 14\cos 40°, -14\sin 40°\rangle$ **14** 109 lb; S78°E

15 $-16\mathbf{i} + 12\mathbf{j}$

16 $\left\langle -\dfrac{12}{\sqrt{58}}, \dfrac{28}{\sqrt{58}}\right\rangle$

17 Circle with center (a_1, a_2) and radius c

18 The vectors $\mathbf{a}$, $\mathbf{b}$, and $\mathbf{a} - \mathbf{b}$ form a triangle with the vector $\mathbf{a} - \mathbf{b}$ opposite angle θ. The conclusion is a direct application of the law of cosines with sides $\|\mathbf{a}\|$, $\|\mathbf{b}\|$, and $\|\mathbf{a} - \mathbf{b}\|$.

19 183°; 70 mi/hr

20 **(a)** 10 **(b)** $\cos^{-1}\left(\dfrac{10}{\sqrt{13}\sqrt{17}}\right) \approx 47°44'$ **(c)** $\dfrac{10}{\sqrt{13}}$

21 **(a)** 80 **(b)** $\cos^{-1}\left(\dfrac{40}{\sqrt{40}\sqrt{50}}\right) \approx 26°34'$ **(c)** $\sqrt{40}$

22 56

23 $10\sqrt{2}\operatorname{cis}\dfrac{3\pi}{4}$ **24** $4\operatorname{cis}\dfrac{5\pi}{3}$ **25** $17\operatorname{cis}\pi$

26 $12\operatorname{cis}\dfrac{3\pi}{2}$ **27** $10\operatorname{cis}\dfrac{7\pi}{6}$

28 $\sqrt{41}\operatorname{cis}\left(\tan^{-1}\dfrac{5}{4}\right)$ **29** $10\sqrt{3} - 10i$

30 $12 + 5i$ **31** $-12 - 12\sqrt{3}i, -\dfrac{3}{2}$

32 $-4\sqrt{2}i, -2\sqrt{2}$ **33** $-512i$ **34** i

35 $-972 + 972i$ **36** $-2^{19} - 2^{19}\sqrt{3}i$

37 $-3, \dfrac{3}{2} \pm \dfrac{3}{2}\sqrt{3}i$

38 **(a)** 2^{24} **(b)** $\sqrt[3]{2}\operatorname{cis}\theta$ with $\theta = 100°, 220°, 340°$
39 $2\operatorname{cis}\theta$ with $\theta = 0°, 72°, 144°, 216°, 288°$
40 47.6° **41** 197.4 yards **42** 235.8 mi
43 53,000,000 mi **44** **(a)** 449 ft **(b)** 434 ft
45 **(a)** 33 mi, 41 mi **(b)** 30 mi **46** 204
47 1 hour and 16 minutes **48** **(c)** 158°
49 **(a)** 47° **(b)** 20
50 **(a)** 72° **(b)** 181.6 ft² **(c)** 37.6 ft

CHAPTER 8 DISCUSSION EXERCISES

4 **(b)** *Hint:* Law of cosines
5 **(a)** $(\|\mathbf{b}\|\cos\alpha + \|\mathbf{a}\|\cos\beta)\mathbf{i} +$ $(\|\mathbf{b}\|\sin\alpha - \|\mathbf{a}\|\sin\beta)\mathbf{j}$

6 **(a)** 1 **(b)** $\pi i; \dfrac{\pi}{2}i$ **(c)** $\dfrac{\sqrt{2}}{2} + \dfrac{\sqrt{2}}{2}i; e^{-\pi/2} \approx 0.2079$

7 The statement is true.

Chapter 9

EXERCISES 9.1

1 $(3, 5), (-1, -3)$ **3** $(1, 0), (-3, 2)$

5 $(0, 0), \left(\dfrac{1}{8}, \dfrac{1}{128}\right)$ **7** $(3, -2)$ **9** No solution

11 $(-4, 3), (5, 0)$ **13** $(-2, 2)$

15 $\left(-\dfrac{3}{5} + \dfrac{1}{10}\sqrt{86}, \dfrac{1}{5} + \dfrac{3}{10}\sqrt{86}\right),$ $\left(-\dfrac{3}{5} - \dfrac{1}{10}\sqrt{86}, \dfrac{1}{5} - \dfrac{3}{10}\sqrt{86}\right)$

17 $(-4, 0), \left(\dfrac{12}{5}, \dfrac{16}{5}\right)$ **19** $(0, 1), (4, -3)$

21 $(-6, -1), (-1, 4)$ **23** $(\pm 2, 5), \left(\pm\sqrt{5}, 4\right)$

25 $\left(\sqrt{2}, \pm 2\sqrt{3}\right), \left(-\sqrt{2}, \pm 2\sqrt{3}\right)$

27 $\left(2\sqrt{2}, \pm 2\right), \left(-2\sqrt{2}, \pm 2\right)$ **29** $(3, -1, 2)$

31 $(1, -1, 2), (-1, 3, -2)$

33 **(a)** $b = 4$; tangent
(b) $b < 4$; intersect twice
(c) $b > 4$; no intersection

35 Yes; a solution occurs between 0 and 1.

37 $\dfrac{1}{4}$; tangent **39** $f(x) = 2(3)^x + 1$

41 12 in. $\times$ 8 in.

43 (a) $a = 120,000, b = 40,000$ **(b)** 77,143

45 $(0, 0), (0, 100), (50, 0)$; the fourth solution $(-100, 150)$ is not meaningful.

47 Yes; 1 ft $\times$ 1 ft $\times$ 2 ft or

$$\dfrac{\sqrt{13} - 1}{2} \text{ ft} \times \dfrac{\sqrt{13} - 1}{2} \text{ ft} \times \dfrac{8}{(\sqrt{13} - 1)^2} \text{ ft}$$
$$\approx 1.30 \text{ ft} \times 1.30 \text{ ft} \times 1.18 \text{ ft}$$

49 The points are on the parabola **(a)** $y = \dfrac{1}{2}x^2 - \dfrac{1}{2}$ and

(b) $y = \dfrac{1}{4}x^2 - 1$.

51 (a) $(31.25, -50)$

(b) $\left(-\dfrac{3}{2}\sqrt{11}, -\dfrac{1}{2}\right) \approx (-4.975, -0.5)$

EXERCISES 9.2

1 $(4, -2)$ **3** $(8, 0)$ **5** $\left(-1, \dfrac{3}{2}\right)$ **7** $\left(\dfrac{76}{53}, \dfrac{28}{53}\right)$

9 $\left(\dfrac{51}{13}, \dfrac{96}{13}\right)$ **11** $\left(\dfrac{8}{7}, -\dfrac{3}{7}\sqrt{6}\right)$ **13** $\left(\dfrac{220}{13}, \dfrac{137}{13}\right)$

15 No solution

17 All ordered pairs (m, n) such that $3m - 4n = 2$

19 $(0, 0)$ **21** $\left(-\dfrac{22}{7}, -\dfrac{11}{5}\right)$

23 313 students, 137 nonstudents

25 $x = \left(\dfrac{30}{\pi}\right) - 4 \approx 5.55$ cm, $y = 12 - \left(\dfrac{30}{\pi}\right) \approx 2.45$ cm

27 $l = 10$ ft, $w = \dfrac{20}{\pi}$ ft **29** 2400 adults, 3600 kittens

31 40 g of 35% alloy, 60 g of 60% alloy

33 540 mi/hr, 60 mi/hr **35** $v_0 = 10, a = 3$

37 20 sofas, 30 recliners

39 (a) $\left(c, \dfrac{4}{5}c\right)$ for an arbitrary $c > 0$ **(b)** \$16 per hour

41 1928; 15.5°C **43** LP: 4 hr, SLP: 2 hr

45 $a = \dfrac{1}{6}, b = -\dfrac{1}{6}e^{6x}$ **47** $a = \cos x - \sec x, b = \sin x$

EXERCISES 9.3

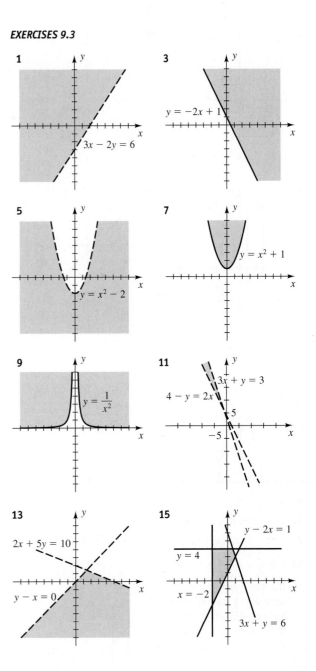

17

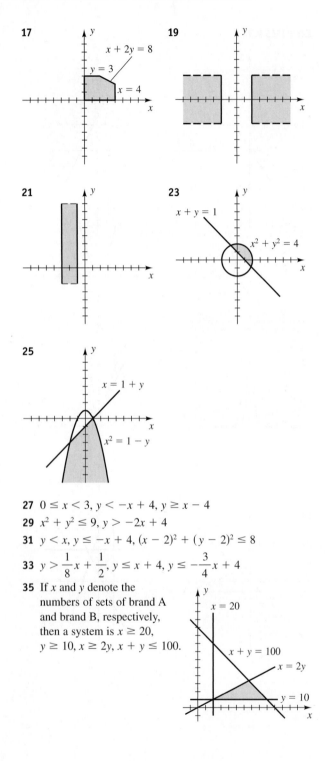

$x + 2y = 8$

$y = 3$

$x = 4$

19

21

23

$x + y = 1$

$x^2 + y^2 = 4$

25

$x = 1 + y$

$x^2 = 1 - y$

27 $0 \le x < 3, y < -x + 4, y \ge x - 4$

29 $x^2 + y^2 \le 9, y > -2x + 4$

31 $y < x, y \le -x + 4, (x - 2)^2 + (y - 2)^2 \le 8$

33 $y > \dfrac{1}{8}x + \dfrac{1}{2}, y \le x + 4, y \le -\dfrac{3}{4}x + 4$

35 If x and y denote the numbers of sets of brand A and brand B, respectively, then a system is $x \ge 20$, $y \ge 10, x \ge 2y, x + y \le 100$.

$x = 20$

$x + y = 100$

$x = 2y$

$y = 10$

37 If x and y denote the amounts placed in the high-risk and low-risk investment, respectively, then a system is $x \ge 2000, y \ge 3x,$ $x + y \le 15{,}000.$

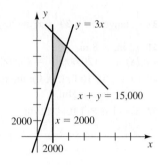

$y = 3x$

$x + y = 15{,}000$

2000

$x = 2000$

2000

39 $x + y \le 9, y \ge x, x \ge 1$

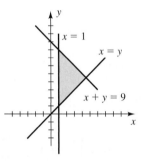

$x = 1$

$x = y$

$x + y = 9$

41 If the plant is located at (x, y), then a system is $60^2 \le x^2 + y^2 \le 100^2, 60^2 \le (x - 100)^2 + y^2 \le 100^2,$ $y \ge 0.$

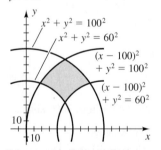

$x^2 + y^2 = 100^2$

$x^2 + y^2 = 60^2$

$(x - 100)^2 + y^2 = 100^2$

$(x - 100)^2 + y^2 = 60^2$

10

10

43 **(a)** Yes

(b)

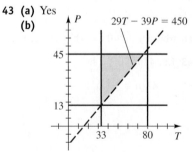

$29T - 39P = 450$

45

13

33 80

(c) Region above the line

EXERCISES 9.4

1 Maximum of 27 at $(6, 2)$; minimum of 9 at $(0, 2)$
3 Maximum of 21 at $(6, 3)$ **5** Minimum of 21 at $(3, 2)$

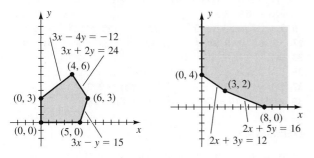

7 C has the maximum value 24 for any point on the line segment from $(2, 5)$ to $(6, 3)$.

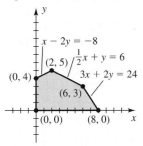

9 50 standard and 30 oversized
11 3.5 lb of S and 1 lb of T
13 Send 25 from W_1 to A and 0 from W_1 to B.
   Send 10 from W_2 to A and 60 from W_2 to B.
15 None of alfalfa and 80 acres of corn
17 Minimum cost: 16 oz X, 4 oz Y, 0 oz Z;
   maximum cost: 0 oz X, 8 oz Y, 12 oz Z
19 2 vans and 4 buses   **21** 3000 trout and 2000 bass
23 60 small units and 20 deluxe units

EXERCISES 9.5

1 $(2, 3, -1)$ **3** $(-2, 4, 5)$ **5** No solution
7 $\left(\dfrac{2}{3}, \dfrac{31}{21}, \dfrac{1}{21}\right)$

Exer. 9–16: There are other forms for the answers; c is any real number.

9 $(2c, -c, c)$ **11** $(0, -c, c)$
13 $\left(\dfrac{12}{7} - \dfrac{9}{7}c, \dfrac{4}{7}c - \dfrac{13}{14}, c\right)$

15 $\left(\dfrac{7}{10}c + \dfrac{1}{2}, \dfrac{19}{10}c - \dfrac{3}{2}, c\right)$

17 $\left(\dfrac{1}{11}, \dfrac{31}{11}, \dfrac{3}{11}\right)$ **19** $(-2, -3)$ **21** No solution
23 17 of 10%, 11 of 30%, 22 of 50%
25 4 hr for A, 2 hr for B, 5 hr for C
27 380 lb of G_1, 60 lb of G_2, 160 lb of G_3

29 (a) $I_1 = 0, I_2 = 2, I_3 = 2$ **(b)** $I_1 = \dfrac{3}{4}, I_2 = 3, I_3 = \dfrac{9}{4}$

31 $\dfrac{3}{8}$ lb Colombian, $\dfrac{1}{8}$ lb Costa Rican, $\dfrac{1}{2}$ lb Kenyan

33 (a) A: $x_1 + x_4 = 75$, B: $x_1 + x_2 = 150$,
   C: $x_2 + x_3 = 225$, D: $x_3 + x_4 = 150$
   (b) $x_1 = 25, x_2 = 125, x_4 = 50$
   (c) $x_3 = 150 - x_4 \leq 150$;
   $x_3 = 225 - x_2 = 225 - (150 - x_1) = 75 + x_1 \geq 75$
35 $x^2 + y^2 - x + 3y - 6 = 0$
37 $f(x) = x^3 - 2x^2 - 4x - 6$

EXERCISES 9.6

1 $\begin{bmatrix} 9 & -1 \\ -2 & 5 \end{bmatrix}, \begin{bmatrix} 1 & -3 \\ 4 & 1 \end{bmatrix}, \begin{bmatrix} 10 & -4 \\ 2 & 6 \end{bmatrix}, \begin{bmatrix} -12 & -3 \\ 9 & -6 \end{bmatrix}$

3 $\begin{bmatrix} 9 & 0 \\ 1 & 5 \\ 3 & 4 \end{bmatrix}, \begin{bmatrix} 3 & -2 \\ 3 & -5 \\ -9 & 4 \end{bmatrix}, \begin{bmatrix} 12 & -2 \\ 4 & 0 \\ -6 & 8 \end{bmatrix}, \begin{bmatrix} -9 & -3 \\ 3 & -15 \\ -18 & 0 \end{bmatrix}$

5 $[11 \quad -3 \quad -3], [-3 \quad -3 \quad 7],$
   $[8 \quad -6 \quad 4], [-21 \quad 0 \quad 15]$
7 Not possible, not possible,
   $\begin{bmatrix} 6 & -4 & 4 \\ 0 & 2 & -8 \\ -6 & 4 & -2 \end{bmatrix}, \begin{bmatrix} -12 & 0 \\ -6 & 3 \\ 3 & -9 \end{bmatrix}$

9 -18 **11** $\begin{bmatrix} 16 & 38 \\ 11 & -34 \end{bmatrix}, \begin{bmatrix} 4 & 38 \\ 23 & -22 \end{bmatrix}$

13 $\begin{bmatrix} 3 & -14 & -3 \\ 16 & 2 & -2 \\ -7 & -29 & 9 \end{bmatrix}, \begin{bmatrix} 3 & -20 & -11 \\ 2 & 10 & -4 \\ 15 & -13 & 1 \end{bmatrix}$

15 $\begin{bmatrix} 4 & 8 \\ -18 & 11 \end{bmatrix}, \begin{bmatrix} 3 & -4 & 4 \\ -5 & 2 & 2 \\ -51 & 26 & 10 \end{bmatrix}$

17 $\begin{bmatrix} 1 & 2 & 3 \\ 4 & 5 & 6 \\ 7 & 8 & 9 \end{bmatrix}, \begin{bmatrix} 1 & 2 & 3 \\ 4 & 5 & 6 \\ 7 & 8 & 9 \end{bmatrix}$

19 [15], $\begin{bmatrix} -3 & 7 & 2 \\ -12 & 28 & 8 \\ 15 & -35 & -10 \end{bmatrix}$

21 $\begin{bmatrix} 2 & 0 & 5 \\ 5 & 3 & -2 \end{bmatrix}$, not possible **23** $\begin{bmatrix} 4 \\ 12 \\ -1 \end{bmatrix}$

25 $\begin{bmatrix} 18 & 0 & -2 \\ -40 & 10 & -10 \end{bmatrix}$

35 (a) $A = \begin{bmatrix} 400 & 550 & 500 \\ 400 & 450 & 500 \\ 300 & 500 & 600 \\ 250 & 200 & 300 \\ 100 & 100 & 200 \end{bmatrix}$, $B = \begin{bmatrix} \$ 8.99 \\ \$10.99 \\ \$12.99 \end{bmatrix}$

(b) $\begin{bmatrix} \$16,135.50 \\ \$15,036.50 \\ \$15,986.00 \\ \$ 8,342.50 \\ \$ 4,596.00 \end{bmatrix}$

(c) The $4,596.00 represents the amount the store would receive if all the yellow towels were sold.

EXERCISES 9.7

1 Show that $AB = I_2$ and $BA = I_2$.

3 $\dfrac{1}{10} \begin{bmatrix} 3 & 4 \\ -1 & 2 \end{bmatrix}$ **5** Does not exist

7 $\dfrac{1}{8} \begin{bmatrix} 2 & 1 & 0 \\ -2 & 3 & 0 \\ 0 & 0 & 2 \end{bmatrix}$ **9** $\dfrac{1}{3} \begin{bmatrix} -4 & -5 & 3 \\ -4 & -8 & 3 \\ 1 & 2 & 0 \end{bmatrix}$

11 $\begin{bmatrix} \frac{1}{2} & 0 & 0 \\ 0 & \frac{1}{4} & 0 \\ 0 & 0 & \frac{1}{6} \end{bmatrix}$ **13** $ab \neq 0$; $\begin{bmatrix} \frac{1}{a} & 0 \\ 0 & \frac{1}{b} \end{bmatrix}$

17 (a) $\left(\dfrac{13}{10}, -\dfrac{1}{10} \right)$ **(b)** $\left(\dfrac{7}{5}, \dfrac{6}{5} \right)$

19 (a) $\left(-\dfrac{25}{3}, -\dfrac{34}{3}, \dfrac{7}{3} \right)$ **(b)** $\left(\dfrac{16}{3}, \dfrac{16}{3}, -\dfrac{1}{3} \right)$

EXERCISES 9.8

1 $M_{11} = 0 = A_{11}$; $M_{12} = 5$; $A_{12} = -5$;
 $M_{21} = -1$; $A_{21} = 1$; $M_{22} = 7 = A_{22}$

3 $M_{11} = -14 = A_{11}$; $M_{12} = 10$; $A_{12} = -10$;
 $M_{13} = 15 = A_{13}$; $M_{21} = 7$; $A_{21} = -7$;
 $M_{22} = -5 = A_{22}$; $M_{23} = 34$; $A_{23} = -34$;
 $M_{31} = 11 = A_{31}$; $M_{32} = 4$; $A_{32} = -4$;
 $M_{33} = 6 = A_{33}$

5 5   **7** -83 **9** 2   **11** 0   **13** -125 **15** 48
17 -216 **19** $abcd$ **31 (a)** $x^2 - 3x - 4$ **(b)** $-1, 4$
33 (a) $x^2 + x - 2$ **(b)** $-2, 1$
35 (a) $-x^3 - 2x^2 + x + 2$ **(b)** $-2, -1, 1$
37 (a) $-x^3 + 4x^2 + 4x - 16$ **(b)** $-2, 2, 4$
39 $-31i - 20j + 7k$ **41** $-6i - 8j + 18k$

EXERCISES 9.9

1 $R_2 \leftrightarrow R_3$ **3** $-R_1 + R_3 \rightarrow R_3$
5 2 is a common factor of R_1 and R_3.
7 R_1 and R_3 are identical.
9 -1 is a common factor of R_2.
11 Every number in C_2 is 0.   **13** $2C_1 + C_3 \rightarrow C_3$
15 -10 **17** -142 **19** -183 **21** 44   **23** 359
33 $(4, -2)$ **35** $(8, 0)$
37 $|D| = 0$, so Cramer's rule cannot be used.
39 $(2, 3, -1)$ **41** $(-2, 4, 5)$

43 $x = \dfrac{cgi - dfi + bfj}{cei - afi + bfh}$

EXERCISES 9.10

1 $\dfrac{3}{x - 2} + \dfrac{5}{x + 3}$ **3** $\dfrac{5}{x - 6} - \dfrac{4}{x + 2}$

5 $\dfrac{2}{x - 1} + \dfrac{3}{x + 2} - \dfrac{1}{x - 3}$ **7** $\dfrac{3}{x} + \dfrac{2}{x - 5} - \dfrac{1}{x + 1}$

9 $\dfrac{2}{x - 1} + \dfrac{5}{(x - 1)^2}$ **11** $-\dfrac{7}{x} + \dfrac{5}{x^2} + \dfrac{40}{3x - 5}$

13 $\dfrac{24/25}{x + 2} + \dfrac{2/5}{(x + 2)^2} - \dfrac{23/25}{2x - 1}$

15 $\dfrac{5}{x} - \dfrac{2}{x + 1} + \dfrac{3}{(x + 1)^3}$ **17** $-\dfrac{2}{x - 1} + \dfrac{3x + 4}{x^2 + 1}$

19 $\dfrac{4}{x} + \dfrac{5x - 3}{x^2 + 2}$ **21** $\dfrac{4x - 1}{x^2 + 1} + \dfrac{3}{(x^2 + 1)^2}$

23 $2x + \dfrac{1}{x - 1} + \dfrac{3x}{x^2 + 1}$ **25** $3 + \dfrac{4}{x} + \dfrac{8}{x - 4}$

27 $2x + 3 + \dfrac{2}{x - 1} - \dfrac{3}{2x + 1}$

CHAPTER 9 REVIEW EXERCISES

1 $\left(\dfrac{19}{23}, -\dfrac{18}{23} \right)$ **2** No solution   **3** $(-3, 5), (1, -3)$

4 $(4, -3), (3, -4)$ **5** $(2\sqrt{3}, \pm\sqrt{2}), (-2\sqrt{3}, \pm\sqrt{2})$

6 $(-1, \pm1, -1), \left(0, \pm\dfrac{1}{2}\sqrt{6}, -\dfrac{1}{2}\right)$ **7** $\left(\dfrac{14}{17}, \dfrac{14}{27}\right)$

8 $\left(\log_2 \dfrac{25}{7}, \log_3 \dfrac{15}{7}\right)$ **9** $\left(\dfrac{6}{11}, -\dfrac{7}{11}, 1\right)$

10 $\left(-\dfrac{6}{29}, \dfrac{2}{29}, -\dfrac{17}{29}\right)$

11 $(-2c, -3c, c)$ for any real number c **12** $(0, 0, 0)$

13 $\left(5c - 1, -\dfrac{19}{2}c + \dfrac{5}{2}, c\right)$ for any real number c

14 $(5, -4)$ **15** $\left(-1, \dfrac{1}{2}, \dfrac{1}{3}\right)$ **16** $(3, -1, -2, 4)$

17

18

19

20

21 $\begin{bmatrix} 4 & -5 & 6 \\ 4 & -11 & 5 \end{bmatrix}$ **22** $\begin{bmatrix} 26 \\ -6 \end{bmatrix}$ **23** $\begin{bmatrix} 0 & 4 & -6 \\ 16 & 22 & 1 \\ 12 & 11 & 9 \end{bmatrix}$

24 $\begin{bmatrix} 0 & -37 \\ 15 & -6 \end{bmatrix}$ **25** $\begin{bmatrix} -12 & 4 & -11 \\ 6 & -11 & 5 \end{bmatrix}$

26 $\begin{bmatrix} a & 3a \\ 2a & 4a \end{bmatrix}$ **27** $\begin{bmatrix} a & 3a \\ 2b & 4b \end{bmatrix}$ **28** $\begin{bmatrix} 0 & 0 \\ 0 & 0 \end{bmatrix}$

29 $\begin{bmatrix} 5 & 9 \\ 13 & 19 \end{bmatrix}$ **30** $\begin{bmatrix} 1 & 0 & 0 \\ 0 & 1 & 0 \\ 0 & 0 & 1 \end{bmatrix}$ **31** $-\dfrac{1}{2}\begin{bmatrix} 2 & 4 \\ 3 & 5 \end{bmatrix}$

32 $\dfrac{1}{11}\begin{bmatrix} 8 & 1 & -2 \\ 5 & 2 & -4 \\ -14 & 1 & 9 \end{bmatrix}$ **33** $\begin{bmatrix} 1 & 0 & 0 \\ 0 & 2 & -7 \\ 0 & -1 & 4 \end{bmatrix}$

34 $\dfrac{1}{37}\begin{bmatrix} -4 & -20 & 15 \\ 3 & 15 & -2 \\ 9 & 8 & -6 \end{bmatrix}$ **35** $(2, -5)$ **36** $(-1, 3, 2)$

37 -6 **38** 9 **39** 48 **40** -86 **41** -84

42 0 **43** 120 **44** -76 **45** 0 **46** -50

47 $-1 \pm 2\sqrt{3}$ **48** $4, \pm\sqrt{7}$

49 2 is a common factor of R_1, 2 is a common factor of C_2, and 3 is a common factor of C_3.

50 Interchange R_1 with R_2 and then R_2 with R_3 to obtain the determinant on the right. The effect is to multiply by -1 twice.

51 $a_{11}a_{22}a_{33} \cdots a_{nn}$ **53** $\left(\dfrac{76}{53}, \dfrac{28}{53}\right)$ **54** $\left(\dfrac{2}{3}, \dfrac{31}{21}, \dfrac{1}{21}\right)$

55 $\dfrac{8}{x - 1} - \dfrac{3}{x + 5} - \dfrac{1}{x + 3}$ **56** $2 + \dfrac{3}{x + 1} + \dfrac{4}{(x + 1)^2}$

57 $-\dfrac{2}{x + 5} + \dfrac{3x - 1}{x^2 + 4}$ **58** $\dfrac{4}{x^2 + 2} + \dfrac{x - 2}{x^2 + 5}$

59 $40\sqrt{5}$ ft $\times 20\sqrt{5}$ ft   **60** $y = \pm2\sqrt{2}x + 3$

61 Inside radius $= 90$ ft, outside radius $= 100$ ft

62 Tax $= \$750{,}000$; bonus $= \$125{,}000$

63 5 mi/hr; 2 mi/hr

64 25 pounds of peanuts and 30 pounds of raisins

65 1325 mi/hr; 63 mi/hr

66 In ft³/hr: A, 30; B, 20; C, 50

67 Western 95, eastern 55

68 If x and y denote the length and width, respectively, then a system is $x \le 12$, $y \le 8$, $y \ge \dfrac{1}{2}x$.

69 $x + y \le 18$, $x \ge 2y$, $x \ge 0$, $y \ge 0$

70 80 mowers and 30 edgers
71 High-risk $250,000; low-risk $500,000; bonds $0

CHAPTER 9 DISCUSSION EXERCISES

1 **(a)** $b = 1.99$, $x = 204$, $y = -100$;
$b = 1.999$, $x = 2004$, $y = -1000$

(b) $x = \dfrac{4b - 10}{b - 2}$, $y = \dfrac{1}{b - 2}$

(c) It gets close to $(4, 0)$.

2 **(a)** $D = [12{,}000 \quad 9000 \quad 14{,}000]$;

$$E = \begin{bmatrix} 0.90 & 0.10 & 0.00 \\ 0.00 & 0.80 & 0.20 \\ 0.05 & 0.00 & 0.95 \end{bmatrix}$$

(b) The elements of $F = [11{,}500 \quad 8400 \quad 15{,}100]$ represent the populations on islands A, B, and C, respectively, after one year.

(c) The population stabilizes with 10,000 birds on A, 5000 birds on B, and 20,000 birds on C.

3 *Hint:* Assign a size to A, and examine the definition of an inverse.

4 AD: 35%, DS: $33\dfrac{1}{3}$%, SP: $31\dfrac{2}{3}$%

5 $a = -15$, $b = 10$, $c = 24$; the fourth root is -4

6 **(a)** Not possible **(b)** $x^2 + y^2 - 1.8x - 4.2y + 0.8 = 0$

(c) $f(x) = -\dfrac{5}{12}x^2 + \dfrac{7}{12}x + 4$

(d) $f(x) = ax^3 + \left(-2a - \dfrac{5}{12}\right)x^2 + \left(-3a + \dfrac{7}{12}\right)x + 4$,
where a is any nonzero real number

(e) Not possible

Chapter 10

EXERCISES 10.1

1 $9, 6, 3, 0; -12$ **3** $\dfrac{1}{2}, \dfrac{4}{5}, \dfrac{7}{10}, \dfrac{10}{17}; \dfrac{22}{65}$

5 $9, 9, 9, 9; 9$

7 $1.9, 2.01, 1.999, 2.0001; 2.000\,000\,01$

9 $4, -\dfrac{9}{4}, \dfrac{5}{3}, -\dfrac{11}{8}; -\dfrac{15}{16}$ **11** $2, 0, 2, 0; 0$

13 $\dfrac{2}{3}, \dfrac{2}{3}, \dfrac{8}{11}, \dfrac{8}{9}; \dfrac{128}{33}$ **15** $1, 2, 3, 4; 8$

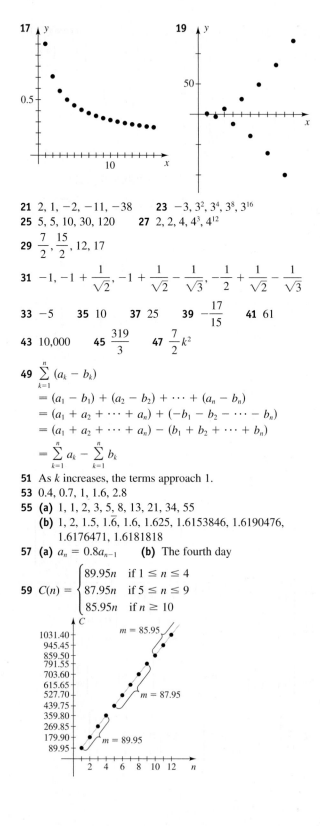

17

19

21 $2, 1, -2, -11, -38$ **23** $-3, 3^2, 3^4, 3^8, 3^{16}$

25 $5, 5, 10, 30, 120$ **27** $2, 2, 4, 4^3, 4^{12}$

29 $\dfrac{7}{2}, \dfrac{15}{2}, 12, 17$

31 $-1, -1 + \dfrac{1}{\sqrt{2}}, -1 + \dfrac{1}{\sqrt{2}} - \dfrac{1}{\sqrt{3}}, -\dfrac{1}{2} + \dfrac{1}{\sqrt{2}} - \dfrac{1}{\sqrt{3}}$

33 -5 **35** 10 **37** 25 **39** $-\dfrac{17}{15}$ **41** 61

43 $10{,}000$ **45** $\dfrac{319}{3}$ **47** $\dfrac{7}{2}k^2$

49 $\displaystyle\sum_{k=1}^{n} (a_k - b_k)$

$= (a_1 - b_1) + (a_2 - b_2) + \cdots + (a_n - b_n)$

$= (a_1 + a_2 + \cdots + a_n) + (-b_1 - b_2 - \cdots - b_n)$

$= (a_1 + a_2 + \cdots + a_n) - (b_1 + b_2 + \cdots + b_n)$

$= \displaystyle\sum_{k=1}^{n} a_k - \sum_{k=1}^{n} b_k$

51 As k increases, the terms approach 1.

53 $0.4, 0.7, 1, 1.6, 2.8$

55 **(a)** $1, 1, 2, 3, 5, 8, 13, 21, 34, 55$

(b) $1, 2, 1.5, 1.\overline{6}, 1.6, 1.625, 1.6153846, 1.6190476, 1.6176471, 1.6181818$

57 **(a)** $a_n = 0.8a_{n-1}$ **(b)** The fourth day

59 $C(n) = \begin{cases} 89.95n & \text{if } 1 \le n \le 4 \\ 87.95n & \text{if } 5 \le n \le 9 \\ 85.95n & \text{if } n \ge 10 \end{cases}$

61 2.236068   **63** 2.4493
65 (a) $f(1) = -1 < 0,\ f(2) \approx 0.30 > 0$ **(b)** 1.76

EXERCISES 10.2

1 Show that $a_{k+1} - a_k = 4$.   **3** $4n - 2;\ 18;\ 38$
5 $3.3 - 0.3n;\ 1.8;\ 0.3$ **7** $3.1n - 10.1;\ 5.4;\ 20.9$
9 $\ln 3^n;\ \ln 3^5;\ \ln 3^{10}$ **11** -8 **13** -8.5
15 -9.8 **17** $\dfrac{551}{17}$ **19** -105 **21** 30   **23** 530
25 $\dfrac{423}{2}$ **27** $934j + 838,265$

29 $\displaystyle\sum_{n=1}^{5} (7n - 3)$ or $\displaystyle\sum_{n=0}^{4} (4 + 7n)$

31 $\displaystyle\sum_{n=1}^{67} (7n - 3)$ or $\displaystyle\sum_{n=0}^{66} (4 + 7n)$

33 $\displaystyle\sum_{n=1}^{6} \dfrac{3n}{4n + 3}$ or $\displaystyle\sum_{n=0}^{5} \dfrac{3 + 3n}{7 + 4n}$

35 $\displaystyle\sum_{n=1}^{1528} (11n - 3) = 12,845,132$

37 24   **39** 12 or 18   **41** $\dfrac{10}{3}, \dfrac{14}{3}, 6, \dfrac{22}{3}, \dfrac{26}{3}$
43 (a) 60   **(b)** 12,780   **45** 255   **47** 154π ft
49 \$1200   **51** $16n^2$
53 Show that the $(n + 1)$st term is 1 greater than the nth term.
55 (a) $\dfrac{8}{36}, \dfrac{7}{36}, \dfrac{6}{36}, \ldots, \dfrac{1}{36}$ **(b)** $d = -\dfrac{1}{36};\ 1$ **(c)** \$722.22

EXERCISES 10.3

1 Show that $\dfrac{a_{k+1}}{a_k} = -\dfrac{1}{4}$.   **3** $8\left(\dfrac{1}{2}\right)^{n-1} = 2^{4-n};\ \dfrac{1}{2};\ \dfrac{1}{16}$
5 $300(-0.1)^{n-1};\ 0.03;\ -0.00003$ **7** $5^n;\ 3125;\ 390,625$
9 $4(-1.5)^{n-1};\ 20.25;\ -68.34375$
11 $(-1)^{n-1}x^{2n-2};\ x^8;\ -x^{14}$ **13** $2^{(n-1)x+1};\ 2^{4x+1};\ 2^{7x+1}$
15 $\pm\sqrt{3}$ **17** $\dfrac{243}{8}$ **19** $\sqrt[3]{3};\ 36$ **21** 88,572
23 $-\dfrac{341}{1024}$ **25** $8188 + 55j$ **27** $\displaystyle\sum_{n=1}^{7} 2^n$
29 $\displaystyle\sum_{n=1}^{4} (-1)^{n+1}\dfrac{1}{4}\left(\dfrac{1}{3}\right)^{n-1}$ **31** $\dfrac{2}{3}$ **33** $\dfrac{50}{33}$
35 Since $|r| = \sqrt{2} > 1$, the sum does not exist.
37 1024   **39** $\dfrac{23}{99}$ **41** $\dfrac{2393}{990}$ **43** $\dfrac{5141}{999}$ **45** $\dfrac{16,123}{9999}$
47 24   **49** 4, 20, 100, 500   **51** $\dfrac{25}{256}\% \approx 0.1\%$
53 (a) $N(t) = 10,000(1.2)^t$ **(b)** 61,917   **55** 300 ft
57 \$3,000,000   **59 (b)** 375 mg

61 (a) $a_{k+1} = \dfrac{1}{4}\sqrt{10}a_k$
(b) $a_n = \left(\dfrac{1}{4}\sqrt{10}\right)^{n-1} a_1,\ A_n = \left(\dfrac{5}{8}\right)^{n-1} A_1,$
$P_n = \left(\dfrac{1}{4}\sqrt{10}\right)^{n-1} P_1$ **(c)** $\dfrac{16a_1}{4 - \sqrt{10}}$
63 (a) $a_k = 3^{k-1}$ **(b)** 4,782,969
(c) $b_k = \dfrac{3^{k-1}}{4^k} = \dfrac{1}{4}\left(\dfrac{3}{4}\right)^{k-1}$ **(d)** $\dfrac{729}{16,384} \approx 4.45\%$
65 \$38,929.00   **67** \$7396.67
69 (a) $\dfrac{2}{5}, \dfrac{6}{25}, \dfrac{18}{125}, \dfrac{54}{625}, \dfrac{162}{3125}$
(b) $r = \dfrac{3}{5};\ \dfrac{2882}{3125} = 0.92224$ **(c)** \$16,000

EXERCISES 10.4

Exer. 1–32: A typical proof is given for Exercises 1, 5, 9, …, 29.

1 (1) P_1 is true, since $2(1) = 1(1 + 1) = 2$.
(2) Assume P_k is true:
$2 + 4 + 6 + \cdots + 2k = k(k + 1)$. Hence,
$2 + 4 + 6 + \cdots + 2k + 2(k + 1)$
$\qquad = k(k + 1) + 2(k + 1)$
$\qquad = (k + 1)(k + 2)$
$\qquad = (k + 1)(k + 1 + 1)$.
Thus, P_{k+1} is true, and the proof is complete.

5 (1) P_1 is true, since $5(1) - 3 = \dfrac{1}{2}(1)[5(1) - 1] = 2$.
(2) Assume P_k is true:
$2 + 7 + 12 + \cdots + (5k - 3) = \dfrac{1}{2}k(5k - 1)$.
Hence,
$2 + 7 + 12 + \cdots + (5k - 3) + 5(k + 1) - 3$
$\qquad = \dfrac{1}{2}k(5k - 1) + 5(k + 1) - 3$
$\qquad = \dfrac{5}{2}k^2 + \dfrac{9}{2}k + 2$
$\qquad = \dfrac{1}{2}(5k^2 + 9k + 4)$
$\qquad = \dfrac{1}{2}(k + 1)(5k + 4)$
$\qquad = \dfrac{1}{2}(k + 1)[5(k + 1) - 1]$.
Thus, P_{k+1} is true, and the proof is complete.

9 (1) P_1 is true, since $(1)^1 = \dfrac{1(1+1)[2(1)+1]}{6} = 1.$

(2) Assume P_k is true:

$$1^2 + 2^2 + 3^2 + \cdots + k^2 = \frac{k(k+1)(2k+1)}{6}.$$

Hence,

$$1^2 + 2^2 + 3^2 + \cdots + k^2 + (k+1)^2$$
$$= \frac{k(k+1)(2k+1)}{6} + (k+1)^2$$
$$= (k+1)\left[\frac{k(2k+1)}{6} + \frac{6(k+1)}{6}\right]$$
$$= \frac{(k+1)(2k^2 + 7k + 6)}{6}$$
$$= \frac{(k+1)(k+2)(2k+3)}{6}.$$

Thus, P_{k+1} is true, and the proof is complete.

13 (1) P_1 is true, since $3^1 = \dfrac{3}{2}(3^1 - 1) = 3.$

(2) Assume P_k is true:

$$3 + 3^2 + 3^3 + \cdots + 3^k = \frac{3}{2}(3^k - 1). \text{ Hence,}$$

$$3 + 3^2 + 3^3 + \cdots + 3^k + 3^{k+1}$$
$$= \frac{3}{2}(3^k - 1) + 3^{k+1}$$
$$= \frac{3}{2} \cdot 3^k - \frac{3}{2} + 3 \cdot 3^k$$
$$= \frac{9}{2} \cdot 3^k - \frac{3}{2}$$
$$= \frac{3}{2}(3 \cdot 3^k - 1)$$
$$= \frac{3}{2}(3^{k+1} - 1).$$

Thus, P_{k+1} is true, and the proof is complete.

17 (1) P_1 is true, since $1 < \dfrac{1}{8}[2(1)+1]^2 = \dfrac{9}{8}.$

(2) Assume P_k is true:

$$1 + 2 + 3 + \cdots + k < \frac{1}{8}(2k+1)^2. \text{ Hence,}$$

$$1 + 2 + 3 + \cdots + k + (k+1)$$
$$< \frac{1}{8}(2k+1)^2 + (k+1)$$
$$= \frac{1}{2}k^2 + \frac{3}{2}k + \frac{9}{8}$$
$$= \frac{1}{8}(4k^2 + 12k + 9)$$
$$= \frac{1}{8}(2k+3)^2$$
$$= \frac{1}{8}[2(k+1)+1]^2.$$

Thus, P_{k+1} is true, and the proof is complete.

21 (1) For $n = 1$, $5^n - 1 = 4$ and 4 is a factor of 4.

(2) Assume 4 is a factor of $5^k - 1$. The $(k+1)$st term is
$$5^{k+1} - 1 = 5 \cdot 5^k - 1$$
$$= 5 \cdot 5^k - 5 + 4$$
$$= 5(5^k - 1) + 4.$$
By the induction hypothesis, 4 is a factor of $5^k - 1$ and 4 is a factor of 4, so 4 is a factor of the $(k+1)$st term. Thus, P_{k+1} is true, and the proof is complete.

25 (1) For $n = 1$, $a - b$ is a factor of $a^1 - b^1$.

(2) Assume $a - b$ is a factor of $a^k - b^k$. Following the hint for the $(k+1)$st term,
$$a^{k+1} - b^{k+1} = a^k \cdot a - b \cdot a^k + b \cdot a^k - b^k \cdot b$$
$$= a^k(a - b) + (a^k - b^k)b.$$
Since $(a - b)$ is a factor of $a^k(a - b)$ and since by the induction hypothesis $a - b$ is a factor of $(a^k - b^k)$, it follows that $a - b$ is a factor of the $(k+1)$st term. Thus, P_{k+1} is true, and the proof is complete.

29 (1) P_8 is true, since $5 + \log_2 8 \le 8$.

(2) Assume P_k is true: $5 + \log_2 k \le k$. Hence,
$$5 + \log_2 (k+1) < 5 + \log_2 (k+k)$$
$$= 5 + \log_2 2k$$
$$= 5 + \log_2 2 + \log_2 k$$
$$= (5 + \log_2 k) + 1$$
$$\le k + 1.$$
Thus, P_{k+1} is true, and the proof is complete.

33 $\dfrac{n^3 + 6n^2 + 20n}{3}$ **35** $\dfrac{4n^3 - 12n^2 + 11n}{3}$

37 (a) $a + b + c = 1$, $8a + 4b + 2c = 5$,

$$27a + 9b + 3c = 14; a = \frac{1}{3}, b = \frac{1}{2}, c = \frac{1}{6}$$

(b) The method used in part (a) shows that the formula is true for only $n = 1, 2, 3$.

39 (1) For $n = 1$,
$$\sin(\theta + 1\pi) = \sin\theta\cos\pi + \cos\theta\sin\pi$$
$$= -\sin\theta = (-1)^1\sin\theta.$$
(2) Assume P_k is true: $\sin(\theta + k\pi) = (-1)^k\sin\theta.$
Hence,
$$\sin[\theta + (k+1)\pi]$$
$$= \sin[(\theta + k\pi) + \pi]$$
$$= \sin(\theta + k\pi)\cos\pi + \cos(\theta + k\pi)\sin\pi$$
$$= [(-1)^k\sin\theta]\cdot(-1) + \cos(\theta + k\pi)\cdot(0)$$
$$= (-1)^{k+1}\sin\theta.$$
Thus, P_{k+1} is true, and the proof is complete.

41 (1) For $n = 1$,
$$[r(\cos\theta + i\sin\theta)]^1 = r^1[\cos(1\theta) + i\sin(1\theta)].$$
(2) Assume P_k is true:
$$[r(\cos\theta + i\sin\theta)]^k = r^k(\cos k\theta + i\sin k\theta).$$
Hence,
$$[r(\cos\theta + i\sin\theta)]^{k+1}$$
$$= [r(\cos\theta + i\sin\theta)]^k[r(\cos\theta + i\sin\theta)]$$
$$= r^k[\cos k\theta + i\sin k\theta][r(\cos\theta + i\sin\theta)]$$
$$= r^{k+1}[(\cos k\theta\cos\theta - \sin k\theta\sin\theta) +$$
$$i(\sin k\theta\cos\theta + \cos k\theta\sin\theta)]$$
$$= r^{k+1}[\cos(k+1)\theta + i\sin(k+1)\theta].$$
Thus, P_{k+1} is true, and the proof is complete.

EXERCISES 10.5

1 1440 **3** 5040 **5** 336 **7** 1 **9** 21
11 715 **13** $n(n-1)$ **15** $(2n+2)(2n+1)$
17 $64x^3 - 48x^2y + 12xy^2 - y^3$
19 $x^6 + 6x^5y + 15x^4y^2 + 20x^3y^3 + 15x^2y^4 + 6xy^5 + y^6$
21 $x^7 - 7x^6y + 21x^5y^2 - 35x^4y^3 + 35x^3y^4 - 21x^2y^5$
$$+ 7xy^6 - y^7$$
23 $81t^4 - 540t^3s + 1350t^2s^2 - 1500ts^3 + 625s^4$
25 $\dfrac{1}{243}x^5 + \dfrac{5}{81}x^4y^2 + \dfrac{10}{27}x^3y^4 + \dfrac{10}{9}x^2y^6 + \dfrac{5}{3}xy^8 + y^{10}$
27 $x^{-12} + 18x^{-9} + 135x^{-6} + 540x^{-3} + 1215 + 1458x^3$
$$+ 729x^6$$
29 $x^{5/2} - 5x^{3/2} + 10x^{1/2} - 10x^{-1/2} + 5x^{-3/2} - x^{-5/2}$
31 $3^{25}c^{10} + 25\cdot 3^{24}c^{52/5} + 300\cdot 3^{23}c^{54/5}$
33 $-1680\cdot 3^{13}z^{11} + 60\cdot 3^{14}z^{13} - 3^{15}z^{15}$ **35** $\dfrac{189}{1024}c^8$
37 $\dfrac{114{,}688}{9}u^2v^6$ **39** $70x^2y^2$ **41** $448y^3x^{10}$
43 $-216y^9x^2$ **45** $-\dfrac{135}{16}$ **47** 4.8, 6.19
49 $4x^3 + 6x^2h + 4xh^2 + h^3$

51 $\dbinom{n}{1} = \dfrac{n!}{(n-1)!\,1!} = n$ and
$$\binom{n}{n-1} = \frac{n!}{[n-(n-1)]!\,(n-1)!}$$
$$= \frac{n!}{1!\,(n-1)!} = n$$

EXERCISES 10.6

1 210 **3** 60,480 **5** 120 **7** 6 **9** 1 **11** $n!$
13 (a) 60 (b) 125 **15** 64 **17** $P(8,3) = 336$
19 24 **21** (a) 2,340,000 (b) 2,160,000
23 (a) 151,200 (b) 5760 **25** 1024
27 $P(8,8) = 40{,}320$ **29** $P(6,3) = 120$
31 (a) 27,600 (b) 35,152 **33** 9,000,000,000
35 $P(4,4) = 24$ **37** $3!\cdot 2^3 = 48$
39 $(2^{16} - 1)\cdot 17$
41 (a) 900
  (b) If n is even, $9\cdot 10^{(n/2)-1}$; if n is odd, $9\cdot 10^{(n-1)/2}$.
43 $n! \approx \dfrac{n^n\sqrt{2\pi n}}{e^n}$

EXERCISES 10.7

1 35 **3** 9 **5** n **7** 1 **9** $\dfrac{12!}{5!\,3!\,2!\,2!} = 166{,}320$
11 $\dfrac{10!}{3!\,2!\,2!\,1!\,1!\,1!} = 151{,}200$ **13** $C(10,5) = 252$
15 $C(8,2) = 28$ **17** $(5!\cdot 4!\cdot 8!)\cdot 3! = 696{,}729{,}600$
19 $3\cdot C(10,2)\cdot C(8,2)\cdot C(4,2)\cdot C(6,2)\cdot 3\cdot 4$
$$= 4{,}082{,}400$$
21 $C(12,3)\cdot C(8,2) = 6160$ **23** $C(8,3) = 56$
25 (a) $C(49,6) = 13{,}983{,}816$ (b) $C(24,6) = 134{,}596$
27 $C(n,2) = 45$ and hence $n = 10$ **29** $C(6,3) = 20$
31 By finding $C(31,3) = 4495$
33 (a) $C(1000,30) \approx 2.43\times 10^{57}$
  (b) $P(1000,30) \approx 6.44\times 10^{89}$
35 $C(4,3)\cdot C(48,2) = 4512$
37 (a) 1, 2, 4, 8, 16, 32, 64, 128, 256, 512
  (b) $S_n = 2^{n-1}$
39 The sum of two adjacent numbers is equal to the number below and between them.

EXERCISES 10.8

1 (a) $\dfrac{4}{52}$; 1 to 12 (b) $\dfrac{8}{52}$; 2 to 11 (c) $\dfrac{12}{52}$; 3 to 10

3 (a) $\dfrac{1}{6}$; 1 to 5 (b) $\dfrac{1}{6}$; 1 to 5 (c) $\dfrac{2}{6}$; 1 to 2

5 (a) $\dfrac{5}{15}$; 1 to 2 (b) $\dfrac{6}{15}$; 2 to 3 (c) $\dfrac{9}{15}$; 3 to 2

7 (a) $\dfrac{2}{36}$; 1 to 17   **(b)** $\dfrac{5}{36}$; 5 to 31   **(c)** $\dfrac{7}{36}$; 7 to 29

9 $\dfrac{6}{216}$ **11** $\dfrac{3}{8}$ **13** 5 to 2; 2 to 5   **15** 5 to 9; $\dfrac{9}{14}$

17 1.93 to 1   **19** $\dfrac{48 \cdot 13}{C(52, 5)} \approx 0.00024$

21 $\dfrac{C(13, 4) \cdot C(13, 1)}{C(52, 5)} \approx 0.00358$

23 $\dfrac{C(13, 5) \cdot 4}{C(52, 5)} \approx 0.00198$ **25** $\dfrac{4}{6}$

27 $(0.674)^4 \approx 0.2064$

29 (a) 0.45   **(b)** 0.10   **(c)** 0.70   **(d)** 0.95

31 (a) $\dfrac{C(20, 5) \cdot C(40, 0)}{C(60, 5)} \approx 0.0028$

    (b) $1 - \dfrac{C(30, 0) \cdot C(30, 5)}{C(60, 5)} \approx 0.9739$

    (c) $\dfrac{C(10, 0) \cdot C(50, 5)}{C(60, 5)} + \dfrac{C(10, 1) \cdot C(50, 4)}{C(60, 5)} \approx 0.8096$

33 (a) $\dfrac{C(8, 8)}{2^8} \approx 0.00391$ **(b)** $\dfrac{C(8, 7)}{2^8} = 0.03125$

    (c) $\dfrac{C(8, 6)}{2^8} = 0.109375$

    (d) $\dfrac{C(8, 6) + C(8, 7) + C(8, 8)}{2^8} \approx 0.14453$

35 $1 - \dfrac{C(48, 5)}{C(52, 5)} \approx 0.34116$

37 (a) A representative outcome is (nine of clubs, 3); 312

    (b) 20; 292; $\dfrac{20}{312}$ **(c)** No; yes; $\dfrac{72}{312}$; $\dfrac{156}{312}$; $\dfrac{36}{312}$; $\dfrac{192}{312}$

    (d) Yes; no; 0; $\dfrac{92}{312}$

39 $1 - \dfrac{10}{36} = \dfrac{26}{36}$ **41 (a)** $\dfrac{1}{32}$ **(b)** $1 - \dfrac{1}{32} = \dfrac{31}{32}$

43 (a) $\dfrac{C(4, 4)}{4!} = \dfrac{1}{24}$ **(b)** $\dfrac{C(4, 2)}{4!} = \dfrac{1}{4}$

45 (a) 0   **(b)** $\dfrac{1}{9}$

47 (a) $\dfrac{304,366}{442,398} \approx 0.688$ **(b)** $\dfrac{344,391}{442,398} \approx 0.778$

49 12.5%   **51 (a)** $\dfrac{1}{16}$ **(b)** $\dfrac{C(4, 2)}{2^4} = \dfrac{6}{16}$

53 $\dfrac{2}{25,827,165}$ (about 1 chance in 13 million)

55 $\dfrac{1970}{39,800} \approx 0.0495$

57 (a) $\dfrac{8}{36}$ **(b)** $\dfrac{1}{36}$ **(c)** $\dfrac{244}{495} \approx 0.4929$

59 (b) 0.76   **61** $0.99   **63** $0.20

CHAPTER 10 REVIEW EXERCISES

1 $5, -2, -1, -\dfrac{20}{29}; -\dfrac{7}{19}$

2 $0.9, -1.01, 0.999, -1.0001; 0.999\,999\,9$

3 $2, \dfrac{1}{2}, \dfrac{5}{4}, \dfrac{7}{8}; \dfrac{65}{64}$ **4** $\dfrac{1}{12}, \dfrac{1}{15}, \dfrac{1}{15}, \dfrac{8}{105}; \dfrac{8}{45}$

5 $10, \dfrac{11}{10}, \dfrac{21}{11}, \dfrac{32}{21}, \dfrac{53}{32}$ **6** $2, 2, 2, 2, 2$

7 $9, 3, \sqrt{3}, \sqrt[4]{3}, \sqrt[8]{3}$ **8** $1, \dfrac{1}{2}, \dfrac{2}{3}, \dfrac{3}{5}, \dfrac{5}{8}$

9 75   **10** $-\dfrac{37}{10}$ **11** 940   **12** -10 **13** $\displaystyle\sum_{n=1}^{5} 3n$

14 $\displaystyle\sum_{n=1}^{6} 2^{3-n}$ **15** $\displaystyle\sum_{n=1}^{99} \dfrac{1}{n(n + 1)}$ **16** $\displaystyle\sum_{n=1}^{98} \dfrac{1}{n(n + 1)(n + 2)}$

17 $\displaystyle\sum_{n=1}^{4} \dfrac{n}{3n - 1}$ **18** $\displaystyle\sum_{n=1}^{4} \dfrac{n}{5n - 1}$

19 $\displaystyle\sum_{n=1}^{5} (-1)^{n+1}(105 - 5n)$ **20** $\displaystyle\sum_{n=1}^{7} (-1)^{n-1}\dfrac{1}{n}$

21 $\displaystyle\sum_{n=0}^{25} a_n x^{4n}$ **22** $\displaystyle\sum_{n=0}^{20} a_n x^{3n}$ **23** $1 + \displaystyle\sum_{k=1}^{n} (-1)^k \dfrac{x^{2k}}{2k}$

24 $1 + \displaystyle\sum_{k=1}^{n} \dfrac{x^k}{k}$ **25** $-5 - 8\sqrt{3}; -5 - 35\sqrt{3}$

26 52   **27** -31; 50   **28** 12

29 $20, 14, 8, 2, -4, -10$ **30** 64   **31** -0.00003

32 1562.5 or -1562.5 **33** $4\sqrt{2}$ **34** $-\dfrac{12,800}{2187}$

35 17; 3   **36** $\dfrac{1}{81}; \dfrac{211}{1296}$ **37** 570   **38** 32.5

39 2041   **40** -506 **41** $\dfrac{5}{7}$ **42** $\dfrac{6268}{999}$

43 (1) P_1 is true, since $3(1) - 1 = \dfrac{1[3(1) + 1]}{2} = 2$.

(2) Assume P_k is true:

$$2 + 5 + 8 + \cdots + (3k - 1) = \frac{k(3k + 1)}{2}.$$

Hence,

$$2 + 5 + 8 + \cdots + (3k - 1) + 3(k + 1) - 1$$
$$= \frac{k(3k + 1)}{2} + 3(k + 1) - 1$$
$$= \frac{3k^2 + k + 6k + 4}{2}$$
$$= \frac{3k^2 + 7k + 4}{2}$$
$$= \frac{(k + 1)(3k + 4)}{2}$$
$$= \frac{(k + 1)[3(k + 1) + 1]}{2}.$$

Thus, P_{k+1} is true, and the proof is complete.

44 (1) P_1 is true, since $[2(1)]^2 = \dfrac{[2(1)][2(1) + 1][1 + 1]}{3} = 4$.

(2) Assume P_k is true:

$$2^2 + 4^2 + 6^2 + \cdots + (2k)^2 = \frac{(2k)(2k + 1)(k + 1)}{3}.$$

Hence,

$$2^2 + 4^2 + 6^2 + \cdots + (2k)^2 + [2(k + 1)]^2$$
$$= \frac{(2k)(2k + 1)(k + 1)}{3} + [2(k + 1)]^2$$
$$= (k + 1)\left(\frac{4k^2 + 2k}{3} + \frac{12(k + 1)}{3}\right)$$
$$= \frac{(k + 1)(4k^2 + 14k + 12)}{3}$$
$$= \frac{2(k + 1)(2k + 3)(k + 2)}{3}.$$

Thus, P_{k+1} is true, and the proof is complete.

45 (1) P_1 is true, since $\dfrac{1}{[2(1) - 1][2(1) + 1]} = \dfrac{1}{2(1) + 1} = \dfrac{1}{3}$.

(2) Assume P_k is true:

$$\frac{1}{1 \cdot 3} + \frac{1}{3 \cdot 5} + \frac{1}{5 \cdot 7} + \cdots + \frac{1}{(2k - 1)(2k + 1)} = \frac{k}{2k + 1}.$$

Hence,

$$\frac{1}{1 \cdot 3} + \frac{1}{3 \cdot 5} + \frac{1}{5 \cdot 7} + \cdots + \frac{1}{(2k - 1)(2k + 1)}$$
$$+ \frac{1}{(2k + 1)(2k + 3)} = \frac{k}{2k + 1} + \frac{1}{(2k + 1)(2k + 3)}$$
$$= \frac{k(2k + 3) + 1}{(2k + 1)(2k + 3)}$$
$$= \frac{2k^2 + 3k + 1}{(2k + 1)(2k + 3)}$$
$$= \frac{(2k + 1)(k + 1)}{(2k + 1)(2k + 3)}$$
$$= \frac{k + 1}{2(k + 1) + 1}.$$

Thus, P_{k+1} is true, and the proof is complete.

46 (1) P_1 is true, since $1(1 + 1) = \dfrac{(1)(1 + 1)(1 + 2)}{3} = 2$.

(2) Assume P_k is true:

$$1 \cdot 2 + 2 \cdot 3 + 3 \cdot 4 + \cdots + k(k + 1)$$
$$= \frac{k(k + 1)(k + 2)}{3}.$$

Hence,

$$1 \cdot 2 + 2 \cdot 3 + 3 \cdot 4 + \cdots + k(k + 1)$$
$$+ (k + 1)(k + 2)$$
$$= \frac{k(k + 1)(k + 2)}{3} + (k + 1)(k + 2)$$
$$= (k + 1)(k + 2)\left(\frac{k}{3} + 1\right)$$
$$= \frac{(k + 1)(k + 2)(k + 3)}{3}.$$

Thus, P_{k+1} is true, and the proof is complete.

47 (1) For $n = 1$, $n^3 + 2n = 3$ and 3 is a factor of 3.

(2) Assume 3 is a factor of $k^3 + 2k$. The $(k + 1)$st term is

$$(k + 1)^3 + 2(k + 1) = k^3 + 3k^2 + 5k + 3$$
$$= (k^3 + 2k) + (3k^2 + 3k + 3)$$
$$= (k^3 + 2k) + 3(k^2 + k + 1).$$

By the induction hypothesis, 3 is a factor of $k^3 + 2k$ and 3 is a factor of $3(k^2 + k + 1)$, so 3 is a factor of the $(k + 1)$st term.

Thus, P_{k+1} is true, and the proof is complete.

48 (1) P_5 is true, since $5^2 + 3 < 2^5$.
  (2) Assume P_k is true: $k^2 + 3 < 2^k$. Hence,
  $(k + 1)^2 + 3 = k^2 + 2k + 4$
  $= (k^2 + 3) + (k + 1)$
  $< 2^k + (k + 1)$
  $< 2^k + 2^k$
  $= 2 \cdot 2^k = 2^{k+1}$

  Thus, P_{k+1} is true, and the proof is complete.

49 (1) P_4 is true, since $2^4 \le 4!$.
  (2) Assume P_k is true: $2^k \le k!$. Hence,
  $2^{k+1} = 2 \cdot 2^k \le 2 \cdot k! < (k + 1) \cdot k! = (k + 1)!$.
  Thus, P_{k+1} is true, and the proof is complete.

50 (1) P_{10} is true, since $10^{10} \le 10^{10}$.
  (2) Assume P_k is true: $10^k \le k^k$. Hence,
  $10^{k+1} = 10 \cdot 10^k \le 10 \cdot k^k < (k + 1) \cdot k^k$
  $< (k + 1) \cdot (k + 1)^k = (k + 1)^{k+1}$.
  Thus, P_{k+1} is true, and the proof is complete.

51 $x^{12} - 18x^{10}y + 135x^8y^2 - 540x^6y^3 + 1215x^4y^4$
  $- 1458x^2y^5 + 729y^6$

52 $16x^4 + 32x^3y^3 + 24x^2y^6 + 8xy^9 + y^{12}$

53 $x^8 + 40x^7 + 760x^6$ **54** $-\dfrac{63}{16}y^{12}c^{10}$

55 $21{,}504x^{10}y^2$ **56** $52{,}500{,}000$

57 (a) $d = 1 - \dfrac{1}{2}a_1$ (b) In ft: $1\dfrac{1}{4}, 2, 2\dfrac{3}{4}, 3\dfrac{1}{2}$

58 24 ft   **59** $\dfrac{2}{1 - f}$ **60** $P(10, 10) = 3{,}628{,}800$

61 (a) $P(52, 13) \approx 3.954 \times 10^{21}$
  (b) $P(13, 5) \cdot P(13, 3) \cdot P(13, 3) \cdot P(13, 2)$
  $\approx 7.094 \times 10^{13}$

62 (a) $P(6, 4) = 360$ (b) $6^4 = 1296$

63 (a) $C(12, 8) = 495$ (b) $C(9, 5) = 126$

64 $\dfrac{17!}{6!\,5!\,4!\,2!} = 85{,}765{,}680$ **65** 5 to 8; $\dfrac{8}{13}$

66 (a) $\dfrac{2}{4}$ (b) $\dfrac{2}{8}$

67 (a) $\dfrac{P(26, 4) \cdot 2}{P(52, 4)} \approx 0.1104$ (b) $\dfrac{26^2 \cdot 25^2}{P(52, 4)} \approx 0.0650$

68 (a) $\dfrac{1}{1000}$ (b) $\dfrac{10}{1000}$ (c) $\dfrac{50}{1000}$

69 $\dfrac{C(4, 1)}{2^4} = \dfrac{4}{16}$; 1 to 3

70 (a) $\dfrac{C(6, 4) + C(6, 5) + C(6, 6)}{2^6} = \dfrac{22}{64}$
  (b) $1 - \dfrac{22}{64} = \dfrac{42}{64}$

71 (a) $\dfrac{1}{312}$ (b) $\dfrac{57}{312}$ **72** 0.44   **73** $\dfrac{8}{36}$

74 5.8125

1 $a_n = 2n + \dfrac{1}{24}(n - 1)(n - 2)(n - 3)(n - 4)(a - 10)$
  (The answer is not unique.)

2 $\ge$; $j = 94$

3 Examine the number of digits in the exponent of the value in scientific notation.

4 The $(k + 1)$st coefficient $(k = 0, 1, 2, \ldots, n)$ of the expansion of $(a + b)^n$, namely $\dbinom{n}{k}$, is the same as the number of k-element subsets of an n-element set.

5 4.61   **6** \$5.33

7 Penny amounts:
  \$237.37   \$215.63   \$195.89   \$177.95   \$161.65
  \$146.85   \$133.40   \$121.18   \$110.08   \$100.00
  Realistic ten dollar amounts:
  \$240.00   \$220.00   \$200.00   \$180.00   \$160.00
  \$140.00   \$130.00   \$120.00   \$110.00   \$100.00

8 11 toppings are available.

9 (a) $\dfrac{1}{146{,}107{,}962}$ (b) $\dfrac{3{,}991{,}302}{146{,}107{,}962}$ (about 1 in 36.61)
  (c) $\dfrac{28{,}800{,}030}{146{,}107{,}962} \approx 0.21$ (d) \$117{,}307{,}932

10 0.43   **11** $0^0 = 1$ **12** The sum equals π.

13 (a) $\tan 5x = \dfrac{5 \tan x - 10 \tan^3 x + \tan^5 x}{1 - 10 \tan^2 x + 5 \tan^4 x}$
  (b) $\cos 5x = 1 \cos^5 x - 10 \cos^3 x \sin^2 x + 5 \cos x \sin^4 x$;
  $\sin 5x = 5 \cos^4 x \sin x - 10 \cos^2 x \sin^3 x + 1 \sin^5 x$

Chapter 11

EXERCISES 11.1

1 $V(0, 0)$; $F(0, 2)$; $y = -2$ **3** $V(0, 0)$; $F\left(-\dfrac{3}{8}, 0\right)$;
$x = \dfrac{3}{8}$

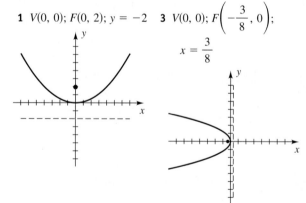

5 $V(-2, 1); F(-2, -1);$
$y = 3$

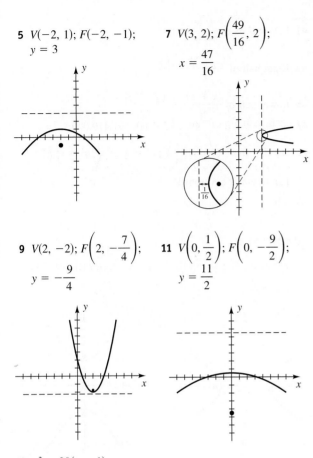

7 $V(3, 2); F\left(\dfrac{49}{16}, 2\right);$
$x = \dfrac{47}{16}$

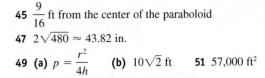

9 $V(2, -2); F\left(2, -\dfrac{7}{4}\right);$
$y = -\dfrac{9}{4}$

11 $V\left(0, \dfrac{1}{2}\right); F\left(0, -\dfrac{9}{2}\right);$
$y = \dfrac{11}{2}$

13 $y^2 = 20(x - 1)$
15 $(x + 2)^2 = -16(y - 3)$
17 $(x - 3)^2 = 6\left(y - \dfrac{1}{2}\right)$
19 $y^2 = 8x$
21 $(x - 6)^2 = 12(y - 1)$
23 $(y + 5)^2 = 4(x - 3)$
25 $y^2 = -12(x + 1)$
27 $3x^2 = -4y$
29 $(y - 5)^2 = 2(x + 3)$
31 $x^2 = 16(y - 1)$
33 $(y - 3)^2 = -8(x + 4)$
35 $y = -\sqrt{x + 3} - 1$
37 $x = \sqrt{y - 4} - 1$
39 $y = -x^2 + 2x + 5$
41 $x = y^2 - 3y + 1$
43 4 in.

45 $\dfrac{9}{16}$ ft from the center of the paraboloid
47 $2\sqrt{480} \approx 43.82$ in.
49 (a) $p = \dfrac{r^2}{4h}$ (b) $10\sqrt{2}$ ft   **51** 57,000 ft^2

EXERCISES 11.2

1 $V(\pm 3, 0); F\left(\pm\sqrt{5}, 0\right)$

3 $V(0, \pm 4); F(0, \pm 1)$

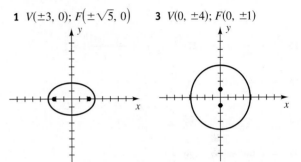

5 $V(0, \pm 4); F\left(0, \pm 2\sqrt{3}\right)$

7 $V\left(\pm\dfrac{1}{2}, 0\right);$
$F\left(\pm\dfrac{1}{10}\sqrt{21}, 0\right)$

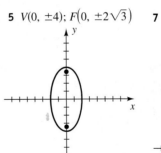

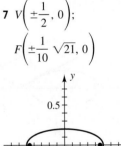

9 $V(3 \pm 4, -4);$
$F\left(3 \pm \sqrt{7}, -4\right)$

11 $V(4 \pm 3, 2);$
$F\left(4 \pm \sqrt{5}, 2\right)$

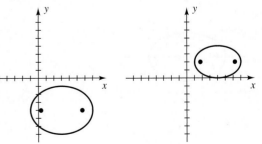

13 $V(5, 2 \pm 5)$;
$F\left(5, 2 \pm \sqrt{21}\right)$

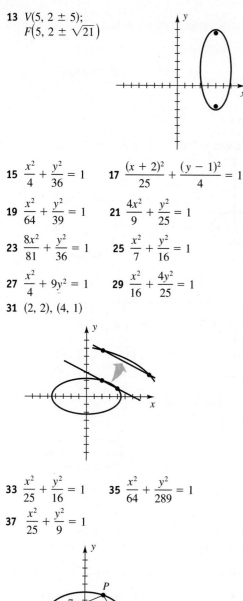

15 $\dfrac{x^2}{4} + \dfrac{y^2}{36} = 1$ **17** $\dfrac{(x + 2)^2}{25} + \dfrac{(y - 1)^2}{4} = 1$

19 $\dfrac{x^2}{64} + \dfrac{y^2}{39} = 1$ **21** $\dfrac{4x^2}{9} + \dfrac{y^2}{25} = 1$

23 $\dfrac{8x^2}{81} + \dfrac{y^2}{36} = 1$ **25** $\dfrac{x^2}{7} + \dfrac{y^2}{16} = 1$

27 $\dfrac{x^2}{4} + 9y^2 = 1$ **29** $\dfrac{x^2}{16} + \dfrac{4y^2}{25} = 1$

31 $(2, 2)$, $(4, 1)$

33 $\dfrac{x^2}{25} + \dfrac{y^2}{16} = 1$ **35** $\dfrac{x^2}{64} + \dfrac{y^2}{289} = 1$

37 $\dfrac{x^2}{25} + \dfrac{y^2}{9} = 1$

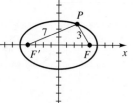

39 Upper half of $\dfrac{x^2}{49} + \dfrac{y^2}{121} = 1$

41 Left half of $x^2 + \dfrac{y^2}{9} = 1$

43 Right half of $\dfrac{(x - 1)^2}{4} + \dfrac{(y + 2)^2}{9} = 1$

45 Lower half of $\dfrac{(x + 1)^2}{9} + \dfrac{(y - 2)^2}{49} = 1$

47 $\sqrt{84} \approx 9.2$ ft   **49** 94,581,000; 91,419,000

51 (a) $d = h - \sqrt{h^2 - \dfrac{1}{4}k^2}$; $d' = h + \sqrt{h^2 - \dfrac{1}{4}k^2}$

    (b) 16 cm; 2 cm from V

53 5 ft

EXERCISES 11.3

1 $V(\pm 3, 0)$; $F\left(\pm\sqrt{13}, 0\right)$;   **3** $V(0, \pm 3)$; $F\left(0, \pm\sqrt{13}\right)$;
    $y = \pm\dfrac{2}{3}x$ $y = \pm\dfrac{3}{2}x$

5 $V(\pm 1, 0)$; $F(\pm 5, 0)$;   **7** $V(0, \pm 4)$; $F\left(0, \pm 2\sqrt{5}\right)$;
    $y = \pm\sqrt{24}x$ $y = \pm 2x$

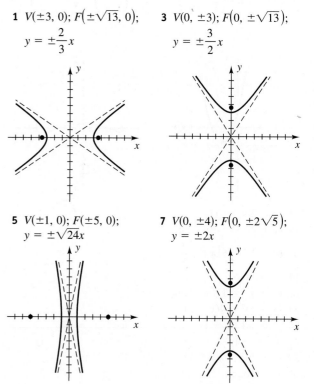

9 $V\left(\pm\dfrac{1}{4}, 0\right)$;

$F\left(\pm\dfrac{1}{12}\sqrt{13}, 0\right)$;

$y = \pm\dfrac{2}{3}x$

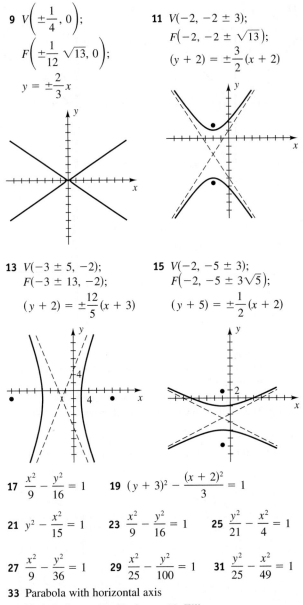

11 $V(-2, -2 \pm 3)$;

$F\left(-2, -2 \pm \sqrt{13}\right)$;

$(y + 2) = \pm\dfrac{3}{2}(x + 2)$

13 $V(-3 \pm 5, -2)$;

$F(-3 \pm 13, -2)$;

$(y + 2) = \pm\dfrac{12}{5}(x + 3)$

15 $V(-2, -5 \pm 3)$;

$F\left(-2, -5 \pm 3\sqrt{5}\right)$;

$(y + 5) = \pm\dfrac{1}{2}(x + 2)$

17 $\dfrac{x^2}{9} - \dfrac{y^2}{16} = 1$ **19** $(y + 3)^2 - \dfrac{(x + 2)^2}{3} = 1$

21 $y^2 - \dfrac{x^2}{15} = 1$ **23** $\dfrac{x^2}{9} - \dfrac{y^2}{16} = 1$ **25** $\dfrac{y^2}{21} - \dfrac{x^2}{4} = 1$

27 $\dfrac{x^2}{9} - \dfrac{y^2}{36} = 1$ **29** $\dfrac{x^2}{25} - \dfrac{y^2}{100} = 1$ **31** $\dfrac{y^2}{25} - \dfrac{x^2}{49} = 1$

33 Parabola with horizontal axis

35 Hyperbola   **37** Circle   **39** Ellipse

41 Parabola with vertical axis

43 $(0, 4)$, $\left(\dfrac{8}{3}, \dfrac{20}{3}\right)$

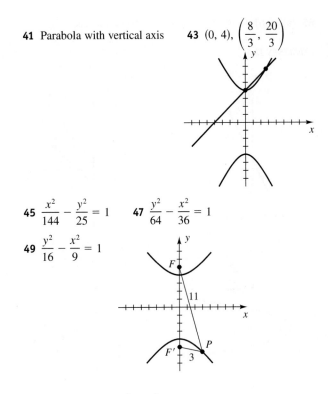

45 $\dfrac{x^2}{144} - \dfrac{y^2}{25} = 1$ **47** $\dfrac{y^2}{64} - \dfrac{x^2}{36} = 1$

49 $\dfrac{y^2}{16} - \dfrac{x^2}{9} = 1$

51 Right branch of $\dfrac{x^2}{25} - \dfrac{y^2}{16} = 1$

53 Upper branch of $\dfrac{y^2}{9} - \dfrac{x^2}{49} = 1$

55 Lower halves of the branches of $\dfrac{x^2}{16} - \dfrac{y^2}{81} = 1$

57 Left halves of the branches of $\dfrac{y^2}{36} - \dfrac{x^2}{16} = 1$

59 The graphs have the same asymptotes.

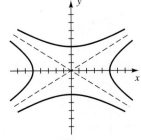

61 60.97 meters

63 If a coordinate system similar to that in Example 6 is introduced, then the ship's coordinates are

$\left(\dfrac{80}{3}\sqrt{34}, 100\right) \approx (155.5, 100)$.

65 (a) $(6.63 \times 10^7, 0)$ **(b)** $v > 103{,}600$ m/sec

EXERCISES 11.4

1 $y = 2x + 7$

3 $y = x - 2$

5 $(y - 3)^2 = x + 5$

7 $\dfrac{(x - 1)^2}{16} + \dfrac{y^2}{9} = 1$

9 $(x - 2)^2 + (y + 1)^2 = 9$ **11** $x^2 - y^2 = 1$

13 $y = \ln x$

15 $y = 1/x$

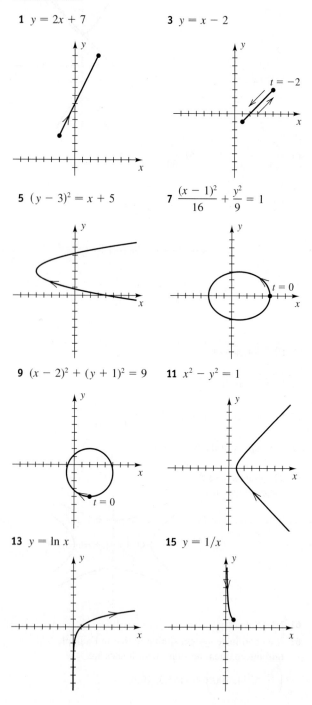

17 $y = \sqrt{x^2 - 1}$

19 $y = |x - 1|$

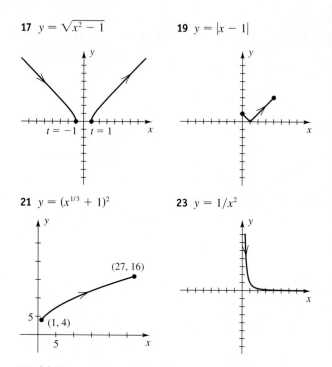

21 $y = (x^{1/3} + 1)^2$

23 $y = 1/x^2$

25 (a) The graph is a circle with center $(3, -2)$ and radius 2. Its orientation is clockwise, and it starts and ends at the point $(3, 0)$.
(b) The orientation changes to counterclockwise.
(c) The starting and ending point changes to $(3, -4)$.

27 C_1 C_2

C_3 C_4

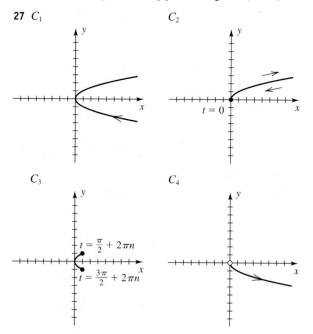

29 (a)

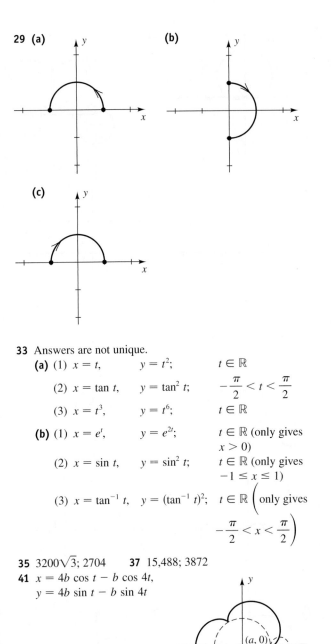

(b)

(c)

33 Answers are not unique.

(a) (1) $x = t$, $y = t^2$; $t \in \mathbb{R}$

   (2) $x = \tan t$, $y = \tan^2 t$; $-\dfrac{\pi}{2} < t < \dfrac{\pi}{2}$

   (3) $x = t^3$, $y = t^6$; $t \in \mathbb{R}$

(b) (1) $x = e^t$, $y = e^{2t}$; $t \in \mathbb{R}$ (only gives $x > 0$)

   (2) $x = \sin t$, $y = \sin^2 t$; $t \in \mathbb{R}$ (only gives $-1 \le x \le 1$)

   (3) $x = \tan^{-1} t$, $y = (\tan^{-1} t)^2$; $t \in \mathbb{R}$ $\left(\text{only gives } -\dfrac{\pi}{2} < x < \dfrac{\pi}{2}\right)$

35 $3200\sqrt{3}$; 2704   **37** 15,488; 3872

41 $x = 4b \cos t - b \cos 4t$,
   $y = 4b \sin t - b \sin 4t$

EXERCISES 11.5

1 (a), (c), (e)

3 (a) $\left(\dfrac{3}{2}\sqrt{2}, \dfrac{3}{2}\sqrt{2}\right)$ **(b)** $\left(\dfrac{1}{2}, -\dfrac{1}{2}\sqrt{3}\right)$

5 (a) $\left(-4, -4\sqrt{3}\right)$ **(b)** $\left(-\dfrac{3}{2}, \dfrac{3}{2}\sqrt{3}\right)$

7 $\left(\dfrac{24}{5}, \dfrac{18}{5}\right)$ **9 (a)** $\left(\sqrt{2}, \dfrac{3\pi}{4}\right)$ **(b)** $\left(4, \dfrac{7\pi}{6}\right)$

11 (a) $\left(14, \dfrac{5\pi}{3}\right)$ **(b)** $\left(5\sqrt{2}, \dfrac{\pi}{4}\right)$

13 $r = -3 \sec \theta$ **15** $r = 4$ **17** $r = 6 \cot \theta \csc \theta$

19 $r = \dfrac{3}{\cos \theta + \sin \theta}$ **21** $\theta = \tan^{-1}\left(-\dfrac{1}{2}\right)$

23 $r^2 = -4 \sec 2\theta$ **25** $r = 2 \cos \theta$

27 $x = 5$ **29** $x^2 + (y - 3)^2 = 9$

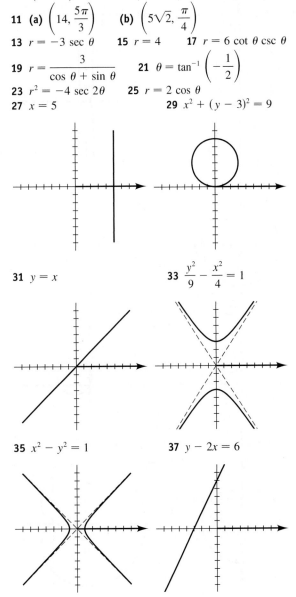

31 $y = x$ **33** $\dfrac{y^2}{9} - \dfrac{x^2}{4} = 1$

35 $x^2 - y^2 = 1$ **37** $y - 2x = 6$

39 $y = -x^2 + 1$

41 $(x + 1)^2 + (y - 4)^2 = 17$ **43** $y^2 = \dfrac{x^4}{1 - x^2}$

45

47

49

51

53

55

57

59

61

63

65

67

69

71

73

75

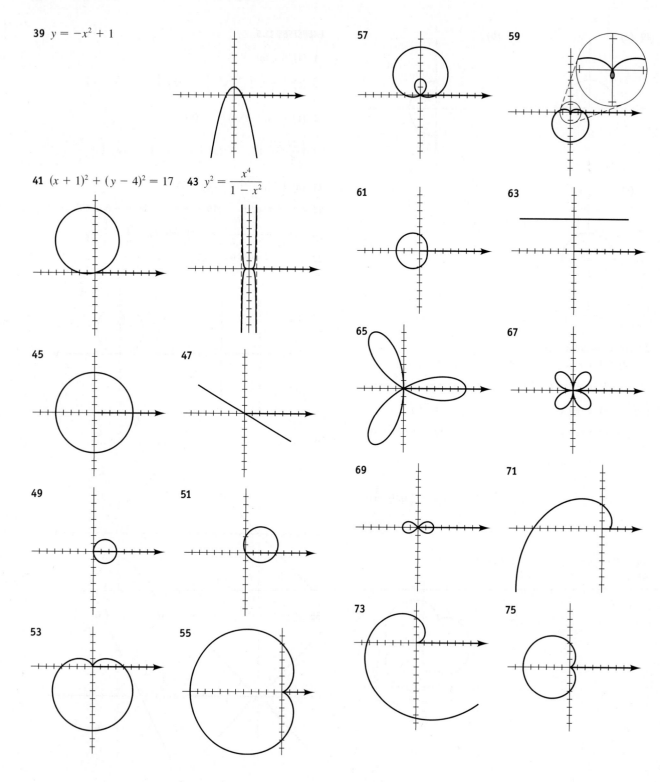

77

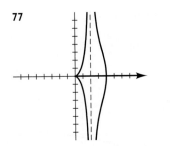

79 Let $P_1(r_1, \theta_1)$ and $P_2(r_2, \theta_2)$ be points in an $r\theta$-plane. Let $a = r_1$, $b = r_2$, $c = d(P_1, P_2)$, and $\gamma = \theta_2 - \theta_1$. Substituting into the law of cosines, $c^2 = a^2 + b^2 - 2ab \cos \gamma$, gives us the formula.

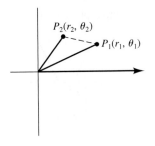

EXERCISES 11.6

1 $\dfrac{1}{3}$, ellipse

3 3, hyperbola

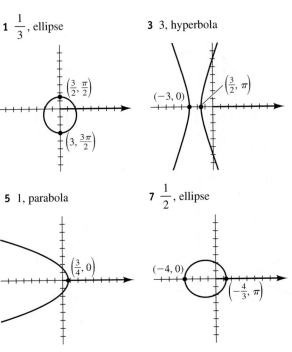

5 1, parabola

7 $\dfrac{1}{2}$, ellipse

9 $\dfrac{3}{2}$, hyperbola

11 1, parabola

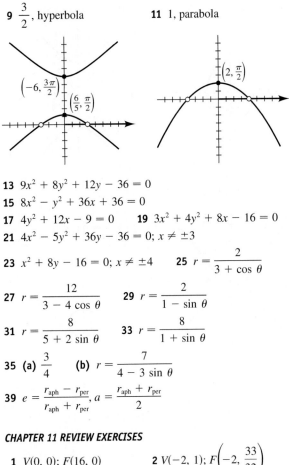

13 $9x^2 + 8y^2 + 12y - 36 = 0$

15 $8x^2 - y^2 + 36x + 36 = 0$

17 $4y^2 + 12x - 9 = 0$ **19** $3x^2 + 4y^2 + 8x - 16 = 0$

21 $4x^2 - 5y^2 + 36y - 36 = 0$; $x \neq \pm 3$

23 $x^2 + 8y - 16 = 0$; $x \neq \pm 4$ **25** $r = \dfrac{2}{3 + \cos \theta}$

27 $r = \dfrac{12}{3 - 4 \cos \theta}$ **29** $r = \dfrac{2}{1 - \sin \theta}$

31 $r = \dfrac{8}{5 + 2 \sin \theta}$ **33** $r = \dfrac{8}{1 + \sin \theta}$

35 **(a)** $\dfrac{3}{4}$ **(b)** $r = \dfrac{7}{4 - 3 \sin \theta}$

39 $e = \dfrac{r_{aph} - r_{per}}{r_{aph} + r_{per}}$, $a = \dfrac{r_{aph} + r_{per}}{2}$

CHAPTER 11 REVIEW EXERCISES

1 $V(0, 0)$; $F(16, 0)$ **2** $V(-2, 1)$; $F\left(-2, \dfrac{33}{32}\right)$

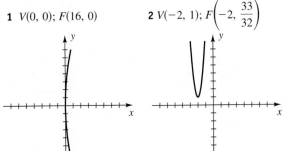

3 $V(0, \pm 4); F(0, \pm\sqrt{7})$

4 $V(0, \pm 4); F(0, \pm 5)$

9 $V(-4 \pm 1, 5);$
$F\left(-4 \pm \dfrac{1}{3}\sqrt{10}, 5\right)$

10 $V(-5, -2);$
$F\left(-\dfrac{39}{8}, -2\right)$

5 $V(\pm 2, 0); F(\pm 2\sqrt{2}, 0)$

6 $V\left(\pm\dfrac{1}{5}, 0\right);$
$F\left(\pm\dfrac{1}{30}\sqrt{11}, 0\right)$

11 $V(-3 \pm 3, 2);$
$F(-3 \pm \sqrt{5}, 2)$

12 $V(5, -4 \pm 2);$
$F(5, -4 \pm \sqrt{5})$

7 $V(0, 4); F\left(0, -\dfrac{9}{4}\right)$

8 $V(3 \pm 2, -1);$
$F(3 \pm 1, -1)$

13 $V(2, -4); F(4, -4)$

14 $V(3, -2 \pm 2);$
$F(3, -2 \pm \sqrt{3})$

15 $V(-4 \pm 3, 0);$
$F(-4 \pm \sqrt{10}, 0)$

16 $V(2, -3 \pm 2);$
$F(2, -3 \pm \sqrt{6})$

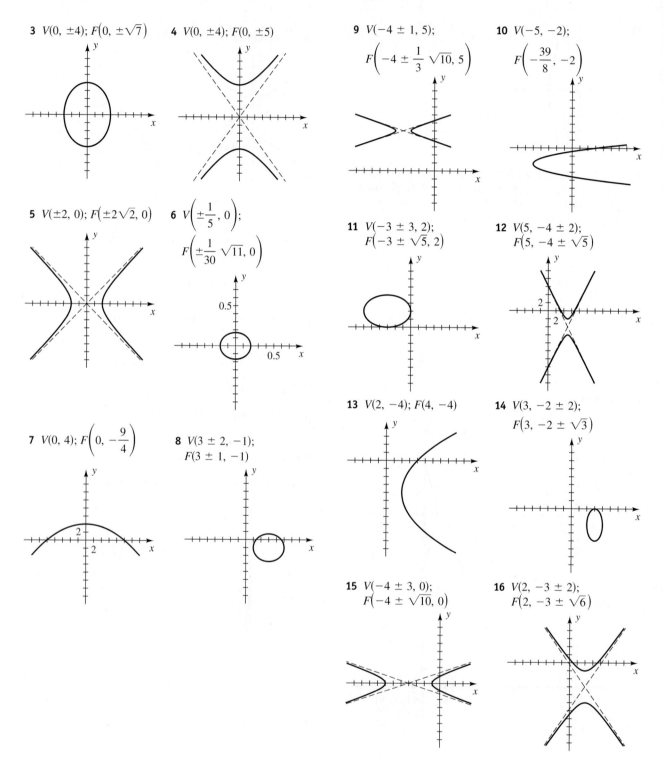

17 $y = 2(x + 7)^2 - 18$ **18** $y = -3(x + 4)^2 + 147$

19 $\dfrac{y^2}{49} - \dfrac{x^2}{9} = 1$ **20** $y^2 = -16x$ **21** $x^2 = -40y$

22 $x = 5y^2$ **23** $\dfrac{x^2}{75} + \dfrac{y^2}{100} = 1$ **24** $\dfrac{x^2}{25} - \dfrac{y^2}{75} = 1$

25 $\dfrac{y^2}{36} - \dfrac{x^2}{\frac{4}{9}} = 1$ **26** $\dfrac{x^2}{8} + \dfrac{y^2}{4} = 1$ **27** $\dfrac{x^2}{25} + \dfrac{y^2}{45} = 1$

28 $\dfrac{x^2}{256} + \dfrac{y^2}{112} = 1$ **29 (a)** $-\dfrac{7}{2}$ **(b)** Hyperbola

30 $A = \dfrac{4a^2b^2}{a^2 + b^2}$ **31** $x^2 + (y - 2)^2 = 4$

32 $2\sqrt{2}$ rad/sec ≈ 0.45 rev/sec   **34** $x = \sqrt{9 + 4y^2}$

35 $x = 4y + 7$ **36** $y = x^4 - 4$

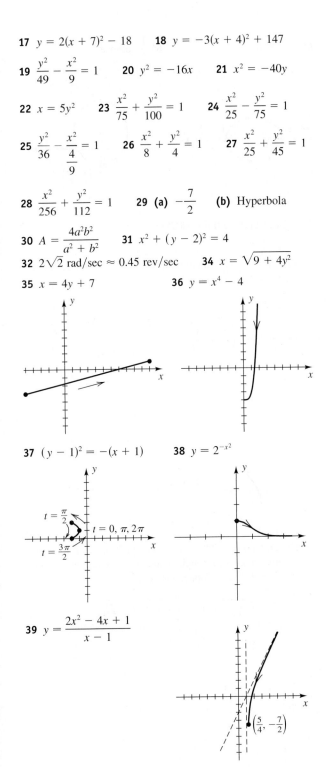

37 $(y - 1)^2 = -(x + 1)$ **38** $y = 2^{-x^2}$

39 $y = \dfrac{2x^2 - 4x + 1}{x - 1}$

$\left(\dfrac{5}{4}, -\dfrac{7}{2}\right)$

40 C_1 C_2

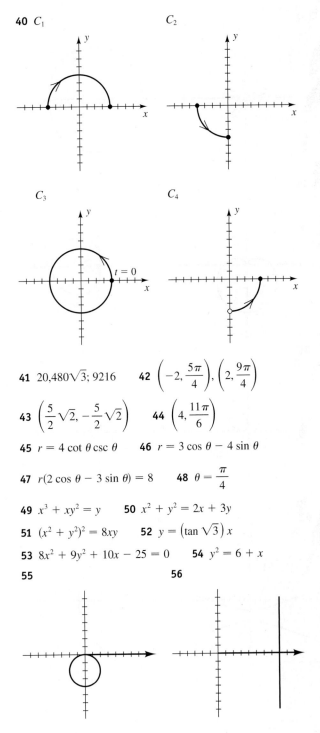

C_3 C_4

41 $20{,}480\sqrt{3}$; 9216 **42** $\left(-2, \dfrac{5\pi}{4}\right), \left(2, \dfrac{9\pi}{4}\right)$

43 $\left(\dfrac{5}{2}\sqrt{2}, -\dfrac{5}{2}\sqrt{2}\right)$ **44** $\left(4, \dfrac{11\pi}{6}\right)$

45 $r = 4 \cot \theta \csc \theta$ **46** $r = 3 \cos \theta - 4 \sin \theta$

47 $r(2 \cos \theta - 3 \sin \theta) = 8$ **48** $\theta = \dfrac{\pi}{4}$

49 $x^3 + xy^2 = y$ **50** $x^2 + y^2 = 2x + 3y$

51 $(x^2 + y^2)^2 = 8xy$ **52** $y = \left(\tan \sqrt{3}\right)x$

53 $8x^2 + 9y^2 + 10x - 25 = 0$ **54** $y^2 = 6 + x$

55   **56**

57

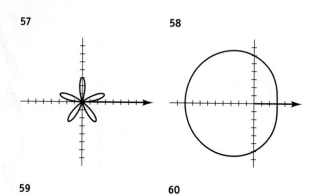

58

59

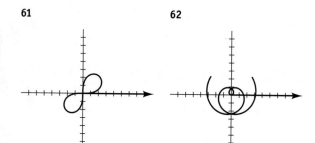

60

61

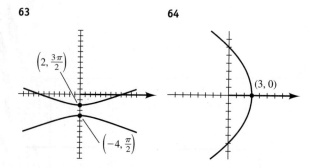

62

63

64

65 $\frac{2}{3}$, ellipse

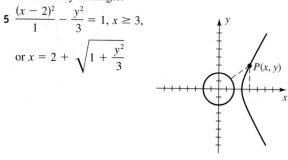

66 $\frac{1}{2}$, ellipse

CHAPTER 11 DISCUSSION EXERCISES

1 $w = 4|p|$

2 The circle goes through both foci and all four vertices of the auxiliary rectangle.

5 $\dfrac{(x-2)^2}{1} - \dfrac{y^2}{3} = 1$, $x \geq 3$,

or $x = 2 + \sqrt{1 + \dfrac{y^2}{3}}$

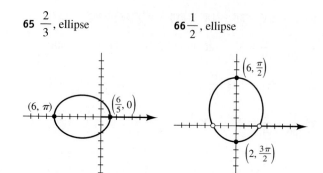

6 $d = \dfrac{1}{4\sqrt{a^2 + b^2}}$ **7** $43.12°$

9 $y = \pm\sqrt{\dfrac{1 \pm \sqrt{1 - x^2}}{2}}$

10 The graph of $r = f(\theta - \alpha)$ is the graph of $r = f(\theta)$ rotated counterclockwise through an angle α, whereas the graph of $r = f(\theta + \alpha)$ is rotated clockwise.

11 $(180/n)°$

12 $y = 2 \pm \sqrt{4 - x^2}$, $y = \pm\sqrt{4 - (x-2)^2}$

INDEX OF APPLICATIONS

INDEX

A

Abscissa, 124
Absolute value, 10, 11, 21
  equations containing, 94
  graph of an equation containing, 180
  properties of, 108
  of a real number, 547
  system of inequalities containing, 585
  of a trigonometric function, 417
Absolute value function, 172
Addition
  of matrices, 614–615
  properties of, 4
  of vectors, 525, 526, 527
  of y-coordinates, 417
Addition formulas, 457, 459, 461, 462
Additive identity, 4
Additive inverse, 4, 615
Adjacent side, 359
Algebraic equation, 55
Algebraic expression, 28–38
Algebraic function, 198
Alternating infinite series, 676
Ambiguous case, 505, 514
Amplitude
  of a complex number, 548
  of a graph, 402
  of harmonic motion, 426
  of a trigonometric function, 402, 403,
    405, 406
Angle(s), 348–355
  acute, 350, 359
  central, 350, 354
  complementary, 350, 422
  coterminal, 348, 349, 393
  definition of, 348
  degree measure of, 348
  of depression, 422, 423
  of elevation, 422–423, 506–507
  initial side of, 348
  measures of, 350–352
  negative, 348
  obtuse, 350
  positive, 348
  quadrantal, 348, 370
  radian measure of, 350
  reference, 393, 394, 395
  right, 350

  standard position of, 348
  straight, 348
  subtended, 350
  supplementary, 350
  terminal side of, 348
  trigonometric functions of, 358–372
  between vectors, 538
  vertex of, 348
Angular speed, 355
Applied problems
  equations in, 61–69
  trigonometry in, 420–426
Approximately equal to ($\approx$), 3
Approximations, 13
Arc, of a circle, 350
Arc length, 483
Arccosine function, 486
Arcsine function, 483
Arctangent function, 488
Area
  of a circular sector, 354
  of a triangle, 126, 472–473, 516
Argand plane, 546
Argument, 178
  of a complex number, 548, 550
  of a function, 156
Arithmetic mean, 667
Arithmetic sequences, 664–668
Arrangements without repetitions, 696
Associative properties, 4
Astronomical unit (AU), 745
Asymptote
  horizontal, 251
  for a hyperbola, 751
  oblique, 261–262
  vertical, 250, 388, 412–413, 415, 485
Augmented coefficient matrix, 600
Augmented matrix, 600
Auxiliary rectangle, 751
Average, 667
Axis (axes)
  conjugate, 751
  coordinate, 124
  of an ellipse, 739
  of a hyperbola, 751
  imaginary, 546
  major, 739
  minor, 739

  of a parabola, 132, 729
  polar, 772
  real, 546
  transverse, 751

B

Back substitution, 599
Bacterial growth, 292
Base, 11, 16
  of an exponential function,
    287–288
  for exponential notation, 16
  logarithmic, 308–310, 331
Bearings, 424, 425, 517
Binomial(s), 28, 686
  multiplying, 30–31
Binomial coefficients, 688
Binomial expansion, 690–692
Binomial theorem, 686–693
Bounds for zeros, 236–238
Branches
  of a hyperbola, 752
  of the tangent, 385

C

Calculators, 12–13
  approximating functions values with,
    362–363, 396, 397, 398, 452–453
Cancellation of common factors, 41
Cardioid, 779, 780, 781
Cartesian coordinate system, 124–128
Catenary, 304
Center
  of a circle, 137
  of an ellipse, 737
  of a hyperbola, 750
Central angle, 350, 353
Change of base formula, 331
Circle, 728
  radius and center of, 137
  standard equation of, 135–136
  unit, 136
Circular arc, 353
Circular functions, 377
Circular sector, 354
Closed, definition of, 3
Closed curve, 762
Closed interval, 103

QUICK REFERENCE CARD

THE SWOKOWSKI • COLE SERIES

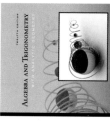

PRECALCULUS: FUNCTIONS AND GRAPHS
Eleventh Edition

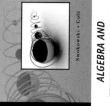

ALGEBRA AND TRIGONOMETRY WITH ANALYTIC GEOMETRY
Twelfth Edition

ALGEBRA AND TRIGONOMETRY WITH ANALYTIC GEOMETRY
Classic Twelfth Edition

BROOKS/COLE
CENGAGE Learning

FORMULAS FROM TRIGONOMETRY

FUNDAMENTAL IDENTITIES

$$\csc t = \frac{1}{\sin t}$$

$$\sec t = \frac{1}{\cos t}$$

$$\cot t = \frac{1}{\tan t}$$

$$\tan t = \frac{\sin t}{\cos t}$$

$$\cot t = \frac{\cos t}{\sin t}$$

$$\sin^2 t + \cos^2 t = 1$$

$$1 + \tan^2 t = \sec^2 t$$

$$1 + \cot^2 t = \csc^2 t$$

FORMULAS FOR NEGATIVES

$$\sin(-t) = -\sin t$$

$$\cos(-t) = \cos t$$

$$\tan(-t) = -\tan t$$

$$\cot(-t) = -\cot t$$

$$\sec(-t) = \sec t$$

$$\csc(-t) = -\csc t$$

ADDITION FORMULAS

$$\sin(u + v) = \sin u \cos v + \cos u \sin v$$

$$\cos(u + v) = \cos u \cos v - \sin u \sin v$$

$$\tan(u + v) = \frac{\tan u + \tan v}{1 - \tan u \tan v}$$

SUBTRACTION FORMULAS

$$\sin(u - v) = \sin u \cos v - \cos u \sin v$$

$$\cos(u - v) = \cos u \cos v + \sin u \sin v$$

$$\tan(u - v) = \frac{\tan u - \tan v}{1 + \tan u \tan v}$$

HALF-ANGLE FORMULAS

$$\sin \frac{u}{2} = \pm\sqrt{\frac{1 - \cos u}{2}}$$

$$\cos \frac{u}{2} = \pm\sqrt{\frac{1 + \cos u}{2}}$$

$$\tan \frac{u}{2} = \frac{1 - \cos u}{\sin u} = \frac{\sin u}{1 + \cos u}$$

DOUBLE-ANGLE FORMULAS

$$\sin 2u = 2 \sin u \cos u$$

$$\cos 2u = \cos^2 u - \sin^2 u$$

$$= 1 - 2 \sin^2 u$$

$$= 2 \cos^2 u - 1$$

$$\tan 2u = \frac{2 \tan u}{1 - \tan^2 u}$$

FORMULAS FROM TRIGONOMETRY

TRIGONOMETRIC FUNCTIONS

OF ACUTE ANGLES

$$\sin \theta = \frac{\text{opp}}{\text{hyp}} \qquad \csc \theta = \frac{\text{hyp}}{\text{opp}}$$

$$\cos \theta = \frac{\text{adj}}{\text{hyp}} \qquad \sec \theta = \frac{\text{hyp}}{\text{adj}}$$

$$\tan \theta = \frac{\text{opp}}{\text{adj}} \qquad \cot \theta = \frac{\text{adj}}{\text{opp}}$$

OBLIQUE TRIANGLE

OF REAL NUMBERS

$$s = t$$

$$\sin t = y \qquad \csc t = \frac{1}{y}$$

$$\cos t = x \qquad \sec t = \frac{1}{x}$$

$$\tan t = \frac{y}{x} \qquad \cot t = \frac{x}{y}$$

LAW OF SINES

$$\frac{\sin \alpha}{a} = \frac{\sin \beta}{b} = \frac{\sin \gamma}{c}$$

LAW OF COSINES

$$a^2 = b^2 + c^2 - 2bc \cos \alpha$$

$$b^2 = a^2 + c^2 - 2ac \cos \beta$$

$$c^2 = a^2 + b^2 - 2ab \cos \gamma$$

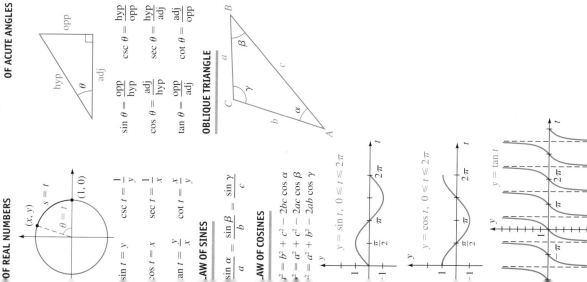

$$y = \sin t, \ 0 \leq t \leq 2\pi$$

$$y = \cos t, \ 0 \leq t \leq 2\pi$$

$$y = \tan t$$

area A perimeter P circumference C
volume V curved surface area S
altitude h radius r

RIGHT TRIANGLE

Pythagorean theorem:
$$c^2 = a^2 + b^2$$

TRIANGLE

$$A = \frac{1}{2} bh \qquad P = a + b + c$$

CIRCLE

$$A = \pi r^2 \qquad C = 2\pi r$$

SPHERE

$$V = \frac{4}{3} \pi r^3 \qquad S = 4\pi r^2$$

RIGHT CIRCULAR CYLINDER

$$V = \pi r^2 h \qquad S = 2\pi r h$$

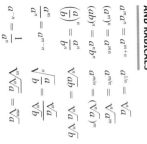

RIGHT CIRCULAR CONE

$$V = \frac{1}{3}\pi r^2 h \qquad S = \pi r \sqrt{r^2 + h^2}$$

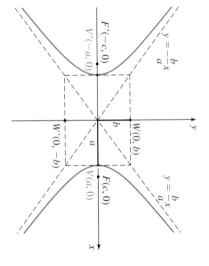

QUADRATIC FORMULA

If $a \neq 0$, the roots of $ax^2 + bx + c = 0$ are
$$x = \frac{-b \pm \sqrt{b^2 - 4ac}}{2a}$$

SPECIAL FACTORING FORMULAS

$$x^2 - y^2 = (x + y)(x - y)$$
$$x^2 + 2xy + y^2 = (x + y)^2$$
$$x^2 - 2xy + y^2 = (x - y)^2$$
$$x^3 - y^3 = (x - y)(x^2 + xy + y^2)$$
$$x^3 + y^3 = (x + y)(x^2 - xy + y^2)$$

EXPONENTIALS AND LOGARITHMS

$y = \log_a x \quad \text{means} \quad a^y = x$

$\log_a xy = \log_a x + \log_a y$

$\log_a \dfrac{x}{y} = \log_a x - \log_a y$

$\log_a x^r = r \log_a x$

$a^{\log_a x} = x$

$\log_a a^x = x$

$\log_a 1 = 0$

$\log_a a = 1$

$\log x = \log_{10} x$

$\ln x = \log_e x$

$\log_b u = \dfrac{\log_a u}{\log_a b}$

EXPONENTS AND RADICALS

$a^m a^n = a^{m+n}$

$(a^m)^n = a^{mn}$

$(ab)^n = a^n b^n$

$\left(\dfrac{a}{b}\right)^n = \dfrac{a^n}{b^n}$

$\dfrac{a^m}{a^n} = a^{m-n}$

$a^{-n} = \dfrac{1}{a^n}$

$a^{1/n} = \sqrt[n]{a}$

$a^{m/n} = \sqrt[n]{a^m} = (\sqrt[n]{a})^m$

$\sqrt[n]{ab} = \sqrt[n]{a}\,\sqrt[n]{b}$

$\sqrt[n]{\dfrac{a}{b}} = \dfrac{\sqrt[n]{a}}{\sqrt[n]{b}}$

$\sqrt[m]{\sqrt[n]{a}} = \sqrt[mn]{a}$

POINT-SLOPE FORM OF A LINE

$y - y_1 = m(x - x_1)$ m is the slope

SLOPE-INTERCEPT FORM OF A LINE

$y = mx + b$ m is the slope

CIRCLE

$(x - h)^2 + (y - k)^2 = r^2$

PARABOLA

$x^2 = 4py$

ELLIPSE

$\dfrac{x^2}{a^2} + \dfrac{y^2}{b^2} = 1$ with $a^2 = b^2 + c^2$

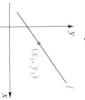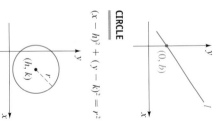

HYPERBOLA

$\dfrac{x^2}{a^2} - \dfrac{y^2}{b^2} = 1$ with $c^2 = a^2 + b^2$

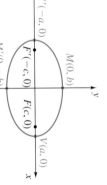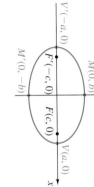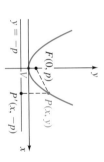

CONIC SECTIONS

PARABOLA

$$x^2 = 4py$$

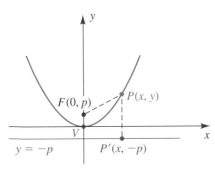

ELLIPSE

$$\frac{x^2}{a^2} + \frac{y^2}{b^2} = 1 \quad \text{with} \quad a^2 = b^2 + c^2$$

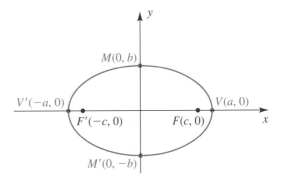

HYPERBOLA

$$\frac{x^2}{a^2} - \frac{y^2}{b^2} = 1 \quad \text{with} \quad c^2 = a^2 + b^2$$

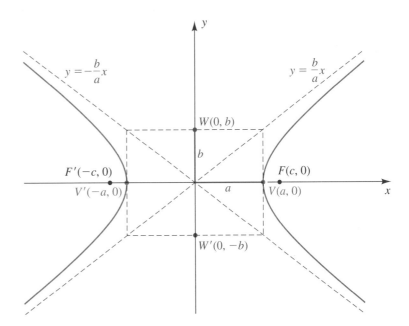

PLANE GEOMETRY

SIMILAR TRIANGLES

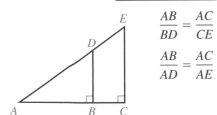

$$\frac{AB}{BD} = \frac{AC}{CE}$$

$$\frac{AB}{AD} = \frac{AC}{AE}$$

CONGRUENT ALTERNATE INTERIOR ANGLES

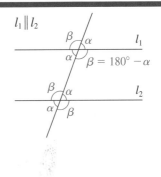

TRIGONOMETRY

TRIGONOMETRIC FUNCTIONS

OF ACUTE ANGLES

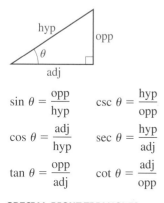

$$\sin \theta = \frac{\text{opp}}{\text{hyp}} \qquad \csc \theta = \frac{\text{hyp}}{\text{opp}}$$

$$\cos \theta = \frac{\text{adj}}{\text{hyp}} \qquad \sec \theta = \frac{\text{hyp}}{\text{adj}}$$

$$\tan \theta = \frac{\text{opp}}{\text{adj}} \qquad \cot \theta = \frac{\text{adj}}{\text{opp}}$$

OF ARBITRARY ANGLES

$$\sin \theta = \frac{b}{r} \qquad \csc \theta = \frac{r}{b}$$

$$\cos \theta = \frac{a}{r} \qquad \sec \theta = \frac{r}{a}$$

$$\tan \theta = \frac{b}{a} \qquad \cot \theta = \frac{a}{b}$$

OF REAL NUMBERS

$$\sin t = y \qquad \csc t = \frac{1}{y}$$

$$\cos t = x \qquad \sec t = \frac{1}{x}$$

$$\tan t = \frac{y}{x} \qquad \cot t = \frac{x}{y}$$

SPECIAL RIGHT TRIANGLES

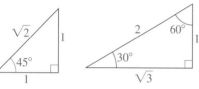

OBLIQUE TRIANGLE

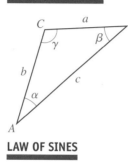

AREA

$$\mathcal{A} = \frac{1}{2} bc \sin \alpha$$

$$\mathcal{A} = \frac{1}{2} ac \sin \beta$$

$$\mathcal{A} = \frac{1}{2} ab \sin \gamma$$

$$\mathcal{A} = \sqrt{s(s-a)(s-b)(s-c)},$$

where $s = \frac{1}{2}(a + b + c)$ *(Heron's Formula)*

LAW OF COSINES

$$a^2 = b^2 + c^2 - 2bc \cos \alpha$$

$$b^2 = a^2 + c^2 - 2ac \cos \beta$$

$$c^2 = a^2 + b^2 - 2ab \cos \gamma$$

LAW OF SINES

$$\frac{\sin \alpha}{a} = \frac{\sin \beta}{b} = \frac{\sin \gamma}{c}$$

SPECIAL VALUES OF TRIGONOMETRIC FUNCTIONS

θ (degrees)	θ (radians)	$\sin \theta$	$\cos \theta$	$\tan \theta$	$\cot \theta$	$\sec \theta$	$\csc \theta$
0°	0	0	1	0	—	1	—
30°	$\frac{\pi}{6}$	$\frac{1}{2}$	$\frac{\sqrt{3}}{2}$	$\frac{\sqrt{3}}{3}$	$\sqrt{3}$	$\frac{2\sqrt{3}}{3}$	2
45°	$\frac{\pi}{4}$	$\frac{\sqrt{2}}{2}$	$\frac{\sqrt{2}}{2}$	1	1	$\sqrt{2}$	$\sqrt{2}$
60°	$\frac{\pi}{3}$	$\frac{\sqrt{3}}{2}$	$\frac{1}{2}$	$\sqrt{3}$	$\frac{\sqrt{3}}{3}$	2	$\frac{2\sqrt{3}}{3}$
90°	$\frac{\pi}{2}$	1	0	—	0	—	1

GREEK ALPHABET

Letter	Name	Letter	Name
A α	alpha	N ν	nu
B β	beta	Ξ ξ	xi
Γ γ	gamma	O o	omicron
Δ δ	delta	Π π	pi
E ϵ	epsilon	P ρ	rho
Z ζ	zeta	Σ σ	sigma
H η	eta	T τ	tau
Θ θ	theta	Υ υ	upsilon
I ι	iota	Φ ϕ (φ)	phi
K κ	kappa	X χ	chi
Λ λ	lambda	Ψ ψ	psi
M μ	mu	Ω ω	omega